D0734418

Context and Meaning
in Cultural Anthropology

A. IRVING HALLOWELL

Context and Meaning in Cultural Anthropology

EDITED BY MELFORD E. SPIRO

IN HONOR OF A. IRVING HALLOWELL

The Free Press, New York

Collier-Macmillan Limited, London

GN8
S67

Copyright © 1965 by The Free Press

A DIVISION OF THE MACMILLAN COMPANY

Printed in the United States of America

All rights reserved. No part of this book may be reproduced or utilized in any form or by any means, electronic or mechanical, including photocopying, recording or by any information storage and retrieval system, without permission in writing from the Publisher.

For information, address:

THE FREE PRESS
A DIVISION OF THE MACMILLAN COMPANY
60 Fifth Avenue, New York, N.Y. 10011

Collier-Macmillan Canada, Ltd., Toronto, Ontario

Library of Congress Catalog Card Number: 65-12858

To A. Irving Hallowell

Teacher, Friend, Colleague

UNIVERSITY of PENNSYLVANIA

PHILADELPHIA

ALFRED IRVING HALLOWELL

Scientist and sage, alumnus of this University, you have been guided and inspired by your great friend and mentor, the late Professor Frank G. Speck.

During a long and notable career devoted to teaching and research in anthropology, you have contributed importantly to our understanding of the development of human nature in the long perspective of evolution and have given us sharpened insight into the connection between personality and social environment.

Your meticulous and painstaking researches, marked by true originality, have aided in bringing anthropology and psychology into a closer and more productive relationship, to the enrichment of both disciplines and to the fuller understanding of man's nature.

Mr. President, I am most happy to present to you Alfred Irving Hallowell, Professor of Anthropology in the University of Pennsylvania, for the honorary degree Doctor of Science.

CITATION ACCOMPANYING THE HONORARY DEGREE OF DOCTOR OF SCIENCE CONFERRED ON MAY 20, 1963

Contributors

Erika Bourguignon
OHIO STATE UNIVERSITY

Robbins Burling
THE UNIVERSITY OF MICHIGAN

Frederica de Laguna
BRYN MAWR COLLEGE

Theodosius Dobzhansky
THE ROCKEFELLER INSTITUTE

Fred Eggan
UNIVERSITY OF CHICAGO

Raymond D. Fogelson
UNIVERSITY OF WASHINGTON

Paul Friedrich
UNIVERSITY OF CHICAGO

J. L. Giddings†
BROWN UNIVERSITY

Ward H. Goodenough
UNIVERSITY OF PENNSYLVANIA

Jacob W. Gruber
TEMPLE UNIVERSITY

Melville J. Herskovits†
NORTHWESTERN UNIVERSITY

Bert Kaplan
RICE UNIVERSITY

† (1909–1964)
† (1895–1963)

Richard Lawless
UNIVERSITY OF KANSAS

George Peter Murdock
UNIVERSITY OF PITTSBURGH

Murray G. Murphey
UNIVERSITY OF PENNSYLVANIA

Dennison Nash
UNIVERSITY OF CONNECTICUT

Ruben E. Reina
UNIVERSITY OF PENNSYLVANIA

Louis C. Schaw
UNIVERSITY OF CALIFORNIA

George Spindler
STANFORD UNIVERSITY

Louise Spindler
STANFORD UNIVERSITY

Melford E. Spiro
UNIVERSITY OF CHICAGO

Anthony F. C. Wallace
UNIVERSITY OF PENNSYLVANIA

Herbert H. Williams
SAN FRANCISCO STATE COLLEGE

Judith R. Williams
SAN FRANCISCO STATE COLLEGE

Laurence Wylie
HARVARD UNIVERSITY

Contents

Part Four
Cultural Dynamics

Part Five
Perception and Cognition

Part Six
Projective Tests

Part Seven
History of Anthropology

RAYMOND D. FOGELSON
AND MELFORD E. SPIRO

Introduction

This volume was conceived as a *Festschrift* for Professor A. Irving Hallowell in recognition of his great eminence within and influence upon contemporary anthropology. Hallowell's contributions to American Indian studies alone would have assured him a position of pre-eminence in American anthropology. From an early interest in Algonkian ethnology, resulting in field research among the Indians of the Northeast, his interests shifted westward to the northern Ojibwa, a people who occupy an important place in the anthropological record largely through Hallowell's writings. In a series of brilliant papers, written over a period of thirty years, Hallowell has described, analyzed, and interpreted various aspects of Saulteaux culture and behavior.

But Hallowell's influence extends much beyond the Americanist field. His work is widely known to scholars who know or care little about the Ojibwa or, for that matter, about any other American Indians. For Hallowell's has been a wide-ranging and pioneering career, exploring new domains that have had relevance not only for anthropology, but for psychology and economics, sociology and psychiatry, history and biology. Within his own field of anthropology there are few contemporary issues—from social organization to social perception, and from behavioral evolution to the evolution of anthropological thought—that have not been influenced, sometimes incisively, by Hallowell's work.

The catholicity of Hallowell's interests and the diversity of his contributions can be gauged to some extent by the variety of topics considered in the present volume. Seemingly a haphazard collection of papers, this variety is a consequence of a conscious and intentional editorial decision that the book reflect the work and the mind of the man whom it honors. Its variegated topics indicate, but do not exhaust, the variegated interests of a fertile mind. If this volume achieves integration—and we believe that it does—it is by virtue of the integration of these diversified strands in Hallowell's own work. Indeed, if one were to seek the underlying aim, the intellectual orientation of his scientific inquiries, integration would probably be its core component. Where others saw chasms—between culture and personality, for example—he sought to build bridges (1937c).[1] What others accepted as discontinuity—between, for example, animal society and human culture—he perceived as continuity (1961). When others were content with discrete variables—values and mental health, for example—he insisted on functional relationships (1950b).

This volume was conceived, not only as a formal recognition of Professor Hallowell's distinguished career, but as a personal testimony to his influence on their own work and thought, by a small number of students, colleagues, and friends. Since a host of scholars, in addition to the contributors to this volume, fit into one or more of these categories, many others might have been invited to contribute; indeed, a number of them offered voluntary contributions when it became known that a *Festschrift* was being planned. Unfortunately, exigencies of space and of cost rendered the desirability of a larger volume impracticable. The present contributors, however, may be taken to be a fair sample of a larger group of scholars who, as students, colleagues, or friends, have been influenced by Hallowell and his work.

II

Born in Philadelphia in 1892, Hallowell received his undergraduate and graduate training at the University of Pennsylvania. Except for a brief period at Northwestern University (1944–47), and visiting appointments at a number of other universities, he was associated with his *alma mater* for his entire professional life. In recognition of his contributions to psychiatric thought, he was appointed professor of psychiatry in the Medical School, in addition to his professorship in anthropology. Upon his retirement in 1963, the University of Pennsylvania conferred upon him the degree of Doctor of Science.

1. All citations to Hallowell's work refer to his bibliography appended to this volume.

A dedicated teacher, Hallowell's classroom demeanor was better suited to graduate, than to undergraduate, teaching. Although the more serious undergraduates were stimulated to high standards of achievement by his vast erudition, his exacting standards, and his searching mind, it was among graduate students that these qualities were best appreciated. Always accessible to students, he combined that balance of criticism and support which stimulates intellectual work without arousing great anxiety. Providing a framework, in lectures and seminars, for the interpretation and analysis of data, he encouraged students to develop and to pursue their own interests. Although an Americanist himself, he made no attempt to convert students to his own field. Ranging over wide intellectual horizons, his lectures and seminars attracted students from such diverse fields as biology and American civilization, psychiatry and intellectual history. Free with comments and suggestions, he never forced his students to adopt his point of view. The results were predictable: students not only respected him for his intellectual powers, but they held him in the greatest affection. Addressed as "Pete"—never Professor Hallowell—by older generations of students, to later generations he was known as "Uncle Pete."

Friend and counsellor to his own students, Hallowell's mentorship was not confined to them. A number of other young scholars—some of them represented in this volume—have experienced his generosity. Ojibwa specialists, Rorschach workers, culture historians, acculturation students, to mention but a few, have sought and received his assistance. For some, field notes were made available; for others, manuscripts were read and criticized; for still others, research projects were discussed and evaluated. All were treated seriously; none was turned away empty-handed.

The honesty and integrity that are apparent in Hallowell's scholarship characterize as well his relationship with people, whether they be students or peers. Although we have known him for many years, we have never heard him engage in the carping and adverse criticism of other scholars that so often characterizes academic conversation. The many offices he has held in a variety of professional organizations is as much a testimony to his personal qualities as to his scholarly contributions. He was elected president, for example, of the American Anthropological Association, the American Folklore Society, and the Society for Projective Techniques. He has been chairman of the Division of Anthropology and Psychology of the National Research Council, and editor both of the Monograph Series of the American Ethnological Society, and of the Viking Fund Publications. He has served on the Boards of the Social Science Research Council, the American Council of Learned Societies, and the International Congress of Anthropological and Ethnological Sciences. In addition, his scholarly contributions have been recognized by the highest honors which the anthropological and scientific worlds have to bestow: the Viking Medal in anthropology and membership in the National Academy of Sciences. He is also a member of the American Philosophical Society.

III

A mature assessment of Hallowell's contributions to anthropology and, more widely, to the behavioral and social sciences is difficult and still premature. His has been a very productive career, and his research and writing—despite his retirement—still continue. A cursory glance at his bibliography reveals publications in such diverse fields as behavioral evolution, material culture, New World archaeology, law, physical anthropology, ethnobotany, kinship, economics, ecology, oral literature, projective tests, cognition and perception, religion, acculturation, ethnohistory, the history of anthropology, and others. It would be too much to expect that his work in all of these fields has been important or distinguished. It is surprising, however, in how many of them his contributions have been innovative, decisive, or both.

For many scholars, including some anthropologists, Hallowell is primarily, if not exclusively, known for his work in culture and personality. For them, publication of *Culture and Experience* (1955), a collection of his most important essays in this field, appeared to be the capstone to a distinguished career in this uncharted no-man's-land between psychology and anthropology. An examination of all the papers in that volume, however, as well as of the items in the bibliography appended to this book, reveals that appearances can be deceiving. His work in other fields, such as acculturation and social organization—prior to *Culture and Experience*—would in themselves have marked a distinguished career. Hallowell's research on changes in kinship usage, to take but one example, was pioneering. In a series of papers dealing, first, with the St. Francis Abenaki (1928a) and expanding later (1928b, 1932, 1937) to include the entire Northern Algonkian-speaking area, he was able to demonstrate the former existence of cross-cousin marriage among people in which it is no longer practiced. These researches represent one of the first attempts to *demonstrate* actual changes in kinship. Speculations about kinship change were present, of course, in the works of the classical evolutionists and others, but Hallowell's hypotheses were based in large measure upon documentary evidence and, where direct historical material is lacking, on reasonable inference from other forms of available data.

But Hallowell's career, as the appended bibliography reveals, is still in progress. Many of his most significant writings postdate *Culture and Experience*, and the bottom of his inkwell is still not in sight. Although he continues, in some of his later work, to pursue and expand his interest in culture and personality, he also—in papers dealing with behavioral evolution (1959, 1960, 1961), for example, or the history of anthropology (1960)—explores frontier areas. It is for this reason that the time is still not ripe to render a proper assessment of his work. It is not only because there is more to come, but because the full impact of his contributions have yet to be felt. Just as many of his earlier articles seem surprisingly fresh today, anticipating later interests in the discipline, so his more recent publications will probably influence and stimulate contemporary and later generations of anthropologists.

Although an assessment of Hallowell's work is premature, it is not too early to characterize its quality. To do so in a few simple statements, however, is not simple. Hallowell must be read to be fully appreciated. His published contributions consistently combine a depth of treatment and insight with breadth in scope and outlook. A not inappropriate metaphor might better capture the flavor of his work. A Rorschach analyst might see in Hallowell's devotion to small print—his footnotes sometimes rival the text in length—evidence of a "Dd," or small detail, "nit-picking" personality. On further inspection a "D," or ordinary detail component, indicative of practicality and reality orientation, would emerge in the strong sense of problem that pervades almost all of Hallowell's writings. (It should be noted that this consistent and conscious emphasis on problem is unusual among the anthropologists of his generation.) Finally, our Rorschach analyst could hardly miss the definite "W," or holistic tendency, revealed in the masterful way in which highly diverse materials are synthesized and related to a larger context. The analogy—like all analogies—lacks precision, but it does serve to show that Hallowell's approach to anthropology defies easy characterization.

Still one more dimension of Hallowell's writings must be noted. Hallowell has demonstrated a high degree of self-awareness about his own work. This trait is reflected in his careful selection, editing, and arrangement of the papers in *Culture and Experience*. Taken as a whole, his corpus of published writings shows a logical sequence of ideas, a direction, and an awareness of general and specific relationships to correlative developments in anthropology and in other disciplines. Clearly Professor Hallowell would make his own best commentator. The present remarks stand only as temporary approximations to be modified and corrected if and when he himself decides to put his own house in order.

IV

Since Hallowell's most important contribution has been in the field of culture and personality, it would be remiss to end this introduction without a few comments about his work in this field. Although it has been widely acclaimed for its seminal quality, not everyone agrees with this evaluation. In his review of *Culture and Experience*, David Aberle (1956) is dubious about the ultimate importance of a psychological approach to anthropology. While praising the obviously solid craftsmanship and scholarly integrity displayed in these papers, Aberle regards Hallowell's efforts as symptomatic of a sterile and misguided development. Although only the action of time's winnowing basket upon Hallowell's ideas will settle this dispute, we would take strong issue with Aberle's suspicions. For us, such notions as, for example, "behavioral environment" (1957), "personal objects" (1958), and "transculturation"

(1963) are not to be regarded as chaff, but as germinal kernels that will spread deep and wide roots in the changing and enlarging field of anthropology. This conviction is best understood from the perspective of the intellectual context within which these notions were developed and in contrast to their conceptual alternatives.

As a corrective for the descriptivism and naïve empiricism that dominated the early decades of twentieth-century anthropology, two important theoretical approaches, each with its own conception of the problems with which anthropology ought to be concerned, took form: structural anthropology and culture-and-personality. Structural anthropology took its task to be the discovery of those principles by which society is organized and the analysis of the social functions which are consequent upon social action as it occurs within different types of social structures. Culture-and-personality was interested, rather, in the principles by which social action is structured and in the analysis of its culturally constituted cognitive, perceptual, and motivational determinants.

Clearly, the problems posed by both approaches were important for scientific progress in anthropology. It was only natural, however, since each was concerned with explaining different things, that they develop different theories. While culture-and-personality was primarily concerned with explaining social action, structural anthropology was content to take it for granted. To the extent that the latter approach was concerned with behavior at all, it aimed not to explain it—behavior, for structural anthropology, was a given—but rather to analyze its consequences (its social functions) for the maintenance of social structure. If not antipsychological, structural anthropology was indifferent to psychological variables—an attitude entirely consistent, it should be noted, with its self-imposed explanatory tasks. It was only when its more polemical proponents argued—or, at least, appeared to argue—that the social functions (consequences) of behavior were the determinants (causes) of behavior, that its *theoretical indifference* to psychology became an *ideological bias*.

Relatively indifferent to the problems of social structure, and primarily interested in explaining social action, culture-and-personality was necessarily concerned with psychological variables. Seeking those determinants which might constitute the set of necessary and sufficient conditions for behavior, culture-and-personality was concerned with, among others, three psychological variables: cognition, perception, and motivation. It assumed, that is, that an explanation for social action requires, as a *minimum* set of conditions, answers to the following three questions: What do the actors *know* about the world? How do they *perceive* the world? What do they *want* from the world? If the anthropologist can answer these questions—and the answers, so it was assumed, were to be found in culturally constituted experience—he might be able to explain both stability and change in social behavior.

Although this field was not confined to Hallowell, it was he who persistently and systematically emphasized this essentially phenomenological approach to the problems of culture-and-personality. Importantly influenced by stimulus-response, and especially by learning psychology, he nevertheless emphasized, even in his earliest writings, that behavior cannot be adequately explained by attending merely to its objective context. Behavior, he insisted—and he was able to demonstrate this in a series of brilliant papers (1938a, 1939a, 1940a, 1941a, 1942c, etc.) dealing with the Saulteaux—is responsive not to stimuli but to their meanings. Whether the stimuli be external (animals, kinsmen, shamans, food, or thunder) or internal (drives of various kinds), it is their meaning for an actor, rather than their objective properties, which governs his response. For Hallowell, then, an actor does not know or perceive *the* world, he knows and perceives *his* world—a world which is mediated, not merely through receptors, but through culturally constituted symbols. For Hallowell the "culturally constituted behavioral environment" is no empty phrase.

But Hallowell has been concerned with the internal, as well as with the external, world. For him the "self" does not respond to external stimulation alone. It also responds to, and is constituted of, the inner stimulation of needs and drives, fears and conflicts, wishes and fantasies. Influenced by psychoanalytic theory, Hallowell sees meaning, not chaos, in this inner world which, like the external world, is mediated through complex symbol systems, both private and public. Going beyond the more conventional analyses, he has shown —using cross-cultural materials—how the latter symbolic systems produce a self which is "culturally constituted" (1954a). The "symbolic transformation of experience" is, for him, not merely a fashionable concept, but a tool by which he illuminates large segments of Saulteaux personality. With these same notions he has been able to show how the self, as a dynamic agent, acts upon the external world, to change as well as to maintain it. Here, his pioneering (an overused word, but how can one avoid it?) work in acculturation has demonstrated the crucial importance of personality variables for the understanding of cultural dynamics (1942a, 1945a, 1950b, 1951b, etc.).

Hallowell (1955, Chapter 8) has expressed these notions in succinct form.

> A human level of existence not only necessitates a unique biological structure and a sociocultural mode of life, it necessitates a peculiar and distinctive kind of psychological structuralization, characterized by a level of personal adjustment and experience in which a unique and complex integration occurs between responses to an "outer" world of objects and events and responses to an "inner" world of impulse, fantasy, and creative imagination. Besides this, a human existence is one in which potentialities for readjustment, reorientation, change, are constantly present.

In sum, while other scholars with different interests may choose to ignore this approach to anthropology, we believe that it represents an important attempt to cope with some of its central and perennial problems. To characterize this approach as peripheral, while understandable, perhaps, in the past, is a mark of inexcusable provincialism today. Largely through Hallowell's own contributions, this "psychological" approach has entered into, and has become assimilated by, the mainstream of contemporary anthropology. Just as a previous generation of personality students had to learn that an understanding of impulse, fantasy, and imagination requires reference to sociocultural variables, contemporary anthropologists have learned that kinship behavior, or religious beliefs, or social functions cannot be fully understood without reference to personality variables.

If it has not effected a fusion of structural and psychological anthropology, Hallowell's work has certainly contributed to an ending of the fission. His concern with context, meaning, and culture—the key terms in the title of this volume—do not exhaust the contents of the anthropological tool kit, but they are certainly among its most important components. The contributors to this volume, sharing this conviction, have attempted to explore different facets of these concepts to whose understanding Hallowell has contributed so importantly.

References

Aberle, D. F.

1956: Review of A. I. Hallowell, *Culture and Experience*, in *American Anthropologist*, **58**, 920 923.

Part One

Ethnology and Social Organization

FREDERICA DE LAGUNA

Childhood among the Yakutat Tlingit

The Indians of Yakutat Bay, who live on the Gulf of Alaska in an area richly endowed by nature, are the most northwesterly of the Coastal Tlingit. Until the early or mid-eighteenth century, the inhabitants of this region were Eyak-speakers, like their relatives to the west at the mouth of the Copper River. Although they are now Tlingit, largely as a result of immigrations from the Chilkat, Sitka, and Hoonah of southeastern Alaska, and have been Tlingit for some two hundred years, the Yakutat population also includes important increments from the Atna of the middle Copper River to the west and from the Southern Tutchone of the Alsek River-Dry Bay area to the east. Yakutat culture, when compared with "classic" southeastern Alaskan Tlingit culture, has, therefore, a distinctive stamp, reflecting not only some local traits peculiar to its geographical position on the Gulf Coast, but also those that show the effects of close ties to the Athabaskans of the hinterland, as well as influences from the Chugach Eskimo of Prince William Sound just beyond the Copper River delta.

In 1949, 1952, and 1954, I carried out ethnological work at Yakutat, accompanied and assisted by students (Edward Malin in 1949, Mary Jane Lenz in 1954) and with the collaboration of Catharine McClellan in 1952.[1] While the general aim of the study was historical and comparative, in that the ultimate objective of this and other related field researches was to trace the development of northern Tlingit cultural patterns within the context of northwestern Indian cultures, and while archaeological and historical materials were also obtained and studied, the Yakutat ethnographic data were gathered without restriction to any specific range of problems. Rather, an attempt was made to cover as much of the culture as possible and to record the information in the informants' own words. This last was possible since almost all spoke English, while our own growing familiarity with Tlingit vocabulary gradually permitted fuller use of native expressions. The material recorded in this fashion relates largely to the world as remembered from childhood, that is, from the mid-1880's and 1890's up to 1910. Our aim was to see and to present Yakutat culture as the people themselves saw it: as the universe into which each one was born and as the way of life through which each one became himself and strove to fulfill himself.

Dr. Hallowell has shown us the rewarding insights to be gained by viewing the culturally patterned world of any people as their "behavioral environment" or *lebensraum*, and equally by asking what it is to be a "person" in such a world and by tracing the individual's experiences from childhood to full adulthood and even to the grave and beyond (Hallowell: 1955; esp. pp. 75–110, 172–182). Although we made no particular efforts to gather data on Yakutat child-rearing, it was interesting to see how much material on this aspect of the life cycle had actually been obtained. This was assembled and written up before I had read Olson's "Channeling of Character in Tlingit Society" (1956), with which it presents interesting parallels and contrasts. Neither of us, I believe, actually observed old-fashioned Tlingit methods of child-rearing, but relied upon the personal reminiscences of a few good informants. This means that differences in the pictures we present will reflect not only those due to tribal (local) differences and to our personal biases as ethnographers, but also to the personalities of our particular informants. It is to these problems that I will eventually return.

At present we may consider the more general questions: *What is it to be a Tlingit child?* To what extent is *childhood* recognized by the Tlingit? In what ways and to what degree are Tlingit children *persons* (incomplete persons, or super-persons)? To what extent are they expected to share the same values, attitudes, and responsibilities as adults? How are these inculcated? By "preachings," by threats, by actual punishments, by rewards? Furthermore, while it is fashionable

1. This work was sponsored and supported by the Wenner-Gren Foundation for Anthropological Research, the Social Science Research Council, the Arctic Institute of North America (with funds from the Office of Naval Research), and the American Philosophical Society, to all of whom I acknowledge my gratitude.

to focus on infant frustrations and gratifications, and on childhood discipline, in order to see how personality is determined, we might well ask what is the actual *content* of what is learned by the growing child? What are the useful skills acquired through games or serious tasks? What knowledge or lore is needed for a person to be at home in the world of men and of "other-than-human persons"? What aesthetic and intellectual outlets make possible the more richly endowed person and the fuller life? And lastly, although we shall certainly not attempt to suggest an answer here, yet because we are anthropologists and archaeology is the ethnology of the past, we should ask: What archaeological evidence is there of childhood? We may keep all these questions in mind, even though we may not find satisfactory answers to any of them in our present data.

For the Tlingit there is no beginning and no end to the life cycle of the individual, since every baby born is the reincarnation of some maternal relative who has died, and each person nearing death is consoled by the prospect of a future incarnation, while his clan and lineage relatives anticipate his rebirth to them again as a baby, and indeed usually perform the magico-religious rites to ensure the return of the departing "soul" (de Laguna: 1954). Babies are welcomed, girls perhaps more than boys, since girls "always raise more kids to increase the family [matrilineal line]," even though the boy will be able to "take care of the family." In former days, only the bastard was unwanted and had a status close to that of a slave; now the fatherless child is a beloved member of the family.

While we regard the newborn child as a completely new person, a "little stranger" who has come to the family, even though we may search his features to discover resemblances to his relatives, for the Tlingit the baby is both more and less of a person. The resemblance to a dead ancestor, the mother's dream, the dying relative's announcement of his intended return, or some other sign, will indicate who the baby really is; the name which he receives confirms and establishes this identity. Many babies are said to recognize the relatives they knew in their former lives, perhaps refusing at first from shyness to suck at their new mother's breast because she is really a sister or a niece. When older, the child may be able to relate details of his former life and manner of death. He is expected to be something like his former incarnation in character and abilities—how far the identity is stressed I do not know, except that very small children used to be given certain foods, or even pipes to smoke, because they had been so fond of them before.

The newborn baby was put into a carrier or pouch, made from a large basket cut in half, covered with skin and lined with soft moss. The rim of the carrier was strengthened by a wythe, "so when they pick it up, it don't get out of shape." This had to be put on neatly, the ends meeting "just right," otherwise, "that cause the baby to stutter." Down the middle of the back was a thin board, "to keep the body of the baby straight, so it won't get disfigured." Over the entire carrier was a skin cover that laced down the front, within which the baby was rigidly confined, leaving only the head free. "It keeps them straight so they don't get broken bones. The body don't get out of shape, and there's also something to keep their ears flat to their head . . . some sort of cap." For the first ten days, the child was kept in the dark, to prevent sore eyes. This was done by putting a basketlike frame, covered with skin (or cloth) over the head, and this protection was removed only when feeding or cleaning the baby. At the end of this period, the mother and child returned from the special birth hut to the regular house.

The moss used as diapers was said to have been changed three times a day, and the mother was careful of its disposal, since if any worm or rat got into it, this might endanger the life of her child. (I suspect she was also fearful that it might be used by witches.) It was apparently carried back into the woods, put under a stump (the symbol of longevity), and burned.

During infancy the baby was never separated from the mother, except when fondled by other loving relatives in the great multifamily house. At night, the baby slept in its carrier under the mother's blanket. "First thing in the morning, you take the baby out before breakfast. Change the baby. About the time you're having breakfast, the baby sleeps. They never let the kids cry. They living so many together at that time; the whole place disturbed when the baby cried." During the day, while the mother worked, the baby carrier might be propped up against a box beside her, but it was more customary to put it into a little hammock or swing, made from a blanket or robe. Later, the child, without the carrier, would sleep in the hammock. "After they feed the babies, they put them in the swing and have a string tied to it and swing them. Then they go to sleep, and the women make baskets." If the baby cries, the mother can tug on the string to rock the hammock. "No trouble for mother. . . . Oh, it's cute! You pull it just once and it rocks itself." Or, if the mother goes outdoors, perhaps to pick berries, she carries the child on her back, the carrier held securely in a fold of the blanket drawn over her shoulders. The baby faced somewhat to the side and to the rear, so that he would not be scratched by bushes. "You can look back [over your shoulder] and see if the baby is all right. And then the father always looks, too. Sometimes the father is carrying the baby."

Grandparents, other adults, and even older children used to carry babies in this fashion, or rocked them to sleep in their arms, hissing "*Ṡ, ṡ, ṡ*," or crooning "*Awwwɛ́*—Love."

The first carrier was used for about three or four months; then a larger one was made in which the child was kept until he was big enough to learn to walk. In the second carrier, the baby began to enjoy more freedom of movement. "First exercise when the baby is about four months old. Take his little hands out.

Then he start to play. . . . Then they make him exercise." But the baby's arms were apparently tucked in again at night.

The baby was given the breast whenever hungry or frightened or even when he was likely to cry. Sometimes he was given a bit of fat to suck, or other food, such as berries that had been crushed in someone's mouth, especially if the baby's spirit was supposed to have enjoyed such fruit in his previous incarnation. A baby was fed "all the time. When it's old enough and the next one coming, they have to wean them. They put something bitter on their breast . . . native pepper." This was a powder made from a plant called "medicine that stinks." It does not hurt the mother. The child was also warned that he would burn his mouth, "and he won't have any more tongue left."

Weaning marked the end of infancy, and from accounts given of small children who tried to suck when their mothers were asleep, or who struggled to push the new baby aside, we may infer that weaning was frustrating and likely to produce sibling rivalry. It was perhaps these experiences that formed the foundation for the sometimes deadly rivalries between brothers, between sisters, or between lineage-mates, leading to accusations of witchcraft, since black magic was believed to be almost always practiced against an envied sibling or fellow-clansman (de Laguna: 1953).

The baby received not only practical care and love, but magical exercises (*hex̣ʷa*) were also performed on his behalf. Thus, if the newborn boy were sickly, the afterbirth might be wrapped up to look like a person, and the baby's hands manipulated to knock it down, while one exclaimed how husky he was. While this was undoubtedly a magical wish, no set formula was required. A model bow and arrow or a miniature gun, made by the boy's father and fastened to his carrier, was supposed also to influence his development.

Most magical treatment of a little boy was intended to make him a good hunter. Thus, the tendon from the hind leg of a wolf might be tied around his ankle so he would be swift when chasing bears and mountain goats. Or a tiny splinter of wolf bone might be broken over his forehead, or his hammock might be made of wolf skin. The slime from a bear's mouth rubbed on a boy would make him brave.

The umbilical cord was dried and sewed into a little flat, round bag, at first fastened to the baby's carrier, later worn around the child's neck, until he or she "is old enough to learn." A restless, mischievous little child was said to have lost this amulet and to be looking for it. The cord was finally disposed of in such a way as would benefit the child in later life. That of a boy might be put into an animal's hole, so that when he was grown he would not be afraid to pursue bears into their dens. Or it might be laid on a game trail, while one uttered the magic wish: "Luck! Let him become a hunter!" The umbilical cord of a girl could be stitched into something her mother was sewing or woven into a basket to make the child skillful. The nail parings of a baby girl might be similarly disposed of, or those of either sex be bound into a paintbrush so that the child might acquire artistic gifts. Most magical rites for a girl were not performed, however, until her first menstruation.

There was also magic for crying babies. A tuft of "Alaska cotton" was wiped around the child's lips for four successive days, then tied up with roots (probably of some magical plant), and buried in the ground. "Or else you put it under your pillow. When you sleep on it, that baby's gonna sleep, too."

When the new baby came, the mother was obviously occupied with him, and care of the small child who had been weaned fell largely upon the grandmother, although the grandfather, paternal cousins and aunts, older siblings, and any other member of the large household also helped. Small children might continue to sleep in the same cubicle as the parents, but a little girl usually slept with her grandmother, and a small boy with his older brother.

Grandparents were and are especially beloved by children. "The grandchild loves the grandmother more than his own mother and father because the grandmother is always there," we were told. "We love our grandchildren better than our own children." This warm relationship is taken for granted as natural.

We secured practically no information about toilet training, probably because this was not a matter of much concern. If a child wet his bed, there was apparently no punishment; instead, various magical remedies were tried. Fine moss was put under him for four nights and then taken back into the woods. If this cure was not effective, the same procedure was employed with the soft shreds of spruce cones left by the squirrels. If even these remedies failed, the child was given to eat "that stringy stuff that grows inside the crab shell." One swallow of this was supposed to be enough, but "if it don't help, eat some more." However, judging by "pet songs" in which the beloved child is called "stinker" or "stinking," we judge that, when small children dirtied themselves, no fuss was made, since this was treated as a condition natural to their age. On the other hand, much more concern was felt for the safety of the child who went out at night to urinate, because of the dangers from kidnapping Land Otter Men or lurking witches. Thus, a watertight basket was kept just inside the door as a chamber pot, and very small children were not allowed outside at night, while their older siblings were cautioned not to go too far. Small boys apparently went just around the corner of the house.

Little children were treated with much indulgence and affection. They could go into any house in which they had a relative and be sure of a welcome. Our informants remember only a few persons in the village of whom they were afraid when they were small, and these were described as ugly old people, feared perhaps because they were comparative strangers or queer and cantankerous. Children were fed whenever they were hungry, to judge from reminiscences, and even today regular mealtimes would not be imposed on

Tlingit children if it were not for school hours. Similarly, while the household usually went to sleep early and rose at dawn, children were not put to bed at regular times when exciting events were taking place. They were expected only to keep quiet and not to interfere.

Children were given as valuable presents as their parents could afford. Today, children are given money to buy candy or soft drinks whenever they ask for it, without a thought that too many sweets may be harmful. It was almost impossible for a grandparent to deny anything to a grandchild. Thus, the myth that tells how Raven obtained the precious stars, moon, and daylight from his "grandfather," simply by crying for them, reflects current Tlingit attitudes and is cited as "explaining" such obvious features of the established order of human relations. Paternal uncles and aunts were also especially generous toward their brother's children.

Children took part in many adult activities, such as potlatches, where they danced in costume, gave and received gifts, and were honored with "big names," formally bestowed. In former times on such occasions, children had their ears pierced and nasal septum perforated by members of the opposite moiety. (The girl's labret hole was made when she emerged from her puberty seclusion.) The splendor of the ceremony and the amount of property given for these services reflected the wealth of the child's sponsors (parents, maternal uncle, or paternal grandfather) and thus naturally taught him his own place in society.

Although our information on aboriginal clothing is scanty, it would appear that children were dressed like adults. Little girls of well-to-do families wore heavy ornaments, made of beads and dentalia, attached to their hair in back. The swinging of these ornaments was supposed to resemble the motion of bushes and young trees in the wind, symbolic of growth, and so promote the growth of the child. Such ornaments might be assumed as early as the age of four or five, be put aside at puberty, and worn again until marriage.

Only a few restrictions were imposed on very small children, and it is hard to tell how severely they were disciplined in former days. On the whole, Tlingit children are far quieter and less mischievous or demanding than white American children of the same ages, even though we recognize great individual differences. "Nowadays people realize children should be active. In the old days they wanted the child to be quiet." When a child cried, the reaction was "Feed them! They find out if they're hungry, or something wrong or not." "They train them so they wouldn't cry for anything they wanted. . . . Gave them a good shaking up, if they know enough [i.e., were old enough to understand]." But things which the children were not supposed to touch were usually secured in boxes, set high above their heads.

Little children had, of course, to learn to avoid such dangerous things as the fire that burned in the middle of the house, hot objects, sharp knives, the swift running river, and the terrible things lurking in the woods. Dangerous things were pointed out to small children. " '*X! X! X!*' we talk to baby to scare them. 'Don't touch! It burns!' That's baby talk. . . . We call it '*Xox!*' when we try to scare the children." We do not know just how children were taught to avoid dangerous places, but one father in the 1880's built a fence along the river bank and made a pond where his children could play safely with their canoe. Stories of Land Otter Men that kidnap people who fall in the water or are lost in the woods, as well as the real fear evinced by adults of such beings, must have prevented all but the most adventurous children from wandering off. In addition, children were taught what words to say to a bear or what protective magic to use against Land Otter Men in case they should encounter such fearsome creatures.

It is difficult to estimate how much physical punishment was given in the old days, although there is no doubt that children feared it. One woman, born in 1900, said that there was "spanking in my days," but that she had never heard of it in former times. Older women, however, spoke of it. Thus, when we asked a woman born in 1884 if children used to be spanked, she exclaimed, "You bet! You get a spanking if you do something wrong. You can't let your child do wrong things. They believe in that a long time ago." Another punishment that she mentioned was to "keep them inside and don't let them out and play until they get over it. . . . If children run around too much, they tie their feet up, trying to make them behave." The last was especially to train children to be quiet. Another woman, born in 1896, was asked what was done if a child said naughty words. "That happened to me. Chase me in the room, stay there. Sometimes they slap their mouth if they [are] using bad words. They don't want it. That's a lower-class people [who speak that way]; they don't have respect for big people. Oh, my mother used to be strict! But that's the way, if you want good kids."

The woman who doubted that naughty children were spanked, said that "They tied their feet together. My mother used to tell me that when people used to settle down by the open fire, that means they're going to tell a story, and the women would get the children and tie their feet together, and then everything would be quiet, so the men could tell the story." But this was more of a precaution than a punishment.

Another said, "I know that when you get fighting with your brother or sister, they tie you together and put water between you, so you won't fight any more. . . . The water was in a bucket. You face each other." The water bucket was evidently so balanced that the children would drench themselves if they did not quiet down.

"In the old days they used to cure spoiled boys and girls who did wrong by putting their heads in urine."

"I was afraid of a spanking and being put in a dark corner. The dark corner is a little room, no light, no window. I don't get that often."

"My mother spanked me," said one woman, "but my father spanked my brothers. . . . I'm not scared of my father—he never put his hand on me, but I'm scared of my older brother. He's quiet but he gets mad."

Children must often have escaped merited chastisement because it was taboo for the mother to punish them when her husband was out hunting (her aggressive acts might be imitated by ferocious bears or cause storms or avalanches), and, by the time the father returned, her anger would have cooled and he might well be too tired to bother with such domestic matters.

Although children anticipated spankings when they were naughty, these were more often threatened than actually administered, to judge from the numerous stories of childish escapades. One woman reported that when she was naughty, her mother reached out as if to scratch her face, "but it's just make-believe. I'm scared they tie me up to the pole and I get whipped." When asked if such whipping were customary, she said, "Yeh. They do that until they promise they won't do it any more. I never see it, but them days they mind their mother better than they do now. . . . They are just strict." She explained that you would fear a whipping "if you tell a lie, and your mother find it out. You got to mind your father, unless you get whipped to death, so I *did* tell the truth."

On another occasion, when the children had helped themselves to some mountain-goat tallow which had been saved for a special occasion, their angry mother told them: " 'Wait till daddy comes home! You're going to get a licking —no fooling!' . . . My father is out seal hunting, my mother can't lick us." However, this time not even the older boys who had been the leaders were punished. On several other occasions when one of the children had been naughty, they were all lined up and asked who had done it. Sometimes the culprit tried to lie, but again usually escaped with only a scolding.

The child's adult joking relatives were often effective disciplinarians, utilizing the same techniques of public ridicule or practical joking that they might employ toward another adult joking relative. The license of this joking must have afforded a welcome outlet for irritations produced by a troublesome child in the big multifamily household, especially since no one, including the victim, was supposed to take offense at the joke. Thus, when a spoiled little girl had made trouble between her father and mother so that their quarrels and her tantrums had disturbed the whole household, one old lady who was the child's joking relative set a basket of urine to boiling, grabbed up the child, and pretended she was going to put her head into the basket. The child was so frightened she stopped crying. Then another woman, the joking relative of them both, picked up the old woman and threatened her in the same way. In her fright, the child upset the boiling urine on the floor, and all the women hastened to snatch up the dishes and clear away the mess. But there seems to have been no ill-feeling in consequence, for the old woman later taught the little girl many useful things, and the latter served her first when her father gave a sugar feast to his relatives.

Joking relatives of the same age were sometimes held up as rivals with whom a child was encouraged to compete.

Another method of disciplining children was to let them suffer the consequences of what they had done, often supplemented by threats. When one woman as a little girl took her mother's sharp ulo without permission, and cut her finger, her paternal (?) aunts, to whom she appealed for help, at first refused to bandage the cut, telling her she would die. On two occasions when she was involved in escapades in which another child in the family was injured, her punishment was to wait upon the hurt child until the latter's recovery. This same woman's mother also seems to have been something of a tomboy when she was small. Once, despite the remonstrances of an older sister, she attempted to walk on a log across a deep pit which had been dug for a cache and fell in. The child could not climb out and began to run from side to side, wailing with fright. The other children notified her older brother, who only laughed. " 'Let her suffer a while,' he said. 'Learn a lesson.' " Her father, however, was afraid she might be caught by a cave-in and rescued her.

Other threats involved bogeymen, that is, creatures which the children were told would punish them. Thus, when our informant was a very little girl and had been naughty, she ran out of the house and refused to come in when it got dark. "Finally my uncle said, 'If you don't come in when I tell you, the Crow is going to *kits̓* you, and you'll drop dead!' I start to squeal, and stand there till he come and take me in. They even say they going to shoot me, but I don't come. But 'Crow is going to *kits̓* you!' was the only thing scared me. I don't even know what it means till recently." It evidently meant that Raven would see-saw with her.

Owls were also invoked to frighten children. "That's why I'm so scared of owls. When I start to cry, they say, 'Keep quiet! The owl will hear you and take you away!' " This informant was familiar with the story of the boy who was stolen by the owl and fed what he thought was delicious food, but what was in actuality ants and other insects that devoured his insides.[2] What makes the threat of owls so effective is that adults are also frightened when they hear the bird hooting, since this is a message of misfortune.

It is evident that myths were used as cautionary tales for children. Thus, the story of the KIKSADI girl who turned into an owl (Swanton: 1909, Tale 37) is used to point a moral. "That's why they always say, 'Never hurt your mother-in-law. You will become an owl.' Tlingit people always says that." Some "crazy girls" don't like their mothers-in-law, because the latter are always watching them. Therefore, girls are warned, and the story is said to be a true one.

And when the children ate their mother's mountain-goat tallow, "that's the time my mother said, 'You mustn't steal anything—take anything without

2. Swanton (1909, Tale 11) records the same story about a Land Otter Man that carried off a crybaby.

asking. See what happened to those girls.' " Then she told the story (Swanton: 1909, Tales 65 and 92) of the two sisters who stole their mother's mountain-goat tallow. The mother scratched out the insides of their mouths and drove them out to marry Mountain Man, and they became owls. "That's why people lick the stuffing out of kids when they do something wrong. . . . That's why my mother and them preached to me." Apropos of another tale: "My parents preached to me about it, so I won't cheat. . . . My grandparents preach to my mother about it."

Apparently there was real concern of being too severe with children. Thus, "My grandfather dared not bawl my mother out when she was scolding me. He loved her too much. But he would scratch his head and make a noise: '$H^{n}A$! $H^{n}A$!' [a complaining grunt]. He used to say to her: '*Xatchdaqet* [her name], you be old like me [some day]. You get some use for your kids, when I'm in the grave. They'll grow up healthy if you don't get after them.' His idea is that they get nervous and excited," if she were too severe, and also that they might turn against her. It is perhaps significant that in the myth about Mountain Man, the daughters who were punished for stealing tallow eventually secured revenge upon their mother.

It is interesting that fathers were often particularly indulgent to their daughters, as the quotation above suggests. One woman reported that her mother used to spank her with a stick or with her hand, but never when her father was present. Her father had told the mother not to punish her, because her older brothers and sisters had died and he wanted the little girl to be happy. (Does this suggest that an unhappy child is especially likely to die?) Another woman said, "My father wouldn't let my mother punish me. . . . He used to tell my mother, 'Don't be mean to my little daughter. She's just the image of my mother. I don't want to see that girl cry!' " The daughter recalls how spoiled she was as a child and how she used to play her father off against her mother. (One wonders whether such a spoiled child represents the Tlingit reflection of the institutionalized "favorite child" among the nearby Athabaskans.)

Although we unfortunately lack full personal reminiscences from now elderly men about their childhoods, the comments made by one about his first trip away from home, when he cried for his mother (see p. 18), suggest a strong emotional bond between mother and son, comparable to that between father and daughter. Today grown men speak of their mothers with greater warmth than of their fathers, even though it was their mother's brothers who became the strictest disciplinarians.

No adequate picture of childhood can be given without mentioning children's games and toys. Reminiscences of childhood include climbing rocks on the beach, going wading, swimming in ponds, paddling small canoes, picking flowers and berries, and so forth. Boys and girls used to make a hole in the sand, big enough to put their heads in, so they could hear the mysterious sounds, music, and whisperings made by the surf. Or they might divide into two teams, one on each side of the hole, and compete to see whether all their members could in turn cross the sand blindfolded without falling in.

Little girls played with dolls, sometimes those bought from traders but more often made by their mothers with a white rock for the head and rags for the body. Boys had puppies or dogs, and children of both sexes also had other animals for pets. These included bear cubs, which would be suckled by the child's mother until they grew so large that they would have to be killed. Then they might be stuffed. One woman recalls having a brown bear cub, a black bear cub, a squirrel, an ermine, and a baby seal, all stuffed. Children caught humming birds with sticky stuff and played with them on the end of a string.

A great deal of children's play imitated the activities of adults. Thus, girls might play house, the "mother" shutting her "adolescent daughter" away in a special puberty hut; or older children might indulge in sexual games, "just play man and wife—nothing wrong." More serious sexual experimentation was, however, forbidden.

Children began to learn practical skills through games and also through imitating their elders. There seems to have been a great deal of individual variation in the amount of formal instruction given. Thus one woman recalled, "I go with my mother all the time. She showed me how to weave baskets. She gave me one [already started?], and showed me. . . . I do one row; she does the next; I do the next. That's why I learn so quick." At the same time, her mother warned her that husband after husband would divorce her if she were lazy. Another woman, however, said, "As the only girl, I had to learn to do all kinds of things. My mother didn't want to teach me, but I watched and learned." This was the child who took her mother's ulo without permission and cut her finger, because she was so anxious to learn how to slice seal fat. Another recalled how eager she was to learn how to cut fish for smoking and how she nearly wept over those she spoiled.

Little girls learned how to cook, not only from helping their mothers, but also because they were given toy pots and dishes to use. They also had toy lamps which would really burn oil and were cautioned to be careful of fire. Little boys were given small bows and arrows with blunt heads to play with and thus learned to shoot. Yet wantonly to kill small animals or birds in their play was taboo, and they had to pray to the animals' "souls" and to the "Spirit Above" for forgiveness or risk the unknown horrors of "Dog Heaven" after death. Little boys and girls also fished with gaffs or with hook and line, and they might have small canoes which they learned to paddle.

It should not be supposed that small boys did not learn many of the arts normally carried on by women. Thus, boys were also taught to cook. In Yakutat today, there are a number of little boys who are just as reliable and competent in caring for small siblings, cooking and washing dishes, and in performing other domestic tasks, as are little girls. Usually it is the oldest child in a well-managed household who can do such things.

In former times, children learned a great deal by listening to the older people talk, especially when the old men gathered in the sweathouse to bathe and chat. Then the children might sit outside and listen to their stories. It may have been characteristic that when one woman was telling us about a monstrous birth, she interrupted her narrative to admonish her ten-year-old granddaughter, who was sitting at the table with us, not to "listen so hard." This was obviously a device for ensuring attention.

Moral education was stressed and children were instructed by lectures and by the recitation of proverbs and stories. In these, correct behavior was explained or illustrated, and the benefits were pointed out, just as the consequences of improper conduct were made explicit. The heroes of mythology, as well as real persons, were held up as models for emulation. What made such moral instruction so effective was that it was undertaken by the house chief or by some other old, wise person and was addressed to all members of the household, not simply to the children alone.

"As soon as a grandchild could talk, the chief tells him what is right and what is wrong. Each person has a power or spirit above you to punish you if you do wrong—same thing as God, only we didn't know about only one god then—so people won't lie and steal." Bad people go to "Dog Heaven," and these include witches. In fact, "Indian doctor says it's people who lie and steal who are witches." So are those who commit incest within the moiety, sib, or close family.

On the other hand, "kindness," that is, gentle speech and manners, was stressed. "Be kind to people. Don't run away with the idea you're above other people. Be as low as you can. . . . Don't brag about yourself. . . . Be kind to your own people and don't insult and bawl them out. Do what you can to help. That's the way to get along with your own people." These moral admonitions are typical examples. "Kindness" and generosity to the poor, to slaves, and to anyone less fortunate marked the true aristocrat. Such kindness was also extended to small animals and wounded creatures. Stories report the miraculous good fortune won by those who befriended a wise slave or injured animal and the disasters that followed the torture of a little bird. Yet, these principles did not prevent the sacrifice of slaves at a potlatch, playing with humming birds, or the use of cruel harpoons in hunting, although there is evidence that some of these practices aroused ambivalent feelings.

Wisdom, sound judgment, industry, and courage were all stressed. The good man or woman was wise, brave, and resourceful and acquired wealth. Frugality was also a virtue. "I hear my grandmother and grandfather talking about it—preaching to my mother about that. 'Don't be careless with grub!' " The story of Salmon Boy (Swanton, 1909: Tales 99 and 100) served as a reminder for those who treated food with disrespect. A true story of starvation was cited as an example of improvidence. "That's why grandmother preached to us. 'Don't say *Iiiiii!* to anything. Eat what you can get!' " Children were also warned not to be greedy. Indeed, the chief of the house and his wife were supposed to set the example of eating very little, first serving the young men who had been out all day hunting or engaged in heavy work before they put anything into their own dishes.

Laziness was equated with poverty, worthlessness, and being pitiful. It was conceived almost as a living thing that sat on the left shoulder of the slothful child, who would turn away his head to the left, "asking his Lazy," when told to hurry on some errand. It also lurked in his pockets or under his armpits, ready to suck his hands and thus condemn him to poverty if he stood around idly, warming his fingers, or slept too late when he should be fetching wood or water. Boys in particular were warned not to loaf and especially not to sit on rocks, for this would make them heavy and slow as hunters. Even when resting, they were to "sit ready to get up all the time," or an old man would switch them on the shins.

The higher the rank of the child, the higher the standards to which he had to conform. The children, grandchildren, and maternal nephews of the sib chief received a more thorough formal education than did ordinary young people. A large part of this was carried out by the stories told at night by the chief or by a wise man "next to him."

"Just like school in those days. People go to school to learn. So everybody listen to them, every night. But when the chief, when he's training his grandchild on his tribe's side [i.e., his son's son in his own sib and his potential successor], when a boy getting smart between 10 and 16 years old [then the chief would ask him]: 'Now you tell me a story about what I been telling you.' . . . So the boy start to tell the story to the grandfather, to the chief. If any place that boy make a mistake, the chief correct him. That's the way they training the grandchild, because it's gonna be the next chief to him. Till it's all correct, the story he tell. Then he begin to tell another story. He want his grandchild to memorize the whole thing. Not only Tlingit stories—Tsimshian, Haida, Aleut stories, and *Tasna-qwan*—that's Eskimo stories. . . . And *T̓oyat* stories—that's Flathead Indians of Washington—their stories. And all the Interior Indians. A person has to learn all the stories before he become to a chief, a tribe leader. No matter how rich he is, a person can't be a chief if he don't know all the stories from the different tribes, unless he knows all the stories from all the tribes in Alaska." He could, however, become a house chief. It is hardly necessary to emphasize that children had to learn all the traditions and ceremonial prerogatives of their own sib, as well as much that pertained to their father's sib, or to others of their relatives.

This same type of training was given to all the children in the house, but was of a less comprehensive nature for those of lesser rank. It continued well past puberty.

"In the evening the chief talks to all the people in the house. He watches the young men to see who is smart. It's like high school or college. Everyone graduates, but there are some stupid ones and some that are smarter than others. The chief notices who is not listening. He notices who is smart. The smart one—the chief sends him away, traveling all over—to southeast Alaska, or to Cordova [among the Eyak]—to learn the stories and songs of other tribes. Then at potlatches, he tries to catch out the other side [by exhibiting greater erudition in ceremonial traditions]. Even if he's not a chief's son, he may become a chief." Thus, promising youngsters were sent away at about the age of 10 to live with foreign chiefs, learning their language, history, stories, songs, and traditions, "just like getting a college education," and the returned youths would become interpreters for the chief, and eventually some of his advisers at councils or ceremonies. From among the group of eligible maternal nephews and paternal grandsons thus trained, the chief would choose as successor the boy who showed himself best-fitted through education, wisdom, sound judgment, and moral virtues.

Other accomplishments which brought respect and which were especially appropriate for aristocrats were skill in hunting, ability to forecast the weather, artistic ability in carving and painting for men, in sewing and weaving for women, and in song composition and dancing for either sex. Children early began to look forward to the time when they could demonstrate these admired traits. Although Yakutat children were certainly not encouraged to brag or show off, as are the children of white Americans, their skills and accomplishments were praised by their elders, and there was always a big audience in the old-fashioned house to applaud the deserving child.

A number of food taboos had to be observed by children, and these seem to have lasted until the girl married or until the boy became a recognized hunter. In the case of the girl, such taboos were intensified at puberty. They included drinking broth made from any meat except that killed by the young hunter himself, or by the woman's husband. Fish skins, marrow, seagull eggs, intestines, bear paws, and so on, were all forbidden. Nor were little girls supposed to drink much water. The penalties were risking heart trouble, getting cold, being sluggish and unlucky hunters, or having chapped hands, losing wealth by "washing it away," or failing to secure a good husband. One informant reported that "We used to say, 'Things the old people want to eat, they don't want the kids to eat.' " Yet many things which we would regard as bad for children were not denied them. Thus, they might be given a taste of whisky, or might eat the liquor-soaked dough used to plug the cracks in a still; some children regularly chewed snuff or smoked a pipe. Indeed, at smoking feasts for the dead, all, even small children, were supposed to participate.

While the magical preparation of the boy for his future life as a hunter was initiated at birth, active training for this role began when he was only six or seven, when he was supposed to leave the house of his parents and live with his mother's brother, that close relative in his own sib whose property he shared, whose titles, wealth, and perhaps wife he was to inherit, and who now became his mentor and disciplinarian. What is most clearly remembered by all our informants is the way in which the small boys were made to take icy baths in order to harden themselves. It was the duty of the uncle to make his nephews plunge in the water early in the morning, "icy water—so they can be strong. If they stay with their mother, they [will be] weak, and they [will be] poor. . . . They sure respect what their uncle says and what their [older] brother says." It is clear from personal reminiscences, however, that not only was this hardening process initiated by the parents (often by the mother), but that many boys stayed at home until marriage, although the uncle seems to have lived next door or near enough to fulfill his functions. It was also his duty to beat the boys with alder switches when they came from their baths and to see that they had nourishing seal fat to eat.

The cutting of firewood was a daily chore for older boys and young men, one preferably performed at that magically optimum hour "before the Raven calls at dawn." A youth seeking good fortune would make a point of going out naked before daybreak to chop wood for his uncles, grandfathers, and later for his father-in-law. He would also bathe and scrub his body in icy water before he came in to eat. Such hardening exercises in the cold dawn not only strengthened the body, conditioned it to endure cold, and supposedly rendered it immune to consumption, but were also purifying and virtuous, and hence were rewarded by good fortune. These exercises were not discontinued with adulthood, but were rather made more severe as the youth became older and stronger, and were considered a necessary preparation for any dangerous or uncertain activity, such as a long hunting trip or war party, the handling of magic herbs or amulets, or even as preparation for a potlatch.

Uncles also helped to teach their small nephews how to hunt and took them on their first hunting trips when they were very small. As one man remembered: "I was lonesome that time. I was little boy. I think of my mother. . . . Sometimes I cry—I think of my mother. Pretty hard staying with my uncle—talking, talking! 'Don't sleep too long! Wake up early in the morning!' Every morning I heard no raven [i.e., they rose before dawn]. It's pretty dark, dark two mornings. 'Make the fire! Make the fire!' my uncle told me. 'Cook some coffee!' " Most of what the boy learned on this sea-otter hunting trip, we gather, was how to handle a canoe, make camp and cook, and what magical rules to follow. This was evidently before he was ten years old. Later, he would be taken hunting by his father, older brothers, or brothers-in-law, but a youth would not go out alone until he was recognized as a skilled hunter, canoeman, and woodsman.

There was no event in a boy's life comparable to the first menstruation of his sister. Yet in former times, his first success as a hunter was a matter for rejoicing by his family and meant an enhancement of his personal status. When a boy killed his first game he was called "master of animals." He was forbidden to eat any of this kill, lest the head of the slain animal bite him in the face. His father would divide up and distribute the game, but whether this was simply given away or cooked for a feast, and who were the recipients, we did not learn. In any case, the act of sharing was supposed to make him lucky the next time he went hunting. The food taboos which had been imposed on him as a child were now lifted with respect to the specific animals which he might hereafter kill.

As children grew older, the brothers and sisters, including the parallel cousins and other members of the sib and moiety considered as siblings, began to be shy of each other, although the rules against looking at or speaking to a sibling of the opposite sex were not strictly enforced until puberty.

By this time, too, children had already acquired a good notion of the ramifications of the kinship system and of the importance of sib and moiety. Thus, they realized that if a playmate were hurt when children of different sibs were together, the affair was likely to be treated very seriously by their elders, for it might necessitate the payment of damages. In such cases, no matter how the injury had been incurred, it would be the children of the opposite moiety who would be held responsible, and their kin would have to pay the maternal relatives of the injured child. Children who found themselves in such scrapes would, if they were wise, keep quiet about the circumstances to protect each other from parental and avuncular wrath.

Older children were well versed in the traditions of their own sib and gave it their allegiance. Although they identified themselves with it, they still proudly boasted of being the "children" of their father's sib. They also knew a good deal about shamanism and witchcraft. In the old days they had probably seen a witch tied up to force a confession and had certainly been present at shamanistic seances and curing ceremonies. Our oldest informants had seen slaves freed at potlatches, and their parents had even seen slaves killed. All had witnessed and taken part in funerals (the laying-out of the corpse, the cremation, and later the inhumation). On the whole, they must have been a great deal more sophisticated than white American children of comparable age, although girls were still supposed to be completely ignorant about intercourse and how babies came. Even our informant, who as a child had crept near a birth hut to listen to the moans of a woman in labor, did not know until after her own marriage that mothers did not find babies on the beach!

Almost the most important event in a woman's life was her first menstruation, for her conduct during her long puberty confinement was supposed to influence not only her own future life for good or ill but also the fortunes of her relatives and of her future husband. For this reason she was surrounded by taboos and enjoined to perform many magical acts. Many of these were to be repeated when she became a widow, and a somewhat similar pattern was followed by anyone taken as a Peace Hostage, for such a man "then became a woman." The restrictions on the girl were not really lifted until she married.

Mothers watched their little daughters carefully from the time they were twelve years old, anticipating the first fateful stains. The little girls had been warned what to expect and that they should promptly report it. They were also aware of the confinement and restrictions they would have to suffer, because they knew what had happened to their older playmates and had perhaps been naughty enough to visit them in their place of seclusion, a dark room in the house. Already when our oldest informants came of age, puberty observances were being modified or omitted because of pressure from the missionaries and from younger, more acculturated members of the tribe. Although it was the ideal to keep girls, especially of rank, shut up for a whole year or even two, none of our informants was confined for more than three or four months.

It is impossible to enumerate all the restrictions, but it may be sufficient to report that the first eight days (symbolizing the "eight bones" of the body) were the most severe. During this time the girl was in theory supervised by her father's sister, that close relative in the opposite moiety whose responsibility it was to render ritual services at all life crises, although in actuality her mother or grandmother usually cared for her. During this period she thirsted and fasted, sitting as immobile as possible, her fingers laced together with string, "so money wouldn't slip through her fingers." At the end of the first two days, water was offered her, but if she reached for it, the basket-cup was spilled. Later she would be given water "in a little basket, the size of your thumb," because to drink much would mean that all luck and wealth would be washed away. Her fast was broken at the end of the fourth day and again at the end of the eighth. Then the utensils used were buried under an old stump.

When the girl broke her fast, all the preserved things in the house were shared around the village in a special feast. This evidently corresponded to the sharing of the first game killed by the young hunter. The girl's dolls were all given to her paternal cross-cousins.

The girl also performed magical exercises during the first eight days. She rubbed a hard stone around her lips and face eight times, and this, too, was buried under a stump. "This makes your tongue and face heavy, so you can't gossip. . . . You can't turn your face around to do bad things." She wore a cap of black loonskin, so her hair would never turn gray. She jerked at evergreen boughs above her head, wishing that riches would shower on her as the needles fell, just as a youth would make a similar wish when snow fell on him when he was chopping wood. She urinated and defecated on rotten wood which was later buried under a stump, so that she would not dirty herself or her bed when she grew old.

After the ordeal of thirsting or the shame of having the longed-for water dashed down, what our informants remember best were the long dreary months that followed. "They had a tent over my bed. Shut me in so I couldn't see daylight. [The baleful glance of a menstruant would bring storms.] It was cruel. My mother slept in that room. . . . Girls of my age were running around and playing, making noise with tin can, and I had to stay shut up under that tent!"

It was during this period that the girl was given various tasks to perform, not only to train her in a practical way, but as magical exercises. For example, "They would rip up clothes—rip up the seams and throw it at you. You have to sew it fast and wish that you be handy." Often, the aunt in charge would rip out the seams and make the girl sew them all over again. Or, the girl would weave baskets, sometimes starting one and twirling it around fast, pretending to weave, so that she would become a swift worker. Food taboos enforced at this time and for several years after prohibited fresh fish (to prevent too great a menstrual flow), beach food (which means poverty), or too rapid eating of dried fish, "so you wouldn't be so hoggish and eat too much."

We must not suppose, however, that all girls docilely observed these and other regulations, for one of our informants told how she did peek out and how she went picking berries before this was allowed (thereby risking palsy in old age). For these and other misdeeds, she was not punished but was merely scolded by her mother, who pointed out that most of the taboos were for her own good.

When the girl was finally released from her confinement, her old clothes were burned and the ashes buried under a stump, so that she would have a long life. She was then dressed in fine new clothing, loaded with ornaments, and long ago would have had a hole cut for her first labret and had her hands tatooed with her sib crest. For a time, her head was covered with a hood, hung with tassels of dentalia, till "she gets used to being seen." When girls come out of the hole, they are white; their hands are like glass." This clear white skin was much admired. Girls who had been confined "can hardly walk or stand when they come out."

However, the girl was not yet really free, for the mother exercised a strict chaperonage over her daughter until the latter married, even accompanying her to the latrine. This period of supervision did not usually last long, since a girl was considered marriageable as soon as her puberty seclusion was ended, and prudent or aristocratic parents took pains to marry her off promptly. Sometimes they even betrothed her while she was still confined. The young girl might not know who her husband was to be, and, even if she did, her strongest wishes might be disregarded in favor of a marriage that was politically desirable for her sib. Similarly, the young man had little or nothing to say about his first mariage but might have to take his uncle's old widow.

The Yakutat adult who exhibited the most desired traits which his training was supposed to have inculcated was loyal to his lineage and sib, versed in its traditions, and proud of them. He was, if of noble rank, courteous and "gentle," since this showed respect for himself and for others. He was proud without being arrogant, careful in speech and manner lest he give offense when none was intended, yet ready to resent any slight and to face death if necessary to defend his honor or to protect his kinsmen. He was rich and generous, skilled as a hunter, and perhaps also as an artist and, above all, secure in the consciousness of his unblemished ancestry (no slaves or witches) and in his affinal connections. The ideal woman shared also in many of his virtues and was wise in her management of the wealth of the household, especially of the stores of food that made possible the potlatching upon which social position depended. Her loyalties were more divided than that of the man, since she had strong ties both to her own sib and to her husband and his people. Women were therefore regarded as especially likely to cause troubles or feuds; a woman who never quarreled was actually honored at a potlatch for her self-restraint.

In comparing Yakutat child-training with that described by Olson (1956, esp. p. 681) for the Chilkat, we are struck with the brutality with which Chilkat children might be punished. There is nothing comparable to the cruel Chilkat practice of putting naughty children in boxes beside a hot fire. We might think this punishment was only a threat, like dousing in boiling urine, had not one of Olson's informants been actually subjected to it. Yet I suspect that these informants may also have exaggerated the severity of the ordeal and the frequency with which it was employed. The Chilkat were an arrogant, hard, warlike people, who depended upon their complete domination of their Athabaskan trade partners and upon their monopoly of this inland trade for their survival. They not only had to be ready to defend their position by actual force, as they did when they burned down the Hudson's Bay post at Fort Selkirk, but they also had to cultivate a reputation for aggressive, unyielding, unflinching character. Even in potlatching they were to be feared (*cf.* Swanton: 1909, Tale 28, p. 71). It was natural for the Chilkat to have made an actual cult of brutality.

The Yakutat, in contrast, have lived in a more isolated and in a richer natural environment. Although they did enjoy a reputation of being "bloodthirsty savages," probably because they destroyed the Russian post at Yakutat in 1805, and although some of their sibs did take part in wars against Chilkat (Swanton: 1909, Tale 32, pp. 161–165) and Wrangell sibs, as allies of their Hoonah and Sitka relatives, yet they seem a somewhat gentler people than the southeastern Alaskan Tlingit. I felt a contrast between them and the Chilkat. It may be significant that a Yakutat potlatch was more an occasion for grief and for honoring the dead than for an arrogant display of sib crests, although this element was also present. It should also be noted that face-saving potlatches or property contests to wipe out insults were very rare at Yakutat. The Athabaskan and Eyak background of part of the population undoubtedly explains this difference, for it is just those sibs that trace their origins to the Tlingit of southeastern Alaska who seem to have exhibited the most typically Tlingit hardness and touchy pride. Others were descended from the more docile *Gunana*, whom the Tlingit were said to have discovered and "organized" for trade.

Yet we should not exaggerate the differences between the various Yakutat sibs or between these people and the Chilkat. All are equally Tlingit, even though Olson and I may have seen somewhat different sides to their characters. While he (Olson: 1956, p. 686) felt that life was rewarding and satisfying to most individuals and that there was little of neurosis or of personality conflicts resulting from childhood experiences, yet I would see the readiness to interpret a careless word as insulting, the warlike rivalry between guest sibs at a potlatch, the fear of being ridiculed for mistakes in dancing and singing, the preoccupation with acquiring more wealth than one's rivals within the same sib or moiety, and the frequent accusations or suspicions of witchcraft within the lineage, as evidence of the jealousies and tensions initiated in childhood and reinforced by the self-discipline and fortitude demanded throughout later life.

References

Hallowell, A. I.

1955: *Culture and Experience* (Philadelphia: University of Pennsylvania Press).

Laguna, F. de

1953: "Some Dynamic Forces in Tlingit Society," *Southwestern Journal of Anthropology*, **8,** 1–12.

1954: "Tlingit Ideas about the Individual," *Southwestern Journal of Anthropology*, **10,** 172–191.

Olson, R. L.

1956: "Channeling of Character in Tlingit Society," in D. G. Haring (ed.), *Personal Character and Cultural Milieu* (3rd rev. ed.; Syracuse: Syracuse University Press), pp. 675–687.

Swanton, J. R.

1909: "Tlingit Myths and Texts," *Bulletins of the Bureau of American Ethnology*, **39.**

GEORGE PETER MURDOCK

Algonkian Social Organization

The magnitude of A. I. Hallowell's contributions to the field of culture and personality has tended to obscure the fact that he has also been one of the most competent and productive men of his generation in the field of social organization. In addition to important ethnographic contributions to the knowledge of kinship and marriage among a number of northern Algonkian peoples (Hallowell: 1926, 1928, 1932, 1937, 1938), he has closely followed developments in other parts of the world and was, indeed, the first to call attention (Hallowell: 1943) to the presence of a system of the Omaha type among the Araucanians of Chile. Moreover, the quality of his courses on social organization at the University of Pennsylvania is attested, not only by the plaudits of his former students there, but also and even more convincingly by the substantial subsequent achievements of many of them in this highly specialized field. It is therefore eminently appropriate that this volume should include a survey of the social systems of the Algonkian peoples—the linguistic stock to the study of whose more northerly members Hallowell has devoted so large a portion of his lifework.

The procedure in this paper will be to present a regional and typological classification of the social systems of all the Algonkian-speaking peoples of North America, derived from a nearly complete survey of the relevant ethnographic literature, and to discuss the essential features of each regional type from both a structural and a historical point of view. Sources not specifically cited may be located readily in Murdock (1960b). Tribal maps are available in Driver (1961), Driver and Massey (1957), Kroeber (1939), and Murdock (1960b).

Ojibwa Cluster

The first structural type was found aboriginally in a cluster of tribes centering around Lakes Huron and Superior—the Ojibwa peoples (including the Bungi or Plains Ojibwa, Chippewa, Saulteaux, etc.), the Algonkian proper, the Ottawa, and the Potawatomi. The principal sources, in addition to Hallowell (1937, 1938), are Densmore (1929), Dunning (1959), Hilger (1951), Jenness (1935), Kinietz (1940, 1947), Landes (1937), Quimby (1940), and Skinner (1913, 1924–27). Except for the Bungi, who were buffalo hunters at the edge of the Plains, all groups subsisted primarily by hunting and fishing, with a subsidiary dependence upon gathering. Only the Ottawa, the Potawatomi, and the Chippewa of Minnesota practiced agriculture to a limited extent.

The tribes of the Ojibwa cluster were organized in politically autonomous, seminomadic bands, which occupied fixed settlements for only a portion of the year. Polygyny prevailed to a limited extent, and the related families which comprised a band were usually aggregated into small, cooperating, extended-family groups. Except among the Rainy River Ojibwa, for whom a bride-price appears to have been customary, marriage involved no transfer of property. However, a moderate amount of bride-service was commonly expected during the usual initial period of uxorilocal residence. Permanent residence was normally patrilocal, usually with uxorilocal or neolocal residence as an optional alternative. A tendency toward local exogamy prevailed in some but not all bands. Where it occurred, patrilocal residence and patrilineal descent operated to give the band a structure approximating that of a patriclan.

With the possible but dubious exceptions of the Bungi and Potawatomi, cross-cousin marriage was preferential or at least permitted in all groups, and kinship terminology was everywhere of the Iroquois type (with special terms for cross-cousins). Exogamous patrilineal sibs were present throughout the area. In general, therefore, the tribes of the Ojibwa cluster exhibited a social system of the classical "Dakota type" (see Murdock: 1949, pp. 236–238). It is probably accidental that their immediate neighbors to the south, the Central Algonkians, also had a patrilineal form of organization, albeit of quite a different type (see p. 29), for the Ojibwa system is better explained as an evolutionary development from the system prevailing among their northern neighbors, the Cree, than as a product of diffusion from the much more complex cultures adjoining them on the south.

Cree Cluster

A second structural type prevailed among the Cree peoples, who resided immediately north and northwest of the Ojibwa cluster, and among the kindred Montagnais and Naskapi to the east and northeast. The principal ethnographic sources are Hallowell (1928, 1932, 1937, 1938), Honigmann (1953, 1956), Lips (1947), Mandelbaum (1940), and Skinner (1913), supplemented by Flannery (1938), Speck (1918, 1927, 1935), and Strong (1922). Occupying a somewhat harsher environment than their southern neighbors, these peoples subsisted primarily by hunting and trapping, with subsidiary fishing and gathering. Only among the Swampy Cree did fishing assume a dominant position in the economy. Agriculture was entirely unknown.

As in the Ojibwa cluster, local organization was into politically autonomous, seminomadic bands, but these were agamous rather than exogamous, and, at least in the east, their lands were typically divided into family hunting territories exploited by small groups of related families. Limited polygyny prevailed, but marriage involved no bride-price except among the Plains Cree after the introduction of the horse. Marital residence was ambilocal—more frequently virilocal in most but not all groups. Preferential cross-cousin marriage and Iroquois cousin terminology are attested in all the fuller ethnographies, but occasional exceptions to both—possibly due to acculturative influences—are reported in fragmentary accounts of some of the southern and interior bands of the Labrador Peninsula.

The most striking deviation from the social organization of the Ojibwa cluster was the complete absence of patrilineal sibs. Descent was strictly bilateral throughout the area. On the whole, the social systems of the Cree and Montagnais-Naskapi peoples corresponded closely in most essential respects to what the author has elsewhere (Murdock: 1960a, pp. 7–9, 14) characterized as the "Carib type" of social organization. From this type of system, an increasing emphasis on virilocal residence and local exogamy could readily have produced, through a gradual and natural transition, the type of social structure found in the Ojibwa cluster.

Maritime Cluster

The Algonkian tribes of northern New England and the Maritime Provinces—the Abnaki, Malecite, Micmac, and Penobscot—had a still different type of social system. For the Micmac we fortunately possess good early descriptions (Denys: 1908; Le Clercq: 1910), but otherwise we must depend upon recent ethnographers, of whom the most helpful are Hallowell (1926), Mechling (1958–59), Parsons (1926), Smith (1957), Speck (1918, 1940), and Wallis and

Wallis (1955, 1957). The Maritime peoples practiced a little agriculture, though probably not until the post-Columbian period in the case of the Micmac. It was, however, a subsidiary activity, like fishing and gathering, and hunting provided a considerably larger proportion of the food supply. The peoples of the Maritime cluster had permanent settlements, which they occupied particularly during the fishing season in the spring and early summer, but they dispersed in migratory bands during most of the rest of the year. In contrast to the peoples previously described, however, the bands were not politically independent but were aggregated into confederations or into subtribal units under chiefs who possessed considerable authority.

Polygyny prevailed to only a limited extent, and the typical residential unit appears to have been an independent nuclear family. The groom paid no bride-price but performed bride-service during an initial year of uxorilocal residence. Permanent residence was usually, though by no means invariably, patrilocal. Families were aggregated into small patrilineal lineages, which, according to Speck, were associated with animal totems, but neither these nor the local bands were exogamous. Marriage was regulated only by kinship. Incest taboos prevented unions between first or second cousins of any kind, thus rendering cross-cousin marriage impossible. Cousin terminology was probably of the Hawaiian type. To be sure, a majority of the sources report Eskimo terminology, but there are substantial grounds for ascribing this to acculturative influences.

The above summary depends rather heavily upon the interpretation of incomplete and often ambiguous source materials. If it is correct, the social systems of the Maritime cluster corresponded approximately to what the author has elsewhere (Murdock: 1949, pp. 235–236) called the "Guinea type" of social organization. Patrilineal descent, however, was at best only incipient, and it is conceivable that what we have interpreted as patrilineages were in actuality only extended families and that at least some of the Maritime peoples had a bilateral form of organization.

The exceedingly fragmentary information on the Algonkian tribes of southern New England, summarized by Rainey (1936), reveals a stronger dependence upon agriculture, a more complex form of political organization, and in general a more highly elaborated culture. With respect to social organization, however, it does little more than to reveal that descent was neither matrilineal nor strongly patrilineal and to leave open the possibility that the social system may have resembled that of their northern neighbors.

Delaware Cluster

The Delaware Indians, who formerly inhabited New Jersey and adjacent eastern Pennsylvania, had a form of social organization closely resembling that of their northwestern neighbors, the Iroquois. They were semisedentary rather than seminomadic in their settlement pattern, and their subsistence depended more upon agriculture than on hunting, fishing, or gathering. The early source materials have been carefully assessed by Herman (1950), Newcomb (1956), and Wallace (1947).

Marriage among the Delaware involved an exchange of gifts but no bride-price. Descent was matrilineal, and residence was normally matrilocal in the long house occupied by the families of the wife's female lineage mates. When polygyny occurred, it was usually in the sororal form. Lineages were aggregated into exogamous matrilineal sibs, and a settlement commonly contained two or more matriclans, i.e., lineages localized in long houses. Each clan had a chief. Though these clan chiefs were perhaps originally autonomous, by the eighteenth century, at least, the Delaware were politically organized in three independent subtribes.

Morgan (1871), who was the first to record the kinship terminology of the Delaware, reports cousin terminology of the Hawaiian type. He obtained his information, however, in 1860—a full century after the Delaware had lost all their lands and after they had been subjected to two centuries of intensive acculturation—and Newcomb (1956) argues that their aboriginal cousin terminology was of the Iroquois type. We unfortunately lack evidence on the rules governing cousin marriage, which conceivably could resolve the problem. If Newcomb is correct in his inference, the original social system of the Delaware conformed in all respects to the classic "Iroquois type."

It is possible that the southeasternmost Algonkian peoples—the Conoy, Nanticoke, Powhatan, and Pamlico tribes of Delaware, Maryland, and coastal Virginia and North Carolina—had social systems akin to that of the Delaware, but the ethnographic information is insufficient to establish more than, at best, a faint presumption that they were matrilineally organized.

Central Algonkian Cluster

The Algonkian tribes of Wisconsin, Illinois, Indiana, and Kentucky, namely the Fox, Illinois, Kickapoo, Menomini, Miami, Sauk, and Shawnee, exhibited aboriginally a type of social organization quite distinct from any of those previously described. The Potawatomi of Michigan, though ordinarily grouped with the Central Algonkian tribes, actually had, as previously noted, a social system more closely resembling those of the Ojibwa cluster. The principal sources are Hoffman (1893), Jones (1913), Keesing (1939), Kinietz (1940), Morgan (1871), Skinner (1913, 1923–25), Tax (1937), and Trowbridge (1939).

The tribes of the Central Algonkian cluster had very diversified economies, depending substantially on both gathering and fishing but usually deriving even more of their food supply from hunting and agriculture. They lived in permanent villages of multifamily bark houses but occupied smaller mat lodges on extended hunting trips during the winter months. Political organization was complex. Villages were politically integrated at least into subtribes, and in many instances the entire tribe acknowledged a single chief, who was normally succeeded by his eldest son.

Marriage was polygynous, usually with a preference for the sororal form, and no source reports a genuine bride-price. However, gifts were often given or exchanged, and the groom might perform bride-service during an initial period of uxorilocal residence, which is specifically reported for the Fox, Illinois, and Sauk and may well have been general. Permanent residence, however, was normally patrilocal. Descent was patrilineal, with exogamous patrisibs. There are suggestions that sibs, or more probably lineages, were originally localized, but whether there were several or only one in a village is unclear, though the latter seems more probable in at least the case of the Menomini. All tribes, with the possible exception of the Shawnee, appear also to have had a moiety organization, but its functions were primarily ceremonial, and the moieties did not regulate marriage. In several tribes, indeed, it was customary to assign the first child to the father's moiety, the second to the mother's, etc. All groups had kinship terminology of the Omaha type, and all of them forbade any kind of cousin marriage. In sum, the Central Algonkians had social systems of the classic "Omaha type."

Hockett (1964), in an admirable application of refined linguistic techniques, attempts a reconstruction of the kinship system of the ancestral Central Algonkians. One of his conclusions is that they practiced cross-cousin marriage. Since this interpretation rests primarily upon evidence from the Ojibwa, Potawatomi, and Cree, where it is supported, as we have seen, by contemporary ethnographic data, it may not actually be pertinent for the group of tribes presently under consideration. Comparative evidence, in the author's opinion, suggests that Dakota and Omaha systems are alternative forms of patrilineal organization and that it is rare for a system of either type to evolve directly into the other. He therefore doubts that the Central Algonkian systems are derived from those of the Ojibwa cluster, or vice versa. If Hockett's reconstruction is correct, the author suggests that the Ojibwa and Central Algonkian clusters have followed separate developmental paths and have independently evolved alternative types of patrilineal systems, on the basis of a single antecedent system which still survives relatively unchanged among the Cree and the Montagnais-Naskapi.

Cheyenne Cluster

The social organization of the Cheyenne and Arapaho, two Algonkian tribes which formerly roamed the west-central Plains, has been well described by Eggan (1937), Grinnell (1923), Llewellyn and Hoebel (1940), and Michelson (1934). Although these tribes did a modest amount of gathering and cultivated a little tobacco for ceremonial purposes, they subsisted primarily by hunting the buffalo—a mode of livelihood which was strikingly intensified after they acquired the horse. They were organized in migratory bands, occupying temporary camps of skin tipis as they followed the buffalo herds. The Arapaho bands were aggregated into four subtribes, whereas the Cheyenne had a unified tribal political system. In general, however, the bands operated independently except for a period during the summer when the subtribe or tribe assembled for a collective buffalo hunt and Sun Dance ceremonial, at which time a military or age-grade society was granted effective police authority.

Marriage took place either by elopement or by a presentation of gifts, which in the late period sometimes amounted practically to a bride-price. Polygyny was common and preferentially sororal, residence was normally uxorilocal, and the nuclear or polygynous families of a woman and her daughters formed an extended family unit which cooperated economically and occupied a cluster of adjacent tipis in camp. Marriage was forbidden with any known cousin, however remote. This resulted in a tendency toward local exogamy since a band was usually, though not invariably, composed of kinsmen. There were, however, no unilineal kin groups of any kind. The only grouping of kinsmen other than the extended family was the personal kindred, an aggregation of an individual's bilateral relatives which functioned at life-crisis ceremonies. Cousin terminology was of the Hawaiian type, sibling terms being extended collaterally to all cousins, at least throughout the kindred and possibly beyond.

The social organization of the Cheyenne and Arapaho was clearly bilateral in character. It resembled the well-known "Eskimo type" (Murdock: 1960a, pp. 6–7, 14) in its complete lack of descent groups and in the presence of bilateral kindreds, but it differed in having extended rather than independent nuclear families, in possessing Hawaiian rather than Eskimo cousin terms, and in the very wide collateral extension of marriage prohibitions. These features are widely characteristic of systems of the "Polynesian type" (Murdock: 1960a, pp. 9–14), but the absence of ambilineal descent and of ramages precludes the classification of the Cheyenne and Arapaho systems with them and suggests the desirability of establishing a new type of bilateral organization with characteristics intermediate between those of the Eskimo and Polynesian types.

Blackfoot Cluster

A somewhat variant form of social organization was found among the Algonkian tribes of the northwestern Plains—the Blackfoot, Blood, Piegan, and Gros Ventre. These groups closely resembled the Cheyenne and Arapaho in their migratory mode of life, in their predominantly hunting economy, and in their political organization, except that the Blackfoot political system may not have transcended the level of the band. The major sources are Flannery (1953), Goldfrank (1945), Hanks and Richardson (1945), Josselin de Jong (1912), Kroeber (1907), Michelson (1916), and Wissler (1912).

The social organization exhibited striking resemblances to that of the Cheyenne and Arapaho in many respects, notably, the prevalence of sororal polygyny, a strong tendency toward local exogamy, cousin terminology of the Hawaiian type, the wide collateral extension of marriage prohibitions, and the complete absence of unilineal kin groups. The most significant difference was a marked preference for virilocal rather than uxorilocal residence. There was also a stronger development of the bride-price, polygynous families were not aggregated into extended families except among the Blackfoot, and personal kindreds, though quite possibly present, have not been specifically reported.

On the whole, the social systems of the Cheyenne and Blackfoot clusters seem to be two variants of a single structural type, differentiated primarily by a preference for either uxorilocal or virilocal residence. Both are clearly bilateral, though differing in significant respects from bilateral systems of the Eskimo type. Both have numerous parallels in other parts of the world (see examples listed in Murdock: 1959, pp. 136–137). These are particularly common in western North America, where, for example, most of the northeastern Athapaskan and Basin Shoshonean tribes reveal a preference for uxorilocal residence, and most of the Plateau and southern Northwest Coast tribes a preference for virilocal residence, but deviate from the Eskimo type in much the same ways as do the Plains Algonkians. It therefore seems advisable to designate this distinctive type of bilateral organization by a separate name, recognizing its variability in regard to rules of residence. Because of its strong representation among the Salishan-speaking peoples, the author proposes that it be called the "Salish type."

Conclusion

The Salish type is more widely distributed in North America than any other type of social organization, and there is reason to suspect that it is the original type from which most other North American systems have arisen by one or two steps of normal evolutionary development. Among the Algonkian peoples, for example, the Maritime and Central Algonkian clusters could readily have evolved their respective Guinea and Omaha systems through a process of patrilocalization and the consequent emergence of patrilineal lineages and sibs, and the Delaware could have developed their matrilineal system through a parallel process of matrilocalization and sib formation. The social organization of the Cree cluster could have arisen very simply through the development of cross-cousin marriage, after which patrilocalization and the emergence of patrilineal sibs would have given rise to the Dakota systems of the Ojibwa cluster.

Despite the variability in social structure of the Algonkian peoples, whose seven clusters exemplify six widely distributed and distinctive types of social organization—Carib, Dakota, Guinea, Iroquois, Omaha, and Salish (with two subtypes), it nevertheless seems possible to account for all the regional variations in accordance with a single comprehensive theory of sociocultural change. This has the additional value of accounting equally well for the distribution of forms of social organization throughout most of the rest of North America and perhaps elsewhere in the world where bilateral systems prevail.

References

Densmore, F.
1929: "Chippewa Customs," *Bulletins of the Bureau of American Ethnology*, **86**, 1–204.

Denys, N.
1908: "The Description and Natural History of the Coasts of North America," in W. F. Ganong (ed.), *Publications of the Champlain Society*, **21**, 399–452; 572–606.

Driver, H. E.
1961: *Indians of North America* (Chicago: University of Chicago Press).

Driver, H. E., & Massey, W. C.
1957: "Comparative Studies of North American Indians," *Transactions of the American Philosophical Society*, n.s., **47**, 165–456.

Dunning, R. W.
1959: *Social and Economic Change among the Northern Ojibwa* (Toronto: University of Toronto Press).

Eggan, F.
1937: "The Cheyenne and Arapaho Kinship System," in F. Eggan (ed.), *Social Anthropology of North American Tribes* (Chicago: University of Chicago Press), pp. 33–95.

Flannery, R.
1938: "Cross-Cousin Marriage Among the Cree and Montagnais of James Bay," *Primitive Man*, **11**, 29–33.
1953: "The Gros Ventre of Montana," *Catholic University of America Anthropological Series*, **15**, 1–221.

Goldfrank, E. S.
1945: "Changing Configurations in the Social Organization of a Blackfoot Tribe," *Monographs of the American Ethnological Society*, **7**, 1–73.

Grinnell, G. B.
1923: *The Cheyenne Indians* (2 vols.) (New Haven: Yale University Press).

Hallowell, A. I.
1926: "Recent Changes in the Kinship Terminology of the St. Francis Abenaki," *Proceedings of the International Congress of Americanists*, **22**, 97–145.
1928: "Was Cross-Cousin Marriage Practiced by the North-Central Algonkian?" *Proceedings of the International Congress of Americanists*, **23**, 519–544.
1932: "Kinship Terms and Cross-Cousin Marriage of the Montagnais-Naskapi and the Cree," *American Anthropologist*, **34**, 171–199.
1937: "Cross-Cousin Marriage in the Lake Winnipeg Area," *Publications of the Philadelphia Anthropological Society*, **1**, 95–110.

1938: "The Incidence, Character, and Decline of Polygyny among the Lake Winnipeg Cree and the Saulteaux," *American Anthropologist*, **40**, 235–256.

1943: "Araucanian Parallels to the Omaha Kinship System," *American Anthropologist*, **45**, 489–491.

Hanks, L. M., & Richardson, J.

1945: "Observations on Northern Blackfoot Kinship," *Monographs of the American Ethnological Society*, **9**, 1–31.

Herman, M. W.

1950: "A Reconstruction of Aboriginal Delaware Culture from Contemporary Sources," *Kroeber Anthropological Society Papers*, **1**, 45–77.

Hilger, I.

1951: "Chippewa Child Life and Its Cultural Background," *Bulletins of the Bureau of American Ethnology*, **146**, 1–218.

Hockett, C. F.

1964: "The Proto-Central Algonquian Kinship System," in W. H. Goodenough (ed.), *Explorations in Cultural Anthropology* (New York: McGraw-Hill).

Hoffman, W. J.

1893: "The Menomini Indians," *Annual Reports of the Bureau of American Ethnology*, **14**, 11–328.

Honigmann, J. J.

1953: "Social Organization of the Attawapiskat Cree Indians," *Anthropos*, **47**, 809–816.

1956: "The Attawapiskat Swampy Cree," *Anthropological Publications of the University of Alaska*, **5**, 23–82.

Jenness, D.

1935: "The Ojibwa of Parry Island," *Bulletins of the Canada Department of Mines, Geological Survey*, **128**, 1–115.

Jones, W.

1913: "Kickapoo Ethnological Notes," *American Anthropologist*, **15**, 332–335.

Josselin de Jong, J. P. B. de

1912: "Social Organization of the Southern Piegans," *Internationales Archiv für Ethnographie*, **20**, 191–197.

Keesing, F. M.

1939: "The Menomini Indians of Wisconsin," *Memoirs of the American Philosophical Society*, **10**, 1–261.

Kinietz, W. V.

1940: "The Indians of the Western Great Lakes," *Occasional Contributions from the Museum of Anthropology of the University of Michigan*, **10**, 1–427.

1947: "Chippewa Village," *Bulletins of the Cranbrook Institute*, **25**, 1–259.

Kroeber, A. L.

1907: "Ethnology of the Gros Ventre," *Anthropological Papers of the American Museum of Natural History*, **1**, 145–281.

1939: "Cultural and Natural Areas of Native North America," *University of California Publications in American Archaeology and Ethnology*, **38**, 1–242.

Landes, R.
1937: "Ojibwa Sociology," *Columbia University Contributions to Anthropology*, **29**, 1–144.

Le Clercq, G.
1910: "New Relation of Gaspesia," in W. F. Ganong (ed.), *Publications of the Champlain Society*, **5**, 1–452.

Lips, J. E.
1947: "Naskapi Law," *Transactions of the American Philosophical Society*, **37**, 381–492.

Llewellyn, K. N., & Hoebel, A. E.
1940: *The Cheyenne Way* (Norman: University of Oklahoma Press).

Mandelbaum, D. G.
1940: "The Plains Cree," *Anthropological Papers of the American Museum of Natural History*, **36**, 155–316.

Mechling, W. H.
1958–59: "The Malecite Indians," *Anthropologica*, **7**, 1–168; **8**, 161-274.

Michelson, T.
1916: "Notes on the Piegan System of Consanguinity," *Holmes Anniversary Volume* (Washington, D.C.), pp. 320-333.

1934: "Some Arapaho Kinship Terms and Social Usages," *American Anthropologist*, **36**, 137–139.

Morgan, L. H.
1871: "Systems of Consanguinity and Affinity of the Human Family," *Smithsonian Contributions to Knowledge*, **17**, 1–590.

Murdock, G. P.
1949: *Social Structure* (New York: Macmillan).

1959: "Evolution in Social Organization," in B. J. Meggers (ed.), *Evolution and Anthropology: A Centennial Appraisal* (Washington, D.C.: Anthropological Society of Washington), pp. 126–143.

1960a: "Cognatic Forms of Social Organization," *Viking Fund Publications in Anthropology*, **29**, 1–14.

1960b: *Ethnographic Bibliography of North America* (3rd ed.; New Haven: Human Relations Area Files).

Newcomb, W. W., Jr.
1956: "The Culture and Acculturation of the Delaware," *Anthropological Papers of the University of Michigan Museum of Anthropology*, **10**, 1–141.

Parsons, E. C.
1926: "Micmac Notes," *Journal of American Folklore*, **39**, 460-485.

Quimby, G. I., Jr.
1940: "Some Notes on Kinship and Kinship Terminology Among the Potawatomi of the Huron," *Papers of the Michigan Academy of Science, Arts, and Letters*, **25**, 553-563.

Rainey, F. G.
1936: "A Compilation of Historical Data Contributing to the Ethnography of Connecticut and Southern New England Indians," *Bulletins of the Archaeological Society of Connecticut*, **3**, 1–89.

Skinner, A.
1913: "Social Life and Ceremonial Bundles of the Menomini Indians," *Anthropological Papers of the American Museum of Natural History*, **13**, 1–165.
1923–25: "Observations on the Ethnology of the Sauk Indians," *Bulletins of the Public Museum of the City of Milwaukee*, **5**, 1–180.
1924–27: "The Mascoutens or Prairie Potawatomi Indians," *Bulletins of the Public Museum of the City of Milwaukee*, **6**, 1–411.

Smith, N. N.
1957: "Notes on the Malecite of Woodstock," *Anthropologica*, **5**, 1–40.

Speck, F. G.
1918: "Kinship Terms and the Family Band among the Northeastern Algonkian," *American Anthropologist*, **20**, 134–161.
1927: "Family Hunting Territories of the Lake St. John Montagnais," *Anthropos*, **22**, 387–403.
1935: *Naskapi* (Norman: University of Oklahoma Press).
1940: *Penobscot Man* (Philadelphia: University of Pennsylvania Press).

Strong, W. D.
1922: "Cross-Cousin Marriage and the Culture of the Northeastern Algonkian," *American Anthropologist*, **31**, 277–288.

Tax, S.
1937: "The Social Organization of the Fox Indians," in F. Eggan (ed.), *Social Organization of North American Tribes* (Chicago: University of Chicago Press), pp. 243–282.

Trowbridge, C. C.
1939: "Shawnese Traditions," in V. Kinietz and E. W. Voegelin (eds.), *Occasional Contributions from the Museum of Anthropology of the University of Michigan*, **9**, 1–71.

Wallace, A. F. C.
1947: "Woman, Land, and Society: Three Aspects of Aboriginal Delaware Life," *Pennsylvania Archaeologist*, **17**, 1–35.

Wallis, W. D., & Wallis, R. S.
1955: *The Micmac Indians of Eastern Canada* (Minneapolis: University of Minnesota Press).
1957: "The Malecite Indians of New Brunswick," *Bulletin of the National Museum of Canada*, **148**, 1–58.

Wissler, C.
1912: "The Social Life of the Blackfoot Indians," *Anthropological Papers of the American Museum of Natural History*, **7**, 1–64.

Part Two

Religion

ERIKA BOURGUIGNON

The Self, The Behavioral Environment, and the Theory of Spirit Possession

In his paper, "The Self and Its Behavioral Environment," Dr. Hallowell opened an area of investigation that had long been neglected by anthropologists. In this paper, he considers the continuity and the maintenance of personal identity in the perception of the self and states: ". . . it can be deduced that psychopathological phenomena that affect the maintenance of personal identity and continuity must necessarily be considered abnormal in any society" (1955, p. 95). I now wish to raise the question whether this comment, by implication, may be applied to those dissociational states variously known in the anthropological literature as "trance" or "spirit possession." I wish to examine this proposition in relation to data on self-perception and self-concepts derived from a study of Haitian peasant society.[1]

1. The Haitian data drawn on in this paper were collected during a field trip to Haiti during 1947–48. The study was supported by a grant from the Graduate School of Northwestern University and the Carnegie Corporation of New York. Comparative material, some of which is drawn on in this paper, was analyzed with a group of graduate students in a seminar held at the Ohio State University during the summer of 1962.

Before approaching the data to be discussed, a few remarks may be in order on the present state of research dealing with the subjects of trance and spirit possession. Quite a large number of recent anthropological publications deal with what appears to be a group of related phenomena. Among these publications are Jane Belo's detailed study (1960) of trance in Bali, Alfred Métraux's study (1959) of the *vodû* cult in Haiti, which includes a lengthy discussion of spirit possession, and M. J. Field's study (1960) of shrine cults in Ghana, which also deals with spirit possession. Other examples of studies in which terms such as "spirit possession" and/or "trance" are used are those by Teicher (1960) on the windigo psychosis as well as those by Leiris (1958), by Messing (1958), and by Haberland (1960) on the *zâr* cult of Ethiopia. In connection with his Ethiopian study, Leiris introduces the concept of shamanism. The question arises whether all these authors are indeed speaking of related matters. Is windigo psychosis in some way similar to spirit possession in Ghana or in Haiti; is the *zâr* cult similar to Siberian shamanism? It is evident that some clarification of concepts and terminology is called for as well as some systematization of what appears to be an extensive and widely dispersed area of investigation. When we ask about the significance of the phenomena of "trance" and "spirit possession" even in a more narrowly defined group of related cultures, as those among whom Afro-American cults flourish, we find wide disagreement. Herskovits tells us (1937, p. 295; 1948, p. 66), that spirit possession is "normal," Dorsainvil (1931) says it is a definite sign of pathology—hereditary pathology at that, while Roger Bastide (1950) prefers to consider the phenomenon as "prophylactic." Métraux (1959), like Leiris (1958) in another cultural context, is impressed by the theatrical aspects of possession.[2]

In spite of the rich source materials available and the evident psychological problems posed by them, it is striking that the subjects in question have not been dealt with in any textbooks, books of readings, or other systematic treatments in the field of culture and personality or psychological anthropology. They have been given only limited attention in cross-cultural studies of religion, where they are usually dealt with in the context of shamanism or "unusual states" (e.g., Norbeck: 1961). Wallace's important paper on hallucination (1959) deals with a neighboring problem. There has been no systematic treatment of this neglected area since T. K. Oesterreich's monumental work in 1921. A preliminary analysis of terms appears to be in order.

We may distinguish, first of all, between the terms "trance" and "spirit possession," which often appear to be used interchangeably. While some types of spirit possession do indeed involve trance, others do not. Conversely, while

2. This list could indeed be lengthened considerably. Note, for example, among the most interesting discussions by nonanthropologists: Sargant (1957), who includes trance states in a discussion of brainwashing, and Gill and Brenman (1961), who compare trance in Bali with hypnosis in their clinical practice. In another context, note also Ernesto de Martino (1962) on tarantism in Southern Italy.

some types of trance are interpreted as possession by spirits, others are not. To put it differently, trance is a psychiatric term, indeed one now rarely used in the clinical literature, while a belief in spirit possession involves a cultural theory, which accounts for a variety of phenomena, often, but not always, those included under the heading of trance. In their well-known dictionary of psychological terms, English and English (1958) define trance as following:

> A sleeplike state marked by reduced sensitivity to stimuli, loss or alteration of knowledge of what is happening, substitution of automatic for voluntary activity. Trances are frequent in hysteria, and they may be hypnotically induced. In extreme form trance resembles (or is) coma. Religious or emotionally marked trances are called ecstasy.

However, Gill and Brenman (1947), in a review of the literature, find hypnosis itself to be a most poorly understood phenomenon, and in a more recent work (1961) they prefer to speak of "altered states of consciousness." The term "hysteria" occurs with greater rarity in psychiatric textbooks; indeed the most recent *Statistical and Diagnostic Manual of the American Psychiatric Association* (1956) dispenses with the term altogether.

In the literature dealing particularly with the shamanism of Northern Asia we find references to epileptic and epileptoid seizures; we hear of cataleptic states in connection with trance and also of multiple personalities and fugues. M. J. Field (1960) in her study of shrine cults of Ghana, in which priests are "possessed," prefers to speak of "dissociation." This she defines (p. 19) as "mental mechanism whereby a split-off part of the personality temporarily possesses the entire field of consciousness and behavior." She states (p. 56) that there appears to be "no reason to suppose that dissociation is *necessarily* hysterical" (Field's emphasis). It is clear that we are dealing here with a complex variable phenomenon, which is perhaps not fully understood.

In contrast to trance, the term "spirit possession" refers to a cultural theory, which exists in diverse forms in many societies, but surely not in all. It holds that certain spirits exist, which may enter the bodies of human beings—sometimes also those of animals and of objects. Trance states may be taken to be evidence for the occurrence of such possession. However, possession may be thought to occur under other circumstances as well. For example, among some American Indian groups given types of mental illness may be interpreted as due to possession by spirits. This is true in certain instances of *windigo* psychosis (Teicher: 1960) and also serves as an explanatory category among the Mohave (Devereux: 1961). However, in neither of these cases is there any reference to states of trance or dissociation.

On the other hand, dissociational states are clearly not limited to those societies in which theories of spirit possession are held. Hysterical and hypnotic states—the one "pathological," the other "normal"—exist in Western society, without, nowadays, any attendant theory of spirit possession. Among "non-inspired" shamans (Loeb: 1929), e.g., among the tribes of California, dissociational states exist, but these involve communication with spirits, rather than possession by them.

It would appear, then, that dissociational states are to be found in all parts of the world, and indeed, perhaps, in all societies. Conceivably, they may represent a very old phenomenon, if we are to believe Eliade (1948) or Kirchner's interpretation (1952) of the "dead man" at Lascaux as a shaman in a trance. Since trancelike states can be produced in animals by restricting their field of attention, we may easily accept the capacity for trance, or better, dissociation, as part of man's psychobiological heritage.

Cultural attitudes toward dissociational phenomena vary widely, from seeking such states to fearing them, from gaining prestige through dissociation to receiving social and even physical punishment, as in many types of exorcism. Where dissociational experiences are valued, techniques for inducing them often exist. These techniques again vary widely, from the breathing patterns of whirling dervishes (Coon: 1951), to the use of drugs (Huxley: 1954), to the use of music, dance, or certain herbs (Verger: 1957). Similarly, "trance" behavior varies widely, from the highly stylized dancing of the Balinese trance dancer (Belo: 1960), to the chaotic howling and running about on all fours in the Kentucky revival (Clark: 1949), to the full-fledged development of secondary personalities among the Yoruba and Fon peoples, as described by Verger (*op. cit.*), and the fugue states of the Ashanti shrine priests (Field, *op. cit.*), to cite only a few contrasting examples.

As there exists a variety of attitudes toward dissociation, a wide variety of attitudes toward possession by spirits is also to be found in those societies where some form of this belief exists. In the Afro-American cults of Brazil and of the Caribbean, spirit possession is usually desired, as it is among the West African peoples, particularly Fon and Yoruba, from whom these patterns derive. Again, among the Pentecostal groups in the United States, who seek "to get the spirit," this experience is sought. On the other hand, in the *zâr* cult of Southern Ethiopia (Haberland: 1960), among the Wataita of Kenya (Harris: 1957), among nineteenth-century East European Jews and medieval Christians, spirit possession is and was undesired, and partial or complete exorcism may be resorted to. In the latter case, spirit possession is used as an explanation for a variety of physical and mental disorders and cure is attempted through the driving out of the spirit. It would be interesting to investigate whether any relationship exists between high evaluation of the trance experience and the desirability of spirit possession and low evaluation of trance experience and undesirability of such possession. Yet in some groups, as among the Pentecostalists of the United States, both types of possession are found, by the Holy Ghost and by devils. In the New Testament, which provides the authority for the Pentecostal groups, we also have evidence of a belief in evil spirits to be driven out—which can possess pigs as well as humans—and in a positive type of possession in the Pentecost.

Spirit possession may then be desired or feared, and in some societies it may be both, depending on the type of spirit and the manner in which its presence is perceived. A study of the geographical distribution of these types should throw some light on possible diffusions. A study of the specific behavior of possessed persons, ritual surrounding possession, and the terminological context should be similarly revealing.[3] This has been done impressively by Simpson and Hammond (1960), who have shown the African antecedents of spirit possession in Jamaica, contrasting these patterns in some detail with those associated with Scottish and United States revivalist possession.

Where spirit possession is diagnosed as the cause of a given disease, reaction to this diagnosis may vary, as may the symptoms. In the example cited from the New Testament, as in many medieval cases of "spirit possession," the presence of evil spirits is seen in the behavioral pathology, and recourse is to exorcism. Some, but not all, of this behavioral pathology may have involved dissociational states. On the other hand, Leiris (*op. cit.*) tells us that in Gondar, Ethiopia, many types of disease and other troubles may be explained as due to possession by a spirit (*zâr*), and trance is induced in the patient in order to question the *zâr* as to his wishes. Induced trance is then part of the cure, where trance need not have taken place during the illness. The induction of such states helps the patient to alleviate his (or her) condition, and in some cases, to become a curer, making use of controlled trance in the performance of the curer's role. Similarly, M. J. Field tells us, concerning the shrine cults of rural Ghana, that shrine priests are people who have learned to "control" trance after an initial illness and often fugue. They are able to induce a dissociational state at will, during which the spirit is believed to use the priest as his vehicle. The priest acts as curer while in trance and by virtue of possession.

The Ghanaian shrine cults and the Ethiopian *zâr* cult are reminiscent of shamanistic initiation in many tribal groups. The California shaman experiences seizures and must learn to control them. Yet these states are not interpreted as possession by spirits but rather as encounters with the spirits, in dreams or visions. Other shamanistic specialists, such as the Saulteaux conjurers (Hallowell: 1942) are similarly of the "noninspired" type (Loeb: 1929) in that the spirits speak to them rather than through them. In the case of the Saulteaux, visions may have existed, but there is no reference to trance states, either in the "call"—which occurred in dreams—or in the conjuring itself.

As to our second question concerning the "normality" of spirit possession,

3. Since completing this paper, the writer, together with Drs. Pettay and Haas, has undertaken to explore some of these problems in greater detail. This research is being made possible by a two-year grant from the National Institute of Mental Health (MH 07463–01).

we must now ask what tangible form this presumed possession by spirits takes, since, as we have already seen, spirit possession and dissociational phenomena are not synonymous. If we ask about the "normality" of trance, it is obvious that this is not a unitary phenomenon either. Certainly, hypnotic trance can be induced in "normal" individuals, and some types of trance associated with theories of spirit possession may be much like hypnotic trance (Belo: 1960; Gill and Brenman: 1961).

While the comment is frequently read that classic cases of hysteria, of the kind described by the French psychiatrist of the late nineteenth century, are rarely met with today (Fenichel: 1945, p. 224; Monroe: 1955, p. 282), it has also been stated that in so-called primitive societies hysteria in its grand form may still be found, but there it occurs often not in a medical context but in a religious one. Thus Arieti and Meth (1959, p. 555) state "It must be kept in mind that hallucinations and delusions, which we consider almost pathognomic of psychoses, are normal and frequent occurrences in many exotic people during their trance states. Hallucinations in these states, however, have a different character and significance from those occurring in psychosis. They are generally benign and not persecutory in content, last only as long as the trance does and are more often visual, not auditory."

Yet these same authors also assert that shamans are often mentally ill, since "they are more apt to achieve the dissociative states of trance and possession which are required in the ceremonies of many primitive people" (p. 554).

Arieti and Meth here combine a discussion of hallucination with one of trance and spirit possession, which are not further distinguished. Wallace (*op. cit.*) has lucidly analyzed this type of terminological confusion. Furthermore, it would appear that the issues raised by Arieti and Meth are not as definitively settled as they suggest. As we have seen earlier, even in the restricted Afro-American field there is wide disagreement among authors on the normality or pathology of spirit possession and/or trance, the two usually not being clearly distinguished in the literature.[4] The Brazilian psychiatrist and anthropologist René Ribeiro (1956) has studied in detail a number of individual cult members in Pernambuco who undergo possession trances. In their case histories he was able to show clearly that the significance of the experience varies from individual to individual and that the blanket statements characterizing trance as "normal," "prophylactic," or "pathological" hardly come to grips with the reality of the situation. What may superficially appear to be the "same" phenomenon obviously implies different things for different people. It is important to realize here that a great deal of individual variation is found in the Afro-Catholic cults of Brazil, Haiti, Trinidad, and other parts of the Caribbean area. These groups

4. See also Jane Belo's discussion of the problem of the normalcy and pathology of trance (*op. cit.*) as well as Verger's (*op. cit.*). Both of these authors review various points raised in the literature.

allow "choice" of the particular deity or deities that will possess the individual and some degree of affinity between the individual and the spirits that possess him is recognized (for Brazil see Bastide: 1958). Such possibilities of accommodation to express the possessed person's individuality leaves much room for the expression of differences in personal history and personal need. Dissociational states of this type must clearly be distinguished from those in other societies, where behavior is far more stereotyped and leaves minimal room for individual differences. Shamanistic trances which require the report of fairly stereotyped visions and no acting out obviously represent quite a different phenomenon in psychological terms.

The foregoing brief discussion may indicate that, to the extent to which the problem of dissociational states has been dealt with in the literature, this has been done in terms of the description and analysis of particular societies, and many of these are indeed excellent. However, so far a framework for comparative analysis has not emerged. Nor has a consensus been reached on the subject of the normalcy or pathology of these states.

It is hoped that it may be fruitful to analyze the phenomenon of dissociation, as institutionalized in the Haitian *vodû* cult, with its attendant theory of spirit possession, from the perspective of the self and its behavioral environment, as formulated by Dr. Hallowell. Such an analysis could provide a framework for future cross-cultural analysis.

Most Haitian peasants, members of the urban proletariat, and some others believe in the existence of a large number of spirits—variously referred to as *loa*, *zanges*, *saints*—who must be attended through ritual and who may choose to appear at such rituals in the bodies of their worshippers. It is said that the *loa* "mounts" his worshipper, who is known as the *loa's* "horse" (*cheval*). The *loa* is also said to be "in the person's head"—the head being the seat of the *loa*—or else to "dance on the person."[5]

A woman among the faithful is addressed by a male *loa* as his wife, and women initiates are referred to as *hunsi* (*Fon*, lit., wife of spirit), although the original sense of this term is probably not understood. The faithful refer to most of the male deities as "papa" (father) and address them as such. Several female *loa* are addressed as "grandmother" (*gran*).

Possession, or "mounting," is manifested by alterations in behavior, speech, voice, facial expression, and motor behavior as well as by changes in clothing and in the manner in which the individual is responded to by others. The

5. The symbolism of this relationship is of interest, as is the fact that the representation of the god and his worshipper as a rider and his horse appears to be very widespread in Africa, far beyond the region of the provenience of the ancestors of the Haitian and other New World Negro populations. The historical problems raised by this observation are, however, far beyond the scope of the present paper. For comparative material, see particularly Nadel (1946), who tells us that the Nyama of the Nuba Hills speak of the spirit "mounting" a shaman, but not riding him, rather "enter[ing] his head." The parallel is astonishingly exact.

observer may be led to believe that a "genuine trance" or dissociation has taken place or that some individuals may be play acting, or he may indeed observe no particular change. There appears to be wide variation in depth of dissociational state from a passing dizziness, in which the individual is said to be made "drunk" by the *loa* (*saoulé*), to total unconsciousness. However, a transitory, childlike state (*éré*) reported for Trinidad, Brazil, and the Yoruba (Simpson: 1962; Bastide: 1958; Verger: 1957) has never been reported from Haiti.

The putative state of possession may last from a few minutes to several hours to, reportedly, several days. When the individual returns to his customary mode of behavior and expression, he claims to know nothing of the intervening events and must be told of the behavior of the *loa*, even to the extent that *loa* leave messages for their "horses"; the cultural tradition demands such ignorance, and in many cases this postdissociational amnesia is undoubtedly genuine. There is thus discontinuity in personal identity. Moreover, a person may be "mounted" by several *loa* in succession, each with different attributes. This is in contrast to belief and practice as found among related peoples in West Africa, such as the Fon of Dahomey and the Yoruba of Nigeria (Verger, *op. cit.*) or Afro-American people of more orthodox West African tradition, or in the cult centers of Brazil (*ibid.*) where possession is by one deity only.[6]

The *loa* which appear in succession may be of the same sex or of different sexes and of the same or different sex as the person possessed. The personality of each of the *loa* may be well differentiated and continuous from one visit to the next. While the "horse" knows nothing of the *loa's* behavior, the amnesia is not reciprocal, and the *loa* is fully informed of his "horse's" behavior, that of his social environment, and of other *loa* possessing the same "horse." Beyond that, he is expected to know what he, the *loa*, has said and done in other manifestations, when "mounting" other "horses" or in his own, nonmanifested identity.

We may briefly examine the theory that underlies such expectations. The *loa* are immaterial spirits who may manifest themselves when and where they choose. In practice, however, this usually means that they appear in response to an expressed human appeal or a clearly felt human need. While each *loa* has multiple manifestations, varying in some detail, there is thought to be continuity, and indeed identity among these manifestations. Therefore, any manifestation of, e.g., the *loa* Guédé, is in some sense continuous with other such manifestations, whether present in the "head" of a particular human vehicle or in his nonmaterial identity. The human being (*chrétien vivant*, lit., a living

6. Another interesting difference between Haitian cult life and that of the other groups mentioned is in the fact that Haitian periods of initiation are very short, lasting no more than a week in the regions with the most complex practices, whereas in West Africa initiations lasting a year have been reported. Verger particularly, while giving few details, speaks of a lengthy process of re-education in which full secondary personalities are developed (*op. cit.*, pp. 71–73).

Christian) consists of a body and two spiritual principles (or "souls"). One of these, the *gros bon ange* (lit., guardian angel) may be displaced by the *loa* "mounting his horse." Thus, the events which occur during the period of putative possession are perceived by the audience and by the subject himself as continuous with the identity of the *loa*, not with the identity of the human vehicle.

Thus, with reference to spirit possession, the Haitian concept of the self clearly involves a continuity of the body and one of the souls, but not a continuity of personal identity, memory, or responsibility for actions carried out by one's body, when it becomes the temporary vehicle and residence of another, more powerful spirit. It is even expected that there will be no continuity in the body's physiological response, since that response is an attribute of the possessing spirit, rather than of its vehicle: A person who is made ill by alcohol is possessed by deities who drink freely; a person crippled by rheumatism will dance with agility, dancing on burning embers will cause no pain or harm, etc. The expectation of physiological discontinuity may go beyond this: Maya Deren (1953) reports the possession of a woman by a male deity, who produced semen! In another manner this loose connection between the body and the self, the individual's identity, is also seen in the widespread belief in *zombis* (Bourguignon: 1959). This involves not only the possibility, on the one hand, that bodies of dead people may be partially revived by sorcerers for their own nefarious purposes, but from the point of view of this discussion, even more interestingly, the possibility that people may be turned into animals. These beliefs, which incidentally are held not only by *vodû* cult members but also by some Catholic and Protestant converts, imply the possibility of a partial continuity of the self in the absence of continuity of memory, sense of identity, or even under circumstances of gross bodily alteration. Indeed, there is more continuity of self in a *zombi*, even in the guise of an animal, than in the case of a man or woman with a *loa* in his head.

The essential underlying theme here is not only that the self and the body are only partially and loosely connected, but even more basically, that appearances may be deceptive and things—people, animals—often are not what they appear to be: An animal may be a person; a snake or a tarantula may be a *loa*; a person, whether seen in waking life or in a dream, may be a *loa*; while familiar people are thus potentially dangerous, strangers are even more so, for they may be *zombis* or sorcerers.

The relation between man and *loa* develops in early childhood. Babies are carried along to ceremonies, and there is no time when they are too young to have witnessed the impersonated presence of the *loa*, or to have heard stories concerning them. Yet, interestingly, there exists no formal mythology. While there are story-telling sessions, in which a rich store of secular folk tales is presented by highly skilled raconteurs, there is no body of sacred myths. Rather, the myths of the gods find their expression in the acting out of possessed individuals who embody the characters of the Haitian pantheon with all their varied individual characteristics which are constantly elaborated. Anecdotes, bits of songs, dreams, accounts of possessions round out the picture.

Early encounters of children with the spirits are instructive. One of my informants, A. C., told as her earliest memory how, as a small child, she had at a ceremony greedily taken food from a dish presented to the *marassa*, the spirits of the twins. Immediately, large numbers of small snakes appeared and frightened her. The *vodû* priest, her father's half-brother, was called and he explained that the snakes were the twins come to punish the greedy child and caused them to go away. Only upon specific questioning did it become clear that the snakes were visible only to the child and, she believed, to the priest; not, however, to others present.

Children play at spirit possession and are encouraged in doing so by their elders. Groups of children may engage in such activities, or a single child may engage adults in its play, as in the following account, taken from my field notes:

> In the afternoon, while her mother, A. C., was boiling water, and her mother's sister, J. C., was roasting coffee, the five-year-old girl, T., began to say she was Papa Ogû and did a pretty good job of imitating a possession, i.e., she made her voice sound deeper, she shook hands with everyone in the typical fashion and started beating herself on the chest and singing the appropriate songs—all to the enormous amusement of the two sisters, as well as their brother who had arrived meanwhile. J. C. responded to the songs, and when T. forgot for a moment that she was playing Papa Ogû, they reminded her teasingly. At one point she burnt herself, and her mother corrected her, saying that *loa* never burn themselves, which T. repeated ten times.
>
> This game was continued on several subsequent days. On the fourth day T. was teased about it by her mother's aunt, who was visiting from another hamlet and who had already heard of T's little game. And a week later:
>
> All evening T. was again playing at possession, mostly Ogû but also Guédé. While T. was playing Ogû her aunt, J. C., kept asking what he, Ogû, thought of his "wife T." and complained that she was no good. With this incitement by her aunt, T. tried to beat herself, and then claimed that since Ogû no longer liked T., he must look for another horse—namely, their neighbor, Altida. Her mother, A. C., kept saying: "show us how you'll mount the head of Altida" and finally, in desperation, and to the great amusement of all, she literally tried to climb on top of Altida.

A number of features of this account are noteworthy. The little girl continued this activity off and on for more than a week. Encouraged by the adults around her, she kept returning to the same game, developing a pattern of activities and alternate identities. Impersonating the *loa* she learned to speak of herself in the third person and was encouraged in this and in criticism of her own behavior; in this she attempted to dissociate her identity as the deity from her identity as a little girl and, furthermore, she attempted to develop a continuity between Ogû mounting the little girl and Ogû "mounting" the neighbor.[7]

Actual dissociation states, considered to be possessions, are rare in children. Typically, first possessions occur among teenagers, although sometimes later. Old people are rarely possessed. It is said that the gods do not wish to tire them. Also, as people acquire more spiritual control over the gods, by gaining esoteric knowledge and by feeding the gods, it is said that they are more rarely possessed. It is not necessary for the officiating priest to go into a dissociational state and V.C., the priest of the family under discussion here, did not go into such states anymore, although he had done so when younger.[8]

A. C., the little girl's mother, claimed that her own first possession occurred during a childhood game, in which she lost consciousness. First possessions are expected to be "wild" (*bossal*) and disorderly, and identification of the possessing deity and subsequent initiation rituals are necessary to bring the "wild" deity under control. For example, *bossal* possessions involve rolling about on the ground, because the *loa*, it is said, have not as yet learned to stand and to dance. For that to happen, they have to be baptized and established in the head of their "horse." Identification is made by the vodû priest, in this case, by V. C., the girl's father's half-brother, who earlier in the subject's life had chased away the punishing snakes. It is clear that, by identifying the possessing god, the priest can influence the choice of the deity to conform with the deities which are worshipped in the subject's family and the priest's cult house. This interpretive and directive role of the priests needs further investigation.[9]

In spite of this potential intervention by the priest, there is considerable room for innovation. Deities vary in their manifestations from individual to individual, in their activities, tastes, demands, tractability, etc. Even totally new deities may appear, either identifying themselves to their elected servant in dreams or through the possession of their servant. Thus the Haitian pantheon is indeed constantly in a state of flux and modification. On the other hand, deities may be inherited, either by the possessing of a new "horse" at the death of a previous one or by having their service taken up by an heir of the deceased servant. In Haitian theory, service of the *loa* is partly at the choice of the *loa*, partially at the choice of their human servants. The pattern of succession has not been studied, but it appears that there is some variety, thus some freedom of choice.

7. Compare Hogg's report of the Convince Cult in Jamaica, in which a photograph is included of a Bongo man, possessed by a spirit, climbing on the back of another man, literally "riding" him (Hogg: 1960).

8. The *hungan* may indeed be possessed, but he need not be. There is great individual variety here, and I would question Ari Kiev's characterizations, contrasting types of possession into those of *hungan* and those of *hunsi* (Kiev: 1961).

9. For a discussion of the role of the priest in identifying deities in the Brazilian cults, see Bastide (1958).

Once the deity is identified, some expectations as to his behavior and his tastes are, of course, developed. The first initiation ritual (*laver tête* or washing of the head) is called a baptism, in which other gods, having "mounted" other people, act as godparents. Cuts are made in the initiate's scalp and the person's principal deity (*maît' tête* or master of the head) is established. By means of this ritual, and of a preparatory retreat, the behavior of the deity is brought under control. The initiation ritual involves a three-day retreat and A. C. spoke of her experience as follows:

> After three days you go home. They are speaking *langage* in your head. You spill a pot (of water) at the threshold and then you tie your head. You go home right away, early in the morning, before the sun beats down.

The pouring of the water represents a customary libation, which is made upon entering or leaving a cult house. *Langage* is the esoteric language of priests and *loa* which laymen and initiates do not know. A. C.'s comment appears to mean that she experienced her own confusional thoughts as words spoken in her head, in an unintelligible language by supernatural beings, housed in her head. *Langage* is more of a supposed esoteric language than a real one, consisting of some African fragments as well as nonsense syllables. However, it is called on as an explanation of phenomena of glossolalia, when these appear in possession states. Also, if people speak incomprehensibly in their sleep, this may be interpreted as a supernatural visitation, in which the *loa* is speaking in *langage*.

As stated above, each of the *loa* is clearly thought to have a personal identity and continuity independent of his "horse" or "horses." Yet certain affinities between the *loa* and their vehicles are believed to exist: On the one hand, a person is thought to be "for" a given deity, whose character traits resemble his own, e.g., a vain and flirtatious woman will be said to be "for" Erzili. Yet it is also recognized that deities may choose "horses" who appear to be their very opposites. In the case of A. C., both propositions appear to hold true: One of her important *loa* was Ogû, a powerful, aggressive male deity, given to drinking, smoking, and angry outbursts, whereas A. C. was a small, shy, apparently quiet and fearful woman. Among her other deities was a Guédé, known for his cowardice.

Like the dreams of the Iroquois (Wallace: 1958), it appears clear that the possessions of the Haitians may express the "wishes of the soul," although the Haitians themselves hardly would formulate matters in this manner. Possessions may occur spontaneously, as protective measures. The emergencies may be physical or emotional. Danger may bring on the dissociational state in which no pain is felt and in which the deity may frighten away the potential aggressor. Like numerous other informants, A. C. too had experienced a frightening encounter with a *zombi*, in which her family deity, Loko, took over by "mounting" her and rendering the suspected *zombi* incapable of harm. The compliant, self-serving nature of the visitations of the *loa* is also clearly seen in the following abbreviated excerpt from field notes, reporting on an occasion in which A. C. wanted me to meet Ogû. This took place on the day after I had told her that I was considering a visit to her kin in a rural area, an announcement which pleased her visibly. I had never previously met Ogû "in her head."

> Having sent her little girl to buy a candle and her neighbor to buy a cigar, A. C. explained to me that she was going to call Papa Ogû to please me. She put some water in a cup and placed it on the floor, the lighted candle and the cigar on a plate beside it. She called her neighbor to sing, tied a red kerchief (Ogû's color) about her head, sat on a chair, resting her arms on the table. Both A. C. and her neighbor began to sing; A. C. explained that Ogû was very busy and it might take as much as three or four songs for him to come. The singing was quite slow and rather sloppy. A. C. stared at the candle, but looked away again; breathed quickly, then heavily, then began to shake her head violently, then calmed down again. Then raised her head with totally altered expression. This was Ogû who began to smoke the cigar, poured the water as a libation. Ogû greeted the two neighbors who were now present and myself, giving me special attention, making me turn about to induce possession, and took three hops backward on each leg. This was repeated toward the four directions. Then Ogû started various songs which the others would pick up, usually the same song repeated for quite a while. After a while he began to talk, in a somewhat altered voice. He talked a great deal in all but it came unevenly, as though he were looking for things to talk about, each time a subject was exhausted. He made me a great many compliments, saying he loved white women, that he did not like his old woman Erzili anymore and might leave her, etc., that it was a good idea for me to go to L. with his *cheval.* He got angry about being called to such a small room but was quickly restrained and calmed by the women. He criticized one of the women and blamed her principal deity, Guédé, for her behavior, insulted Guédé and warned me against him, saying that he was jealous, etc. After about 20 minutes he decided to depart after profuse leave-taking. At that, A. C. sat down, with her head on her arms on the table. She was breathing heavily, then quietly. After about two minutes she began to talk quickly, in a high voice, unintelligibly. One of the women removed the red kerchief and a few moments later A. C. got up, with a changed expression, laughing and hopping about. She was now possessed by Guédé. Their neighbor quickly got a cigar and clairin which Guédé downed quickly. He began by complaining about Ogû and people who malign him, i.e., Guédé, saying that it was Ogû who was the vagabond, while he himself could speak French, Spanish, and anything else. He insisted it was he rather than Ogû who would protect me. After some banter he said he had to leave so he could accompany me past the cemetery on my way, and with some affectionate leave-taking he departed. A. C. sat down as when Ogû had left. When she came to she inquired about Papa Ogû's visit and was surprised to hear that Guédé, too, had come.

Here we see that the ritual with which the *loa* are invited may be of a highly abbreviated sort, outside the context of any ritual occasion, indeed, for purely personal purposes, in this case "to please" the fieldworker. There is great readiness here for dissociation, a readiness established at least in part by frequent dissociations on earlier occasions. A preparatory mood was well established prior to my arrival, and while all of the specific elements which helped to establish it are not known to me, the motivation for the calling of the *loa* was clear: A. C. wished to confirm me in my plan of going to the country with her, and apparently felt that the *loa* would help me make up my mind to do so. She also expressed the idea that it would please me to meet them.

The act of calling Ogû, by songs, by symbolic dressing of the part, if only in token fashion, the preparation of an offering in the form of a candle, a cigar, and water indicate a conscious desire to take on Ogû's identity, to let him speak for her. Some degree of control is exercised in carrying out the preparatory steps. Yet where Guédé is concerned, this control is lacking. He appears seemingly uncalled, spontaneously. It is up to the neighbor's initiative to remove the red kerchief of Ogû and provide the necessary offering. Yet the neighbor's presence is incidental—indeed, accidental. Guédé's arrival seems to be prompted by Ogû's uncomplimentary reference to him, and he responds by criticizing Ogû and claiming me in opposition to Ogû. Yet while some conflict is expressed between these spirits, this does not appear to touch on any intrapsychic conflict in A. C.; rather the conflicting spirits reinforce each other and her own everyday self in their attempt at persuasion.

As far as awareness is concerned, Ogû knows about me and my plans and about the neighbor's behavior and her relation to Guédé. Guédé, in addition, knows about Ogû's visit. A. C., on the other hand, upon returning from the dissociated state, knows about neither visit.

The identities of the gods reveal another aspect of the Haitian behavioral environment, that of a class-structured society. The attributes of the gods identify them as members of the several classes: Ogû powerful, dominant, at times drinking rum and speaking French;[10] Guédé, the lower-class individual, parodying upper-class pretensions, drinking clairin, eating lowly foods. He lives in the cemetery and represents the dead and the cemetery, yet he is obscene and is associated with fertility and birth. Indeed, he helps at difficult deliveries. There are others, such as Erzili, the light-skinned woman with straight hair, who flirts with all the *loa* except the lowly Guédé; Zaca, called "cousin" rather than "Papa" like the other male gods, the peasant with his peasant costume and his ignorance of city ways, etc.

10. Haitian *loa* frequently attempt to speak in foreign tongues, the most frequent of which are French, English, and Spanish. One middle-class subject was reported to have been possessed by the Archangel Gabriel who spoke Hebrew, the spirit himself explaining to bystanders what language he was speaking! Another phenomenon discussed by May (1956) also occurs in Haiti; these are *phonations frustes*, the production of inarticulate sounds while in trance. A. C., at one ritual occasion, was possessed by a Guédé who could not speak and who desperately attempted to communicate by *phonations frustes*.

It is interesting that the gods are approached with a very considerable mixture of banter and respect. There is respect, indeed, reverence and awe, in asking the gods for help, yet it is recognized that when they come during ceremonies, they wish to enjoy the drums and the dancing, the food and drink, and generally to have a good time, and a great deal of ribald talk and banter takes place. Not only do the spirits themselves approach their faithful in this manner, but they accept and expect such talk in return. Religious activity is not a solemn-faced affair, but one in which there is a good deal of humor and verbal fencing, aspects of behavior which are not foreign to everyday, human, social interactions.

While spirit possession with its dissociated behavior and amnesia shows discontinuity of memory and personal identity, in the example under discussion there seems to be obvious continuity of motivation. This is also seen clearly in another incident in A. C.'s life. When the father of her children, with whom she was living in consensual union (plaçage) had become ill, some two years before this field work, Erzili, possessing A. C., undertook to cure him. In order to do so, Erzili required that the man marry both her and her "horse," A. C. The man complied, to the extent of marrying Erzili, i.e., Erzili while "in the head" of A. C., in a vodû ceremony.[11] However, he later refused to marry A. C. It appears clear that possession by Erzili and Erzili's demands were strictly in accordance with A. C.'s wishes. Indeed, in Erzili's offer to cure him, may there not be A. C.'s (unconscious) wish that he get well only on condition that he marry her? Yet the motivation was not questioned; it was Erzili who was involved, not A. C., even though it was A. C.'s presence that impersonated the deity.

The self-enhancing nature of possession is not limited to this case, where motivation admittedly appears to play almost too obvious a role. A. C.'s father, for example, is a mild-mannered man, generally ignored and pushed around by his kin. Yet he has one of the most powerful deities of the family, and when possessed, he is given great deference by his wife, who has left him, by his children, by his successful half-brother, and by others. Significantly, his possession on ceremonial occasions appears to linger on longer than most others. One of his half-brothers is considered somewhat dim-witted, yet his principal deity is crucial to the annual ritual at Christmas and without him, the brother who is a successful vodû priest could not conduct his ritual.

I do not wish to claim that all cases of possession show such obvious continuity with conscious motivation. Cases are cited where the gods punish individuals, so that the possessed person inflicts pain and harm on himself or does things which the individual upon returning to his ordinary state of consciousness considers to be contrary to his will or interests. An example of this is found in people who are possessed although they do not wish to be. Women

11. For a discussion of such ceremonies and the resulting marriage contract between men and female deities, see Rigaud in Deren (1953) and Métraux (1959).

claim that by tying their hair in a particular manner they can prevent possession; reasons for this vary from the observation that possession is tiring to a desire not to spoil one's clothes and are usually rather superficial. Yet it is also believed that if the individual attempts to prevent the gods from coming, they may come with much greater violence, so violently as to kill the "horse." The presumed greater violence of undesired possessions is interesting. One would suspect that a closer inspection would reveal continuity of motivation in such apparently negative cases also.

Impersonation of the *loa* involves the possibility of assuming other social roles, of dressing the part. This theme of disguise and role playing goes beyond the ceremonial impersonations which are taken seriously. Here the gods are believed to come and conscious impersonation is feared as sacrilegious in genuine ceremonies. Yet there is some elasticity in this situation. I recall a ceremony performed for a visiting American who wanted to have a set of drums baptized. Not only was the ceremony much abbreviated, but the officiating priestess took advantage of the situation to impersonate a possession by the frequently foul-mouthed Guédé to let loose a stream of obscene talk at the expense of the visitor, to the great glee of the participating members of her cult house.

The theme of impersonation, disguise, and role playing runs through much of Haitian life, be it the impersonation of carnival, the dressing up of Rara bands during Holy Week, or of the Guédé for All Saints Day. The same pattern of impersonation is expressed in the art of the raconteurs, where voices are imitated and performance verges on the theatrical.

It is interesting that the themes of disguise, mask, and costume appear frequently in Haitian Rorschach records (Bourguignon and Nett: 1955, p. 124). In the analysis of the content of projective test protocols, such disguises have been discussed under the heading of "distanciation" (e.g., W. Klopfer: 1954), which is said to represent an indirect expression of psychological themes. Holt and Havel have suggested the term "remoteness" about which they say:

> When an unacceptable impulse is expressed in a response, it may be made more acceptable if S puts distance between himself and the response by making the latter remote in time, place, person or level of reality (Holt and Havel: 1961, p. 299).

In the Haitian context, impersonation and disguises make it possible to act out impulses which, when carried out in one's own name and with one's own identity are socially unacceptable. Where dissociation occurs and the gods are assigned the responsibility for such behavior, the social significance of the behavior is changed. Where disguise may make behavior excusable, "possession" and its attendant dissociation will give it prestige and authority. Since the actions were carried out by gods, by entities not only other than the self but more powerful than the self, no fear or guilt or shame or social censure attaches to them. While dissociations do in fact entail discontinuity of the self, in the sense of personal identity, memory, and responsibility, may they not be thought of as *enlarging* the field of action of the self, rather than restricting it? Even if it is not I myself who did this, it is the Ogû in my head—who healed my child, who protected me from zombis, who let me not feel pain, who expressed wishes that I harbor—secretly or unconsciously. Can we not speak here indeed of "dissociation in the service of the self," much as Ernst Kris (1952) speaks of "regression in the service of the Ego?"

Kris directed his attention particularly to regression in the context of artistic creation and inspiration. In the Haitian case, there is some evidence that some, though not all, innovation in the religious field is channeled through the medium of dissociation. New deities may manifest themselves, as well as variations of familiar ones. They may make new demands and institute new ritual traditions or enlarge their sphere of activities. Other sources of innovation are dreams and the interpretation of supernatural demands by vodû priests and priestesses. Possessed individuals may engage in what appear to be untraditional activities. In one vodû shrine, in the region of Léogane, the walls were covered with painted hand prints, at least superficially reminiscent of those of Upper Paleolithic art. The only information about these that I was able to elicit was that these prints had been made by a *loa*, that is, a possessed person. There seemed to be no explanation available, except that it had been the desire of the *loa* to make these prints. The Haitian primitive painter Hyppolite, who was himself a *hungan*, claimed that his paintings were not executed by him, but by St. John the Baptist in his head. While there is reason to interpret this as a bit of clever publicity, the statement itself remains in the context of a vodû world view, in which the *loa* are creative innovators.

The Haitian peasant does not consider states of "possession" to be abnormal, in the sense that the discontinuity of personal identity is not thought of as pathological or evaluated negatively. Rather, it is a sign of the choice of the gods, of their approval. This, however, does not mean that the mechanisms encountered here are other than those familiar to us from psychopathology. There is dissociation: Actions are carried out, many, if not all, of which are unacceptable to the self in its everyday social roles; frequently they are unacceptable to the social group, if carried out by the individual on his own responsibility. The group, in requiring that certain actions may be carried out by gods but not by men, plays a significant role here. Yet the aims that are furthered in the dissociated states may be clearly the aims of the self. This was illustrated by the examples from the life of A. C. cited above, as well as from the experience of others. The actions of the deities are frequently—perhaps always—self-enhancing to the "horse." Yet their self-enhancing nature is clearly dependent on the social consensus, on the shared perception by the impersonator's group of the situation as one involving supernatural beings. Where group support fails, such people clearly become pathological. Examples of such unsupported, pathological dissociations are quoted by the Haitian psychiatrist Louis Mars (1947). However, admittedly, the relationship between those dissociational states which have group support and those which do not requires further investigation.

Conclusions

So far as the relation between "trance" and "possession" is concerned, several points may be noted in the Haitian case: In the ritual context, "possession" is always expected to involve "trance," i.e., postdissociational amnesia, anesthesia, etc., although degrees of dissociation vary from profound states of unconsciousness to dizziness to theatrical involvement to outright faking. Yet speaking in one's sleep is thought of as a sign of possession and people seen in one's dreams are thought of as possessed by spirits. Once more, then, the terms "trance" and "possession" should not be thought of as synonymous. On the other hand, in contrast to some of the examples discussed in the introductory portion of this paper, spirit possession is not used as an explanatory or diagnostic category for mental disease. That is to say, spirits may *cause* insanity or illness, by sending it, by confusing the individual, etc., but a person is not said to be ill because a spirit is *possessing* him.[12] Patients may be taken to vodû priests for cures, but these cures do not involve exorcism, as the illness does not involve possession. In this respect the Haitians and apparently other Afro-Americans are different from many East and West African groups. In the Haitian context, while possession is a prerequisite for becoming an initiate and later a priest, illness and cure is not such a prerequisite, as it is in many parts of Africa as well as in classical Asiatic shamanism.

Discontinuity in personal identity, the temporary substitution of other "selves" in the context of a belief in ritual possession by spirits, cannot be considered deviant in the reference system of Haitian culture. While such discontinuity surely does not represent the statistical norm, it does represent the opportunity for acting out certain positively evaluated social roles, and does provide the individual with a wider field for social action and social effectiveness.

12. Métraux (1959, pp. 274–281) speaks of "possession" by the dead as causes of illness and insanity. This is behaviorally and conceptually distinct from the ritual possession trances discussed in this paper. A sick person whose illness is thought to be due to such "possession" by the dead does not exhibit impersonating or trance behavior. The state is thought to be brought about by the activity of a sorcerer, who sends a dead person (or a zombi) against the victim. While the dead is said to be "on" the patient, he is not said to "mount" the patient, to be "in his head" or to "dance on" him, all expressions used with ritual possession by the *loa*. Nor is the patient the dead person's "horse." The dead have no volition or personal characteristics and diagnosis serves to identify the sender, not the identity of the "possessing" dead, nor does it involve a questioning of the dead person himself. A person who thinks, as A. C. did, that a dead person (or zombi) is sent against him by someone, may have encounters with living persons that are interpreted as encounters with the attacking dead.

It lends the individual support for varieties of actions and enhances his self-esteem.

Yet even within the limited range of Haitian society, I believe, there are considerable individual differences in the motivations leading to the assumption of dissociational roles. Thus the person who uses the capacity for dissociation, together with other talents, to become a vodû priest or priestess, one who literally "makes a career" of it, acquires power in the "real" world outside the ritual context, and in local terms, wealth as well—such a person surely must represent a personality organization different in significant respects from that of A. C., discussed in the preceding pages.

Admittedly, dissociation, supported by the group and its world view, may turn the individual away from "realistic" solution to his problems or keep the dissociated desires and behaviors "split off" from the everyday roles of the self. Prince (1964) has argued that possession behavior of the Yoruba is not integrated into the personality of cult members. Yet in the Haitian examples cited above, the self-serving nature of the supposedly "dissociated" wishes and desires is perhaps their most notable aspect. I should like to argue that ritualized dissociation provides the self with an alternate set of roles, in addition to his everyday inventory of roles, in which unfulfilled desires, "unrealistic" in the context of the workaday world, get a second chance at fulfillment, a fulfillment which is surely not merely vicarious because the glory goes to the possessing spirit rather than to the "horse." As in the admittedly unsuccessful case of A. C., the supernatural role may influence the "real" behavior of others toward the "horse" and the unwilling common-law husband, to cite only one example, may be pressured into legal marriage. Furthermore, the dramatic enactments of ritual are more than theater, since the roles are not merely "played", but are lived: All the participants consider the events of the ritual drama as real or more so than the events of everyday life. And there is no skeptical, dispassionate, incredulous audience. In a world of poverty, disease, and frustration, ritual possession, rather than destroying the integrity of the self, provides increased scope for fulfillment.

References

American Psychiatric Association

1956: *Statistical and Diagnostic Manual for Mental Disorders*, prepared by the Committee on Nomenclature and Statistics (2nd ed.; Washington, D.C.: American Psychiatric Association).

Arieti, S., & Meth, J. M.

1959: "Rare, Unclassifiable, Collective and Exotic Psychotic Disorders," in S. Arieti (ed.), *American Handbook of Psychiatry* (2 vols.) (New York: Basic Books).

Bastide, R.
1950: *Sociologie et Psychanalyse* (Paris: Presses universitaires de France).
1958: *Le Condomblé de Bahia* (*Rite Nagô*) (Paris–The Hague: Mouton).

Belo, J.
1960: *Trance in Bali* (New York: Columbia University Press).

Bourguignon, E.
1959: "The Persistence of Folk Belief: Some Notes on Cannibalism and Zombis in Haiti," *Journal of American Folklore*, **72**, 36–46.

Bourguignon, E. & Nett, E. W.
1955: "Rorschach Populars in a Sample of Haitian Protocols," *Journal of Projective Techniques*, **19**, 117–124.

Clark, E. T.
1949: *The Small Sects in America* (rev. ed.; Nashville, Tenn.: Abingdon-Cokesbury Press).

Coon, C. S.
1951: *Caravan: The Story of the Middle East* (New York: Holt, Rinehart and Winston).

Deren, M.
1953: *The Divine Horsemen: The Living Gods of Haiti* (New York: Thames & Hudson).

Devereux, G.
1961: "Mohave Ethnopsychiatry and Suicide: The Psychiatric Knowledge and the Psychic Disturbances of an Indian Tribe," *Bulletins of the Bureau of American Ethnography*, **175.**

Dorsainvil, J. C.
1931: *Vodou et Névrose* (Port-au-Prince, Haiti: Imprimerie La Presse).

Eliade, M.
1948: *Le chamanisme et les Techniques Archaïques de l'extase* (Paris: Payot).

English, H. B., & English, A. C.
1958: *A Comprehensive Dictionary of Psychological and Psychoanalytic Terms* (New York: Longmans, Green).

Fenichel, O.
1945: *The Psychoanalytic Theory of Neurosis* (New York: Norton).

Field, M. J.
1960: *Search for Security: An Ethno-psychiatric Study of Rural Ghana* (Evanston, Illinois: Northwestern University Press).

Gill, M., & Brenman, M.
1947: *Hypnotherapy* (New York: International Universities Press).
1961: *Hypnosis and Related States: Psychoanalytic Studies in Regression* (New York: International Universities Press).

Haberland, E.
1960: "Bessessenheitskulte in Süd-Äthiopien," *Paideuma, Mitteilungen zur Kulturkunde*, **6**, 142–150.

Hallowell, A.
1942: *The Role of Conjuring in Saulteaux Society* (Philadelphia: University of Pennsylvania Press).
1955: *Culture and Experience* (Philadelphia: University of Pennsylvania Press).
Harris, G.
1957: "Possession 'Hysteria' in a Kenya Tribe," *American Anthropologist*, **59,** 1046–1066.
Herskovits, M. J.
1937: *Life in a Haitian Valley* (New York: Knopf).
1948: *Man and His Works* (New York: Knopf).
Hogg, D.
1960: "The Convince Cult in Jamaica," in S. Mintz (ed.), *Papers in Caribbean Anthropology: Yale University Publications in Anthropology*, **58,** (New Haven: Yale University Press).
Holt, R. R., & Havel, J.
1961: "A Method for Assessing Primary and Secondary Process in the Rorschach," in M. A. Rickers-Ovsiankina (ed.), *Rorschach Psychology* (New York: Wiley).
Huxley, A.
1954: *The Doors of Perception* (New York: Harper).
Kiev, A.
1961: "Spirit Possession in Haiti," *American Journal of Psychiatry*, **118,** 133–138.
Kirchner, H.
1952: "Ein archäologischer Beitrag zur Urgeschichte des Schamanismus," *Anthropos*, **47,** 224–286.
Klopfer, W. G.
1954: "Interpretative Hypotheses Derived from the Analysis of Content," in B. Klopfer, M. D. Ainsworth, W. G. Klopfer, & R. R. Holt (eds.), *Developments in the Rorschach Technique* (Yonkers, New York: World).
Kris, E.
1952: *On Inspiration: Psychoanalytic Explorations in Art* (New York: International Universities Press).
Leiris, M.
1958: "La possession et ses aspects théâtraux chez les Éthiopiens de Gondar," *L'Homme, Cahier d'Éthnologie, de Géographie et de Linguistique*, **1** (Paris: Plon).
Loeb, E. M.
1929: "Shaman and Seer," *American Anthropologist*, **31,** 60–84.
Mars, L.
1947: *La Lutte Contre la Folie* (Port-au-Prince, Haiti: Imprimerie de l'État).
Martino, E. di.
1961: *La Terra del Rimorso* (Milan: Il Saggiatore).
May, L. C.
1956: "A Survey of Glossolalia and Related Phenomena in Non-Christian Religions," *American Anthropologist*, **58,** 75–96.

Messing, S.
1958: "Group Therapy and Social Status in the Zâr Cult of Ethiopia," *American Anthropologist*, **60,** 1120–1126.

Métraux, A.
1959: *Voodoo in Haiti* (New York: Oxford University Press).

Monroe, R.
1955: *Schools of Psychoanalytic Thought* (New York: Dryden).

Nadel, S. F.
1946: "A Study of Shamanism in the Nuba Mountains," *Journal of the Royal Anthropological Institute*, **76,** 25–37.

Norbeck, E.
1961: *Religion in Primitive Society* (New York: Harper).

Oesterreich, T. K.
1921: *Die Bessessenheit* (Halle: Wendt & Klauwell).

Prince, R. H.
1964: "Indigenous Yoruba Psychiatry," in A. Kiev (ed.), *Magic, Faith, and Healing: Studies in Primitive Psychotherapy Today* (New York: Free Press).

Ribeiro, R.
1956: "Possessaô-Problema de Etnopsicologia," *Boletim do Instituto Joaquim Nabuco de Pesquisas sociais* (Pernambuco, Brazil), **5,** 5–44.

Sargant, W.
1957: *Battle for the Mind: A Physiology of Conversion and Brainwashing* (New York: Doubleday).

Simpson, G. E.
1962: "The Shango Cult in Nigeria and in Trinidad," *American Anthropologist*, **64,** 1204–1229.

Simpson, G. E., & Hammond, P.
1960: Discussion of M. G. Smith, *The African Heritage in the Caribbean*, in V. Rubin (ed.), *Caribbean Studies: a Symposium* (Seattle: University of Washington Press).

Teicher, M. I.
1960: "Windigo Psychosis: A Study of a Relationship Between Belief and Behavior Among the Indians of Northeastern Canada," in V. Ray (ed.), *Proceedings of the 1960 Spring Meeting of the American Ethnological Society, Seattle.*

Verger, P.
1957: "Notes sur le culte des Orisa et Vodun à Bahia, la Baie de tous les Saints au Brésil et à l'ancienne Côte d'Esclaves en Afrique," *Memoires de l'Institut Français d'Afrique Noire* (Dakar), **51.**

Wallace, A. F. C.
1958: "Dreams and the Wishes of the Soul: A Type of Psychoanalytic Theory Among the Seventeenth Century Iroquois," *American Anthropologist*, **60,** 234–248.
1959: "Cultural Determinants of Response to Hallucinatory Experience," *American Medical Association Archives of General Psychiatry*, **1,** 58–69.

THEODOSIUS DOBZHANSKY

Religion, Death, and Evolutionary Adaptation

Religion is one of the cultural universals of mankind. A great variety of religions, living and dead, are known. Tylor, Frazer, Malinowski, Durkheim, Levy-Bruhl, Lowie, Hallowell, and many other anthropologists have made important contributions in the field of comparative study of religion. It is not my purpose to review their work, even briefly. What emerges from their studies is, however, of interest to an evolutionist. The universality of religion indicates clearly enough that religion satisfies some deep-seated and vital need of the human psyche. An evolutionist is driven to enter the ground "which angels fear to tread." What are the evolutionary origins of this need so obviously inherent in human nature?

The philosopher Whitehead said that the lives of individuals may seem to be "passing whiffs of insignificance" (1900). Hartshorne, another philosopher, describes religion as "man's acceptance of his own fragmentariness" (1962). Man overcomes his transience and insignificance by becoming, at least in his imagination, a part of some sublime and eternal life. Does, then, life really have some meaning? There may never be a convincing, definitive, doubt-proof answer to this question. An influential school of philosophy cheerfully proclaims that the question is meaningless. People nevertheless persist posing this question. I agree with Brinton that to urge them to stop doing so is as pointless as to ask them to do without sex relations.

It can neither be proved scientifically nor rigorously ruled out that man's existence, and that of the world in which he lives, is meaningful or meaningless. Neither biology nor science as a whole is engaged in asking such questions. Scientific hypotheses must be submitted to tests before they can be either accepted or rejected. There is simply no way to put to a test the hypothesis that the world is or is not meaningful. Should a biologist at this point declare: Full stop? I do not think so. As biologists, we are constrained to inquire how and why it came about that man, individually and collectively, persists in asking questions about the meaning of things. It is a most extraordinary fact that one of the, at least, two million existing biological species, a peculiarly made-over ape called mankind, has started to ponder such difficult, and perhaps insoluble, problems. This fact does fall within the province of evolutionary biology and anthropology. The present essay is a tentative attempt to examine the evolutionary implications of this fact.

Whether or not religion can be regarded an evolutionary adaptation is a meaningful problem. Its solution is to be sought in the consequences of man's refusal to accept "his own fragmentariness." A refusal constitutes a rebellion against life, which invites a biological, as well as a spiritual, disaster. An analysis, unexcelled in the world literatures, of the consequences of such a rebellion is that given by Dostoevsky in *The Possessed.* Kirillov, the rebel, can find no sense or meaning in the world he knows. The world is only "a devil's vaudeville." And yet, in the midst of this world there is a being, Kirillov, who understands that the world is senseless. And he realizes that he happens to be, without his consent, placed in the role of an actor in this "devil's vaudeville." There is no escape other than self-destruction. A freely arrived at decision to commit suicide is the only road Kirillov sees toward assertion of his "new awesome freedom." He not only kills himself, but does this in a way which assists a bunch of scoundrels to perpetrate the crime of killing another person whom Kirillov pities and respects. But why worry if we are caught in a devil's vaudeville anyway!

The adaptive function of religion has been described very aptly by Feibleman (1963), a psychiatrist with a philosophical bent. In his words: "Theologies are qualitative response systems which promise survival. Irrespective of their truth or falsity (and since they conflict, no more than one of them can be true), the overwhelming statistics as to their prevalence indicate that they are necessary for some need-reduction in the human individual. The need is, of course, the need for survival, for ultimate security, for the escape from the pain of death. The human individual knows that he must die, but has thoughts larger than his fate. . . . Religion is an effort to be included in some domain larger and more permanent than mere existence." The inclusion does not necessarily imply a belief in a personal immortality. This is most obvious in Buddhism, which regards the release from the cycle of rebirths, i.e., from the incarnations and reincarnations, the greatest spiritual achievement open to man. A person's individual existence may then be ephemeral; what really matters is that this existence is believed to be a part of something that endures eternally. Emotional responses elicited by hopes of participation in a life everlasting are sometimes strong enough to overcome the fear of death itself.

Socrates maintained that "True philosophers are ever studying death." It is debatable whether this is, or was, true of all philosophers, or only of the "true" ones. There is, however, no question that every human being, above the idiot level and past the age of childhood, knows that death is sooner or later inevitable. Man lives in the awareness of the certitude of death. Some people contemplate the prospect with a composure mixed with awe, others with fear and dread. A coolly rational acceptance is feigned more often than achieved. Tolstoy, in one of his stories, has a poignant description of a person's predicament in the face of death. A man begins to realize that his death is near. He tries to be sensible about it; he recalls an example of syllogism in a textbook of logic: "All men are mortal; Gaius is a man; Gaius must die." Suddenly he recoils from this logic: "What does all this have to do with me, I am not Gaius."

Living creatures other than man are also mortal. Man is, however, unique in knowing that he will die. This is difficult to prove rigorously, especially since philosophers like Whitehead (1900) and Hartshorne (1963), and biologists like Rensch (1959), argue that everything, down to atoms, contains some spark of life, spontaneity, and freedom. It may just as well be imagined that all animals, and even all organisms, have a trace of some kind, however faint, of a foreboding of death. I fail to see any basis, or any advantage, in such a speculation. However that may be, this much can hardly be questioned—man's awareness of the inevitability of death is uniquely and unambiguously clear.

Most informed people now accept, albeit not a few of them a bit grudgingly, the story of the evolutionary origin of mankind from animal ancestors. There is nevertheless some hedging on the part of certain theologians and philosophers. Man's body is a product of evolution, but evolution has allegedly nothing to say about the essential human nature, sometimes designated the *humanum*. Man's awareness of his transience, with all the intellectual and spiritual consequences of this awareness, unquestionably belongs to his *humanum*. The evolutionary origins of this awareness are indeed a difficult, and strongly challenging, problem. I believe that this problem nevertheless does fall within the competence of the evolution theory.

Mankind, the human species, has evolved from ancestors that were not human. A being who knows that he will die thus arose from ancestors who did not know. The appearance of this new kind of being was an evolutionary event certainly unprecedented on earth, possibly and even probably unprecedented in the cosmos. Where, when, and how this event took place is conjectural. This may never be known, since human thoughts are not preserved in fossil condition. Fortunately, some of the products of these thoughts are preserved, and from them the nature of the thoughts may with some plausibility be inferred. Only man buries his dead, and a burial is a sign of some reverence for death, which can hardly be felt by anyone who does not know that he too will die. There are some hints of concern with death in humans as ancient as Peking man, a representative of the species *Homo erectus*, presumed to be ancestral to *Homo sapiens*. With the Neanderthal race of *Homo sapiens*, the evidence becomes unambiguous. Veneration or fear of the dead is, of course, common if not universal among primitive peoples, and the remains of ancient civilizations are mute testimony of a great intensity of these emotions.

It is not likely that an awareness of one's mortality would be a help, and a lack of such awareness a hindrance, to the so-called instinct of self-preservation. This is a misleading designation anyway, since there is no such "instinct." True enough, all organisms, from the highest to the lowest, react to some stimuli of their environments in ways which tend to maximize the chances of their survival, either as individuals, or as species, or (usually) both. The reactions are, however, not automatically and unconditionally beneficial; the organism does not always "know" what is good for it. By no means all environmental agents elicit objectively beneficial reactions. It is chiefly environments which the species had encountered regularly and frequently in its evolutionary history that evoke beneficial reactions termed ("modifications" by Schmalhausen [1949]). Reactions to novel or unusual environments are far from always beneficial. Examples of unadaptive responses (Schmalhausen's "morphoses") are not difficult to find. Moths are attracted to bright lights, where many of them burn to death. The tanning of the human skin by sunlight is an adaptive modification, but X-rays may cause morphoses—burns and cancers. The beneficial reactions obviously do not result from an instinct which "knows" what is or is not useful for preservation of health and of life; such reactions are built into the genes by natural selection in the evolutionary past in the species.

Attempts to understand the origin of the death-awareness by itself are futile; considered in isolation from other human attributes, its origin in human evolution is inexplicable. Evolutionary changes are shaped by natural selection in response to the challenges of the environments in which the species lives. Changes induced by natural selection are adaptive, at least in the environments which prevail where and when they are selected. In short, they are selected because they are adaptive. An ability to recognize the approach of a danger is evidently useful if one can do something to avoid that danger. If such an ability is even in part genetically conditioned, natural selection promotes its development. But what is the advantage of knowing that death is inevitable?

An escape from the impasse may be found if the death-awareness could be shown to have been a by-product of some other evolutionary change directly advantageous to the species. The hypothesis to be considered is that the death-awareness is a sequel to self-awareness. That self-awareness is adaptive in man is fairly obvious. The argument in favor of this view has been stated most clearly by Hallowell (1953): ". . . psychological functioning at a level of self-awareness is as important for rational personal adjustment as it is for the functioning of sociocultural systems." Only having developed the ability to see himself as an object among other objects, did man gain a perspective in which he could begin to understand the relations between processes and events, including the consequences of his own actions. Some understanding of these relations is obviously indispensable for survival in human environments, at even the most primitive cultural levels. A concomitant of self-awareness is, however, death-awareness. The adaptive value of death-awareness was at best doubtful, at least until man had reached the stage when a parent could begin making provisions for the maintenance of his progeny in anticipation of his own demise.

The reasons why useless and even harmful traits can become established in evolution controlled by natural selection must be made unambiguously clear. First of all, let it be understood that a "trait" is not a genetic or a biological unit but rather a semantic device. An organism is not an aggregate of independent traits; we make it seem to be such an aggregate when we describe it in words. The height, or weight, or color is not an entity separable from the body which is measured or weighed or viewed. Apart from semantics, different "traits" have to be distinguished because different operations are performed to investigate them; the trait "head length" is measured with a pair of calipers, while the "blood group" is discovered by observing the agglutination of erythrocytes. Moreover, there is no one-to-one correspondence between a gene and a trait; expressions like "the gene for eye color" are metaphors. Finally, natural selection does not select, eliminate, or promote separate genes; it does not even select genotypes; it operates only when individuals which carry certain genotypes survive more often, and leave on the average more progeny, than do carriers of other genotypes.

No genetic endowment is best in all environments. The Darwinian fitness is not an intrinsic property of a genotype; it is contingent on the environment in which the carrier of a genotype happens to live. A genotype may confer a high adaptive value on its carriers if it gives them some important advantage in some respect. What must be stressed here is that such an advantage may compensate for one or several minor disadvantages. Probably no organism is ideal in all respects, and it remains alive because its weaknesses are compensated by its strong points. As an example of such a compensation, consider the grossest unadaptive feature of human physiology, the difficult childbirth. How could such a biological absurdity have become established in human evolution? It certainly could not possibly have been selected by itself, on its own merits. Difficult childbirth appears, however, to be a concomitant of the erect body posture. The erect body posture is, in man, an obviously adaptive feature; it has permitted the development of hands capable of handling tools and performing operations which would be at least difficult for appendages used also for walking. Women suffer childbirth pains because they (and also men) are bipeds instead of quadrupeds.

According to Hallowell (1960), "A human social order implies a mode of existence that has meaning for the individual at the level of self-awareness. A human social order, for example, is always a moral order. If the individual did not have the capacity for identifying the conduct that is his own and, through self-reflection, appraising it with reference to values and social sanctions, how would a moral order function in human terms?" Since man controls his environment by means of his social and moral order, and since self-awareness is a key, or even the key, to his social and moral order, it follows that self-awareness, or rather its genetic basis, is a product of adaptive evolution. A by-product of self-awareness is, however, death-awareness. Man has discovered his transitoriness and mortality, and he had to learn to live with the consequences of his discovery. He strove to do so presumably ever since he became recognizably human, but never fully succeeded. Is this what Socrates meant by his assertion that philosophers "are ever studying death"? Man's struggles with his death-awareness belong, of course, to the cultural rather than to the biological level of existence. Cultural events have, however, biological consequences, and vice versa. Some of the consequences of death-awareness are biologically adaptive and others unadaptive. Quite certainly, they are important to man.

Since man knows that he is mortal, the strategy of "eat, drink, and be merry, for tomorrow we die" seems to be the simplest to adopt, and therefore a most popular solution. Unfortunately, this is a meretricious and illusory solution. It does not make it easy to accept the certitude that the eating, drinking, and merriment will presently end. World literatures are forever busy with this vexed problem. Existentialists of all varieties, from Kierkegaard to Sartre, have made human anxiety in the face of the problem of death the keystone of their philosophies. This anxiety is probably species-wide in man, although its pitch varies greatly. It intrudes more upon the consciousness when the primary needs for food, drink, sex, and safety are satisfied than when they are not. It is stronger in those whose hold on life is weak than in those more secure, higher among the unwell than among the healthy. There probably exist also constitutional, very likely genetically conditioned, differences among people which make them more or less anxiety-prone.

The problem of anxiety has received a great deal of attention of psychoanalysts, from Freud to the present day. Erich Fromm (1959) has expressed some ideas, the implications of which are particularly interesting to a biological evolutionist. Man is a being who "even if all his physiological needs were satisfied, he would experience his state of aloneness and individuation as a prison from which he had to break out in order to retain his sanity." People consequently strive for a union with, and for relatedness to, other human beings. A union may, according to Fromm, be sought by submission to others, or by domination, or finally by love of others. The first two methods are misguided, because only "in an act of loving, I am one with all, and yet I am myself, a unique, separate, limited, mortal human being. Indeed, out of the very polarity between separateness and union, love is born and reborn." If Fromm's view is valid, it would seem to follow that a biologically unadaptive trait (anxiety-proneness), which is itself a by-product of an adaptive one (self-awareness), rebounds to yield another highly adaptive one (love).

Love and devotion to one's progeny are easiest to understand, introspectively as well as biologically. Although an individual's life is transitory, yet he may hope that a trace of himself will somehow be perpetuated in his children, and the children's children, and so perhaps forever. Parental care is, of course, by no means limited to man, but only in man is the relatively weak instinctual component reinforced by striving for the relatedness and love; and only in man is the parental devotion liable to produce a disappointment, a parent finding in his children alienation and rejection instead of continuity and love. It is also true that self-sacrifice by the parents on behalf of their progeny is not unknown among animals, including insects. In some species of birds and mammals, an individual may place itself in a position of danger from an enemy's attack, shielding from peril the young who may or may not be the defender's progeny. Whether this objectively self-sacrificing behavior is comparable to human altruism is quite another problem. It is likely that the genetic endowment of the human species is a necessary (though certainly not sufficient) condition for the manifestation of altruism.

Identification can be established with groups larger, and presumably more enduring, than one's offspring and one's family. A clan, a tribe, a nation, and finally mankind as a whole may abide much beyond the span of an individual's life, even unto eternity. Hopefully, so may an enterprise, such as science or art, a movement such as a church or a sect, and an institution such as a political party or a community. Time after time, people have shown themselves to be willing to sacrifice their lives for real or imaginary benefits of groups or "causes" which continue to exist when the individual who sacrifices himself is dead.

The human ability to acquire identification with groups, movements, and institutions evidently confers a cohesion upon the latter. The importance of this cohesion in human cultural evolution is difficult to exaggerate. It makes human history different from biological history. In man, the group cohesion is predicated upon his self-awareness. It is therefore different from the cohesion of a herd, a flock, or an anthill, which stems from instincts handed down through the genes. This greatly enhances the biological adaptive value of self-awareness as a human genetically conditioned trait. Whatever might have been the adaptive significance of self-awareness when it first arose in man's evolution, it became vital with the development of human social organization to which the self-awareness is the key.

Social cohesion based on self-awareness suffers, however, from a weakness from which the instinctual cohesion of the anthill is free. No institution and no enterprise has an obvious and unconditional meaning or utility not subject to doubts and misgivings. Identification with groups or enterprises which endure beyond an individual's lifetime does not confer upon this life a value that cannot be called in question. Everything may be only "vanity and a striving after wind," everything including the universe itself. And it is science that is alleged to have suggested, or even demonstrated, the meaninglessness of everything. Is this allegation warranted?

It cannot be gainsaid that science has made necessary serious alterations in the world image inherited by Western civilization from its more ancient predecessors. Nor can it be denied that the prescientific world view was in some ways more comfortable and snug than is our present one. God was believed to have created the world as recently as 5724 years ago, and moreover, to have created it expressly for man to live in and to enjoy. Even though man misbehaved and was banished from God's proximity, God has lost interest neither in mankind nor in each individual person. He watches every one of us constantly from His dwelling somewhere above the clouds. He is open to our prayers and entreaties.

The scientific image is cold and detached. In expanding the world immeasurably science has seemingly deflated man. After Copernicus it appears ludicrous to suppose that the vastness of the cosmic spaces was devised for man, even if he becomes a cosmonaut. Darwin allegedly completed what Copernicus and Newton had begun. Instead of having been created in God's image, man has only recently departed from a monkey's image. Instead of a pre-established moral order, science can see in the world, and even in living bodies, an only slightly mitigated molecular disorder. Freud has attempted to give a *coup de grâce* to man's self-exaltation; far from being good by nature, we are bundles of subconscious strivings, mostly of rather contemptible sorts, kept in check only with difficulty by something called the "superego." Is it, then, not ridiculous to presume that the God of the universe billions of light-years across may set some store by the doings of a human person, an evanescent speck on the surface of a minor planet whirling around a second-rate sun? Has science added to our self-awareness, first a death-awareness, and then an awareness of being unwilling actors in the Dostoevskian "devil's vaudeville"?

The above "scientific" world image is neither as full nor as compelling as we have been assured by some writers that it is. It overlooks the most essential contribution to human thought made by Darwin and by the evolutionists who followed him. Whatever else the world in which we live may be, it is certainly not an unchanging world. It is an evolving world. Regardless of what man's ancestors were, and regardless of whether the present state of mankind is or is not satisfactory, man is not unalterable. This is what makes the Darwinian world so completely different from the Newtonian world. The world of Newton was a marvelously well-ordered, high-precision mechanism. It did not, however, have either much of a past nor, presumably, much of a future. Its very perfection precluded improvement with time. Darwin's world is the antithesis of stability. Even the billiard ball-like atoms of classical physics have been split and shown to have arisen in a process of cosmic evolution. Life is a relative newcomer; it arose on earth perhaps two billion years ago, and the existing living creatures are very different from their ancestors. Man, with his consciousness, self-awareness, and death-awareness, is a much more recent arrival, his period of existence being a mere flash on a cosmic time scale.

The Darwinian world is on the move. Whither is it going? Where will it be when we are no longer here? These are questions to which there may possibly never be clear and incontrovertible answers. And yet seek for answers we must, even in the face of the admonitions that the questions may be meaningless. This is, indeed, man's "ultimate concern," which cannot be abandoned unless we have lost interest in our own existence. A gallant attempt to outline a new set of answers to these questions has been made in the works of Teilhard de Chardin. Teilhard's views must be considered here, of necessity very briefly, because they bear on almost every issue alluded to in the present essay. Teilhard was a thoroughgoing evolutionist; he regarded biological evolution as a prolongation of the cosmic, and human cultural and spiritual evolution as a prolongation of the biological. The whole universe is, to him, one vast evolving system, in which the human species is the main growing point. Hallowell has described man's distinctive character as follows: "Man, unlike his animal kin, acts in a universe that he has discovered and made intelligible to himself as an organism not only capable of consciousness but also of self-consciousness and reflective thought" (1960). Teilhard expressed himself in almost identical words. But he goes much beyond this; to him, man not merely accepts but overcomes his fragmentariness when he realizes that his individual existence is a part of an existence more enduring. The destiny of man is to be the leading part of the progressive evolution of his species, the living world, and the cosmos.

Teilhard's writings have met with a mixed reception, ranging from hero-worship to outright hostility. The nature of his work and his message is frequently misunderstood.[1] Teilhard was a Christian mystic as well as a scientist. His insights were those of a man trying to assimilate the discoveries of science into his mystical vision of the dazzling and formidable universe, not to build a scientific substitute for his vision. He often tries to speak about the ineffable. This can be attempted only by means of poetic imagery if it can be done at all; poetic imagery does not, however, fare well if it is mistaken for a scientific discourse. And yet not all scientists despise poetry, or succeed in keeping it wholly separate from their science. The interest and significance of Teilhard's thinking lies precisely in the synthesis which he was able to achieve. Some scientists, e.g., Julian Huxley (1959), have claimed the ability to state Teilhard's doctrine in purely scientific terms (or even to have discovered it before Teilhard). The result can most charitably be compared to a *Hamlet* without the Prince.

Teilhard's synthesis does not have the force of a scientific demonstration; in this respect it is not at all comparable to Darwin's work, as some of Teilhard's overenthusiastic followers are ready to claim. The intellectual grandeur of this synthesis may, however, be recognized even by those who are not fully convinced by it. Teilhard sees the universe as a product of evolution and an evolving whole. The center of his doctrine is that the evolution has a discernible direction or trend. It is a struggle between "the unified Multiple and the unorganized Multitude." And: "Man, the center of perspective, is at the same time the center of construction of the Universe. And by expediency no less than by necessity, all science must be referred back to him" (1959). The whole evolution is seen as a continuous progression, or an ascent, from atoms, to atomic compounds, to megamolecules, to living organisms of increasing complexity, to differentiation of nervous systems, to the origin and growth of consciousness, to formation of the noösphere (the "thinking layer"), to "a harmonied collectivity of consciousnesses equivalent to a sort of super-consciousness," to an eventual confluence in the Point Omega, which is Teilhard's symbol for God.

Teilhard's evolutionism is cosmic and at the same time frankly anthropocentric. He has stated this splendidly as follows: "Man is not the center of the Universe as we naïvely believed, but something much more beautiful, Man the ascending arrow of the great biological synthesis. Man alone constitutes the last-born, the freshest, the most complex, the most subtle of the successive layers of life" (1959). The immensity of the universe does not contradict the evolutionary centrality of man. The evolutionary process has a destination in

1. Strange to say, it was misunderstood by Teilhard himself, who begins the preface to his *The Phenomenon of Man* by the following statement: "If this book is to be properly understood, it must be read not as a work on metaphysics, still less as a sort of theological essay, but purely and simply as a scientific treatise" (1959). How completely erroneous is this bidding is shown by the other writings of Teilhard, which expound much the same doctrine as *The Phenomenon of Man* and make no claim of being science pure and simple. Teilhard's self-deception proves only how difficult it is to keep one's mind divided in compartments the contents of which are not allowed to contaminate each other.

the Point Omega, and man is its greatest achievement so far. An individual man passes; mankind, however, not only abides but forges ahead; mankind is not merely one of the many independent and equivalent evolutionary lineages but the vanguard of the evolution of the cosmos.

The evolutionary vision of Teilhard is not derived from biology or from science, but it includes science as a component part. It is a vision of a religious mystic, but of a mystic not only familiar with the evolutionary doctrine but one to whom this doctrine is of paramount importance, as shown clearly by the following statement: "Is evolution a theory, a system, or a hypothesis? It is much more—it is a general postulate to which all theories, all hypotheses, all systems must henceforward bow and which they must satisfy in order to be thinkable and true" (1959). This situation is frequently misunderstood by Teilhard's proponents and by his opponents. The proponents like to think that since Teilhard was a scientist, he was able to give a scientific demonstration of his mystical vision, and Teilhard's above-quoted preface to his great book seems to show that at least for a moment he himself nurtured such an illusion. The opponents (among whom G. G. Simpson [1964] has given the best-reasoned critique) rightly point out that the vision does not necessarily follow from the scientific evidence.

I think that the proponents and the opponents are equally in error, because they mistake a part for the whole. The greatest interest of Teilhard's work is that it represents a synthesis of science, and metaphysics, and theology; this synthesis is stated, as such a synthesis can only be stated, in a language of poetic inspiration. Now, the validity of a synthesis depends on the validity of every one of its components, although the components do not necessarily validate or invalidate each other. Teilhard's synthesis need not be taken for a completed structure; on the contrary, it doubtless should and will be revised and improved as the different branches of human thought which have contributed to its construction achieve improved knowledge and insight.

From the biological side such a revision is patently necessary; Teilhard was insufficiently familiar with the theories of biological evolution which were current when he was writing his works, not to speak of the changes since then. It would be out of place in the present article to enter upon technical biological criticism of Teilhard's works. One point must, however, be mentioned, at least briefly, since it may cast Teilhard's thought in a wrong perspective. Teilhard lays great stress on the evolutionary history of the universe being a directional process. This is, indeed, the key postulate in his synthesis. To him, the directionality is evident in the cosmic (inorganic), in biological, cultural and spiritual evolution. This directionality he repeatedly calls "orthogenesis." Now, orthogenesis is a technical term in biology. It signifies that the evolution is impelled by internal forces residing in the organism itself, rather than by natural selection which is a challenge-response mechanism involving interaction between the organism and its environment. Orthogenesis is a unilinear evolution, unfolding or unveiling something that has been preformed and preordained. Orthogenesis may be interpreted mechanistically, but more often it has been conceived as involving some transcendental, spiritual, or divine guidance.

Orthogenesis never was more than a minority opinion among biologists, and at present its adherents are not at all numerous. Majorities are not always right, and what is more relevant here is that the notion of orthogenesis is so clearly uncongenial to the general tenor of Teilhard's system of views that one cannot help wondering whether the author himself realized its implications. Orthogenetic evolution is in the last analysis a spurious evolution; nothing genuinely new is permitted to arise, and no room is left for creativity or freedom. Orthogenesis envisages the evolution of the living world as something like the operation of a music box, the spring of which was wound up at some time in the past, and which gradually sends forth the program stored in it.

Evolution can well be directional without being orthogenetic. That biological evolution does have a discernible over-all trend or direction is substantiated by evidence; the evidence comes mainly from paleontology, the discipline with which Teilhard was personally most familiar. The trend has been, without doubt, on the whole progressive. Although a satisfactory definition of what constitutes progress in biological evolution has never been formulated, it is a fact that the most ancient organisms were less complex, and especially that they had much less developed nervous systems than the more recent organisms, especially the vertebrates. Man is, on the geological time scale, a very recent arrival indeed. The noösphere is accordingly more recent than the biosphere.

Orthogenesis is a possible, but neither necessary nor even a very plausible, explanation of the progressive trend observed in the history of the biosphere, culminating in the emergence of the noösphere. The explanation preferred by most evolutionists is philosophically more interesting, as well as more in accord with the spirit of the Teilhardian system. Its main advantage is, of course, that it is well supported by the evidence accumulated in biology and paleontology. Very briefly, it is held that living species respond to challenges of their environments by adaptive alterations; these responses, mediated by natural selection, are the building blocks of the evolutionary changes. Adaptation and progress are not predestined and not automatic; they have to be struggled for. The struggle leads often, but not always, to success; however, the evolution is sometimes regressive. Adaptive changes may be opportunistic, making the organism highly fit in environments which are only temporary. Such changes may cut off the ability of the organism to respond to further environmental challenges, and thus result in extinctions. A living species may be described, somewhat metaphorically, as groping for ways to widen and improve its hold on its environment. It may "discover" new and advantageous paths, but it may also become stranded in blind alleys.

The universe is an evolving product of an evolutionary process. It is not an accident; it is an enterprise. Life has an important place in this enterprise; it is, in Teilhard's words, "the spearhead of evolution." Mankind is the spearhead of life, because it is the product of evolution which is becoming conscious of its role in evolution. Again in Teilhard's words: "Mankind as an organic and organized whole possesses a future: a future consisting not merely of successive years but of higher states to be achieved by struggle. Not merely survival, let us be clear, but some form of higher life or super-life." An individual human is conscious of his own fragmentariness. However, it is up to him, to some extent at least, to make his existence something more than a "passing whiff of insignificance." He can, if he so chooses, contribute toward the achievement of a higher life for himself and for the world of which he is a part.

References

Feibleman, J. R.
1963: *Mankind Behaving* (Springfield, Illinois: Charles C. Thomas).

Fromm, E.
1959: "Value, Psychology, and Human Existence," in A. H. Maslow (ed.), *New Knowledge of Human Values* (New York: Harper).

Hallowell, A. I.
1953: "Culture, Personality, and Society," in A. L. Kroeber (ed.), *Anthropology Today* (Chicago: University of Chicago Press).
1960: "Self, Society, and Culture in Phylogenetic Perspective," in S. Tax (ed.), *Evolution after Darwin*, Vol. 2 (Chicago: University of Chicago Press).

Hartshorne, C.
1962: *Man's Fragmentariness*, Virginia Wesleyan College Lecture (unpublished).
1963: "Real Possibility," *Journal of Philosophy*, **60**, 593-605.

Huxley, J.
1959: Introduction to P. Teilhard de Chardin, *The Phenomenon of Man* (New York: Harper).

Rensch, B.
1959: *Evolution above the Species Level* (New York: Columbia University Press).

Schmalhausen, I. I.
1949: *Factors of Evolution* (Philadelphia: Blakiston).

Simpson, G. G.
1964: *This View of Life* (New York: Harcourt, Brace).

Teilhard de Chardin, P.
1959: *The Phenomenon of Man* (New York: Harper).

Whitehead, A.
1900: Quoted by Hartshorne (1962).

RAYMOND D. FOGELSON

Psychological Theories of Windigo "Psychosis" and a Preliminary Application of a Models Approach[1]

Windigo disorder among the Northern Algonkian-speaking Indians has attracted much attention in the anthropological literature as an example of a seemingly ethno-specific type of mental derangement. Most interpretations of the disorder emphasize functional, rather than possible organic, factors relevant to the etiology and symptomatology of the windigo syndrome. Physiological reactions—possibly produced by drastic dietary change, chronic or periodic mineral or vitamin deficiency, or, perhaps, consumption of toxic food substances—may underlie, or at least be partially responsible for, the behavioral manifestations which these Indians classify as windigo. Correlatively, in the Northern area where small breeding populations are the norm, one cannot *a priori* dismiss the possibility that certain genetic factors may predispose particular individuals to windigo reactions. However,

1. My interest in the subject of windigo was first aroused as a student in Dr. A. I. Hallowell's course, Psychology and Culture. Later, at Eastern Pennsylvania Psychiatric Institute, I was given the opportunity to review the windigo literature as part of a project directed by Dr. A. F. C. Wallace. A shortened version of this report was read at the 1962 American Anthropological Association Meetings.

sufficient data to generate, let alone test, specific physiological and genetic hypotheses are not readily available. This report, then, will concentrate on psychological aspects of windigo.

In the first part of the paper, various psychological explanations that attempt to comprehend certain facets of windigo ideology and behavior will be reviewed and synthesized. Very little of what will be presented can qualify as formal psychological theory but, instead, largely represents impressionistic observations and interpretations offered by travelers, missionaries, and anthropologists. The second portion of the paper contains a preliminary application of a simple model approach as an effort to define some of the parameters of a windigo disorder in terms of logical types inferred from illustrative case materials.

Review of Implicit and Explicit Psychological Theories Concerning Windigo

The earliest reported cases of windigo (although not given that name) are recorded in the Jesuit Relations. Le Jeune's Relation of 1634–35 contains an account of a crazed Indian (probably Micmac) who threatened to kill and eat his sisters and brother-in-law. The brother-in-law noted: ". . . this man is half mad; he does not eat; he has some evil design" (Thwaites: Vol. 8, 1901, pp. 31–33). Fathers Drueillete's and Dablon's "Journal of the First Journey Made to the North Sea" contains an account of fatal cannibalistic madness suffered by their Cree deputies during the winter of 1660–61.

> Those poor men (according to the report given us) were seized with an ailment unknown to us, but not very unusual among the people we were seeking. They are afflicted with neither lunacy, hypochondria, nor frenzy; but have a combination of all these species of disease, which affects their imaginations and causes them a more than canine hunger. This makes them so ravenous for human flesh that they pounce upon women, children, and even upon men, like veritable werewolves, and devour them voraciously, without being able to appease or glut their appetite—ever seeking fresh prey, and the more greedily the more they eat. This ailment attacked our deputies; and, as death is the sole remedy among those simple people for checking such acts of murder, they were slain in order to stay the course of their madness (Thwaites: Vol. 46, 1901, pp. 263–265).

These two accounts substantiate that a kind of cannibalistic insanity was already known in the Northeastern area during the seventeenth century. However, these cases are not definitely linked with the evil Windigo spirit. The first account mentions certain prodromal symptoms common to windigo "psychosis" as described in many later accounts. As Teicher notes (1960, p. 77), the case of the crazed deputies is unusual in that it is one of the few examples of epidemic-like group cannibalistic frenzy. Some of the other implications in these two reports will be elaborated more fully in conjunction with later case materials.

At this point, it seems wise to consider some of the earliest references to, and connotations of, the term "Windigo" (including its close cognates). The late Father Cooper uncovered early documentary material which suggests that Windigo, or Witiko, designated a malevolent spiritual being among the Cree (1934). A clerk (who Cooper thinks was either Charles Swaine or Theodore Swaine Drage) spent the winter of 1746–47 at Fort Nelson (York Factory) and left the following pertinent data concerning the religious notions of the neighboring Indians.

> They "are not without the Sense of a Deity. It is a received Opinion amongst the *Indians* in those Parts, that there are two Spirits, one whom they call *Manitou*, to which Spirit, they attribute all the Perfections of the Deity, the other Spirit they call *Vitico*, and that Spirit they imagine to be the Cause of all the Evil with them. These Juglers [conjurers] pretend to an Intimacy with Vitico." Drage then goes on to describe the conjuring tent and its rite, ascribing to Vitico seemingly the leading role of spokesman therein. "Nor do the *Indians* make any likeness of *Manatou* or *Vitico*, or have they any Temples or Altars. Neither do these People worship *Manatou*, but to *Vitico* sometimes they make an Offering; where there is wanted a Removal of a present Evil, or to avert a future one."
>
> "In a time of great Scarcity or Sickness," there was a type of dog sacrifice to *Vitico*, with a prayer for "Health, or, as the Case is, more Plenty. They have a Notion of a Personal Appearance of *Vitico* . . ., but not of *Manitou*." When drunk, they used to go out of their tents to shoot Vitico dead with their guns (quoted from Cooper: 1934, pp. 54-55).

This account is corroborated by Ellis, who also spent the winter of 1746–47 in the York Factory area, and by Wales, who resided in the Churchill district for thirteen months in 1768–69. A detailed account written by Umfreville, who spent eight years at the York Factory between 1771 and 1782, sheds further light on our problem.

> Exclusive of these superstitious ideas (he has just described "the Devil" in terms that evidently identify him with the Witiko), the religious sentiments of these people, though confused, are in many respects just. They allow that there is a good Being, and they sometimes sing to him; but not out of fear or adoration, for he is too good, they say, to hurt them. He is called *Kitch-e-man-e-to*, or the Great Chief. They further say, there is an evil Being, who is always plaguing them; they call him *Whit-ti-co*. Of him they are very much in fear, and seldom eat any thing, or drink any brandy, without throwing some into the fire for *Whit-ti-co*. If any misfortune befals them, they sing to him imploring his mercy; and when in health and prosperity do the same, to keep him in good humour. Yet, though obsequious sometimes, at others they are angry with him, especially when in liquor; they then run out of their tents, and fire their guns in order to kill him. They frequently persuade themselves that they see his track in the moss or snow, and he is generally described in the most hideous forms. They believe that both the

good and the bad Being have many servants; those of the former inhabiting the air, but those of the latter walking on the earth (quoted from Cooper: 1934, pp. 56–57).

These sources strongly imply that Windigo may have represented an evil deity in aboriginal Algonkian religous conceptions.[2] The good deity, Manitou, although beneficent, seems remote, abstract, nonintervening in human affairs, and thus unneedful of propitiation. The evil deity, on the other hand, was more earthly and substantive and subject to human attention. The evidence of his tracks, his hideous form, the fact that he had servants (perhaps transformed humans?), and his association with "juglers" suggest later facets of the windigo complex. However, more interesting to note is the absence in these early accounts of characteristics which were later associated with the Windigo being: as his gigantic stature, his anthropophagous propensities, and his symbolic connections with the north, winter, and starvation.

Several recorded instances of windigo disorder survive from the late eighteenth century. Alexander Henry encountered a Cree youth who was found guilty of eating his uncle, aunt, and their four children under winter starvation conditions. Henry comments:

> The Indians entertain an opinion that the man who has once made human flesh his food will never afterward be satisfied with any other. . . . He ate with relish nothing that was given him; but, indifferent to the food prepared, fixed his eyes continually on the children which were in the Indian lodge, and frequently exclaimed, "How fat they are!" . . . his behavior was considered, and not less naturally, as marked with the most alarming symptoms; and the Indians, apprehensive that he would prey upon these children, resolved on putting him to death. They did this the next day with the single stroke of an axe, aimed at his head from behind, and of the approach of which he had not the smallest intimation (quoted from Quaife: 1921, p. 201).

Two basic Indian beliefs about cannibalism are expressed here: (1) Once human flesh is tasted, insatiable craving for more is established; and (2) because of this antisocial appetite, cannibals had to be killed as a menace to the group.[3] The

2. This assumption runs counter to the principal arguments of Father Cooper, who favors aboriginal monotheism in the form of a single Northern Algonkian Supreme Being (1934). However, it should be noted that bicephalous religious systems headed up by a good and a bad deity (often brothers) are widespread in aboriginal Eastern Woodland cultures.

3. Substantially the same beliefs are recorded for the late eighteenth-century Western Woods or Swampy Cree. Samuel Hearne stated ". . . when any of their tribe has been driven to the necessity of eating human flesh, they become so fond of it, that no person is safe in their company. And though it is well known they are never guilty of making this horrid repast but when driven to it by necessity, yet those who have made it are not only shunned, but so universally detested by all who know them, that no Indians will tent with them, and they are frequently murdered slyly" (quoted in Curtis, Vol. 18, n.d., p. 63).

These beliefs were also recorded for the nineteenth century Ojibwa [viz. Jones: 1861, pp. 69–70; Hind: 1860, p. 65].

first point contains some subtle psychological implications. It is felt that once the tabu against eating human flesh has been broken, the violator will have no scruples against repeating the act. As is evident in some of the later accounts, the cannibal himself frequently suffers such a loss in self-esteem and depersonalization that he no longer feels he has sufficient control over his own behavior to avoid future recurrences of anthropophagous acts. In another light, windigo cannibalism is viewed as a character flaw in which an individual manifests moral weakness under the pressure of extenuating circumstances. Jenness has mentioned that among the Parry Island Ojibwa that individuals who appear gluttonous and have abnormal appetites for fats are considered as having a predisposition to windigo "psychosis," the assumption being that such persons under the stress of starvation will be the first to lose control and resort to cannibalism (Jenness: 1935, p. 40).

David Thompson, whose *Narrative* spans the period from 1784 to 1812, reports some native beliefs about "Weetigoes" or man-eaters. After noting that the ailment seems to be limited to the Nanathaway and Chippeway Indians, and unknown to the Plains tribes and the Dinnae, Thompson writes,

> The word Weetigo is one of the names of the Evil Spirit and when he gets possession of any man (women are wholly exempt from it) he becomes a man eater, and if he succeeds; he no longer keeps company with his relations and friends, but roams all alone through the forests, a powerful wicked man, preying upon whom he can, and as such is dreaded by the natives. Tradition says, such evil men were more frequent than at present, probably from famine. I have known a few instances of this deplorable turn of mind, and not one instance could plead hunger, much less famine as an excuse, or cause of it . . . (Tyrrell: 1916, p. 261).

Thompson also presents two detailed cases of windigo in which the sufferer is killed and his body burned to ashes to forestall resurrection of the Evil Spirit.

Thompson raises a number of interesting points. He sees Weetigo and the Evil Spirit as identical and considers transformation into human Weetigoes as resulting from possession by the Evil Spirit. The windigo evil deity identity has already been discussed, but this is the first clear statement that spirit possession is an important native explanation for human transformation into windigoes. Thompson's assertion that the disorder is limited to men is not supported by Teicher's survey, which reveals an approximate 4:3 ratio between reported male and female cases (Teicher: 1960, p. 108). Thompson also maintains that hunger or famine is not a necessary prerequisite for setting off a windigo reaction; this assumption *is* supported by later case materials. The cremation of the corpses of known Windigos occurs in several actual cases and in most windigo folk tales. The burning of windigo corpses is accounted for by the native belief that Windigos possessed hearts of ice (sometimes homuncular) which had to be melted in order to prevent reincarnation and insure permanent departure of the malevolent soul.

The artist Paul Kane visited the Saulteaux in 1846 and makes the following general statements about windigo belief and treatment.

> The Weendigoes are looked upon with superstitious dread and horror by all Indians, and any one known to have eaten human flesh is shunned by the rest; as it is supposed that, having once tasted it, they would do so again had they an opportunity. They are obliged, therefore, to make their lodges at some distance from the rest of the tribe, and the children are particularly kept out of their way; however, they are not molested or injured in any way, but seem rather to be pitied for the misery they must have endured before they could be brought to this state (Kane: 1859, pp. 60 61).

This quotation again stresses the addictive quality of human flesh, but suggests an alternative handling of Windigoes by social ostracism rather than the usual death penalty. This social isolation and avoidance, as will be seen later, doubtlessly exerted a profound influence on the man-eater's subsequent behavior. If the individual was not particularly abnormal prior to his real or supposed act of cannibalism, segregation from his fellows would be likely to encourage eventual asocial behavior.

Lieutenant William Hooper, who searched for the remains of the last arctic explorer, Sir John Franklin, reports an incident that reveals the personal feelings of an Indian who openly confessed to having eaten human flesh under the threat of starvation.

> I was told here of an Indian of the Beaver tribe who, after having experienced with many others the horrors of starvation in 1849, visited in the spring of the following year the fort at Dunvegen. The gentleman in charge of the post offered him his hand in greeting, but it was declined, as were also the salutations of other Indians present. When asked the reason of his strange demeanour, he replied, "I am not worthy to shake hands with men; I am no longer a man, for I have eaten man's flesh. It is true I was starving, was dying of hunger; but I cannot forgive myself; the thought of the act is killing me, and I shall die soon, and with contentment, for although I still exist I cannot any longer consider myself a human being." He had, as I understood, since died (Hooper: 1853, pp. 404 405).

The tremendous sense of guilt over his actions had sapped this Indian's will to live. Having tasted human flesh, he felt that he had forfeited his membership in the human race. There is no hint of imminent punishment by others for his misdeed, only a willful desire for self-destruction; he felt he could never regain self-respect or dignity in his own eyes. Hooper also notes the contrast of this pattern with other Athabaskan groups where starvation cannibalism is accepted as a fact devoid of enduring personal or social stigma.

J. G. Kohl's *Kitchi-gami* (1860) is a rich source of windigo material. In addition to providing valuable case material, Kohl makes some rather acute psychological statements, a few of which will be quoted and commented upon. Kohl says the following about Indian attitudes toward cannibalism.

> But even these cases of unnatural attacks on one's own brethren, produced by unspeakable want, are only exceptions to a rule. The Indians here, on the contrary, have always returned to a state of natural repugnance against cannibalism, and they have indeed, a decided aversion from those who have committed the crime, even when in extreme want, and almost in a state of rabid frenzy. They give the opprobrious name of "Windigo," which is nearly synonymous with our cannibal and it is quite certain that if a man has ever had recourse to this last and most horrible method of saving his life, even when the circumstances are pressing and almost excusable, he is always regarded with terror and horror by the Indians. They avoid him, and he lives among the savages like a timid head of game.
> Any one that has once broken through the bounds does so easily again, or, at least, the supposition is rife that he can do so. Hence he becomes an object of apprehension, and must live retired from the rest of his fellow men. He does not enjoy their fraternal assistance, and thus his hostile position towards society soon drives him back into the same difficulty and temptation. In this manner, or nearly so, a class of windigoes is called into existence (Kohl: 1860, pp. 355–356).

Here again, the terror and fear associated with cannibalism, the belief that once having tasted human flesh the act is repeated more easily, and the social ostracism of known Windigoes are reiterated. Kohl is explicit in suggesting that social isolation fosters subsequent antisocial acts and cannibalism.

In another place, Kohl presents an interesting hypothesis concerning the origin of human Windigoes:

> It is very natural that in a country which really produces isolated instances of such horrors [cannibalism], and with a nation so devoted to fancies and dreams, superstition should be mixed up in the matter, and that at last, through this superstition, wonderful stories of windigos should be produced, as among us, in the middle ages, the belief in witches produced witches. Just as among us some people really did unusual things through electro-magnetism and spiritualism, and performed incantations; and as superstition endowed these magicians and witches with greater and more dangerous powers than they really possessed, and people grew at last into giving themselves out as witches and magicians—here, too, some men have become windigos by necessity; in the same way fear has caused some gloomy-minded people to be regarded as windigos; and, worst of all, this fear and the general opinion have so worked upon some minds, that they believe themselves to be really windigos, and must act in that way. In all physical and mental diseases incidental to humanity, there is a certain epidemic tendency, and a spontaneous self-production and propagation. It is just like the "Sorrows of Werther." First, there is a Werther in real life, whom the poets render celebrated, and at last the nation is inoculated with Werthers.
> It is a universal tradition among the Indians that in the primitive ages there were anthropophagous giants, called Windigos. The people's fancy is so busy with them, as well as with the isolated cases of real cannibalism, that they begin to dream of them, and these dreams, here and there, degenerate to such a point that a man is gained over to the idea that he is fated to be a windigo.

> Such dreams vary greatly. At times a man will merely dream that he must kill so many persons during his life; another dream adds that he must also devour them; and as these strange beings believe in their dreams as they do in the stars, they act in accordance with their gloomy suggestions (Kohl: 1860, pp. 357–358).

The gist of this hypothesis, stripped down to its essentials, is that isolated occurrences of cannibalism plus highly developed cultural fantasies about cannibalism conspire to bring about or call into existence human Windigos. Additionally, dreams serve as one of the direct vehicles by which fantasy is conveyed into the realm of accepted reality. Kohl's statements foreshadow some of Hallowell's interests in the role of cultural factors in perception and also anticipate (by about one hundred years) Teicher's principal thesis that windigo belief determines windigo behavior (Teicher: 1960, pp. 110, 113).

Kohl was aware of the distinction between prodromal and terminal symptoms in windigo disorder and the generality of windigo classification in native usage. After reporting a case in which a man kills several people because of a dream message, but does not devour them, Kohl comments:

> The story of the man I have told who struck down others in consequence of a dream, is not actually cannibalism. But a case of the sort is frequently connected with cannibalism, and, at any rate, depends from the entire chain of superstition I describe here, and of which the windigo forms the termination. The windigo mania rarely breaks out spontaneously; it must have its predecessors and degrees. If a man live much apart and out of the world, if he appear to be melancholy and is tortured by evil dreams, then people begin to fear he may end by becoming a windigo, and he is himself attacked by fatalistic apprehension, and is driven towards a gloomy fate (Kohl: 1860, p. 360).

Here, Kohl stresses the social (or asocial) nature of windigo disorder. The man who is out of step with his fellows becomes feared by society. Fairly soon he internalizes the society's image of him, and the process of becoming a Windigo is accelerated. Kohl also recognizes the connection between Windigos and evil spirits and notes the existence of windigo women—*des femmes windigo* (Kohl: 1860, p. 363).

Moving now to some of the material collected in the twentieth century, we see additional implicit and explicit psychological interpretations of windigo disorder. Father Saindon reported an instance of mental breakdown among the James Bay Cree in which the sufferer was unable to manage or reduce dissonance between contradictory stimuli. This case might be interpreted in terms of the recent "double-bind" theory of schizophrenia (viz. Bateson *et al.*: 1956).

> F. had the Windigo malady. She did not want to see anyone except her husband and her children, because strangers became metamorphosed in her eyes into wild animals—wolves, bears, lynxes. These animals are dangerous to life. To protect herself she was driven by the desire to kill them. But this was repugnant to her because these animals are human beings.

> She fought against the obsessing idea that found lodgement in her consciousness. She wished to kill and she didn't. The idea became stronger and more compelling. As a solution of her conflict, she fled from reality and took the stand of not wishing to see anyone or to speak with anyone. Walled up in her tent, she was resigned to her condition. She was taciturn. She almost always held her eyes cast down. She struggled against this situation. She couldn't sleep (Saindon: 1933, p. 11).

In this case, Mrs. F. struggles with two orders of information—that one should kill wild animals, but that one should not kill human beings. Normally these two cognitions are not contradictory, but they become so when the sufferer experiences perceptual disorientations that prevent her from discriminating between human beings and animals. Mrs. F. attempts to resolve her difficulty by withdrawal from the conflict via minimal interaction with other people and downcast eyes. The eventual outcome of the case is not indicated.

Father Cooper also tends to see the essence of "Witiko psychosis" as a kind of double-bind phenomenon. After mentioning the reality of historic traditions of starvation cannibalism, Cooper continues,

> Driven to desperation by prolonged famine and often suffering from mental breakdown as a result thereof, the Cree would sometimes eat the bodies of those who had perished, or, more rarely, would even kill the living and partake of the flesh. The solution, however, of the conflict between hunger and the rigid tribal taboo [against cannibalism] often left, as its aftermath, an "unnatural" craving for human flesh, or a psychosis developed in men or women who had not themselves previously passed through famine experience (Cooper: 1933, p. 21).

Here, the double-bind consists of the physiological need for nourishment and the culturally inculcated horror of anthropophagy, a situational conflict which Cooper feels is likely to produce mental disorder.

Hallowell views windigo disorder as a complex of cultural and physical factors. The most prominent of these factors are the physical symptoms of the individual, the native interpretation of these symptoms, the attitudinal interplay between the patient and the group, and the psychological reality of witchcraft. According to Hallowell:

> . . . the initial mental phase of the "Wihtigo psychosis" appears to be a morbid state of anxiety on the part of the subject, directly traceable to the native interpretation of certain physical symptoms. These are the distaste for ordinary types of food, nausea and perhaps vomiting. When these symptoms continue to manifest themselves for several days or more, anxiety develops, and, if they fail to disappear, rapidly reaches a climax. This is because repugnance to food is construed as positive evidence that the person is becoming a "wihtigo," i.e., a cannibal. This state of anxiety in the subject is further excited by the general fear of cannibalism which is shared by everyone in the community. In no time the whole camp will be agog with the news because everyone knows everybody else's business. The

> person afflicted with anxiety, therefore, soon becomes the object of the projected fears of a number of other human individuals. But on the part of the subject there is another reason for agitation. This is the fear that he or she has been "bewitched" and the general belief in witchcraft is so potent that the conviction that such is indeed the case is enough to give anyone the "jitters." Besides all this, the condition of the subject is further conditioned by a negative fact. This is the failure to rationally consider alternative causes of the physical symptoms, a possibility unconsidered on account of the cultural attitudes engendered by the positive emphasis imposed by the witchcraft belief and the association of the symptoms with the *wihtigo* concept. Individual experience is immediately shunted into a vicious circle of belief patterns from which there is no escape. The individual affected is usually watched day and night by some relative and, in former times, a medicine man would probably be consulted. If there were no improvement, the afflicted one would often ask to be killed and this device was usually gratified (Hallowell: 1934, pp. 7–8).

Hallowell disagrees with Cooper over the classification of the windigo condition as necessarily "psychotic" or "pathological."

> . . . My point is that all reputed cases of this "psychosis" may not be pathological and even those which are may be, perhaps, of varying psychiatric classification on closer inspection. I did hear of the case of a man who actually killed his wife and children and ate them and not under the pressure of starvation. He was also considered a *wihtigo*. . . . This one [case], and others similar to it, might perhaps be considered as morbid states of anxiety exaggerated by cultural factors and by the attitudes of their contemporaries who treat the subject as a potential social menace (Hallowell: 1934, p. 9).

Hallowell also stresses the necessity of distinguishing the initial phases of the disorder from the terminal phases in which cannibalistic fantasies and urges are acted out. In most of the Berens River cases reported in the 1934 article and in subsequent articles (1936 and 1938), the sufferer experienced only the prodromal symptoms and frequently was cured. Such cases, perhaps, more closely approximate severe anxiety neuroses than full-blown psychoses. Hallowell calls for the collection of additional case data to demonstrate that disorders labeled as windigo do not share a common etiology and should be differentially diagnosed.

Speck feels that the amount of cannibalism attributed to the Naskapi by earlier writers has been exaggerated. The few authenticated instances of cannibalism were brought upon by starvation conditions and involved whites as well as Indians. Speck reports no cases of "psychotic pathology" that are attributed to windigo. Nevertheless, the windigo concept is quite strong in native belief. *Wihtigo*, the cannibal spirit, is said to wage war against the Great Man (soul-spirit) of a weaker person and, if victorious, devours the vanquished person. Human beings could also become Windigos. According to the native belief,

> When a man had eaten human flesh, he became a *wi'tigo*, and by having eaten so powerful a form of "game," his spirit, or *Micta'peo*, would grow so strong that they [other members of the group] would be afraid to attack him, so a conjuror could destroy him only by sorcery. He would then try to get the wi'tigo spirit into his power by luring it to a fight. The conjuror having succeeded in this, the man would be doomed (Speck: 1935, p. 43).

Here, the notion of windigo and cannibalism are closely linked, but the status of windigo is achieved only after the anthropophagous act has been consummated. Thus, the windigo belief serves the Naskapi as *post hoc* explanation for cannibalism. There are no advance warnings, pathological or otherwise, that an individual is in danger of becoming a Windigo.

Ruth Landes has written much about the psychological aspects of windigo disorder among the Ojibwa, and her contributions warrant extended discussion. Landes agrees with Hallowell in considering windigo to be a cover term embodying several clinical diagnoses and also in seeing at least two phases in the windigo syndrome. She says:

> Windigo . . . manifests itself differently in different persons, but the Ojibwa regard it as a unit. The onset is withdrawal into melancholia. . . . He lies inert, said to be brooding over the possibilities of cannibalism, wanting to eat men and yet afraid. His family around him looks to him like luscious beavers heavy with fat. In his lucid moments he describes himself as sad because he wants to eat them but is not motivated strongly enough to get them. He neither eats nor sleeps and seems insensible to all about. The next stage is that of violence, which may follow almost immediately or only after a considerable period. . . . This is commonly a compulsive carrying out of his cannibalistic desires (Landes: 1938a, pp. 25–26).

The perceptual disorientation described here is comparable to that reported by Cooper and Saindon for the Cree.

Landes lists three principal modes by which a person can become a Windigo. A person may contact the Windigo Spirit through a dream or vision quest. If the person does not renounce Windigo as his guardian spirit, he will become a cannibal. People also become windigos under starvation pressures. The starvation may be real: where an actual lack of food forces the person to feed on his fellows; or, in some cases, tremendous anxiety over the fear of imminent starvation may bring on symptoms of windigo disorder. The third route to windigo disorder is through sorcery, real or imagined, direct or indirect. By indirect sorcery is meant the efforts of a sorcerer to influence the weather or remove the game and thereby bring starvation to the cursed party. The sorcerer can also work directly by inducing the Windigo Spirit to possess the victim. Landes gives a vivid description of Windigo Spirit possession:

> The Ojibwa say that these sufferers [in the violent stage] are possessed by the Windigo spirit sent upon them by a sorcerer and that the victim must serve the windigo's appetites as his own. He ceases to brood on defeat, and all his internal conflict yields to the one fixed idea: that meat be supplied him. He kills his family quite coolly, as he does any usual food object, and eats them. The home supply lasts a long time though he has an inordinate appetite, and when he has exhausted that supply, he wanders for more. Only his death can restore safety to the community, and the windigo sufferer in this stage invited his own doom. Some people so afflicted even command their relatives, in their lucid moments, to burn them as windigos upon the pyre. Windigos in this phase of their sufferings are to the Ojibwa a greater terror than the evil shaman, for insane cannibalism is the ultimate monstrosity (Landes: 1938a, p. 26).

Landes has also recognized three variations from the typical windigo syndrome. The first variation does not manifest the usual initial melancholia, and, sometimes, the open aggressiveness associated with the terminal stage is absent. Landes notes:

> There are occasional instances of windigo cannibalism among the Ojibwa that are not regarded as due to the malevolence of a sorcerer. Persons so afflicted are not known to suffer any acute melancholia. They are quiet and retiring and execute their murders without show, perhaps through craftiness, perhaps simply in a depressed, dissociated mood (Landes: 1938a, p. 27).

A second variation involves windigo disorder among shamans. According to Landes:

> Windigo insanity among shamans, since they in contrast to ordinary mortals have the power with which to fight defeat, takes a somewhat different course. If a shaman is defeated—and at least temporary defeat is implied in every windigo affliction—his very life is forfeit, so that a conflict is necessary to the death. For this reason the Ojibwa regard windigo in a shaman as incurable unless he himself throws it off in a great conflict with his enemy.
>
> The onset of windigo in a shaman is the same as in the case of an ordinary mortal. He is unsuccessful on the hunt in his winter trapping grounds, and he believes that the game has been frightened away by a rival shaman, whom he sees as balls of fire (will-o'-the-wisp) and bears as the hooting of owls and barking of dogs. He too falls into a melancholia and sees his family as good eating in the disguise of beavers. He cannot eat or sleep—and it is interesting to observe that, though he is a visionary under other circumstances, this involuntary fast does not provoke compensatory visions. When the violent stage ensues, he may, however, strike out against his persecutor and in fortunate cases vanquish him (Landes: 1938a, p. 28).

From Landes' material, and also from Hallowell's, another variant windigo pattern can be recognized. In this class, the patient suffers only the initial melancholic symptoms and is considered curable.

> Windigo insanity in non-shamans does not necessarily proceed to violence and obsessive cannibalism; the affliction is not thought to be as severe as it is among shamans. With non-shamans assiduous nursing and loving care during the period of melancholia will persuade the sufferer to face life again (Landes: 1938a, p. 27).

Landes sees windigo disorder as ultimately rooted in the dominant Ojibwa ethos that conditions interpersonal behavior.

> Ojibwa ethos . . . is saturated with anxiety, which has a realistic basis in the often recurring periods of starvation. To alleviate this anxiety an Ojibwa may not depend upon the support of his fellows, whom he characteristically regards with envy and suspicion and from whom he expects similar unfriendly emotions. The individual who gains prestige is one who exerts power for his own private ends; and when he is successful, he is regarded not as having gained security, but as having become more vulnerable. The neuroses and psychoses which flourish in such soil are conditioned by this ethos (Landes: 1938a, p. 24).

This picture of Ojibwa anxiety and interpersonal fear has been observed by several other investigators of Ojibwa personality. Landes goes on to construct a differential male-female ethos; on this basis she argues that men are more liable than women to windigo attacks, particularly in reaching the cannibalistic phase. She feels ". . . the culturally inculcated masculine pursuit of power, the ideas of personal reference, the penalizing of success—those things which make a capable man only the more conspicuous target for envy, are the aspects of Ojibwa male ethos which underlie the marked neuroses and psychoses which are termed windigo" (Landes: 1938a, p. 33). Although noticeable differences in Ojibwa sex role patterning are not to be denied, Landes' hypothesis seems misdirected, since the evidence mentioned previously does not indicate a significantly differential male-female incidence of windigo disorder.

Landes favors a cultural explanation of windigo disorder over explanations based solely on environmental or economic factors. This point she illustrates by reference to the Eskimo, who generally are conceded to live in a harsher environment with slimmer food resources, but among whom the obsessive anxiety, preoccupation with cannibalism, and pathological windigo states are absent. In seeing the genesis of windigo belief in Ojibwa ethos, Landes seems to be invoking an implicit Freudian displacement hypothesis, based upon a *pseudo*-hydraulic analogy. Direct channels for the expressions of normal interpersonal aggression and hostility are blocked by a dam of customary deference and avoidance patterns, and the main flow of aggressive and hostile feelings is diverted into devious side branches of sorcery and gossip. This hypothesis is consistent with many of Hallowell's observations, and Flannery also interprets the matter similarly when she speculates ". . . the cannibal giant (windigo), as this character functions in northern Cree and Montagnais folklore may serve as a release for the fear, anxiety, and hatred which are fairly well blocked by social convention" (Flannery: 1947, p. 400).

Seymour Parker recently has advanced a psychoanalytic interpretation of windigo disorder that emphasizes Ojibwa primary and secondary institutions and the correlated basic personality structure (1960). Parker believes that the ontogenesis of "Wiitiko psychosis" is rooted in the distinctive Ojibwa character structure, particularly the strong oral fixation which is felt to result in permanent dependency cravings. Despite the absence of any direct evidence, Parker goes so far as to suggest that the prototype of the Wiitoko monster is the mother figure. He notes the wide range within which disorders labeled windigo may fall, and he follows Landes in postulating the influence of divergent male and female *ethea* responsible for a supposed differential incidence rate of male and female sufferers. Parker's argument that Ojibwa fixation at the oral stage of psychosexual development underlies windigo disorder is not a sufficient explanation. By and large, practically all North American Indians, with the possible exception of the Pueblo peoples, have been characterized by culture-and-personality specialists as having strong oral dependency needs. If these characterizations are valid, the question arises as to why windigo "psychosis" is restricted to the Northern Algonkian-speaking Indians.

Morton Teicher's monograph, *Windigo Psychosis* (1960), contains a comprehensive compilation of actual windigo cases plus a representative sampling of Algonkian myths and folktales concerning Windigo. Teicher's key thesis is that windigo "psychosis" is explained best as an example of belief determining behavior. Teicher interprets the natural history of the windigo concept in the following fashion:

> The windigo belief was built up by inductions from actual experiences of starvation and cannibalism. It was embellished by fearsome stories until the belief became a fact of life. It entered the mainstream of the belief system to the point where it was traditional and dominant. It stood as an unquestioned and widely held concept, occupying a foremost position in the belief system of every individual who shared the culture. As a fundamental cultural generalization, the windigo belief provided a basis for ready deductions leading to action. Thus, it may truly be said that the windigo concept determined behavior (Teicher: 1960, p. 110).

This line of argument is essentially similar to J. G. Kohl's analogy, presented earlier, that belief in witches eventuated in the production of self-confessed witches during the Middle Ages. The attempt to assign primacy to either belief or behavior seems rather artificial, since the two variables, if legitimately isolated as such, seem dynamically reciprocal or bidirectional in their mutual influence. Despite seeming theoretical shortcomings in his monograph, Teicher has performed a great service by assembling a nearly exhaustive compilation of recorded windigo cases. This collation provides a basis from which to examine some of the prevailing demographic features concerning windigo disorder. As was mentioned previously, the supposed differential male-female incidence of windigo disorder is *not* supported by Teicher's material. Additionally, the fact that only seventy fairly well-authenticated cases of windigo disorder have found their way into the literature—from a population of about thirty thousand over a period of three centuries—suggests strongly that windigo disorder may be a relatively rare phenomenon, notable more for its spectacular features than for its chronicity.

Before attempting to construct a typology of various types of windigo disorder from cases reported in the literature, it might be well to recapitulate briefly some of the major or pervasive psychological explanations that have been advanced to account for windigo "psychosis." Four nonmutually exclusive psychocultural approaches toward comprehending the genesis of windigo disorder can be discerned. The first kind of explanation might be termed the "belief-determines-behavior" approach, of which Kohl and Teicher are the principal advocates. A second closely related approach can be labeled "the reciprocal effect," in which a physical symptom becomes exaggerated into actual mental disturbance through a complex interaction between symptom interpretation (generally colored by beliefs about sorcery) by other community members and the detrimental feedback of such interpretation upon the sufferer. This point of view is developed most elaborately by Hallowell. A third major approach may be designated as the "double-bind" theory. Here the sufferer is overcome by a tremendous urge to cannibalistic behavior, usually via distorted perceptions of human beings as animals, yet recognizes and shares the highly charged cultural abhorrence of cannibalism. Cooper and Saindon most clearly represent this approach. Finally, the fourth approach takes it cues from psychoanalysis. The psychoanalytic interpretation is represented in two ways: (1) through the mechanism of displacement in which direct expression of aggression is blocked by the ethos of the Northern Indians (Landes); and (2) by viewing the etiology of windigo disorder as rooted in the oral character structure of these Indians (Parker).

Types of Windigo Disorder

In this section a models approach will be followed for analysis of selected cases of windigo "psychosis" in an attempt to discover whether or not the phenomena labeled windigo by the Northern Algonkians can be reduced to a finite number of logical types. In addition to facilitating the description and definition of various types of windigo disorder, it is hoped that this preliminary effort may prove useful as a first step in reconciling the native psychiatric classification with Euro-American systems of psychiatric diagnosis. A more distant hope is that the method employed here may contribute ultimately to the comparison of the formal structural features of windigo with those of other supposed ethno-specific mental disorders reported elsewhere in the world.

In reviewing the literature, it became obvious that several different syndromes were incorporated by the Indians under the term windigo. Hallowell, in his disagreement with Cooper over the classification of all windigo disorders as psychotic, was the first to stress that at least two types of pathology were involved: (1) the full-blown "psychosis" characteristic of the advanced case in the final phases; and (2) a milder form in which only prodromal symptoms were manifest and which was considered capable of treatment. Landes' work has helped clarify additional types of windigo. It is hoped that the following operations will afford a logical framework for the definition of recognizable types of windigo disorder.

The model to be employed was developed by Anthony F. C. Wallace and his collaborators (including the present writer) at the Eastern Pennsylvania Psychiatric Institute in 1959. The model was devised originally as a conceptual tool to aid in the investigation of patients' theories about the nature and course of their own mental illnesses. Wallace has demonstrated the applicability of the model in a cross-cultural context by analyzing the changes in affective states undergone during the process of becoming a diviner in Zulu society (Wallace: 1961). The analytic technique has been labeled the "N-U-P model" in reference to the three principal states or phases delineated by the model. Basically, the model contains three aspects: (1) the specification of various *states* or *phases* (depicted as various lettered boxes with [N] standing for "Normality," [U] for "Upset," [P] for "Psychosis," [T] for the "Treatment" phase, and [I] for "Innovated Personality"); (2) the *transfer mechanism* by which the individual passes from one state to another (indicated by directional and reversible arrows); (3) the *program* of illness and/or recovery which is encompassed by the whole system (the entire paradigm) (Wallace: 1961, pp. 278–279).

Before proceeding, one methodological point requires discussion. Models such as the "N-U-P" scheme can be constructed from several vantage points. The point of view may center on the patient's own theory of his symptoms and condition. Secondly, the point of view may represent that of the wider culture shared to a greater or lesser degree by members of the particular local community. Finally the point of view may be that of psychiatrically trained or untrained non-native observers. The following chart demonstrates the relevance of varying points of view with reference to a type of mental illness known in our own culture.

Point of view	Patient's own theory and description	Theory and description given by relatives, friends, community (gen. culture)	Professional observers but nonspecialists with no psychiatric involvement	Interpretation by professional psychiatrist or psychologist
Type of explanation or interpretation	Rationale of behavior usually stressing reality of symptoms or denial of illness	Content of symptoms emphasizing those that appear strikingly deviant or abnormal	Objective description of selected symptoms phrased in quasi-professional language	Objective synthesis and categorization
Illustration	"I'm upset sometime. People don't realize I'm Jesus or they wouldn't want to kill me"	"Sometimes he talks O.K. but then he goes off his rocker and thinks we're staring at him and going to hang him on a cross"	"He has delusions of grandeur and feels people are persecuting him"	Paranoid schizophrenia

In the typology that follows, the model will be applied primarily from the viewpoint of the general cultural interpretation of the illness as expressed by members of the local community. It might have been preferable to construct the paradigms from the sufferer's *own* picture of his illness, but the majority of the reported windigo cases lack sufficient detail to reconstruct the patient's private theory of his illness. Presumably, however, the patient's own theory and interpretation of symptoms should show a high degree of correlation with the general theory and expectations prevalent in the culture of which he is a member.

The five basic types of windigo disorder isolated by means of the "N-U-P" model are presented in the form of paradigms with appropriate illustrative cases and comments.

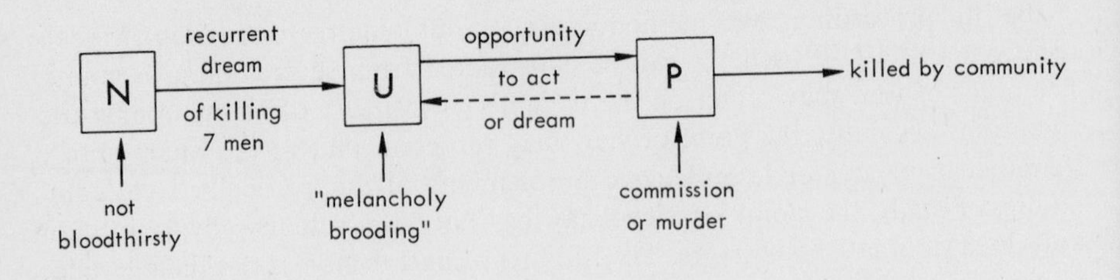

Type 1.—Classic Three-Stage

Illustrative Case—"Some few years back a man lived here who dreamed that he must kill seven men during his life, and would not be suffered to stop till he had completed that number. He was naturally not at all blood-thirsty or of murderous propensities; merely the dark destiny in which he believed drove him to such deeds of horror. He had dreamed of it, perhaps several times: the dream made him melancholy and brooding, but he must obey it, and so soon as an opportunity offered, he killed a fellow-being. Thrice he had already thrust his knife into the heart of his innocent brethren, when punishment or destiny overtook him. He had not been caught committing one of his murders, not one of his crimes could be proved by testimony, and yet suspicious signs repeatedly pointed to him as the source of all the misfortune preying on the community. He had also friends cognizant of his dreams, for such poor tortured dreamers can rarely keep their secret entirely to themselves. A gloomy cloud hung over him, rumor had long before branded him, and so, as he was sitting one day with his back to a tree, brooding and solitary, an axe cleft the wicked dreamer's head asunder. A few of his victim's friends had joined together to put him out of the way. They did so, and the whole community applauded them for freeing them from such a monster" (Kohl: 1860, pp. 358–359).

Comments—Although this case does not involve cannibalism, it is still considered windigo according to Kohl. The native interpretation of the disorder is that the murderer became possessed of the evil Windigo spirit through the medium of dreams. There does not seem to be any sorcery involved in this case, although frequently in other models of this general type the dominant transfer mechanism is the evil designs of a sorcerer. There is also a hint of oscillation between [U] and [P] (indicated by the dotted arrow), as it is stated that "a gloomy cloud hung over him," after the violent state [P] had been reached and murders had been committed.

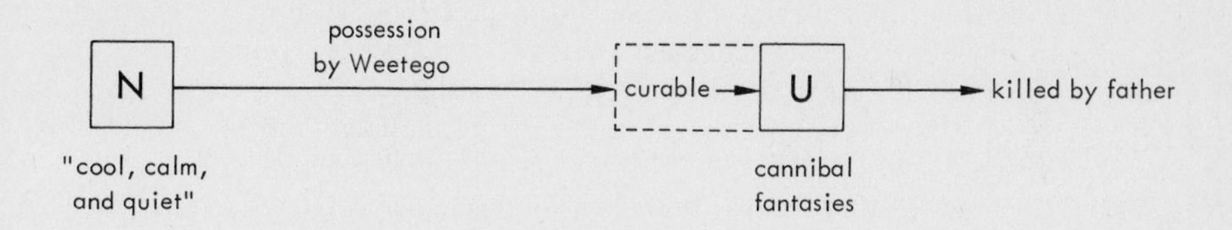

Type 2.—Two-Stage in Which Sufferer Is Killed in [U] Phase

Illustrative Case—"One morning a young man of about 20 years of age on getting up, said he felt a strong inclination to eat his sister; as he was a steady young man, and a promising hunter, no notice was taken of this expression; the next morning he said the same several times in the day for a few days. His parents attempted to reason him out of this horrid inclination; he was silent and gave them no answer; his sister and her husband became alarmed, left the place and went to another camp. He became aware of it; in other respects, his behavior was cool, calm and quiet. His father and relations were much grieved; argument had no effect on him, and he made them no answer to their questions. The camp became alarmed, for it was doubtful who would be his victim. His father called the men to a council, where the state of the young man was discussed, and their decision was, that an evil spirit had entered into him, and was in full possession of him to make him become a Man Eater (a Weetego). The father was found fault with for not having called to his assistance a Medicine Man, who by sweating and his songs to the tambour and rattle might have driven away the evil spirit before it was too late. Sentence of death was passed on him, which was to be done by his father. The young man was called . . . [and] . . . informed of the resolution taken, to which he said, 'I am willing to die'; the unhappy father arose, and placing a cord about his neck strangled him, to which he was quite passive; after about two hours, the body was carried to a large fire, and burned to ashes, not the least bit of bone remaining. This was carefully done to prevent his soul and evil spirit which possessed him from returning to this world and appearing at his grave; as they believe the soul of those who are buried can, and may do, as having a claim to the bones of their bodies. It may be thought that the council acted in a cruel part in ordering the father to put his son to death, when they could have ordered it by the hands of another person. This was done to prevent the law of retaliation; which had it been done by the hands of another person, might have been made a pretext of revenge by those who were not the friends of the person who put him to death. Such is the state of society where there are no positive laws to direct mankind" (From David Thompson's narrative, quoted in Hallowell: 1936, pp. 1308–1309).

Comments—There are two unusual aspects to this case. The intermediate stage ([U]) is devoid of the usual symptoms of melancholia, nausea, and refusal of food. Also this case took place during the summer, when, presumably there was no threat of starvation. The dotted lines preceding the [U] stage, labeled curable, are inferred from the statement that the youth might have been cured, but that they had waited too long. The native interpretation holds that the boy was possessed by a Weetigo Spirit, but it is not clear by what agency this spirit was contracted—by a dream, vision quest, or through the malevolent actions of a sorcerer. Most probably the spirit was contracted via a dream, since the opening statement reads, "One morning a young man . . . on getting up, said he felt a strong inclination to eat his sister."

The case of Mrs. Cochran, although different in emotional content, would also qualify as a two-stage example.

"Mrs. Cochran felt that she was becoming windigo: the people around her looked like beavers and she wanted to eat them. She ordered her brother-in-law to strait-jacket her, stun her with an axe, and then set fire to her and her tent. While this was done, her husband and children looked on, for she had an undisputed right to dispose of herself as she chose" (Landes: 1937, p. 101).

Here the sufferer had awareness of her condition and wished to be killed before she actually acted on her obsessive thoughts. The case may be diagramed as follows:

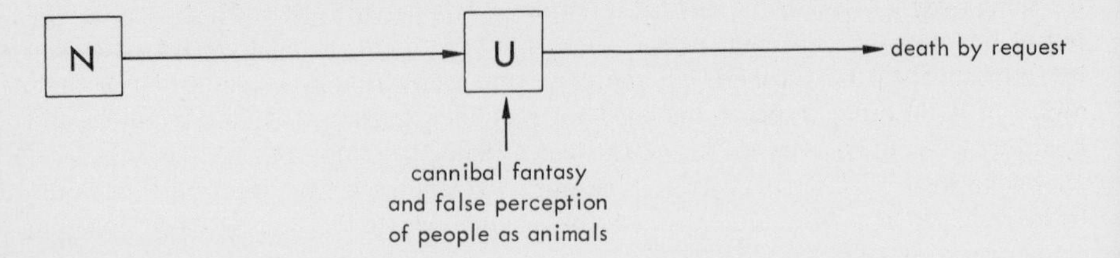

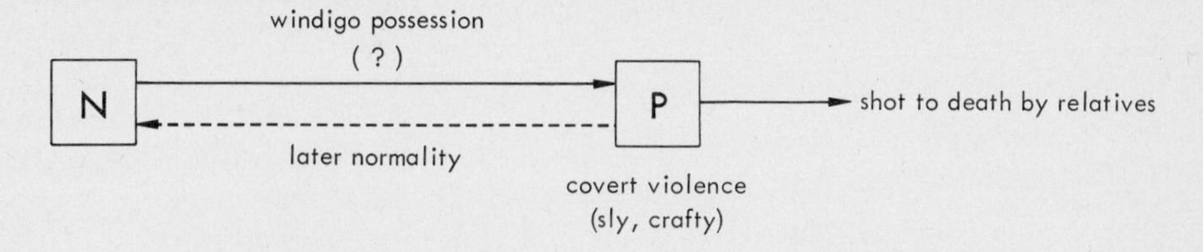

Type 3.—Nonmelancholic Two-Stage (No [U] Stage)

Illustrative Case—"This is a story of a young man named Shaywayko and his parents. They went back into the bush to hunt and snare rabbits and they stayed there quite a while. One day when his father was away, his mother said to him, 'My son, I want to ask you if you would kill your father when he comes back,' and he said, 'all right.' He waited along the road for his father and when his father came, he shot and killed him, and they ate him up. He had a sister older than himself, and brothers and sisters younger. His older sister helped him while he killed his younger brothers and sisters, and ate them up too. His mother was the last one they ate. They did not eat them all up, but they ate only the good parts. When they had nothing more to eat, Shaywayko told his sister that they would go away and try to find some Indians (to eat); so they went. When night came they stopped, and he got so hungry that he killed his sister and ate some of her. When morning came, he started off again. He took the rest of his sister's body with him, and ate her as he went along. Then he came to a place where his uncle named Nahko and his family were camping. He went into their wigwam. His uncle asked him why he was coming alone, and he said, 'oh, they all died of starvation and I came away and killed a porcupine along the road, and that is what I ate.' He took a chunk of meat out of his sock, and showed it to them. It was the meat of his sister, but they did not know what it was. When night came they all went to bed. He slept with his cousin, who was a young man like himself. The young man became afraid, for Shaywayko kept feeling around his body (to see if he was fat enough). The young man got up and said to his father, 'I wonder why my cousin is feeling around my ribs? And he also stinks so bad!' So the old man got up and started to commune with the supernatural, and rattle and sing and while he was singing (a shamanistic process which summons the aid of supernaturals) he had a vision of his nephew's killing his sister and his mother and his father. Then he knew for sure that his nephew had become *windigo* and had eaten up his own people. He stopped singing, and asked his nephew just what had happened, why it was that he was the only one that had not starved. Then Shaywayko answered, 'Well, it was my mother who first said that I should do this, and eat up our father. We had lots of other things to eat, but she wanted to eat father very badly. So I shot him.' After he told that, they were very frightened. The old man said to his family, 'Get ready, we will move from here and go where there are some Indians.' They all got ready that day, and they moved. This old man had two sons, and these two boys went along ahead with their cousin. Shaywayko would run on ahead and then stop and wait for his cousins; he would stop by the side of the road and hide, and the young men were afraid of him.

"At last they came to a place where some Indians were camping; the *windigo's* mother's brother was camping there with some other Indians. It was almost spring now, and nothing happened there. The *windigo* was just like a harmless (i.e., normal, ordinary) man now. But anyway the Indians were afraid of him. They used to fish on the lake with hooks. They made holes in the ice and caught jackfish, and the *windigo* too would roast a jackfish and eat it (having tastes, now, like a normal person). When the lakes were just about opened up, all the Indians decided to move to Warroad (the summer village) to fish, and all the young men went to hook some jackfish to take along with them to eat on the way. Shaywayko also went and caught some jackfish and roasted them. They were to move the next day, and they were all busy. Shaywayko helped carry the bundles and wooden drum to his toboggan and then he returned to the wigwam for his jackfish. The rest of the people (who were his relatives: uncles, aunts, cousins) had already planned to shoot him, and his closest uncle waited for him to return. And as he came up the hill he was shot dead on the road. The rest of the men ran back and set fire to his body. (Evil shamans and *windigos*, who are their brothers in evil, are cremated instead of buried. This is done to destroy the material and spiritual selves of the deceased. In the case of the *windigo*, there is the additional belief that the ice skeleton nucleus of a *windigo* can be destroyed only by burning, that is, by applying fire to melt the ice.) When his body was almost burned up, they found a chunk of green stuff on his back (this is some evil spirit). They never knew what it was. So they burned him all up. They were afraid that if he lived through the summer he would become worse again in the winter. That was why they killed him while he was harmless (to kill a *windigo* at the time of his winter strength is supposed to be a difficult feat). Then they moved to Warroad for the spring" (Landes: 1938b, pp. 221–222).

Comment—In this case, Shaywayko does not appear to have suffered any melancholic or withdrawal symptoms [U] which usually serve as a prelude to windigo violence. He also seems to have returned to a normal state in the early spring while with his uncle's group. However the fear that he might again become windigo the following winter forced his relatives to execute him. The cultural explanation of his disorder and cannibalism appears to be that he was possessed by Windigo spirit, although the precise manner in which the possession took place is not clear.

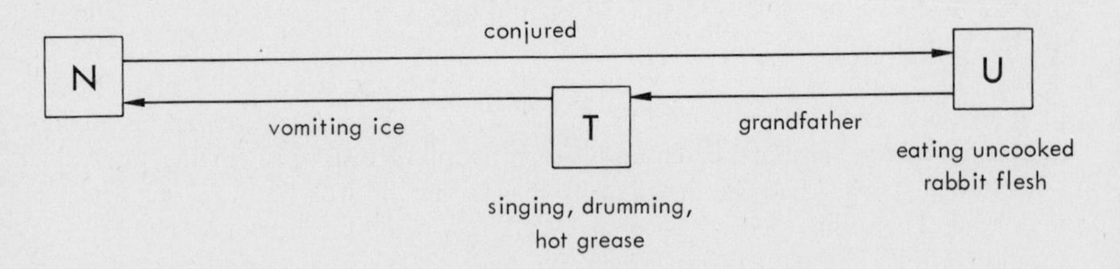

Type 4.—Curable

Illustrative Case—"One story was told me about an aged Waswanipi Indian whom I met several years ago but who has since died. He had in earlier life trespassed another man's hunting ground. The other man conjured him and he began to eat uncooked rabbit flesh. At last he nearly turned into a Witiko. In the nick of time, his old grandfather sang and drummed to cure him, and gave him a little hot bear grease. A short while after swallowing the grease, the conjured man vomited a lot of clear ice which was then thrown into the fire. This marked the turning point and the victim escaped becoming a Witiko" (Cooper: 1933, p. 22).

Comment—Here the sufferer reaches a [U] stage, but is saved by the ministrations of his grandfather. Sorcery is the mechanism by which the man was transferred from [N] to [U]. The sorcery presumably involved dispatching a Windigo to possess the man who had trespassed. However, the possession, symbolized by the ice, had not fully crystallized and the man was able to be saved from complete windigo transformation. From the material presented, it seems as if the man did not undergo any permanent personality change, but was returned back to his old normal self [N].

A variant of the Type 4 model can be seen in a case reported by Landes (1938a and b) in which the patient recovers but emerges from treatment [T] with a slightly different personality than she had before the windigo attack. This model, including the innovated personality [I], can be diagramed as follows:

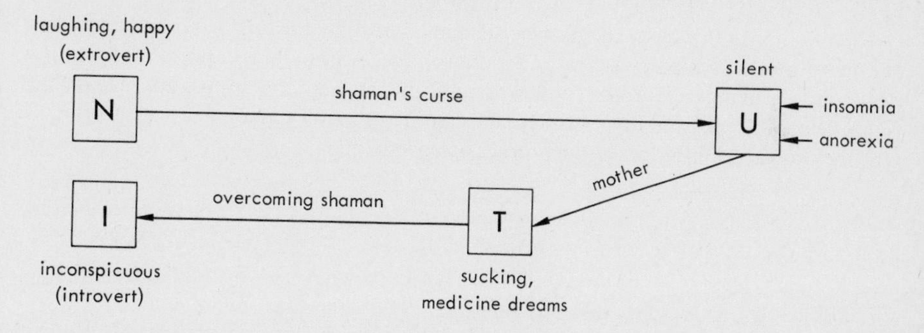

Type 4.—(Variant)

Illustrative Case—"Sioux Woman had been taken captive from the Dakota Sioux by a Cree warrior, and had lived happily with him as his wife for about ten years. 'She was there over ten years and her mother was also there with her. They went out walking one time, and one old Cree man ('old man' in this connection means sorcerer) was sleeping. She and her mother passed him, and they were talking. She used to laugh very loud. This old man woke up suddenly (startled by her laugh, annoyed that he had been awakened), and heard her laughing. He jumped up for he thought that she was making fun of him. He got mad and said, 'This winter you will eat many Indians' (i.e., become insane, windigo). But of course she did not hear him. Sure enough that winter before Christmas she got sick and crazy. She used to sit in one place for a long time . . . not a word out of her, and she did not sleep or eat or do anything at all. The people were frightened: they knew she was going to be a *windigo*. For twenty days she did not eat anything. Then her mother started giving her medicine; she smoked medicine on her, and used the sucking cure. She made a long speech when she started to cure by sucking, and made signs with her hands. All the children were taken away, and some of the grown people went away too. Only a few stayed there to watch her. One day the old woman told her son-in-law to get a frog or snake.

The man asked some old people for a snake, and he got a little snake meat. The old woman made medicine out of it, and gave it to her daughter to drink. She also gave her dried blueberries and Indian rice to eat. This was to stop her from becoming a *windigo*. Sioux Woman was like that for a long time. The old woman kept on with her *manito kazo*. She fought for her daughter (against the shaman who must have been persecuting Sioux Woman), and she finally got the best of him. After he was beaten, he got sick and died in four days. Then Sioux Woman got better. She never was out of her mind. When this old man died, everybody was glad, for he was a very bad old man. He had destroyed lots of people by his medicine. The Sioux old woman was the first one to outdo him by her drams and put an end to him. After her daughter got better, her grandchildren all came home, and they lived happily after that" (Landes: 1938b, pp. 194–195).

In another place, with reference to the same case Landes says: "But she never regained her easy gaiety; she wanted only to be inconspicuous, dreading the consequences of her former happiness" (1938a, p. 27).

Comment—In this case, the disorder is sent directly by the outraged shaman. Sioux Woman's mother's medicine finally overcomes the evil conjuror's power causing his death and her daughter's recovery. The significant thing to note in this account is that Sioux Woman's personality is different after her recovery than before, showing a tendency toward inhibition of her former extroversion.

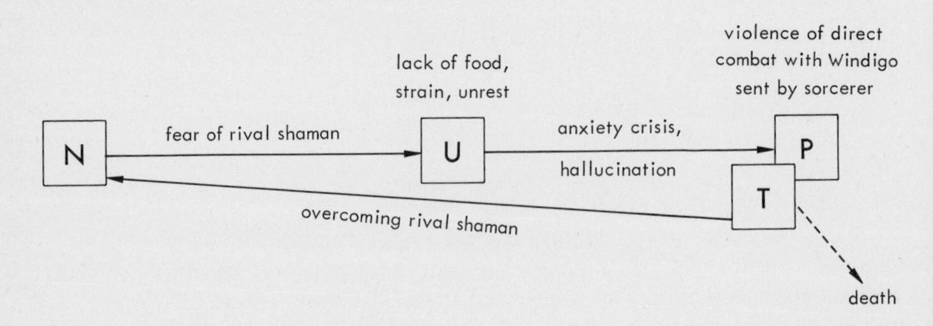

Type 5.—Windigo in a Shaman

Illustrative Case—"Bombay (a shaman) had been under a great strain, caused partly by starvation and partly by a feeling of unrest resulting from the fact that his daughter had slighted her husband, son of another shaman. In true paranoid fashion he sought for some explanation in his inability to command food and weather, and found it in the sorcery of the rival shaman, who was in this way avenging the insult to his son. Finally Bombay's anxiety reached a crisis, and he experienced the hallucination of combat with his imagined tormentor" (Landes: 1938b, p. 196).

"He strode out into the woods to fight with the windigo set upon him at his enemy shaman. He heard the monster in the wild glades cracking the branches and in the groaning of the earth that gave under the windigo's tread, while the whole atmosphere darkened. Armed with his gun and a stout oak branch he went out to slay the monster. . . . In the woods he lost his senses, and, when he revived, he knew he had fought and won. The ground was torn up, branches were broken and scattered, the air was still and the sun shone palely. His gun was nowhere in sight; looking for it, he found a porcupine. . . . After that he found all the game he wanted" (Landes: 1938a, p. 28).

"His belief in his interpretation of events was strengthened when he was able to find game after he had thus in fantasy defeated his enemy, and when he found later that the other man had actually died at about the time of their shamanistic combat" (Landes: 1938b, p. 196).

Comment—The case of windigo sickness among shamans differs from that as found in the general population, since the shaman is armed with medicine, prayer, and power by which he can defend himself. Such a power struggle between two shamans is a serious affair, since it will generally result in the death of one or the other.

I had some difficulty in deciding whether to classify the shamanistic combat fantasy as [U] or [P], but I took the latter alternative in that the fantasy was said to be hallucinatory and in the fantasy open aggression was expressed, as well as the statement that Bombay "lost his senses." I feel that in terms of the "objective" results of this combat—the finding of game and the death of the rival—the Ojibwa would feel that the "fantasy" was real. Also to be noted in the diagram is the overlapping of [P] and [T]. This was done because the shamanistic combat could be alternatively thought of as terminal violence (active state) or as a form of treatment, albeit an extreme form but the only one possible.

Conclusions

In the first portion of this paper various psychological theories and hypotheses concerning windigo disorder were reviewed, critically evaluated, and synthesized into four basic approaches. Some degree of continuity was found in the speculative hypotheses of early travelers, traders, and missionaries as compared with the more theoretically oriented explanations of windigo disorder offered by anthropologists. One persistent problem encountered in the literature was whether the mental disturbances labeled windigo were a unitary phenomenon or whether windigo was a general term encompassing several syndromes that would be differentially diagnosed by a Euro-American clinician.

In an effort to sketch the parameters of the disorder and to delineate logically separable types of windigo, the "N-U-P" model was applied to selected case materials reported in the literature. Five basic types of windigo disorder, with some subtypes, were identified. It would have been desirable to classify a larger sample of windigo case materials by means of the model so that relative frequencies of the deduced types could be ascertained. Unfortunately, the available case material is for the most part too fragmentary and deficient in pertinent detail to permit rigorous application of the model on a wider scale. Nevertheless, the five basic types of the disorder seem sufficient to classify most cases of windigo, if more detailed information were available. It is possible, however, that one or two additional types might emerge with additional data.

From the results of this study, it would be premature to attempt a direct translation of native-recognized windigo manifestations into Euro-American psychiatric equivalents. However, it does seem evident that the native windigo category incorporates several different disorders recognized in Euro-American psychiatry. It is suggested that these disorders probably range from mild and severe episodes of anxiety neurosis to full-blown psychoses.

Finally, it is hoped that the usefulness of the "N-U-P" model in the analysis of windigo disorder may stimulate other investigators to apply similar models to other exotic forms of mental disorder as a small step forward toward a truly transcultural psychiatry.

References

Bateson, G., *et al.*

1956: "Toward a Theory of Schizophrenia," *Behavioral Science*, **1,** 251–264.

Cooper, J. M.

1933: "The Cree Witiko Psychosis," *Primitive Man*, **6,** 20–24.

1934: *The Northern Algonquian Supreme Being* (Washington, D.C.: Catholic University of America).

Curtis, E. B.

n.d.: *The North American Indian*, Vol. 18 (Norwood, Massachusetts: Plimpton Press).

Flannery, R.

1947: "Algonquian Indian Folklore," *Journal of American Folklore*, **60,** 397–401.

Hallowell, A. I.

1934: "Culture and Mental Disorder," *Journal of Abnormal and Social Psychology*, **29,** 1–9.

1936: "Psychic Stresses and Culture Patterns," *American Journal of Psychiatry*, **92,** 1291–1310.

1938: "Fear and Anxiety as Cultural and Individual Variables in a Primitive Society," *Journal of Social Psychology*, **9,** 25–47.

Hind, H. Y.

1860: *Narrative of the Canadian Red River: Exploring Expedition of 1857 and of the Assiniboin and Saskatchewan Exploring Expedition of 1858*, Vol. 1 (London: Longman, Green, Longman & Roberts).

Hooper, W. H.

1853: *Ten Months among the Tents of the Tuski with Incidents of an Arctic Boat Expedition in Search of Sir John Franklin as Far as the Mackenzie River, and Cape Bathurst* (London: Murray).

Jenness, D.

1935: "The Ojibwa Indians of Parry Island," *Bull. 78, Anthropological Series 17* (Ottawa: National Museum of Canada).

Jones, P.

1861: *History of the Ojebway Indians* (London: A. W. Bennett).

Kane, P.

1859: *Wanderings of an Artist among the Indians of North America* (London: Longman, Brown, Green, Longman & Roberts).

Kohl, J. G.

1860: *Kitchi-gami, Wanderings round Lake Superior* (London: Chapman & Hall).

Landes, R.

1937: "The Ojibwa of Canada," in M. Mead (ed.), *Cooperation and Competition among Primitive Peoples* (New York: McGraw-Hill).

1938a: "The Abnormal among the Ojibwa Indians," *Journal of Abnormal and Social Psychology*, **33**, 14–33.

1938b: *The Ojibwa Woman* (New York: Columbia University Press).

Parker, S.

1960: "The Wiitiko Psychosis in the Context of Ojibwa Personality," *American Anthropologist*, **62**, 603–623.

Quaife, M. M. (ed.)

1921: *Alexander Henry's Travels and Adventures in the Years 1760–1776* (Chicago: Lakeside Press).

Saindon, E.

1933: "Mental Disorders among the James Bay Cree," *Primitive Man*, **6**, 1–12.

Speck, F. G.

1935: *Naskapi* (Norman: University of Oklahoma Press).

Teicher, M. I.

1960: "Windigo Psychosis," in V. F. Ray (ed.), *Proceedings of the 1960 Annual Spring Meeting of the American Ethnological Society* (Seattle: University of Washington Press).

Thwaites, R. G. (ed.)

1901: *The Jesuit Relations and Allied Documents*, Vols. 8 & 46 (Cleveland: Burrows Brothers).

Tyrrell, J. B. (ed.)

1916: *David Thompson's Narrative of His Explorations in Western America* (1784–1812) (Toronto: Champlain Society).

Wallace, A. F. C.

1961: "Mental illness, Biology, and Culture," in F. L. K. Hsu (ed.), *Psychological Anthropology* (Homewood, Illinois: Dorsey Press).

MELFORD E. SPIRO

Religious Systems as Culturally Constituted Defense Mechanisms

Introduction

Since the range of beliefs, values, and rituals related to supernatural beliefs and events is enormous, it is obvious, as Durkheim observed long ago, that no belief, value, or ritual is intrinsically identifiable as "religious." Since the "religious," on the contrary, is a quality capable of being attached to almost any instance of these three dimensions of religious systems, the latter, to use a modern idiom, are in large measure projective systems. It is this characteristic of religion that poses a problem which has long confronted its students, and which comprises the problem of this paper: If religious systems are indeed projective in character, how can we be sure that religious behavior is not abnormal behavior, requiring psychiatric, rather than sociocultural, analysis?

Anthropology, as is well known, has adopted a fairly uniform stance with respect to the cross-cultural variability which characterizes notions of the good, the true, and the beautiful. This stance, so far as the normal-abnormal distinction is concerned, was given classic expression by Benedict (1934), who maintained that judgments concerning abnormality are necessarily relative to intracultural standards. What is judged to be abnormal in one cultural setting may be properly characterized as normal in other cultural settings. This relativistic approach continues to provoke somewhat heated controversy, not only within the anthropological fraternity, but within the social sciences in general.

In a series of seminal papers Professor Hallowell has offered us important conceptual vehicles by which we can avoid the Scylla of nihilistic relativism and the Charybdis of ethnocentric absolutism. His concept of a "culturally constituted behavioral environment" (Hallowell: 1955, Chapter 8) allows us to view behavior relative to its cultural setting and, at the same time, to assess its functional consequences in terms of pancultural scientific criteria. I should like to examine the relationships between religion, abnormality, and relativism in the light of these conceptual tools. Although only these concepts are explicitly taken from Hallowell, this entire paper is heavily indebted to his work. Indeed, it is difficult to say when his ideas end and mine begin.

The persistent controversy over cultural relativism has been confounded by implicit disagreements concerning its proper antithesis. Some scholars conceive of (what I shall term) "universalism" to be the antithesis of relativism, while others take (what may be termed) "absolutism" to be its antithesis. The logic of relativism is quite different, depending upon which of these two alternative conceptions is taken to be its antithesis; indeed consensus concerning one or the other antithesis would mitigate, if not resolve, the controversy. I should like to propose absolutism as the valid antonym for relativism, and universalism as the antonym not for relativism, but for what might be called "particularism."

Universalism vs. Particularism

The question entailed by this distinction is whether a particular belief or behavior pattern found in our society—and which a clinician would characterize as pathological—occurs in all societies, in some societies, or only in our own society. This is an empirical question, concerned exclusively with the *occurrence* and relative *incidence* of a certain type of behavior. Correspondingly, the answer to this question must also be empirical, rather than judgmental. Whatever the answer to this question may be, the research task—once the answer is provided—is to identify those causal or antecedent conditions which produce the behavior or which account for its differential occurrence. In the older arguments for relativism, in which sociocultural variables were adduced as foils for, or as antidotes to, biological variables (usually, but not always, associated with racism), relativistic theorists turned to sociocultural determinants in order to explain the differential occurrence of different types of behavior. Particularism, as I shall label this variety of relativism, interprets the differential occurrence of a certain type of behavior as relative to, because determined by, differential sociocultural conditions.

Anthropological data—and, one might add, historical and sociological data as well—are unambiguous so far as the universalistic-particularistic dichotomy is concerned. The occurrence and relative incidence of certain types of behavior which, when occurring in our society, are labeled as schizophrenic, hysterical, paranoid, etc., vary not only from society to society, but they vary as well within the same society at different periods in its history, and among different social groups (class, ethnic, religious, etc.) within the same historical period. This empirical finding is independent of any judgment by which these types of behavior may be evaluated.

Absolutism vs. Relativism

This, rather than the former, dichotomy raises the genuine relativistic question, viz., can certain types of behavior which are designated as pathological when they occur in our society be properly designated by the same label when they occur in other societies? The concern here is not with the question of the differential occurrence of beliefs and practices—this is taken for granted—but with their clinical assessment. Absolutism holds that certain types of behavior are properly designated as pathological wherever and whenever they occur. Relativism holds that judgments concerning pathology are necessarily relative. There are different types of relativism, however, differing according to what these judgments are conceived to be relative to. One type, which we may label "social relativism," holds that judgments concerning pathology are relative to intra-societal criteria, because there are no panhuman criteria by which cross-cultural judgments can be made. A second type, which may be termed "cultural relativism," holds that the criteria for judging pathology are panhuman, but that judgments based on these criteria are relative to the cultural context in which the action occurs. I should like to examine these two types of relativism, and their respective subtypes.

Social Relativism—Social relativism holds that judgments concerning pathology can only be based on intrasocietal—and, as we shall see, quantitative—criteria. One subtype, which might be termed "objective social relativism," insists that judgments concerning the pathology of some type of behavior must be relative to its incidence in the society (or some social group within a society) in which it occurs. Hence, behavior is properly judged to be pathological if (but only if) it is statistically rare; if, that is, it deviates from the statistical norms for that society. According to this subtype, "schizophrenic" behavior is pathological in our society because it characterizes a minority; if schizophrenics were to become a majority, schizophrenia would be normal. For this subtype, then, the abnormal represents social deviation.

"Subjective social relativism" holds that behavior may be judged to be pathological if it is deemed to be pathological by the members of the society in which it is found; it is not pathological if they deem it to be normal, or, at least, if it is positively rather than negatively evaluated by them. If, according to objective social relativism, judgments concerning pathology are relative to the incidence of some type of behavior within a society, according to subjective social relativism they are relative to its evaluation by the members of society. For the former, pathology represents deviation from statistical norms discovered by the anthropologist; for the latter it represents deviation from evaluative norms held by the society.

Although their criteria differ, both subtypes of relativism agree that there can be no panhuman criteria by which judgments concerning pathology can be established. Hence, behavior which is properly labeled "paranoid" when found in our society is "normal" if found among the Kwakiutl; hysteria is normal in the case of St. Theresa, but abnormal in a contemporary middle-class woman; the belief that most of mankind is doomed to eternal hell-fire is normal for a Calvinist, but abnormal for a Buddhist, and so on.

In my opinion both subtypes of social relativism are untenable. In the first place, since man (even *homo religiosus*) is a biological organism, there are I would suggest panhuman *biological* criteria by which behavior may be judged. If the majority in a given society have cancer, are we to say that they, the majority, are biologically normal, while those who do not have cancer, the minority, are biologically abnormal? This crude analogy suggests the fallacy inherent in the first subtype of social relativism. Judgments concerning biological normality or abnormality (health and illness) are indeed relative; but they are relative to specified criteria for the functioning of healthy organisms, criteria which are—or, at least, biological science takes them to be—universally applicable. Only two of the criteria which are relevant for the problem of behavioral pathology need be mentioned here: adaptation and optimum functioning.

Any organic characteristic which, like cancer, produces death, and which, if generalized, precludes the survival of the group—i.e., any maladaptive characteristic—is biologically abnormal. Furthermore, any characteristic which reduces efficient functioning—efficient relative to the potentiality of either the organ or the organism—is biologically abnormal. Thus, impaired vision or hearing, let alone blindness or deafness, are abnormal because they reduce the optimum functioning of these organs and, ultimately, of the organism. In short, maladaptive and inefficient functioning are, for the physician and biologist, panhuman criteria by which the presence of biological abnormality may be assessed; this assessment is independent of the incidence of these characteristics in a society or of their evaluation by its members. If we are prepared to accept these criteria it would seem to follow that any condition which produces these effects—whether it be a characteristic of the organism or a characteristic of behavior—is pathological. Hence, if it is the case that a religious belief or a religious ritual is maladaptive and/or reduces optimum biological functioning, such a belief or ritual is, biologically viewed, abnormal.

But man is not only a biological, he is also a psychological and a social animal. For psychological, as for biological processes, the homeostatic principle, tension→tension-reduction, holds: tension stimulates action which is intended to reduce tension. Hence the persistence of tension is abnormal. Most psychological tension stems from conflict, either between one's moral values and/or one's self-image, or between those desires which violate the one or the other (or both). Since the tension induced by such conflict is painful, the typical actor —in accordance with the homeostatic principle enunciated above—attempts to resolve the conflict and, hence, to reduce tension. This is usually accomplished by a number of maneuvers, termed "mechanisms of defense," which defend the ego against the pain induced by the tension. Although these defense mechanisms may reduce the tension, thereby satisfying the homeostatic criterion of normality, they may have other pathological consequences. Any resolution of conflict, however successful in reducing tension, which results in the impairment of psychological, social, or cultural functioning may be taken to be a universal index of pathology.

"Impairment of psychological functioning" refers to distortions of three important modes of action. (1) Cognitive distortion: This refers to any cognitive behavior in which a demonstrably false belief is held to be true. (2) Perceptual distortion: This refers to any perceptual behavior in which stimuli are perceived to be other than what they are. (3) Affective distortion: This refers to any emotional behavior which, relative to the stimulus condition, is characterized by hyper- or hypoaffectivity. "Impairment of social functioning" refers to any condition of the actor which precludes the performance of social roles. "Impairment of cultural functioning" refers to any condition of the actor which precludes compliance with cultural norms and rules.

The three psychological criteria of pathology are panhuman because, if satisfied, the reality-testing function of the ego, the agent of man's adaptation (to nature) and adjustment (to society), is impaired, and the consequence of such impairment may be either individual or social disruption. The last two sociocultural criteria of pathology are panhuman because, in the absence of adequate social and cultural functioning, the survival of the individual—and, if generalized, the survival of the group—is jeopardized. No society could persist if the behavior of its members was characterized, for example, by genuine schizophrenia or genuine paranoia. Hence any religious belief or religious ritual which is characterized by, or which leads to, these three types of impairment is properly characterized as abnormal, regardless of its incidence and regardless of its evaluation by the members of society.

Cultural relativism—Despite these animadversions on social relativism, its rejection does not entail the acceptance of absolutism. According to absolutism certain forms of behavior and certain kinds of beliefs are pathological wherever or whenever they may be found. Thus, for example, if a religious belief or ritual in a non-Western society is phenotypically similar to a belief or behavior pattern characteristic of a Western psychotic, the former, according to absolutism, is also abnormal. This position is as untenable as social relativism. Although the criteria by which behavior is judged may be universally applicable, it does not follow that all instances of phenotypically identical behavior or belief, when evaluated by these criteria, will lead to the same judgment. Although the criteria are panhuman, the judgments based on these criteria are necessarily relative to the sociocultural context within which behavior occurs. Distortion, for example, implies the existence of some reality relative to which a cognition is false, a perception is skewed, an affect is misplaced. But this reality, as Professor Hallowell has so cogently shown, is not a universal "given." Different cultures structure reality in different ways. For any actor reality is mediated through the world view and behavioral environment constructed by his culture. Hence, judgment concerning the existence of distortion must be based on the culturally constituted world view and the behavioral environment of the actor whose behavior is being assessed. For a Western man to believe that he is the reincarnation of some ancestor is to commit severe cognitive distortion; a Buddhist who holds the same belief commits no distortion. In short, the same criterion, applied to two identical acts, yields different judgments because the judgment—but not the criterion—is relative to the sociocultural context within which action occurs.

Social and cultural inadequacy must be assessed in the same manner. Whether a particular condition does or does not permit normal social and cultural functioning is necessarily relative to the repertory of social roles and the set of cultural norms which are found in the actor's, not the observer's, society.

If the preceding discussion is sound, it may then be concluded that beliefs and rituals which characterize the behavior of religious actors in non-Western societies, although phenotypically identical with beliefs and behavior which may characterize abnormal individuals in our society, are not necessarily (or even usually) abnormal when sanctioned or prescribed by the religious systems of the former societies and taught to the actors as part of their cultural heritage. There are a number of reasons for this conclusion. (a) The religious actor acquires his beliefs and rituals, as he acquires other aspects of his cultural heritage, through the usual techniques of instruction and imitation. Hence these beliefs and rituals are expressions, rather than distortions, of (his culturally constituted) reality. They are consistent with, rather than obstacles to, social and cultural functioning. Psychotic beliefs and behavior, on the contrary, are devised by the actor himself, as an attempt to reduce the painful tension induced by inner conflict. This attempt is necessarily based on his private distortion of (culturally constituted) reality, resulting in serious impairment of his social and/or cultural functioning. (b) Since religious beliefs and practices are derived from tradition, they are frequently compulsory; but since they are not created by the actor himself to defend against forbidden or shameful impulses, they are not compulsive. Psychotic beliefs and practices, on the contrary, are not compulsory—indeed they are usually prohibited—but as attempts to reduce tension, they are compulsive. (c) Although not devised by the actor to resolve conflict, religious beliefs and ritual may be used for that end. When so used they may not only resolve conflict, but as "culturally constituted defenses" (Spiro: 1961, pp. 472–497) they are consistent with, rather than distortions of, reality; they comprise culturally sanctioned, rather than culturally prohibited, behavior; they protect the individual and his society from the disruptive consequences both of his shameful and/or forbidden needs and of his private defensive maneuvers. Conflict may also be resolved by psychotic beliefs and practices; but these idiosyncratic resolutions produce those psychological distortions and sociocultural impairments which, as I have argued, are properly characterized as abnormal. I should like to examine these propositions in the context of one empirical situation—Burmese Buddhist monasticism.

Burmese Monasticism[1]

In Burma, one of the centers of Theravada Buddhism, the monastic vocation is the most venerated of all patterns of life. Almost every village contains at least one monastery with at least one resident monk. The monk, in theory at least, lives an exclusively otherworldly existence. His monastery is outside the village gates, and his interaction with the layman is confined to occasional ritual situations. The monk is prohibited from engaging in any form of physical labor, including any economic activity. All of his wants are attended to by the laymen, who provide his daily meals, his robes, and other necessities. Except for teaching young children, the monk's official responsibilities to the laymen are restricted to chanting of "prayers" at funerals and to public recitation of the Buddhist precepts on the "Sabbath" and other sacred days. His primary responsibility is to himself and to his attempt to attain nirvana. The latter goal is achieved through the study of Scripture and through various techniques of Buddhist meditation. These activities are believed to be instrumental to the attainment of Release from the round of rebirths because they lead to ultimate comprehension of the true characteristics of existence, viz., impermanence, suffering, and the absence of an ego. This comprehension, in turn, is believed to lead to the severance of all desire for, and cathexis of, the world. With the destruction of desire or "clinging" (*tanha*), the basis for rebirth is destroyed. Nirvana, whatever else it may be, is the cessation of rebirth.

The true monk, then, is completely absorbed in his own "salvation." Although living in a state of absolute dependence on the laymen, he has with-

1. Materials in this section are based on field work carried out during 1961–62; I am grateful to the National Science Foundation for a research fellowship which made the research possible.

drawn both physically and psychologically from the physical and social world, and even—in states of trance (*dhyānas*)—from his own self. This extreme withdrawal from reality is similar to that withdrawal behavior which, in our society, would be taken as symptomatic of severe pathology, most certainly schizoid, if not schizophrenic. Is the Burmese monk to be similarly characterized? Such a judgment, in my opinion, would be grossly in error. Phenotypically, the behavior of the monk and that of the schizoid or schizophrenic patient may be very similar. Genotypically and functionally, however, they are importantly dissimilar. All of the criteria suggested in the previous section for assessing pathology are applicable to the schizophrenic; none is applicable to the monk.

In the case of the schizophrenic the actor resolves his inner conflict by constructing private fantasy and action systems; in the case of the monk, however, the actor uses culturally constituted fantasy and action systems (Buddhism) to resolve his inner conflicts. This difference not only provides the primary basis for a differential diagnosis of monk and schizophrenic, but it also provides, parenthetically, an important insight into the nature of religion. Culturally constituted religious behavior not only is not a symptom of pathology but, on the contrary, it serves to preclude the outbreak of pathology. The schizophrenic and the Burmese monk, alike, are characterized initially by pathogenic conflict, and schizophrenia and monasticism may each be interpreted as a means for resolving conflict. But this is where the similarity ends. Although schizophrenia and monasticism are both symptomatic of pathogenic conflict, the former represents a pathological, whereas the latter represents a nonpathological, resolution of the conflict. Let us examine these claims.

An analysis of monastic personality, based on the Rorschach records of a sample of Burmese Buddhist monks, and without reference to their (monastic) behavioral environment, would surely lead to a diagnosis of severe pathology. Dr. James Steele (1963), who has analyzed these records, finds the following "pathological" features, among others: (1) a very high degree of "defensiveness"; (2) "pathologically regressed" expression of aggressive and oral drives; (3) cautious avoidance of "emotionally laden" situations as a means of obviating the necessity of handling affect, for which there are no adequate resources; (4) a "hypochondriacal self-preoccupation" and "erotic self-cathexis," instead of a cathexis of others; (5) latent homosexuality; (6) above-average fear of female- or mother-figures.

One of the significant characteristics of the Rorschach protocols of these monks, according to Steele, is their similarity to the records of Burmese laymen. It is not that the monastic records do not differ from those of the laymen; but the difference is one of degree, not of kind. Monks differ from laymen, not because they have different problems, but because they have more of the same problems. The monk, in other words, is a Burman *in extremis*. Burmese laymen (like Burmese monks) are constricted, ruminative, defensive, anxious about females, distrustful of others, and, perhaps, latently homosexual. The monks differ from the laymen only in that, for all these characteristics, they are *more so*. Monks are *more* constricted, *more* ruminative, *more* . . . , etc. For other characteristics, however, monks are *less so*. Compared to laymen, monks are ". . . less phallic, less self-confident, less striving, and less impulsive." In summary, Burmese monks not only appear to have "more of the basic problems" which characterize Burmans in general, but they also seem to be characterized by a "more constricted adjustment." It is the latter feature, still quoting Steele, which makes them "less accessible to social interaction with the protection that this provides."

This picture of the Burmese monks is surely a picture of pathology. Are we to conclude then—holding in abeyance a specific psychiatric diagnosis, and assuming that the Rorschach test is a reliable instrument—that these monks are abnormal? If personality existed in a social and cultural vacuum, the answer would be an unqualified "yes." Acute psychological conflicts and attendant intrapersonal tensions are marked. That these conflicts have produced defensive distortions of various kinds—perceptual, cognitive, affective—is clearly indicated. That social impairment is a most likely consequence of these conflicts, tensions, and distortions can hardly be doubted. In brief, if personality existed *in vacuo* one would probably conclude that Burmese monks resolve their conflicts in a manner which issues in severe pathology (perhaps paranoid schizophrenia).

But the proviso, "if personality existed *in vacuo*," is crucial. Although Steele's analysis of their Rorschach records is remarkably similar to my clinical impressions of these monks, impressions derived from intensive participant-observation in a score of monasteries, and from personal interviews with more than twenty-five monks—thus providing a dramatic test of the reliability of the instrument and of Steele's skill in its use—I did not ever feel that these monks, with but one exception, were pathological or, specifically, schizophrenic. Nor is this a paradox. The psychological analysis (based on Rorschachs and clinical impressions) provides a set of statements concerning the emotional problems of the subjects; it also provides, to a somewhat lesser extent, a picture of their idiosyncratic defenses, i.e., of those defenses which the subjects have constructed for themselves, in an attempt to resolve their problems. That these defenses are hardly adequate to the task is obvious from the Rorschach analysis. Left exclusively to their own inner resources many of these subjects would have become, I believe, genuine psychotics.

But personality does not exist *in vacuo*, and Burmese males, characterized by the problems described, are not confronted with the necessity of solving these problems by means of their own resources. In addition to their private resources, they are able to utilize a powerful cultural resource for their solution, i.e., they can solve their problems by recruitment to the monastic order. By utilizing the role-set prescribed for this institution as a culturally constituted defense, Burmese monks can resolve their conflicts with a minimum of distortion. Since, moreover, the performance of the roles comprising this role-set satisfies their prohibited and/or shameful needs and reduces their painful fears and anxieties, these potentially disruptive psychological variables, rather than provoking socially disruptive behavior, provide the motivational basis for the persistence of the most highly valued institution—monasticism—in Burmese society. As a culturally constituted defense, the monastic institution resolves the inner conflicts of Burmese males, by allowing them to gratify their drives and reduce their anxieties in a disguised—and therefore socially acceptable—manner, one which precludes psychotic distortion, on the one hand, and criminal "acting-out," on the other. Hence, the monk is protected from mental illness and/or social punishment; society is protected from the disruptive consequences of antisocial behavior; and the key institution of Burmese culture—Buddhist monasticism—is provided with a most powerful motivational basis. Space permits only a brief examination of these assertions.

The monastic rules which interdict *all* labor, and those Buddhist norms which guarantee that the laity provide monks with *all* their wants, combine to satisfy the monk's "regressed oral drives." The monastic life, moreover, makes no demands, either social or psychological, which might render the monk's weak "phallic-orientation," his low degree of "striving and impulsivity," and his lack of "self-confidence" nonviable modes of adjustment. Quite the contrary, the physical isolation of the monastery, and the monastic norms proscribing social participation, preclude the stimulation of "disruptive affect." At the same time, the monk's "self-preoccupation" and "erotic self-cathexis" is wonderfully expressed and institutionalized in the prescribed techniques of Buddhist meditation. Latent "homosexual" needs can be satisfied in the exclusively male setting in which the monks live. Finally, the strong interdiction on interaction with females provides little opportunity for encounters with them and for the consequent fear attendant upon such encounters. Buddhist monasticism, then, is a highly efficient means for coping with the psychological problems of many Burmese men. The differences between a monastic and a psychotic resolution of these problems are instructive.

1. In general the genesis of the psychotic's conflict is idiosyncratic, while the genesis of the monk's problem is rooted in modal features of his society. That is, the source of the monk's conflict—which we cannot discuss here—is to be found in culturally constituted experiences which the monk shares with many other members of his social group. The monk differs from other Burmans in one of three ways: his potentially pathogenic experiences are more intense than those of other males; other Burmans utilize alternative, non-Buddhist, institutions for the resolution of equally intense problems; still others (a minority)

develop idiosyncratic methods of conflict-resolution (in extreme cases, these take the form of mental illness or criminal behavior).

2. The psychotic resolves his problems by means of idiosyncratic, private, defenses; the monk resolves his problems in an institutionalized manner, by utilizing elements of his religious heritage as a culturally constituted defense. The difference between these two types of defense accounts for the following differences between the psychotic patient, on the one hand, and the normal monk, on the other.

3. The behavior of the psychotic is incompatible with any normal social role within his society, and inconsistent with important cultural norms of the larger society. The psychotic is *psychologically incapable* of performing social roles or of complying with those cultural norms which he violates. The behavior of the monk, on the other hand, is entirely appropriate to—indeed, it is the enactment of—a most important and honorific social role. The monk may be psychologically incapable of performing nonmonastic roles, but he is ideally suited for performing the monastic role.

4. As a corollary of the above, the behavior of the psychotic is bizarre in the eyes of, and disapproved by, his fellows. The behavior of the monk is not only approved by the other members of his society, but it is most highly valued.

5. Following from the last point, the behavior of the psychotic alienates him psychologically from his fellows. The behavior of the monk, on the contrary, though isolating him physically from his group, serves to integrate him psychologically into the group; for in his behavior he expresses the most cherished values of Burmese culture.

6. The world view constructed by the psychotic represents a dramatic distortion of reality, as the latter is structured by the world view of his culture; and the cognitions and perceptions that are derived from his idiosyncratic world view are highly distorted, relative to the behavioral environment in which expected social interaction of his society takes place. The world view of the monk, on the other hand, rather than being constructed from his private fantasies, is taught to him as an integral part of the cultural heritage of his society. The private world view of the monk corresponds to the public world view of his society; his world view, in brief, is a culturally constituted world view. The Buddhist world view, of course, may be false, a distortion of reality, relative to the world view of modern science; but it is true, relative to the knowledge available to Burmese society. True or false, however, the monk's cognitions and perceptions are consistent with, rather than distortions of, reality, as the latter is structured by the world view and behavioral environment of his society. The perceptions and cognitions, the fantasies and emotions experienced by the monk in the course of Buddhist meditation and concentration may never be experienced by other Burmans—because the latter do not meditate or concentrate—but they are experiences consistent with the conception of reality

which all Burmans hold, and they are vouchsafed to any Burman who is prepared to enter into these spiritual disciplines.

7. The psychotic sustains social relationships neither with the normal members of his society, nor with other psychotics. Psychotics, in short, do not participate in the society of which they are members, nor do they comprise a social group, distinct from the larger society, but nevertheless viable for its constituent members. Burmese monks, on the other hand, although socially isolated from Burmese society, are yet psychologically part of it. Moreover, although the monk may find difficulty in participating in the larger society, and in forming social relationships within it, he does enter into social relationships with other members of the monastic order. Monks are members of increasingly larger concentric groups, beginning with other members of the local monastery and extending to the entire order of monks. In short, while psychotics comprise a typological class, the monks constitute a social group. The psychotic cannot live as a member of a social group, even if it be but a subgroup of the larger society.

8. Finally, and as a corollary of the last point, the behavior of the psychotic is anomic; it violates many of the rules of his society. The monk, on the other hand, not only exemplifies the rules of Burmese society, but he must, in addition, comply with the 227 rules of the monastic order (as outlined in the *Vinaya*). Should he violate these rules, he is expelled from the order as a charlatan, regardless of whatever wondrous visions he is alleged to have had, or miraculous powers he is supposed to possess.

In summary, then, a psychiatrically diagnosed psychotic is not only incapable of participating in his own society, he is incapable of participating in any society. An American psychotic would function no better in a Buddhist monastery than in an American city. A Buddhist monk, to be sure, while not capable of functioning in every cultural environment, functions very well indeed within *his* cultural environment. This is hardly surprising, since the latter environment is so structured that it satisfies his needs and resolves his conflicts. That he cannot function in a radically different environment does not render him "sick," nor his adjustment precarious. Typically, differential sets of human needs are differentially satisfied in different types of cultural milieux. It is doubtful if the typical Burmese peasant could adjust to an American urban environment, or a typical American to a Buddhist monastery. For neither is the new environment capable of satisfying the needs and resolving the conflicts which were produced by the old.

Summary and Conclusions

Burmese monks, as Rorschach data and clinical observations agree, are characterized by serious emotional conflicts. Their religious heritage, however, provides them with institutionalized means for resolving conflicts, and, moreover, for resolving them in a manner which satisfies none of the five criteria suggested in the first section of this chapter as panhuman indices of abnormality (psychological distortions and sociocultural impairments). Employing the monastic system as a culturally constituted defense obviates the necessity for Burmese males to erect private defenses which, necessarily, would lead to one or more of these distortions and impairments. Monasticism, in short, has important psychological functions for individual actors. By the same token, however, the psychological problems of these actors have the important cultural function of helping to perpetuate the monastic system; that is, these conflicts are not only resolved by means of the monastic system, but they provide the motivational basis for recruitment to the monastery and, hence, for the persistence of the system. The existence of the monastic system, moreover, not only permits the resolution of emotional conflict (the latent psychological function of the monastery), but by serving this function it reduces the probability of the occurrence of other, nonsanctioned means by which these conflicts might be expressed and resolved (latent social function of the monastery). If this culturally constituted defense were not available for the resolution of conflict, the consequent persistence of tension might lead to defenses of a psychotic nature, psychosomatic disorders of various kinds, or many types of antisocial, i.e., criminal behavior. I would suggest that a study of Burmese crime, including dacoity and insurgency—both of which are, and have been, endemic in Burma—would reveal that a large percentage of dacoits and insurgents are recruited from the ranks of those for whom the monastic life is not (for reasons still to be determined) a psychologically viable means for resolving emotional conflict.[2]

The monastic system, in short, not only serves the important personal function of precluding psychotic breakdown, but it also serves the important social function of allowing potentially disruptive, antisocial drives to be channeled into culturally approved (institutional) behavior. Since the monastery, moreover—for reasons beyond the scope of this paper—is the most integrative institution in Burmese society, the social function of psychological conflict, when resolved in this fashion, cannot be overestimated.

If the foregoing analysis is correct, then—to return to the more general problem of this paper—abnormal behavior can be expected to appear under one of three conditions: (1) when emotional conflict is idiosyncratic, so that cultural means are not available as potential bases for culturally constituted defense mechanisms; (2) when emotional conflict is modal, and cultural means are available for conflict resolution, but these means have been inadequately taught or inadequately learned; (3) when, under conditions of rapid social change,

2. This generalization excludes those—and I have met them—for whom insurgency and dacoity are romantic, adventurous activities to be given up when the adventure palls. It also excludes those whose emotional conflicts are idiosyncratic, rather than culturally patterned, and for which there are no cultural institutions by which conflict can be resolved.

culturally constituted defense mechanisms are unavailable, either because older institutions have been discarded or because the new situation creates a new set of conflicts. These three conditions, however, are necessary, but not sufficient, conditions for abnormal behavior. Although emotional conflict is potentially pathogenic, it need not produce pathology. Emotional conflict issues in pathology only if it is not resolved, or if it is resolved in a manner which is characterized by psychological distortion and/or sociocultural impairment. The latter resolutions are characteristic of neurotic and psychotic resolutions.

But neurosis and psychosis are not the only means for resolving conflict. Other private defense mechanisms may be constructed which are perceptually, cognitively, and affectively consistent with the behavioral environment of the actors, and which, moreover, constitute no obstacle to adequate sociocultural functioning. Finally, there is a third category of defense mechanisms—culturally constituted defenses—which are not only not disruptive of, but rather serve to perpetuate, the sociocultural system. Conflict, in short, may indeed produce pathological defenses; but it may also produce normal defenses, either private or culturally constituted.

In most traditional societies, where religious beliefs and practices continue to carry conviction, religion is the cultural system *par excellence* by means of which conflict-resolution is achieved. In such societies, in which religious behavior is appropriate to, rather than disruptive of, the behavioral environment of the actors, and in which a religious world view is consistent with, rather than a distortion of, "reality," religion serves as a highly efficient culturally constituted defense mechanism.

References

Benedict, R.
1934: *Patterns of Culture* (Boston: Houghton Mifflin).

Hallowell, A. I.
1955: *Culture and Experience* (Philadelphia: University of Pennsylvania Press).

Spiro, M. E.
1961: "An Overview and a Suggested Reorientation," in F. L. K. Hsu (ed.), *Psychological Anthropology* (Homewood, Illinois: Dorsey Press).

Steele, J.
1963: *A Preliminary Analysis of the Burmese Rorschachs*. Unpublished ms.

Part Three

Social Character

PAUL FRIEDRICH

An Agrarian "Fighter"

The Problem

Just as kinship and linguistic theory depend on studies of particular kinship systems and languages, so no theory of individual psychology can have validity without the systematic study of human beings in different cultures. Although such men and women are unique and continuously change in their organization of motives, sentiments, and thought, they still illustrate and even epitomize human types and universal problems.

In the present paper my first goal has been to examine one leader, Nicolás Gomez of Durazno, Mexico, and show, in what has been called a "topical life history," how a person of his status is related to the patterns of the two institutions with which he has been primarily concerned: village politics and government. This sheds light on the dynamics of the individual, notably, in this case, on his cooperative and aggressive tendencies, and also on the dynamics of the two, closely related institutions. Since Nicholás has been singularly responsive to the traditions and changing ways of his community, I have focused on the adaptive and nonadaptive political shifts in Durazno and made them a coordinate subject of my presentation; just as the analysis of culture change cannot avoid the concept of personality, so the study of individual character cannot ignore economic, social, and political change.

My second goal has been to infer or at least give intimations of one man's character and to show, in particular, how his unique and partly deviant traits fit into the total network and into the folkways and recent history of his village; valid understanding is only possible if one relates the changing profile of a man to his human environment. In the cogent words of A. Irving Hallowell, "It is only through the study of affective experience in a number of different societies that the role of cultural variables can be thoroughly understood. Comparative data of this sort may also indicate that individual deviations themselves take on characteristic forms in different societies" (1955, p. 265).

The "Fighter": An Introduction[1]

The appearance of Nicolás Gomez gives intimations of his central role in the recent political history of his village. The comparatively tall figure is still physically lithe and well-coordinated. His facial structure is heavy, his cheekbones prominent, and his forehead slopes back sharply to the white hair of his circular cranium, a perfect fit for the small, pointed peak of his broad-brimmed sombrero. During the months that I knew him, Nicolás invariably wore blue denim or khaki jeans, cheap, ankle-length boots, and a white shirt and white cotton jacket, always with some dry earth caught in the seams. In cold weather he would don an aviator-style jacket with a collar of artificial fur. Stubble covered his face so habitually that one would make a mental note on seeing him clean-shaven.

In formal contexts the man was called Nicolás, or even "Don Nico," but friends usually referred to him and addressed him as Nico. He often seemed to effuse a personal brand of grimness, his grey eyes clouded and hostile, or mirroring what I took to be some distant purpose or suppressed intent. Characteristically he would sit or stand before the town hall, the focus of political life, with his athletic back erect, his jaws clenched, and stare off into space. Unlike most other leaders, he could think or daydream for half an hour or more without moving any part of his body. Almost in caricature, his elegant gestures of hand and the precise articulation of his fingers exemplified the style with which Tarascan Indians punctuate any emphatic personal opinion. His gentle, almost pressureless handshake symbolized the Tarascan desire to minimize bodily contact.

1. Eighteen months were spent in Mexico during 1955–56, fourteen of them entirely in Durazno and Tiripendo. The last year of field work was largely devoted to politics and government. The present article is one of ten comparable life histories that constitute the sixth chapter of my doctoral dissertation (Friedrich: 1957). The remaining nine, for which I have Rorschachs, will be published separately as a monograph. I am most grateful to Lore Friedrich, Robbins Burling, Robert Laughlin, and David Schneider for their critical reading of this manuscript, and to Sidney Mintz for his advice during the field work and the organization of earlier drafts of the thesis.

Yet to some of his fellow villagers this same man was "an assassin" (*asesino*), and many Mexican outsiders would rank him as the worst gunman in a town of killers (*matones*); an American psychiatrist who read some of my field notes went so far as to class him a "criminal psychopath." His career of violence had been launched at the age of twenty-two when he joined the faction that won the agrarian revolt. Since 1920, he had killed at least eight men, and wounded many others in ambush, skirmish, and drunken brawl. Some people insisted that he had accounted for twelve to fifteen deaths if one included the unrecorded assassinations in other villages. These facts, together with certain deviant acts to be described, had earned him the sobriquet of "Bones" (*Huesos*), used with certain off-color intimacy by his friends, or with hostility by his enemies.[2] One townsman waxed sarcastic about his ambushes: "Bones never shot anyone until they gave free rein to criminality. He has killed many, but always from behind. A turkey in a flock never acts alone." Another intelligent but equally biased informant cracked that Bones "kills them, goes to the wake, and drinks coffee with the bereaved." Bones had been wounded several times and twice riddled by would-be killers. All of the fighting had been part of agrarian politics, although some was simultaneously connected with struggles over a woman, or with fear and aggression of a more personal sort.

The evaluation of Nico's moral stature within the moral order of the pueblo is no simple matter, however. To many villagers he was an agrarian fighter (*luchador*), with a distinguished record of very early participation in an almost universally approved reform. More than that, he was thought of as manly, and brave (*valiente*), the sort who resorts to homicide in politics, and who may get dangerous when drunk. Bones, then, illustrated the excess of a trait which his own villagers feel to be human rather than despicable; man has a passionate, violent streak and his emotions may at times be expressed through a state of rage, or *coraje*. I have seen two villagers who, when enraged, became as though disconnected from the world, their eyes out of focus, breathing in deep gasps. Bones may have acted like this during some of the killings to be described. Others when enraged grow cold, and may shoot down a man from ambush as though he were a coyote. I imagine that Bones has gunned down some of his political enemies in this fashion. The men most known for such expressive homicide are, like Bones, comparatively soft-spoken and polite, and habitually reserved. I have no evidence that Bones sadistically protracted people's deaths, or enjoyed their brief pain. At best, therefore, he was to his fellows simply an agrarian fighter and a man of passion.

Bones has, in fact, grown old in a town with a name for violence. Between 1920–26 his and two neighboring villages carried out an agrarian revolt that became a test case for agrarian reform in Michoacán. In the twenty years of

2. Following village usage I have generally named him Nico, reserving Nicolás for more formal contexts and Bones for the sections involving his violence.

factional strife that followed the three pueblos attained a unique notoriety as "the slaughterhouse" (*el rastro*) of the state: a total of seventy-seven political homicides have interrupted its life during the past thirty-six years and during the bad years of 1937 to 1939 alone, twenty-one politically motivated homicides and several times more armed encounters disturbed the superficially peaceful-seeming community. Durazno leaders have organized violence and have assassinated opponents in other parts of the state. In the entire period since 1920, there have been eight other fighters with as great a propensity to homicide, and with records equalling or exceeding Nico's; two of them collaborated with him for almost twenty-five years. The town, with a population of 1000 to 1500 has always contained five to fifteen or more "valiant fighters," just as quick to act, and a match for Bones in armed encounter, although most of them more interested than he in agriculture and their families. In addition, there have always been between fifteen to forty or more active or potential agrarian fighters. In 1956, for example, four living leaders had killed or participated directly in the killing of at least eight enemies apiece, eight others had killed three or four each, and a total of at least twenty-nine had at some time taken part in a homicide. Bones is no braver than dozens of other villagers, including many younger men. Self-help is still needed for defense and punishment, and a man, to be normal, must be prepared to kill in certain contexts. Bones has never stood alone for violence.

Life History and Political Role: The Formative Years (1898–1920)

When Nicolás was born fifty-eight years ago, most of the people of his village spoke only the Indian language, and felt a strong identity with the Indian customs. The town included only two families that could be called *mestizo* (non-Indian Mexican), and they had lived there for several generations, spoke Tarascan, and owned land. Otherwise, the town was suspicious and hostile toward outside mestizos and Spaniards. As Nicolás himself recalls, "before 1925, we didn't like to have people of reason (*gente de razón*) settle here. We used to get drunk and then someone would want to kill a *turísUni.*[3] That is why there are still so few of them in Durazno." Even in 1956, the village contained only five per cent mestizos, and the mestizos of the region identified "those from Durazno" by their more consistently Indian traits of race (*por la raza*).

Nicolás, however, had mestizo parents. His father came from a mestizo hamlet and, in a certain sense, had learned broken Tarascan in order to survive; the son still remembers with amusement some specific errors of pronunciation. Nico's mother, from a nearly adjacent mestizo settlement, was unable to speak the native language. In sum, the boy learned Tarascan not from his parents but from his companions (*compañeros*). To my knowledge he was the only

3. *TurísU* is the Tarascan for mestizo, that is, a non-Indian.

villager of his generation who grew up in such a divided world, although several of the agrarian leaders did come from families that were fully bilingual, and about a third of the leaders in 1956 had had mestizo fathers who deserted Durazno while their sons were still young. The peculiar linguistic split between Nico's parents and his community, especially his young friends within the community, must have engendered certain conflicts and dichotomies within his own mind that were later paralleled by conflicts in agrarian politics. The linguistic facts make it reasonable to assume that he learned the local culture imperfectly or atypically, facilitating his later rejection of certain parts of it. In 1956, he still spoke Tarascan fluently and frequently seemed more at home in it than in Spanish. He felt that it set him off from "the people of reason." After the first six months he always used to greet me in Tarascan, and enjoyed swapping a few phrases, usually terminated by a *double entendre* that I could not understand.

Nicolás' infancy and childhood were marked by extreme physical deprivation. About ten years before his birth most of the best land in the valley—a great marshy swamp lying north of the village—had been seized by a Spanish company directly backed by the national government. This was part of the "rape of the pueblos" by mestizos and foreigners then taking place in many parts of Mexico. The resulting social disorganization in Durazno was conjoined with national inflation and generally chaotic economic conditions during the first decade of this century. In this particular case, the Spaniards were collaborating with local mestizos, including the two families within Durazno mentioned above. The lands were drained and extraordinarily productive plantations were created. By the same token, the population was no longer able to get fish, fowl, and the superb rushes from the marsh, and the majority, including Nico's parents, were forced to eke out a subsistence as hired peons for the new landlords. More often, they made periodic migrations to the great sugar cane fields to the south, near the Pacific Ocean. Nico's father was one of these landless, wage-earning peons, and he usually made the trek to the "hot country" several times a year. He was accompanied by his wife and children, who were carried along into the disturbing and poverty-ridden environment of the labor camps. One of Nico's brothers died in childhood. His father perished of fever when the boy was ten, and his mother died two years later. After these deaths he lived with an older sister and three other, older brothers, two of whom soon died of fever. The Gomez family may be said to have typified the new proletariat of the village; above all, the children of this have-not class suffered from sickness and early death through malnutrition, and tropical diseases (malaria is mentioned most often).

Certain conflicts and frustrations during these years may account for the later aggressive behavior of Bones Gomez and the large contingent of youths and adult men who subsequently made up the notorious, "red-boned" agrarian faction of Durazno. But the infancy and childhood of the man do not appear to have differed greatly from those of dozens of others, and the overt acts which we now stigmatize as "aggressive" were more than uniquely personal in origin. Unlike many other leaders, Nicolás never complained to me of having suffered as a child, or of having eaten "nothing but tortillas."

Until agrarian reform, the children of poorer villagers received little formal education. Nicolás never attended the tiny elementary school that functioned in the village before the Mexican Revolution of 1910. Being thus deprived may at first have made him responsive to the ideals of education set forth by the agrarian leaders. But, in later years, the uncomfortable awareness of his illiteracy provoked hostility to outsiders and particularly to schoolteachers. During his adolescence Nicolás rode herd for the new landlords of the valley and for one of the two wealthy mestizo families. He generally slept in the stables of the latter as a sort of attached servant; old women still think of him as a former stableboy. With this background he became the expert horseman he remains to this day, and during the same years he formed the friendships and animosities that were to govern his later conduct. In particular, I suspect that he began to resent or hate his mestizo employers.

The Mexican Revolution, from 1910 to 1920, created hardships for the village. Since it lay on one of the great east-west roads and rail-lines, army detachments and bands of marauding guerrillas repeatedly passed by. Sometimes they shot or threatened leaders believed to be politically hostile. Women often fled into the sierra to escape mistreatment, including rape. From his twelfth to twenty-second year, Nicolás, the orphaned stableboy, saw or heard of many acts of violence and challenges to the foundations of society. He personally remembers how agrarian unrest germinated during the decade of the national revolution as the ideas of Emiliano Zapata and Francisco Villa slowly trickled into the town. Mestizo peons from the new plantation often molested Durazno women. In 1912, when Nico was fourteen, a mob of enraged Indians with slings and spears attacked a party of drunken mestizo peons, killing six. Nicolás recalls with pleasure how the local priest was later encouraged to leave. The chaotic times and his own underprivileged status made him susceptible from the start to the ideology of agrarianism and the violence necessary to achieve it. Yet, I have no evidence or even suggestion that he was known for violence until the onset of the agrarian revolt itself.

Bones' First Conversion (1920)

One of the most significant experiences in Nico's life was his early and unwavering identification with the agrarian hero, Primo Tapia. Tapia differed fundamentally from Nico, and yet their personalities and social roles were complementary. Because of a generous uncle, Tapia had had the good fortune to receive excellent secondary school training in a Catholic seminary, before going off to the United States in 1907, where he spent fourteen years as a migrant laborer in the mines and farms of the West. Because of the agrarian unrest already stirring in his own village, Tapia was attracted to the peculiar blend of philosophical anarchism and idealistic socialism then being propounded by the Flores Magón brothers, "the ideological precursors of the Mexican Revolution." He spent two years studying and associating with the Magons in Los Angeles, before entering the anarchist International Workers of the World where he organized or participated in several strikes. Returning to Durazno in 1920, aged thirty-six, he needed only a few months to pull together the agrarian movement in the valley, despite the legal toils and armed militia of the local landlords. Within Durazno he organized a "shock brigade" of about twenty core "fighters," and some fifty additional partisans. His success as an indigenous revolutionary depended on a combination of ideological sophistication with a dead-sure intuitive sense of local customs and situations that permitted effective communication with potential "fighters" such as Nicolás. In the absence of such leaders and "fighters," agrarian revolts sputtered out or never were kindled in many parts of Mexico.

One of Nico's many positive emotions is his abiding gratitude to Tapia for ideological orientation. "Primo used to explain everything to us, that such-and-such ideas were wrong, that such-and-such ideas were right, and that it was a pure lie that we would be sent to Hell for taking part in agrarianism (*el agrarismo*). He understood everything and he used to explain it well." In Tarascan? "Yes, he always talked to us in Tarascan. He could speak Tarascan, Spanish, and . . . and . . . English! Ever since I joined him I have never gone to church. I never go in *there*. I am still with Primo out here" (*Y me tiene aquí todavía*). These boasts are not vain. Nico has not used his political authority to acquire large amounts of land, being content with his plot in the communal lands. And he remains a staunch atheist. "Primo organized us, and explained everything. He was one of us." From the writer's point of view, Tapia brought to Durazno an articulate, comprehensive, and effectively communicated world view, and Nicolás Gomez was one of the most susceptible, perhaps *the* most susceptible of the new "coreligionaries."[4]

An Original Agrarian (1920–26)

During the agrarian revolt Nico functioned as one of Tapia's young fighters; although not one of the inner core of leaders, his place in local history as an "original fighter" has been attested without qualification by persons of all political affiliation, including his worst enemies. A pregnant way of putting this is, "He was one of the first who sided with Primo" (*Era uno de los primeros que andaban con Primo*). His part in the often nocturnal violence between 1920 and

4. From a psychoanalytic viewpoint, Nico's sudden conversion suggests that agrarian reform functioned as a "screen for aggressive impulses."

1925 cannot be precisely determined, aside from his own vague admission that there was "a lot of killing, but I don't like to think about that any more." His enemies allege that he carried out various assassinations and even robberies. Certain it is that he spent much time hiding out in the sierra south of Durazno in order to avoid retaliation from federal troops and the hacienda militia. In 1924, the men of Primo Tapia, to quote Nico, "ran the opposition out of town, and they couldn't return without signing the agrarian census. They were foolish (*tonto*), reactionary. We were getting the ejido lands for the good of the town, and they opposed us." Nico's position is rational: under the circumstances, agrarian reform was an adaptive change. Later the same year, the agrarian factions won the struggle against the Spanish landlords. The Indians of Durazno obtained rights over almost fifteen hundred acres of black soil which they organized as an ejido of collectively owned and administered agricultural lands. Until the death of Tapia, all phases of production and distribution were communalistic.

During these stressful years, Nicolás emerged as one of "Tapia's well-known killers." In August of 1924, at the age of twenty-six, he definitely shot and killed a member of one of the five land-owning families which had been supporting the landlords; the face-to-face political homicide was catalyzed by sugar cane brandy. In 1925 a group of agrarians, including Nico, ran the leading witch out of town. Later that year he participated in a gun battle on the streets of the county seat, where three Durazno agrarians lost their lives. Agrarian reform, viewed as an adaptive social change, had required and, in turn, fostered a certain social status, that of "fighter," for which personalities such as Nico's were singularly well fitted.[5]

But on April 26 of the following year, 1926, Primo Tapia was kidnaped by federal agents under direct orders from the national president, and lynched the same evening by his guards. Nico and three agrarian comrades dashed off by horse to the state capital, making inquiries, and attempting to secure a federal safe conduct. Two days later they bore home the horribly mutilated body for burial in Durazno. The sadistic lynching of Primo Tapia outraged Nicolás Gomez.

A Fighter in Village Factionalism (1926–47)

With the death of Tapia, regional control disintegrated as the local chieftains in the agrarian communities turned against their neighbors. The peasants had become so involved in the new goals of land and local leadership that they now turned on each other with scarcely abated resolve. During the summer of 1926 the Durazno agrarians split, headed in each case by large groups of more or less related men: the Rocas and the Casos. These factions were divided on the sub-

5. Connections such as this presumably underlie Spiro's (1961) argument that personality and social systems intersect in the role.

stantive issue of land usufruct. The "reactionary" Rocas wanted to have the communal ejido divided into separate plots for each family, and to admit families that had not fought under Tapia. The "revolutionary" or "Bolshevik" agrarians wanted all phases of land use to be communalistic, and did not want to admit any of the new, mestizo families or other ex-White Guards. An aggressive young fighter like Nicolás had to choose sides; Nico opted the Caso faction. It seems most likely that the Rocas had wounded his *amour propre* or had somehow thwarted his egoism (*egoismo*). He now claims to have opposed them because "they offended me," and "refused to recognize my worth, to respect me." More important, he was related to several Casos by intimate friendship, the main bond between political leaders who are not actually relatives. Nicolás, especially when in the company of his partner, Jaime Caso, was already a heavy drinker, and ugly in his cups: "He used to be very much of a murderer when he got drunk," as one old-timer put it. But he was also "very fast and alert" (*muy listo*), and escaped from two ambushes. On January 18, 1929, he killed a member of the Roca faction in a drunken brawl. Three years later he and several Caso agrarians assassinated a man in revenge for the murder of one of their number.

As has been noted, Durazno was strongly ethnocentric in the first decades of the century, and the ethnic factor functioned to rally the Indians during the agrarian revolt. Immigrant mestizos like Nico had to adjust to the local version of Tarascan culture. But agrarian politics, although directed against an external foe, did not increase communal solidarity. On the contrary, it split the village, and agrarian factions have been splintering ever since. By the late 1920's political ambition had come to outweigh cultural solidarity, since both of the agrarian Indian factions within the village had alliances in adjoining mestizo villages. For example, Nico's group in the 1929 assassination was led by a mestizo who represented the vigorous support of the Casos by mestizo squatters who hoped to get land under the laws and statutes. In such troubled waters and shifting currents of power Nico has survived and even succeeded.

Three years later, as the Casos were emerging victorious, Bones again notched the record with a killing that, though accidental, is always mentioned with lowered voice and undertones of horror. A member of the Roca faction had stolen and eaten his cow. Such immediate causes may trigger off a homicide that is congruous with the larger frame of politics. Shortly afterwards Nicolás, somewhat intoxicated, asked the thief to come and "discuss a little matter on the edge of town." They walked out together, followed by a friend of the culprit. On reaching the railroad tracks on the outskirts, both men drew their pistols, but, being at close quarters, almost side by side, they grappled and went down together. The thief's wife had been informed and came running up and tried to interject herself between her husband and Nicolás, who had gone wild. As she was twisting herself between the men, Nicolás got his pistol free and mortally wounded her with a shot into the mouth. Some split seconds later, his adversary was shot in the stomach just as the friend, who had been waiting his chance, shot Nico through the back, beneath the kidney. Both of the men left town shortly afterward and have never returned.

The Durazno woman and child should not suffer violence through politics. Although a woman may be deceived or abducted, she is axiomatically precluded as the victim for a vendetta. This may derive from the sacredness of a man's relation to his mother; since almost all women do become wives and mothers, the murder of one defending her son or husband appears fearsome and somehow even perverse. The same taboo partly explains the fearless abandon with which women interject themselves between their fighting men. Durazno history shows, at several points, how obscene references to someone's mother can trigger off a political homicide. Thus, the accidental shooting of a woman added a somber hue to the reputation of Bones Gomez.

Like most Mexicans, all men of Durazno were riders, and some rode very well; a man was judged by his horsemanship, and any man could recognize at a great distance the horse of any other villager. "In those days one wanted to own a fine horse," and fine horses were remembered for decades. Nicolás, who had spent his youth as a cowhand, was and remains particularly sensitive to these values. With the new affluence of the ejido, he was not long in buying a fine bay mare that is still recalled with admiration by some old-timers. It was only natural for him to join the mounted militia in the early 1930's. He soon became the outstanding performer at riding erect while straddling two horses, or at leaping from one horse to another while at full gallop, or at jumping from horse to ground and back again, and other equestrian feats. Buses and other means of transportation were subsequently introduced by the through highway, but the equestrian orientation remains strong to this day; to have been the best rider in Durazno is no mean accomplishment. Nico's horsemanship was part of a community-wide pattern: many of the best athletes have avoided politics, but almost all the noteworthy leaders and fighters have excelled at some sport—riding, racing, basketball, billiards, or the native game of *palillos*. Nico's horsemanship also points to a salient personal trait: superb physical coordination. His seemingly complete relaxation, when at rest, is combined with swift and sure body movements once he is called into action.

In the 1930's, local militias of the peasantry were closely tied to the army units stationed in the state. The Durazno militia, which included several Caso and Roca leaders still alive today, was often instructed by officers and sergeants from the cavalry detachment in the county seat. It distinguished itself at several large affairs, once winning a state-wide contest in Paracho. The local militias of Michoacán, composed of peasants like Nicolás, were a key factor during the abortive uprisings of conservative, pro-clerical movements, and later during the intensified, pervasive factionalism of 1932–36; candidates who could bring a few thousand armed peasants into the streets of the capital stood better chances in the elections. The dissolution of all local militias by the national government in the early 1940's signalled the end of an era in Mexican politics, and demonstrated that a stable and centralized control had been achieved by the "Center" in Mexico City.

Since about 1932, the Rocas had been collaborating with the governor's faction, but the latter perished in 1935 almost immediately after the inauguration as national president of the state's leading politician, to whom the Casos had remained unswervingly loyal. The Rocas' external buttresses collapsed and they had to give up within the pueblo, some thirty families emigrating forever.

In the ensuing atmosphere of factional victory, Bones' virtues were formally recognized through his "election," though he was still illiterate, to the office of town judge. For two critical years during mopping-up operations against the defeated Rocas, he rendered valuable service by ignoring the derelictions of his comrades while, on the contrary, summoning the municipal police or even military detachments in cases against the local opposition. Such interdependence between law and the power struggle, implicit in all cultures, becomes particularly obvious in the Mexican provinces at times of stress.

Shortly after relinquishing these legal responsibilities, Bones reverted to a more familiar role. In June, 1937, he killed a member of a new opposition faction by the method known as "treachery" (*de traición*). Just one year later he participated in a similar bushwhacking of three mestizos from a neighboring hamlet. In contrast to the earlier case of collaboration between Indians and mestizos, described above, this was one of Indian fighters from Durazno helping their various allies in the neighboring mestizo villages. A few months later Bones was threatened by a drunken Durazno peasant who had taken up residence in the county seat. "In order to anticipate" (*para anticipar*) the move, he bushwhacked the man a week later. The episode illustrates how a local fighter may expect aggression from some quarters and at any given time may be planning on how to "anticipate it." Thus, political and highly personal motives may be interwoven; violence in a fighter often derives from intense political ambition, and aggressiveness in the streets may well outweigh forensic shortcomings at the town meetings.

The reason for Bones' renewed violence was a new schism within Durazno. The Casos had taken over a good land surplus, were in the enjoyment of "full legal guarantees," and were led by two first cousins who were similar in personality and political orientation. But the cousins differed profoundly in other ways. Pablo had fought through the regional agrarian reform and had then become a fairly prominent state leader serving as head of the Confederation of Labor for three years (1932–35). The other had only returned in 1926, a few months before the death of the agrarian hero, but had since then become the dominant leader within the community. In 1937, the two men split over "a question of egoism," and a specific "question of skirts" (the hostility between their mestizo wives). The majority of the adult Casos sided with the local cousin, as did the majority of the top fighters, including Nico. But value conflicts were insoluble. Alcoholism sharply increased among many leaders and fighters. After 1937 the village entered a new and terrible phase, with politically motivated killings between former friends, relatives, and even compadres. Nico's compadre, Jaime Caso, is most often named as the "bad man" of the town (*hombre malo*), but his own words for the epoch were: "That was no longer the agrarian struggle. That was pure politics, with death, orphans and widows. We entered in a time that was bad, bad!" The leaders and fighters who fought out this struggle gradually became disillusioned (*decepcionados*).

Because so many of the better men had gone against him, Pablo, the increasingly professional politician, operating from the state capital, had hired two mestizo thugs known as Jorge and Lucás. By the same token he broke with the still vital tradition that homicides should be done by one's fellow villagers; the use of outside mercenaries both suggested his weakness within the pueblo and appeared to threaten village unity. The following year (1937) his two unsavory myrmidons, together with a local fighter, assassinated a precandidate for state congressman while he was plowing his plot in an adjacent agrarian community. In 1939 Jorge and Lucás ambushed Nico as he was walking through the plaza—quite drunk, by one account—and gravely wounded him through the arm, shoulder, and abdomen. The nearly successful murder unleashed a whirlwind of rage (*coraje*) among his comrades in the Caso faction: within two hours Jorge had been hunted down and riddled where he was hiding in the tall maize of the ejido, and one brief hour later Lucás was dispatched by Jaime in a head-on encounter on a side-alley known as "The Street of the Dead."

These happenings point up the dichotomy between "fighter" (*luchador*) and "gunman" (*pistolero*). The fighter such as Jaime or Bones is somewhat more habituated to carrying a pistol, and is comparatively more prone to the ambush and assault that punctuate the perennial vendetta, the relations between local factions, and the killings over women. For example, of the ten leaders and fighters who accompanied the dominant cacique on a campaign tour in 1956, only Bones had mounted a .45 Colt in a large holster (beneath his aviator-style jacket), although several others had hung smaller pistols inside their pants. Had the need arisen, Bones would have been able to bring the heaviest caliber bullets into play the fastest. But even egregious killers such as Bones have remained dirt peasants, tilling the soil with their own hands, and enjoying the network of friends and kinship that is one's best defense. To put it somewhat differently: while playing all the roles normal to a man, they somewhat exaggerate the political one. For these reasons it seems wise to follow the local classification and to distinguish between a fighter, that is, a local peasant who has been outstanding in political violence, as against the opprobrious epithet of *pistolero* (professional thug or hired gun), so apt in this case, for the ill-fated (and homosexually linked) Jorge and Lucás.

Among other things, Nico has been very lucky. In 1939 he emerged from his narrow brush with death augmented in prestige, and enjoying the greater attachment of his comrades. But these were troubled times. The presidential elections in 1940 were marked by national unrest, and in Durazno at least eight leaders and fighters in the fallen faction openly opposed the candidate for president who had been designated by the outgoing chief executive. Their enemies now claim that they "retreated into the sierra," either to await reinforcements and start a revolution, or simply to escape the intensified dangers of life in the village. Several of the men insist that no one ever "retreated into the sierra." In either case, they appear to have left the village for some time; under the Agrarian Code anyone who leaves ejido lands fallow for one year falls subject to expropriation, and anyone who fails to cultivate it for two years may be deprived of rights; by the same token, anyone who does cultivate a plot for two years acquires full rights. During late 1940, therefore, the Casos resolved to expropriate the eight opponents, most of them "original agrarians," like Nico, with far more right to the land than any newer claimants.

Early in 1941 Nicolás Gomez was elected president of the ejido (*comisariado ejidal*); the other three ejidal posts were also filled by veterans of the mounted milita. Upon them devolved the precarious job of advancing the claims for expropriation and of holding off the old ejidatarios. In 1942, Bones, in a state of rage (*coraje*), shot dead one of the eight; one enemy alleges that the man had done nothing but steal a liter of Nico's brandy, but the death fit well into the political framework. By the time of his retirement in 1943, the reclamation had been effectively blocked and the new ejidatarios had acquired rights in perpetuity by virtue of having worked the land for the necessary minimum. Just as when he was judge during the expulsion of the Rocas, Bones' tenure in the major office of ejidal president symbolized the full institutionalization of violence during these stressful years. By 1943 the transition had been made from true agrarian reform to the comparatively barren struggle among leaders and fighters for a half-dozen contested plots. On June 3, 1944, Bones and several other Caso fighters, some of them new ejidatarios, outbluffed the expropriated men as they were trying to enter their former lands.

During 1945, political unrest broke out all over the state, concomitant with the election of a new governor; in neighboring Tiripendo the ejidal president was shot and killed. On false charges Nico, together with two friends, was arrested for the first time in his life and briefly detained. A few weeks after his release the opposition faction, staring defeat in the face, made two desperate efforts. First, three of the dominant cacique's peons were butchered in the sierra. Second, a band of mestizos from a neighboring hamlet tried to ambush the cacique himself on his way home from the town hall. In typically swift retaliation, the formidable trio of Nico, Jaime, and Carlo ambushed and killed two of the fallen cacique's lesser supporters as they were walking up the highway toward the county seat the following afternoon; of the premeditated forms of homicide, ambush has always been preferred, although face-to-face assault remains in favor because it enhances the assailant's repute for valor.

By 1947, the Caso faction had won, although some terrible episodes were yet to come: In the same year Nicolás was accomplice to the murder of a nephew to the fallen cacique; he was shot through the back while trotting home from the fields on his donkey. His three-year-old son, riding in front, was also seriously wounded.[6] Injury to children as a part of politics is opposed by strong feelings in Durazno, although it conflicts with a potential extension of blood vengeance. Taken together with his shooting of a woman, Bones' involvement in the deviant shooting of 1947 reinforced the tendency of many in the fallen faction to mentally segregate him and Jaime Caso as "criminals" and "assassins," prone to disregard the moral code that has been shared and transmitted through all the years of factional strife.

Bones' Second Conversion

Power, starting with reasonably malleable stuff, had begun to corrupt Nicolás. One evening later in the same year of 1947, while wandering along the main street of town, besotted, brandishing his pistol, and threatening to kill so-and-so, he met the newly elected mayor, a respectable, determined little peasant who, like the great majority in Durazno, had been peacefully tilling the soil and bringing up his sons during the entire period of factional contention. Now Nico, the drunkard and politician, swayed up to him and exclaimed, "You think, because you are mayor, that you're a big shot . . . you . . . son of the fucked one. . . ." The mayor retorted, "*¿Y tú qué?*" pulled out his own pistol and shot Nico several times in the stomach and abdomen.[7]

During the long convalescence that followed both friends and doctors remonstrated, and Nico pondered his heavy drinking and the stomach wounds. Too drunk for defense, he had nearly been killed by a man "without valor" in the kind of homicidal exchange that counts for much. He resolved never to touch liquor again, and may have come to other important decisions in what appears to have been a rather spontaneous turning point in his life. Since 1947 he has shot nobody, and in 1956 he was still careful to steer clear of drinking groups or, if the pressure to conviviality grew too imperious, would imbibe the Pepsi-Cola sedulously ordered by an understanding friend. As a form of

6. The son was still alive in 1956.

7. This exchange, like all the other political data, was reported to me in Spanish. Durazno is now almost entirely bilingual, many younger leaders know Spanish much better than Tarascan, and many persons under twenty know very little Tarascan. The leaders use the indigenous language mainly for comical or personal communications.

moral lesson, the little ex-mayor who had shot him down was still prospering, the head of a patriarchal household with the ideal defense: three grown sons.

Nico's Role in Local Intrigue (1952–57)

Nicolás has remained politically ambitious, and prone to envy (*envidia*). He never forgave the Casos for accepting his help over twenty-five dangerous years, only to join public opinion in declaring that the little mayor had acted in line of duty, and even jesting about their valiant warrior. Nico's vengeful sentiments were prompted by a genuine threat to his own person, and by the explicit awareness that the Casos *had failed to respect him*; "making oneself respected" as a man is a major factor in village politics.

While his election to the important office of mayor in 1952 seemingly prolonged the Caso hegemony, it was in reality the beginning of a third fission among the members of the dominant faction; by the year in question many villagers and at least two-thirds of the leaders had grown restless and resentful toward the "interminable cacique" and his four faithful nephews.[8] Even personal friends and compadres of the ruling family had come to abominate the cacique's obese and spiteful (mestizo) wife. The majority of the pueblo, including Nico, was culturally estranged from seven of the top leaders, partly because the latter had mestizo wives, most of them former teachers, who were hostile and resentful toward the village in which they were forced to reside. And the personal egoism of the least educated and most Indian leaders was galled by the spectacle of the top Casos operating in state politics; by 1951, the eldest nephew was elected alternate (*suplente*) to the national senator from the state.

After the expiration of Nicolás' term in office the new opposition, although loosely put together, was sufficiently cohesive to back Jaime Caso for the post of mayor in 1952. Because of his blood ties this notorious fighter seemed to ensure the continued domination of the ruling oligarchy. But beneath these probabilities lay the fact that Jaime had never been adequately rewarded with political office and that he, more than anyone, despised the obese wife of the cacique. He began openly to form a third party with pretentious projects for material improvements and revitalization "in the spirit of Primo Tapia." In formulating this new ideology he was aided and guided by his son, a superior public speaker and a left-wing law student in Mexico City. The new faction accused the Casos of "never having done anything for the pueblo," and itself carried out major tasks such as the construction of a short road and the building of a bridge in the ejido lands.

But beneath the idealism of the son and the ambitions of the father, and the

8. *Cacique* is a pejorative term for a forceful ruler, or a tyrant in a village or state. *Caciquismo* is usually related to active factionalism, and to a comparatively "reactionary" or "revolutionary" ideology. Unlike the neighboring agrarian communities, Durazno has had a long, unbroken *cacicazgo*.

allegiance of several families, there lay the financial cupidity of many other supporters (among whom Nico cannot be numbered). They embezzled funds, sometimes running to several thousand pesos, and took over certain contested plots of land during these same years. Not actually trusting Jaime because of his close kinship with the Casos, they planned to have him bear the brunt of the reprisals if their bid for power should fail, or to eliminate him and his son after the Casos had been overthrown. By 1954, at the height of the Jaime Caso fission, three local factions were being led by three separate splinters of the old Caso faction of 1934. All three of the new factions depended on the essentially identical agrarian ideology, and the shaky loyalty of the many villagers, including Nico, who were basically hostile toward *all* the outstanding representatives of the abnormally discrete political life that had evolved. The personal hostility grew most acute between the purely local fighter, Nicolás, and the eldest of the Caso nephews, a comparatively educated politician, who once exclaimed, during an argument in 1954, "All right, Bones, let's go to the edge of town or before the ejidal assembly, and see who comes out the dirtiest!"

Jaime's bid for power was broken through the influence of higher authorities, and several touches of violence; he was wounded in the heel during an ambush from which he and his son were fortunate to escape alive. They retreated to Mexico City. But equally decisive were the machinations of the town secretary, a nephew of the cacique. He first undermined Nico's faith by suggesting that Jaime, though a compadre and old comrade-in-arms, would have him assassinated as soon as victory had been assured; there is enough of backbiting and threats *in absentia* to give credulity to intrigues of this ilk. Many defects in the so-called "plan for material improvements" were then explained. Although he had been born and bred in the village, Jaime's young son, the law student, was depicted as a man from the city "who could not understand the problems of Durazno." But perhaps the small and indirect bribes were most persuasive; every time after the civil authorities had "done justice," the town secretary would refuse any part of the fine on the grounds that his private income was sufficient, insisting that Nico accept now ten, now twenty pesos as his just due. Within a short time Nico allegedly became "very fond" of the young secretary (*me tenía mucho cariño*), let him run the court, and soon reneged against the rebellious faction of Jaimie in order to redeclare his loyalty to the Casos. The story of petty bribery is probably true, but the more decisive factor may have been that Nico began to appreciate Jamie's ineptitude as a community leader, in contrast to the *savoir faire* and the outside connections of the Casos. He therefore switched for reasons of expediency without making a personal break with his long-time comrade-in-arms. By 1954, the slogans of anticlericalism and material improvements of political parties were still a potent means of mobilizing loyalty. But they had been largely replaced at the communal level by comparatively amorphous alignments of power within which every man showed either a primary concern for fleeting personal advantages or for the deeper and more enduring bonds of kinship and friendship. In 1956, Bones and Jamie reciprocated in citing each other as friends and compadres.

Nico as a Senior "Prince" in 1956–57

Nico, in 1956, was one of the eight or nine leaders in the dominant faction who met secretly on occasion to make decisions affecting the entire community. In his function as judge, Nico was often in the town hall during 1955–56, and aways attended the full sessions. Because of the disputes over ejidal plots, and the unremitting attempts of some dozen expropriated ejidatarios to regain their land, the meetings of the ejidal government were often witnessed and even addressed by delegates from the Agrarian Department in Mexico City. Durazno leaders followed the letter of the Agrarian Code rather closely partly because they were politically prominent and ideologically explicit agrarians, partly because written denunciations by the fallen faction provoked regular visits by government inspectors. On such occasions the federal delegates were very careful to turn to Nicolás, and two or three others, as if they held the deciding vote.

By regional and national standards the overt political life of Durazno was hyperactive; the town hall was usually open, and leaders were always congregating there in the evening for informal discussions. The civil and ejidal governments usually convened once every month or two. But despite such opportunities, Nico seldom spoke in public and then only in a few awkward sentences. The guarded quality of his behavior was probably connected with a disillusionment over the great schism of 1937 and his resentment at the overweening political ambitions of the caciques, at the entire tradition of political hegemony under one family. At least from 1952 onward he was overtly playing along with the dominant wing of the Casos, while remaining in cautious collusion with those intriguing for an overthrow.

Sometimes Nico did wax fluent in conversation if the subject touched on politics. During 1956, politics suddenly became quite "hot" when most communities in the valley opposed the nomination of Durazno's cacique as state congressman. During these weeks Nico often entered into the arguments with short but relevant sentences on the need for Durazno to retain "control" (*control*).

Nico also spoke out on another occasion of moral portent. One of two brothers had seduced a young wife and had been carrying on a liaison. One Sunday afternoon the mother-in-law of the girl started a public scene with the adulterous brother, and slapped him several times. In the ensuing brawl the two brothers nearly knifed her other son, a minor leader. All parties involved were summoned to the town hall for a general discussion. Nicolás, who was then judge, eventually "took the word," as they say, and began pouring forth proverbs and many fixed or hackneyed phrases. He blamed those who stimulate an outbreak of passion while the contestants are still in control of themselves, that is, those who precipitate rage; the man who triggers off rage is more guilty than the man who acts violently when in a state of rage. Most of the villagers would agree to some extent with this legal notion. By the same token, the two brothers were let off with a mild admonition, whereas heavy blame was heaped on the mother of the man who had nearly been knifed.

During the same hearings Nicolás talked at some length about human passion and the eruption of rage, exculpating such acts in terms of his partly mestizo and partly Tarascan values. He then went on to say that the defendants and all of the Durazno community should outgrow its hard-earned reputation of containing only killers (*puros matones*), and should settle deep grievances in the town hall, and "not in the fields." Here as elsewhere it would be a mistake to think that his social role has been a disguise or mask for his real self; Nico has consistently played himself, and, in this sense, been true to himself.

A perceptive and educated observer once remarked, "the great majority in Durazno are like a herd of sheep, docile and pacific." But in fact there is no sharp dichotomy between the leaders and the led, between the elite and the mob; on the contrary, the political role of most men varies greatly through time and according to context. A more accurate view would recognize a scale of political status. At the lower extreme stand about fifty to seventy men who are inactive and have never held office, and are not prone to homicide. At the other end stands an approximately equal number of leaders and fighters. But "leader" and "fighter" do not mean the same thing; on the contrary, the relation between the two statuses is precarious. Several villagers have actually left because they lacked the toughness to play their designated role. Others are sensitive and educated enough to make excellent leaders, but lack the necessary valor or the flair for intrigue. On the other hand, some with the valor and vengeance obligations to be fighters lack the leadership ability to be "princes." For example, "Pancho the Squirrel" García, killer of three and local expert in folk songs, is frequently named in accusations but was never considered for office. Several minor leaders are simultaneously reckoned dangerous fighters, notably the courteous but temperamental *Turís* ("The Mestizo"), and the taciturn Juan Flores.[9] At present all but one of the nuclear princes of the ruling faction are also fighters, including, of course, Nicolás.

Character and Culture: Marital History

Sex and politics are closely linked in mestizo Mexico in the sense that a politically ambitious man usually has many affairs with women and exploits his political power to satisfy what has been called his "limitless sexual deficit" (Wolf: 1959, p. 239). Although partly Indian, the caciques and outstanding

9. Both these men are of mestizo origin, but have grown up within the village.

"fighters" in Durazno and the neighboring agrarian pueblos have had the lions' share of liaisons. More than any other leader, Nicolás has interwoven politics and sex.

In 1919, at the comparatively advanced age of twenty-one, he eloped with a young relative of one of the two most prominent fighters of the agrarian revolt. Nicolás and his have-not parents-in-law lacked the minimum for a wedding in the traditional style, and so the couple just joined, *Así, no más*. Moreover, the disturbed times were not conducive to marital fidelity, and Nicolás, as has been remarked, spent much time after 1920 in the sierra avoiding retaliations. He deserted the first wife in 1922, after three years, at the height of the agrarian revolt. Two years later his friend and ex-father-in-law was killed with ox-goads by five antiagrarians. Shortly thereafter, Nicolás joined in common-law marriage with a woman. She bore him four children; one son who reached maturity is now a minor leader.

Abandoning the second wife after six years, he drifted during the thirties, associating simultaneously or in succession with numbers of Durazno and Pazuca women. A friend, when asked about his affairs, grinned and responded, "*Mil amores*"; most of the "thousand loves," especially the longer relationships, seem to have been with Tarascan-speaking women. Documents and interviews for the 1930's contain occasional references to a "woman" in Nico's house; certainly the available widows and faithless wives are quicker to surrender to such a leader. Several enemies accused him of having seduced or assaulted the wife of a political enemy. While it would be absurd to interpret Durazno politics as primarily a struggle over the connubium, there is no question but that the opposition of both factions is steeled by real or fancied threats to the womenfolk.[10]

When sex is the subject, Nico knows few inhibitions. Once when discussing premarital relations he casually remarked, "We begin to fuck at fourteen." With whom? "With whomever we can lay our hands on, with a widow, or a girl friend." When do relations begin with the bride? "After the capture, and before it too." He is given to trite *double entendres*. One day a friend in the Caso faction remarked on a woman peddler across the street. What had been her wares, vegetables? Nico answered in the affirmative and touched off a general guffaw by playing on the word for a kind of wild green (Spanish *quelite*, Tarascan *shakuá*), which, in the dialect of another region, also means vulva.

During the second week of March 1956, a Tiripendo girl was abducted and raped in the sierra by three adolescents. Such sexual violations, occurring every year or two, invoke profound value conflicts; the women, the priest, and some of the more moral men are variously upset or outraged, whereas the majority of

10. From a psychoanalytic point of view we might deduce that Nico's well-known promiscuity between 1924 and about 1945 may have been connected with his failure to find emotional satisfaction in any woman.

the men are either resigned or even see something to joke about. In this case it was decided in Tiripendo that one of the boys would have to marry the girl. Nico and five companions talked at length about it while seated before the town hall; while recognizing the gravity of the act, they also jested a few times about the young men taking such good advantage of their opportunities.

On another evening in 1956, Nicolás and a group of leaders were lounging on the plaza in the great tourist center, Pátzcuaro. Someone saw a local girl pass by and noted, "She is pretty," in Tarascan, at which the old goat, Nico, chuckled and said, "Bite my cheek." Laughing harder all the time, he continued with, "Bite me on the cheek, Give me a kiss, Grab me and squeeze my breasts, Embrace me, darling, with your legs pointing upwards" (*katsípakurini, malesíta, tsíkajtekua jimbó*). He finished bent over, shaking with mirth.[11] Incidentally, Nico's scurrilous humor always referred to ventroventral heterosexual intercourse. His naturalism about sex, which he sees as an often humorous form of physical pleasure, is probably related to his lack of anxiety about death and his resignation to the homicidal rage in man. I could never detect in him signs of what might be called "moral anxiety"; *chercher la femme* was part of life, and factional enmity was a cause of death. In some ways, Nico's amatory and homicidal exploits had generated, if not affection, then at least sporadic amusement, even comic relief, in a culture where "Indian humor" can sometimes laugh at physical pain as well as broken crockery.

Perhaps the truest index of a naturalistic sexual past are his present relations with older women in their fifties, with whom he often seems to be on the verge of jest or horseplay; I sometimes watched him at a distance, conversing with such a Durazno matron, breaking into a chuckle, or buckling over and shaking his head in a gesture that contrasted sharply with his usual iron reserve. The contempt and vilifications of Nico's political enemies must be weighed in the balance against his joking and friendship with so many of the women who have grown old along with him, even if their shabby attire and often unkempt hair suggest the demoralizing effects of the past forty years. I have discussed Bones at some length with women in their sixties and seventies; several hated him as "bad," but the consensus was that he *used to be* "wild," and "one of the brave ones," but unquestionably belonged "with the community."

A few years ago Nicolás joined in common-law marriage with a much younger Tarascan woman who struck me as cheerful and fairly attractive. At fifty-eight, he appeared to have settled down. But he threw back his head and laughed out when someone remarked that men remain sexually active until their death. He often absented himself from the town hall for a week or ten days, sometimes simply to relax in his cozy, one-room adobe house near the plaza,

11. Such conversations may give the reader some idea of Nico interacting with his fellows on a subject of mutual interest; I had to make mental note en route under conditions where mechanical recording devices would constitute, at best, a hapless pedantry.

enjoying the company of his wife and two elderly female in-laws. At other times he would remain away in order to cultivate his ejido plot, or a few small patches of beans; unlike some leaders he did not hire peons, preferring to till the land himself. Although faithfully anti-clerical, he compromised with the folk religion to the point of participating in such pagan fiestas as the "Day of the Dead," and "Tacari Day"; until very recently, the leaders and fighters, including Nico, were fond of dressing up on "Tiger Day" in tiger suits and deer-head masks, and carrying out butting and mock wrestling matches on the nearby "Mountain of the Moon." In 1956, he and a group of friends spent five hours watching "The Last Supper" and "The Trial of Jesus in the Sanhedrín," as part of the Easter mysteries annually staged in Tiripendo. Such religious adjustment, like his tilling of the soil, goes far toward clarifying his status within the moral order of the community.

Nico's sexual and marital history fits in with the range of behavior that some Durazno villagers regard as normal, and to which others are simply resigned. One or two men out of ten are actually chaste at marriage,[12] and over half of the weddings result in permanent and reasonably harmonious unions. But it is also true that the majority of young men have their first experiences between fourteen and sixteen, and that young, married men manage two or three extra-marital adventures a year, in a municipal whorehouse, if nothing better. With precedents such as Pablo Caso, the leaders have long been noteworthy for their marital infidelity, although the homes of almost none have disintegrated because of separation. Several have even maintained mistresses within the village, or absconded with the wives of fellow villagers. During the protracted drinking bouts that follow the ejidal harvest it is common for small groups of two or three to terminate the night with a visit to a widow or some other woman apt to give satisfaction. On the one hand, no evidence could be obtained for homosexual relations between men, except for a few hapless youths seduced by Jorge and Lucás. On the other hand, there was little evidence of anxiety on the score of homosexuality; adolescent masturbation was regarded by all as inevitable and something of a joke. A contemptuous smile was provoked in Nico by the imputation of adult homosexuality to several prominent mestizo politicos. On the campaign tour during 1956, mentioned above, the cacique, who appears to have been influenced by life in the capital, told a rather raw joke about professional fellatio; the young lawyer present laughed heartily, but the ten "fighters" from Durazno stared stonily into space. Other students of the Tarascans, such as Beals (1946: p. 177), working in Cherán, have made similar observations.[13]

12. In the independent judgment of several reliable men.

13. The same patterns apparently obtain among the Aztecs. By way of contrast, I was surprised at the amount of homosexual joking that could be observed during just three hours with the mestizo workers in the lunchroom of the Pazuca factory.

Relations with Children and Men

As noted, Bones was involved in the unique wounding of a small child as a part of politics. In light of this shocking event and his other "grim antecedents," one might be struck by the tenderness and concern he displays for tots. He was often seen cuddling and kissing his baby granddaughter in public, something not too usual for a Durazno man. Once I saw him walk half the length of the plaza to pick up a little boy, move him back from the street, and warn him to be careful. Nico's affection toward children is probably linked to his friendly dealings with mature women, and his jocular attitude toward old, senile men (*viejitos*). No one of these three categories threatens him; some of the old women and children respect him as the ranking agrarian and town official, and even address him as "Don Nico." By way of contrast, his occasionally expressed hostility or suspicion toward adolescent and adult males probably symbolizes an anticipation of strife or envy from this quarter of the population.[14]

In 1956, Nico had one son, and a step-son by the same wife. Both men were married, in their mid-twenties, and formed a joint fraternal family in one large house. They struck me as intelligent and capable, and both were important young leaders who already held office in the civil or ejidal administration. Yet they displayed the most extraordinary reserve toward their father; in hundreds of observed cases I hardly ever heard a word pass directly between the two generations. No other sons displayed such filial distance and respect. I assume that this expressed extreme ambivalence. The sons, lesser leaders in the same faction, felt an axiomatic loyalty toward their father, but they had been embarrassed by his earned reputation as a drunkard and killer, and by his treatment of their mother, and perhaps by other acts within the home that I could not discover. In them has developed to a noteworthy degree the "respect" that marks all son-father relations. On his side, Nico was unquestionably fond of both sons, and their presence in the town may well have influenced his sharp *volte face* in 1947; since that time he had neither drunk a drop of liquor, nor shot a man.

Nico's own closeness and reserve stem in part from his illiteracy; he is the only illiterate leader. And unlike others for whom Tarascan was or remains the first language, he has had little contact with Spanish-speaking Mexico; I believe he has never even left Michoacán, and I know he has never been to the United States. This "lack of education," as he terms it, has caused him anxiety. He was the only leader whom I could not persuade to take a Rorschach test, on the few occasions when such a request seemed appropriate; all others whom I asked agreed readily, although I admit I did not feel like asking either of the

14. Nico was more reticent about himself than any other leader, so that the life history presented here had to be pieced together like a mosaic from other people's statements or from such brief disclosures as emerged naturally or could be cultivated for five or ten minutes during a conversation on other subjects.

main caciques.[15] Several persons have, with considerable justification, accused Nico of persecuting the schoolteachers. Once in the early 1950's, he and two other, relatively uneducated stalwarts threatened with drawn pistols a recently arrived *and politically ambitious* young pedagogue. During the first months of my field trip Nico was cold and even uncivil. But then he began asking questions in Tarascan and laughing in response, and our mutual relations improved noticeably after a lengthy interview on housebuilding. Once I was telling a small group before the town hall about translations of the Bible into Tarascan by nearby missionaries. I wound up by handing over a copy of the gospel according to Saint John. Nico took it like the tail of a rat suspected of carrying the bubonic plague, and swung it around in a semicircle, keeping it away from his body, before passing it on to one of the Caso cousins. The gesture may well have symbolized hostility to religious literature.

Nico's Primary Groups

Central to both the social structure and individual psychology of Durazno are the several kinds of primary or intimate groups that surround every individual. These primary groups have somewhat specialized functions for the leaders. Thus, the fathers, sons, and brothers of one's families of birth and marriage are obligated to political loyalty and blood vengeance. A certain number of one's cousins, nephews, and other relatives form a kindred of strong political allies. Moreover, every leader has from about four to eight compadres, or ceremonial coparents (parents and godparents of the same child); in the ideal, and usually in practice, the compadre relationship is marked by mutual respect, year-long familiarity, economic support, and often great emotional interdependence. Leaders are normally bound outwards to lesser leaders or nonleaders by such ritual bonds. Finally, most men have four to seven or more "friends of confidence" (*amigos de confianza*), with whom they drink and confide their troubles. Such friendship is the main bond between the many leaders who are not natural relatives.

The primary ties of friendship, and ceremonial or natural kinship, are one's most immediate and meaningful integration with the community, and one's optimal form of political security. Kinship, in the broadest sense, remains one of the most vital institutions and has, if anything, been invigorated by the factionalism of the past forty years; every time a man acts politically in the name of such bonds he is reaffirming his belief, and recommitting himself to live by their implicit principles. Our evaluation of Nicolás' deviant behavior must therefore depend heavily on the picture of his primary group relations. Much

15. Fortunately, the fallen cacique returned to Durazno during my field trip. But because of his frequent absences from the village, he was difficult to pin down even for the two long interviews that I did obtain. As with almost all the leaders, I was on a reciprocal *tú* basis with the dominant cacique, but he grew noticeably cool during my last months in the field.

can be inferred about a human being from his patterns of accepting and rejecting others, and from the congruity of these patterns with those of the village.

In light of Bones' political trajectory one feels edified to learn that he is genuinely liked by a wide circle and, in his own opinion, has many friends. Most of the leaders in the dominant faction named him as a "friend of confidence," and Nicolás, when questioned on the subject (in private, of course), stretched out his arms inclusively, and said, "Many," before listing eleven, with the implication that he could name a few more; most men carefully list about a half dozen and seem very certain that there is a boundary line, and where to draw it. Nicolás is well liked and confident in his friends, partly because of the down-to-earth understanding that he shows in conversation, and partly because of his inveterate proneness to ribald jest and salacious (if unoriginal) puns.

Nicolás' ties of friendship contrast strongly with those of kinship; after fifty-eight years of almost constant residence in Durazno he turned out to be the godfather of the wedding for several of the younger leaders, but could name only three men linked to him by the respectful status of baptismal compadre (ritual coparent). On the one hand, this gap in his personal network reflected a long and sometimes off-color career as an agrarian fighter, and, in particular, as an agrarian atheist who scrupulously avoids entering a church. On the other hand, his compadres were Jaime and two other leaders in the abortive Jaime Caso fission that has been described earlier. Neither the dominant cacique, nor any of the latter's close nephews were named as either compadres or close friends, except for one, his former comrade-in-arms, who did not reciprocate in naming Nico a "friend of confidence." Nico's position thus indexed rather accurately the chthonic hostility he had borne the Casos ever since they betrayed him in 1947.[16] I was not surprised to learn by subsequent correspondence with a very reliable informant that Nicolás had been partly responsible in 1959 for the successful ambush of another leading fighter, which precipitated the temporary fall of the Caso hegemony. And one suspects that he was equally implicated in the successful assassination of the Caso cacique one year later, in 1960.

Nicolás' natural kindred within Durazno has always been very limited. Neither of his immigrant mestizo parents gave him any kinship ties, of course, and most of his siblings died in infancy or childhood, as has been detailed. His brother-in-law by his first marriage was a leading fighter, but Nicolás was soon divorced, and then this affinal ally was killed. One son of the dead brother-in-law did serve as secretary in the 1940's and remains a respected if minor young leader. Finally, Nicolás has a son and step-son who support him politically and

16. Such sociometric patterns taken together with psychological variables cannot be used to make specific predictions about the course of politics, because of the great number of other variables and even other types of causation that determine political life.

are minor leaders in the same faction. As against these positive if limited ties, Nicolás' only living brother split with him during the schism of the late 1930's and has ever since followed a publically acknowledged if undistinguished role in the rank and file of the opposition faction; to my knowledge this opposition of two blood brothers is unique in the recent history of the village (although I may have missed some other cases). Blood brothers are generally the least divisible block in Durazno politics.

I therefore conclude that Nicolás is locked squarely but not too fairly in the three-dimensional system of primary groups: He is friendly and has friends, but the reciprocal tie is extraordinarily diffuse, much closer in fact to the norms of mestizo peasants; he has abnormally few compadres, and the ones he does have are rather glaringly related to his recent political intrigues, and were sealed in spite of his genuine atheism and hostility to any priestly ritual; he has only a handful of primary and secondary relatives, and his only blood brother is a factional enemy. Only one other leader depends less on the intense support of others; Nico is a comparatively free agent in the play of factional opposition. In any case, I think Nico's history demonstrates how a man can be deviant but still acceptable in a changing cultural system, and how the particular mode of his deviancy is tightly articulated with the norms of his group.

Conclusions

From a certain perspective, Nico's influence on local history has been conservative and egalitarian. The communalistic ejido which he so enthusiastically supported was revolutionary in overthrowing the clergy and landlords, and subconsciously as well as explicitly associated with Communism. But the same reform actually revitalized an archaic, prehistoric Indian system of land use that is economically backward in its extreme local autonomy and lack of mechanization. It is true that Nico favors basic education; both his sons have finished primary school, and are functional literates. But since 1945 he and others like him have unobtrusively but successfully opposed an increase of the school staff, and the completion of a small school of arts and crafts. They have also prevented the immigration of mestizos, the development of local industries, and other moves calculated to change Durazno from a community of poor, semiliterate ejidatarios.

Nico and his friends have weakened the power of the supernatural; the contempt for witchcraft and religion typical of the leading protagonists in the factional struggle has implied a liberation from some of the most powerful social controls in a Tarascan village.[17] But notions of supernatural sanctions still universally shared by the women may have influenced Nico's 1947 conversion from alcoholism and violence. And his opposition to the clergy, although

17. I suspect another reason the agrarians opposed sorcery is that so many of its expensive specialists reside outside the pueblo (notably in Cherán, San Andrés, and Pazuca).

phrased in terms of atheism, has functioned to exclude an exploiting power that might contribute to economic and political change. Durazno and Nicolás also have been consistently hostile to the change prosetylized by Protestant missionaries in the Tarascan area during the long regime of the dominant leader in the state. But although he has opposed outside religious specialists, he has not fought certain parts of the local "folk religion," and still reminisces with affection about Tapia's acting in the mystery plays over thirty years ago.

If we discount the months of refuge in the sierra during the agrarian revolt, then Nicolás has spent less time outside the village than any other leader. He has never worked as a migrant, leaving the village only a few times in 1955–56, and then only to go to an adjacent village, always accompanied by comrades. Clearly, this man identifies strongly with his town, and the great majority of the villagers—who are certainly in the best position to judge—accept him for what he is and deal with him on those grounds. Nico is mestizo by parenthood and he has ranged wide within certain local mores, but he is far less "acculturated," far more Indian, in fact, than most of the other leaders.

I have little doubt that Nico felt and still feels certain culturally defined sorts of inadequacy—his mestizo origin, his former poverty, his lack of education. Some of these inadequacies were resolved through *egoismo*, the struggle for political office. But Nicolás' conservatism is related to a personal modesty more acceptable to most villagers than the comparative wealth, education, and fine clothes of some of the more ambitious leaders. A lack of acquisitiveness is suggested by the limitation of his private property to a small, one-room house, with neither electricity nor running water. His acceptance of small bribes of ten to thirty pesos fits within the normal limits, whereas no one accuses him of the large-scale embezzlements running to thousands of pesos that have marred the incumbencies of a few other leaders. He has only two bean patches in addition to his ejido plot of five acres: like most of the village he adheres closely to the Agrarian Code. The one luxury of Nico, a spirited and carefully groomed roan mare, indicates an adherence to conservative, local values. Finally, his presence as judge functioned at least in 1955–56 to maintain peace in the community, despite the vilifications of the partisans of Pablo against the "assassin in the town hall." Thus one is led to the concluding observation that Bones Gomez, former alcoholic, killer, and philanderer, by 1956 had become a teetotaller living in monogamous union and actively enforcing law and order, more by the strength of his reputation for "valor" than by the use of his old .45 Colt which, as he proudly and somewhat truthfully claimed, he no longer needed to carry.[18]

18. A most vivid memory of Nicolás goes back to a moonlit night when, as passing alone through the Durazno plaza, I was stopped by a slightly inebriated man, unknown to me, who launched into an extended harangue in Tarascan that I simply could not follow. Suddenly Nico appeared, gliding swiftly down the long porch before the town hall, staying in the shadow. He took my interlocutor by the arm and led him away, bantering the while. As he left I saw the .22 pistol in its small holster over the small of his back.

References

Beals, R.
1946: *Cherán: a Sierra Tarascan Village* (Publication 2, Washington, D.C.: Smithsonian Institution, Institute of Social Anthropology).

Casagrande, J. B. (ed.)
1960: *In the Company of Man: Twenty Portraits by Anthropologists* (New York: Harper).

Dollard, J.
1935: *Criteria for the Life History* (New Haven: Yale University Press).

Friedrich, P.
1957: *Cacique: The Recent History and Present Structure of Politics in a Tarascan Village*. Unpublished Ph.D. thesis, Yale University.
1962: "Assumptions Underlying Tarascan Political Homicide," *Psychiatry*, **25**, 4.
1965: "A Mexican Cacicazgo," *Ethnology* (in press).

Hallowell, A. I.
1955: *Culture and Experience* (Philadelphia: University of Pennsylvania Press).

Kluckhohn, C.
1945: "The Personal Document in Anthropological Science," in L. Gottschalk, C. Kluckhohn, & R. Angell, *The Personal Document in History, Anthropology and Sociology* (New York: Social Science Research Council Bulletin 53), pp. 79–174.

Linton, R.
1936: *The Study of Man* (New York: Appleton-Century-Crofts).

Spiro, M.
1961: "Social Systems, Personality, and Functional Analysis," in B. Kaplan (ed.), *Studying Personality Cross-Culturally* (Evanston, Illinois: Row, Peterson), pp. 93–129.

Wolf, E.
1959: *Sons of the Shaking Earth* (Chicago: University of Chicago Press).

MURRAY G. MURPHEY

An Approach to the Historical Study of National Character[1]

Ever since Thucydides first called us to the scientific study of the past, historians have been struggling to find reasons for the varying fates of human societies. That Athens, or Rome, or England should wax powerful and carry all before it, and then, for some occult cause, should decline and fall, posed for the historian more, and more subtle, problems of human behavior than he could well deal with. Faced with such unsearchable mysteries, the historian retreated to all too simple answers. The fate of nations was declared subject to climate, or topography, or race, or destiny, or any one of a number of similar factors, scrutable or inscrutable. Often these determinants were regarded as inducing in the members of the society certain common psychological characteristics which were thought to be relatively stable from generation to generation, due either to constant environment or to transmission through heredity. So, in an era before modern genetic theory, one often finds race and nationality combined, and historians speak of the English race or the German race, meaning

1. I am greatly indebted to Catherene Morton who served as my assistant in the research and preparation of this paper.

really no more than that Englishmen seem to have certain traits in common and that this community outlasts a generation (Fiske: 1902, pp. 207–238). Similarly, the interpretation of our own history has long labored under the curse of Turner's frontier, to whose ubiquitous presence all characteristics of Americans have been attributed (Turner: 1948). Thus historians have long been wedded to concepts of national character, meaning by this that character, or set of characteristics, common to a given national group. Yet these concepts, however useful, have remained always at an intuitive and poetic level, and so have never been refined into instruments serviceable for a scientific theory of human behavior.

Meanwhile the social sciences have come of age. The comparative study of cultures soon led anthropologists to the recognition that there are characteristic psychological differences between societies; consequently in the 1930's Benedict (1934); Linton and Kardiner (1939), and others turned their attention to the study of group personality.[2] It may be admitted that in its early years this field of study was not characterized by precision, but this defect has been substantially remedied. The definition of group personality as the modal personality of the group substituted a statistically exact notion for an intuitively vague one (Linton: 1945), and by so doing redefined the entire area of study. The concept of basic personality structure as expressed by Kardiner (1939), and the demonstration of the relation of child-rearing techniques to adult personality structure, hypothesized by Freud and confirmed and extended in modern studies such as that of Whiting and Child (1958), have clarified the problem of intergenerational transmission by substituting the laws of learning for ill-defined and false conjectures regarding heredity or simple environmental determinism. Hallowell (1955), Spindler (1955), and others have used the Rorschach to identify distinctive psychological constellations characteristic of particular groups, and have examined the fate of such personality constellations under acculturation. Moreover, Hallowell (*op. cit.*, pp. 75 ff.) has succeeded in integrating modal personality with world view by pointing out the psychological significance of the basic orientations which the world view affords to the individual. Thus the last thirty years have witnessed a rapid development in the study of the relations between personality, culture, and society, and the general principle that there are personality characteristics common to the members of groups is no longer seriously challenged.

The characteristic concern of anthropologists with preliterate societies has directed their attention away from problems of historical reconstruction, since obviously such societies have left no written records on the basis of which such a reconstruction might be undertaken. Some anthropologists however have been concerned with historical problems. Hallowell (*op. cit.*, pp. 125 ff.), for

2. For general reviews of the literature, see Inkeles and Levinson (1954) and Duijker and Frijda (1960).

example, used the accounts of the early Woodland Indians contained in the *Jesuit Relations* to attempt a reconstruction of the aboriginal Woodland Indian personality—a reconstruction ingeniously confirmed by comparison with contemporary Woodland Indians under varying degrees of acculturation, and now widely accepted by both historians and anthropologists. Other social scientists have also turned their attention to historical problems. The psychologist David McClelland (1961) has attempted to investigate levels of need achievement in historical populations and the relation between such need strengths and other aspects of the sociocultural system. Similarly, David Riesman (1950) has written a highly controversial book which attempts to utilize a triadic personality typology in the interpretation of American history. It is notable that all these attempts to apply modern culture and personality theory to historical material have been made by social scientists—not by historians. The historians themselves have been loath to enter upon this uncharted sea, and there are reasons why this is so.

Modal personality is a statistical concept, and if one is to apply this concept to a particular society, then, as Inkeles and Levinson (*op. cit.*, p. 981) have so clearly pointed out, statements about modal personality must be supported by reference to a sample of individuals drawn from the society in question. Where one is dealing with the history of a preliterate society this is *a priori* impossible: those who cannot write leave no written records. But even in the case of a highly literate historical society, such as the United States in 1800, there are very serious problems involved in obtaining samples from which any generalization can be made. Furthermore, one cannot give Thomas Jefferson a psychiatric interview. If we are to investigate questions of group personality in America in 1800, the investigation must be made through such evidence as now survives. And so far as documents which give intimate personal information are concerned, we are really limited to letters, diaries, and autobiographies. Whether, and to what degree, the relevant information can be obtained from such documents, is a question which requires careful consideration.

We may conceive of a given historical population as a set N of n individuals, and we may conceive of the set of all those members of N for whom the data relevant to our questions now exists as a subset K of N. It is obvious that we can draw random samples from K, but whether such random samples of K are random samples of N depends upon whether or not K itself is a random sample of N. Unfortunately our knowledge of the processes of record formation and preservation is quite sufficient to assure us that K is not a random selection out of N. The probability that a record was ever made depends upon many variables such as literacy, educational level, occupation, class, degree of prominence or notoriety in the society, and a number of ill-understood psychological variables controlling the proclivity to commit the record of one's affairs to paper. And the probability that a record once made will survive for any given period depends upon further variables such as the material on which the record was made, the number of copies made, the interest which family or friends or enemies may have felt in preserving such records, and the physical dangers to which the records were exposed (fire, flood, loving daughters, bombing raids, mold, rot, riot, revolution, and invading hoards, to mention only the most obvious, have all taken their toll). Such factors do not select at random, and the result of their selection is a sample which must be regarded as grossly biased. Moreover, the selective processes involved are so complex that no reasonably exact quantitative estimate of the bias is possible. We therefore confront a situation which makes the application of statistical concepts such as model personality to historical data extremely difficult.

A similar situation was confronted by Inkeles and Bauer in their study *The Soviet Citizen* (1959). Since they did not have access to the Soviet citizens themselves, they were forced to work with refugees who either had fled from the Soviet Union or had been forced by the Nazis to leave it and had subsequently chosen not to return (*ibid.*, p. 25). This situation is precisely analogous to that confronted by the historian: an inaccessible population concerning which information is desired, and a biased subset concerning which information can be obtained. Yet by adroit use of their data Inkeles and Bauer did obtain considerable information about the citizenry of the Soviet Union. To do this, they used their knowledge of the direction of the bias to interpret the significance of their findings. Thus they found their sample to be strongly in favor of state ownership of heavy industry. Since the sample is biased against the Soviet regime, yet favors this particular Soviet policy, it is reasonable to assume that people within Russia also favor it (*ibid.*, pp. 26 f.). Again, they found in the sample that degree of hostility to the Soviet regime increased as one descends the class scale. They therefore held that

> It is reasonable to assume that whatever selective factors account for the anti-Soviet bias of our sample operate relatively uniformly on all the subgroups in our sample, and that comparable groups in the Soviet population will stand in the same *relationship* to each other as do the members of our sample (*ibid.*, p. 27).

This approach is equally applicable to historical problems. The chief difference is that the historian will rarely, if ever, confront so simple and clear-cut a problem of bias as that which Inkeles and Bauer had, and he will therefore have to take more and subtler biases into account.

The failure to achieve randomness in historical sampling calls into question the applicability of the statistical techniques of hypothesis testing and estimation. These techniques do require randomness, and accordingly Inkeles and Bauer carefully avoided their use. But there is an important sense in which such techniques are fully applicable even in this case. If, for example, the historical population under study is the American people in 1860, there may remain to us data concerning several thousand individuals from that population. It is unlikely that all of this data can be utilized, but it can be sampled, and if this is done intelligently estimation and hypothesis testing can be used to generalize from the sample to the set of all those for whom the data now remains. And this generalization, while it does not take us to the original historical population, is nevertheless important and should be made, for it is clearly worth knowing whether our findings hold for fifty or five thousand people. But when we wish to generalize from the 5000 to the original historical population classic statistical inference fails us and we must now include intuitive estimates of the bias. Thus one may summarize a major difference between history and the social sciences as follows: For the social scientist in the general case sample bias can be eliminated by the use of an adequate methodology, while for the historian sample bias is inescapable and must therefore be taken into account in the formation and testing of his generalizations.

But sampling is not the only problem facing the historian; he must also face certain inevitable limitations imposed by the nature of his data. It seems reasonable to assume that information concerning personality is most likely to be available in those documents in which the author speaks with greatest freedom about his own actions, thoughts, and feelings—what we may call "personal documents." The chief classes of such documents concerning historical individuals are private letters, diaries, and autobiographies; since the latter category is the only one utilized in this paper we may limit the discussion to it. An autobiography may be defined as a document in which an individual writes a history of his own life from birth. Such documents are therefore not life histories in the sense of Murray (1962, pp. 412 ff.) or Dollard (1949); rather, what one finds in an autobiography is an account of those events and experiences which the author remembers or has been told about, considered significant, and is willing to let the village gossips know. Thus an autobiography rarely gives data concerning the author's weaning or toilet training, because the author cannot remember those experiences, usually has never been told about them, and would generally consider them too private for discussion if he did know about them. Similarly, in the autobiographies used in this paper there are no accounts of sexual experience, presumably because the authors did not regard such matters as proper for public revelation. Consequently the information available from these sources is highly selective, and the criteria of selection are not those we should have chosen.

With such data, what kinds of questions about personality can we hope to answer? Specifically, can we investigate problems of the relation of child-rearing practices to adult personality? Clearly, the autobiographies will give us no data on infant rearing, but they do give considerable information concerning childhood, early upbringing, and discipline (i.e., after age five or six), parental roles, and the author's attitude toward his parents. Is this enough, or must we also have precise data on infancy? The answer, of course, is that the more data the better, but some information is better than none. After all, the great importance of such infantile experiences as weaning and toilet training lies in the fact that they are the child's first experience with the discipline of impulse and that the patterns of behavior and the attitudes learned in these experiences are enduring and are subsequently generalized into characteristic modes of response to similar needs (Kardiner, *op. cit.*, pp. 467 ff.). But what has been learned can be unlearned. If we conceive personality as a dynamic structure developing continuously through time, it is clear that the persistence and generalization of these infant patterns depend upon the existence of continuity and consistency in the whole child-rearing pattern from cradle to adulthood. There is no time at which the personality can be said to be "fixed," although it does seem likely that infantile experience is disproportionately influential. We should therefore expect to find that disciplines imposed at any time will have an effect upon subsequent patterns of behavior and attitude.

There is a further way in which the autobiographies can be used to investigate the problem of the relation of child rearing to adult personality. Although we cannot obtain information regarding the infantile experiences of the specific persons whose autobiographies we have, we can generally obtain information about the child-rearing practices prevailing in the society into which these people were born. We may therefore pose to ourselves the following types of problems: Supposing such and such a child-rearing pattern prevailed in this society, what attitudes would we expect the people so reared to have toward their parents and toward their parents' discipline; what kind of account of their childhood would we expect these people to leave; are attitudes toward parents generalized to others of the same sex or age, and so forth? We may then regard the autobiographies as a sample of individuals drawn from the society, and test our expectations against the data they afford.

Two sets of hypotheses are under examination in this paper: The first set concerns the child-rearing practices prevailing in the Middle Atlantic region during the early nineteenth century; the second set concerns the relation of those practices to certain adult personality characteristics in the population so reared. The generalizations about child rearing which compose the first set must be regarded as hypotheses because our knowledge of those practices is not sufficient to permit positive assertion. Nevertheless, these hypotheses are supported by considerable qualitative data, and to explain both their origin and their plausibility it will be necessary to review briefly what is known about child rearing in this period.

Few studies have been done on early American child rearing, and the results to date are far from conclusive. What is known is derived from two kinds of data: accounts of foreign travelers, and manuals on how to rear children addressed to the parents of the time. Such data are of course biased. Foreign travelers chiefly saw the urban upper classes and saw them at best fleetingly. The manuals are also addressed chiefly to the urban upper classes and represent, not descriptions of actual practice, but prescriptions as to what practice ought to be. Nevertheless, the picture of child rearing which emerges from these disparate sources is fairly consistent, and needs to be briefly stated.

Virtually all European travelers in the early nineteenth century comment on American children, and it is clear that they found them very puzzling. There are four characteristics of the children which they particularly stress. First, they were startled by the familiar and affectionate relation existing between parents and children. Second, they all remark upon what they call the lack of discipline of American children. Under this heading they include the rarity of corporal punishment, the extreme permissiveness of the parents, the absence of attitudes of deference and submissiveness in the children, and the corresponding lack of authority of the parents. Third, they were astonished by the independence of American children. This is not to be equated with lack of parental restraint; rather, it means that the children were capable of taking care of themselves, of doing things for themselves, and of thinking and talking for themselves. Fourth, they remark on the precocity and early maturity of the children (Berger: 1943, pp. 82–84; Calhoun: 1960, Vol. 2, pp. 52–70; De Tocqueville: 1957, Vol. 2, pp. 202–211; Martineau: 1837, Vol. 2, pp. 268–280; Mesick: 1922, pp. 83–84). To the traveler, these children appeared to acquire the attitudes and behavior of adults so early that one writer claimed they were born middle-aged (Calhoun, *op. cit.*, p. 56).

The Europeans were clearly puzzled by these children, and one suspects that the root of their puzzlement was the fact that this seemingly indulgent and permissive method of child rearing produced, not the spoiled, dependent, pampered, child they expected, but rather a highly self-reliant, self-sufficient, precociously mature child. Yet that such was in fact the case they all agree.

The description of child-rearing practices given in the manuals is generally consistent with that given by the travelers but differs from it in some particulars. The manuals point out, as the travelers do not, the differences in parental roles. Early child rearing, until perhaps the age of six, seems to have been almost exclusively the mother's function. She was responsible, not only for the child's physical care and training, but also for his early moral and religious training. Although family religious services were conducted by the father, individual moral and religious training was the mother's task, and the conscience is even described as the internalization of the mother's voice (Kuhn: 1947; Sunley: 1955, pp. 151 ff.). In the phrase of the day, "The mother sways the dominion of the heart, the father that of the intellect" (Kuhn, *op. cit.*, p. 3). The father's role receives little discussion in these manuals, since they are chiefly concerned with the child's early years. The father's primary task appears to have been providing for the family as a whole. He was, however, expected to administer corporal punishment to the child when the need for it arose and, as the child grew older, to assume the responsibility for his education and for preparing him to make his way in the world (Kuhn, *op. cit.*, pp. 4–10; Sunley, *op. cit.*, pp. 152 f.).

The manuals do not give a very precise picture of the specific rearing practices used in infancy. Breast feeding was evidently the rule. There was apparently little attempt to impose feeding schedules and the child was fed whenever it was hungry. Weaning occurred sometime between the eighth and the twelfth month and was probably gradual. The manuals complain of children being overfed both before and after weaning; consequently, the general picture of oral training appears to be one of indulgence. The facts respecting anal and sexual training are not so clear. Toilet training was undoubtedly early, but just how early we do not know. Since the manuals express disgust with the child's soilage and stress cleanliness, anal discipline may well have been severe. Similarly, although detailed information on sexual discipline is not available, the vigor with which masturbation is condemned and sexual purity is praised suggests that training in this area may also have been strict. Independence training was evidently inaugurated early and given considerable emphasis, both in practical and in moral and religious respects. The objective was to make the child "at an early age a self-maintaining moral being" (Sunley, *op. cit.*, p. 162). But the stress on independence did not involve any inhibition of maternal affection. The importance of mothering is uniformly emphasized: direct physical contact between mother and child was regarded as desirable and the mother was enjoined to care for all the child's needs herself and to give freely of love and affection (Calhoun, *op. cit.*, p. 133; Kuhn, *op. cit.*, pp. 160 f.; Sunley, *op. cit.*, pp. 150–163).

In his study of the child-rearing literature of this period, Sunley found three distinct theories of child rearing expressed. The first and apparently most prevalent was the Calvinist theory which regarded the child as innately depraved and therefore emphasized severe discipline, obedience, and "breaking the child's will." A second and less prevalent theory, stemming from Locke, viewed the child as an innocent creature born into a corrupt society and emphasized severe child-rearing practices which would "harden" the child against the demoralizing influences around it. The third theory, which was apparently widespread, emphasized gentle treatment.

> The child was to be led, not driven; persuaded to the right, not commanded. Consistency and firmness were counseled, but with understanding and justice to the child. Encouragements and rewards should be offered; beatings, reproaches, slaps, dark closets, and shaming were to be avoided. Punishment and reward were to be administered not according to the consequences of the child's act but according to the motives. . . . Corporal punishment was undesirable, partly because it did not bring about the desired results, partly because the child was felt to be too tender for such treatment. . . . The child was ignorant of right rather

than bent to wrong. Consequently, the fear of indulging the child and of being dominated by it was not marked, nor was it imperative to "break the will." A firm stand by the parents eliminated obedience problems (Sunley, *op. cit.*, pp. 161 ff.).

These three theories are not wholly exclusive: It is notable that a group among the Calvinist writers advocated a modified view which had much in common with the gentle treatment theory.

How accurate is the picture presented by the manuals? We must accept the fact that these books contain an urban upper-class bias. Nevertheless, the picture of the parental roles is undoubtedly accurate for both farm and city. Owing to the division of labor which prevailed on the farm, the child was in the mother's care until he was old enough to go to work in the fields—usually at seven or eight years of age. Thereupon his childhood freedom was ended, and he worked under his father's direction as a regular member of the labor force. In the city more or less the same pattern existed, and although there was no such abrupt transition as that involved in going into the fields, the father's direction of the child certainly increased as the child matured. With respect to specific infant-rearing practices we have no independent data upon which to assess the accuracy of the manuals, but since the severity of these practices should be a function of the general child-rearing theory held, we can inquire which of these general theories was dominant. In view of the large number of adherents that the various Calvinist denominations had in America—particularly in New England—there can be no doubt that the Calvinist theory was widespread and was probably practiced with rigor by the devout. On the other hand, it is clear that a strong group within the Calvinist clergy itself was propounding a modified theory not unlike the gentle treatment theory, although we do not know how many adherents this liberal version had. Outside the Calvinist denominations there is no reason to believe that such severity was enjoined or practiced. Indeed, if we admit the accounts of the foreign travelers as evidence, we can hardly avoid the conclusion that the gentle treatment theory was all but universal. Although the travelers had biases of their own and are hardly to be regarded as trained observers, nevertheless the unanimity of their reports is impressive. Accordingly, it seems quite likely that outside the hard-core Calvinist ranks, and possibly outside New England, the prevailing theory and practice approximated the gentle treatment theory.

On the basis of these reflections, one may hazard the following hypotheses concerning child rearing in early nineteenth century America, at least for the Middle Atlantic region.

1. Early child rearing was conducted chiefly by the mother and was affectionate, used mild discipline, and attempted to lead the child by love rather than to drive it by fear or force.

2. Corporal punishment was usually administered by the father.

3. Early moral and religious training was effected chiefly by the mother.

4. The child was trained for early independence.

5. After six or seven the father's direction of the child increased and was usually more severe and exacting than the mother's, particularly in the areas of work and practical knowledge.

If these hypotheses concerning child rearing are true, what effects would we expect these practices to have upon the people so reared? Specifically, what would we expect to find in autobiographies written by people raised in this fashion? It seems clear that the following hypotheses ought also to be true.

1. The mother should be idealized and described in terms of such qualities as lovingness, tenderness, kindness, solicitude, etc.

2. Attitudes toward the mother should be more favorable than those toward the father.

3. Religion and morality should be particularly associated with the mother.

4. Father's discipline should be perceived as more severe than mother's discipline, and should be more resented.

5. Resentment of father's discipline in childhood should be correlated with adult aggressiveness toward other males in situations of threat.

6. Aggression toward women should rarely occur.

7. There should be no relation between resentment toward mother's discipline and adult aggressiveness toward males in situations of threat.

The first four hypotheses essentially translate the five hypotheses concerning child-rearing practices into a form in which they can be tested against the autobiographical data. If the child's perception of the parents corresponds at all to the actual behavior of the parents toward the child, it is very difficult to see how the child-rearing hypotheses can be true and the first four hypotheses above be false.

The reasoning underlying the fifth hypothesis is somewhat more complex and is based upon the following argument. First, it seems clear that to the degree that the father's discipline is more severe than the mother's discipline, it should be perceived as frustrating, and that when this difference is very large, the father's discipline should be perceived as aggressive. It is well known that anger, hostility, and aggression are likely to be aroused by frustration, and are even more likely to be aroused by aggressive acts (Buss: 1961, Chapters 1 and 2; Dollard *et al.*: 1939). These three responses are not equivalent: anger is an emotional response having the properties of a drive state which may serve as the drive for aggression (Buss, *op. cit.*, pp. 9–11); hostility is an enduring attitude which arises as a conditioned anger response and which does not possess drive properties (*ibid.*, pp. 12–15); aggression is a behavioral response which "delivers noxious stimuli to another organism" (*ibid.*, p. 1). These responses can occur separately, but in the case here considered it is clear that they should occur together. Accordingly, one would expect that the greater the difference in severity between father's[3] and mother's discipline, the more likely it is that anger, hostility, and aggression against the father will be aroused in the child.

Second, the more intense these responses are, the more likely it is that they will be elicited by other comparable stimuli. The usual explanation for this is afforded by the classic stimulus generalization model, according to which if a stimulus S evokes a response R, other stimuli similar to S will also evoke R, in direct proportion to their similarity to S. Hence if the threatening and frustrating father evokes anger, or hostility, or aggression, other males in similar situations may be expected to provoke a similar reaction (Buss, *op. cit.*, pp. 62 ff.; Miller: 1948, pp. 155–178). The generalization of aggression, however, may be given an alternative explanation in terms of the effects of anger on the thresholds for aggressive responses. On this model, the existence of an anger state has the effect of lowering the threshold for aggressive responses, so that noxious or annoying characteristics of stimulus objects, which under ordinary circumstances would not be sufficient to elicit aggression, now do so. Thus a child who is angry at its father kicks its dog for a trivial reason which under ordinary circumstances would elicit no such response (Buss, *op. cit.*, pp. 60 ff.). The two models may be combined: we may explain the generalization of anger by stimulus generalization and the occurrence of aggression in the substitute situation by lowered thresholds. But whichever of these models one adopts, the result should be that the child who is intensely angry, hostile, or aggressive toward the father should display anger, hostility, or aggression more frequently and against a wider class of stimulus objects than the child who is not.

While the father may not be aware of the child's anger and hostility, he will certainly be aware of its direct aggression and will punish the child for such acts. Such punishment, or the expectation of it, will produce aggression anxiety in the child which will inhibit direct aggression.[4] In his classic paper on stimulus generalization and displacement, Miller showed how the approach-avoidance model can be applied to this situation to explain the displacement of aggression to other stimulus objects. If the generalization gradient of avoidance is steeper than that for approach, but such that the two gradients intersect, direct aggression will be inhibited over the domain of stimulus objects for which the avoidance gradient lies above the approach gradient, but not for those objects for which the avoidance gradient lies below the approach gradient. Under these circumstances, Miller showed that aggression will be "displaced" to the point where the avoidance gradient cuts the abscissa, since the net approach strength is maximum at that point (Buss, *op. cit.*, pp. 65 ff.; Miller: 1948; Miller and Kraeling: 1952, pp. 217–221). Miller's construction is wholly in terms of the

3. We are considering here what Buss calls "angry aggression."

4. The effect of punishment on aggression is highly complex. Punishment can serve as an added frustration which may temporarily increase the degree of aggressiveness. Cf. Sears, Whiting, Nowlis, Sears (1953) and R. Sears (1961).

stimulus generalization theory, but it is easy to see that a similar result will follow in terms of the threshold model. The lowering of thresholds will be offset within the domain of stimulus objects for which the inhibitions exist, and so will lead to increased aggression only outside that domain. In either case, one has the displacement of aggression from one class of stimulus object to another, the difference being that in Miller's model the substitution depends upon similarity to the original while for the threshold model it depends upon increased sensitivity to noxious or annoying characteristics of the substitute. On either model, therefore, one would expect the child to displace his aggression against the father to substitute objects against whom it can be expressed with less danger. Whether in this case anger or hostility is also displaced depends upon the particular situation: the displacement of aggression does not require the displacement of anger or hostility but merely their generalization (Buss, *op. cit.*, p. 60). Nevertheless, for convenience in the present discussion and to avoid cumbersome locution, we may speak of "anger and aggression being displaced from S to S′," meaning that anger is either generalized or displaced from S to S′ and that aggression is displaced from S to S′.

The choice of model is not irrelevant to the question of what objects can serve as substitutes, but both models agree that displacement of anger and aggression should occur against other males who are to some degree threatening or frustrating to the child. On either model, therefore, we may expect anger and aggression against a male in threat situations to occur more frequently for displacing subjects than for nondisplacing subjects. This is so not only because the drive strength—the amount of anger—should be greater for displacers, but also because the strength of the habit of making aggressive responses in threat situations should be greater for displacers. There are several grounds for the latter expectation. The simple occurrence of aggressive responses in threat situations will not lead to the formation of a habit of so responding unless there is reinforcement, and such reinforcement must inevitably be partial, but for a constant ratio of reinforced to nonreinforced trials, the greater the number of trials the greater the habit strength should be (Hull: 1952, pp. 135 ff.). Furthermore, there is some reason to believe that the reinforcement for displacing subjects may be greater than that for nondisplacing subjects. To see this, consider two subjects confronting a stimulus sufficiently noxious to elicit anger and an aggressive response, and suppose one subject is also displacing anger and aggression from another source against this stimulus. Then we should expect the level of anger of the displacing subject to be higher than that of the nondisplacing subject, i.e., that the anger components summate. If both subjects now make the same aggressive response, both will experience catharsis, i.e., a drop in the anger level, and this catharsis serves as the internal reinforcement for the response. Now is the catharsis equal for the two subjects? It would seem reasonable to suppose that the catharsis for the displacing subject should involve both diminution of the anger aroused by the present stimulus and diminution of the displaced anger, and if that is so the total reinforcement of the aggressive act should be greater for the displacing subject than for the non-displacing subject. If this supposition is correct, it follows that the strength of the habit of making aggressive responses to such stimuli should be greater for the displacing subject (Buss: 1961, pp. 57 ff. and Chapter 5), and this effect should hold whether the stimulus generalization model or the threshold model is used. Accordingly, we may conclude that for displacing subjects the probability of responding to threat situations by aggressive acts will be greater, by an amount proportional to the amount of the anger displaced, than for nondisplacing subjects.

If such a difference in the behavior of displacing and nondisplacing subjects were once created, it ought to be enduring. The hostility toward threatening males should be stronger in displacers than in nondisplacers, and so one would expect that even after the parent's death the amount of anger aroused by the threat stimuli should remain greater for the displacers than for the non-displacers (Buss, *op. cit.*, pp. 15 f.). Similarly, the habit strength of the displacers should remain higher than that of the nondisplacers. It thus appears that if such differences were established in childhood, they should continue into adult life, and this yields the fifth hypothesis.[5]

The expectation that there will be few acts of aggression against women stems from several factors, among which the cultural prohibitions against such behavior and the relative mildness of the maternal discipline are the chief. Indeed, the cultural factor alone is here so powerful that one would be astonished if many such acts were recorded. On the other hand, the mother does exercise discipline over the child, and the child must inevitably develop a certain amount of frustration and anger against her (P. Sears: 1951; R. Sears: 1961; Sears *et al.*, 1953). If this frustration and anger were sufficiently strong, it might be expected that resentment to maternal discipline would be significantly related to aggression in threat situations by a construction similar to that outlined above. It is our expectation here that the relative mildness of maternal discipline is sufficient to prevent this from occurring, and this yields the final hypothesis.

The sample used in this study consisted of twenty-three autobiographies written by men born between 1794 and 1830 in the states of New York, Pennsylvania, New Jersey, and Delaware. New England was excluded because it could

5. It is assumed above that the relation between anger, hostility, and aggression and difference in severity of parents' discipline is linear. In fact, it probably is not (Buss: 1961, p. 58; Sears, Whiting *et al.*: 1953). But it is doubtful if the curvilinear relation could be expected to appear in our data. Where severity of discipline is so intense as to produce such curviture, it probably results in repression of the feelings of anger and hostility, and so these would not appear in any overt way in autobiographical data. In fact, one case in the sample very strongly suggests just this phenomenon; the man was clearly terrified by his father, yet he inordinately idealized him and shows no overt resentment against his discipline.

be assumed that the Calvinist views of child rearing were more prevalent there, and the South was excluded because the known differences between northern and southern society in this period are sufficient to require that they be treated separately. The occupational distribution of the sample was as follows: 5 businessmen, 2 editors, 3 teachers, 3 political figures, 2 doctors, 2 lawyers, 2 ministers, 2 farmers, 2 writers. The upper-class urban bias of the sample compared with the total population is obvious. On the other hand, the sample is probably representative of the total population of writers of autobiographies. Men who write the story of their lives have generally not been failures and they are apt to be better educated than the average. The occupational distribution of the fathers of the sample members is as follows: 15 farmers, 2 doctors, 1 mechanic, 1 cartman, 2 ministers, 1 politician, 1 surveyor. The father's distribution, while still skewed, is much closer to that of the general population for this period than is the distribution of the sample itself, and this fact indicates that although most members of the sample were successful in attaining high status they did not begin with it. Six of the parents were members of Calvinist denominations; the others were non-Calvinist.

Not all of the twenty-three cases were equally usable, since several did not give the information necessary to answer some of the questions asked. There are, for example, two cases of men who give no information concerning either parent. Unfortunately, little can be inferred from such silence: it may reflect hostility to the parents but it may also reflect merely a strong sense of privacy. Such cases had therefore to be excluded from the sample used for that particular question.

The analysis of such data to obtain expression of value and attitude requires the use of some form of content analysis. The obvious choice for this case appeared to be the method of value analysis developed by Ralph K. White (1951). This technique is designed to reveal the goals of the writer of the document and the standards of judgment used by the writer in evaluating other people (*ibid.*, p. 13). Moreover, White himself applied this method to the analysis of autobiographical data, and his results indicated that the needed information could be so obtained (White: 1947). Unfortunately, experience in working with the method has revealed certain difficulties. Although White's scheme is partly derived from Murray's needs, he includes no distinction between press and response (Murray: 1962, pp. 115–123), and without this distinction it was found impossible to make a meaningful analysis. Accordingly, the analytic scheme was readapted by classifying situations in terms of the press which they exhibited, and then classifying the responses to those press in terms of White's categories.

If the first hypothesis is true we ought to find that in the descriptions of the mother the most frequently occurring categories in White's scheme are G and Lo (givingness and family love). This is in fact the case.

Number of Mothers for Whom the Most Frequently Occurring Categories Are

G and Lo	*Other than G and Lo*
14	2

This difference is significant at the .002 level by the binomial test.[6]

To test the second hypothesis, a rating was made for each autobiography which gave the necessary information as to which parent was most favorably described. The results were: mother more favored than father, 8; father more favored than mother, 3; parents equally favored, 5. The difference in favor of the mothers is significant at the .11 level using the sign test.

The third hypothesis was tested by determining which parents are described as giving the religious instruction. The results are:

Parent(s) Giving Religious Instruction

Mother	*Father*	*Both*
9	3	4

It is not clear how to interpret the cases in which both parents are said to have given religious instruction. Since the father normally did take some part in religious instruction, e.g., he conducted the family religious services, it is impossible to tell whether this response is consistent with the hypothesis or not, and accordingly these cases should probably be ignored. If this is done the difference is significant at the .07 level by the binomial test.

The fourth hypothesis asserts that resentment to the father's discipline should occur more frequently than resentment to the mother's. The results are:

		Mother's Discipline	
		Resented	*Not Resented*
Father's Discipline	Not Resented	1	14
	Resented	0	6

The sign test permits the rejection of the null hypothesis at the .06 level of significance.

To test the fifth hypothesis we require a measure of aggressiveness, which was obtained as follows. We examined all situations in the autobiographies where the press was a threat. For each book, the responses to such press were categorized on White's plan and the results tabulated to determine the frequency with which each class of responses occurred. Then, for each book, the responses were ranked in order of frequency of occurrence. An individual was judged high aggressive if aggression was above the median for his list of res-

6. For tests used in this section, see Siegal (1956).

ponses, and low aggressive if aggression was at or below the median for his list of responses. Using this definition, the test result is:

		Aggressiveness	
		High	*Low*
Father's Discipline	Not Resented	0	13
	Resented	4	2

This difference is significant at .004 by Fisher's exact test.

The sixth hypothesis is confirmed by the fact that no instances of aggression against a woman were recorded. Finally, the last hypothesis is confirmed by the result

		Aggressiveness	
		High	*Low*
Mother's Discipline	Not Resented	3	13
	Resented	0	1

This difference is significant at the .82 level by Fisher's exact test.

There are several points about these results which require particular comment. First, the sample is obviously too small to permit these results to be regarded as more than suggestive. Nevertheless, some of the relations are strong, particularly that between resentment to father's discipline and aggression, and all the results are in the expected direction. Second, the sample is clearly biased toward the urban upper classes. But the distribution of father's occupations is only slightly so biased, and it is the father's occupations which are relevant in determining the relation between class and the child rearing of members of the sample. Since two thirds of the fathers were farmers, and most were at best middle class, it is unlikely that there is any appreciable class or urban bias involved. What does represent a biasing factor is of course the fact that these children succeeded, but it is not clear that this bias should vitiate the generality of any of these results.

Third, the sample yields a very low percentage of high aggressives and of resenters of father's discipline. This is, I believe, the result of errors of measurement. The criterion used to separate high and low aggressives turned out to be far stronger than was anticipated. Our high aggressives therefore represent, not the most aggressive half of the sample, but the extreme aggressives in the sample. Unfortunately, the fact that absolute numbers of responses could not be compared from book to book made it necessary to stay with this criterion. Similarly to qualify as a resenter of the father's discipline, one had to specifically and overtly express resentment in unambiguous terms. Had more indirect measures been employed, the number of resenters would certainly have been increased. What the figures give us is the relation of very extreme aggressives to very strong resentment. There is no reason to expect a reversal of the relation as the intensity is decreased.

Fourth, the bare descriptive categories of the content analysis do not convey the variations in intensity of the data. This is particularly true of the descriptions of the mother. For example, the most aggressive man in the sample writes of his mother as follows:

> Beautiful in person, cultivated in mind, gentle in heart, sober and sure in judgment, she was to me an incarnation of the qualities which the mothers of the all-absorbing Anglo-Teutonic race have almost unconsciously developed and transmitted to the best and noblest of its sons. She was companion and friend, joy, solace, and delight to every member of her family, and when in 1878, after a long life devoted to their happiness, at the ripe age of seventy-four, she died surrounded by her children, calm, fearless and triumphant, something was taken from their lives which changed the tenor of their thoughts forever (Wistar: 1937, p. 7).

Such rhapsodic descriptions indicate a degree of idealization of the mother which is strikingly different from even the most favorable descriptions of the father.

Finally, it may be asked whether the data supporting the first, second, and fourth hypotheses are not more simply explained by the Freudian oedipal theory. The data are certainly consistent with that theory, but that fact does not vitiate the approach used here. Even if the oedipal theory is a correct description of certain universal features of the psychological development of male children, there are still variations in that development from culture to culture which remain to be explained. It seems clear that these variations must be related to specific child-rearing practices obtaining in those cultures, so that some theory of the relation between these specific practices and psychological development is necessary in any case. Whether such a theory is sufficient is perhaps another question.

To the student of nineteenth-century American social history it would seem utterly banal to remark that American men of that time worshiped God, home, and mother—not necessarily in that order—and were highly aggressive. But as historians we have been prone to accept these traits simply as given, or, if we have sought explanations for them at all, to explain them by vague reference to "the requirements of the frontier" or to some similar irrelevancy. That this extraordinary idealization of the mother might be connected to the high levels of intermale aggression through structural relationships within the family and child-rearing practices has not even been suggested. Yet if these traits were as general as most historians believe they were, it seems reasonable to conclude on the basis of current theories of personality formation that they must be rooted in child-rearing practices. And it is therefore a nontrivial problem for the historian to determine whether or not such practices and processes can be investigated with the data and methods at his command. The purpose of this exploratory paper is to suggest that such investigations are possible.

References

Benedict, R.
1934: *Patterns of Culture* (Boston: Houghton Mifflin).

Berger, M.
1943: *The British Traveller in America 1836–1860* (New York: Columbia University Press).

Brooks, J. G.
1908: *As Others See Us* (New York: Macmillan).

Buss, A.
1961: *The Psychology of Aggression* (New York: Wiley).

Calhoun, A. C.
1960: *A Social History of the American Family* (3 vols.) (New York: Barnes & Noble).

De Tocqueville, A.
1945: *Democracy in America* (2 vols.) (New York: Knopf).

Dollard, J.
1949: *Criteria for the Life History* (New Haven: Yale University Press).

Dollard, J., Doob, L., Miller, N., Mowrer, O. H., & Sears, R.
1939: *Frustration and Aggression* (New Haven: Yale University Press).

Duijker, H. C. J., & Frijda, N. H.
1960: *National Character and National Stereotypes* (Amsterdam: North Holland Co.).

Fiske, J.
1902: "The Races of the Danube," in *Darwinism and Other Essays* (Boston: Houghton Mifflin), pp. 207–238.

Hallowell, A. I.
1955: *Culture and Experience* (Philadelphia: University of Pennsylvania Press).

Hull, C.
1952: *A Behavior System* (New Haven: Yale University Press).

Inkeles, A., & Bauer, R.
1959: *The Soviet Citizen* (Cambridge: Harvard University Press).

Inkeles, A., & Levinson, D.
1954: "National Character: The Study of Modal Personality and Sociocultural Systems," in G. Lindzey (ed.), *Handbook of Social Psychology*, Vol. 2 (Cambridge: Addison-Wesley), pp. 977–1020.

Kardiner, A.
1939: *The Individual and His Society* (New York: Columbia University Press).

Kuhn, A.
1947: *The Mother's Role in Childhood Education: New England Concepts 1830–1860* (New Haven: Yale University Press).

Linton, R.
1945: *The Cultural Background of Personality* (New York: Appleton-Century-Crofts).

Martineau, H.
1837: *Society in America*, Vol. 2 (New York: Saunders & Otlay).

McClelland, D.
1961: *The Achieving Society* (New York: Van Nostrand).

Mesick, J.
1922: *The English Traveller in America 1785–1835* (New York: Columbia University Press).

Miller, N.
1948: "Theory and Experiment Relating Psychoanalytic Displacement to Stimulus-Response Generalization," *Journal of Abnormal and Social Psychology*, **43**, 155–178.

Miller, N., & Kraeling, D.
1952: "Displacement: Greater Generalization of Approach than Avoidance in the Generalized Approach Avoidance Conflict," *Journal of Experimental Psychology*, **43**, 217–221.

Murray, H. A.
1962: *Explorations in Personality* (New York: Science Editions).

Riesman, D.
1950: *The Lonely Crowd* (New Haven: Yale University Press).

Sears, P.
1951: "Doll Play Aggression in Normal Young Children: Influence of Sex, Age, Sibling Status, Father's Absence," *Psychological Monographs*, **65**, No. 6.

Sears, R.
1961: "Relation of Early Socialization Experience to Aggression in Middle Childhood," *Journal of Abnormal and Social Psychology*, **63**, 466–492.

Sears, R., Whiting, J. M., Nowlis, V., & Sears, P. S.
1953: "Some Child-Rearing Antecedents of Aggression and Dependency in Young Children," *Genetic Psychology Monographs*, **47**, 135–236.

Siegal, S.
1956: *Nonparametric Statistics for the Behavioral Sciences* (New York: McGraw-Hill).

Spindler, G.
1955: *Sociocultural and Psychological Processes in Menomini Acculturation* (Berkeley: University of California Press).

Sunley, R.
1955: "Early Nineteenth Century American Literature on Child Rearing," in M. Mead & M. Wolfenstein (eds.), *Childhood in Contemporary Cultures* (Chicago: University of Chicago Press).

Turner, F. J.
1948: "The Significance of the Frontier in American History," in *The Frontier in American History* (New York: Holt).

White, R. K.
1947: "Black Boy: A Value Analysis," *Journal of Abnormal and Social Psychology*, **42,** 440–461.
1951: *Value-Analysis: The Nature and Use of the Method* (Society for the Psychological Study of Social Issues).

Whiting, J. M., & Child, I. L.
1958: *Child Training and Personality* (New Haven: Yale University Press).

Wistar, I.
1937: *Autobiography of Isaac Jones Wistar, 1827–1905* (Philadelphia: Harper).

LAURENCE WYLIE

The Life and Death of a Myth*

In 1950 two of my criteria for deciding on a rural community in France where I might live and gain an idea of French life at the grass roots were that in politics and religious behavior the population should represent the majority of the French people. That is, the community should be predominantly Catholic but not ardently so; politically it should be divided with a majority

* One evening in September, 1948, I timidly made a telephone call to Professor Hallowell. He did not know me, but with his characteristic cordiality and patience he listened to my plea: How could I, a French teacher with a doctorate in Romance Languages and Literature, learn to look at French culture today as anthropologists might?

I did not realize how important this telephone conversation was to be for me, for it led to my participating in the Hallowell seminars on personality and culture and on community studies. There I discovered a world of new ideas, became aware of complicated relationships and subtle implications in human behavior, learned to look at culture with more method and perspective, acquired techniques for field work.

Since then Professor Hallowell has continued to advise me and lend me his support. In 1950, largely through his encouragement, I undertook my first field work, living for a year with my family in a Vaucluse village. When that study was published I moved on to the investigation of a contrasting community in western France, Chanzeaux, which is the subject of this paper.

voting to the center and to the left. The town of Roussillon, in the département of the Vaucluse, satisfied these requirements.

After making the study of Roussillon I was eager to find a village that would be like it in many respects—land tenure, patterns of economy, kinship structure, social organization—but which would be its opposite in religion and politics, that is, politically conservative and ardently Catholic. Such a comparative study might be made in several parts of France, but the Basques, Bretons, Alsatians, and Flemish seemed unrepresentative of French culture as a whole. In a not very well-known area called the Mauges, roughly the south-western quarter of the former province of Anjou and the present département of the Maine-et-Loire, I found precisely what I wanted.

French students of the sociology of religion have made a map of the religious practice of the rural population, and it is striking to see how clearly certain areas of western France, including the Mauges, are differentiated from the rest of France in their religious behavior. Professor Le Bras writes:

> If you travel from Luçon to Bayeux, following rather closely the line of the *bocage*, you have constantly on your left seventy to ninety-five percent of the population who go to mass regularly and on your right a maximum of twenty percent. I have taken several of these trips myself to establish the points of geographical separation. Sometimes in a village divided by a small stream, you have on the right bank twenty percent and on the left bank ninety percent of the population practicing Catholics. And this proportion is generally maintained over an area of fifty or one hundred kilometers in depth (Le Bras: 1944, p. 226).

Within this strongly Catholic area of the Mauges, twenty miles southwest of the city of Angers, is the village of Chanzeaux, a community of some 1150 people, where I settled with my family for a year's study. Of the 200 children of school age in the community only 15 were enrolled in the public school maintained by the State, and although our two sons, then nine and eleven, had been in a Quaker school at home, they were accepted by both the priest and teacher as regular pupils in the Catholic school of the village. This was particularly important from my point of view, since I had decided to concentrate my study on the forces determining the behavior of these good Catholics and strong conservatives, so different from the lukewarm Catholics and the Socialist-Radicals and Communists I had known in the Vaucluse. It seemed reasonable to expect that the child training in these two communities must be noticeably different to produce adults so unalike in their relationship to authoritarian political and religious institutions.

It did not take long to realize that this informal hypothesis was wrong. The children of Chanzeaux were raised in no more authoritarian a manner than the children of Roussillon. Indeed, if I had had to make a generalization on the point I should have said—and would still say—that the Chanzeans seemed in many ways less authoritarian than the Roussillonnais. Except that in Roussillon the parents may have appeared less doting and in Chanzeaux more attention was given to teaching religious forms and ceremonies, the differences in bringing up children were less marked than the similarities. In both communities children were wanted and loved; they were raised in an atmosphere of affection but taught respect for tradition and manners. Once the social rules were accepted by a child, he was allowed considerable latitude in his thoughts and sentiments. In both communities even the social restraints were relaxed, for the boys especially, during later adolescence.

In effect, the people of both Roussillon and Chanzeaux were bringing up their children in the same way, and the effect was fundamentally the same. Regardless of political labels and religious practice the two communities were essentially conservative in that they were conserving their own particular tradition. With this insight the focus of my study inevitably changed to an attempt to understand the difference between the traditions that each community was conserving. Instead of child training and education, the history of Chanzeaux and its effect on the behavior of the present population became my principal consideration. The hypothesis I chose to work from was that the traumatic effects of the Vendée Rebellion had been basic in shaping the patterns of behavior in the region. There was evidence that the events of 1793 to 1795 were still a part of daily life in Chanzeaux. It seemed that these events and the communal memory of them held the key to the conservative voting habits and devout religious practice in the Mauges which contrasted so markedly with the political and religious behavior in the Vaucluse and in France generally. How had the nightmare of the Vendée War been made bearable? How had a myth evolved which could give continuing guidance and direction to community life?

The most obvious fact of Chanzeaux's history is that the village lies on the border of the area known as the *Vendée militaire*, which revolted against the Republican revolutionary government of Paris in 1793. First as a center of sedition, then as a bastion in the final defeat, Chanzeaux suffered the worst rigors of the struggle against Republican authority. In the first months of the revolt the Vendeans seemed invincible as they successfully dominated the towns in the region and then swarmed through the cities of Cholet, Saumur, and Angers. Eventually, however, the Republican forces were effectively strengthened and the Vendée Rebellion was suppressed, but with the usual horrors of civil war; the suppression was extreme and pitiless. The whole area of which Chanzeaux is a part was pillaged and burned by Republican soldiers. In Chanzeaux over a third of the people living in the community in 1793 had, two years later, died or disappeared. Only three of the houses in the village were intact. The chateaux were destroyed. The fields and woods were burned. Of the church only the burned-out tower remained. This traumatic episode in the history of the town obviously shaped many of the beliefs and attitudes of the people for a long time to come. But how and to what extent?

The traditional answer to the question of why the Vendeans revolted against the Republican government is that the Republicans had tried to suppress religious practice, and the Vendée, more devout than the rest of France, revolted for the sake of religious freedom. Abundant reminders of the belief in this heroic stand surround the inhabitants of the village today. The tower of the old church still stands in the center of the square, repaired and made a part of the church which was built in 1900. In the new church the stained glass windows are dedicated to the memory of "our glorious ancestors who gave their lives for *Dieu et la patrie*." One window shows the defense of a group of survivors in 1795 who took refuge in the church tower only to be burned out by the Republicans. The priest is shown lifting the chalice at the moment it is hit by a Republican bullet which then buries itself in the breast of the priest. By his side is the sexton, Ragneau, who led the defense and who, it is said, was killed a few moments after the priest. In the church there is also a mural of the massacre of the women and old men of the village by Republican soldiers which, according to tradition, was ordered when two women defied the orders of the Republican general to remove flowers they had put on the altar. The martyrs are shown singing the "Salve Regina" as they are marched to the mill bridge and shot into a common grave.

The memory of those days is seen not only in formal monuments. Across the street from the church lives a descendant of Ragneau, the sexton. The present Ragneau is also sexton, and his family is proud of saying, "We have been bell ringers for three hundred years." Other people in the community are well aware of their connections with the old Vendean warriors. The models for the mural in the church were all descendants of the martyrs.

Books about the Vendée Rebellion are abundant, too abundant. For the last one hundred and seventy years apologists for the Vendeans and for the Republicans have piled volume upon volume in defense of their respective parties. Unfortunately, nothing could be less convincing than most of these apologies. The black is only black, and the white is white. Happily, most of these authors refer to source material, which may still be consulted in the archives of the Maine-et-Loire in Angers; microfilming makes it possible to examine at leisure the hundreds of documents that bring back to life the Chanzeaux of 1793.[1]

What actually brought about the rebellion of 1793? It is obvious now that the image of the peasants of western France rising spontaneously and unanimously

1. Harvard undergraduates have become interested in this material and have brought to the surface treasures of information. Suzanne Textor, under the guidance of Professor Philip Dawson, wrote her senior thesis on the social situation in Chanzeaux from 1780 to 1795, and she has continued her research in the archives in Angers. Guides to this new research, the works of two contemporary scholars, Paul Bois's *Paysans de l'Ouest* and Charles Tilly's *The Vendée*, have both driven a wedge of truth deep into the prejudice on which most Vendée histories have been based.

in defense of their king, their nobles, and their priests who were being persecuted by the Republican government is a deceptive cliché. Just as inaccurate is the conception of eighteenth century western France as an isolated region, devoted entirely to agriculture, where peasants lived in harmony with their priest and local noble (according to the Vendean thesis) or under the heel of their priest and noble (according to the Republican historians). Tilly points out that, contrary to the general belief, a region once industrialized may still revert to agriculture. Because there was little industry in the Mauges in the nineteenth century we have assumed that it was uniquely agricultural in the eighteenth century. This was not the case. In the eighteenth century the manufacture of cloth was transforming the economy and social structure of the region. Home weaving—because of the extension of the putting-out system—was important throughout the Mauges. A rural proletariat had emerged, as well as the prosperous group of bourgeois who ran the cloth industry, importing raw materials, putting them out to local weavers, collecting the manufactured cloth, and exporting it from the region.

Although most of these new industrialists continued for practical reasons to live in the villages and small towns, they were in taste, education, and business interests closely allied with the people of the cities. They were not the only bourgeois in the small towns, of course. In each community they had friends whose backgrounds and training were similar—the notaries, judges, doctors, tax collectors, and civil officers. The parish priest and his vicars were their equals socially, but they were largely recruited from and more directly concerned with the majority of their parishioners—not just the peasants but the numerous artisans and small merchants who served the rural community. The aristocracy for the most part lived in the city and knew the rural population only through overseers, who actually managed their estates, and through servants who were recruited from the country. It was only in the following century that the nobles developed a sentimental attachment to their country estates.

It appears that these rural groups had been living in relative harmony until the reforms of the Revolution exaggerated differences which had already been intensified by economic problems. In the 1780's there was a depression in the cloth industry, and many weavers were out of work. Bad weather had ruined many of the crops. Two thirds of the vines of Chanzeaux were reportedly frozen by the great cold of 1788. There was no social violence, however, until the priests—traditional leaders of the rural communities—were deprived of much of their power and eventually driven out. As the small group of people most closely identified with city ways—the manufacturers, wholesale merchants, government employees, and professional men—in turn acquired this power, all the potential conflicts of interest between the city-oriented and rural populations emerged with rapidly growing and terrifying violence.

Many of the causes of conflict had no essential relationship to religious issues; unfortunately most of them had, if only quite indirectly, religious implications. The distribution of charity, for instance. Because of poor harvests and industrial depression there were even more than the usual number of people dependent on the alms traditionally dispensed by the priest. But the Revolutionary government had decreed that poverty was a public responsibility and should be corrected through publicly dispensed charity. The government, however, did nothing to make the necessary funds available. At the same time the priests were made public employees and paid a salary instead of living from the tithe so that with their reduced incomes they could not help the poor even when they wanted. The poor were then able to blame the government for the loss of the support they had traditionally received from the church. In Chanzeaux this meant that the small group of city-minded people who were now running the town could be blamed for depriving the poor of the charity they had always received from the patriarch of the community, the priest Blondel de Ris.

The same mechanism functioned in almost every instance to permit the people of the village to reproach the revolutionary authorities and their small group of followers for the evils besetting the community and to claim that the trouble came from curtailing the role of the priest. There had been no complaint when the government decreed the sale of church properties, but because most of the land was bought by the city-minded people who were in charge of the sales, the transaction was made to symbolize the persecution of the church. The more prosperous farmers who might have hoped to acquire the land they were working were usually unable to compete successfully in the bidding. Even the poorer peasants who had no hope of buying their own farm had a serious stake in the transfer of property from the church to bourgeois landlords. Traditionally they had worked under the surveillance of overseers with whom viable arrangements were possible. Now, instead of the representatives of distant and impersonal monasteries and convents, the managers of their farms would be the owners themselves, bourgeois living in the neighborhood.

Whether we consider charity, the sale of lands, taxation, law making or the enforcement of new laws, the situation was always the same: a small group of city-minded people was pitted against the more rural traditionalists, and the church was involved to some degree. Since it is natural for people to clothe their grievances in as holy a garb as possible, the issue of the church became more and more central as all conflicts polarized around it. The poor man, no longer receiving charity, was able to speak not of his own plight but of the wickedness of the men who had reduced the income of the clergy. An unsuccessful bidder for church lands might piously blame the successful bidder for profiting by the spoilation of the church. The closing of surplus chapels and churches, although decreed by diocesan authorities before the Revolution, could be blamed on godless republicans. The unpopularity of price-fixing and requisitioning of crops to feed the city people fell on these same local officials charged with enforcing the government decrees.

By the spring of 1791 the old fissures in the social structure were so widened and the feelings were so charged with religious sentiment that reconciliation would seem to have been impossible. When the priests were called to swear allegiance to the Republic their parishioners would have rejected their leadership had they taken this step toward reconciling the community with the revolutionary government. The alternative was no more positive a step, however, for when a priest refused to take the loyalty oath his parish was declared vacant and, according to the new Constitution of the Clergy, it was for the active voters to elect new bishops and priests. Since only those men who had taken an oath of allegiance had the right to vote, the election of new priests fell into the hands of the same small group of revolutionary leaders—those who had proved themselves least religious in the traditional sense and most imbued with eighteenth century rationalism. Finally, when the priests who refused to take an oath and refused to leave their parishes were arrested and taken by members of the National Guard to Angers either to be deported or executed, the revolutionary cliques remained in control—but their control was precarious.

In Chanzeaux even the moderate members of the Town Council had deserted the revolutionary cause. The five remaining members wrote pathetically to the district authorities asking for protection:

> In Chanzeaux the five undersigned citizens are the only people faithful to the Constitution. We cannot hold out against the rest of the people together with those of the neighboring parishes who are also determined to kill the patriots. We run the greatest risks and can no longer leave our houses and speak freely of the benefits of the Constitution (Archives of the Maine-et-Loire, L 365).

Throughout the Mauges it seemed only a matter of time until serious conflict broke out. The occasion for the eventual outbreak of the rebellion was the government's attempt in March 1793 to enforce the draft law. Young men throughout the region rebelled, and having gone so far they could not draw back. The counterrevolutionary war had begun.

We know something of several of the young rebels in Chanzeaux and a good deal about another young man, a Republican leader whose murder actually touched off the rebellion locally. The Republican was Claude Godelier, the town surgeon. Descended from a long line of surgeons—his father practiced in the neighboring town of Saint-Lambert—Godelier had been trained in Angers. In 1789 when he began practice in Chanzeaux the town council had been so grateful to him for coming that they had petitioned the government to pay him to remain in the community. Godelier's practice must have flourished, for we find that in 1791 he was able to purchase some of the lands belonging to the parish of Chanzeaux. By 1793 he was serving as town prosecutor and "Colonel of the National Guard of Chanzeaux." He had become a leader among the town's most influential men, not only wealthy landowners like Crestault de la Mothe and Thibault-Chambault with city ties and departmental responsibilities in the new government, but also humble people like Durand, the cobbler, Rozé, the clerk, Picherit, and the constable, Hamon, a shopkeeper from a neighboring hamlet which had the reputation of being staunchly revolutionary. To this group it was obvious that the new constitutional policies, representing the modern, enlightened point of view, could not be put into effect until the "religious fanaticism" of the traditionalists had been suppressed, and the group did its best to stop the illegal religious processions and ceremonies that were taking place in the community. But the harder Godelier and his gendarmes tried to break up the religious demonstrations, which represented not only piety but all the stored-up resentments from nonreligious irritations, the more defiantly the people flaunted their religion.

Among the leaders of the opposing majority was René Forest, one of the twelve children of the innkeeper and related to many of the old families in the community. Forest had served for a time as the valet to Monsieur Gourreau de Chanzeaux and had even gone into exile with him in Germany. There Forest had undoubtedly seen the fine troops of the Allies but had heard how ridiculously prepared and ill-equipped the Republican troops were. For some reason he chose not to accompany his master, who went on to England and eventually emigrated to Kentucky. Instead Forest returned to Chanzeaux, but as a former émigré he remained in France under penalty of death.

Forest was far from being the only outlaw in Chanzeaux, however. One of his best friends was René Fougerai, a young man outlawed for desertion from the Republican army. Fougerai had volunteered for service in the first batallion of recruits from the Maine-et-Loire to be sent to the eastern front. He witnessed what in French history has become known as the Mission of the Virgins of Verdun. This unsavory episode gave him as low an opinion of the Republicans as Forest had from his experience with the émigrés. According to the legend the leading citizens of Verdun, unsympathetic to the Revolution and loath to see their city made a battlefield between Prussian and French armies, sent their loveliest maidens to the Prussian camp to use their wiles on the enemy generals. This is a considerable exaggeration of the actual incident, but it is true that the city of Verdun did surrender without a battle, and the disgraced revolutionary general, Beaurepaire, killed himself. (Or was he murdered when he tried to prevent the surrender?) The Republican army dispersed, and Fougerai returned to Chanzeaux, bringing with him stories of how the people of Verdun had eagerly turned away from the revolutionary leaders and embraced the enemy at the first opportunity. The men of Fougerai's batallion were called back into service at once, but Fougerai refused to report. He remained at home instead and was condemned to death as a deserter.

Other friends of Forest were also in trouble with the law. The five Godillon brothers had suffered the heavy fine of five hundred pounds for participating illegally in religious processions. Ragueneau, the weaver and sexton, had been deprived of his church job because of his loyalty to the nonjurant patriarch, Curé Blondel de Ris. But it was difficult to live in Chanzeaux without breaking the law. Most people had sheltered an outlawed priest or at least knew where one was hiding and failed to inform on him. Many refused to have their babies baptized, their young people married, their dead buried by other than outlawed priests. People even refused to register these facts with the civil authorities, who had now taken on this function. The possession of guns was forbidden, but most families had hidden weapons. Some people flaunted their illicit loyalties more openly by not wearing the prescribed tricolor cockades; instead they wore white ribbons and Sacred Hearts.

Hostility toward the government was intensified by the anxiety many families felt for close relatives who were priests either in hiding or in prison. René Forest's brother, Jean-René, was the most distinguished member of this large family. As a child he had studied with the priest in the next village and had then gone to Angers to prepare for the priesthood; not content to take a parish when he was ordained, he went to Paris where he received his doctorate in theology in 1788. In 1791 he was in prison in Angers, and his family was naturally concerned for his safety. Rumors repeatedly circulated throughout the countryside that the imprisoned priests were about to be deported or executed, and at each rumor his father, the innkeeper of Chanzeaux, would dash to Angers. The only hope for the Forest family—like that of most of the people in Chanzeaux—was that the revolutionary government might be overthrown. René Forest and his friends easily found popular support for their defiant stand.

In March 1793, when the young men refused to answer the draft, violence broke out for the first time. The surgeon Godelier, leading two gendarmes to stem the outbreak, came face to face with Forest, Ragneau, the Godillon brothers, and other young men of Chanzeaux. Godelier was shot by Ragneau, and since he was not killed outright, François Jouslain finished him off with a pitchfork. Now there was no possibility of reconciliation with the Republican minority. Bands of young men from the many communities caught in the same kind of predicament joined forces. Their first acts were to burn the official records that bore proof of seditious actions. The Vendée Rebellion had begun.

What actually happened in this war is of consequence here only as it gives us an understanding of the myth of the Vendée as it has been elaborated over the decades. It is a fact that is still remembered, but it is the evolution of the memory of it which has been a shaping force in the community. The myth began to grow as soon as the basic issues in the conflict were linked to the question of religious freedom. The nonreligious problems, as we have seen, were overlooked or interpreted only in the light of their religious connotation which made it possible for the rebels to act self-righteously.

The first official statement of the myth was made after three months of fighting when the Vendée rebels were able to unite and form a rudimentary government. One of the first acts of the rebel council was to issue a statement on June 1, 1793, justifying their position:

> We, commander of the Catholic and Royal Armies, having taken up arms only to uphold the religion of our fathers and to render to Louis XVII, our only legitimate sovereign, the luster and soundness of his throne and his crown, desiring to reestablish everywhere peace and harmony of all hearts, openly proclaim that if, in spite of our good and loyal intentions and in contempt of their oaths, the Republican clubists and all other disturbers of the public peace succeeded in taking up arms against the Catholic religion and against their king, we should return to punish them most severely. Our policy in their regard should convince them that peace and harmony are the objects of our will and that the general good is the single aim of our common efforts (Statement of Rebel Council, 1793).

This statement is typical of those the rebels continued to issue during the civil war. In their generation the myth developed no further except as it was reinforced by tales of Republican atrocities. Stories were told of Republican soldiers collecting the ears of Vendée victims. It was said that a Republican bibliophile in Angers had had a book bound in the skin of a Vendean priest. There was talk of "Republican marriages": Instead of shooting or guillotining the nuns and priests they wished to execute, the Republicans were rumored to have tied them together by pairs, naked, facing each other, and then drowned them in the Loire estuary. All of these stories obviously intensified the belief in the Mauges that the Republicans were indeed instruments of the Devil whom the Vendeans should destroy for the sake of God.

Although the major conflict in the rebellion was over in 1795 its spirit had grown so strong that the Vendeans took advantage of every new provocation to revolt again—in 1797, 1799, 1814, and 1815, and even in 1832. During this time both the spirit of revolt and the myth of the Vendée were nourished principally by the die-hard veterans, the families who could not forget their suffering, the priests who had managed to survive, and the aristocratic émigrés. As this generation gradually disappeared the spirit of the myth grew less powerful. As a social force it might have died with the death of its veterans in the nineteenth century, if new intellectual and political movements had not seized upon the myth and adapted it to their purposes.

The Vendée revolt had many features to endear it to the Romantic writers in the first half of the nineteenth century. Men wearing Sacred Hearts on their sleeves and fighting in the name of religion could not fail to appeal to a country in which there was a revival of religion, or at least of religiosity. This was also the period of the Gothic revival, a time of enthusiasm for historical novels and of yearning for a return to a more natural, and, therefore, it was thought, more virtuous, life. It was imagined that the Vendée rebels were all peasants, men of the earth, nearer to nature and less corrupted than people from the cities. Furthermore, it was imagined that these people had been living in a medieval society, a remnant of feudalism which had defended itself against the modern world. The example of peasants protecting their priests, their nobles, and their king was infinitely appealing to the apologists for the Bourbons who were trying to restore the joint rule of Altar and Throne to France. Just as the French had become aware of their nationality during the Revolution, so the regions became conscious and proud of their individuality in the nineteenth century. In this time of nascent regionalism, it seemed right that the Vendeans had defended their *pays* against the encroachments of Parisian government. Finally, in the age of the Romantic hero the Vendée Rebellion furnished the example of simple people rising to heights of heroism against overwhelming forces. Napoleon himself had called the Rebellion a War of Giants. The Vendeans lost, but they had faced the task laid upon them by Providence. The subject attracted the most popular Romantic novelists of the day. Balzac wrote *Les Chouans*. Dumas wrote a whole series of Vendée novels. Hugo wrote *Quatre-Vingt-Treize* and Trollope *La Vendée*. Thus the outside force of cultural history strengthened and at the same time popularized the myth of the Vendée.

By chance the community of Chanzeaux found its own Romantic historian who gave new life to the myth of its past. His name is as romantic as the life he wanted to lead—Count Théodore de Quatrebarbes. Born in 1803 in the Mauges, he went to military school and became a career officer in the army. In 1830 he was fighting in Algeria when news came of the July Revolution and the accession to the throne of Louis-Philippe. Quatrebarbes, unwilling to serve under a bourgeois king who called himself not King of France but King of the French, broke his sword over his knee, resigned his commission, and returned to Anjou. For a while he participated in plots against the government, but when in 1832 he married the heiress of the Gourreau de Chanzeaux family he transferred to this village the frustrated devotion he felt for the cause of the Bourbons.

In 1840 Quatrebarbes rebuilt the chateau Renaissance style. He managed the twenty-four farms belonging to the estate and served as arbitrator when his subjects quarreled. He built a boys' day school and a girls' boarding school. In 1848 he served briefly as mayor of the town. When the plague broke out in the neighborhood, Quatrebarbes worked side-by-side with the priest and doctor, caring for the ill and burying the dead. Unable to serve in war as a knight should, this modern Bayard chose to serve God and King by living out the feudal ideal in Chanzeaux.

Quatrebarbes also worked to popularize his ideals. He wrote a book defending the temporal power of the Pope and another celebrating a fifteenth century noble who had come to be known as Le Bon Roi René d'Anjou. He commissioned a statue of René, from David d'Angers, for the square in front of the Angers chateau. In Chanzeaux he leased a building on the national highway to an innkeeper on condition that the inn be called the "Auberge du Bon Roi René."

His best and most popular book was *Une Paroisse Vendéenne sous la Terreur*, a romantic account of the Vendée Rebellion as it affected Chanzeaux, and it was this book that consecrated the myth for successive generations of Chanzeans. The tone of the work is set by a quotation from the Book of Maccabees:

> Judas said unto them: Take up your arms and fill yourselves with courage. Make yourselves ready for tomorrow morning in order to fight against the assembled nations who have come to destroy us and overthrow our religion. . . .
> For it was better to fall in combat than to see the ills of their people and the destruction of all holy things.

As one would expect, Quatrebarbes describes the idyllic life of the people of Chanzeaux before the Revolution:

> Like most of the communes of our Anjou, Chanzeaux was for a long time surrounded with a happy obscurity. Its land had never been the theater of either a tragic or glorious memorable event; and had it not been for the unanimous war cry which shook the Vendée, its history would still be composed only of the simple description of the virtues of its priests, the charity of its gentry, and the pure and laborious customs of its peaceful peasants (Quatrebarbes: 1837, p. 20).

Then come the glorious feats of the Vendeans and the suffering at the hands of the villainous Republicans, depicted in great detail on the basis of the eyewitness accounts of people still living in the community when Quatrebarbes moved there. In conclusion, he says that in the nineteenth century the spirit of those days still lives in the people of Chanzeaux, who find in it their inspiration:

> God has taken into account the labors and sacrifices of Chanzeaux and has blessed its grief. The blood of martyrs, the tears of orphans, the laments of their mothers have not been in vain. To wipe out the traces of the unbelievable disasters which ravaged its land and taken away half of its people, only a quarter of a century have sufficed. Thanks to its zeal and to its patriarchal society the Vendée has again become one of the richest and most populated provinces of France. Its unconquerable resistance has covered with glory the tomb of the Bourbon monarchy. And if it seems to have failed, if it has not reestablished the dynasty whose banner it sought to hold on high, it has on its own ruins brought about the triumph of religion and faith. That is its great, its immortal victory, and that is why its children took up arms and died (*ibid.*, pp. 312–314).

Beneath the ideal picture of Chanzeaux as Quatrebarbes describes it one finds as little basic truth as in the picture he painted of the Rebellion. By delving into the archives of the town and into the papers of the Quatrebarbes family we find that in fact life in Chanzeaux in the nineteenth century was not so ideal.

Whether Quatrebarbes acknowledged it or not, the Revolution had taken place, and life did not go on as in the feudal world of his dreams. Instead, we find instances of frequent conflict between Quatrebarbes and the priest and between Quatrebarbes and the people of Chanzeaux. His rebuilding the chateau entailed razing a mill, moving the town laundry and horse trough, and building a huge wall around the chateau grounds that forced people to travel an extra kilometer to reach the national highway. The Chanzeans retaliated as best they could. When Quatrebarbes missed the annual auction of church seats his elaborate pew was awarded to a commoner. It took the influence of the bishop himself to restore the pew to the Quatrebarbes family. When the Town Council spurned his offer of a new location for the horse trough, he could only weakly accuse them of ingratitude and repeat his wife's threat that for some time they had been thinking of abandoning the village and moving to Rome.

At the day-to-day level of existence it is certain that Chanzeaux and Quatrebarbes did not always live up to the ideal he had described in his statement of the Vendée myth. There is no doubt, however, that the myth had an important function in giving the people a sense of identity that they expressed in their religious and political behavior. Chanzeaux remained a community where everyone remained attached to the church. In the quinquennial reports of the priest to the bishop during the nineteenth century it is reported that every inhabitant of the community went to Mass and took communion at least once a year. After 1848, when universal suffrage was introduced in France, the Chanzeans habitually voted for conservative and royalist candidates. In that first year, however, Quatrebarbes did not trust the voters and gave marked ballots to all his tenant farmers and made sure they voted as he had indicated!

Quatrebarbes died in 1871, and at about the same time the chances for a Bourbon restoration in France died, too. France began to live under a Republic, and slowly people became accustomed to the idea. The appeal of the old Vendée myth steadily weakened. By 1890 there were very few people in Chanzeaux who had lived under the Bourbons, or even under the Orléans. Under the Second Empire people had not suffered; indeed, until the military catastrophe of 1870 took place, it had brought them prosperity. The Third Republic did little to change their existence and certainly brought no reform to frighten them. It had made no antireligious gesture, and the Catholic schools of Chanzeaux were prospering. The farmers were prospering, too, for the Méline tariff protected the farmers of France from the giant producers of wheat and beef in eastern Europe and in the Americas. As the people became reconciled to the Republic the Church took conciliatory steps. The Pope, in his encyclical *In the Midst of Solicitudes*, called upon the French people to accept the Republic. This action seemed to destroy the old alliance of Altar and Throne, and the royalist pretender to the throne was even led to denounce the action of the Pope as "foreign intervention which the French people could not accept." The very basis of the myth of the Vendée, the loyalty to both Church and King, seemed to be disintegrating.

Once again, however, the myth was given new life, and again outside forces created the fear that traditional local values were threatened. The religious controversy that broke out in the 1890's culminated in the enactment of anti-clerical legislation between 1899 and 1905. Although there were riots in some villages when government agents came to evaluate the confiscated church property, there were no riots in Chanzeaux. The trend toward reconciliation with the Republic was broken, however. The few Royalists remaining in the commune were once more justified in asserting that a Republic was inevitably antireligious. The Republicans, who in 1892 had even elected a mayor, were discredited in the eyes of the majority of the people. For the first time since the Concordat of 1801 the government withdrew financial support for the church and Catholic schools. In Chanzeaux this meant that the greatest burden fell on those most able to pay, the wealthy landowners who had remained most faithful to the ideals of the myth of the Vendée. As they became the principal support for the religious and educational institutions in the community their influence grew proportionately.

Curiously enough there was a better chance in the twentieth century to make a reality of the ideals of the myth than there had been either in the eighteenth century or at the time of the Comte de Quatrebarbes. The idea of noble and priest leading a community to the fulfillment of its destiny was as nearly realized in the first decades of the twentieth century as it had ever been. Since Quatrebarbes had died without an heir, the chateau was inherited by a distant cousin of Madame de Quatrebarbes, a young lady who had married a career army officer, Monsieur d'Hattecourt. Just as Quatrebarbes as a matter of principle had left the army in 1830, so Monsieur d'Hattecourt broke his sword and retired from the army in 1905 rather than serve a "godless government." He, too, withdrew to Chanzeaux and made his life there. Within a short time he was elected mayor and served in that office until his death in 1939. It was largely with Quatrebarbes's money, inherited by the d'Hattecourts, that the new church was built, the schools were enlarged, the priest and teachers supported, and a parish recreation hall constructed. A tall, imposing man with a kind heart and a strong sense of justice, d'Hattecourt seems to have been loved and respected by the people as the aristocrat of the Vendée myth should have been.

In 1919 d'Hattecourt was joined by Abbé Chupin, who had the bearing and character to play the role of the mythical priest. He was a patriarch who knew when to loose his thunderbolts against deviant parishioners and when to accept their weaknesses as pardonable aspects of the human condition. With him the myth of the Vendée was as powerful a moral weapon as the Bible for the Catechism. It is said that he never missed a Sunday without referring to the "martyred ancestors who died for their religion" as constrasted with their descendants, his parishioners, who failed to measure up to the Christian standards in the many ways he described in his sermons. Abbé Chupin was the curé in Chanzeaux until his retirement in 1955.

Meanwhile the faith in Altar and Throne, renewed in Chanzeaux by the reaction to the anticlerical campaign of 1899–1905, had been weakened again by outside forces impinging on the community. Belief in the Altar remained strong, but the experience of two world wars fostered a sense of common interest between the people of Chanzeaux and the French Republic. The men who served in the army became reconciled to the idea of Republic as they joined with men from all parts of France in a common cause. The anxiety of families at home, the bond of death or the threat of death, privations shared by everyone, all drew people together. In the First World War this unity found expression in the *Union Sacrée*, which suspended the old conflict between Royalists and Republicans. In the Second World War there were serious political divisions but there was no serious disagreement over the ultimate goal of saving *la patrie*.

Just as the myth of the Vendée had been adapted to the changed political reality of the nineteenth century, so did it bend with the winds of the twentieth century. In 1954 when the Abbé Body died—he was a native of Chanzeaux who had clung to the legend of the town's history—he left his little fortune to the church of Chanzeaux to memorialize the Vendée War. It was Curé Chupin who arranged for appropriate stained glass windows to be designed and installed. On one of the windows under the heading *Martyrologie de Vos Ancêtres Qui Sont Morts Pour Défendre la Religion et la Patrie* is a list of the families martyred during the Rebellion. The idea of *patrie* had become so hallowed by the two world wars that Curé Chupin seems to have been quite unaware of the irony and anachronism of using this phrase, but the ancestors whom he was honoring must have turned in their graves. If there was one thing they died in the hope of destroying it was *la patrie*! In the days of the Rebellion this term was synonymous with *République*; the members of the hated revolutionary clique in the village were called *patriotes*. The sound of this word gave rise to the insulting and more commonly used epithet, *pataud*s, "bloated city dogs." But for the *patriotes*, the *patrie* was a new religion, and the *patriotes* had their own saints—Cincinnatus, Brutus, Wilhelm Tell—for whom their children, *les enfants de la patrie*, were named.

Many decades, and above all the two great wars, had passed between the Vendée Rebellion and the installation of the stained glass windows in Chanzeaux in 1955. The idea of the *patrie* had become so acceptable to the Chanzeans that they had even erected a monument to the dead who had given their lives in 1914–18 and 1940–45. They now assumed that their ancestors, too, must have died for *la patrie* as well as for religion. An essential part of the myth, the ideal of loyalty to a king as a contemporary social force, had been lost. In modern

Chanzeaux only a few people, the remaining aristocrats and a few descendants of the Vendean leaders, remained faithful to the ideal, and their role was inconsequential.

By 1955 the myth was losing still another source of strength. Even the Catholic Church, feeling the need to strengthen its popular base, was ready to forgo union with an aristocratic tradition. The older priests—Body, who had left money for the stained glass windows, and Chupin, under whose guidance they were designed and installed—were still motivated by the ideal of the myth. Curé Chupin must have received a painful shock, however, when the new Bishop, Monseigneur Chappoulie, came to dedicate the windows. Somewhat more gently, but in substance the Bishop said in his address:

> What your ancestors did was magnificent. You have every right to be proud of them and to honor them as you do today. It is time, however, to give up feelings that divide you from your fellow citizens. The old political quarrels are ended. We must, in the church, forget the traditional feuds and unite with all Frenchmen and with Christians everywhere for the glory of God.

For thirty-five years Curé Chupin had reminded the Chanzeans that they were or should be different from other Frenchmen and defend their peculiar ideals against the enemy. It must have hurt the old curé to be told by his bishop that what he had devoted his long career as a priest to fostering was neither a firm nor proper base for the future.

Before his retirement Curé Chupin had begun to organize a pageant as a final reminder to parishioners of the heroic example set for them by their ancestors. The young curé who replaced him, Abbé Bonsergent, was in sympathy with the new ideas of the Bishop, but plans for the pageant were so far under way that he felt they ought to be carried out. Since the people of Chanzeaux like nothing better than amateur dramatics, there was enthusiastic cooperation. The pageant, which was given in the church itself, was a great success and undoubtedly gave great pleasure to Monsieur Chupin, who returned for the performance. The new cureé must also have gathered from the popular enthusiasm that the myth of the Vendée was still a strong motivating force among his parishioners.

Two years later, in 1957, it was not surprising that as a newcomer to the community I, too, should have thought that the Vendée myth was still a force in the lives of the people. I was overly impressed, however, by the material evidence of the myth which overwhelms the newcomer. Contrary evidence was too weak to arouse my doubts, and it took months for me to see that the myth was in fact dying. The infrequent disparagement of it was easily ignored. Very few people talked about it as the barber did one day as I was having my hair cut:

> Don't take too seriously all this talk you hear about the glorious ancestor business. My grandmother says that her grandmother told her that the people burned out

of the church tower by Republican soldiers got what they were asking for. The Republicans happened to be marching through the village on their way home at the end of the war. Ragneau was stupid enough to frighten people into going up and trapping themselves in the tower. Then he started shooting at the Republicans, and that started the trouble. This talk about martyrs!! Why couldn't they mind their own business and let the Republicans mind theirs?

Since barbers are often inconoclasts I did not take these words seriously. As far as I knew the barber was alone in expressing such sentiments.

In the past five years, however, this point of view has become current in Chanzeaux, and undoubtedly it was more generally held in 1957 than I realized. Only recently I learned about the reaction in the parish to a Vendée play produced in 1956. Because the Vendée pageant had been such a success, the Catholic School Committee had decided the following year to produce it as a play in the parish recreation hall as a benefit performance for the schools. The teacher of the younger boys wrote the script, leaning heavily on Quatrebarbes's book and on a short story entitled *Les Sonneurs de Cloche*.[2] The result is an extravagantly romantic melodrama, as one can see from this sample of the dialogue in the scene at the siege of the tower:

Banchereau. (gasping) Monsieur l'Abbé . . . I am going . . . to die.

Abbé Blanvillain. (giving him absolution) Lord, receive his soul. (removing the silver chalice from its case) May his sacrifice and our own be acceptable to Thee . . . (he is wounded) Oh! Heavens!

Ragneau's wife. Monsieur l'Abbé, you are wounded.

Abbé Blanvillain. The ball that pierced the chalice hit me, too . . . Ragneau, perhaps we ought to surrender . . . haven't we done more than our duty?

Ragneau. What are you saying, Monsieur l'Abbé? Should you beg for your life? . . . God is giving you an opportunity to seek bliss through martyrdom. . . . Pray for us and show us how to keep our courage. As for me, never . . . never shall I surrender to these Republican wretches. This tower has been my cradle; it will be my tomb.

Abbé Blanvillain. You are right, Maurice. May God forgive me for this moment of weakness. May my death be the expiation of my sin. (he gives the chalice to Mlle. Petit) Take this chalice, my daughter. I can hold it no longer. Oh Mary, refuge of sinners, give us eternal peace. (he falls into the flames rising in the tower)

When the pageant was given before the altar it had been received respectfully. In the parish hall the enthusiasm was high, but the spirit of the audience was very different: The lightness with which everyone looked upon the Vendée

2. I have seen this story only in the pages torn from a book so I am unable to give the proper bibliographical reference. No one in Chanzeaux or in the Angers bookshops knew who had written the story.

legend was easily apparent. The slightest *faux pas* set off laughter, and the *faux pas* were numerous. The teacher who had written the play had given himself the role of René Forest, the young man who led his friends into the fight for freedom. In an eloquent speech urging them to revolt he ended with a battle cry:

> The best way to serve our country is to kill off these mad dogs who seek to drown France in rivers of blood.
>
> It is time, it is high time, to act! The more cowardly we are, the bolder they become.
>
> SOLDIERS! Henceforth, I shall call you "soldiers" since you do me the honor of choosing me as your leader.
>
> SOLDIERS! God and France need you!
>
> God and France need your heroism to stamp out wickedness.
>
> For God and for France we shall win or we shall die! . . .
>
> The Holy War is begun! Forward, Soldiers of God!

The young actors were wearing the broad-brimmed hats that the Vendeans are always pictured as having worn, but these were made of paper painted black. When Forest uttered his immortal words, "We shall win or we shall die," he whipped off his hat to point to the road they all must travel. As he thrust his arm full length, the hat went sailing over the heads of the audience. From then on the audience showed the fun they could have laughing at the deeds of their ancestors.

Jean Brillet, a sharp-tongued farmer who had been one of the Vendeans in the play, ended his account to me by saying, "You know, we don't care about this Vendée stuff any more. You won't find many people around here interested in our martyred ancestors."

"Why not?"

"What could the people of Chanzeaux have gained by fighting against the Republic, anyway? Probably the truth was that they were forced to fight by the nobles who had them in their power."

This was the same idea expressed in 1957 by the barber, but now one of the town's most respected young farmers was saying the same thing. Clearly the myth had lost prestige in a few years. The ideas of what had actually happened during the Vendée War had always been vague in the minds of the people I had asked about it. Usually they remembered only a detail here and there, and often these were inaccurate, but still they had seemed to believe that the Vendeans had fought only for *Dieu et patrie*. Now they had become skeptical of that.

Even the Catholic schools have reduced the emphasis on the Vendean tradition. In the general history book used in the classes in Chanzeaux the rebellion is mentioned only in passing. The little book on Angevin history and geography has but four of its one hundred and four pages devoted to the revolutionary period, the summary of which the children must memorize:

> Anjou was not displeased by the beginning of the Revolution and sent to the States General deputies who almost all favored reform.
>
> But the Civil Constitution of the Clergy stirred up the people who on the whole were very religious. So in 1793 the Vendée War broke out. First the Vendée was victorious, but then it was defeated in a series of hard fights. The war was prolonged by partisan struggles called the Chouannerie.
>
> Because of the Vendée Rebellion the Terror was more violent in Anjou than elsewhere and ended only by the spontaneous reestablishment of Catholic worship under the Directoire. (Civrays: 1958, p. 41).

But how much of even this brief, formal explanation did the children actually remember? And what did they pick up from family traditions and from the archaeological evidence in their surroundings? To help me find the answer to these questions the teachers agreed to give the following assignment to the older children:

> An American child comes to visit Chanzeaux. He knows nothing about the Vendée War or about what happened at Chanzeaux during the Revolution. Tell him what happened. Explain why it happened and how it all ended.

Unfortunately the teachers did not take my request seriously to give the children no help in writing the themes. There were too many details that most of the boys mentioned and which none of the girls included and too many details that the girls mentioned which the boys omitted: the teachers must at least have given the children a few guideposts to the story of the Vendée and of Chanzeaux's past. Nevertheless the themes are instructive because even with the help of the teachers the children show no real knowledge of these past events and certainly no curiosity about them. The best of the themes show only a vague awareness of a heroic past; the worst are simply unintelligible. The children's ignorance of this episode certainly reflects the growing indifference of their parents and teachers.

At this point I pause to consider the hypothesis which involved me in the study of Chanzeaux's past. I went to Chanzeaux because I wanted to understand why most people went to Mass and why politics were preponderantly conservative. I had assumed that Chanzeaux's religious and political behavior might be explained by the myth of the Vendée. Now I find that although this is true, the myth has lost its effectiveness as a social force, and even these patterns of behavior have changed.

Eighty per cent of the population of Chanzeaux still go to Mass regularly every Sunday, and as in the past this differentiates them from people living a few miles to the north and to the east. (We know the statistics precisely because the diocesan authorities have tabulated the religious behavior of each household in the diocese on IBM cards.) But in the last five years the number of people attending Mass regularly has diminished by five per cent. Instead of being distressed by this drop, the most ardent Catholics, who belong to the Catholic Action groups and who not only go to Mass but take Communion every Sunday, express a sense of satisfaction. They disapprove of perfunctory attendance and say that many of the Chanzeans, if not most of them, have been going to Mass simply to conform, and it would be better if they did not go at all rather than sit whispering in the back of the church.

The priests in the Mauges generally agree with this point of view. They are not impressed by the large attendance at Mass because they say that real religious devotion is not usual—perhaps even as rare as it is in communities like Roussillon where only five per cent of the people are regular attenders. In the Vaucluse the people of Roussillon do not go to Mass because in that *pays* one does not go to Mass. In Chanzeaux, on the other hand, going to Mass is the thing to do. The habits encouraged by the myth of the Vendée still linger even though the myth has lost its creative force.

I felt sure that in a political situation, however, one might still observe the full force of the myth. Surely in an election the conservative candidates, spiritual heirs of the royalists, would bring out the old bunting and sound the clichés of the Vendée to win votes with slogans of the past. In November 1962 I went to Chanzeaux for the national elections. For two weeks I listened to campaign speeches, interviewed candidates, talked to voters—and recorded a great deal of all this on tape. To my amazement the Vendée tradition was never once mentioned. Everyone was concerned with issues of immediate interest—the Common Market, *la force de frappe*, Algerian refugees, price controls. Even the question of the government's support of Catholic schools, which would have seemed a natural concern and one easily supported by references to the Vendean martyrs, was not mentioned.

So in politics, too, the content of the myth has lost its interest and its force. People still vote conservatively, but again largely from habit. In the Mauges, de Gaulle received ninety-five per cent of the votes in his plebiscites, and in the election of 1962 the Gaullist incumbent won easily in Chanzeaux in the first round:

Hauret (Gaulliste)	369
Lesieur-Desbrières (Indépendent)	45
Bégault (Conservative without affiliation)	24
Poujade	27
Gohard (Socialiste)	8
Mahias (Communiste)	16

In politics as in religion the forms of the tradition have been maintained even though belief in the tradition itself is lost. People vote to the right because the weight of the past impels them in that direction, just as it impels them toward church on Sunday morning.

Other lingering effects of the tradition are equally misleading. In 1957 the young people had organized two folk dance groups. On Sunday afternoons they practiced their dances, and frequently they dressed in regional costumes to take part in regional folk festivals. This seemed evidence of an interest in tradition. But now the local church officials have ceased to frown on modern dancing, and the young people rock'n'roll or madison at the dance hall on Saturday night. The folk dance groups have all but ceased to function. Obviously the young people were not really interested in history!

Yet people often express a certain pride in their past. They say rather whimsically, "*Nous sommes des fils de chouans ici!*" in the same way that French history books speak of "*nos ancêtres les Gaulois.*" Apparently this gives a vague assurance of identity. But the vagueness is in fact emphasized by their misuse of the word *chouans*. The ancestors of the Chanzeans were Vendeans, not *chouans*, who were actually guerrilla fighters north of the Loire. The accuracy of the term matters little, however. The expression used by Balzac as the title of his first novel evokes a more romantic and therefore more desirable past with which people like to be associated.

It is ironic that many people in Anjou who call themselves descendants of the *chouans* are, if they only knew or were willing to admit it, descendants of the bourgeois who fought bitterly in the 1790's to establish the new Republican government. As these families prospered under the Republic and acquired new wealth and status during the nineteenth and twentieth centuries, they married into the families of former aristocrats and have deserted their Republican heritage. The largest landowner in Chanzeaux is a *monsieur bien pensant* living in the neighboring community. His ancestor was an enthusiastic Republican leader who was able to purchase a great deal of church property, but today it is hardly tactful to remind Monsieur Charvet that he is not descended from the *chouans*.

The true descendants of the Vendeans are the farmers, artisans, and storekeepers whose ancestors formed the backbone of the rural rebellion against city domination. These people continue to go to Mass and to vote for the most conservative parties, but they are indifferent to the Vendée rebellion and the martyrdom of their ancestors. In 1793, 1830, and 1905 the myth had a function: it justified the position of the people of Chanzeaux who felt alienated from the rest of France. The continued belief in the myth depended on a mythmaker. With no function and with no mythmaker the myth loses its momentum. Only a few habits and romantic notions linger on.

References

Archives of the Maine-et-Loire, L365

Bois, P.
1960: *Paysans de l'Ouest* (Paris-La Haye: Mouton).

Civrays, T.
1958: *Histoire et Géographie de l'Anjou* (Angers: Siraudeau).

Le Bras, G.
1944: in André Siegfried (ed.), *Aspects de la Société Française* (Paris: Librarie générale de droit et de jurisprudence).

Quatrebarbes, T. de
1837: *Une Paroisse Vendéenne sous la Terreur* (Angers: Launay-Gagnot).

Statement of Rebel Council, 1793
1917: *Andégaviana*, **19**, 378.

Tilly, C.
1964: *The Vendée* (Cambridge: Harvard University Press).

Part Four

Cultural Dynamics

J. L. GIDDINGS

A Long Record of Eskimos and Indians at the Forest Edge

Ever since A. I. Hallowell showed us that bear ceremonialism was a basic idea, with a spread across the boreal zones of two continents (Hallowell: 1926), we have wondered how to get at the dating of bear worship and other similarly distributed traits. Possibly the precise time scale for cultural change that we are beginning to see in the Bering Strait region can be of use. With this scale, we may even be able to decide, before long, when the Eskimo cultural entity began to separate itself from an older boreal base.

The Arctic treeline has long been recognized as a boundary between Eskimos and Indians. We are accustomed to read that Eskimos "venture" to the forest edge for tent poles and that the Chipewyans "retreat" after a caribou hunt on the barren grounds to the "safety" of the trees. This sharp distinction between forest dwellers and coast and tundra dwellers holds true only in some parts of the Eskimo range. In others, it tends to lose its meaning. Those who have worked at the forest edge along the shores of the northern Bering Sea, Kotzebue Sound of the Chukchi Sea, and inland along the forested streams know that speakers of the Eskimo language have long been entrenched as far

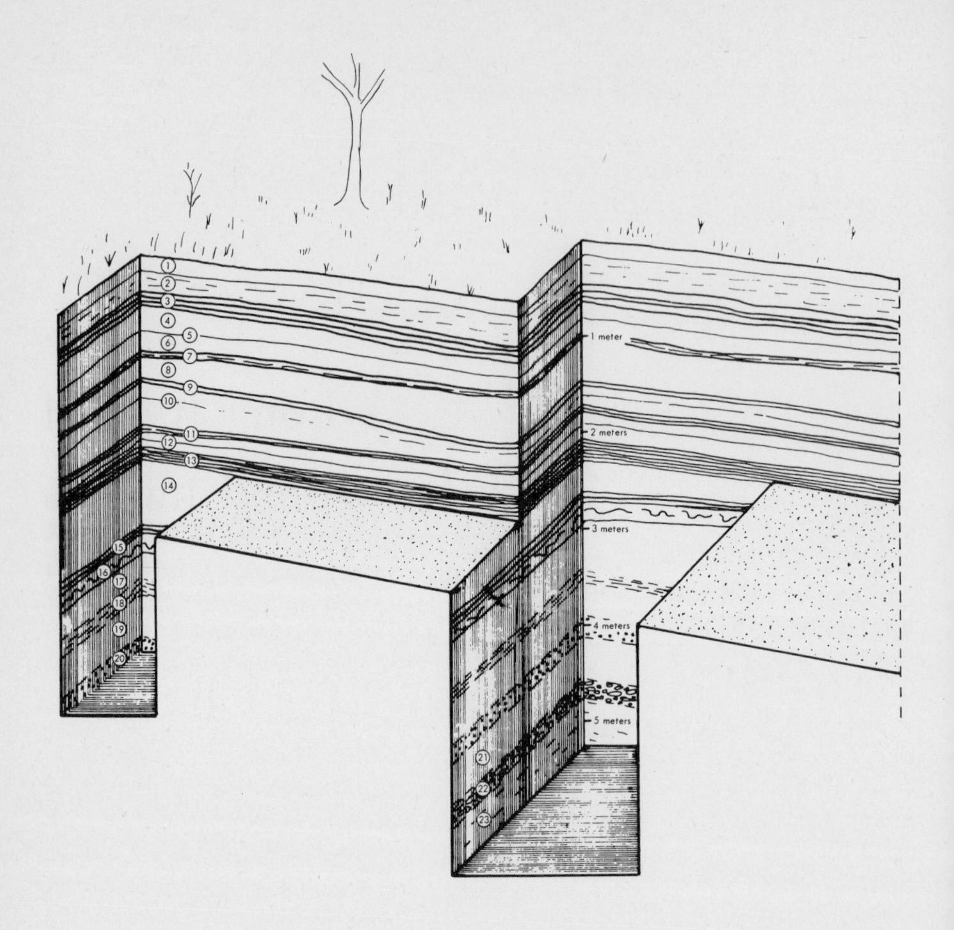

Figure 1.—Stratigraphy in the Onion Portage site, Kobuk River

1. turf
2. sandy loam, with Thule to recent inclusions
3. "middle" band—lower layers Norton Culture
4. light brown sandy loam
5. thin layer—chips
6. yellow sandy loam
7. "old hearth" band—2-3 layers
8. mottled brown sandy loam
9. Denbigh Flint complex—2-3 layers
10. light brown sandy loam
11. "obsidian" band—3 layers
12. gray-brown sandy loam
13. "wide" band—9-12 culture layers
14. brown to reddish sandy loam, banded with red streaks toward bottom
15. grey band—thick charcoal at middle
16. solifluction band—clay, marbled with charcoal and red ocher
17. chocolate brown sand
18. gray, clayey sand
19. chocolate brown sandy silt
20. small pebbles in brown sandy silt
21. brown sand
22. heavy gravel—like river beach
23. brown-gray, banded sand

as 200 miles within the forest. If it were not for language, there might be some question about the cultural affiliation of the people who have lived in recent centuries along the Kobuk River, the lower Yukon River, and intervening streams.

The Arctic Woodland Culture

After three seasons of archaeological work between 1940 and 1946 in the Kobuk Valley just north of the Arctic Circle, I found it difficult to place the 700-year continuity of people there in either the Eskimo or the Indian category. The people whom I interviewed along the upper Kobuk spoke a Malemiut dialect and wore the parkas of coastal Eskimos; yet, like their Athapaskan-speaking neighbors, the Koyukuk River Tena, they folded birch bark into baskets and boats, and had a similar overlap in nearly every aspect of material culture and folklore.

The archaeology, likewise, was split between things Indian and Eskimo. After a close study of the artifacts from five tree-ring dated sites and other undated ones, I concluded that it would have made little difference to the material culture what language was spoken along the Kobuk at any given time, as the people living there would still have employed many of the circumpolar traits that had been put together in the "sea, river, and forest hunting" archaeology. I called this combination the Arctic Woodland culture and judged it to be even older than the sites we had discovered and a material culture that would "outlive the physical appearance, the speech, and many of the social practices of its participants" (Giddings: 1952, p. 118). If languages had actually changed their boundaries along the river, while the techniques of fishing, hunting, and tool-making remained essentially the same, I felt that this material culture might be prejudiced by assigning it a linguistic label. It seemed unwise to ask archaeology to cast light upon early ethnic and linguistic groupings. In recent months, however, five newly discovered sites have disclosed a whole new range of Kobuk River archaeology that clearly shows a long record of surges of influence alternately from the interior and from the coast. One is tempted, therefore, to reintroduce the terms "Eskimo" and "Athapaskan" and to draw conclusions about the antiquity of these groups.

Onion Portage

Some of the newly emerging Kobuk River archaeology is orderly almost beyond belief. At the Onion Portage site about halfway (125 miles) between the coast of Kotzebue Sound and the present Athapaskan Indian country, the stratigraphy lies in undisturbed layers (Figs. 1 and 2), at least 28 of which are identified between the surface and a depth of nine or ten feet. Each culture layer, as one exposes it horizontally, divulges not only the camp sites of caribou hunters, but deposits of charcoal more than adequate for radiocarbon dating.

Figure 2.—Onion Portage stratigraphy. Photographic detail of area shown in the center of diagram of Figure 1

Obsidian, rare in sites of the coast, is found here in all but the earliest and most recent levels thus far exposed. Quite probably some of the deepest levels that contain charcoal will prove upon wide-scale excavation to extend the archaeology back into Wisconsin times. Before we look closely at the findings at Onion Portage, however, I should mention the narrow margin by which I missed its full significance in 1941. Vital changes might have come to Arctic interpretations had we excavated the site then.

Earlier Excavations

I first saw the old site—a favorite Eskimo camping place at the head of swift water at a great bend of the Kobuk—in the late summer of 1940. A luxuriant ground cover of redtop grass and fireweed under a poplar grove on a gentle slope above a gravel beach of the river indicated at once that the site had been frequently visited in recent decades. Also on this slope were three older house pits. Others, numbering nearly thirty, lay concealed by birches on the hillside and by spruce trees and alder thickets on the river bank where it turned away from the slopes. Trees growing in some of the pits were two or three hundred years old.

The following year, Onion Portage was a major goal, and I returned there for excavation with a student assistant and a crew of Eskimos. When we arrived at the site, however, in that unusual summer of continuous rain and a flooding river, we found that the frost had retreated little below the moss and sod on the surface. As the four house pits that we stripped the first day thawed slowly down to the bottoms of floors and tunnels, we realized that the timbers were too rotten for tree-ring dating. This knowledge led us to move elsewhere as soon as we had exposed the four floors. Ordinarily, we should have tested well below the floor of any house, but at Onion Portage there seemed little likelihood of our finding anything more in the sandy loam, even if we were to wait for the ground to thaw. I had almost no doubt that we were correct in moving to the site of Ekseavik nearer the seacoast, where I knew that frost in the ground had preserved logs of an early period.

There was one small doubt, however, and it grew during the next twenty years into a certainty that we had not yet found the earliest horizon at Onion Portage. This doubt centered on four flints that we had recovered from the floor of House 1 on our final day there in 1941. These were three microcores and a microblade.[1] They had been a source of immediate speculation when we found them. At that time, such carefully made, wedge-shaped cores were known mainly from the Campus site at the University of Alaska near Fairbanks. The abundant microblades and cores from the Campus site had been compared by N. C. Nelson to his collections from the Gobi desert of Mongolia and pronounced nearly identical in form (Nelson: 1937). The Campus site was thought to be extremely old—perhaps even of the Mesolithic age attributed by Nelson to the Gobi desert finds. The Onion Portage specimens, on the other hand, had been lying upon the floor of a house like those of coastal Eskimos, the other contents of which proclaimed it to be not much older than 700 years. Microblades had been reported by Froelich Rainey in a recent Indian village site of the far interior (Rainey: 1939) and microblades were known to be an element of the Dorset culture of the eastern Arctic, then assumed to date well within the Christian era. My first conclusion, then, was that the small Onion Portage blades and cores marked the persistence of a technique still useful in the Arctic forests and other isolated regions of North America, whatever might have been their original source. Another explanation might have been that the Onion Portage householders knew of a place where they could collect flints deposited by earlier people.

With the discovery in 1948 of the old Denbigh Flint complex (Giddings: 1964) on the coast of Bering Sea and the later discoveries of Denbigh or related cultures both on the shores of Alaska and in the far interior at mountain passes

1. They are illustrated in Giddings, *op. cit.*, Plate 46, pp. 14–16, 19.

near the treeline, there came an inevitable review of old sites and their clues. Might not the microblade and cores from Onion Portage be as old as objects they resembled in the Denbigh horizon? Could we have missed stratigraphy at Onion Portage? I felt quite certain that the three house pits we had excavated on the steeper hillside had not been built into earlier cultural deposits. The other (House 1), on the other hand, lay on the gentler slope within the grassy area in the poplar grove. Since we had excavated this house only to the limits of frost each day, stopping at the marks of decayed timbers clearly visible in the sand, the signs of stratigraphy beyond the house might have been missed. To say simply that they had been missed, however, understates the oversight. It is as though we had excavated a haystack in search of a needle without seeing the elephant hiding there.

Later Work at Onion Portage[2]

In mid-summer of 1961 I left our archaeological base at Cape Krusenstern on the Chukchi Sea to go to the upper Kobuk by air and to paddle down the river in a rubber kayak. Among other clues to be tested was the one suggesting that stratigraphy might be found at Onion Portage. House 1 now looked dry in the sunlight that filtered through the trees, and it took only a moment to test the thawed ground below the house floor and find there a culture layer that clearly had nothing to do with the people who had built the deep houses. After this promising disclosure, I arranged to spend the last ten days of the 1961 season excavating the site with a crew of five. We laid out a grid over the grassy part of the area and opened three test trenches at intervals, one of which encompassed the old pit of House 1. In each unit we saw an incredible stratigraphic order, apparently the same in all three unconnected pits. Each stratum, the remains of an old, stable ground surface, lay above another of the same character, and this was repeated again and again as our tests moved downward.

Except for House 1, few of the layers had been marred by ancient excavations. As we cleaned a surface of its earth cover, we came to campsites—probably tent sites—in which bones, chips, and stone tools lay in the vicinity of well-defined hearths, the whole often covered by traces of birch or spruce bark. In some levels we recognized artifacts of types well-known in the coastal region, while in others we saw only unfamiliar forms. By the end of the ten days we had exposed a great deal of one particular early level that lay just above the frost line and immediately under the floor of House 1 and had found traces, in thawed spots, of even deeper layers. A study of the materials secured that season indicated that we were down to a level deposited about 2000 B.C. and a culture more immediately referable to the Indian country than to the coast. Yet neither this nor the levels above supplied a firm answer to the meaning of the microcores and microblade in House 1. It was now evident that those

2. The 1961 work is reported in detail in Giddings (1962).

objects belonged to none of the phases of culture exposed in 1961 but to some aspect of the Denbigh Flint culture, no trace of which had yet been found in the forested interior.

For the 1963 season I was invited to excavate with a Danish National Museum group in Greenland. My colleagues there understood, however, the urgency of getting further answers at Onion Portage, so after digging half the season in Godthaab Fjord, I returned to Copenhagen and proceeded to Alaska with my son, James, as assistant. We traveled the air polar route to Anchorage and reached the Kobuk River in mid-July of the past season.

After an exploratory trip to the headwaters of the Kobuk, we settled down with Eskimo assistants to the further excavation of two pits opened in 1961. The ground was now completely thawed and we had only to proceed cautiously with the trowel so as not to destroy any part of the thin culture layers. Only one and a half feet below the bottom layer of 1961 we encountered a hard, claylike surface, grayish in color. This reminded me of the culture-bearing top of a dense soil layer on which the Denbigh Flint complex had been discovered at the type site. Within a short time we encountered the stones and charcoal of a hearth and, lying about it, the characteristically minute chert and obsidian chips of the Denbigh Flint culture. Artifacts included fine, diagonally flaked arrow points made on already small microblades, microblades themselves, burins and burin spalls, and other definitive types that we knew from Denbigh sites both on the coast and in the mountains.

Immediately below this was a second layer and, in some places, a third, also containing microblades. Deeper by another foot or more lay another series of three claylike layers, each, presumably, marking an old ground surface. In it were found quantities of chips as well as artifacts of obsidian along with objects of chert and similar stone. A square-based spear point of obsidian, widest near the tip (Fig. 4, No. 1), introduced a new farm to the region. In none of these layers was found a microblade or burin.

As the excavations went deeper, we came to still another band of closely sandwiched layers, this time numbering between nine and twelve. In four of these were found hearths and artifacts sufficient for a first definition of the culture phase. Side-notched points predominated, and, with them, coarse choppers made by striking large, thick flakes from boulders and broadly chipping one end into the shape of an ax. Hearths in these layers usually lacked a concentration of stones, but their fires had been laid on beds of powdered red ocher. Again, among the hundreds of flakes and artifacts recovered from this range—temporarily called the "Wide" band—we found no trace of microblades or burins. While this series of culture-bearing levels is the lowest in which flints thus far occur, it seems highly probable that as a greater area is tested in future seasons charcoal in some of the lower layers will prove to be that of campfires.

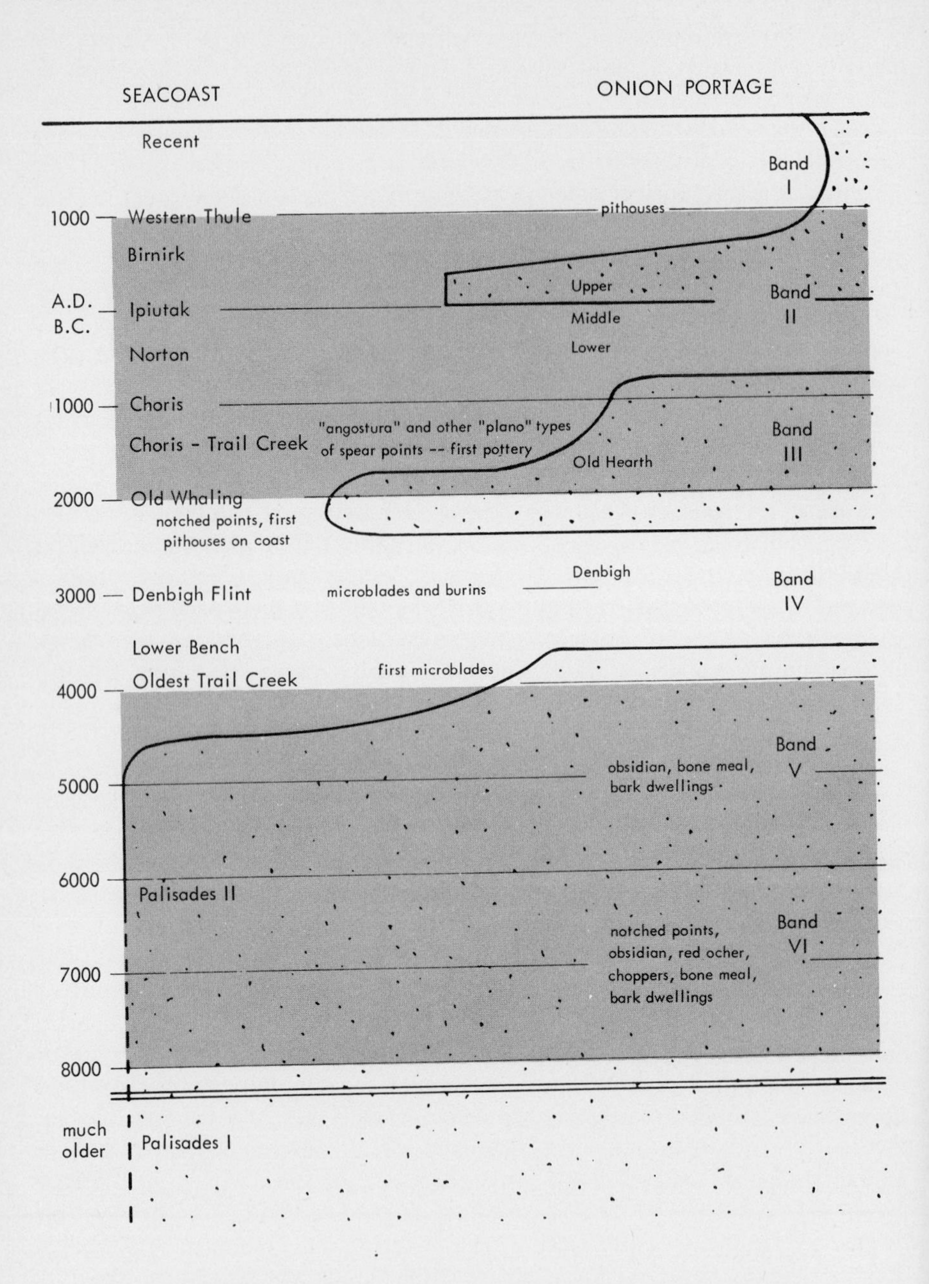

Figure 3.—Estimated chronology and cultural comparison between Kotzebue Sound and Onion Portage site, Kobuk River. The stippled zones reflect the inland influence (presumably Indian) along the river and on the coast

The next stratum below, ranging between seven and eight feet below the present ground surface, contains, first, three well-defined layers—the center one thick with charcoal—and then, immediately below these, a zone of dense, fine-grained loam or clay. Throughout this zone are streaks of charcoal and red ocher. These streaks differ from all other strata, however, in showing the effects of strong solifluction—that is, folding under, as mud does when saturated with moisture and partly freed by retreating ground ice. This solifluction relates to some change—probably climatic—in the manner of deposition at Onion Portage. One possible answer, suggested by a visiting geologist, is that the river was repeatedly dammed by glaciation, causing a thick deposit of fine-grained materials to accumulate at a time when extreme cold caused deep ground frost.

Below this band, and continuing to the bottom of two deep pits, are layers of sand or sandy loam interspersed with layers containing pebbles or heavy beach gravel. We ceased digging at about eighteen feet because of the danger in working in quarters so confined, where sloughing might take place.

Once more the season ended before we were able to plumb the strata at Onion Portage. Certain facts are clear, however. At least twenty-eight distinct cultural levels in the form of hard, old ground surfaces have been exposed, on each of which there is either an extensive deposit of cultural material or the promise, through charcoal and chips, that as the excavations expand, camp sites will be found. Beneath these definite culture-bearing layers a more than reasonable chance exists that somewhere in the site we shall encounter the cultural remains of glacial age people. Although bones are poorly preserved in the lower levels and must be hardened with chemicals as soon as they appear, we may expect that some of the bones of caribou, sheep, and beaver thus far identified will be accompanied by the bones of animals now extinct. It will be reasonable, also, to look for some human bones in a site of this magnitude.

Comparison with the Seacoast

The soils at Onion Portage appear, on the whole, to have accumulated gradually. The thin layers of fine-grained earth that occur by twos and more in a band seem to represent stable and long-lasting ground surfaces. The layers of white sand that separate some layers may, on the other hand, have been brought by single wind storms. Nevertheless, the sandy loam that makes up the body of the deposit is nearly identical in color and consistency with the soil of the neighboring wooded slope and signs are strong that this material has increased the depth of the site through slow and regular accumulation which is proportional to the lapse of time. This is shown diagrammatically in Fig. 3. To the right are arranged the bands of layers at Onion Portage in approximately their order of deposition (see Figs. 1 and 2). To the left are shown a scale of time and cultural phase names based upon coastal sites stretching from Cape Denbigh around Cape Prince of Wales and northward to Point Hope. The dating is based in part upon radiocarbon dates, most of which are not yet published,[3] and, especially, on a series of 114 successive beach ridges at Cape Krusenstern with their horizontally stratified cultural deposits. This sequence and its dating have been described in considerable detail (Giddings: 1960, 1961a; Giddings and Bandi: 1962).

In 1961 there was little reason to question either the relative order or the approximate dating of all the coastal cultures here shown, at least from the time of the Denbigh Flint culture to the present. While I felt confident of my relative placement of the Palisades cultures, the oldest Trail Creek, and Lower Bench, it could be questioned by those who base their dating on long-range cross-comparison with dated sites in the eastern United States or on estimated chronologies from undated and unstratified sites in central Canada and interior Alaska. It will be necessary now to remind ourselves briefly of the nature of the named cultures and phases of Kotzebue Sound and of some points of difference in the interpretation of cultural trends. First, let us consider the cultural phases from early to late, beginning with the estimated earliest:

Palisades I. A group of artifacts and flakes from a high bench on the hillside behind the Cape Krusenstern beach ridge sequence separated from Palisades II of the same bare-topped site only on the basis of a chemical change throughout the material. After separation on this basis, Palisades I was found to consist solely of percussion-flaked objects of relatively large size: flakes, large axlike implements resembling certain "chopper" tools of Asia, and one bifaced projectile point or knife possessing a single-shouldered stem. The transformation of the stone after these specimens were made and the absence of similar change in other objects in this part of western Alaska led me to believe that this assemblage was much older than Palisades II and presumably of glacial age.

Palisades II. A collection of encrusted flints including many small, side-notched projectile points or knife blades, large, parallel-edged, unifaced blades, and the fragments of large bifaced spear points with straight bases, among less definitive traits.

Lower Bench Site. Closer to the water's edge on the same steep hillside as the Palisades site. It contains many microblades and a few other objects suggesting an early phase of the Denbigh Flint culture. The artifacts presumably date with those from the bottom levels of the Trail Creek caves, excavated by Helge Larsen (1951; 1963), wherein microblades like some of those of Lower Bench were found near slotted arrowheads of antler similar to examples from Mesolithic Europe.

3. The dated samples awaiting publication originate at the laboratories of the University of Pennsylvania, the National Museum in Copenhagen, and The University of Michigan. Published samples are in Froelich Rainey and Elizabeth Ralph, "Radiocarbon Dating in the Arctic," *American Antiquity*, **24,** 365–374 (1959).

Denbigh Flint Culture. Now known from six coastal sites of the North Bering Sea and Kotzebue Sound and several closely related sites of the Brooks Range. Characterized by an abundance of microblades, burins, and burin spall artifacts and by the extremely delicate diagonal flaking of small weapon tips and edges, this is now the best-known of the early Alaskan cultures.

Old Whaling. A single site on Beach 53 at Cape Krusenstern includes the remains of five deep, winter houses and five summer houses built on the surface. This village was the home of a sealing and whaling people who worked flint, rather than slate, but whose harpoon heads and certain other objects were closely similar to those of quite recent Eskimos.

Choris and Choris-Trail Creek. Found thus far only at the Kotzebue Sound sites and the middle level of Trail Creek caves and characterized by many spear points nearly identical in form and appearance to those known to be much earlier along the western slope of the Rocky Mountains and elsewhere in the United States proper.[4] Here occurs the first pottery, impressed with cord marking (the earlier phase) and with linear stamping (the later phase). Choris people lived in great, oval houses and show few continuities with any of the cultures preceding them.

Norton Culture. Continues certain Choris traits, but has also inherited some of the artifact types and complexes of the old Denbigh Flint complex.

Ipiutak. Continues many Norton traits but is by no means a direct descendant of it, and becomes even more Denbigh-like in its use of small, bifaced side blades and end points.

Birnirk-Western Thule-Recent. Essentially modern Eskimo in a cast of culture breaking sharply with previous cultures, but proceeding in an unbroken continuity across all of Arctic coastal America and a sizable part of adjacent Asia.

Two objections to this proposed sequence of events have been made by archaeological theorists, some of whom are also Arctic field workers.[5] First, it had not been expected that the forms of spear points of early postglacial sites far to the south would be nearly duplicated in Arctic sites dating later than 5000 years ago. One or two workers had even gone so far as to place their collections in serial order, largely on the basis of the resemblance of a few spear points to forms dated in regional chronologies of the western states. Second, a few side-notched points from sites of the interior had been estimated by their excavators to belong with later materials such as pottery, and this viewpoint was upheld by the relatively late appearance of side-notched points

4. Detailed comparisons of these spear points appear in Giddings (1963).

5. See especially papers by H. B. Collins, J. M. Campbell, W. N. Irving, R. S. MacNeish, and J. B. Griffin in F. H. West (ed.), *Early Man in the Western American Arctic* (*Anthropological Papers of the University of Alaska*, **10,** No. 2, College, Alaska, 1963) and in J. M. Campbell (ed.), *Prehistoric Cultural Relations between the Arctic and Temperate Zones of North America* (*Arctic Institute of North America*, Technical Paper No. 11, Montreal, 1962).

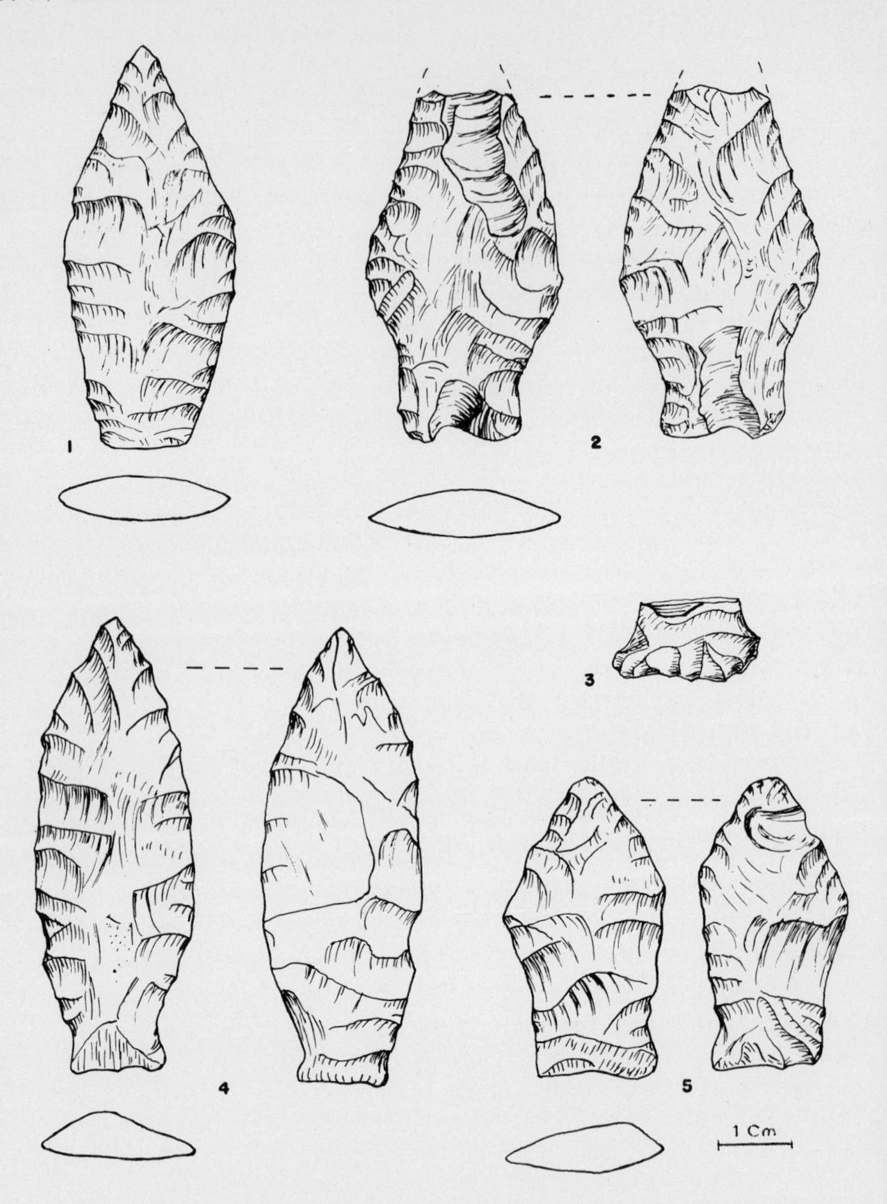

Figure 4.—Projectile points from lower levels, Onion Portage

1. Obsidian spear point, basal edges, and base ground (Band V of Figure 3).
2. Notched obsidian point (Band VI, layer 1 of Figure 3).
3. Base of notched chert point (Band V or VI of Figure 3).
4 and 5. Notched chert points (Band VI, layer 4 of Figure 3).

in the Archaic horizons of the Great Lakes region and the eastern United States. Furthermore, other theorists guessed, on the basis of proposed datings from distant places in Asia, that burins and microblades preceded, rather than followed, notched points in the Arctic area.

While each of these viewpoints could be upheld on a theoretical basis, there appeared to me to be no definitive site in the region that could counter the strong stratigraphic and serial evidence from Cape Denbigh and Cape Krusenstern—that is, that the two Palisades assemblages had preceded both microblades and most of the paleo-Indian forms of projectile points.

Now let us examine the Onion Portage column of Fig. 3 with a view to calculating its relationship to the coast. Beginning with the oldest cultural levels, the nine to twelve old culture-bearing ground surfaces of Band VI, we find the following traits: side-notched[6] points of chert (Fig. 4, Nos. 2–5), coarse choppers reminiscent of, but not closely like, those of Palisades I, rather large bifaced knife blades of chert and obsidian, and a wide variety of end scrapers. These were associated with numerous flakes that appear to outline areas within the bounds of bark tents of some kind. Here the traces were especially clear of birch bark or spruce bark lying directly on top of most of the hearths and the adjoining ground. The red ocher of these hearths seems to have been obtained in great quantities and powdered before distributing as a base for the fireplace. Hearths here are not customarily surrounded by stones.

In Band V was found a straight-based point (Fig. 4, No. 1) of obsidian. Obsidian was also generously used here for side scrapers, end scrapers, and large bifaces. The hearths contained, as they had in Band VI, quantities of bone fragments, mainly of caribou, that had been crushed into a "bone meal" of rather uniformly small size similar to that reported for recent Athapaskan sites of the interior. This was then burned in the fire. Bone meal does not distinguish any of the cultures of the coastal region in which hearths have thus far been located. In both Bands V and VI occurred artifacts of slate ground only on one edge. Some of these appear to have been implements used for the grinding of side notches on points found in the lower levels. Although hundreds of flakes were recovered from Bands V and VI, none indicated that their makers had a knowledge of either microblades or burins.

Band IV contained, in two or three layers, classic Denbigh Flint culture with microblades, burins, burin spall artifacts, and other definitive pieces. Its hearths, while containing most of the key artifact types of the Denbigh Flint culture, also displayed bone meal and layers of bark, as did the hearths of earlier bands. Fired pebbles or cracked stones lay within the hearths just as

6. While three of the specimens illustrated in Fig. 4 (2, 4, and 5) might also be described as "stemmed," each has been strongly edge-ground from 2 millimeters or more above the base, evidently by abrasion with a narrow grindstone, effecting shallow notches. Bases are also ground to some extent.

they did in the coastal sites of Denbigh culture, perhaps indicating that meat was boiled in baskets.

Most of the artifacts of Band III came from a single layer. We call the culture simply "Old Hearth." This material forms a sharp contrast to the preceding Denbigh. Obsidian artifacts, large bifaces, bone meal in the hearths, and other traits form a continuity with the pre-Denbigh horizons at the site. Most artifact types are very different from those of the Denbigh Flint culture, resembling in their thickness and certain specific forms artifacts known from the emerging early archaeology of central Alaska. Nearly the only connection with the Denbigh culture appears to be a bifaced side blade and a few crudely executed microblades, none with more than two facets. The bone meal in the hearths appears identical with that in Band VI.

In Band II, the lower charcoal-bearing strata show strong continuities with the Norton culture of the coast in materials used and in forms, which include side blades; end blades; scrapers; polished, burinlike instruments; thin whetstones; and others. The middle layer contains flints similar to those of Kayuk culture of Anaktuvuk Pass. The upper layer, however, departs sharply from the pattern of the lower ones. It is characterized by small flint weapon tips, thick and diamond-shaped in cross section, and by the extensive use of a unique material. This is a completely opaque obsidian. Light does not enter even the edges of thin flakes. This obsidian thus forms a horizon marker without parallel. Materials of this upper layer of Band II seem to relate more closely to those of the Old Hearth band than to the lower layers of its own band. The artifacts are unlike those known from coastal sites.

Finally, in Band I, the Thule-related culture of modern Eskimos enters the picture at Onion Portage. In its latest stage, as shown by an eighteenth century site on the upper Kobuk[7] and by ethnographic studies (Giddings: 1961b), a trend toward a more Indian-like culture had set in.

Indians or Eskimos?

The relationships of the sites of Kotzebue Sound to the layers at Onion Portage are indicated in Fig. 3 by the heavy, meandering line that separates some of the culture layers from others. Where a stippled space bounded by this line opens to the right, influence from the interior dominates the scene at Onion Portage. Spaces outside the line to the left indicate greater continuity of Onion Portage with coastal sites. Thus, Bands VI, V, all of III, and the upper part of II open to the interior, suggesting that a basic culture (or related cultures) has existed there since at least the end of last glaciation—a culture distinct in many ways from the coastal cultures of the last five or six thousand years. If we allow these spaces to stand for Indian languages, in contrast to

7. The Ambler Island site. See Giddings (1952).

another language at the coast, then we see strong continuities: the use of a great deal of obsidian, the only known source of which, in northern Alaska, is the Koyukuk River; the building of bark dwellings on the surface; the production of bone meal in hearths; the intensive use of red ocher, especially in the earliest period, but persisting in all periods; and the production of artifacts more nearly resembling those of early sites in the far interior of Alaska than those less than six thousand years old on the coast.

On the other hand, traits like those of the interior seldom occur on the coast after oldest Trail Creek and the Lower Bench at Cape Krusenstern. Rather, traits of the highly distinctive Denbigh Flint culture become dominant both on the coast and along the Kobuk River. The refined microblade technology of the Denbigh Flint culture probably entered the continent at Bering Strait at the time of Onion Portage Band IV and continued unbroken into the interior and then all the way along northern Canada to the northern tip of Greenland. Certain continuities—but not those of microblades, which end on the coast with the disappearance of the Denbigh Flint culture—are seen from the Denbigh into the Norton and Ipiutak cultures. A few different Denbigh traits appear in the Choris and Middle Trail Creek horizons. Only the Old Whaling culture is anomolous at present, containing, as it does, quantities of notched points, both large and small, but differing in most other respects from sites of the interior. It gives the impression of somehow having inherited notched points from the Palisades sequence and of developing along lines sharply distinct from the Denbigh-Ipiutak-Recent line of the coast.

Few areas exist in which a chronology is firm enough to be compared with that of Cape Denbigh, Cape Krusenstern, and Onion Portage, nor are there many parts of the world where sites occur on a natural borderline as broad as the forest edge of the Kobuk River region. The evidence thus far amassed from Kotzebue Sound and the Kobuk River strongly indicates that an inland influence dominated the cultural cast of peoples both of the Kobuk River and the coast from the end of the Wisconsin period to the time when microblades appeared on the coast. One might surmise that the introduction of microblades to this part of North America represents essentially an extension of the Mesolithic period of Europe (as Henry B. Collins (1960) has believed for some time[8]) and thus a microblade trail possibly older than most of the microblade phases of the Siberian "Neolithic." After the first microblades, however, the cultures in the Bering Strait region appear to have evolved locally, waxing and waning, producing specialties and losing them, down through at least four thousand years before the pattern we recognize as definitely Eskimo appears full-fledged on the coast and along the edge of the forest. Throughout all this time and earlier, the language spoken in the far inland forests appears to have been Indian. Who knows that it might not have been Athapaskan? The next

8. A recent statement on this point is found in Collins (1960).

seasons of excavation should, at any rate, provide more details, in precise chronological order, about the give and take between two contrasting ways of life. This has not previously been possible in so long a sequence in North America. It perhaps helps to fulfill Professor Hallowell's long-held hope for an "intercontinental perspective" in American culture history (Hallowell, *op. cit.*, p. 163).

In the meantime, we may recall from Onion Portage that people of all the bands from VI through II apparently resided there only temporarily and for the same explicit purpose: to meet the annual fall migration of caribou and to slaughter, butcher, and render oil until the hunt was over, just as more recent people have done, and, with modification in hunting methods, still do. If the application of linguistic labels to the inland people and those of the coast becomes too much of a burden, we can always fall back on the Arctic Woodland culture and guess that whatever language is spoken or whatever cultural advances or regressions are made in art or manners, people will come to Onion Portage again and again to repeat the patterns of hunting and living worked out by their first predecessors in the Kobuk Valley.

References

Collins, H. B.

1960: "Recent Trends and Developments in Arctic Archaeology," *Actes du VIe Congrès International des Sciences Anthropologiques et Ethnologiques*, Tome II (1er vol.) (Paris: Musée de l'homme), 373–377.

Giddings, J. L.

1952: *The Arctic Woodland Culture of the Kobuk River* (Philadelphia: University Museum), p. 118.

1960: "The Archeology of Bering Strait," *Current Anthropology*, **1**, 121–138.

1961a: "Cultural Continuities of Eskimos," *American Antiquity*, **27**, 155–173.

1961b: *Kobuk River People*, University of Alaska Studies of Northern Peoples, **1** (College, Alaska: University of Alaska Press).

1962: "Onion Portage and Other Flint Sites of the Kobuk River," *Arctic Anthropologist*, **1**, 6–27.

1963: "Some Arctic Spear Points and Their Counterparts," in F. H. West (ed.), *Early Man in the Western American Arctic* (Anthropological papers of the University of Alaska, **10**, 1–12).

1964: *The Archeology of Cape Denbigh* (Providence: Brown University Press).

Giddings, J. L., & Bandi, H.-G.

1962: "Eskimo-archäologische Strandwalluntersuchungen auf Kap Krusenstern Nordwest-Alaska," *Germania*, **40**, No. 1.

Hallowell, A. I.

1926: "Bear Ceremonialism in the Northern Hemisphere," *American Anthropologist*, **28**, 1–175.

Larsen, H.

1951: "De Dansk-amerikanske Alaska-ekspeditioner 1949–50," *Geografisk Tidsskrift*, **51**, 63–93.

1963: "The Trail Creek Caves on Seward Peninsula, Alaska," *Proceedings of the 34th International Congress of Americanists, Vienna*, 1960, 284–291.

Nelson, N. C.

1937: "Notes on Cultural Relations between Asia and America," *American Antiquity*, **2**, 267–272.

Rainey, F. G.

1939: "Archaeology in Central Alaska," *Anthropological Papers of the American Museum of Natural History*, **36**, 364–371.

DENNISON NASH AND
LOUIS C. SCHAW

Achievement and Acculturation: A Japanese Example[1]

Introduction

Does personality in an acculturation situation undergo change; if so, to what extent and in what directions, and what are the factors which cause such change? This, according to Hallowell (1955, pp. 307–309), is one of the important questions in the study of the psychological dimension of culture change. In order to answer this question Hallowell (1955, pp. 333–366) undertook an ingenious study of Ojibwa indians living at different levels of acculturation. Later, Spindler (1955), working in the same culture area, applied a refined research design to the same question. Although the importance of Hallowell's contribution is beyond dispute, we think that, like many pioneering ventures, it may have led to an increasingly one-sided view of acculturation—a view which we believe may be traced to the research design employed. In this essay we shall try to broaden the view of the acculturation process by

1. The study was made possible by a University of Connecticut Research Foundation grant. We are indebted to officials of the American and Japanese embassies in Havana who helped Nash to get the field work under way and to A. I. Hallowell, Jerold Heiss, and Benson Saler for critical comments on the manuscript.

using a different (but by no means fully adequate) research design which permits the consideration of an alternative explanation of observed personality changes in situations of culture change.

The procedure used by Hallowell and Spindler to show if, and how, personality change is related to acculturation is to demonstrate an association between acculturative categories and group personalities at a single point in time. Thus, Hallowell (1955, pp. 345–357) presents three groups of subjects which are drawn from Inland (least acculturated), Lakeside, and Flambeau (most acculturated) locations, and Spindler (1955) a series of groups on an acculturative continuum extending from native-oriented to elite-acculturated. The fact that the group personalities differ or do not differ in the various acculturative categories is taken to prove the effect of acculturation on personality. But a consideration of this method of proof will reveal that such a conclusion may be unwarranted. The inadequacy of this method is due, mainly, to its inability to discriminate effects which are the result of selection out of some traditional population by different acculturative situations from those which have been brought about through the process of learning in the acculturation situation. Still, both Hallowell and Spindler would regard differences in group personalities in the various acculturative categories as effects of acculturation. Thus, Hallowell (1955, p. 345), with his usual flair for putting the crucial question, asks, "Are the people at Flambeau, e.g., psychologically identifiable as Ojibwa despite their high level of acculturation? Or have they been psychologically transformed?"[2]

The question of causation here is a delicate one. A population in an acculturative category may exhibit a personality difference from that of a traditional category, but is this difference due to a selection of pre-existing traits by the situation or to a transformation of personalities through the process of learning in the situation? In both cases change would have occurred —change which has been caused. However, the processes of causation are different. A failure to differentiate between these two kinds of causation could have serious effects on our judgment about the plasticity of human personality under different conditions.

An appropriate experimental design for proving what Hallowell and Spindler claim to prove, i.e., the effects of acculturation on personality, is entered in Table I. It would be desirable to construct an experiment which would assess the group personalities of an acculturative (experimental) group and a traditional (control) group, both of which constituted representative

2. Such a question may be asked and answered in studies of this kind only if one of two assumptions is made: (1) The aboriginal population was homogeneous as to personality type; (2) the populations in the different acculturative categories began as representative samples of the aboriginal population. Both Hallowell and Spindler appear to have made the first assumption.

samples of some traditional population. Since the sampling procedure would rule out selection as a factor causing any differences in the personalities observed in the two groups, any differences in group personalities could be attributed to acculturative learning.

Table I.—Traditional Population Group Personality

Population 1[a]	*Population 2*[a]
ACCULTURATIVE (EXPERIMENTAL)	*TRADITIONAL (CONTROL)*
Group personality	Group personality

[a] Both populations 1 and 2 constitute representative samples of the traditional population.

Studies of immigrants seem to offer an excellent opportunity for such experimentation. Although it would be difficult to obtain groups with background and personality representative of a traditional population, it would be possible to mark their selectivity and thus assess the effects of selection in the first generation. The existence of a second, mature, immigrant generation would (were the effects of aging known and discarded) facilitate the charting of trends through time and the identification of factors associated with personality change or stability. In such studies it would be preferable to have similar aims, techniques, and specific foci of concern for each population.

In this article we will set up a natural experiment of this general type which will follow a specific personality trait, i.e., achievement motivation, through an immigrant-acculturation situation in an attempt to account for changes in its character. Our experiment deviates from the ideal model depicted in Table I. It sacrifices control and discrimination to the possibility of conducting such an experiment at all. Instead of an acculturative and traditional group there are two acculturative groups—Japanese immigrants to different acculturation situations—whose selection from the traditional (home) population could not be controlled. Accordingly, any differences between them may be not only the result of different acculturative experiences, but also selection from the traditional Japanese population. The schema is depicted in Table II.

Table II.—Traditional Population (Japanese) Group Personality

Population 1[a]	*Population 2*[a]
ACCULTURATIVE (EXPERIMENTAL) GROUP	*ACCULTURATIVE (EXPERIMENTAL) GROUP*
Group personality	Group personality

[a] The sampling of populations 1 and 2 from the traditional population was not controlled.

The two immigrant populations—each having two mature generations—are on the Isle of Pines, Cuba, and in Chicago, United States. The Isle of Pines group, which was founded by Issei migrants who came to the island between

1915 and 1930, was studied by Nash in field trips in 1956 and 1958. The Chicago group, begun by migrants from relocation camps between 1943 and 1946, was studied by Caudill and his associates in the period 1947–50 (Caudill: 1952).[3] The personality trait to be examined, i.e., the achievement motive, was elicited by the Thematic Apperception Test (TAT). It is supposed to be central to Japanese personality and was studied in the Chicago Japanese in a separate monograph by Caudill and DeVos (1956).

Murray defines the achievement need elicited by the TAT as "an active, persistent striving to accomplish something creditable" (1943, p. 9). This need appears to be roughly equivalent to the well-known *yamato damashii* or "Japanese spirit" which has been reported by a number of scholars (e.g., Benedict: 1946; Haring: 1946). It appears to be a distinctive Japanese trait (see McClelland: 1961, pp. 77–78). To trace the achievement motive through successive generations of Japanese immigrants to the New World, therefore, will be to inquire into the fate of one of the touchstones of Japanese identity abroad.

Acculturation Situation and Japanese Adaptation

The Isle of Pines Japanese live on an island which is 60 miles south of the Cuban mainland. This group is the largest single concentration of Japanese in Cuba. In 1958 it numbered 130 in a total Isle of Pines population of about 11,000—a population which, for the most part, is scattered thinly over the northern half of an island 30–40 miles across.

Although predominantly rural and agricultural, the Isle of Pines never has had big money crops such as sugar cane, tobacco, or coffee. Missing, too, since the heirs of Spanish crown grants sold out to American entrepreneurs around the turn of the present century, has been the large-scale hierarchical form of rural Cuban social organization known as the *latifundia* with its landed aristocracy dependent upon the labors of a numerous peasantry. No truly large-scale economic organization ever has developed on the Isle of Pines. The small, struggling agricultural enterprise has been typical.

Because the Isle of Pines is, politically, a part of Cuba, the history of its Japanese must be considered within the broader Cuban context. Significant Japanese migration to Cuba began during World War I. The immigrants came mostly from rural Japan. It was usual for an immigrant to enter Cuba as a contract laborer; then, when the contract was completed, to find work in agriculture or some service occupation. If successful in these endeavors he

3. Most of the Chicago Issei lived on the Pacific coast of the United States prior to relocation. They are said to have come to the United States "during the early part of the century" (Caudill and DeVos: 1956, p. 1102). We take this to mean that the time of immigration, being roughly the same in both immigrant groups, may be ruled out as a variable related to differences between them.

would acquire his own farm or business or return to Japan. This pattern is similar to that of the Japanese immigrants on the west coast of the United States (see Broom and Kitsuse: 1956).

The number of Japanese in Cuba increased to a peak of nearly 1000 between 1925 and 1930, then declined to 589 in 1955. The principal reasons for this decline appear to be economic success, which permitted a return to Japan, and barriers to further immigration, such as the loss of economic opportunities during the depression and the enforcement of an old immigration law against foreign workers in 1939. Unfortunately, we do not know how many Japanese returned to their homeland.

Japanese economic achievements in Cuba were said by informants to have been considerable, but the incarceration of all adult males during World War II tended to destroy their attainments. Upon release, these men found that they had lost much of their property and wealth and were faced with the prospect of beginning anew in their various enterprises. Their general economic condition again rose, but at the time of the field study, according to an official of the Japanese embassy, they still had not returned to their prewar level.

Japanese immigration to the Isle of Pines reflects the immigration pattern common to all of Cuba. Most of the Issei in the present colony arrived during the period 1915–30. With one or two exceptions, they came from a rural farm background. This should be compared with the larger urban component of Caudill's Chicago sample, only 62% of whom had a rural farm background (Caudill: 1952, pp. 77–78). Most of the Isle of Pines Issei came directly to Cuba, worked briefly on the mainland, then immigrated to the island. Their reception was favorable. In their life histories many of the Issei remark the friendly attitude of Pineros and contrast this with the attitude of mainland Cubans, who sometimes mistook them for Chinese against whom some prejudice and discrimination existed.

Anyone familiar with the Isle of Pines could have predicted the favorable reception of the Japanese and a toleration of their racial and cultural differences. Corria, for example, says that "*todos los prejuicios y odios originados en creencias y tradiciones de castas pierden en Isla de Pinos toda significacion*" (1959, p. 354). His view that there has been no significant prejudice may be a bit optimistic, especially where Negroes are concerned, but it is clear that discrimination because of racial and cultural differences does not appear to have hindered Japanese adaptation on the Isle of Pines.

The cultural cleavage between Cuban and American ways of life may have posed an adaptive problem for the Japanese by presenting them with a difficult choice of host models. The "American Way" was represented by a small but powerful group of residents, tourists, businessmen, and politicians who have been interested in the Isle of Pines through the years. The Cuban culture, which was maintained by the vast majority of Pineros and by most of the people encountered by the Japanese, was changing slowly in the general direction of American norms. The Japanese, therefore, were offered two lines of acculturation-assimilation. An extensive treatment of this choice and the reaction of the Japanese to it is included below.

Because of the low density of population, the favorable attitude toward squatting, and the customary small farm type of enterprise on the island, it was not too difficult for an Issei—after some success as a laborer and the subsequent acquisition of a wife from Japan—to begin the family farming enterprise for which he was so well prepared. Whatever success he then achieved was not at the cost of direct competition with the hosts. This may be attributed to the easy-going attitude of Pineros with whom he competed indirectly, the isolation from other families in the country, and the general looseness of an economic system which never was played for high stakes and which was controlled by a distant and only slightly comprehensible market in Havana and the United States. The Japanese are competitive, but the situation was not the kind to turn such competitive tendencies to their disadvantage as it did in Peru (see Tigner: 1954, pp. 582–625).

To measure objective achievement requires a knowledge of the values of the achiever. This is difficult in an acculturation situation where standards may be changing; but in Chicago it was made less difficult by the compatibility of the values of immigrants and hosts. Thus, Caudill and DeVos could use traditional measures of American achievement: education and occupational standing (1956, pp. 1103–1105). On the Isle of Pines where there is a comparatively slight division of labor these measures are less satisfactory. Achieved wealth is what counts. Still, one notices a shift in the avenue of achievement from the Issei to Nisei generation. Of 37 Issei males, 26 at the time of the study were in agriculture; 21 of these owned or operated their own farms and 5 of these 21 employed men from outside. Only 3 Issei were in commercial business (one of these also owned the largest Japanese farming enterprise). Of 25 Nisei males aged 13 or over, 17 worked in agriculture, 7 in commercial businesses, and 1 in skilled, nonagricultural labor. These data suggest an acculturative trend toward the urban mode of achievement followed by the Japanese in Chicago. The Isle of Pines immigrants, however, were only beginning the transition from a rural-agricultural to an urban-commercial-industrial existence while their Chicago counterparts were firmly established on the urban occupational ladder (Caudill and DeVos: 1956, p. 1105). The testimony of both Issei and Nisei Isle of Pines informants indicates their belief in the superiority of the urban line of achievement, but unless the economic character of the island changes drastically in the coming years the urban achievement pattern can be continued only at the cost of the disappearance of the colony by emigration to Havana or elsewhere. At the time of the last field trip several Nisei were considering such a move.

Although the Japanese as a group had, at the time of the study, no more than a slight edge in wealth over their Cuban neighbors, the Nisei outstripped the Cubans in formal education. Japanese parents saw schooling as essential to their children's success in life and felt that the most valuable education could be obtained at the American school on the island. The Nisei who attended this school and Cuban schools acquired a reputation for working hard at their studies. There is no evidence that this offended their Cuban and American schoolmates. Their teachers were delighted. This same pattern was found among the Nisei in Chicago. There, their formal education exceeded that of a control sample of Chicago Americans (Caudill and DeVos: 1956, p. 1104).

The Japanese colony on the Isle of Pines was spread out and loosely organized. At the time of the study there was only one formal association, a recently organized "Japanese Society" to help the sick and destitute, provide legal assistance, maintain the collective grave, and organize the few collective activities of the colony. None of the extrafamilial forms of social organization reported for *Suye Mura* by Embree existed (1939, pp. 112–177). In economic affairs the Japanese were almost as likely to cooperate with Cubans or Americans as among themselves. One gained the general impression of weak Japanese solidarity and considerable assimilation with Cuban hosts. These social facts were marked by the marriage of 3 Issei males and 2 Nisei females with Cubans (only those living on the Isle of Pines at the time of the study being counted) and the acquisition of Cuban citizenship by many of the Issei males.

The erosion of traditional Japanese culture in the enclave was marked by the near-disappearance of Buddhism and the yearly cycle of festivals found in *Suye Mura* by Embree as motivating and organizing forces (1939, pp. 135–137), the decline in the use of Japanese as the preferred language among the Nisei, and the disappearance of many Japanese items from the diet. Familism still remained, but only 13 of 56 Issei males had families on the Isle of Pines. Among the Issei there was a tendency to acquire Cuban, rather than American, traits in place of Japanese traits which were lost. Although they preferred American ways they were faced with the necessity of day-to-day contacts with Cubans. This required a certain "Cubanization." The greater social distance from Americans, also, seems to have made them less significant as models to the Issei.

The remaining facts about the colony may be told quickly. As in Chicago there was a bimodal age distribution of Issei and Nisei (see Caudill: 1952, p. 20) with the oldest Nisei only slightly behind their Chicago counterparts in beginning adult careers. As in many immigrant groups the first generation consists mostly of single males. Only 12 of 47 Issei males were married and living with spouses (3 with Cubans); 8 of 9 Issei females were married and living with spouses (all with Issei). Among the Nisei the sex ratio is fairly evenly balanced, but the lag of the males in establishing adult careers has caused a number of the females to look to the Cuban population for mates. One of 38 Nisei males and 6 of 35 Nisei females were married (3 of the latter with Cubans). In the period covered by the two field trips there was negligible emigration and immigration.

In summary, with the exception of their incarceration during World War II, the Isle of Pines Japanese were not hampered by discrimination in the pursuit of their goals. This fact may have contributed to the weak solidarity of the enclave and the comparatively advanced stage of acculturation-assimilation (see Warner and Srole: 1945, pp. 283–296). The undifferentiated economic system and the limited economic opportunities have retarded vertical mobility. As a consequence the cultural gap and associated conflict between the generations appears not to be so great on the Isle of Pines as in Chicago where the vertical mobility has been more rapid (Caudill: 1952, pp. 65–66). Finally, the existence of two host models—one more desirable and one more necessary—posed a problem of adaptation for the Issei which may not have been faced by their Chicago counterparts (see Caudill: 1952, p. 17).

Japanese Achievement Motivation as Revealed by the TAT

A shortened version of the TAT used by Caudill in his study of a sample of Chicago Japanese (Caudill: 1952) was administered in Spanish and English to 10 Isle of Pines Issei, 8 Nisei, and 15 Cuban males who were neighbors of Japanese. Males were selected to reduce the scope of the study and to facilitate the rapport with the fieldworker (Nash), who made an effort to cover all sectors of the Japanese colony, but who did not obtain representative samples. The Japanese group probably is selective of the more acculturated and intelligent men since the few who could not speak Spanish adequately or comprehend the task were not approached. The Issei "sample" constitutes about 21% of Issei males, the Nisei "sample" about 35% of Nisei males aged 17 or more. The ages of both groups seem to be representative of their respective universes. The median age of the Issei is slightly older than of Caudill's males (56.5 to 53.5); that of the Nisei, somewhat younger (22.5 to 28.7). In general, the Isle of Pines Nisei had not yet established their identity as adults while the Chicago Nisei appear to have done so. Problems of interpretation and comparison arising from this fact will be discussed below.

It would have been preferable to give the TAT to the Issei in Japanese rather than Spanish. There were some language difficulties in the administration. With the Nisei there were no language problems. The completed protocols were given to Schaw without translation. He knew beforehand only the general breakdown into Issei, Nisei, older and younger Cubans. His approach to the data was that of a clinical psychologist. He sought salient features of the personalities of the different groups in order to construct the "core personality" of each. His intensive analysis will be used to supplement the manifest content of the protocols as related to achievement.[4]

Caudill and DeVos used Cards 1 and 2 of the TAT series to assess the frequency of achievement motivation in their samples. Our discrimination of achievement-oriented responses follows their procedure (see Caudill and DeVos: 1956, pp. 1109–1112) and is reported (with comparative data from Chicago) in Table III. In it we see the frequency of achievement responses in the different

Table III.—Positive Achievement Responses (PAR) on TAT Cards 1 and 2 and Self-Motivated Responses (SM) on Card 1 of Isle of Pines and Chicago Japanese

	Isle of Pines		*Chicago*[a]	
	ISSEI	*NISEI*	*ISSEI*	*NISEI*
Totals (N)	10	8	30	40
Card 1				
PAR	3 (30%)	8 (100%)	20 (67%)	17 (43%)
SM	2 (25%)	5 (62.5%)	28 (93%)	25 (62%)
Card 2[b]	1 (10%)	7 (87.5%)	25 (83%)	22 (55%)

[a] The Chicago totals constitute representative samples. Those for the Isle of Pines do not.
[b] Self-motivated achievement responses were not scored on Card 2.

samples. We have not measured the strength of such responses in the manner of McClelland and his colleagues (1953). Our data indicate only the number of people whose achievement was sufficient to dictate the appropriate responses on Cards 1 and 2. In this regard the pattern is clear. On the Isle of Pines the frequency of achievement responses is very low among the Issei and high among the Nisei. In Chicago it is high among the Issei and declines somewhat among the Nisei. Typical stories given by the Isle of Pines Japanese, together with the psychological interpretation and comparison with the Chicago data, are given below.

Card 1 (showing a boy contemplating a violin)

Response of Issei male, aged 64 (translated): A child, no? A boy or girl child. He is looking at this—what is it called?—a part of this violin. It looks like there is something the matter with it. And this child is looking at it to find out what is wrong. Nothing more. His look is here [he indicates the violin]. (What is he thinking?) He understands how to play the violin well. He knows how to play it. (?) I don't know what he is thinking, but it is about the violin. (What will happen?) He will speak to his father so that he will look for another violin. He certainly doesn't like this one.

4. Nine cards of the TAT were used (Murray: 1943). The cards were: 1, 2, 3BM, 4, 6BM, 16, 17BM, 19. These were the cards which Caudill (who tested both males and females) had used for his male subjects. Schaw's analysis of the protocols follows the line taken by Henry (1947) in his discussion of the TAT in personality and culture studies.

Interpretation and comparison: No Positive Achievement Response was scored for this story. It is in marked contrast to the Issei example given by Caudill and DeVos (1956, p. 1110) in which the boy "in the end, because he holds steady, becomes a good player." Not only does the Isle of Pines example not reveal achievement, but it points out a defect which may or may not be remedied with outside assistance. What the subject seems to be saying is that the hero may or may not hold his own by the time the episode is over. This response, which may in part be a function of advancing age, illustrates the tentative, often fearful approach of most of the Issei and their very limited aspirations.

Response of Nisei male, aged 30: He is thinking of studying how to play the violin. Yes, he wants to study how to play the violin. He wants to go into the theater where there are many people. He also is thinking of going to various parts of the world. Also, he is thinking of studying. Yes, he will study. (What will happen?) He will be a great man. He will study well and later he will be a great musician.

Interpretation and comparison: This story shows the hero attaining success through his own efforts (particularly through education). There appears to be little doubt about the attainment of a goal if the individual applies himself. All of the Nisei show a similar achievement pattern—one that is shared by only 3 of 10 Issei, by none of 9 older Cubans, and by 2 of 6 young Cuban adults.

In Chicago, while most of the Nisei see the boy as positively achieving and self-motivated, significant numbers, according the Caudill and DeVos (1956, p. 1110), "see him as assigned a task and in conflict with his parents." Although the incidence of positive achievement responses is about the same in the two groups of Nisei, the Isle of Pines protocols indicate less conflict between generations in the area of achievement. The individual is self-motivated but in the framework of the collectivity. In Chicago this traditional Japanese orientation appears to be breaking down under the impact of a different mode of achievement (Caudill and DeVos: 1956, p. 1117). A typical Isle of Pines Nisei response to another card may be used to illustrate further the place of the group in individual achievement.

Card 7 BM (showing an older and younger man)

Response of Nisei male, aged 30 (translated): This fellow is talking with his father about some big business which will make him rich, but his father doesn't seem to like it. He thinks that he's going to ask for a lot of money. His father tells him over and over that he shouldn't spend too much. (What will happen?) The fellow for sure is going to become rich and work hard. He will build a house for his father and for himself. (What advice is the father giving him?) Not to fail in business.

In summary, achievement motivation, which almost disappeared among the remaining Isle of Pines Issei, is revived among the Nisei. In Chicago it is characteristic of both generations, but there is a decline in its incidence among the Nisei. Our problem is to explain why the frequency of this important Japanese trait takes a different course in the two acculturation situations.

At this point it is well to recall that the experimental model depicted in Table I requires that migrant populations to different acculturation situations have the same group personalities and background. However, the Issei in Chicago and on the Isle of Pines who remained to be studied in these situations *do not have* exactly the same backgrounds. More of the Chicago Issei come from urban, upper-status milieus (Caudill: 1952, pp. 77–78), and since McClelland's data (1961, p. 379) suggest that higher achievement motivation is associated with such status in Japan, this indicates that the different frequencies of achievement orientation are at least in part due to differential selection of this trait in the two migrant populations. In addition, we would speculate that achievement-motivated Issei tend to seek out and succeed in areas with greater economic opportunity. Chicago has been such an area. The Isle of Pines, as we have seen, is not. We believe that at least some of the difference in the frequency of achievement motivation in the two Issei populations may be explained in terms of these two kinds of selection.

Unfortunately, we do not have the data to tell us whether achievement motivation (as measured here) may be lost or gained in adults. From McClelland's (1961, pp. 336–390) emphasis upon the family of orientation as a source of achievement motivation, it would seem that radical changes in adulthood would be unlikely. There is a remote possibility, however, that some of the Isle of Pines Issei may have lapsed from a posture of achievement because of certain incompatibilities in their acculturation situation. In the process of assimilation-acculturation an immigrant group uses host models as guides. There may be several potential models, in which case the immigrant must make a choice. One of the factors in making this choice probably stems from the necessity of taking the role of the other in his daily contacts. Another may be the appearance to the immigrant of a compatibility with his own values (see Caudill: 1952, p. 17; Kluckhohn: 1953, p. 354; Ruesch: 1953, p. 133). On the Isle of Pines the latter factor would dictate the choice of Americans rather than Cubans as host models. But although the Japanese had important early contacts with Americans as employees they required some "Cubanization" to get along in what was for them a predominantly Cuban world. Thus, in entertaining a desirable (American) model and a necessary (Cuban) model they may have laid themselves open to conflict resulting from the incompatibility of the two. In turn, such conflict might have led to a lapse of striving in some of the Issei. Our interviews indicate that the Japanese tend to admire Americans but not Cubans. We know also that there were more contacts with, and less social distance from, Cubans. Whether this situation led to conflict and a lapse of striving, however, is an hypothesis which we cannot test with the data at hand.

Just as the data for the first generation of immigrants represent a selection from those for some traditional population, the data for the second generation are a selection from the first. On the Isle of Pines this selection appears to be related to achievement motivation among the Issei. Who are the Issei who produce Nisei—all of whom, in our sample, show achievement motivation? They tend to be found among the more successful. This may be understood if we recall that it was customary for the Japanese immigrant not to marry until he had acquired some wealth and prospects. These attainments, therefore, were prerequisites for marriage and the production of offspring. In turn, a family was an economic asset which furthered the success of the originally successful and led them to further reproduction. This circular course of events resulted in the most successful Issei having the largest families. Now, since it is our impression that on the Isle of Pines the most successful male Issei are achievement-oriented, a pattern of "differential reproduction" appears to exist which makes it more likely for a son to be born of an achievement-oriented Issei. Thus, selection by social success becomes an important factor to consider in explaining the radical change in the frequency of achievement motivation from the Issei to the Nisei group.

Earlier, we suggested that an incompatibility of values may have led to personality conflict which resulted in a lapse from striving among the Isle of Pines Issei. It may be that the same principle will account for the decline in the incidence of achievement motivation among the Chicago Nisei. As Caudill and DeVos (1956, p. 112) put it, "The Japanese values and adaptive mechanisms learned from the Issei help the Nisei in . . . achievement, but they cannot both live up to the expectations of the American world and, at the same time, fulfill their obligations to their parents." Coupled with this problem is the tabu on the traditional mode of tension release in physical indulgence among the more acculturated Nisei (Caudill: 1952, p. 32). The incompatibility of host and parental values, coupled with the disappearance of a previously effective tension release, could account for the many passive-masochistic adjustments found by Caudill (1952, pp. 75–76) and for the concomitant decline in the frequency of achievement motivation. In Chicago mobility and acculturation lead to an exposure to incompatible values which may result in psychological conflict and a lapse from achievement. On the Isle of Pines the tempo and direction of mobility and acculturation appear not to have been sufficient to produce such incompatibilities. Since achievement does not threaten Nisei values there is no reason to give it up.

So far we have discussed differences in the incidence of achievement motivation. It is possible to use the term "change" to cover the differences between generations in the same population providing that such change is conceived to be the effect of both selection and acculturation. But a consideration of such change should not obscure the broader problem of survival of the trait. Why has the achievement motive survived—and even spread—in the acculturation situations? The evolutionist would answer an analagous problem in terms of the principle of adaptation. We think that this principle, if properly qualified, may be used in situations of acculturation.

Although the process of adaptation in all acculturation situations is a "two-way street," the existence of power differences between the parties involved puts the burden of adaptation on subordinates. The Japanese immigrants to the Isle of Pines were subordinate to both Cuban and American hosts. Their adaptation would be a function of their ability to create a role which would enable them, not only to cope with the new environment, but also to avoid discrimination by the more powerful hosts. To the extent that the achievement motive would contribute to such a role it would be compatible with the new situation.

An immigrant will avoid discrimination if he plays a role which does not violate host values. The Japanese as an achiever in Chicago and on the Isle of Pines apparently has not hampered his adaptation by eliciting discrimination. Indeed, Japanese achievers frequently are admired. In Chicago, American employers praise them for traits which probably are related to achievement orientation (e.g., efficiency, punctuality, willingness to work overtime) (Caudill: 1952, pp. 22–23). On the Isle of Pines most Americans display a similar attitude, and most Cubans (who, in terms of those tested, only infrequently show achievement motivation on the TAT) praise them for their hard work and for their economic attainments in the face of obstacles.

If status is taken as a measure of immigrant effectiveness in coping with their new environment, then achievement orientation appears to be related to this aspect of adaptation in Chicago and on the Isle of Pines. Japanese achievers in Chicago have shown remarkable vertical mobility which may result, paradoxically enough, in a decline in adaptation among the Nisei. On the Isle of Pines, the performance of Issei achievers and their families has led to their pre-eminence in the colony. We thus conclude that achievement motivation contributed to a role which enabled the immigrants, not only to cope with their new environment, but also to avoid discrimination by the more powerful hosts. It was therefore compatible with the new situation.

In conclusion, we should make clear that our discussion of the achievement motive and adaptation is based on the assumption that the use of defensive measures tends to hinder adaptation. The more defensive measures which are required to deal with internal or external conflict in the new situation the less energy will be available to cope with the environment. If the adaptive role violates the immigrant's values, or if the role he chooses to play violates those of the hosts, he may have to resort to defensive measures to maintain himself. The pre-existence of, or the ability to acquire, personality traits compatible with the new situation would minimize defensive measures and thus promote adaptation. In the case of the Japanese immigrants the compatible trait, i.e., the achievement motive, appears to have pre-existed in the migrating groups.

The Revival of the Achievement Motive among the Isle of Pines Nisei

So far we have been concerned with the frequency of the achievement motive in the various groups: We have not investigated its other dimensions nor its "fit" in the context of individual personalities in a changing social situation. The Isle of Pines Nisei are particularly interesting subjects for such deeper probing. It will be recalled that among them the achievement motive experienced a revival after suffering near-eclipse in the first generation Issei.

Schaw, in his analysis of the Nisei TAT records, divided the Nisei into two groups: one in which an adult identity had been attained, and the other in which it was not yet established. Among the "late-adolescents" are two further categories of persons: one in which achievement motivation is tenuous because a large part of the individual's energy is devoted to defensive measures, the other in which a maximum amount of energy is available for coping with the external world through achievement. We shall concern ourselves with the four Nisei in the latter group. They are very close to what we consider to be ideal adaptors in this situation.

The Achievement Motive in the Four Nisei Adaptors—In the personalities of these young men the achievement motive establishes the principal line of fulfillment and plays the major part in the organization of personality. Achievement for them involves a rational mastery of things rather than persons, i.e., what Parsons has called "instrumental activism." In the service of future accomplishment, strong but flexible controls are mobilized to postpone gratification. Although the four Nisei show the uncertainties and conflicts associated with a late-adolescent identity crisis there is a basic confidence in their ability to handle future situations. A generalized set of values enables them to remain detached from specific situations and therefore increases their range of adaptability.

Although these Nisei feel responsible as individuals for their fate, they tend to view the older generation as reasonable authorities who collaborate in projects for the benefit of themselves and their family. There is some intergenerational conflict which tends to be resolved in accord with broad parental expectations, giving the individual much leeway in which to establish an identity. The result is a strong but "benevolent" system of controls in the service of the gist of traditional Japanese values and considerable personal autonomy for the individual Nisei. As a result the individual is not threatened with the possibility of alienation from his family as in Chicago. On Card 2, which was used by Caudill and DeVos to elicit possible conflict related to achievement, the problem of leaving the farm does not arise for the Isle of Pines Nisei. In

Chicago, on the other hand, 60% of the Nisei saw the heroine leaving the farm and 25% saw her "leaving negatively" (Caudill and DeVos: 1956, p. 1112).

The Achievement Motive in the Changing Social Context—The four Nisei adaptors come from families which illustrate "the Japanese spirit" in action, i.e., ceaseless, collaborative efforts by all in the direction of economic achievement. In this family environment, we surmise, lies one source of their achievement motivation.

What models for achievement orientation existed outside the family? Within the colony there were the leaders who had particularly adaptive personalities (see Nash and Schaw: 1962–63). But the influence of these men probably was weakened by the looseness of enclave structure. Among the hosts the Cubans were not taken seriously as models by most Japanese. A comparison of the TAT records of Japanese leaders and Cubans suggests why. Where the Japanese postpone gratification, the Cubans want immediate gratification. The Japanese tend to active mastery; the Cubans to passive mastery. The Japanese have strong controls; the Cubans, weak controls. Where the Japanese lean toward an active manipulation of things, the Cubans tend toward a passive manipulation of others, including the supernatural. While the Japanese feel responsible for their individual and group attainments, the Cubans feel that external forces, e.g., God, fate, which can be manipulated wishfully, are mainly responsible for their destinies. Among the Japanese the generations collaborate to achieve common goals; among the Cubans they sabotage one another by mutual seduction. Both groups would like to become rich, but the systematic, purposeful pursuit of this goal is beyond the Cubans. In the Japanese leader-model, therefore, we see an image which we have come to associate with the Protestant Ethic in Western society. The Cubans are very close to the polar opposite.

That Americans were taken as models by the Japanese is indicated by the fact that Americans frequently are pointed out to Japanese children as exemplars of desirable behavior. The high value put on an American education also suggests this. Unfortunately, no sample of TAT protocols was obtained from Isle of Pines Americans, but interviews and association with many of them who have been in contact with the Japanese point to a core personality not unlike that believed to be associated with small-town and rural North America, i.e., a sober, reliable, hard-working, practical, individualistic, rational man of action with limited horizons—a sort of low-keyed example of the Protestant Ethic.[5]

5. The field investigator (Nash) did not realize that Americans might be significant models until too late. He was under the mistaken impression that the Japanese eventually would have to become like Cubans whether they liked it or not. But the pluralistic atmosphere on the Isle of Pines, the direction of culture change, and the desire of the Japanese did not make such a course inevitable (except, perhaps, in the children of those Issei who married Cubans). This error emphasizes the importance of ascertaining the immigrant definition of the situation in predicting assimilation-acculturation.

The favorable attitude of the Japanese toward Americans was reciprocated, but the social distance between Japanese and Americans—which may be due largely to differences in economic status—tended to prevent contacts with them. Japanese and Cuban countrymen, however, often spoke of themselves as belonging to the same group, i.e., *guajiros*, and there was less social distance between them.

In summary, models for the Isle of Pines Nisei were found in their families, among the Japanese léadership, and in the American colony. In addition, the Cubans constituted a necessary, if not desirable, model. Some Isle of Pines Issei maintain that the Nisei have become "just like Cubans." In dress, language, modes of recreation, and religion (more specifically, no religion), this is quite true. But these are only externals. On the deeper level of personality an identity is worked out somewhere between the collaborative mode of striving of the Japanese leaders and the more individualistic mode of Americans.

The Achievement Motive and Adaptation—With the exception of a brief wartime interlude, the Nisei adaptors grew up in a society where Japanese were accepted and even admired. We have invoked the principle of selection to account for their early exposure to an achievement-oriented (family) environment. Their "choice" of extrafamilial Japanese and host models would be in line with this orientation. But the Nisei, although appearing as imitations of their achievement-oriented models in a statistical table, have personalities which give them a considerable range of personal autonomy somewhere between Japanese-traditional and urban-industrial culture. According to our schema for classifying adaptive types of personality in a changing situation they are *Autonomous Men*, i.e., individuals who show a detachment from crippling involvements, a secure identity, and a broad, differentiated, and flexible emotional repertoire (Nash and Schaw: 1962–63).

It is because these Nisei are achievement-oriented *Autonomous Men* that they are well-prepared for the certain rationalization of Cuba. Although dramatic developments have followed the Castro revolution, the basic current of change established under American hegemony continues. In situations of rapid social change the autonomous type of personality is an asset. Further, achievement-orientation, as McClelland (1961, p. 262) has indicated, may flourish in either Communist or capitalist countries. Thus, the Nisei appear to have as favorable expectations as any in the new Cuba.

Conclusion

In this study of Japanese personality in an immigration situation we designed a crude natural experiment to follow the course of achievement motivation among successive generations in two immigrant populations. The group on the Isle of Pines, Cuba, has received most of our attention.

In accounting for the survival and changes in achievement motivation in the immigrant populations we have implied that adaptive traits tend to survive and spread in an immigrant population. Adaptation was seen to be a function of the ability of the immigrants to create a role which would enable them not only to cope with the new environment, but also to avoid discrimination. Personality traits which contribute to such a role could be called compatible with the situation. The existence of such traits in an immigrant population could come about by selection or by learning in the acculturation situation. The principle of compatibility as used here is an elaboration of the definitive conception provided by the Social Science Research Council (1954, pp. 983–984). Such an elaboration may dampen the enthusiasm of those who would use this principle indiscriminately to account for adaptation. An examination of Caudill's "compatibility" hypothesis concerning the adaptation of the Chicago Japanese will prove instructive in this regard.

The reason for the resounding success of the Japanese in Chicago is, according to Caudill (1952, p. 9), the compatibility of Japanese and American middle-class values and the resulting similarity of psychological adaptive mechanisms. This compatibility, which appears to center around achievement, enabled the Japanese to play a role which not only coped admirably with the new situation, but also was favorably evaluated by the hosts. However, a compatibility of values does not always lead to success in both aspects of adaptation (nor does Caudill say that it does). In the case of the Jews in the United States, for example, a compatibility of values again centering on achievement led to coping behavior by the Jews but discrimination by the hosts (see Simpson and Yinger: 1958, pp. 314–321). In the case of the Japanese in Peru a lesser compatibility of values resulted in coping behavior by the Japanese and discrimination by hosts (see Tigner: 1954, pp. 619–625). Thus it appears that the adaptivity of both aspects of the role which reflects a personality trait or value should be considered if its compatibility is to be assessed. In addition, structural (e.g., competition) and demographic (e.g., size of immigrant group) factors must be considered in predicting adaptation. In Chicago, according to Caudill (1952, p. 8), and on the Isle of Pines these factors were favorable.

The problem of personality change and stability in a changing situation also has been illuminated by our data. If change is measured in terms of the disappearance of old, and the acquisition of new, traits in individual personalities —such change being marked off against some premigration base line—then the dramatic "flip-flop" phenomenon on the Isle of Pines may have involved very little change. Because of a somewhat improved (but by no means adequate) research design we were able to suggest selection, not learning through acculturation, as a factor associated with the decline in the frequency of achievement motivation among the Issei and increase among the Nisei there. The student of personality change must be alert to changes which simply are a matter of selection of pre-existing traits as distinct from those which occur in acculturation. It is our impression that previous studies—perhaps influenced by Hallowell's fascinating pioneering work—have tended to assert the latter factor without considering the former. This appears to be because traditional populations in the past have been *assumed* to be relatively homogeneous. Recently, Wallace (1961) and others have pointed to the considerable variability of personalities in primitive societies, and it is quite possible that *all* of the differences noted by Hallowell and Spindler in their different acculturative categories may be due ultimately to the selection of different types from the range available in the aboriginal societies.

Our study of the Japanese immigrants to the Isle of Pines and Chicago has raised, not settled, the problem of selection vs. acculturative learning. Consequently, this investigation has not produced hard results concerning the plasticity of personality. We were, however, able to suggest an hypothesis concerning personality changes in which selection, not acculturative learning, plays a major role. Further evidence about the distribution of achievement motivation in the traditional population and in the immigrant populations shortly after arrival would help us to weigh the effect of each factor and to make some definitive statement about personality change or stability in a specific range of acculturative experience. The ultimate experiment, of course, would be a longitudinal study incorporating the design on Table I. The difficulties of carrying out such a natural experiment may prove to be insurmountable, but until it is done we shall have nothing better than plausible hypotheses concerning personality change in acculturation situations.

References

Benedict, R.
1946: *The Chrysanthemum and the Sword* (Boston: Houghton Mifflin).
Broom, L., & Kitsuse, J.
1956: "The Managed Casualty," in *Culture and Society*, Vol. 6 (Berkeley: University of California Press).
Caudill, W.
1952: "Japanese-American Personality and Acculturation," *Genetic Psychology Monographs*, **45**, 3–102.
Caudill, W., & De Vos, G.
1956: "Achievement, Culture, and Personality: The Case of the Japanese-Americans," *American Anthropologist*, **58**, 1102–1126.
Corria, F. R.
1959: *Excerta de una Isla Magica*, Mexico, D. F.: Editorial Olimpo.
Embree, E.
1939: *Suye Mura: A Japanese Village* (Chicago: University of Chicago Press).
Hallowell, A. I.
1955: *Culture and Experience* (Philadelphia: University of Pennsylvania Press).

Haring, D.
1946: "Aspects of Personal Character in Japan," *Far Eastern Quarterly*, **6**, 12–22.

Henry, W. E.
1947: "The Thematic Apperception Technique in the Study of Culture-Personality Relations," *Genetic Psychology Monographs*, **45**, 3–135.

Kluckhohn, F.
1953: "Dominant and Variant Value Orientations," in C. Kluckhohn, H. Murray, & D. Schneider (eds.), *Personality in Nature, Society and Culture* (rev. ed.; Cambridge: Harvard University Press), pp. 342–360.

McClelland, D.
1961: *The Achieving Society* (New York: Van Nostrand).

McClelland, D., Atkinson, J., Clark, R., & Lowell, E.
1953: *The Achievement Motive* (New York: Appleton-Century-Crofts).

Murray, H. A.
1943: *Thematic Apperception Test* (3rd rev. ed.; Cambridge: Harvard University Press).

Nash, D., & Schaw, L.
1962 63: "Personality and Adaptation in an Overseas Enclave," *Human Organization*, **21**.

Ruesch, J.
1953: "Social Technique, Social Status, and Social Change in Illness," in C. Kluckhohn, H. Murray, & D. Schneider (eds.), *Personality in Nature, Society, and Culture* (rev. ed.; Cambridge: Harvard University Press), pp. 123–136.

Simpson, G., & Yinger, J. M.
1958: *Racial and Cultural Minorities* (rev. ed.; New York: Harper).

Social Science Research Council
1954: "Acculturation: An Exploratory Formulation," *American Anthropologist*, **56**, 973–995.

Spindler, G.
1955: "Sociocultural and Psychological Processes in Menomini Acculturation," *University of California Publications in Culture and Society*, Vol. 5 (Berkeley: University of California Press).

Tigner, J.
1954: *The Okinawans in Latin America* (Washington, D.C.: Pacific Science Board, National Research Council).

Wallace, A. F. C.
1961: *Personality and Culture* (New York: Random House).

Warner, W. L., & Srole, L.
1945: *The Social Systems of American Ethnic Groups* (New Haven: Yale University Press).

RUBEN E. REINA

Cultural Duality and Behavioral Integration: The Human Skulls Ritual among the Lowland Maya of Northern Guatemala

Yearly, the inhabitants of San José in the Department of Peten, Guatemala, hold a ritual using three human skulls.[1] This ritual, an important celebration in the Catholic calendar of the community, constitutes a key for understanding the community culture, and permits the simultaneous exploration of three areas of theoretical interest to anthropologists. These are (1) the cultural synthesis which resulted from the acculturation of the Maya under Spanish domination; (2) the continuity of a ritual in early Maya periods, related to specific myths but changed by the Spanish conquest; and (3) the ritual's prevailing association with the present dual "folk-urban" orientation as well as its theoretical implications for understanding current culture change. "Acculturation," "ritual and myth," and "folk-urban" are, then, the concepts in the foreground of this paper. Because this work is not concerned with a critical review of these concepts I should only like to draw attention to the

1. The ethnographic investigations which yielded the information for this ritual were carried out during a fifteen-month period of field work in 1961–62 under the sponsorship of the National Science Foundation of Washington.

classic discussions of Redfield, Herskovits, and Linton (1936) for the concept of acculturation; the excellent treatment of myth and ritual by Kluckhohn (1942); and the writings of Redfield (1941) and Miner (1952) for the folk-urban concepts. Furthermore, we need to make special mention of the important methodological and theoretical contribution on these subjects of acculturation and myth made by Dr. A. Irving Hallowell. His valuable contributions began in the year 1921 and after publishing numerous papers, he prepared his book *Culture and Experience* (Hallowell: 1955), presenting the essence of his thinking. This work has guided and inspired innumerable students of the behavioral sciences around the world.

The history of the Peten has unique features when compared to the history of the rest of Mesoamerica (Reina: 1961). The Peteneros are descendants of the Maya of Yucatan; more specifically descendants of the Itza, whose origin is not clear but who migrated into the Peten perhaps as early as the thirteenth century (see Cowgill: 1963). Many attempts to conquer these people were made from both north and south, but they were unsuccessful until 1697, a relatively late date when compared with the conquest of Highland Guatemala in 1524. Subject then to a delayed colonization program, these people came under experienced Franciscan and Dominican fathers from Yucatan, who undertook the Peten's spiritual conquest. However, the distance of the Peten from Mérida, strenuous conditions of travel through the tropical rain forest, feelings of isolation and destitution among the clergy, poverty, and frequent political unrest caused many settlements to be only periodically indoctrinated, and frequently left unattended for prolonged periods of time.

These first groups of Itzas were later joined by people from Yucatan, who had already had two centuries of exposure to Spanish program of colonization. The remaining migratory groups spread into the Peten during the course of two centuries, and, as a consequence, the spectrum of Yucatan's population is well represented throughout the villages and towns of the department. The community of San José, located on the shore of Lake Peten Itza, is 99% Maya, and most of the inhabitants are predominantly descended from the early Itzas encountered by Hernan Cortez in 1525.

In the many dramatic encounters between the clergy and the natives of the New Spain, it has been evident that "It is easy to dismember men with cannons; it is more difficult to tame their minds" (Wolf: 1959, p. 167). The clergy had difficulty in establishing the new religion, and on many occasions made use of its political power to eliminate what it did not approve by means of inquisition. It is uncertain, however, how "Indians from Yucatan began to combine some elements of Christian worship with their old idolatrous practices, but we learn of an Indian of rank of Zotuta by the name of Don Andres Cocom who, about the year 1585, was convicted, not only of idolatry, but also as a perverse dogmatizer and inventor of new abominations among Indians" (Roys: 1943, pp. 202–203). This harsh treatment of the natives by means of inquisition caused the depopulation of villages. The acuteness of the problem resulted in a re-evaluation of church policy. A Royal command (*Real Cédula*) of the eighteenth century ordered every Spaniard to do whatever possible, in a peaceful way, to bring back the Maya from the forest and get them to live in villages. The clergy in Peten and Yucatan became more tolerant of some of the natives' views and rituals. As a result, there is a great deal of the early Maya religious element in the Catholicism currently practiced.

One finds nowadays that most corporate Indian communities introduced to Catholic practices after the conquest hold a ritual on November 1 to aid the souls of departed relatives. Redfield and Villa Rojas (1934: p. 202) report that in Chan Kom, Yucatan, "all souls of the dead return to earth for an annual visit and depart . . . tables are arranged at midnight . . . to invite the dead in. Chocolate, bread and several lighted candles [are placed] on the table . . . one *jícara* of chocolate, one piece of bread, and one lighted candle [are] set in [the] doorway for souls with no living kin."

In the Highlands of Guatemala, Catholics of Mayan descent prepare themselves for the visit of the souls of relatives on the same date. There are insignificant variations from village to village as to the time, length, and elaboration of the event. The Pokomam-speaking people of Chinautla,[2] which is located only nine miles from Guatemala City, take food to the cemetery. Much of it is placed at the head of the tomb and left there. Offerings include liquor, cigars, or sweets liked by the dead. The grave is outlined by many dozens of small, lighted candles awaiting the return of the soul. Relatives spend most of the day feasting and exchanging food with each other. At sunset the people feel that the souls will leave, and the women end the event by dramatizing the departure with expressions of grief. For seven years after a death, this practice is important to living people because it is a way to gain favor with the souls, who can do "god-like or devil-like actions" to people on earth. There is no elaborate myth, nor a purely non-Catholic explanation for this nowadays, although progressive people tend to explain their doings in a theological manner, to some extent in accordance with Catholic doctrine. No human skulls are used in the Highlands, as far as is known. San José, Peten, is the one community where the human skulls play a central role in the November ceremony.

November 1st Celebration with Human Skulls

The use of the skulls, the reactions of the people, and the history in the community of this ritual provide the basis for the following description.

Located conspicuously in the left-hand corner of the main church altar

2. Chinautla was studied by the author in 1955–56 (see Reina, 1960).

were three human skulls without the lower jaws. They showed no sign of ever having been buried. Each one was identified by a distinctive mark of gum pasted on the forehead.[3] According to local legend, they have been there since time "immemorial." The oldest people today remember their grandparents' saying that they belonged to *gentes muy finas* (fine people), *priostes* (stewards), but, they add, who knows (*a saber*). The skulls' actual identity has been lost, and there is no old myth to support their meaning and power.

November marks the end of the rainy season. Storms are not as frequent and as rhythmical as in the previous months, and the night of the ritual in 1961 was clear, bringing out the silhouettes of the people gathered in the streets. They were patiently awaiting the important hour. A few young men from the nearby community of San Andres were conspicuous for their boisterousness; they are the "uninvited" guests, year after year. "They are not here for devotion," remarked a San Joseño, "but for eating and drinking." The priest had been invited from the nearby town to say a mass early in the evening, but only a small group of twenty women and children attended the service. The majority of San Joseños do their utmost to be in town on this night, leaving their temporary residences in the forest and chicle camps. The gathering for the celebration would appear to be conducive to the customary heavy drinking. However, San Joseños do not drink on this night.

There is an elder in the town, a *prioste*, in charge of the organization of the celebration.[4] The *prioste* exerts a very quiet leadership throughout the ritual. Early in the day, only one of the skulls is placed in a newly decorated position on the main altar of the church. The *prioste* is informed at the beginning of the year of the families who are willing to receive the skulls in their homes. In 1960 there were nine families on his list. Among the reasons given by the families wishing to honor the skull were illness, an experience which brought the person near to death, the death of a son, desire for protection, devotion and faith.

It was nearly midnight. One of the church bells—dated 1718—announced the departure of the procession from the church. Some of the people in the streets joined it, while others went to their homes or remained behind. There is the belief that when a person joins the procession he must continue until its completion. Otherwise, his indifference is punished. A young man with a large crucifix of wood hanging from his neck led the procession. Cradled in his left arm he held the tin plate on which the skull rested, and he held a homemade candle in his right hand. Three young boys preceded him with a large wooden cross and two tall candleholders. The group of prayermakers, reciting an old liturgy of the church for the occasion, followed them.

3. For the purpose of rotation, the skulls are identified as 1, 2, and 3. The numbers are formed with gum and pasted on the skulls' foreheads.

4. There is no active *cofradía* organization in San José or in any other Peten community.

The party moved slowly through the streets, stopping at the patio of the first household on the list. There were relatives and invited friends awaiting the arrival. Everyone was in complete silence. The young wife, dressed in a new silky dress, her hair combed in the characteristic Yucatecan style, walked with her husband from the door of the house toward the man with the skull. They carried long, black, homemade candles in their hands. The plate with the skull was received by the wife, who invited the participants in the procession to follow her into the home. She delicately placed the plate with the skull on a home altar where hot food, candles, and a container with water had been set for the skull alone. It is a hot meal with *tamales*, *bollos*, and a soup made of pheasants and wild pigeons. For the lonesome souls, without relatives on earth, food was placed outside the house in an isolated place.

The emotions of the group upon the arrival of the procession were evident. The couple and the guests appeared tense. An informant stated that although one sometimes forgets the relatives and even their place in the cemetery, the arrival of the skull means the arrival of their souls. "One feels weak and like crying," he added.

After the household prayers, the special guests of the family were served a small glass of wine, *tamales* and *bollos* made of black corn, and *ixpasha*' or *atole* for drink. The rest of the people were served *tamales* and *atole* afterward. After forty-five minutes, the woman very sadly took the skull from the table for the departure. It was handed to the same leader of the procession. The group, singing a church song, departed for the second household.

The conclusion of the visiting came about sunrise, when the skull was returned to the church. The same skull will not be removed from the church for a period of two years. A priest was invited to conduct the mass of the souls (*misa de los difuntos*). Each family sent representatives to request and pay for the responses of the priest to help the souls of relatives through this church ritual.[5]

There are a number of requirements for those directly involved in the ritual. They include specific rules covering the quality of food, the manner of its cooking, the new pottery for containers, the new containers made from the gourd tree, and the candles. The man handling the skull must select a prayer-maker, who comes to church daily for forty days after the ceremony to pray and to light a traditional candle to the three skulls. Those who promise and hold the reception in devotion cannot be involved in fights, quarrels, or in sexual matters. To be at peace with the world is a prerequisite for the success of the ritual on this day.

5. On October 29, each family observes the Day of the Little Angels (*angelitos*) or those who died while still children. A similar celebration takes place in each house, without the human skull.

Testing the Validity of the Ritual

While awaiting the hour for the procession with the skulls, there was an opportunity to talk about this *costumbre*. The statement of a middle-aged man showed his ideological bent. "The skulls," he said, "were spiritual men of ancient times. My grandfather told me that they were important, and his grandfather said the same thing. They are more important than the saints because the saints are made of wood. The skulls have been human beings and have been alive. They are of real bones just as ours are." A liberal and up-to-date political leader proudly indicated that only San José had been left with this unique celebration in the entire Peten and Yucatan.

The statements of these men disclosed something of the mythical content behind the ritual. The soul (*ánima*) returns to the earth on this night and looks forward to being properly attended. "This we know also from our ancestors. My grandfather used to say that there was once an old man who became very mean and skeptical about the celebration. He went to the church alone before the day of the ritual to take care of some repairs, and while there, he heard many voices of people talking. No one was there, but the voices were discussing familiar places and names of people because they wanted to visit them on the night of November 1. He realized that they were souls. The old man doubted no more."

There is also the legend of another man who failed to observe the ritual. He ordered his wife not to make new pottery (as is done for the occasion) and to stop any preparation. He did not gather wild beeswax for the traditional candle-making, a task of the men. He argued with his wife that the celebration was no longer needed. On the day when everyone was busy with the preparation for the ritual, he went into the forest to work as usual. He returned late in the afternoon, ate, and after closing the doors of the house, the family retired to their hammocks. The rest of the town went on quietly with the celebration. Suddenly he heard loud, strange noises, and out of the confusion someone was clearly saying, "What shall I do, and where shall I go?" The old man and his wife realized that it was the voice of a dead son. The husband failed the ritual no more and was very devoted thereafter.

Many more incidents are told of families who reluctantly have undertaken the celebration only to find that because of their poor attitude the ceremonial food had spoiled before it could be presented to the table of the souls. "These are very old cases but illustrate the importance of continuing the ritual," stated a literate "son of the pueblo" who has traveled to Yucatan, Belize in British Honduras, and to Guatemala City.

No one can forget the action of a mayor in the '30's who prohibited the celebration upon the recommendation of a governor (*jefe político*), a Ladino from the Guatemala Highlands, because the world crisis was affecting the area and chicle was not in demand. Many families had promised to receive the skull in their home that night, and there was confusion, but the official order was obeyed. The town was in silence when at the "heavy hours of the night" some people heard the church bells tolling mysteriously but forcefully. A few brave men went outside and experienced something very strange. They reported seeing a multitude of people in a procession behind a human skull. It was like something real, they said, but it was over the calm waters of the lake.

"We have known all along that the celebration is like a law, and although we live in modern times, this is not something to be disregarded." As to its origin, they have deduced that it must be Maya, because the Spanish clergy does not approve of it. The current clergy is strongly opposed to the ritual. There is the recent incident of a priest who offered a free Mass to bury the three skulls. Said one man, "He requested that we forget this pagan practice. We had no choice but to tell him to leave the skulls on the main altar or to leave town himself. He chose to leave town. The present priest, however, is more understanding. He tells us that he hopes we will forget it all eventually. He does not understand that this old thing (*cosa antigua*) cannot be discarded unless one has a reason for doing so. He comes from the land of Spain and does not understand our customs."

The San Joseños' frequent use of the concept *costumbre* alone is not a sufficient explanation for an event which requires much energy and a total expenditure of approximately $1500.00 from the community.[6] Although the legend of the Popul Vuh, or any other myths of the classic Maya period supporting the use of skulls did not survive the time, one thing is clearly seen today: the consequences of failure to carry out the ritual with the skull constitute new mythological reasons for its continuation.

Skulls in the Maya Past

It is not a historical accident that the use of human skulls for ancestor worship was specifically reported among the Cocoms in Yucatan in the sixteenth century, and that now, in the twentieth century, three human skulls are part of the November ritual in the community of San José. The ritual of the skull is not altogether a strange phenomenon if we take into account that San Joseños distinguish themselves in the area for having endured total cultural breakdown in the struggle with the conquistadores.

When one consults both the history of religious expansion in Mesoamerica and the well-informed clergy, one feels that the profound religious devotion of the San Joseños to the skulls in the Catholic ritual should be attributed to an inheritance which goes beyond the European Catholic indoctrination. There is no doubt, however, that to disentangle the present complex in San José is a delicate methodological problem. Specific generalizations can be

6. For description and illustration see Reina (1962a); Spanish version, Reina (1962b).

based only on circumstantial archaeological evidence. In the European tradition, skulls are the symbol of death, and one could assume that the toleration by a priest of a native skull ritual could have resulted in the present synthesis.[7]

On the other hand, in Maya archaeological tombs, for instance, there is a strong indication that Mayas in the classic period had a very special interest in preserving heads or other parts of the body. A recent excavation at Tikal (Shook and Kidder: 1961) confronted the archaeologists with a headless and handless skeleton laid out at full length in an impressive painted tomb of the early classic period (A.D. 456). The authors interpreted this evidence of an early ritualistic handling of human skulls to mean that people wanted to preserve a token of a person because of "his enormous status and spiritual power in the community" (*ibid.*, p. 4). Gann (1918, p. 87), having found forty human skulls, concluded, "These skulls would seem to have been either the result of secondary interments or the remains of sacrificial victims whose bodies were either eaten or burned elsewhere . . ." Thompson (1954, p. 48) reported that in burials of the formative period at Uaxactun" . . . the thigh bones had been removed . . . the skull had been sawed across so that all the facial bones had been removed . . . the custom of removing the facial bones of a dead chief, and on them modeling in gum or some other plastic substance the deceased's features, was practiced in Yucatan until the coming of the Spaniards."

In the Popol Vuh (1950, pp. 117–120) the human skull had a predominant place in one legend, in which the head of Hun-Hunahpú, after decapitation, was placed in a tree. The fruitless tree was soon covered with fruits. The miracle went even further, when the daughter of Lord Cuchumaquic visited the tree, and the skull, which was among its branches, spoke up and said, "What do you wish? These round objects which cover the branches of the tree are nothing but skulls." During the conversation the maiden was invited to stretch out her hands, and in that instant, the skull let a few drops of spittle fall, making her pregnant.

In the drama of Rabinal-Achi, reference is made to a skull which was to be converted into a cup and carved and decorated inside and out so that when

7. *Time* (Feb. 22, 1963): Reproduction of Zurbarán's painting of St. Francis praying in front of a book supported by a human skull. Also, in a church located in Guatemala City, 10th Avenue and 10th Street, the front church wall has a human-size statue of a monk holding in his hand a human skull.

John L. Stephens, in his *Incidents of Travel in Yucatan* reported many cases in 1841 where skulls were given ritualistic treatment in Southwest Yucatan. In the Church of Ticul, built by the Franciscan monks, "One of the altars was decorated with human skulls and cross-bones, and in the rear of the Church was a great charnel house. It was ended by a high stone wall, and was filled with a collection of skulls and bones, which, after the flesh had decayed, had been dug up from the grave of the cemetery of the Church" (Vol. 1, pp. 155–156). More references to skulls and to the "ancient Maya custom of digging up bones" can be found in Vol. 1, Chapters V, IX, XIII, and XV. I am indebted to Dr. Beate Salz for these references.

trading "... my sons and my vassal shall say: There is the head of our ancestor, of our father. Thus my sons and my vassals will repeat it in memory of me, as long as the sun shall shine . . ." (Tozzer: 1941, p. 120, footnote 548).

Historical evidence also exists in Landa's most vivid description of skull handling among the Cocom family, rulers of Mayapan, Yucatan (Thompson, *op. cit.*, pp. 222–223). "They cut off the head of the dead chief, boil it to remove the flesh, and then saw off the back part. On the front half they model the features of the dead man with a kind of bitumen, and, what is more, they keep these permanent portraits of their ancestors in their household shrines, and offer food to them on all their festivals."

Although the early Maya relationship between the ritualistic practice and its myth most likely has been lost forever, the numerous findings of skulls specially treated or carefully located in tombs cannot be dismissed as an artistic expression of the time. The evidence is circumstantial, and our knowledge is insufficient to establish precisely the place of the ritual and myth in their culture.

The San Joseños' Dual Cultural Orientation

The San Joseños' use of human skulls in a Catholic context should be taken, not only as a distinctive complex in its own right, but also as an expression of the dual nature of the community culture after acculturation. The old and the new orientations appear here in a very special way.

The ninety-five San Joseño families are known as the Mayeros of Peten. This distinction is based upon their indisputably Maya ancestry. Peteneros in general know the historical relationship between San José and specific areas of Yucatan which can be shown ethnohistorically and by such family names as Pech, Moo, Batab, Cohouj, Cocoms, Colli, Tezucum, and Zuntecum. Furthermore, they continue to speak Yucatecan in their homes although the speech is sufficiently distinct that San Joseños find the Northern Yucatecan accent amusing but easy to imitate.

As a result of the forceful acculturation process, their village, economy, technology, clothing, decorations, and political organization have much in common with their non-Mayero neighbors. In appearance they are indistinguishable from the folk non-Maya population of the nearby settlements and from the poorer families of Flores City, capital of the Department. The similarities are such that in the 1950 National Census, San Joseños were classified as Ladinos.[8]

The steady diffusion of outside elements has been possible through the contacts made with non-Peteneros, particularly Mexican and Belizeño Negro

8. The Indian-Ladino division of the Highlands is officially used, but it does not convey the same sociocultural distinction as in the Highlands of Guatemala. The concept of Indian is equated here with the Lacandones.

Labor, Syrian merchants (*los turcos*), and Spanish, British, and North American entrepreneurs who relied on the native population for the exploitation of natural resources. People from Tenocique, Campeche, Mérida, Belize, Cobán, Guatemala City, and lately Mexico City have migrated to Peten, and their cities are places of reference for those San Joseños who have been there and for those who have heard about them. Contact has taken place along trade routes since the time the white man settled there. Natives were sent out to bring in the mail and products of primary necessity including salt, oil, sugar, rice, flour, and kerosene. Furthermore, the operation of lumber camps in the latter part of the nineteenth century and the beginning of the twentieth century was followed by the exploitation of rubber and chicle, archaeological digging, and geological surveys for oil. These operations hired local labor and necessitated much travel just for their maintenance.

San Joseños have not stayed behind by viewing all these business enterprises from a distance. They have learned to use, and consequently have acquired rapidly, such items as an outboard motor for dug-out canoe, or a short-wave battery radio, holiday clothing or a modern bridal dress, perfumes, permanent waves, modern medicines, or a planned vacation-style air trip to Belize or Guatemala City. Significant is the fact that a machine is seldom taken for granted. San Joseños are noted for their inquisitive minds, ability to learn facts, and for their ability to relate them to some logical analysis of the functioning of the parts of a machine. The community itself has advanced equipment, including a small electric plant, a modern school building, a water storage tank for rain water and a dance hall (approximately 80 feet by 45 feet) constructed of modern material flown from Guatemala City at the cost of $12,000 saved from chicle revenue. Moreover, the use of Spanish in all official and city dealings, participation in national political parties, and the discussion of national issues or international issues, such as Kennedy vs. Nixon when they were candidates for the United States presidency, are matters which concern the male population and frequently filter down to some of the women. The sophisticated "up-to-date and matter-of-fact" constitute a modern cultural layer which is functional in dealing with officials, outsiders, or businessmen, as the case may be. I found much in common to talk with the San Joseños, and if a comparison may be permitted, they are more up-to-date than the inhabitants of the Pokomam-speaking village of Chinautla, located only a few miles from Guatemala City.

However, in the light of all these profound changes and accommodations, it is interesting to note that the main portion of their livelihood continues to derive from the forest. Milpas, supplemented by hunting, gathering, and fishing, and the extraction of chicle are activities of major importance. The land is nationally controlled; therefore, San Joseños must request official permission to exploit the land and its resources. Despite the complications in dealing with the administrative officials or agencies, all San Joseños have maintained rights to the use of forest land within the *municipio* and have been able to continue their elaborate rotation of fields.

But the moment a San Joseño puts on his working clothes, takes a dug-out canoe, his machete, tumpline, and his dog, he appears, at first glance, inconsistent with the modern features described so far. In the forest, his ideas about nature and man are distinctly prescientific. Mysterious events of the forest do not require an empirical explanation based upon observable facts. Their explanation lies in the behavior of the guardian of the forest, the *duendes* (goblins), wandering souls, the x-tabay (supernatural being in the form of a beautiful woman), spirits who may appear as fireballs and luminescent birds flying over the lake, gigantic animals which are enclosed in mysterious caves and produce thundering noises, evil winds which will bring sickness, and *espantos* (frights) that cause paralyses. The "heavy hours of the night" are avoided because all those things, souls and ghosts, are actively at work, seeking to contact human beings in various ways. During these hours, it is safest to be asleep under a good roof and enclosed by walls, with doors and windows well shut.

For several months I visited frequently with the most learned man in the community. He had been educated under a well-known teacher from Guatemala City early in the century. Well-trained, he became the teacher and secretary of his own community and nearby communities. Lately, he has been an expert in law (*uisache*), and has defended many cases in Flores and other villages in the court of *Primera Instancia*. His reputation as a "lawyer" is good. His father figured prominently in the nineteenth-century history of Peten, receiving a high military title for his public service. He assisted the governors in the exploration of the forest and helped them during revolutionary periods. He was a real Mayero.

One evening, the community received a wire from Flores. It was for this teacher. His little granddaughter, residing in another town, was seriously ill. Upon his arrival in her town, he questioned the mother about the physical condition of the child and her diet, medicines, doctor's and herbalist's prescriptions. Everything was considered, but an explanation for the illness was not found. Why should the child be sick? His daughter-in-law then told him that the night before she had dreamed of the child's deceased father. There was a sudden change in the grandfather's gestures. He became tense and anxious. "So it is," he said, "her father's soul is lonesome and unhappy; he is visiting the household to take the daughter's soul with him." It was no longer a matter of struggle between the illness and modern medicine; it was a problem beyond medicine. It was a matter between them and the soul of the father. The appeasement of the father's soul, his comfort by some formula, would, it was felt, return the health of the child. Devotion to the human skull was promised for the next November 1st ritual. The girl became well, but died four months later of a real illness. As the grandfather said, "This time she had pneumonia."

Final Implications

San Joseños use old Maya techniques to care for illnesses believed to be caused by acts of supernatural power. By the same token, the ways of the Mayas provide them with techniques, knowledge, and safety when they are in the forest. While the man is in the forest, the family, knowing the risks of a man alone in the jungle, has ways of aiding him from the village through private rituals, and there is confidence in the success of an enterprise, or there is a suitable explanation when failure occurs. The skulls, and their relation to the souls of ancestors, and much of the San Joseños' conceptualization of the universe are bound together in this specific context. Today, in the general context of a modern world, the ritual and its symbol, and the myth which supports them offer a way of "making the influence of the past effective in the present" (see Kroeber: 1962, p. 83). It would seem a paradox to a Westerner from an industrial society to find the two ends of Redfield's continuum coming together to constitute a common frame for the cultural organization. I do not have the impression, however, that one is dealing here with a "marginal man" caught in-between two opposite forces or contradictory sets of assumptions. These people are equally proud of those elements classified as old (prescientific) and those called modern (scientific). Their competence and skill in both, as they face the elements of the forest and city, are to be commended. Therefore, it is not surprising to find the continuity of an old symbol (the human skulls) into the present supported by a reasoning which is the product of the Americanization of Catholicism. Nor is it surprising that on several nights following the ritual of November 1 one of the modern man-made satellites put into orbit was spotted and followed through the sky, with the comment that "men of science, perhaps Russians or Americans, had been able to accomplish this." They are talking, asking questions, and looking forward to the day when men can reach the moon. This interest contrasts with the views of some of the more citified and intellectual men of the Peten, who feel that it would be against the law of God and nature, and predict that it will not be possible.

It is interesting that, historically, the Peteneros were exposed to a late colonization, and were spared a traumatic conquest, as well as the seventeenth century depression; that they were never dominated by the *hacienda* system with its typical patron-client relation of the eighteenth and nineteenth centuries. As a result, we find the opposite of the general pattern for most of Mesoamerica. In Peten are communities making up a society with a middle class and proletariat which ideally believes that this is the only area of Guatemala and Mexico where true democratic principles have been at work, the place where everyone is considered equal and respected for his inner personal qualities. Mayan-Peteneros, Yucatecan-Peteneros, Mexican-Peteneros, and Peteneros have been mutually dependent for survival during economic crises when crops failed, and through years of depression. It was the life and orientation of the Mayeros which showed the non-Mayeros how to live almost self-sufficiently when the outside failed them. They have, therefore, a mutual respect for each other's views, and I noted an avoidance of expressing social prejudices. The ritual of the skulls in San José is well-known throughout Peten, and many outsiders have attended it. Aside from the clergy there is no intention to direct a change; and the general respect shown toward this religious practice is interpreted in the community as implicit support.

The human skull complex is just one of many aspects which belong to that section of the San Joseños' culture which is proudly recognized as having been handed down to them by their earliest ancestors. Because of the particular dual cultural orientation used in separate contexts, the matter of cultural dynamics sometimes takes a unique form in which changes come about by the abandonment of an entire complex. Cases of abandonment are related to the feeling that the abandoned culture complex had too serious consequences. For example, a ritual for the protection of *milpas* is said to have meant death for anyone trespassing on the protected property, including friends and other well-intentioned visitors. Because it was too effective, and therefore harmful, this ritual was literally abandoned. Another important example concerns the *primicia*, a public ritual to express gratitude to the deities and to request the recovery of good health. "The family believed that during the conduct of a *primicia* the deities would be overwhelmed by the quantity of offerings and the emotional intensity of participants and could cure the ill person. The deities, in full control of the forces of the universe, demanded the offering of ceremonial food and orations, but most of all they required the highest mental concentration in group units, utmost solemnity and propriety throughout the twenty-four hour ceremony conducted by the Maya wise man (Reina: 1961, p. 221). The crucial point in the ritual was that errors would not be tolerated by the dieties. By 1942 sufficient cases of failure demonstrated that careless persons had gone ahead with the *primicias* and the deities had punished them with death. Nowadays, San Joseños conceive the ritual to be an impossible task for human beings to handle, and the people's reasoning behind the abandonment is as simple as this: "It is preferable to take a minor damage, one death, rather than expose ourselves to much danger because of failure of participants to observe the things prescribed in the ritual . . ." (*ibid.*, p. 223).

As already indicated, some San Joseños, on their own volition, have experimented with the abandonment of the skull ritual, but so far the results in these cases have only reinforced the community's belief that its continuation is essential.

The dual orientation has its advantages when the abandonment of a ritual takes place, because the new pattern, having existed alongside the old one for some time, has already been explored, practiced, and accepted. A nativistic movement here, and serious factionalism, frequently the result of fast acculturation, are hardly the case. San Joseños are not afraid of change when it comes about in the fashion described, and so far there has been no apparent struggle between the prescientific and the scientific culture.

Finally, the implications of this case study reach a variety of interests in the field of social sciences. Perhaps the human skulls, exposed by archaeologists and by ethnographers, may stand as a demonstration of the fact that the form of a ritual more readily traverses time unchanged, while the accompanying myth is modified to accommodate the demands of civilization. Furthermore, the basic orientations of both classic folk-urban or nonscientific typology are held in common by one group of people. Each orientation, however, has come to serve the people in separate contexts. Curiously enough, this arrangement may account for the absence of disturbance in the face of culture change. The use of human skulls is unique in San José, but I tend to think that cultural duality is not necessarily a way of life uniquely held by San Joseños alone.

References

Cowgill, G. L.

1963: *Postclassic Period Culture in the Vicinity of Flores, Peten, Guatemala*, Harvard University Ph.D. thesis (unpublished).

Gann, T. W.

1918: "Maya Indians of Southern Yucatan and Northern British Honduras," *Bulletins of the Bureau of American Ethnology*, **64.**

Hallowell, A. I.

1955: *Culture and Experience* (Philadelphia: University of Pennsylvania Press).

Kluckhohn, C.

1942: "Myths and Rituals: A General Theory," *Harvard Theological Review*, **35,** 45 79. Reprinted in W. A. Lessa & E. A. Vogt (eds.), *Reader in Comparative Religion: An Anthropological Approach* (New York: Row, Peterson, 1958).

Kroeber, A. L.

1962: "Anthropological Horizons: Report on a Symposium," *Current Anthropology*, **3,** No. 1.

Lothrop, S. K.

1933: *Atitlán: An Archaeological Study of Ancient Remains on the Borders of Lake Atitlán, Guatemala*, Publication No. 444 (Washington, D.C.: Carnegie Institution of Washington).

1940: *The Maya and Their Neighbors* (New York & London: Appleton-Century-Crofts).

Miner, H.
1952: "The Folk-Urban Continuum," *American Sociological Review*, **17**, 529–537.
1953: *Timbuctoo, The Primitive City* (Princeton, New Jersey: Princeton University Press).

Popul Vuh, The Sacred Book of the Ancient Quiche Maya
1950: English version by D. Goetz & S. G. Morley (Norman: University of Oklahoma Press).

Redfield, R.
1941: *The Folk Cultures of Yucatan* (Chicago: University of Chicago Press).

Redfield, R., Herskovits, M., & Linton, R.
1936: "A Memorandum on Acculturation," *American Anthropologist*, **38**, 149–152.

Redfield, R., & Villa Rojas, A.
1934: *Chan Kom, a Maya Village*, Publication No. 448 (Washington, D.C.: Carnegie Institution of Washington).

Reina, R. E.
1960: *Chinautla, A Guatemalan Indian Community: A Study in the Relationship of Community Culture and National Change*, Middle American Research Institute, Publication No. 24 (New Orleans: Tulane University Press).
1961: "The Abandonment of Premicias by Itza of San Jose, Guatemala and Socotz, British Honduras," in *Tikal Reports* No. 10 (Philadelphia: Museum Monographs, University of Pennsylvania Press).
1962a: "Significado cultural de tres calaveras en San Jose, Peten," *Guatemala Indigena*, **2**, 21–46.
1962b: "The Ritual of the Skull in Peten, Guatemala," *Expedition*, **4**, 26–36.

Roys, R. L.
1933: *The Book of Chilam Balam of Chumayel*, Publication No. 438 (Washington, D.C.: Carnegie Institution of Washington).
1943: *Indian Background of Colonial Yucatan*, Publication No. 548 (Washington, D.C.: Carnegie Institution of Washington).

Shook, E. M., & Kidder, A., II
1961: "The Painted Tomb at Tikal," *Expedition*, **4**, 2–8.

Stephens, J. L.
1963: *Incidents of Travel in Yucatan* (New York: Dover).

Thompson, J. E.
1939: *Excavations at San José, British Honduras*, Appendix by A. O. Shepard, Publication No. 506 (Washington, D.C.: Carnegie Institution of Washington).

Part Five

Perception and Cognition

ROBBINS BURLING

How To Choose a Burmese Numeral Classifier[1]

In a number of his papers, Professor Hallowell has shown an interest in the way in which the concepts of space and time are handled by people whose cultures differ radically from our own, and in the varying manner in which they deal with measurement. He has used data from the Ojibwa Indians to explore these problems, and in these papers, as in others, he has shown a sensitivity to the terminology of the Indians and has used their systems of terminology as a means of investigating the way in which Indians classify the phenomena of their world. In this paper I try to follow Professor Hallowell's lead by investigating a set of terms which constitute a measuring system, and which serve in part to express ideas of time and space, though the terms come

1. My interest in Burmese classifiers arose while in Burma as a Fulbright lecturer at the University of Rangoon in 1959–60. Many of the basic data for this paper were collected at that time. Freedom to work up the material in its present form was provided by a grant from the United States Office of Education under the National Defense Education Act. I am indebted to both of my sponsoring agencies for making this research possible. I am also indebted to Henry Hoenigswald and Paul Friedrich for their critical comments on earlier versions of the paper.

from a language spoken on the opposite side of the world from Ojibwa. In Burmese, measurement of all kinds is expressed through the system of numeral classifiers, although classifiers are also used in a wider set of situations than is true of our terms of measurement. In the following pages, the Burmese numeral classifiers will be described, and a number of aspects of the system discussed.

In many of the languages of Southeast Asia, a number is never used without being accompanied by one of the special class of morphemes, known as numeral classifiers. The choice of classifier depends upon the type of object which is being counted. Thus, typically, a special classifier is used for counting people, and it is never enough simply to say the equivalent of "one woman," but instead, one must also include the classifier for people. The resulting phrase has three morphemes: noun to be counted, number, and classifier. Languages differ in the order in which the elements of a numeral phrase must be given, but the manner in which the phrases are used is remarkably uniform in a large number of languages. Numeral classifiers are found throughout Southeast Asia, in languages of all genetic affiliations—Thai, Mon-Khmer, Tibeto-Burmese, and Malayo-Polynesian—and they are even found in the easternmost Indic languages—Bengali and Assamese—and in Chinese. Burmese has about 200 classifiers, and somehow the speaker must choose just one of these each time he uses a number. The specific question posed in the following paper is: "How is this choice among classifiers made?"

Semantics and Syntax

An interesting feature of numeral classifiers is the difficulty of deciding whether they constitute a lexical or a syntactical set. That is, in some ways the choice of which numeral classifier to use in a sentence seems similar to the choice among nouns: one picks the term which corresponds to the extra-linguistic situation, the situation in the world to which one wishes to refer. In other ways, however, the choice of numeral classifier more closely resembles the choice among grammatical markers such as the choice of the particular form of the plural in English, where the speaker is constrained by the internal syntactical rules of the language, and the alternatives convey no distinction in meaning whatever.[2] This rather ambiguous position makes numeral classifiers somewhat difficult to cope with, but strategic to investigate if one hopes to clarify that most slippery of linguistic problems, the relation of structure to meaning.

In this paper I shall first attempt to clarify the contrast between semantic and syntactic requirements and show what sort of knowledge the speaker of

2. I must make clear that I use the term "meaning" to stand for the relation of linguistic forms to the nonlinguistic environment. A word "means" something because it has a relationship to something in the world outside of language. I am not sympathetic to the extreme structuralist view that attempts to reduce meaning to linguistic distribution.

Burmese needs when he chooses among classifiers. I shall then go on to give a rather long list of classifiers, together with some of the characteristics which invite and limit their uses, and I shall conclude by considering certain problems of semantic analysis.

The class of all classifiers can be given a clear syntactical definition: in Burmese it includes all morphemes which follow directly and in close juncture *béhna-*, "how many," or the numbers *ta-*, "one," *hna-*, "two," *θôun-*, "three," etc., up to *kôu-*, "nine."[3] In Burmese the noun is regularly given first and followed by the number and then the classifier. Open juncture separates the noun from the number; in the examples which are given below the noun is set off by a space. The number and classifier, in conformity with the close juncture between them, are written with no intervening space.

Perhaps the most common position taken by linguists toward classifiers has been to regard them as markers which categorize the nouns of the language into classes somewhat akin to the noun classes of Bantu, or even to the gender classes of Indo-European. Thus, the Burmese nouns *khwêi*, "dog," *shín*, "elephant," *myîn*, "horse," *nwâ*, "cow," and many others, can all be said to belong to the same noun class because in counting, they are all commonly accompanied by the same classifier: *-káun*. *Khwêi hnakáun*, "two dogs," *nwâ lêikáun*, "four cows," etc. Such a view has been implied in occasional suggestions that in a dictionary of a language like Burmese, each noun entry should include a notation of what classifier accompanies it. If this were done in a Burmese lexicon, then the word *khwêi*, "dogs," for instance, would be accompanied by a note indicating that it belongs to the class of nouns which take the classifier *-káun*. One might object that this information is a trifle superfluous since *-káun* is used for all animals, from mosquitoes to elephants, and for nothing else. If one simply knows that *-káun* is used for all animals, it need hardly be repeated every time an animal is listed in the dictionary. Strictly speaking, however, this objection is quite irrelevant, for it assumes that the speaker knows which nouns stand for animals, and this type of semantic knowledge is supposed to be taboo when working out grammatical rules. That is, we can set up structural classes only by structural criteria, and it is only a stroke of luck when the classes have semantic correlates. Even a very close semantic correlation does not allow us to define the class in the first

3. The structural features of Burmese classifiers were briefly described by Cornyn (1944) and more fully by Haas (1951), though neither dealt at all extensively with the particular problems treated here. Sadly, my transcription of Burmese is not identical to either of these authors, though it differs from Cornyn's in only two respects: (1) *q* has been substituted for syllable initial *ʔ* to avoid confusion with the entirely separate syllable final glottal stop; (2) the wholesale, but completely automatic assimilation across syllable boundaries in close juncture is not shown. By ignoring this assimilation, morphemes can occur uniformly in the same graphic form which should lend clarity to a paper such as this. Both these modifications, together with some others more suitable for pedagogical purposes than for a technical paper are incorporated into some of Cornyn's more recent publications.

place by semantic criteria. From a strict structural point of view, it would be better to say that we know that *khwêi* is an animal because it is used with *-káun* than to say we use it with *-káun* because it is an animal.

Nevertheless, other problems present themselves if we insist that the choice of classifier depends strictly upon the noun class of the noun with which it is used. Perhaps the most evident problem is that a single noun can, on different occasions, be accompanied by different classifiers, usually with more or less variation in meaning. Thus, to give an extreme example: *ŋapyóθî talôun*, "one banana"; *ŋapyóθî tamyôu*, "one variety of banana"; *ŋapyóθî tashé*, "ten bananas"; *ŋapyóθî taweʔ*, "one half of a banana"; *ŋapyóθî tatwê*, "a bunch of bananas"; *ŋapyóθî takháin*, "one big bunch (arm) of bananas"; *ŋapyóθî taphî*, "a small bunch (15–20) of bananas"; *ŋapyóθî tathân*, "one shoulder-pole load of bananas"; *ŋapyóθî tapèiθâ*, "a viss (about 3½ pounds) of bananas". Similarly *lóunji*, "Burmese saronglike skirt," can be variously classified with *-thé*, which can be used for any article of clothing, or with *-kwîn*, which is used for things which can encircle something else, while pairs of these skirts are classified with *-qouʔ*, a common usage, since they frequently are sold in pairs. Probably no other word in Burmese regularly occurs with this unique trio of classifiers. Each noun listed in the lexicon would have to be followed by not just a single notation of the class to which the noun belongs, but by a list of several classifiers, any one of which might be used with that noun. Certain tricks, it is true, might reduce the complexity of the entries. It can be seen that many of the classifiers that can be used with "banana" are units of volume or weight. These, as well as some others, are used so widely that it might be possible to list them separately in the grammar along with the generalization that they could be used with any of several classes of nouns which are defined by other classifiers. The classifier *-myôu*, "kind, variety," is an extreme example, for it can be used with every noun in the language, making it unnecessary to list it separately with all the nouns in the lexicon. Still, the parallelism of the use of various classifiers with sets of nouns has its limitations. For instance, while *-káun* is used for all animals, and *-šîn* is used for pairs of certain animals, *-šîn* can by no means be used with all the nouns that take *-káun*. *Nwâ tašîn*, "a pair of oxen," and *cwê tašîn*, "a pair of buffaloes," are entirely proper phrases, but *-šîn* cannot be used with the word for "horse" let alone that for mosquito, so it is impossible to make any generalization which would allow *-šîn* to be used with all nouns that can take *-káun*; *-šîn* simply defines a separate although overlapping class of nouns than *-káun*. It happens that *-šîn* is used only with names of animals which are used in teams, and the Burmese do not happen to use teams of horses. If this semantic knowledge is irrelevant, the only structurally sound thing to do would be to note in the lexicon under *nwâ*, "cow," that it can be classified not only with *-káun*, but also with *-šîn*. To omit *-šîn* would be to give the spurious rule that, whenever *nwâ* was enumerated, it would be accompanied by *-káun*. We are then forced to list with each noun entry all the possible classifiers that can be used with it. To do this is to open oneself up to a truly formidable prospect. Informants say with complete conviction that it is possible to say *ceʔ tatâun*, "a basket of chickens," but not **nwa tatâun*, "a basket of cows." Although this makes perfectly good semantic sense, this reasonable semantic information is supposed to be excluded from structural considerations. Must we, then, coldly indicate that *-tâun* is used with *ceʔ* but not with *nwâʔ*. By this time most anthropologists and possibly even most linguists would probably feel that we have gone too far and that the exclusion of *"a basket of cows" is not the kind of limitation that we want to build into a grammar. The difficulty is, however, that if we do not build in the exclusion of **nwâ tatâun*, "a basket of cows," why should we exclude **êinjí takwîn*, "a circle of a shirt," and still include *lóunjí takwîn*, "a circle of a skirt?" Even worse, why should we exclude **lú takáun*, in which *lú*, "people," is erroneously classified with the classifier for animals? Why, indeed, should we exclude any combination of noun and classifier?

The possibility of using several different classifiers with a single noun is not, however, the only problem raised when we attempt to specify the choice of classifiers on syntactical grounds. Classifiers are also regularly used with no antecedent noun whatever. *Lêiyauʔ sâjínté*, "four people wish to eat," is an entirely proper and unambiguous Burmese sentence, but the fact that it is people, rather than animals, who wish to eat is indicated only by the choice of *-yauʔ* as the classifier. If one desired to be more specific and say, for instance, "four women wish to eat," a noun would have to precede the numeral: *mêinmà lêiyauʔ sâjínté*, but if such precision is not required, then it is unnecessary and a bit redundant, though not forbidden, to introduce the sentence with a noun such as *lú*, person. After realizing that no antecedent noun need be present, the only possible way to salvage the view that the choice of classifier is governed by that noun is to suggest that the noun can be zeroed out after its required classifier is introduced. Such a view is awkward, since upon hearing the sentence *lêiyauʔ sâjinté*, it is quite impossible to judge what particular noun has been zeroed out. It could have been *lú*, "person," *mêinmà*, "woman," *yauʔcâ*, "man," *khalê*, "children," or any number of other nouns. Even if one surmounts that difficulty, what is to be done about the few classifiers which never take an antecedent noun: *-yeʔ*, "day," *-paʔ*, "week," etc. With no antecedent noun at all to govern the choice of some classifiers, it becomes increasingly difficult to regard any classifiers as grammatical markers whose use depends primarily upon the grammatical features of the noun.

The examples given here make clear that the choice among Burmese numeral classifiers carries a far greater semantic load than such purely syntactical categories as the choice among plural forms in English. The phrases given above which include the word *ŋapyóθî*, "banana," do not mean the same thing, and the wide variety of meanings is imparted only by the choice of classifiers. If classifiers do carry this much meaning, does it not make better sense to say that **nwâ tatâun* is incorrect because it is such nonsense to speak of "a basket of cows," rather than because it violates some structural principle of the grammar? Similarly, is not **êinji takwîn* incorrect because shirts do not encircle the body in the unambiguous way that Burmese skirts do? Is it not even reasonable to say that **lú takáun* is incorrect because people are not animals, rather than because the noun *lú*, "person," falls into a grammatical class defined by its use with the classifier *-yauʔ*, while only such nouns as *nwâ*, "cow," are classed with *-káun*?

The choice of what morpheme a speaker is to use at any moment is dependent upon both the syntactical requirements of the language, and his semantic intention. The linguist's traditional role has been with the syntactical part of the choice, and it is possible, for instance, to state with great accuracy the syntactical rules by which one chooses among English plural markers, because the choice is solely dependent upon intralinguistic variables. On the other hand, we hardly try to predict what noun will be used as the subject of a sentence, because this choice is dependent almost entirely upon extralinguistic, i.e., semantic, considerations. The choice of classifier may not be quite as free of intralinguistic, syntactical limitation as the choice of the subject of a sentence for **lú takáun*, "person one-animal" does seem so dubious as to be even syntactically questionable. Certainly Burmese cringe upon hearing this phrase. For the most part, however, the Burmese speaker's choice of classifier is governed by extralinguistic requirements—the avoidance of nonsense—rather than the intralinguistic requirement of avoiding nongrammaticality. The real question that must be raised is "how much do we want to build into the syntactical rules of grammar and how much do we want to leave to meaning?" At what point on the continuum from **mans* (as a plural of *man*) to **he went tomorrow*, to **a basket of cows*, do we want to draw the line and say that the rest is grammatically correct but semantically nonsense? Since the study of syntax has been far more successful than the study of semantics, linguists have tended to push the scope of syntax as far as they could and even to dismiss "meaning" as a matter of distribution, and thus exclude by definition any consideration of the relation of language to nonlinguistic phenomena and to render quite meaningless the term "meaning." It is in this way that the suggestion is made that the choice of classifier should be syntactically specified as governed by the antecedent noun. To work out fully the limitations on co-occurrence of nouns and classifiers as a syntactical phenomenon would be enormously complex, and, in the final analysis, not particularly interesting. One could prove conclusively that mosquitoes, dogs, cats, elephants, and snakes belong to one syntactical class, but that women, children, shopkeepers, carpenters, and beggars belong to another. Certainly, as a practical matter, such information is quite useless. One who is learning the language finds it relatively easy to learn the appropriate classifier for any situation, precisely because they make such good semantic sense. No Burmese would ever hesitate about which classifier to use for a new animal upon hearing its name for the first time.

In the end, the problem resolves itself into whether it is simpler to specify the criteria of choice by the linguistic or by the nonlinguistic environment. I feel that there is no doubt that the latter is more promising. The remainder of the paper constitutes an attempt to specify the extralinguistic conditions under which various classifiers are used, or in other words, to show what the classifiers mean.

For several reasons it is not possible to consider every single Burmese classifier. For one thing, certain groups of morphemes can be used as classifiers but are also used as members of some other form class. An important example is the set of classifiers used in counting various parts of plants. These classifiers are formally identical to nouns which stand for the same part of the plant, e.g., *sabâ tahnán*, "a stalk of paddy"; (*hnán* noun, "stalk"; *sabâ* noun, "paddy"). This does not make *-hnán* any less of a classifier, for in this phrase it is used in precisely the same manner as any other classifier, but like a number of other items *-hnán* occurs as a member of two different major form classes, in this case that of noun, as well as that of classifier. Many other items occur both as verbs and classifiers, and one occurs both as a number and as a classifier. This does not imply that classifiers do not form an entirely separate class, for most nouns cannot occur as classifiers and many classifiers can occur in no other way. It does mean that to describe fully the use and meaning of all items which can occur as classifiers would require a foray into the semantics of such areas as botanical nouns which would lead very far afield. Even excluding such terms as the botanical items, the class of classifiers is not strictly limited. New classifiers are occasionally coined or borrowed from other languages. There are also dialect differences and a few specialized classifiers are not used by all speakers. For instance, a large group of classifiers is used in astrology, but nonastrologically skilled Burmese may be vague about their exact meaning. To try to list every single classifier, therefore, would go beyond the idiolect of any one speaker; inevitably in such a case the repertory of even a single speaker is not easy to define precisely, since he may understand and accept some forms which he does not use, or he may use a form for the first time under the stimulus of linguistic interrogation.

Finally, one whole structural subclass will be considered only briefly. Most classifiers, and all of the commonest ones, are entirely different in form from the nouns with which they are used. Members of an extensive class, however, are identical in form to the noun, or to one syllable of the noun, or to the head of the noun phrase, with which they are used, e.g., *yéitwîn tatwîn*, "one well"; *qéin taqéin*, "one house"; *myòu tamyòu*, "one city."[4] Structurally, the simplest way of handling these "echo" classifiers is to consider them all to be allomorphic variants of the same morpheme, the particular allomorph being structurally determined by the form of the antecedent noun. Burmese has many such classifiers and each one applies only to a narrowly restricted set of nouns, usually to a single noun only. The determination of whether an echo classifier is appropriate, and if so, what form it should take, depends less upon semantic considerations than any other aspect of the choice of classifier. However, many of the nouns which can be echoed can also be accompanied by the classifier *-khù* (the use of which will be considered in detail below), and the collective meaning of the echo classifiers can be considered to approximate that of *-khù*. Some classifiers can be used both with nouns different in form from themselves and *also* with nouns identical to themselves. These are included among the other classifiers in the lists given below. A few of the classifiers used only as echos are listed, but no attempt is made to deal fully with them.

The Burmese Classifiers

The lists on the following pages include a large majority of the classifiers used in the Burmese language and an overwhelming majority of those which would be found in any sample of speech. In conformity with the conclusions of the last section they are defined by the meaning of objects which they classify, rather than by a list of nouns with which each can be used. The classifiers are grouped under rough but reasonably transparent semantic categories.

Animate and Sacred Objects or Groups (*Group 1*)—This first set includes classifiers used for animals, people, and various types of supernatural beings.

-shú Buddhas, images of the Buddha, stupas
-pâ Kings, queens, monks, nuns, novices, parents, spirits
-qû Respected people
-yauʔ People of all kinds, women, girls, barbers, and beggars, except royalty or members of the holy orders
-káun Animals of all kinds, from elephants to fish, birds, and mosquitoes; also various mythological animals and near-animals: ogres, dragons, ghosts
-ceiʔ Groups of ten men, or ten Buddhas
-sóun Couples, a man and his wife, lovers

4. Cornyn (1944) recognized this as a special type of classifier and called it "type 2." His "type 1" consists of classifiers used with various nouns, while "type 3" includes those classifiers not preceded by any noun. His types 1 and 3 are both considered in this paper, while type 2 is mentioned only briefly.

-šîn Yokes of animals, teams; used with oxen and buffaloes, but not with elephants or horses; occasionally used for twins, or very close friends

-qouʔ Groups of people or animals: herds, flocks, crowds

Objects with Dimension in Time or Space (*Group 2*)—Several of the most commonly used classifiers roughly indicate the shape of the object or show that some event occurs in time.

-châun Long, slender objects: pencils, spoons, rulers, sticks, needles, knives, cotton yarn (not wool), keys, rope, small pieces of bamboo, umbrellas, pieces of sugar cane, bamboo tie strips, pieces of firewood, horns, tails, braids of hair, etc.

-pín Long slender living, or recently living things, which are vertical or perpendicular to the object to which they are attached: trees, plants or stalks of plants, blades of grass, hair, strands of woolen yarn

-táin Vertical slender objects which are not living: posts, candlesticks

-kwîn Hoops, loops, rings, bracelets, sarongs, rubber bands

-chaʔ Thin, flat objects: carpets, mats, mirrors, plates, trays, loops of pineapple as found in tins, slices of bread, bricks (which were thinner and flatter in traditional Burma than in some countries)

-yweʔ Very thin and flat objects: leaves, paper

-lôun Spherical or cubical objects: boxes, pots, chairs, houses, fruit, cups, loaves, eyes, mountains, bags, pills, seeds, grains, etc.

-pheʔ Objects which come in symmetrical pairs: body parts such as eyes, hands, ears, nostrils; shoes, sides of paper (i.e., "pages" in which the two sides of the same sheet are counted separately)

-pauʔ Holes: windows, doorways (not the door itself), entrances to caves, holes in paper or cloth

-khá Events or actions which take place in time: the number of times that something is done: *takha*, "once," *hnakha*, "twice," etc.

-khauʔ Trips or motions, occurring in time, as "he came here three *times*"

-pyaiʔ For storms of rain and wind

Objects with Use (*Group 3*)—Another commonly employed set of classifiers show something about the use of the object which they classify.

-thé Things worn on the body: trousers, sarongs, shirts, handkerchiefs; not used for shoes or for hats

-sîn Tools or machinery which are used for transportation or for cutting: ships, boats, automobiles, knives, saws, arrows

-sî	Things ridden: elephants, horses, carts, automobiles, airplanes
-sáun	Things which can be read: letters, tickets
-leʔ	Hand tools: knives, guns, umbrellas, hammers, spectacles, brooms
-kôun	For looped objects which can be worn: garlands, necklaces
-sháun	Livable places: houses, apartments; used especially for the apartments of the various queens in the traditional Burmese royal palace
-θwé	(Rare) geographical connections; roads, rivers

Residual Category—Objects (*Group 4*)—The classifier *khù* has a unique role in the Burmese language. It can be most simply understood as belonging where no other more specific classifier is appropriate. Its use and meaning will be considered more fully below.

-khù	Used whenever nothing else is appropriate; implies nothing of shape, or use, but it does show at least that the item counted is not animate or sacred and that it is an individual object: spectacles, chairs, houses, stories, moons, tails, etc.

Numbers (*Group 5*)—All classifiers convey something about the amount or number of the object classified. Those in groups 2–4 and most of those in 1 indicate that single individual objects are being counted, but the remaining classifiers indicate that some other unit or quantity or amount is being counted. Important among these are classifiers with the meanings of the powers of ten: 10, 100, 1000, etc., up to ten million. Burmese is peculiar in its treatment of numbers divisible by ten (including 20, 30, 150, 3620, etc.), for when indicating these numbers it is impossible to use most of the classifiers. One cannot say the equivalent of "cows twenty-animals," as one would say *nwâ θôun káun*, "cows three-animals," but must instead say *nwâ hnashé*, "cows two-tens." Cornyn in his *Outline of Burmese Grammar* describes the situation by saying, "Tens, hundreds, and so on are not followed by a classifier" (Cornyn: 1944, p. 27). However, by the definition of classifiers which he himself gives (". . . nouns which occur immediately after numerals, or *bêhna-*, 'how many' ") these words for "ten," "hundred," etc., are themselves clearly classifiers. Except for *-shé*, "ten," these morphemes, e.g., *-yá*, "hundred," *-θâun*, "thousand," never occur except after a number, precisely the defining frame for classifiers; moreover the semantic area covered by these classifiers is not unlike certain other classifiers which mean such things as "half," "dozen," and "pair."

Shé, "ten," to be sure, can be used either as a number or as a classifier, though not both at the same time. Thus one can translate "ten women" as *mêinmà tashé*, "women one-ten," or as *mêinmà shéyauʔ*, literally "woman ten-people." One cannot say **mêinmà tashéyauʔ*. The simplest interpretation of these alternatives is that *-shé*, like many other classifiers, can also occur as a member of another form class (in this single instance as a number), but the *-shé* of the first example is still most naturally considered to be a classifier. We are therefore left with a group of classifiers which specify the powers of ten. Complex higher numbers are formed by a succession of numbers with classifiers: *lú ŋâtháun hnayá šiʔshé ŋâyau*, "5285 people," literally, "people five-thousands two-hundreds eight-tens five-people." The classifiers for the powers of ten are unique in that they can be used both for people, etc., and for inanimate objects, i.e., one can count either people or houses with the same classifiers. They can be grouped together with a few others with related meanings.

-weʔ Half
-shé Ten; used for counting groups of ten objects
-dázín Twelve; used primarily but not exclusively for packaged goods of European style, as a "dozen tins of condensed milk"; *-dázín*, unlike other classifiers, for higher numbers, is never used with people or animals
-yá Hundred
-tháun Thousand
-θâun Ten thousand
-θêin Hundred thousand
-θân Million
-gadéi Ten million

Weights and Measures (*Group 6*)—A large set of Burmese classifiers are used much as are the units of weights and measures of English. They show the quantity of an object as measured along some dimension: length, area, volume, time, weight, or value. By using these classifiers, it is possible to construct phrases which are close equivalents of such English expressions as "five pounds of coffee," "two drops of water," "one minute," "three miles," etc.

Length

-shámjí (Rare) a hair width
-thauʔ The length of a grain of rice
-leʔmaʔ The width of the thumb, "inch"
-thwá Span; the distance from the outstretched thumb-tip to the tip of the middle finger
-maiʔ Distance from the end of the outstretched thumb to the opposite side of a clenched fist; used especially in measuring cloth and rope
-béi An English "foot"; used especially in building construction
-táun The distance from the elbow to the tip of the extended middle finger; "cubit"

-táunsouʔ The distance from the elbow to the end of the doubled fist

-kaiʔ A yard; considered to be two *táun*; used especially in measuring cloth

-lán Arm span; considered to be four *táun*

-phálóun An English furlong; $\frac{1}{8}$ mile

-máin An English mile

-táin An archaic measure of distance; about two English miles

Area

-éikà Acre; this seems to be the only unit of area

Volume

-pyí A small measure of volume, usually for dry foods, and especially uncooked rice

-tîn Sixteen *pyí*; the amount held in a basket of standard size

-seʔ Drop; used for any liquid

-gálán Gallon; used especially for gasoline

Time

-maniʔ Minute

-náyí Hour

-yeʔ Day

-baʔ Week

-là Month

-hniʔ Year

-sheʔ Generation

-θeʔ Lifetime

-bawà Existence (i.e., one round in the Buddhist cycle of existences)

Weight

-ywéiléi A very small measure of weight, used only for jewels and gold

-ywéijí Two ywéileí

-bízawá A small unit of weight used only for precious stones, especially for diamonds

-bêθâ $\frac{1}{16}$ tikal

-mûθâ $\frac{1}{8}$ tikal (when used with *ŋâ*, "five," *ŋâmûθâ* means $\frac{1}{2}$ tikal, illogical though this may be)

-maʔθâ $\frac{1}{4}$ tikal

-caʔθâ One tikal; 1/100 of a viss; the weight of a silver "kyat" or rupee

-páun One English pound; used especially for European-type goods; coffee, English tea, sweets

-pèiθâ One "viss"; equivalent to about $3\frac{1}{2}$ English pounds

Value

-pyâ Smallest unit of the Burmese monetary system; 1/100 of a "kyat"

-maʔ 25-*pyâ*

-mû Used only with the numeral *ŋa* "five" the combination meaning 50-*pyâ*

-caʔ One "kyat," the Burmese monetary unit, officially equivalent to about U.S. $.21

Weights and Measures: Relative (*Group 7*)—Many units of weights and measures are less precisely fixed in value than those in Section 6. They vary in some degree with the measuring device and show something of how the measuring is done: a span, a stone's throw, the height of a man, a load. An important subgroup of these are words for containers. Any name for a container can be used both as a noun referring to the object, and as a classifier denoting the amount that can be held in the container. In this manner, one can form such expressions as *θajâ tazûn*, "a spoon of sugar," *zabâ tatâun*, "a basket of rice," of *zûn tatâun*, "a basket of spoons."

Distance

-kán The distance of an arm length, especially the distance that something may be passed from hand to hand; a reach

-pyiʔ A stone's throw

-khó The distance one can call

-pyà The distance between corner gables on a palace, and by extension, a "block"

Height

-yaʔ The height of a man—used in measuring heights of trees, buildings, etc.

-pháun The height that a man can reach with arms stretched upward

Girth

-thwâzái The circumference around which the outstretched fingers of two hands can reach

-pheʔ The circumference around which the two arms can reach

Volume

Containers—as classifiers these indicate the amount which can be held in such a container.

-bû Box, tin

-zûn Spoon

-louʔ Mouth

-shouʔ	Hand
-pagán	Plate
-tâun	Basket
-chîn	A rough type of basket
-qeiʔ	Bag
-hleiʔ	Cartload
-khweʔ	Cup, bowl, glass
-palîn	Bottle
-qôu	Pot, jar
-khayâ	Kettle
-sí	Tank, drum
-bôun	Bucket, kerosene tin (which, in Burma is often used for other things than kerosene)

Weights, Loads

-pwèi	An armful; used for firewood, flowers, vegetables
-paiʔ	An armful; synonomous with *pwèi*
-thân	Amount carried in the two loads of a shoulder pole
-yweʔ	Amount that can be carried on the head

Vague Amounts (*Group 8*)—A few classifiers show an amount of something along a particular dimension in a manner somewhat analogous to the units of weights and measures but in a much less precise manner. They simply suggest an indefinite quantity of distance, time, or weight.

-paʔ	A circuit; the distance around a circle, as the distance around the waist, the arm, a traffic roundabout, or even the distance around a city
-céin	A period of time of indefinite length; *-céin* is also sometimes used to indicate actions in time, especially for the number of bows made to a monk
-swê	An indefinite unit of weight

Residual Category—Amounts (*Group 9*)—Two classifiers indicate even less about the object counted and can be considered to occupy another residual category. These show nothing of dimension or method of measurement or precise amount.

-chòu	Some, used only with the number *ta-*, "one"
-póun	Part; used in constructing fractions such as "of four parts, three parts," i.e., $\frac{3}{4}$, but *-póun* does not in itself indicate any specific fraction

Pieces, Sets, Parts, Portions, Piles, Bunches (*Group 10*)—Like weights and measures, the members of this large and heterogeneous group specify amounts of something and do not point to a single individual object. They show something of the manner in which the amount is measured or calculated, but they are even less precise than the relative weights and measures.

-sóun	Pairs, complete assortments; pairs of shoes, sets of clothes, sets of dishes, cutlery, or furniture
-yán	Pairs of personal ornaments and clothing, earrings, bracelets, bangles, shoes
-pwé	A serving of food, usually complete with rice, curry, etc.; a course
-qouʔ	A pair of sarongs
-póun	Piles of anything: firewood, clothes, sand, food, etc.
-sî	Tied-up bunches: flowers, firewood, vegetables
-thoʔ	Wrapped-up bunches: a serving of food wrapped in a leaf, a packet of salt, a deck of cards, a bundle of clothes
-twê	Tied-together bunches, such as keys: a train carriage, possibly because it consists of a connected series of compartments
-sîn	A bunch of hair added to the natural coiffure to give bulk: chignon
-pyiʔ	Sections of thatch which are cut by a special technique known as *pyiʔde* in Burmese
-khauʔ	Folds
-tùn	Gathers
-sà	Pieces
-tân	Rows of things such as trees, chairs, etc.
-lâin	Rows or lines of things: trees, chairs, flowers
-leiʔ	Rolled-up things: rolled mats, cigarettes, cigars, rolls of paper or cloth
-khín	Hanks of rope or wool
-khwéi	Coils of rope: wreaths of flowers
-pâin	Cross-sectional pieces of bamboo, fish, logs; used especially for sections of long, slender things, but also for such things as tables, houses, and even stories of a building; often, but not necessarily, *pain* means "one-half"
-chân	A slice, usually length-wise, of fruit, fish, bamboo; often, but not necessarily, means one-half, or one of two parts, even if the parts are not equal
-seiʔ	A slice, especially of fruit, which is ambiguous as to the direction of the slice; indicates a piece smaller than half and usually only one-fourth or less
-shìn	Layers such as those of a food carrier which can be taken apart; shelves, i.e., sections which can be stacked one on top of another
-taʔ	Layers, stories

-tôun Blocks, cakes, or pieces of more or less homogeneous substances such as soap, ice, meat, charcoal, gold
-pauʔ A bit of liquid; usually more than a drop, but an indefinite amount
-kweʔ An area, usually a wet area; a puddle; a paddy field
-kwîn A field for crops or for playing games
-chán A field for flowers or fruit trees, especially the latter
-wâin Compounds

Language Units (*Group 11*)—A number of classifiers are used for segments of written or spoken language of various lengths: songs, words, paragraphs.

-pouʔ Songs, poems
-khûn Words, occasionally for sentences or utterances
-paiʔ Verses, paragraphs
-câun Sentences, lines of poem
-lôun Small bits of speech or letters of the alphabet
-pâin Parts of a story

Plant Parts (*Group 12*)—A fairly extensive and unique set of classifiers are used for parts of plants. These classifiers are often homonymous with nouns designating the same part. Thus, *seiʔ*, "joint, node," can act as a noun, but in *weʔ hnaseiʔ*, "two joints of bamboo," it acts as a classifier.

-kháin Branches, especially branches containing fruit or flowers: arms of bananas (whole stalk)
-kâin Branches
-phî Hands of bananas; used for nothing else
-kheʔ Small branches, twigs, especially small sprigs of flowers
-twê Bunches of fruit, such as grapes, or branches laden with grain
-hnàn Stalks of grain, especially paddy
-pwìn Single flowers
-ŋóun Buds
-phû Buds
-qù Edible roots and tubers
-seiʔ Joints or nodes, as of bamboo, sugar cane, or the joints of fingers
-hmwá Sections of fruit, as of an orange or of a jackfruit
-tô Forests; used with species names of trees, as "a forest of pine"

Myôu (*Group 13*)—One classifier is unique in its ability to occur with all nouns in the language.

-myôu Kinds, varieties, sorts

Echo Classifiers (*Group 14*)—Only a sample of echo classifiers is given here, but even a short list may indicate their character. *Khù* may be substituted for all of these, though it is often felt less elegant than the more specific classifier.

-caun	Schools	*-câ*	*Lancâ*, lanes, paths
-tháun	Jails	*-lân*	Roads
-qéin	Houses	*-twîn*	*Yeidwin*, wells
-yôun	Courts	*-tâun*	Baskets
-khân	Rooms	*-thân*	Paddles, oars
-ywá	Villages	*-póun*	*Dâpóun*, photographs
-myòu	Towns, cities	*-bêin*	Wheels
-né	Districts	*-sín*	Stages, shelves
-pyí, pyéi	Countries	*-youʔ*	Dolls
-kán	Lakes	*-lâun*	Corpses
-cûn	Islands	*-hmaʔ*	Marks
-chán	Gardens	*-shwê*	Drawers
-pwê	Ceremonies	*-yiʔ*	Grooves, as on a screw
-hlân	Steps	*khún*	Skin, peel
-câun	Straight lines, rulings on paper		

Semantic Structure

Having claimed that the choice among Burmese classifiers is made on a semantic, rather than a syntactic basis, and having provided an extensive list of classifiers, we may still raise the question of what degree of semantic structuring can be found within the system of classifiers. The list of classifiers that has been given is analogous to a list of kinship terms in which each term is roughly defined and in which the terms are grouped into handy, but not necessarily precise, categories, such as "blood," "in-law," and "step." No student of kinship terminology is any longer satisfied with such a list and, among other things, kinship analysts have looked for important semantic "dimensions," such as sex, generation, or lineage membership, which apportion the terms into categories and by which the terms can be defined (Goodenough: 1956). It may be interesting to see whether or not analagous distinctions can also illuminate the set of numeral classifiers. A few possibilities will be considered here and some of the difficulties of an attempt at this type of analysis will be examined.

Individuals vs. Amounts—Many of the classifiers are used to designate single individual objects. Of course, the number with which the classifier is used may be higher than one, but this simply shows that several of these individuals are grouped together. In *lú ŋâyauʔ*, "five people" (literally, "people five-people"), *-yauʔ* clearly indicates individual people. All the classifiers which show something of shape or use, and the residual category classifier *khù* (groups 2, 3, 4) are clearly of this type, as are some, though not all, of those used for animals, men, and gods (group 1). On the other hand, classifiers which indicate higher numbers, weights, and measures, piles, bunches, etc. (groups 5–10), and a few of those which stand for animals and people, just as clearly show that the things counted are not single individuals but are groups, or parts, or amounts, measured out from some substance. This semantic distinction is close to one found in English, since in English the amounts must usually be explicitly mentioned when counting, while we have no equivalent at all for the classifiers for individual objects. Such English expressions as "a pound of rice," "a foot of cloth," "a pair of oxen," "a basket of corn," "a slice of pineapple," "a branch of pine," all correspond closely to Burmese phrases which include classifiers that show an amount. One could define a semantic class of mass nouns in Burmese which can be classified *only* by classifiers indicating amounts: *yéi*, "water" may be classified with *-seʔ*, "drop," *-gálán*, "gallon," *-khweʔ*, "cup," etc., but all of these indicate amounts, and there is no way to enumerate water without some indication of amount. The converse, however, is not true. Nouns which can be classified by individual classifiers can typically be classified by those indicating amounts, as well.

The distinction between individuals and amounts seems to be of considerable importance in Burmese, and we might be tempted to hope that this distinction could constitute a semantic dimension which would run across the system, much as the dimension of sex runs throughout many systems of kinship terminology. However, the attempt to pursue such a distinction too far and to try to turn it into a precise and systematic dimension like the sex distinction in kinship, leads to some peculiar questions. Should a classifier like "branch" be considered as a "part" (of a tree or plant) which shows the amount of the substance counted, or is a "branch" an object in its own right? The apparent triviality of such a question may even lead one to doubt the good sense of pursuing such distinctions, for surely the meaning is obvious without forcing it into one side or the other of this dichotomy. Piles, bunches, and the classifiers for units of language raise similar problems. One must say therefore that Burmese includes some classifiers clearly indicating single individuals, others clearly denoting amounts, and still others which are ambiguous along this dimension, though it is not even easy to say clearly when ambiguity is present. Is a "pair" clearly an amount? If so, what about "slice"? Perhaps the distinction between individual and amount is not trustworthy until such questions are answered.

Specified vs. Unspecified Amounts—Those classifiers which show something about the amount of the object being counted seem to fall into two types which vary in the degree of precision with which the amount is indicated. Some which can be said to "specify" the amount either show the exact number of objects or give an amount along a particular dimension, or state that the unit considered is enough to fill a container or to be used in some manner (groups 5, 6, 7, and a few in 1). Other classifiers do not specify the amount, even though they show that amounts rather than individuals are being counted (groups 8, 9, 10, and a few in 1), e.g., "crowd," "circuit," "some."

"Cultural" vs. "Noncultural"—Many classifiers show the shape of the object or indicate the size or amount of the units counted but imply nothing of the way in which the object is made or used. If "noncultural" is used to stand for these classifiers, then "cultural" can indicate those classifiers which show something about the manner of use, or of the general cultural context of the object counted. These "cultural" classifiers can be taken to include those for individual objects which show how the object is used (group 3), the units of weights and measures which show the method of measurement (group 7), and also the miscellaneous category of parts, pieces, sets, etc. (group 10). One might also suggest that the units of language should be considered "cultural." However, the decision in a number of cases as to whether a particular classifier should be considered to be "cultural" or not is difficult, and perhaps in the end quite arbitrary. "Bunch of tied-up hair" (*sîn*) seems quite clearly "cultural," but what about *seiʔ*, "slice"? Once again, the attempt to push a particular type of analysis too far seems to lead to foolish questions.

Indication of Dimension—Many classifiers show something about shape or dimension. These include not only those in group 2 (objects with dimension), but also the units of weights and measures (groups 6 and 7), since all weights and measures are measured along some particular dimension. Moreover, many of those listed under "piles," "bunches," etc., show something about shape: row, hank, slice, etc. (group 10). However, it is difficult to decide in some cases whether a particular classifier really says enough about shape or dimension to make it significant (layer, fold, cross section) and again, a distinction that seems clear in some cases breaks down when pushed too far.

Residual Categories—The classifier *khù* is clearly recognized to have a unique role in the Burmese language. Burmese speakers readily advise a learner of the language to use *khù* when in doubt, and I have heard children use *-khù* in situations in which an adult would probably use a more precise classifier. *Khù* should never be used for people, animals, or sacred beings (group 1), so it clearly indicates the absence of these characteristics. It shows nothing at all about the shape of the object and nothing at all about its use, but it is specifically used only for single individual objects and never for amounts. It appears that systems of numeral classifiers generally include a residual category classifier. Perhaps the things which people count are of such diverse character that it is impossible to divide them neatly enough to leave no ambiguities. A residual category classifier is necessary to take up the slack.

Many objects can be used only with *-khù*, but in other cases either *khù* or some other classifier can be freely used. With still others *-khù* has varying degrees of awkwardness, and to use *khù* with objects such as people would be clearly improper. It is, therefore, impossible to draw a sharp line around those objects which can be classified with *-khù*, but the term covers a very wide area. Objects which regularly take *-khù* include: moons, clocks, typewriters, noises, omens, cakes, tails, scratches, chairs, tables, and dozens of other items. Those which can take *-khù* but can alternatively be used with other classifiers, as well, include: stories, tickets, mats, pots, and others, while people, animals, pagodas, autos, fruit, rings, and many others never take *-khù*.

Syntactically, *-khù* is in no way distinct from other classifiers, and its obviously unique characteristics can be understood only on the basis of its semantic position. Burmese speakers sometimes include *-khù* in the same series as the classifiers for the powers of ten: *shé*, "ten," *yá*, "hundred," *tháun*, "thousand," etc. This is entirely understandable on the basis of their meaning. Neither *khù* nor the others indicate anything of dimension or use of the object counted. They differ from each other primarily in the size of the group indicated, *-khù* indicating only one individual object (units), *shé*, "groups of ten," etc. They also differ, however, in that *-khù*, unlike the others, *cannot* be used when another classifier is clearly more appropriate, while the powers of ten can be used for anything for which a group of that size must be specified.

A second residual category consists of terms which do not specify amounts and which show nothing of use, shape, or dimension. A term which indicates a vague amount and shows nothing of the use or shape of the object it counts, conveys very little, and in fact, means approximately the same as "some" in English. Such a classifier exists in Burmese, but since it makes no sense to talk of "two somes" or "three somes," this classifier is unique in being used only with the number for one: *tachòu*, "some." Structurally this is like any classifier phrase except that other numbers cannot be substituted for *ta-*. Burmese dictionaries usually list *tachòu* as a separate lexeme, thereby masking its structural and semantic similarities to classifier phrases. Another classifier, *-póun*, means "part," and hence also refers to an unspecified amount in which nothing of the shape or use is shown.

Having outlined certain possibilities for arranging the sets of classifiers, the problem of how to organize the classifiers within each set remains to be explored, though only a few possibilities will be suggested here.

Dimensions—It is tempting to consider the distinctions among classifiers which specify dimension in time or space (group 2), as similar to the distinctions among weights and measures (groups 6 and 7). Classifiers for events which occur in time and others for objects occurring in space are found in both types. Some of the commonest of those for objects in space are those which are used for long, slender objects (analogous to measures of length), thin, flat objects (analogous to measures of area), and globular objects (analogous to measures of volume). There is even a classifier for loop-shaped objects (analogous to measures of girth) and one for vertical posts (analogous to measures of height).

The comparison is not perfect, however, as the reader may verify by comparing the various lists. Certain distinctions are found in each set, which are not found in the others. It is difficult to know how far an analyst is justified in pushing such a comparison, and the particular way in which the distinctions among the various classifiers in these categories are arranged is open to a wide number of alternatives.

Groups and Parts—It might be tempting to recognize a distinction within certain categories between classifiers for parts of things, and those for larger amounts, than a single individual. This looks particularly appealing for the miscellaneous category (group 10), where pieces, bunches, sets, etc., need to be distinguished. It might also be useful in the residual category (group 9), since it contains a classifier meaning "some" and another meaning simply "part." In many cases it is difficult to tell whether an object is a part of something else or not. A "clump of thatch" is a collection of pieces of grass but a part of a roof. Folds, gathers, rows, hanks, servings, piles, and bunches are similarly obscure.

Prestige—Among the classifiers for animate objects there seems to be a reasonably clear hierarchy of prestige, or perhaps of relative sanctity. Animals rank below men, ordinary men rank below kings, monks, and nuns, and even these exalted people rank below Buddhas. Supernatural beings are assimilated into this rank order. Ghosts, which the Burmese view as rather vulgar and mean beings, are classified along with animals, whereas spirits rank just below the Buddha and along with monks and royalty.

Miscellaneous—One can easily point out many other distinctions which divide the meaning of one classifier from another. No particular description need recognize them all, and yet many would have to be recognized if every classifier were to be allotted a separate semantic space in a manner analogous to the dimensional analysis of kinship terms. Some weights and measures are obvious borrowings from other languages and are still used largely to classify imported goods (e.g., *dázín*), and these could be considered as falling into a separate category. Any number of ways could be devised to distinguish among the classifiers for plant parts, speech parts, etc. Clearly there are scores, and even hundreds, of conceivable semantic dimensions that could be recognized.

Conclusions

A number of semantic distinctions have now been considered. Some looked promising at first but the attempt to find pervasive semantic dimensions which unambiguously apportion the entire set of classifiers into clear subsets has hardly been successful. Repeatedly, semantic distinctions which seemed useful for some classifiers proved difficult to interpret when pushed to other areas, and the attempt to pursue the kind of analysis so illuminating for kinship terms led to such silly questions as whether a branch should be considered an object or an amount.

I argued in the first part of this paper that the choice among classifiers must be made on semantic, rather than syntactical grounds, and I will not modify that conclusion. Yet the techniques of semantic analysis which anthropologists have applied with considerable elegance to other terminological areas seem to fall down here. Perhaps kinship terminology has something special about it and perhaps anthropologists should not assume that techniques developed there will be usable elsewhere. Of course, in spite of these difficulties, Burmese do learn to speak to each other and even foreigners can learn to use classifiers without undue difficulty. Seeing the problems which arise in the attempt to bring order into the set of classifiers, one may feel that the best available "analysis" so far is simply the list of classifiers with their definitions. If there is such a thing as "semantic structure" in a language, then this list ought to be reducible to some more orderly arrangement, but it seems doubtful that componential analysis is up to the task. Systematically minded anthropologists are welcome to take the data presented here and try to organize them in a more satisfactory way. Perhaps other techniques can illuminate classifiers as much as componential analysis has illuminated kinship terminology.

References

Cornyn, W.
1944: *Outline of Burmese Grammar*. Language Dissertation No. 38, supplement to *Language*, **20,** No. 4.

Goodenough, W. H.
1956: "Componential Analysis and the Study of Meaning," *Language*, **32,** 195–216.

Haas, M. R.
1951: "The Use of Numeral Classifiers in Burmese," *Semitic and Oriental Studies, University of California Publications in Semitic Philology*, **11,** 191–200.

WARD H. GOODENOUGH

Personal Names and Modes of Address in Two Oceanic Societies[1]

One's identity as a person and as a member of society is an object of universal human concern. Hallowell (1955, p. 74) has observed, "Self-awareness is a psychological constant, one basic facet of human nature and of human personality." He added (*idem*) that "it is becoming increasingly apparent that this peculiarly human phenomenon is the focus of complex, and functionally dependent, sets of linguistic and cultural variables that enter into the personal adjustment of human beings as members of particular societies." In other words, all men are concerned with their identities, but the directions and emphases of their concern vary from individual to individual and modally from one social group to another.

This variation is conditioned by differences in two major sets of factors. One consists of the ways in which social relationships are culturally organized; the other consists of the prevailing circumstances in which these cultural organizations find expression. Both sets of factors in combination produce

1. This paper expands on an idea to which preliminary formulation has been given elsewhere (Goodenough: 1963, pp. 191–193).

the actual social arrangements in which people find themselves. These social arrangements directly affect the way people feel about themselves, individually and collectively, and thus influence the direction of their identity concerns. To find a workable *modus vivendi* with these arrangements and concerns, regardless of how they vary, is a universal human problem. In every society we should expect to find at least some institutions and customary practices functioning in ways that, among other things, help people to deal with this problem.

Customs relating to personal names and modes of address recommend themselves as among those most likely to be intimately linked with identity concerns. In this respect, two Oceanic communities in which I have made field studies offer a remarkable contrast. One is in Truk in the Caroline Islands and the other in Lakalai (West Nakanai) on the north coast of New Britain.[2]

Truk

It is evident that before the introduction of European and Japanese names in Truk, no two persons ever had the same personal name (*jita-n*, "his name"); nor were the same ones given knowingly as of 1947. The genealogies recorded on Romonum Island at that time (Goodenough: 1951, charts 3–22) contain the names of 793 individuals (excluding foreign-born) over as many as ten generations (Table I).[3] Of these about 133 individuals have names that are

Table I.—Personal Names Recorded in Truk

	Number of Individuals Named	*Number of Names*
Names of native origin	660	660
Names of foreign origin	133	129
Totals	793	789

certainly or apparently of foreign origin (all born after 1900), and 660 bear Trukese names. In all, only four names appear more than once, and each of these twice only. These four names—Aryko, Siro, Teriwo (from Japanese) and Jeniisa (from German *Elise*)—are all of foreign origin and in at least three instances involve persons born on different islands in Truk's lagoon. If only 8 individuals of 133 with foreign names share their name with another person, and at least 6 of these do so by accident, it seems evident that even in the

2. Field work in Truk was undertaken in 1947 as a member of a research team from Yale University under the leadership of Professor G. P. Murdock and sponsored by the Pacific Science Board of the National Academy of Sciences-National Research Council and the Office of Naval Research. Work in Lakalai was undertaken by a research team from the University of Pennsylvania in 1954 under the joint auspices of the Department of Anthropology and the University Museum with additional financial support from the American Philosophical Society and the Tri-Institutional Program for the Pacific (Bishop Museum, University of Hawaii, and Yale University). For this paper I have drawn on data for Lakalai collected by Dr. Ann Chowning and Dr. C. A. Valentine in addition to those that I obtained personally.

3. The genealogies were collected jointly by G. P. Murdock and the writer in 1947.

giving of Christian and other alien names, duplication has been avoided. Thus we have the remarkable situation that for 793 individuals there are 789 distinctive personal names.[4]

We should observe, moreover, that women's names are frequently marked as such in Truk by an initial element *Jine-* or *Neeji-*, as in *Jinewin* and *Neejitiw*. Sex distinctions in Christian and Japanese names are regularly preserved in Truk also.

In address, people regularly use personal names. People do not ordinarily address one another by kinship terms. Little children may use special kin terms of address to their parents, but soon abandon this practice in favor of addressing their parents by name. On ceremonial occasions a chief may be addressed by title, but otherwise people address him by name. Teknonymy (identifying a person through his child), moreover, is as strange in Truk as in the United States. The one serious restriction arises in the brother-sister relationship. Brothers and sisters do not normally address each other at all, being in a classic "avoidance" relationship; but on those occasions when they may, they do so by name. In short, the right and proper way to address another on virtually all occasions when social intercourse is permitted is by personal name.

A short form of the personal name may be used in address, at least on some occasions. Nicknames descriptive of some personal attribute are common, but are not usually used in the presence of those to whom they apply. I heard nicknames used in address only rarely and then in the context of deliberate teasing or joking.

In summary, with rare and accidental exceptions, every individual in Truk has a distinctive personal name that he shares with no one else, living or dead, and he expects to be addressed by that name and in no other way by everyone on almost all occasions.

Lakalai

Nothing so simple can be reported for Lakalai. The great majority of individuals have more than one name. Nearly everyone shares his name or names with someone else. There are no sex distinctions in names; even such a name as Taurikau ("Rikau Man") is held by a woman as well as by a man. Finally, the use of names is hedged by tabu, terms for kin and other relationships are used widely in address, and teknonymy (identifying a person through his child) is common in address and reference.

Personal names (*la-isa-la*, "his name")[5] are of several types. First, each person has what may be called a primary name (*la-isa-la sesele*, "his true or

4. That almost all of these names were supplied from memory by Simiron of Romonum, with only a handful of corrections having to be made later, is noteworthy in itself.

5. In Lakalai all nouns are marked as such by a prefix *la-* or, in the case of personal nouns, names of persons and places, and a few other nouns, by *e-*, which is optionally dropped in many contexts and regularly dropped in direct address.

proper name"). He may also have a secondary name (*la-tohilovula*) and a defecation name (*la-tohilovula-la-tatahe*). The coming of Christianity has now added baptismal names. Cutting across these distinctions in part is another one. Some names carry with them obligatory other names that must be given to one's first child, regardless of its sex. Thus Sege must name his (her) first child Samila, and Samila must name his first child Bubu; Uoso must name his first child Babo, who must name his first child Golumu, who must name his first child Kautu. As these examples imply, there are fixed sequences of names of this type, each sequence forming a cycle in that at some point it closes on itself with a return to the same name with which it started. All such cycle names, as I shall call them, serve as primary names, but not all primary names are cycle names. Some individuals may have more than one cycle name, also, because of the way in which names are given. Some individuals, on the other hand, lack a cycle name. While most primary names are cycle names and most other names are not, the correlation is not perfect.

In naming children, a man whose primary name is a cycle name will give the corresponding cycle name to his first child. If he has no cycle name, his first child will be named according to his wife's cycle name. When both husband and wife have cycle names, then the first child may be named according to the father's name and the second child according to the mother's. The mother's cycle name may be ignored, however, only the father's being honored; or the first child may be named according to the father's cycle name if it is a boy and according to the mother's if it is a girl.[6] When a person has more than one cycle name, his first child will be named according to one and a subsequent child according to another.

If a man has more than one wife—polygyny is common—then his first child be each wife must bear the name that goes with his cycle name. The firstborn (*la-posolagu*) occupies a special place in Lakalai values. It is a father's duty to celebrate each step in the child's maturation and socialization with a feast. Any injury to a first child requires the payment of special indemnity to his parents. Subsequent children are not accorded such special attention. The definition of a firstborn, however, involves both parents simultaneously: the first child a man has by each different wife is a firstborn, and the first child a woman has by each successive husband is also a firstborn. The equivalence of a man's several firstborn children by different wives is emphasized by the requirement that they all bear the same primary name, whether they received it in consequence of the father's cycle name or not. Figure 1 provides an actual example from the genealogies. Uoso's firstborn Babo had two wives, Solamomo and Kaula, the latter herself one of a pair of firstborns by her father's two marriages. Babo's two firstborns, both sons, were each named Golumu, in

6. Only the first of these usages was reported to me. The others were reported as alternatives to C. A. Valentine.

accordance with Babo's cycle name. One Golumu married Mape and died while she was pregnant with his first child. This child was named Kautu according to his father's cycle name. Golumu's half brother, the other Golumu, married the widowed Mape, and named his first child by her Kautu in accordance with his own cycle name. The latter Kautu is conveniently distinguished from the former by his baptismal name, Paulus.

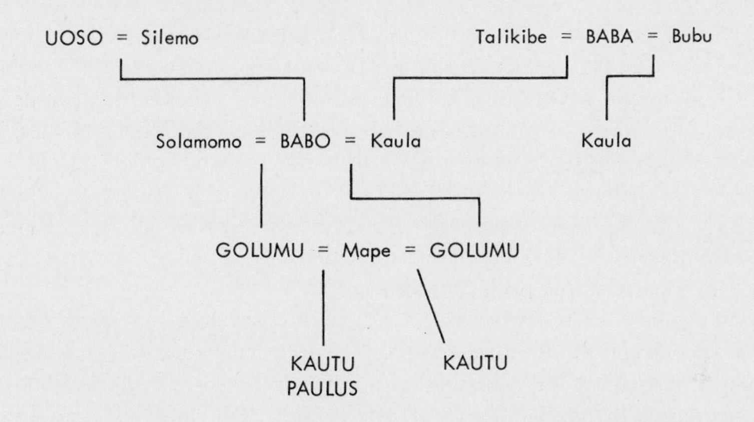

Figure 1.—Sequence of firstborns under polygyny in Lakalai

Key: The names of men are given in capitals and those of women in lower case. Marriage is indicated by =.

People like to have their names given to younger persons and thus kept in use. It is wrong for a parent to give his child his own name; but people frequently request that a grandchild or the child of some other relative be named for them. This leads to a special namesake relationship in which the junior may request favors and the senior is obligated to grant them. Children are also frequently named after deceased relatives, and famous sibmates from the past.[7] These practices provide a means by which other than firstborn children acquire primary names that are cycle names; but firstborns may also be named in this way, thus acquiring two cycle names, one in accordance with their parent's cycle name and the other as a relative's namesake.

A result of these practices is that full siblings may have the same primary name. A daughter and a son of one couple are both named Bubu, for example, each having been named for a different relative. Similarly, a son and two daughters of another couple were all three named Ragi.

Other practices include naming children for their sib, or for the place, time of year, weekday, or other event or circumstance associated with their birth. Examples are Garua (from the sib of that name), Talasea (name of the

7. Every Lakalai belongs to a matrilineal, named, totemic sib (*la-maratatila*).

Government seat), Gauru ("Path"), Sárere ("Saturday"), Hura ("Rain"), and Kalakulu ("Breadfruit Leaf," on which the newly born was laid).

The foregoing naming methods are not mutually exclusive. It is common to give children more than one name. Thus, someone may receive the obligatory cycle name Gaa, the noncycle name Tausulu ("Sulu Man") after a dead relative of that name, and the noncycle name Mahuma ("Garden") for the place where his mother gave birth to him.

Individuals may also acquire nicknames descriptive of a personal characteristic or physical feature. Examples are Haremasile ("Torn Mouth"), Matakea ("Blind"), Vahasaa ("One Leg"). Once established, a nickname becomes part of what is handed on to a namesake, who receives all the names of the person he is named for. Thus a man who was ordinarily referred to as Toho had been named after a man called Gelu (Toho's primary and cycle name), who after falling down at the foot of a mangrove tree received the nickname Bulatoho, "Base-of-Mangrove." The nickname, shortened to Toho ("Mangrove"), had been handed on with the primary name.

Lakalai men, but not women, have a highly developed sense of shame in relation to defecation. Because so many people have one or more names in common, it frequently happens that an adult man shares a name with an infant in his household or hamlet. To say of the infant, "Oh, look,——had a movement!" within hearing of a man of that name is to shame the latter so as to give him cause for suicide—at least so the Lakalai allege.[8] To avoid any possibility of embarrassment, therefore, infants are referred to by their baptismal name or some other convenient nickname that belongs to no one who is likely to be shamed. These defecation names go out of use after a child has reached about ten years of age. Needless to say, the Lakalai sometimes name a child (for one of his names) after a European for the precise purpose of providing a convenient defecation name and an opportunity to insult the European in the extreme while pretending to honor him.[9]

What one of his several names a person will be commonly known by depends on several considerations. If there are others in his hamlet who share his primary or cycle name, it may be convenient to call him by a secondary name or nickname. Of the twenty-five individuals recorded in the genealogies with the cycle name Kautu, for example, secondary names were also recorded for nine, most of whom were referred to by both names at once, e.g., Kautu e-Susu, Kautu Guluve, Kautu Karoki, etc. Two persons with the same name may also be distinguished by adding the word "big" (*uru*) to the name for one of them, as with Tokile and Tokileuru.

8. In Lakalai, anyone who by his actions causes another to commit suicide is guilty of manslaughter.

9. By no means all instances of naming for a European are with this purpose in mind. Usually, the intention is honorable.

Of great importance is the widespread prohibition of the use of personal names in address and reference. There are several special "partner" relationships into which people may enter, all of which require the partners to refrain from using one another's names, in referring not only to one another, but to any one else of the same name. Persons do not refer to one another by name, moreover, if they happen to have the same one. And there are several kin categories whose occupants may not be mentioned by name. Thus if a man's cycle name of Kautu requires that his firstborn be named Kaveu, and Kaveu happens to be the name of his father-in-law, then he cannot refer to his firstborn by his primary name, but instead must use a secondary name or nickname. Others may refer to him as Kaveu, or they may follow the father's lead, so that the child gets to be known generally by a secondary name, rather than his primary one.

A common circumlocution is to name a person teknonymously. Thus, Kautu may be referred to or addressed as *tama* (*tila*) *le-Kaveu*, "father (mother) of Kaveu," or simply as Kaveu. The system of cycle names makes it possible to use teknonymy even with small children, the names of whose firstborns are already determined.[10]

As the foregoing suggests, kinship terms and the terms for special partner relationships are frequently used in address. Even in relationships in which there are no name tabus, kinship terms are commonly used when addressing senior members of one's immediate kindred.[11]

Discussion

Truk and Lakalai are in remarkable contrast. Customs relating to personal names and personal address in Truk all serve to emphasize individuality and to give it explicit recognition. Customs of naming and address in Lakalai, on the other hand, emphasize one's place in a procreational chain or in formally structured kin and social relationships. These customs pointedly ignore one's place in the social order in Truk and even more pointedly call attention to it in Lakalai.

To assume that Trukese society is more individualistic in its values than Lakalai society, however, would be a serious mistake. Indeed, the fallacy of inferring general values from specific customs or institutions without reference to all the others in a society is clearly illustrated here.

10. When a woman marries, she is named by teknonymy according to her husband's cycle name rather than her own, because her husband's name will now determine the name of her first child.

11. The kindred in Lakalai is one's circle of kinsmen, regardless of how they are related genealogically, and is not to be confused with one's matrilineal sib or lineage. All noncasual social relationships are structured either in kinship or partnership terms. The resulting elasticity to one's circle of kinsmen leads the Lakalai to distinguish close kin and hamlet mates, who together form one's immediate kindred (Goodenough: 1962), from nominal kin, who comprise one's extended kindred. Senior close kin are addressed by kinship terms, whereas senior nominal kin are not, except when kinship is being specifically emphasized.

In Truk corporate descent groups (matrilineal lineages) are highly developed, and it is virtually impossible for an individual ever to be fully independent of the one into which he was born. Most of his rights, privileges, and immunities in the larger community derive from his membership in a lineage. The lineage is the principal agent of social control over his behavior and the principle defender of his rights. Within the lineage authority is based on relative age. Since the individual must always subordinate his private interests to those of his lineage, his lineage elders have the power to veto any of his private plans, a power they frequently exercise. To take independent action, to seek to dissociate oneself from one's lineage in any way is publicly disapproved as contrary to one's most important and binding social obligation, which is to promote the solidarity and well-being of one's sibling group and lineage, itself conceived of as a sibling group. This value is clearly expressed in the marital relationship. Whenever the joint interests of husband and wife are in conflict with the interests of their respective lineages, the former must be sacrificed. In any dispute a woman is obligated to take her brother's side against her husband, and even to terminate the marriage if the dispute is not resolved. A person's individual social worth is largely measured in terms of the prestige of his lineage and his own position within its age hierarchy. He can achieve personal recognition only through the knowledge and skills he acquires in a craft or magical speciality, but even his right to learn these is limited by the rules of eligibility, which rest largely on lineage membership and the paternal relationship.[12]

In this way I infer from the cultural ordering of social relationships in Truk, and from the values implicit in its principles and expressed by them, that individualistic values are suppressed in favor of corporate ones and that there is little opportunity for a person to acquire value in the estimation of others and a corresponding sense of his own worth purely and simply as an individual. It would appear that the social order and the public values[13] it expresses frustrate any desire for individualistic expression and individual worth that Truk's people may harbor in their private sentiments.

To the extent that they do have such desires and to the extent that they are frustrated, we should expect to find compensating institutions. Extramarital courtship, a striking preoccupation of Truk's young adults, seems to be, among other things, an important avenue to such compensation.[14] The adulterous

12. For an extended discussion of Truk's social organization and the inheritance of property rights, see Goodenough (1951).

13. Public values are to be understood as the principles implicit in the priorities that are expressed by the way in which rights and duties are defined and differentially distributed in publicly recognized social relationships. See Goodenough (1963, pp. 96–97), and Goodenough (ms.).

14. For accounts and interpretations, see Goodenough (1949); Gladwin and Sarason (1953, pp. 100–117); Swartz (1958).

lover relationship, condemned in public as an infringement of marital privilege, provides an opportunity for people to experience themselves as objects of value to others without reference to their position in the social order. The frustration one's lover is willing to endure and the risks he (or she) is willing to run in order to achieve an assignation are vivid demonstrations of one's importance as a person to someone else. The addiction that so many younger people in Truk seem to have for this elaborate and highly formalized, though illegal, game of courtship is thoroughly consistent with the idea that it symbolizes what is for many people an unresolved identity problem.[15]

In the light of these considerations, I infer that Truk's naming and address customs compensate in another way for the suppression of individuality in Truk's social system. A person's name emphasizes his uniqueness as a person, and whenever anyone addresses him, his individuality is acknowledged.

In Lakalai the public values emphasize individual achievement. Sibling solidarity is stressed, with the elder having authority over the younger, but siblings can and often do go their separate ways. The set of siblings with which a person operates is not so rigidly determined by birth as it is in Truk; choices are available.[16] There are matrilineal lingeages under the leadership of their eldest male member, as in Truk, and as in Truk they are associated with land ownership. But in Truk the lineage (or large sublineage) and the matrilocal extended family based on its women are the principal units of collective action and the lineage is the immediate political constituent of the larger community, whereas in Lakalai the lineages have very few corporate functions. Instead, hamlets made of a group of people related to one another by either birth or marriage in a variety of ways are the principal units of collective action and the immediate political constituents in the larger community. People can and do change their hamlet affiliation, and the villages are organized essentially as confederations of hamlets, which can and do secede.

Leadership roles in the functionally undeveloped lineages are based on seniority alone. Seniority is prerequisite to leadership roles generally, in that opportunity to assume leadership increases with age. But age alone is not enough. To be a leader a man must establish a reputation as a hard and productive worker. He must gain a following of younger kinsmen who entrust their wealth to him, rather than to someone else; he must acquire wealth through

15. For the hypothesis, and supporting evidence, that games symbolize and express the emotional requirements for different kinds of roles that people must play and that game involvement and game addiction are directly related to emotional conflict about these roles, see Roberts, Arth, and Bush (1959); Roberts and Sutton-Smith (1962); and Sutton-Smith, Roberts, and Kozelka (1963). If one looks at extramarital courtship in Truk as a kind of game—and there is good reason to do so—then this hypothesis regarding game involvement should apply here.

16. For an account of the formation of sibling sets in Lakalai, see Goodenough (1962). For other aspects of Lakalai social organization, see Chowning (1958), and Chowning and Goodenough (ms.).

trade and the astute manipulation of social relationships; he must cultivate a reputation as a brave and skillful warrior, and as a bold man of action. He must compete with other emerging leaders by staging large and lavish festivals, which concretely demonstrate his capacity to mobilize the productive labor of an army of followers, who work for him because they are obligated to him for past favors and support, and dependent on him for favors and support in the future. The highest political offices and the positions of highest prestige and authority in Lakalai society are conferred only upon persons who have successfully outdistanced all rivals in such competition for recognition as a "big man."

In both Truk and Lakalai virtue lies in rendering loyalty to one's senior kinsmen, in working hard, in honoring one's obligations, and taking proper responsibility for the affairs of one's dependents, a responsibility that increases with age. But there is no reward in Truk for practicing these virtues other than maintaining one's membership in a lineage and community in good standing. One avoids censure but earns nothing. Personal recognition for skill as a warrior or craftsman does not alter one's position in the seniority hierarchy; only the death of one's elders can do that. In Lakalai, on the other hand, the rewards of virtue are great and positive: personal honor, and expanding personal voice, authority, and power. To achieve it a Lakalai must enter into active competition with his fellows. Traits of temperament that go with a competitive spirit are positively valued and encouraged (Valentine: 1963). Indeed, the Lakalai are such "rugged individualists" in the competition for personal recognition that wealthy men are said to have their surplus wealth destroyed at their death, so that no one, not even one's own children, can present himself as a wealthy and important man without having earned the privilege of doing so by his own effort. The Lakalai, then, emphasize individual competition as the avenue to self-realization. They link this closely with the virtues of hard work, loyalty to elders, and honoring of debts and obligations, as well as to bravery and boldness, but the cooperation and mutual dependability that is essential to the conduct of social affairs in Lakalai is tinged with wariness, with the knowledge that one's fellows in one context are one's competitors in another.

This tension between competition and cooperation is expressed in family relations. Sibling solidarity is highly valued and cultivated, but at the same time parents frankly and openly exhibit favoritism among their children and encourage their children to compete with one another for parental indulgence. Study of the political process in Lakalai reveals the same tension between conflicting values, with villages and hamlets continually breaking up and reforming in response to the changing relative strength of their opposing pressures in concrete situations (Chowning and Goodenough: ms.).

From this viewpoint, I infer that naming customs and modes of address in Lakalai function to offset competition by serving as continual reminders that people are, after all, part of a social order, inextricably tied to others by obligations deriving from birth and contract. Competition is fine, but it must follow the rules and not go so far as to make cooperation and loyalty among kinsmen and peace among neighbors impossible.

In both Truk and Lakalai, then, conventions regarding names and address function as constant reminders to people of things about their identities. In Truk, they are things most people want to be reminded of. In Lakalai, they are things about which most people want to remind their fellows. In Truk, they appear to cater to a widespread desire in private sentiment that is frustrated by a monolithic set of public values in which the individual is consistently subordinated to his group. In Lakalai they serve to reinforce one set of public values that are in opposition to another set of public values. These customs deal primarily with private needs in Truk and primarily with social needs in Lakalai.

In each society, naming customs and modes of address appear to counterbalance the effect that the workings of the social system tend otherwise to give to people's images of themselves and of others. I do not infer from this that such customs are always to be interpreted as functioning in this way. Rather, I would remark that modes of address—and personal names insofar as they are involved in address—are used many times a day in the normal course of life's routine in every society. Whatever form they have, they cannot help but communicate over and over again things about the self and about self-other relationships. Different naming and address customs necessarily select different things about the self for communication and consequent emphasis. In some instances what is selected for emphasis will reflect and reinforce dominant public values; in others what is selected will reflect personal concerns; and in yet others it may reflect something else. In any event, it will be something about which people are concerned, something about their own identities or the identities of others that they *want* to emphasize. What it will be depends on the nature of the identity problems their social circumstances prevailingly create for them.

References

Chowning, A.
1958: *Lakalai Society*. Unpublished Ph.D. dissertation, University of Pennsylvania. Available in microfilm and in Human Relations Area Files.

Chowning, A., & Goodenough, W. H.
Lakalai Political Organization. Unpublished ms.

Gladwin, T., & Sarason, S. B.
1953: *Truk: Man in Paradise*. Viking Fund Publications in Anthropology, No. 20 (New York: Wenner-Gren Foundation for Anthropological Research).

Goodenough, W. H.

1949: "Premarital Freedom on Truk: Theory and Practice," *American Anthropologist*, **51**, 615–620.

1951: *Property, Kin, and Community on Truk*. Yale University Publications in Anthropology, No. 46 (New Haven: Department of Anthropology, Yale University).

1962: "Kindred and Hamlet in Lakalai, New Britain," *Ethnology*, **1**, 5–12.

1963: *Cooperation in Change: An Anthropological Approach to Community Development* (New York: Russell Sage Foundation).

1965: "Rethinking 'Status' and 'Role': Toward a General Model of the Cultural Organization of Social Relationships," in M. Banton (ed.), *The Relevance of Models for Social Anthropology* (London: Tavistock, in press).

Hallowell, A. I.

1955: *Culture and Experience* (Philadelphia: University of Pennsylvania Press).

Roberts, J. M., Arth, M. J., & Bush, R. R.

1959: "Games in Culture," *American Anthropologist*, **61**, 597–605.

Roberts, J. M., & Sutton-Smith, B.

1962: "Child Training and Game Involvement," *Ethnology*, **1**, 166–185.

Sutton-Smith, B., Roberts, J. M., & Koselka, R. M.

1963: "Game Involvement in Adults," *Journal of Social Psychiatry*, **60**, 15–30.

Swartz, M. J.

1958: "Sexuality and Aggression on Romonum, Truk," *American Anthropologist*, **60**, 467–486.

Valentine, C. A.

1963: "Men of Anger and Men of Shame: Ethnopsychology and Its Implications for Sociopsychological Theory," *Ethnology*, **2**, 441–477.

ANTHONY F. C. WALLACE

Driving to Work

Introduction

It was A. I. Hallowell who pointed out to me, when I was a student of his, that cognitive maps were an interesting object of study for an anthropologist. He spoke of "the self" as an object of human awareness, developing along with man's moral capacity in the long reaches of human evolution, and of the unique "behavioral environment" that in each culture man has created for himself by a process of selective attention to his total environment. These ideas were of importance to me in developing the concept of "mazeway," by which I mean the sum of all the cognitive maps which at any moment a person maintains, of self, of behavioral environment, and of those valued experiences or states of being which attract or repel him.

This paper is devoted to an effort to describe in some detail one segment of the mazeway of one individual in one culture. The technical background for the train of thought represented here may be found in several of the writer's publications (*vide* Wallace: 1961a, 1961b, 1962). But for the documentation of the empirical data to be presented, no informant, no authority can be cited beyond the writer himself. This paper is simply an introspective account in which the anthropologist uses himself as his own informant. In it, the informant-anthropologist seeks to describe the cognitive operations he carries out in performing a task which, in a sense, is "required" by the culture in which he lives: driving an automobile from home to work.

For the anthropologist to act as his own informant presents some interesting methodological problems. At first glance, it would appear that the issue is simply one of "introspection" versus objective description of behavior by an "outsider" observer. Introspection, indeed, has little or no value as a source of information about certain sorts of psychological processes, or even about the finer details of processes for which it has some value as an initial method of observation. But, nonetheless, it is unavoidable, and the anthropologist derives a large proportion of his information by the simple procedure of asking an informant to introspect: to say, or write, what he is thinking about a certain subject. Thus for the anthropologist to record, by writing or by dictating, his own thoughts about his own culturally relevant behavior involves only a minor difference in method from standard procedure. And, as in this case, when the technique is used as a means of approach to certain theoretical problems, it has the advantage of permitting a high degree of thoroughness of inquiry and of directness of approach to "psychological reality."

But, one may legitimately inquire, would not the faithfulness of recall of a task like driving to work be improved by lessening the time span between actual behavior and introspective recall of that behavior? Would it not be better, for instance, to have the informant dictate to a portable tape recorder while he is carrying out the task? There are two strong reasons why this would be, in balance, positively undesirable. First of all, the purpose of the investigation is not to describe one day's experience, but the mental pattern, the cognitive map, or mazeway, which is the ever-changing product of many days' experiences. Since not all of that mazeway will be evoked by the circumstances of one day, it is evident that only an introspective process can approach the complexity of the mazeway as it exists even on a single day. And second, requiring the informant to "inform" while he is carrying out the task would change the very psychological processes which are the object of description. Memory, for all its well-known fallibility, is at least *a* record of the actual experience; requiring the informant to record data while he is supposedly doing something else would change the experience itself. We have here another instance of the awkward principle of behavioral complementarity, akin to the principle of complementarity in physics, which may be more serious for the behavioral sciences than for the physical.

Thus, the description of the process of driving to work will depend upon the introspective consultation of memory by an anthropologist-informant, sitting at his writing table, recalling patterns of experience in specific activity which he has personally experienced approximately five hundred times.

The Route

The route to work—or at least certain features of it—is displayed in brief in Fig. 1. The map shows the general compass orientation of the roadway, the turns at intersections or choice points (but not all intersections where the route continues straight ahead), the location of all stop signs and traffic lights, certain environmental landmarks (including origin and destination), and the names of several major roads and highways which are followed for part of the way. The map was drawn from memory on September 15, 1963.[1] The

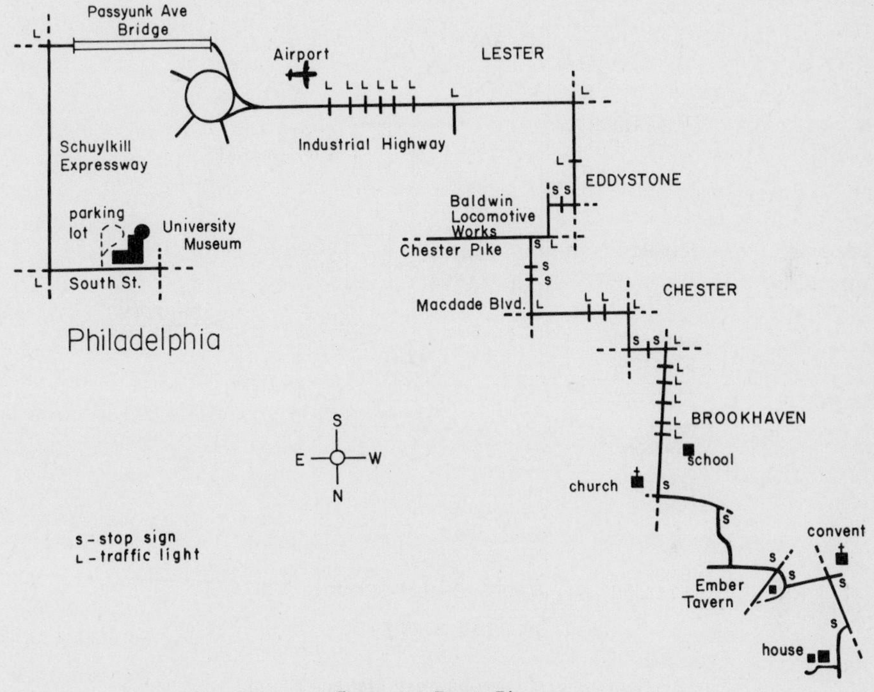

Figure 1.—Route Plan

total driving distance is about 17 miles. Any section of it (i.e., any stretch between any pair of turns, stop signs, lights, or landmarks) can be "blown up," in memory, into sufficient detail to characterize the major type of construction, minor landmarks, road surface, and miscellaneous features of approximately 100-foot units of distance. Thus, for instance, the stretch

1. I checked the Route Plan for accuracy after drawing it from memory. Two too few lights were inserted in the industrial highway sequence; one too many in the Brookhaven segment.

between the first and second traffic lights is a distance of about 300 yards (see Fig. 2). Although from memory it is not possible for me to list and describe in order every building and every intersecting alley or road, nevertheless the character of the area, its major type of construction, its traffic and parking pattern, and the pedestrian activity to be expected are generally available to recall. Effort to recall this detail mobilizes dozens of specific memories of particular incidents: stopping at the drug store (on the way home) to ask for directions; parking along the highway to let a child off at the school; visiting

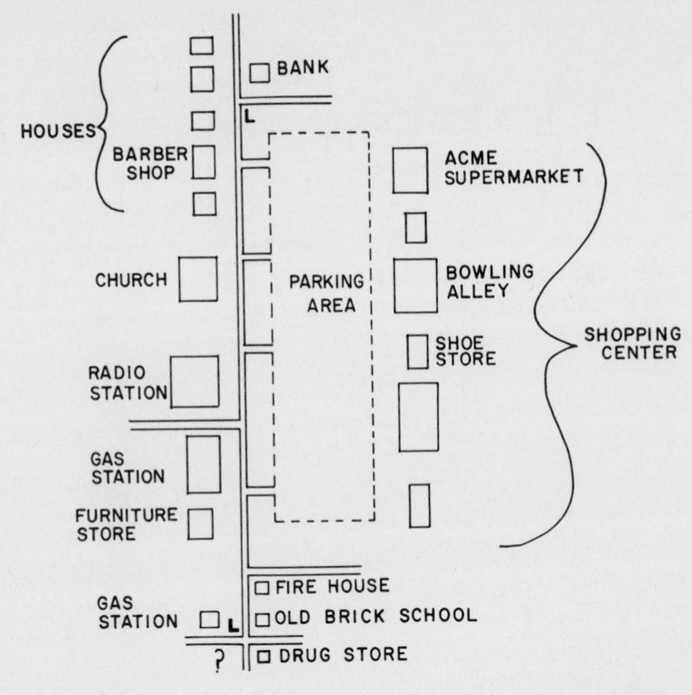

Figure 2.—Route Plan section between first and second traffic lights

the shoe store and the bowling alley; stopping for gas at the second gas station; being held up in traffic at the second light behind a car with a torn fan belt, and so on to less vivid, more selective images of past impressions. The possible maximum speed in this area is about 40 miles per hour; the legal limit is 35; one must watch out for children at the drug store and the school, and for cars entering and leaving the shopping area. The pavement is concrete, traffic markings are apt to be arbitrary (cross-walks are now painted Kelly green, for instance, no doubt by an overly zealous police department), and the surface may be slippery when wet—it is an old, smooth, concrete road.

Traffic is single lane, although the pavement is wide enough for two lanes in each direction, because of cars and trucks parking or stopping on the right, and because the highway has not been painted for two-lane traffic, thus encouraging drivers to wander slowly between the curb and the center line. This strip is somewhat over-patrolled by police: I was arrested once (going the other way) for passing on the right, but discharged by the magistrate because the traffic markings and signs were misleading; foot-police control traffic at market rush hours. The town has a curfew for teenagers. In general, the atmosphere is one of disorganization in the face of suburban inundation by a neighboring industrial city, with local authorities attempting to control the tide, including traffic, by heavy police coverage. All this dictates cautious driving.

The number of times I have driven this route is on the order of five hundred, spread out over a three-year period. The length of time varies between forty-five minutes, as a minimum, and an hour (barring unusual mishaps, such as car trouble or a traffic jam), as a maximum. Usually the drive is made in the morning, leaving the house between eight-thirty and nine-o'clock, and arriving at work between nine-thirty and ten. Earlier travel tends to run into heavy traffic on the industrial highway when it is crowded by workmen hurrying to get to their plants by eight or eight-thirty. By now, I feel, as the saying goes, that I could drive this road in my sleep.

Driving Rules

There are a number of standard driving rules (what in military jargon used to be called "standard operating procedure" or "SOP") which constitutes a set of instructions for what to do under various circumstances. The rules to which I refer are *my* rules, which may or may not conform to the legal regulations for driving; in general, however, these rules are intended to effect a reasonable compromise between, on the one hand, considerations intended to maximize speed and comfort while driving and, on the other hand, considerations intended to minimize the likelihood of accident or arrest by police. These rules govern the following major matters: the pattern of spatial distance between my car and other objects; speed; and response to signals and written instructions on, or at the side of the road. The rules are as follows:

Rule 1: Aim car along route, keeping to right side of road and changing direction as required by Route Plan in order to keep car moving along route toward goal, and go as fast as possible consistent with Rule 2.

Rule 2: Do not exceed posted legal speed limits by more than ten miles per hour except in an emergency (e.g., in order to avoid collision, or in order to get a sick person to a hospital).

Rule 3: Obey all traffic signals and written instructions (e.g., traffic lights, stop signs, painted guide lines on road surface, instructions to slow down, emergency slowdown blinkers at obstructions, etc.).

Rule 4: Reduce speed when visibility is poor, road surface is slippery, traffic is heavy, road bends, or in general whenever current speed is greater than that permitting safe driving.

Rule 5: Maintain visual pattern characterized by safe distance between own car and cars proceeding and following, and equal distance between own car and the lane (especially opposing traffic lane) on left and road shoulders (or lane marker) on right.

Rule 6: Pass vehicles proceeding ahead in same direction as own car but more slowly than own car by turning out to left of these vehicles and accelerating; return to original lane when passing is complete.

Rule 7: Use turn signals to indicate major changes in direction of own car.

Rule 8: At all times be able to control the vehicle and to monitor relevant information; if control and information monitoring functions are seen to be nearing a limit of minimal adequacy, slow down and if necessary stop.

Rule 9: Under all circumstances and by any means, including means which violate any of the other rules except rule 8, avoid collision between own car and other cars, pedestrians, and large objects or obstructions; this implies automatically giving other vehicles the right of way whenever a collision is liable to occur if both own and other vehicle continue in present course.

While each of the terms included in these nine rules can be given further definition, to spell out the meaning of all terms would be a long and tedious task and will not be attempted here. Suffice it to say that there are criteria for judging whether or not visibility is "poor," traffic is "heavy," etc. (rule 4); whether a distance is "safe" (rule 5); whether, because of speed, the condition of the car, or whatever, one is approaching a point of no control of the vehicle (rule 8); whether, in general, a specific operation must be performed in order to follow the route plan and to remain in compliance with the rules.

Operations

In order to travel along the route from home to work, and to follow the driving rules, I must perform various operations. These involve, in general, two kinds of activity: moving various parts of the car in order to control its motion; and moving various parts of the car, or my own position in the car, in order to maintain myself in a comfortable condition for driving.

Control of Direction and Speed of the Automobile—The automobile which I am describing is a 1962 Volkswagen. It has twelve mechanical controls which must be adjusted in order to direct the car safely, legally, and efficiently in a given direction, at the appropriate acceleration, and at the optimal velocity, in conformity with the Driving Rules. These controls are: the ignition switch; the steering wheel; the clutch pedal; the brake pedal; the accelerator pedal; the gearshift; the horn; the emergency brake; the headlight switch; the headlight beam control; the turn signal; and the windshield wiper. The ignition switch starts and stops the motor. It is managed by the left hand and turns "on" clockwise a quarter turn; if the car stalls, the switch must be turned counterclockwise first, and then clockwise, in order to start again. The steering wheel, which faces the seated driver at chest height, is normally grasped by both hands; turning it clockwise turns the car right, turning it counterclockwise turns the car to the left; in a central position the car moves straight ahead. It can normally be turned, or held steady, by one hand. The "settings" are not marked and the correct position must be judged by the directional movement of the car. The steering wheel must be held in the correct position by one or both hands at all times, and minor adjustments in its position must be made almost continuously—at least once every second or two on the average—in order to correct drift caused by wind, irregularities in the road surface, or slight error in the previous wheel setting. Major movements, involving turns of the wheel of 90% amplitude or more, in order to avoid obstacles and follow turns in the route, generally require the use of both hands. The accelerator pedal is pressed down with the right foot in order to make the motor go faster; when the foot is off the pedal, or resting so lightly that the pedal is not depressed, the motor idles at a minimum speed. The speed of the car can be increased by stepping on the accelerator pedal; it can be decreased, at a low negative acceleration, by reducing the pressure on the accelerator pedal. The brake pedal is also controlled by the right foot; it slows down the car, when in motion, and prevents it from moving when it is stopped. Because both the accelerator and the brake are managed by the right foot, it is not possible (without an awkward movement of the left foot) to operate so as to increase motor speed and to brake the car at the same time. The clutch pedal is managed by the left foot; when it is depressed, it is possible to operate the gear shift so as to connect the rear wheels with the motor in one or another gear position. The gear shift is operated by the right hand. There are six positions: neutral, in which the motor does not drive the wheels; reverse, in which the motor drives the car backward; and four forward-driving positions, within approximate velocity ranges: respectively, 0–20, 10–30, 20–50, and 30 to the maximum speed of about 85 miles per hour. The gear shift can be moved from any position to any other, provided the clutch pedal is depressed and the velocity of the car is within shifting range. The horn ring is located inside the circumference of the steering wheel and sounds when pressed by either hand. The emergency brake, for use when the foot brake fails or (more usually) to hold the car when it is stopped or parked, is operated by the right hand; pulling up the lever from a horizontal position sets the brake, letting it drop releases the brake. In order to let the lever drop, a button in the end must be pressed by the thumb. A switch on the instrument panel controls the outside lights. It is managed by the right hand; pulling it out one notch lights the front and rear parking lights (used, actually, most often for driving in twilight); the second notch sets the headlights on, for driving at night; and rotating the knob brightens or dims the light on the instrument panel. The button on the floor near the left foot sets the headlights to high-beam or low-beam; stepping on it shifts the beam from high to low or low to high, depending on where the beam is set at the moment. The outside turn signals are turned on to indicate a right or left turn by moving a lever on the steering column, below the wheel, with the left hand; clockwise a few degrees for a right turn, counterclockwise for a left turn. Finally, the windshield wiper, for driving in rain, snow, or mist, is located on the instrument panel and is operated by pulling by the right hand.

The twelve major controls are thus managed by four limbs. The steering wheel and the horn are managed by both hands, or either one. Of the other nine, two are managed by the left foot (clutch and headlight beam button); two by the right foot (accelerator and brake); two by the left hand (ignition switch and turn signal); and four by the right hand (gearshift, lights, windshield wiper, emergency brake). Evidently the right limbs are given both more, and more responsible, assignments than the left; the three controls of critical importance to safety are all handled, optionally or exclusively, by the right side of the body (steering wheel, brake, and accelerator).

Control of Comfort and Convenience—In addition to the twelve critical direction-and-speed control devices, there are thirteen others (or rather, thirteen classes of others) which the driver operates to maximize his comfort and convenience while driving. These do not require the continuous high-priority attention given to the first twelve; they are apt to be adjusted before, or in the early part of the trip, and then are given occasional attention during relaxed stretches when critical decisions are occurring with minimal frequency. These comfort-and-convenience devices are: the sun visors (two); the rear-view mirrors (two: one inside and one outside); the window open-shut controls (four); seat position levers (two); dome light switch (one switch with three positions); the heater valve handle (a wheel); the ventilator controls (four); cigarette lighter; radio (six); clock (one wheel control); and antifogging cloth. Of these twenty-five discrete devices, nineteen can be managed by the driver while driving: one by the left foot; five by the left hand; and thirteen by the right hand. These controls in general can be said to be important, without being critical, because they enable the driver to maintain an uninterrupted flow of information via windows, mirrors, sun visors, and antifogging cloth; keep him from being too hot or too cold (ventilators and heat valve); permit him to select the least fatiguing posture (seat position); and make it easier and safer to light cigarettes (electric lighter).

The controls in both groups, with a few exceptions, operate by simple motions: pushing, pulling, releasing, and rotating. The electric controls tend to be of a binary, on-off type; the mechanical controls tend to have continuous settings, so that the precise position has to be selected by estimation and corrected from feed-back information. None permit, or require, heavy muscular effort except, occasionally, the brakes. And no more than three, in addition to the steering wheel, can be manipulated at the same time.

Monitoring

I make decisions as to which control to operate, and how, in order to follow the Route Plan in conformity with the Driving Rules, on the basis of a continuous influx of information. This information is gathered via many sensory modalities: sight, sound, smell, temperature, pressure (measuring acceleration and deceleration), equilibrium (measuring angular momentum and slope), internal situations of various kinds. In general, for routine decisions, sight is the principal modality and sound a somewhat distant second; but in extreme emergency, or in case of trouble with the car itself, sound and the other modalities may become as important as sight. We may classify the data monitored into three regions of origin: the space outside the car; the car itself; and the driver.

The Space outside the Car—From outside the car, by sight and sound, I acquire a great deal of information which is relevant to decisions concerning the operation of the vehicle. Most obviously, of course, I keep my eye on the road almost all of the time, matching its course with the configurations of the cognitive map of the route, and turning, slowing down, speeding up, and so forth, as I recognize successive points for which standard instructions are provided by the map itself. I constantly check the road for vehicles: vehicles ahead, vehicles behind, vehicles approaching on the other lane, vehicles which may be entering my traffic lane, vehicles parked beside the lane. I check for bicyclists, for pedestrians, for animals, and for obstructions like slow-moving vehicles, excavations, accidents, and so on; for traffic lights, official instructions in signs, flares, and painted road markings. I monitor the state of the road with respect to its width, the condition of the surface (dry, wet, snow, ice, leaves), its physical smoothness (ripples, pot-holes, etc.), the condition of the shoulders, its composition (concrete, asphalt of various kinds, gravel, wind, etc.), its grade. I note the wind conditions and I monitor the efficiency of the monitoring itself, noting the lighting conditions outside (dawn, dark, bright, cloudy, foggy, rainy, snowy), the clearness of vision through the windows, the noise level from wind, air turbulence, machinery, and other sources.

The Car Itself—Within the car, there are certain instruments which must be checked from time to time, changes in the reading of which indicate the need for control operation. These include the speedometer, the gasoline gauge, the oil pressure light (which shines green when pressure is low), the generator light (which shines red when the generator is not charging the battery), the clock, and the odometer (mileage indicator). Any variation in the sound of the motor from the expected pattern; the smell of gasoline, of burning rubber, of burning electrical insulation or cloth; unusual vibration in the body; a constant pulling or swaying of the car unaccountable by wind or road conditions: all of these indicate probable trouble with motor, gasoline supply, brakes, or tires. And, of course, I must monitor the current setting of the control devices in order to know what action to take in response to information.

The Driver—I, the driver, must also monitor my own state. I must recognize sleepiness, undue fatigue, slow reaction time, distracting pain or discomfort, any difficulty with any of my own sensory equipment, and any motivational state which is prompting me to such behavior as excessive speed, excessive caution, irritability, competitiveness with other drivers, or inattention, any one of which may interfere with efficient driving.

Attention Control

The nature of the monitoring activity in general seems to me to involve several principles in the control of attention which are, insofar as they are applied to driving, the product of experience rather than of explicit instruction. One of these principles is the control of the angle of the cone of visual attention. When driving routinely, the attention is scattered over a wide visual field, shaped like a cone with perhaps 120° of arc from side to side, and covering a considerable distance ahead of the car—where visibility is unhampered, perhaps a quarter of a mile. When, however, data are available to indicate that a decision has to be made on the basis of further information as the situation develops, an "alert" instruction is invoked and the cone of attention is narrowed to an acute angle of perhaps 10° of arc, so that the other data are relegated to the periphery of consciousness. Such a condition will occur if, for instance, a car suddenly appears at a side street, a hundred yards ahead. Will it stop? Attention focuses on that car, in order to glean all possible data relevant to the decision on whether or not to slow down, turn, stop, or sound horn.

Another feature of attention control is the way in which it is distributed over the various control devices inside the car, and over the various regions and types of data monitored. Some parts of the system function almost autonomously and will continue to function satisfactorily even when conscious attention is directed elsewhere. This is particularly true with respect to the subsystem of visual extravehicular data, responsive control of the steering wheel, and maintenance of all other controls at "steady." This system can, as it were, be forgotten and, as long as no disturbance of routine driving occurs, be left to operate by itself while attention is devoted to other monitoring data and controls, or to thinking about other matters: a paper one is writing, a problem at home or at the office, or whatever. Furthermore, most of the stream of monitored data, although it is being received and processed, leads to no executive action at all; the process of sensory intake and semantic evaluation of the data occurs without consciousness. Only when its nature suddenly invokes an executive responsibility does one become conscious of it. Thus the sound of the motor is constantly being funneled into the ear; but only when the motor begins to miss, or clank, or whine, or whatever, does conscious attention suddenly focus on it. The process is similar to that in the well-trained radio operator who can sleep soundly beside his open receiver, ignoring all the radio traffic until his own call letters are transmitted; he wakes up suddenly and completely as soon as these come over the air.

A third feature of attention control might be referred to as a cyclical ranging of conscious attention. "Every so often" I check the speed by glancing at the speedometer rather than by simply assessing the revolutions per second of the motor from its sound; I check the rear-view mirror for following traffic, and look to the left for cars on the left, particularly in the blind spot over the left shoulder; I note the time; check the gasoline gauge. This flickering passage of conscious attention over various types of monitored data supplements the non-conscious readiness to respond to certain cues by directing attention to these sources of data which cannot be judged accurately without conscious attention, which require additional data, or which fall outside the cone of visual observation. The rate of this ranging would be difficult to estimate; I would guess that every second or two, for a fraction of a second, conscious attention shifts from a stream of conscious thinking or talking about nondriving matters to monitor some datum or other, and among these flickers of attention, every twenty or thirty seconds, the ranging process turns on.

Organization

The simplest model of how this total process operates is to consider the driver as a cybernetic machine. Diagrammatically, one might represent the system as follows (see Fig. 3):

This diagram does not, of course, adequately reflect the complexity of the system of information and control. Some minimum estimate of this complexity is implicit in the simple enumeration of the classes of monitored data which must be meshed with the classes of control responses. At any choice point in the route—such as a traffic light—data from all three regions of information must be screened. The observed combination defines the current situation as

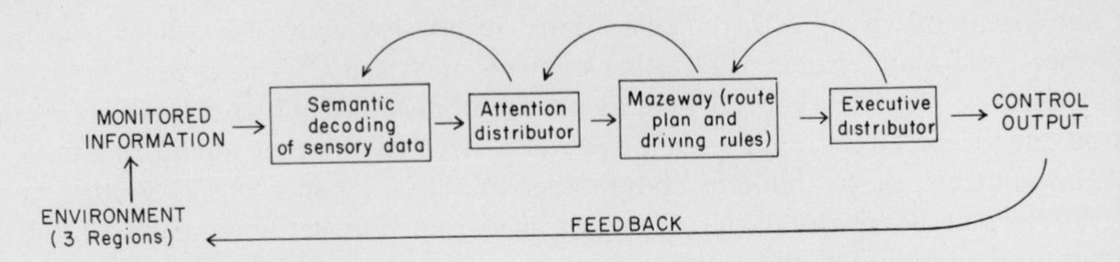

Figure 3.—Mazeway functions in information-and-control system for driving

one of several types, corresponding to which is one combination of the several possible control responses. That one response combination must be the output. The control responses, which are fewer in number, may be analyzed first.

Let us assume that at route choice points, only major responses involving one or more of the twelve primary controls are allowed. The recognition that the situation involves a route choice point may be regarded as Phase 1. The initial response to this recognition is an alerting function, in which Mazeway instructs Attention Distributor to scan for data relevant to major response. Phase 2 involves the selective scanning of the monitored data, according to a setting of the Attention Distributor; the recognition of the situation as belonging to situation type such-and-such (defined according to criteria selected for attention) by Mazeway; and the selection of response type so-and-so, onto which the situation type maps according to instructions from Mazeway.

With respect to route choice points, data concerning the interior state of the car and the condition of the driver must be considered temporarily irrelevant. Certain aspects of the space outside the car are relevant, however. Let us say that the immediate dimension of importance, and the one which alerted the driver, is approach to a traffic light. The outside-of-car dimensions and values listed in Table I are relevant and must be scanned consciously:

Table I.—Outside-of-Car Dimensions

Dimension	*Values*
A. Traffic light	a_1 red; a_2 yellow; a_3 green
B. Route direction	b_1 turns right; b_2 straight; b_3 turns left
C. Traffic (preceding)	c_1 no car in front; c_2 car in front too close; c_3 car in front distance safe
D. Traffic (following)	d_1 no car following; d_2 car following too close; d_3 car following distance safe
E. Road surface	e_1 slippery; e_2 normal
F. Cross traffic	f_1 object entering from right; f_2 no object entering from right
G. Closeness of light	g_1 within stopping distance at current speed; g_2 not within stopping distance at current speed

The matrix of possible states of the system resulting from the combination of these criteria contains $3 \times 3 \times 3 \times 2 \times 2$, or 216 cells. The possible combinations of action at such a choice point, however, are more limited. Ignition switch, clutch pedal, gearshift, emergency brake, headlight switch, turn signal, and windshield wiper may be considered temporarily irrelevant. The control operations listed in Table II—again defined as dimensions and values—are relevant:

Table II.—Control Operations

Dimension	*Values*
V. Steering wheel	v_1 turn left; v_2 hold steady; v_3 turn right
W. Accelerator	w_1 press; w_2 release
X. Brake	x_1 press; x_2 release
Y. Horn	y_1 press; y_2 do not press
Z. Clutch	z_1 press; z_2 do not press

There are, thus, no more than $3 \times 2 \times 2 \times 2 \times 2$ or 48 combinations of actions each to be considered as a unitary response. But, as a matter of fact, there are fewer than this, because the combination w_1 x_2 is impossible (not absolutely impossible, but nearly so, for the left foot has standing instructions not to touch the brake) so that the number reduces to 24.

Now we can see that the large matrix of situations, under the alerting rubric *traffic light*, which is on the order of 216, is mapped onto a much smaller matrix of outputs, on the order of 24. But we also must recognize that the defining of the situation must be performed repeatedly, at intervals of time considerably less than a second, because the situation changes as a result of the motion of the car, the (possibly) changing setting of the traffic light, movement of traffic and the action of the driver on the controls.

Now a sequence of events comparable to the one just illustrated is initiated whenever the monitoring system receives a signal which means "choice to be made." The map of route (Fig. 1) illustrates major classes of choice points: traffic lights; stop signs; turns from one road or street onto another; start of journey; end of journey. The foregoing list of classes of data to be monitored includes as a minimum some 29 dimensions of relevance to the 24-cell accelerate-slow-down-stop matrix previously listed. But the complexity of the whole system—whose measure reaches very large numbers indeed, when one includes all the second-order dimensions relevant to comfort, convenience, and the maintenance of the car itself—is made manageable by two factors: first, its division into a hierarchical, branching taxonomy of situations and responses, governed by the Driving Rules; and second, by the serial invocation of parts of the taxonomy according to the actual situation revealed by the monitoring process. Thus the actual behavior sequence, following the general TOTE model of Miller, Galanter, and Pribram (1960) (where T represents the information input selected by the attention distributor and O the control response output), must resemble the following (in which we add the symbol A for the Alert Signal to invoke a particular subsection of the monitoring matrix):

A_1	O_1					T_2						
a_1	v_2	w_2	x_2	y_1	z_2	a_1	b_2	c_1	d_2	e_2	f_2	g_1
T_2							O_3					
a_1	b_2	c_1	d_2	e_2	f_2	g_1	v_2	w_2	x_1	y_1	z_1	
T_n							O_n					A_2
a_1	b_2	c_1	d_2	e_2	f_2	g_1	v_2	w_2	x_1	y_1	z_1	a_3

From this standpoint, indeed, it would appear that what I have been referring to as "The Mazeway" can in part be regarded as an extremely large system of related monitoring and operation taxonomies, matching portions of which are invoked serially (and to a lesser extent simultaneously, where several systems are operating at the same time) at fraction-of-a-second intervals. Higher order codings, such as the alerting and motivational or value signals, are contained in the Route Plan and Driving Rules, and serve to "switch on" or "alert" the portion of the taxonomy relevant to the task at hand. The magnitude of the total logical net is, of course, very large indeed; but the size of the monitoring and operational segments in use at any one time is very much smaller.

The possibility, of course, does exist that situations can develop whose relevant defining matrices are extremely large, too large for convenient and rapid matching with the appropriate response matrices, and the result in such cases should be confusion, indecision, and possibly disaster. As we all know, such disasters do occur.

Conclusion

In the foregoing passages, I have attempted to delineate in some detail the system of cognitive maps—or portion of mazeway—which I, as one informant, use in driving to work. It is a minimal description, in the sense that not only are there, probably, additional categories to be added at the level of analysis which I have been using, but also other categories, both more abstract cover categories and less abstract subordinate categories, which have not been mentioned. Nonetheless, this statement does describe, with reasonable adequacy I feel, a portion of mazeway of a kind which it is necessary for a person now in my society to learn, maintain, and use in order to drive himself to work. Thus I have been describing also a piece of culture.

I have also been interested in questions of the magnitude of the logical complexity of culturally institutionalized tasks (see Wallace: 1961b). The exploration of this one technical operation, which involves only a moderate degree of skill and experience for its successful performance, suggests that there is a class of technical tasks in which the complexity of definitions of the situation exceeds the complexity of the available response repertoire. In the case used for illustration, for instance, we can observe a scale of complexity somewhat as follows (see Table III):

Table III.—Orders of Complexity

Category	*Complexity*
Matrix of sensory input	Maximal
Matrix of sensory input attended to	
Matrix of conscious attention	
Matrix of definition of situation	
Matrix of available responses	Minimal

The matrix of responses made available under the particular alerting signal used in the illustration is well within the 2^6 rule discussed in an earlier paper (Wallace: 1961b), but the matrix of definitions of the situation is much larger, on the order of 2^{10}. While obviously arithmetic observations based only on a single example intended to illustrate the probable form of a general process cannot be offered as quantitative evidence, they may be of interest in suggesting that the human organism is more restricted in the complexity of its pattern of output of meaningful behavior than in the complexity of the pattern of meaningful perception. This is certainly true of individual neurons, which can receive and discriminate within a complex pattern of stimuli, but can only respond dichotomously, by firing or not firing. Perhaps a similar process occurs in mazeway and, therefore, in culture, namely, that far more subtle perceptions of situations are possible for men than their available neurological, muscular, and technical apparatus can permit them to recognize in response.

Finally, it may be suggested that the model employed for describing this mazeway segment may be more generally useful in formulating psychologically real, cultural descriptions of technological tasks. The model for driving to work involves five categories of descriptions and analysis: Route Plan (the specification of the origin state, destination state, and intervening transitional states at which instrumental choices must be made); Driving Rules (the specification of general rules for making choices among alternative actions); Control Operations (the specification of the minimal behavioral responses available to the actor); Monitored Information (the specification of the types of data relevant to choice of response); and Organization (the pattern of interpretation employed in relating data to action). Those categories may, more generally, be labeled as Action Plan; Action Rules; Control Operations; Monitored Information; and Organization. This model should be adequate to describe such technical tasks (including physical action) as transportation, manufacture, hunting, warfare, and the like. Whether a homologous frame of analysis would be applicable to behavior in social organization remains to be seen.

References

Miller, G. A., Galanter, E., & Pribram, K. H.
1960: *Plans and the Structure of Behavior* (New York: Holt).

Wallace, A. F. C.
1961a: *Culture and Personality* (New York: Random House).
1961b: "On Being Just Complicated Enough," *Proceedings of National Academy of Sciences*, **47**, 458–464.
1962: "Culture and Cognition," *Science*, **135**, 351–357.

Part Six

Projective Tests

BERT KAPLAN AND RICHARD LAWLESS

Culture and Visual Imagery: A Comparison of Rorschach Responses in Eleven Societies

One notes with a certain amount of wonder the close association between what has come to be known as the culture and personality field and the somewhat strange and esoteric personality test known as the Rorschach technique. It is perhaps not the least of A. I. Hallowell's contributions that he was one of the first anthropologists to take up the Rorschach test and to recognize its significance for the developing of the culture and personality area. Not only did this test provide a specially appropriate technique for use in cross-cultural studies of personality, but also, and perhaps more importantly, it made possible a rudimentary quantification of personality variables and thus introduced the idea that rigorous hypothesis testing studies could be conducted in this difficult and complicated field. Hallowell's own early Rorschach studies of acculturation in the Ojibwa (1942) provided important models for a considerable number of subsequent studies. Although from our present perspective more than twenty years after these early studies we are inclined to be slightly more dubious than Hallowell was about extensive dependence on the Rorschach, nevertheless Hallowell did demonstrate clearly that a number of the most significant theoretical issues in anthropology itself could be approached through Rorschach studies.

This paper is devoted to one of these issues. Hallowell was naturally concerned with the question of variability of personality reactions from culture to culture. His chief empirical effort was a study of the effects of the acculturation process as they manifested themselves in Rorschach responses. However, in a paper entitled "Popular Responses and Cultural Differences: An Analysis Based on Frequencies in a Group of American Indian Subjects" (1945), he also conducted a cross-cultural comparison in six American Indian groups of one type of Rorschach response. In this study he recognized that the so-called "popular" response in the Rorschach test was of special significance to anthropological theory. Rorschach workers had long noted that certain responses occurred with great frequency in our own society and they labeled perhaps a dozen to fifteen of these frequently given responses as "popular." These responses were thought to represent images which occur to almost everyone taking the Rorschach test and therefore to represent tendencies which members of a group have in common.

Hallowell's paper was devoted to the question, natural enough to an anthropologist, whether such popular responses vary from one cultural group to another or are common to all cultural groups. He said "It may very well turn out in the case of the popular responses to the Rorschach figures, that we are presented with the problem that has analogies to the functioning of perception generally." In other words, he was approaching the question of whether the perceptual process was similar enough in cultures around the world so that certain objective forms were recognized universally and responded to in a universal manner. Hallowell recognized that the Rorschach test offered the possibility of dealing with this question rigorously and experimentally. Hallowell's study was concerned with only six cultures, all in the same part of the world. He was not able to provide a conclusive answer to the question he raised but found that there were actually three categories of popular responses: one of universal populars or at least universal among the six cultures that were studied; then a second group of "common" populars which were found in several of the six cultures but not in all of them; and finally a group of "unique" populars which were present in only a single culture. Hallowell recommended that further study of these questions on a larger scale was necessary and fully anticipated that such studies would follow his own pioneering effort.

Strangely enough there have been only a few real cross-cultural Rorschach studies subsequently. Where cross-cultural studies have been done they have been for the most part comparisons of pairs of cultures or perhaps of two or three neighboring or associated groups. There has, as yet, been no attempt to conduct a comparative study on a broader scale so that the results will permit conclusions not only about the differences or similarities among the particular group studied but about the nature of variability generally. In the last decade the development of the Microcard publication, *Primary Records In Culture And Personality* (Kaplan, 1955, 1956, 1962, 1963), has made available projective test data, including Rorschach's, from many cultures in different parts of the world, and it is now a relatively simple matter to conduct a comparative study on a broader scale than was possible at the time of Hallowell's preoccupation with the Rorschach. In the present study, Rorschach responses from eleven cultures from several different parts of the world are examined. While it is obvious that this small number does not even approach being a representative sample of the world's cultures, the present analysis may be regarded as a step in the direction of a more comprehensive and definitive cross-cultural study.

The Rorschach test, despite the fact that it probably is the most widely used technique of personality study in clinical psychology, is by no means as well understood as clinicians would like. What seems very clear is that the interpretation by subjects of these rather ambiguous ink blots results in a series of visual images which subjects then describe verbally. These images are commonly used by clinicians as the bases of inferences about the characteristic motivational structures in the subject. However, the relationship between cognitive and motivational processes has many difficult aspects and one does not feel completely confident with the simple (perhaps simple-minded would be a more appropriate word) view, that the cognitive product is nothing more than a reflection of underlying motivations. My own opinion is that the classic division of the psychic life into cognition, conation or motivation, and emotion, which we can trace back as far as Plato and which has dominated Western psychological thought for 2500 years, is in need of serious reconsideration.

Culture and personality theory has tended to underestimate the importance of cognition in favor of regarding motivational processes as the significant variables on the individual's side of the culture-personality relationship. The usual formula is a simple one. The proper functioning of social systems, and of the social institutions which constitute their subsystems, is dependent on the performance of the variety of roles that comprise these systems. Appropriate role behavior of individuals, which constitutes the basis of societal functioning, is dependent on the presence in individuals of motivations that lead them to want to perform in compliance with social role expectations. The neat isomorphism between social requirements on the one hand and individual needs on the other is regarded as the optimum situation both from individual and societal perspectives and when it occurs the main condition for a stable and orderly individual-social system relationship is present. This concentration on the motivational process as the significant human variable in the culture and personality interaction has not seemed incorrect to psychologists and anthropologists versed in modern psychodynamic personality theories. Almost without exception, in such theories, motivational processes occupy the central position. Other processes in all of these theories tend to be regarded as subordinated to the vicissitudes of the motivational processes.

In the last few years Anthony Wallace, working in what is recognizable as the Hallowell tradition, put forward the view that the psychic unity of human groups is based, not on shared motivational structures, but rather on shared cognitive orientations (1961). Wallace states that the basis of orderly cultural participation does not lie in the realm of human needs but in a common universe of learned "meanings" to which individuals are oriented. Hallowell himself (1954) points out that "selves" tend to be organized around one or another of a very small number of conceptions that are present as part of the cultural tradition. Erickson has made very much the same point in regard to the question of "identity" formation (1950). The culture concept itself is closely associated with the notion of "shared *meanings*" and thus the reality of culture may with good reason be thought to be found somewhere in the realm of cognition.

My own position on this issue is that the traditional distinction between cognition and motivation has been carried much too far and that psychological realities everywhere have both a motivational and a cognitive aspect. We would expect, therefore, to find lurking within cognitions some motivational element and within those phenomena we call motivations, a cognitive aspect. Rorschach responses appear in consciousness as visual or perceptual images, but these images also have what may be regarded as motivational or purposeful aspects. The "meanings" of the blots are actively "meant" in that they are put forward or constructed within the psychic life of the individual. This position, which may be recognized by some readers as that of phenomenology, suggests that the comparative study of the psychic life of persons in different cultural groups can indeed be approached through the analysis of the kind of visual imagery that is found in Rorschach tests, and that these images may properly be understood as the characteristic mental structures that are present in members of particular cultures.

In the present study Rorschach data from eleven cultures are analyzed and a series of questions are asked with respect to the nature of the variability of perceptual processes in different cultures and in different parts of the world. The general import of these questions is that on the one hand they are concerned with the relative magnitude of the variability and on the other of the homogeneity that is found in the Rorschach responses and consequently in the perceptual processes of these different peoples. It is anticipated that these results will contribute to the clarification of the cultural influences on perceptual processes and indirectly of their influences on personality. Our analysis will be testing the null hypothesis: that no significant differences are found in the Rorschach percepts of people in different societies. If the data appear to support the null hypothesis we would tend to believe that the so-called pan-human cognitive apparatus dominate the process of perception, with the implication that the universal aspects of the perceptual process shape human realities and form the basis of widely shared psychological structures. If, on the other hand, there is considerable variability in what people in different groups perceive in these Rorschach blots we shall be forced to infer that the concrete circumstances of life in different parts of the world so dominate psychological reality that the latter is shaped into numerous separate and distinct streams. We do not wish to suggest that the present analysis can settle this large and overwhelmingly important issue. These data, however, do have a bearing on this question and may contribute along with other similar analyses to our seeing in what direction the answer may lie.

Procedures

The eleven sets of Rorschach records that comprise the data for the study were obtained from *Primary Records and Culture and Personality* (Kaplan, 1955, 1956, 1962). They include all of the sets of adult records in which the sample size was greater than ten. The names of the groups, sample size, sex distribution, and the name of the collector of the materials are given in Table I. Since women's records were included in only eight of the samples,

Table I

Culture	*Number*		*Collector*	*Area*
	MEN	*WOMEN*		
Navaho	33	17	Bert Kaplan	American Indian
Menomini	55	31	George D. Spindler	American Indian
Mescalero Apache	34	30	William T. Ross and Golda Vanbuskirk Ross	American Indian
Montserrat (B.W.I.)	33	28	Theodora M. Abel	West Indies
Black Carib	26	18	Ruy Coelho	West Indies
Palau	45	30	Francis B. Mahoney	Western Pacific
Ifaluk	35	36	Melford E. Spiro	Western Pacific
New Ireland	16	4	Sally Lewis	Western Pacific
Bhil	27	0	G. Morris Carstairs	Indian
Hindu	50	0	G. Morris Carstairs	Indian
Pakistani	14	0	John J. Honigmann	Indian

we were faced with the choice of confining our analysis to these eight groups or including all eleven groups but eliminating women's records; the latter course was chosen. However, in Tables II to XI, data from the women's records are included so that the reader may have the opportunity of evaluating for himself the importance of the sex factor.

The tabulation of the Rorschach responses proceeded in three steps. First, all of the responses given by members of each culture were placed in a single table. Second, the number of persons who gave each different response was determined. Third, the number of persons who gave these responses in all of the other groups was obtained. Since few responses were absolutely identical to each other, the decision that two responses were the same involved a number of arbitrary criteria; only similar responses to the same blot area of the same card were called identical. Action and other qualifiers were ignored so long as the basic percept was the same: thus bat, black bat, flying bat, and resting bat were all grouped together. Different animals seen in the same blot location were also grouped, e.g., lion, tiger, hyena. Since there were a great many idiosyncratic responses that were given by only one person, the inclusion of such responses would have distorted our statistical analysis and left us with a spurious similarity in that it would have been based on the fact that a particular response was not found in ten of the eleven other groups. It was, therefore, somewhat arbitrarily decided to include only responses which occurred in 2% of persons in the whole table. This step had the effect of eliminating a very large and interesting portion of the original data, a portion, however, that is not amenable to statistical treatment.

The eleven cultures were classified into four distinct culture areas: the American Indian, the West Indies, the Western Pacific, and India. While each area contains too few cultures for our comparisons to be very reliable they do allow us to give a very provisional and tentative answer to the question of whether the differences between areas account for part of whatever variance we find among our eleven groups.

Results

Does the proportion of subjects giving particular responses vary from culture to culture? Tables II through XI describe, for each of the ten Rorschach cards, the frequencies of all responses that were given by at least 2% of the eleven samples taken in toto. Table XII lists the twenty-three responses that were given most frequently in these tables. The reader will recognize that these are, by and large, the popular responses that Hallowell considered in his earlier study and that they are responses which are generally regarded as popular in our own society. The chi-square analyses presented in Table XII indicate that for twenty of twenty-three of these responses, reliable differences between cultural groups are present. Sixteen of them are significant at not less than the .001 level, indicating that there is considerable variability among the different cultures in the frequency with which their responses are given. In what way do differences between different geographical areas contribute to this variability? In order to bring information to bear on this point, the data of the groups within each geographical area were pooled and chi-square tests were performed to determine whether reliable differences existed between the four areas. The results of these analyses are also shown in Table XII. Taking the twenty responses for which reliable differences were found among cultures, we note that in eighteen there is also a reliable difference between geographical areas. On the whole, it seems that a significant portion of the variance between the cultural groups can be accounted for by area differences. At the same time it should be noted that in most instances a substantial portion of the variance is not to be accounted for solely in terms of area variability. This analysis is limited seriously by the fact that only a small portion of the response categories could be analyzed and this small portion is of a special type namely the most frequently occurring or

Table II.—Percentage of Various Rorschach Responses in Eleven Cultures: Card I

	NA.		*MEN.*		*MES.*		*MONT.*		*B.C.*		*PAL.*		*IF.*		*N.I.*		*BH.*	*HIN.*	*PAK.*
	M	*F*	*M*	*F*	*M*	*F*	*M*	*F*	*M*	*F*	*M*	*F*	*M*	*F*	*M*	*F*	*M*	*M*	*M*
Bat W∧	27	6	11	16	38	60	36	46	39	17	40	40	0	0	0	0	0	14	14
Butterfly W∧	18	12	6	7	21	13	18	14	23	33	9	3	0	0	13	0	0	10	14
Human Form D1∧	9	6	7	3	44	17	9	4	8	22	0	0	9	3	25	25	11	8	7
Clouds W∧	6	6	0	0	9	0	0	7	8	0	4	0	34	14	0	0	0	2	0
Bird W∧	3	12	13	7	3	3	6	7	4	11	2	10	14	3	6	0	0	2	7
Sea Animal W∧	9	0	0	0	3	3	9	4	0	0	4	0	0	0	6	0	22	2	0
Hu. Anatomy W∧	0	6	15	3	0	7	3	0	0	0	7	10	3	0	13	25	0	6	7
Geog. Area W∧	0	0	9	0	6	3	9	4	0	0	7	7	3	17	6	0	0	4	7
Birds D2∧	0	0	13	13	0	0	0	0	8	0	0	0	0	3	0	0	0	4	14
Hu. in Action D1∧	0	0	11	16	21	13	0	0	4	0	0	0	0	0	0	50	0	2	0
Wing D2∧	0	0	2	3	0	0	0	4	12	6	0	0	0	0	19	0	0	2	0
Bear D2∧	3	0	9	10	12	7	0	0	0	0	0	0	0	0	0	0	0	2	7
Land W∧	9	0	0	0	0	0	0	0	0	0	0	0	11	14	13	0	0	0	0
Hands d3∧	3	0	0	7	12	7	0	0	0	0	0	0	0	0	13	0	0	2	0
Flying Fox W∧	0	0	0	0	0	0	0	0	0	0	0	0	0	0	25	25	0	4	0
Animal Head W∧	12	6	4	3	12	3	0	0	0	0	0	0	0	0	0	0	0	0	0
Animals D2∧	6	6	0	0	3	3	3	0	8	0	0	0	0	0	0	0	0	6	0
Bat W∨	15	0	0	0	0	3	0	0	0	0	0	0	0	0	0	0	0	10	0
Clouds D2∧	3	6	0	6	3	3	0	0	0	6	0	0	6	8	13	0	0	0	0
Flying Insect W∧	9	0	0	0	3	3	6	4	0	0	2	0	0	0	0	0	0	2	0
Bug D1∧	9	0	4	10	3	7	0	0	0	0	0	0	0	0	6	0	0	0	0
Tree, Flower W∧	3	0	2	3	0	0	0	0	0	0	2	0	3	17	0	0	0	2	7
Mountain W∧	3	0	0	0	0	0	0	4	4	0	0	0	3	17	0	0	0	2	7
Birds D2∧	0	0	7	3	3	10	0	4	0	6	0	0	0	3	0	0	0	0	7
Hu. in Action W∧	6	0	4	7	6	0	0	0	0	0	0	0	0	0	0	0	0	0	0
Mountain D2∧	0	0	0	0	0	0	0	0	4	0	0	0	11	3	0	0	0	0	0
Animal D4∧	0	0	4	7	0	3	0	0	0	6	0	0	0	0	6	0	0	4	0
Human Face W∧	0	0	0	0	9	13	0	0	0	0	0	0	0	0	0	0	0	2	0
Animal Skin W∧	3	6	0	0	6	0	0	0	0	0	0	0	0	0	0	0	0	0	0
Sea Animals D6∧	0	0	7	7	0	0	0	0	0	0	0	0	0	0	0	0	0	0	0
Hu. Figure d3∧	0	0	6	0	0	0	0	0	0	0	0	0	0	0	0	0	0	2	0
Flying Fox W∨	0	0	0	0	0	0	0	0	0	0	0	0	0	0	0	0	0	8	0
Anatomy D6∨	0	0	0	0	0	0	0	0	0	0	0	0	0	0	0	0	0	8	0
Sex Anatomy d5∨	0	0	0	0	0	0	0	0	0	0	0	0	0	0	0	25	0	8	0
Birds W∨	0	0	7	3	0	0	0	0	0	0	0	0	0	0	0	0	0	0	0
Airplane W∧	0	6	0	0	3	0	0	7	0	0	0	0	0	0	0	0	4	0	0
Animal D2∧	0	0	6	7	0	0	0	0	0	0	0	0	0	0	0	0	0	0	0
2 Animals W∧	0	0	2	0	0	0	0	14	4	0	0	0	0	0	0	0	0	0	0
Crab D6∧	0	0	6	7	0	0	0	0	0	0	0	0	0	0	0	0	0	0	0
Animal Anat. W∧	3	0	0	0	0	0	0	0	0	0	0	0	0	0	0	0	0	2	0
Clouds D2∧	0	0	0	0	0	0	0	0	0	0	0	0	3	8	0	0	0	0	0

Table III.—Percentage of Various Rorschach Responses in Eleven Cultures: Card II

	NA.		*MEN.*		*MES.*		*MONT.*		*B.C.*		*PAL.*		*IF.*		*N.I.*		*BH.*	*HIN.*	*PAK.*
	M	*F*	*M*	*F*	*M*	*F*	*M*	*F*	*M*	*F*	*M*	*F*	*M*	*F*	*M*	*F*	*M*	*M*	*M*
Hu. Figures W∧	15	0	15	13	35	27	3	7	23	17	7	0	0	3	19	0	26	12	14
Bears W∧	3	6	46	16	12	3	0	0	8	0	4	0	0	0	0	0	0	30	7
Animals D3∧	3	12	20	13	6	10	9	0	4	11	0	0	3	0	0	0	7	12	7
Animals-Action W∧	3	6	15	19	0	3	0	4	8	0	9	0	3	0	0	0	0	6	14
Animals-No Act. W∧	3	6	2	0	0	0	3	36	4	0	0	0	0	0	6	0	7	16	0
Fowl D2∧	0	0	2	0	6	0	12	4	4	0	0	0	0	0	6	0	0	8	0
Hu. Anatomy D1∧	6	0	2	3	3	0	0	0	4	0	0	0	0	0	13	50	7	2	0
Dogs, Heads D3>	15	0	11	3	9	7	0	0	0	0	0	0	0	0	0	0	0	0	0
Hu. Anatomy W∧	9	0	0	0	6	0	6	4	0	0	7	10	3	0	0	25	0	2	0
Sea Animal D1∧	0	0	0	0	0	0	0	4	4	0	0	0	0	0	25	0	0	0	0
4 Leg Animals D2∧	0	0	2	0	0	0	3	0	4	0	0	0	3	3	6	0	0	4	7
Hu. Anatomy D2∧	0	6	2	3	6	13	3	0	8	6	0	0	0	0	0	25	0	10	0
Hu. Anatomy D3∧	3	0	0	0	3	0	3	0	0	0	0	0	0	0	0	0	7	10	0
Fire W∧	0	0	2	3	0	3	9	11	4	0	0	0	11	19	0	0	0	0	0
Birds D2∧	0	0	2	3	3	3	0	4	8	6	0	0	3	6	0	0	0	0	7
Butterfly D1∧	0	0	0	13	6	7	0	0	8	0	0	0	0	0	0	0	0	0	7
Clouds D2∧	0	0	0	0	0	0	0	0	0	0	0	0	14	22	6	0	0	0	0
Fire D1∨	6	6	9	3	3	13	0	0	0	0	0	0	0	0	0	0	0	0	0
Animal Head d4∧	3	0	4	7	0	0	0	0	0	0	0	0	0	0	0	0	0	4	0
House D1∧	0	0	0	0	0	0	0	0	0	6	0	0	11	6	0	0	0	0	0
Fire D1∧	3	12	4	13	3	10	0	0	0	0	0	0	0	0	0	0	0	0	0
Arrowhead D1∧	3	18	2	0	0	13	0	0	0	0	0	0	0	0	0	0	0	0	0

Table IV.—Percentage of Various Rorschach Responses in Eleven Cultures: Card III

	NA.		*MEN.*		*MES.*		*MONT.*		*B.C.*		*PAL.*		*IF.*		*N.I.*		*BH.*	*HIN.*	*PAK.*
	M	*F*	*M*	*F*	*M*	*F*	*M*	*F*	*M*	*F*	*M*	*F*	*M*	*F*	*M*	*F*	*M*	*M*	*M*
2 People W∧	36	12	75	61	79	67	12	25	39	6	27	20	0	3	56	25	0	2	7
2 Non-Hu. Figures D8 or W∧	6	24	4	7	3	3	9	0	4	11	0	0	6	3	13	50	26	22	7
Animals D2∧	3	6	4	0	3	0	9	7	19	0	0	0	0	8	31	25	4	12	7
Fish D5∧	9	6	2	0	9	10	3	0	0	0	0	0	3	6	6	50	4	28	21
Hu. Body W∧	0	0	0	0	0	0	6	7	0	0	0	0	3	0	13	25	48	2	0
Butterfly D1∧	0	0	26	19	15	20	0	0	15	0	0	0	0	0	0	0	0	0	0
Birds D2∧	0	0	6	7	6	3	3	14	0	0	0	0	0	11	0	0	22	12	7
Head d2∧	0	6	0	3	0	3	3	4	0	0	0	0	0	0	25	0	7	12	0
Bow Tie, Ribbon D1∧	6	0	9	23	18	17	0	4	4	0	0	0	0	0	6	0	0	0	0
Monkeys D2∧	0	0	4	0	3	10	3	11	0	0	0	0	0	3	13	0	15	0	0
Birds D6∧	6	24	7	0	3	0	3	0	8	0	0	0	0	3	6	0	0	2	0
Birds D8 or W∧	12	6	4	7	0	0	0	7	4	0	0	0	0	0	0	0	11	0	0
Rock, Rd., Valley W∧	12	0	0	0	6	7	6	4	0	0	0	0	0	3	6	0	0	0	0
Hu. Anatomy D1∧	3	6	0	0	0	0	3	0	0	0	0	0	0	0	0	0	0	16	0
P. of Wood D5∧	0	6	0	0	6	7	0	0	0	0	0	0	0	0	6	0	0	0	7
Hu. Figures W∨	6	0	0	0	9	13	0	0	0	0	0	0	0	0	0	0	0	0	0
Hu. Heads D4∨	3	0	0	3	6	7	0	0	0	0	0	0	0	0	6	0	0	0	0
Bird Head d2∧	9	6	0	0	0	3	0	0	0	0	0	0	0	0	0	0	4	0	0
Monkeys W∧	0	0	0	0	0	0	0	11	8	0	2	0	0	0	0	0	4	0	0
Pottery W∧	0	0	0	0	12	20	0	0	4	0	0	0	0	0	0	0	0	0	0
Hu. Anatomy W∧	3	0	0	0	0	0	0	4	0	0	2	0	0	0	6	0	0	0	0
Animals W∧	0	0	0	0	0	0	0	7	12	6	0	0	0	0	0	0	0	0	0
Birds D2∨	0	0	6	10	0	0	0	0	0	6	0	0	0	0	0	0	0	4	0

most popular responses. It is clear through inspection of the data in Tables II through XI that there are many additional findings of interest. It may be noted, for example, that many responses were given with a high frequency in only one of the eleven cultures; for example, sex anatomy at the small d5v on card I in the New Ireland group. Certain responses were commonly given by all of the groups within a particular cultural area but not by groups from

Table V.—Percentage of Various Rorschach Responses in Eleven Cultures: Card III

	NA.		*MEN.*		*MES.*		*MONT.*		*B.C.*		*PAL.*		*IF.*		*N.I.*		*BH.*	*HIN.*	*PAK.*
	M	*F*	*M*	*F*	*M*	*F*	*M*	*F*	*M*	*F*	*M*	*F*	*M*	*F*	*M*	*F*	*M*	*M*	*M*
Animal Skin W∧	73	29	33	32	35	57	3	0	12	6	20	10	0	0	0	0	0	22	7
Bat, Bird W∧	6	12	2	7	3	7	15	4	12	11	4	3	9	0	0	0	4	6	21
Sea Animal W∧	6	0	0	0	3	7	15	18	19	0	0	0	0	0	6	0	7	2	0
Tree W∧	0	0	0	0	3	0	6	11	0	0	4	0	26	36	0	0	0	0	7
Animal Skin W∨	24	6	0	3	15	3	0	0	4	0	0	0	0	0	0	0	0	2	0
Animal W∧	0	0	0	0	0	7	12	7	0	0	2	7	0	0	0	0	11	2	14
Bat W∨	9	0	0	0	21	13	0	0	0	6	0	0	0	0	0	0	0	8	0
Sea Animal D1∨	0	0	0	0	3	0	0	0	4	0	0	0	0	0	31	0	0	0	0
Feet D2∧	3	0	0	13	12	13	0	0	19	0	0	0	0	0	0	0	4	0	0
Hu. Anatomy W∧	0	0	2	0	0	0	0	0	12	17	2	0	3	0	6	25	0	8	0
Clouds W∧	3	0	0	0	0	0	3	0	4	0	7	3	14	3	0	0	0	0	0
Animal Anat. W∧	0	0	6	0	3	0	0	0	0	0	13	10	3	0	0	0	0	0	0
Butterfly W∧	0	0	2	0	0	0	0	0	20	0	0	0	0	0	0	0	0	0	0
Frog W∧	0	0	2	0	0	0	15	0	0	0	0	0	0	0	0	0	0	2	0
Land W∧	12	35	0	0	0	0	0	0	0	0	2	0	0	0	0	0	0	0	0
Bear W∧	0	0	2	10	0	0	0	0	0	0	0	0	0	0	0	0	0	0	7
Sex Organs d2∧	0	0	0	0	0	0	0	0	0	0	0	0	0	0	6	75	0	0	0
Mountain W∧	0	0	0	0	0	0	0	0	0	0	0	0	3	14	0	0	0	0	0

Table VI.—Percentage of Various Rorschach Responses in Eleven Cultures: Card V

	NA.		*MEN.*		*MES.*		*MONT.*		*B.C.*		*PAL.*		*IF.*		*N.I.*		*BH.*	*HIN.*	*PAK.*
	M	*F*	*M*	*F*	*M*	*F*	*M*	*F*	*M*	*F*	*M*	*F*	*M*	*F*	*M*	*F*	*M*	*M*	*M*
Bat W∧	33	35	31	39	38	27	18	14	39	6	38	23	0	0	0	0	0	0	7
Bird W∧	24	18	2	7	3	10	21	18	15	22	9	10	49	31	13	25	4	10	36
Butterfly W∧	21	18	15	58	35	40	9	7	31	50	9	3	0	0	13	0	0	6	0
Butterfly W∨	15	0	27	10	18	7	0	14	0	0	0	0	0	0	0	0	0	0	0
Sea Animal W∧	0	0	0	3	0	0	24	11	8	0	2	0	3	0	6	0	4	2	7
Flying Fox W∧	0	0	0	0	0	0	0	0	0	0	0	0	0	0	25	25	7	20	0
Animal W∧	0	0	0	7	0	0	3	0	0	0	9	3	0	3	6	0	7	8	14
Bat, Flying W∧	9	0	4	0	9	13	0	0	0	0	0	0	0	0	0	0	0	26	0
Animals, d3∧	12	24	6	10	3	3	0	0	4	0	0	0	0	0	0	0	15	4	0
Rabbit D2∧	3	0	0	0	9	7	0	0	0	0	0	0	0	0	0	0	0	0	7
Cross W∧	0	0	0	0	0	0	18	11	0	0	0	0	0	0	0	0	0	0	0
Guitar W∧	0	0	0	0	0	0	15	4	0	0	0	0	0	0	0	0	0	0	0
Snakes d1∨	3	0	0	0	0	0	0	0	0	0	0	0	0	0	0	0	0	10	0
Hu. Head, Body D1∧	9	6	0	0	3	10	0	0	0	0	0	0	0	0	0	25	0	0	0
Animal D2∧	0	0	0	0	0	0	0	4	4	0	0	0	6	0	0	0	0	2	0
Tree W∧	0	6	2	0	0	0	0	0	0	0	0	0	6	14	0	0	0	2	0
Bird W>	3	0	4	0	3	10	0	0	0	0	0	0	0	0	0	0	0	0	0
Animal W∧	3	0	0	3	0	0	0	7	0	0	0	0	0	0	0	0	4	2	0
Cloud W∧	0	0	0	0	0	0	0	0	0	0	0	0	3	11	6	0	0	0	0
Cow (extended) W∧	0	0	0	0	0	0	0	0	0	0	4	7	0	0	0	0	0	0	0

other geographical areas. For example, two people W-V on card VII, is present in all of the American Indian groups with some frequency. On the other hand one finds responses that are given by two or more groups from different geographical areas but that are not given by all of the groups within the same geographical areas.

Table VII.—Percentage of Various Rorschach Responses in Eleven Cultures: Card VI

	NA.		*MEN.*		*MES.*		*MONT.*		*B.C.*		*PAL.*		*IF.*		*N.I.*		*BH.*	*HIN.*	*PAK.*
	M	*F*	*M*	*F*	*M*	*F*	*M*	*F*	*M*	*F*	*M*	*F*	*M*	*F*	*M*	*F*	*M*	*M*	*M*
Animal Skin W∧	24	6	15	42	47	37	3	0	8	0	4	3	0	0	0	0	0	4	14
Turtle W∧	15	0	0	3	3	3	9	4	15	0	0	3	0	0	6	0	22	8	0
Tree W∧	0	0	0	0	0	0	0	4	0	0	4	0	11	25	13	0	11	0	14
Sea Animal W∧	6	12	2	0	0	3	15	4	15	0	2	0	0	0	0	0	0	0	0
Skin of Animal W∨	9	0	15	0	12	7	0	4	0	0	0	0	0	0	0	0	0	4	0
Animal Skin D1∧	15	0	6	0	9	23	0	0	0	0	0	0	0	0	0	0	0	8	0
Church, Cross W∧	0	0	0	0	0	0	18	11	0	0	0	0	0	3	6	0	4	4	0
Bird W∧	0	0	2	0	0	0	0	4	4	6	0	7	0	0	6	0	4	6	7
Cross D2∧	0	0	4	0	0	0	3	0	12	6	0	0	0	0	6	0	4	0	0
Insect W∧	0	0	0	0	0	0	3	4	0	6	0	0	0	0	0	0	0	16	7
Insect D2∧	0	6	7	6	6	3	0	4	4	0	0	0	0	0	0	0	0	0	7
Tree D2∧	0	6	0	0	0	0	9	0	4	0	0	0	3	17	0	0	0	0	7
Animals W∧	0	0	0	7	0	0	6	7	4	6	0	0	3	6	6	0	0	2	0
Bird D2∧	3	6	2	7	6	10	0	4	4	0	0	0	0	0	0	0	0	0	0
Animal Head d2∧	6	0	0	7	0	0	6	0	0	22	0	0	0	0	0	0	0	2	0
Animal Skin D1∨	0	0	13	3	0	0	0	0	0	0	0	0	0	0	0	0	0	0	0
Cement W∨	0	0	0	0	0	0	0	0	0	0	0	0	11	0	0	0	0	0	0
Mountain W∧	0	0	0	0	0	0	0	0	0	0	0	3	11	0	0	0	0	0	0
Totempole D2∧	0	0	2	19	0	0	0	0	0	0	0	0	0	0	0	0	0	0	0

Table VIII.—Percentage of Various Rorschach Responses in Eleven Cultures: Card VII

	NA.		*MEN.*		*MES.*		*MONT.*		*B.C.*		*PAL.*		*IF.*		*N.I.*		*BH.*	*HIN.*	*PAK.*
	M	*F*	*M*	*F*	*M*	*F*	*M*	*F*	*M*	*F*	*M*	*F*	*M*	*F*	*M*	*F*	*M*	*M*	*M*
Cloud W∧	15	0	11	0	6	3	0	0	39	0	24	10	46	28	19	0	0	0	0
Geog. Area W∧	3	6	9	0	3	3	9	0	4	6	22	3	6	11	0	0	0	0	0
People W∧	0	0	6	0	6	17	3	21	4	6	9	0	0	0	19	0	4	2	0
2 People D4∧	12	0	2	10	9	7	0	0	12	0	0	0	0	0	13	50	0	0	0
2 People W∨	9	0	11	10	24	27	0	0	0	0	0	0	0	0	0	0	0	0	0
2 Animal D4∧	12	12	7	23	0	17	0	0	19	17	0	0	0	0	0	0	4	0	0
Elephant D2∨	24	6	6	7	3	3	0	0	0	0	0	0	0	0	0	0	0	4	0
2 People D4∨	15	0	0	0	9	10	0	0	0	0	0	0	0	0	0	0	0	4	7
Animals D3∧	12	0	4	10	3	0	0	0	4	0	0	0	0	0	0	0	0	0	7
Land W∧	6	0	0	7	0	3	0	0	4	0	0	0	3	11	0	0	0	4•	7
2 Animals W∧	3	0	0	3	9	17	0	0	4	0	0	0	0	0	6	0	0	0	0
Elephant, An. Head D2∧	3	12	6	7	0	3	3	0	0	0	0	0	0	0	0	0	0	6	0
Tree W∧	0	0	0	0	0	0	3	4	0	0	0	0	11	19	0	0	0	2	0
Fowl D2∧	0	0	2	0	0	0	0	0	8	0	0	0	0	0	0	0	4	0	0
Map W∨	0	0	0	0	3	7	6	14	4	0	0	0	0	0	0	0	0	0	0
Animal D3∨	9	6	0	0	3	0	0	0	0	0	0	0	0	0	0	0	0	0	0
Hu. Anatomy W∧	3	0	0	0	0	0	0	0	0	0	7	10	0	3	0	0	0	2	0
Rocks, Mt. W∨	0	0	0	0	0	0	6	7	4	0	0	0	0	0	0	0	0	0	0
Clouds W∨	0	0	0	0	0	0	3	11	0	0	0	0	0	0	0	0	0	4	0
Fowl D3∧	0	0	0	3	0	0	0	0	0	0	0	0	0	0	0	0	4	2	0

Table IX.—Percentage of Various Rorschach Responses in Eleven Cultures: Card IX

	NA.		*MEN.*		*MES.*		*MONT.*		*B.C.*		*PAL.*		*IF.*		*N.I.*		*BH.*	*HIN.*	*PAK.*
	M	*F*	*M*	*F*	*M*	*F*	*M*	*F*	*M*	*F*	*M*	*F*	*M*	*F*	*M*	*F*	*M*	*M*	*M*
Animals (spec.) D1∧	70	82	22	19	15	3	24	14	69	67	2	3	9	22	25	25	15	52	43
Rodentlike An. D1∧	3	12	4	32	6	7	58	57	12	17	2	0	9	3	19	0	0	12	36
Unspec. Animal D1∧	6	0	27	26	12	10	6	11	8	6	7	10	0	0	13	0	7	20	21
Monkeys D1∧	0	0	0	0	0	0	3	7	4	0	18	3	37	22	0	0	11	4	14
Tree D3∧	0	0	4	19	0	0	0	0	8	0	0	0	6	3	0	0	26	18	7
Animal D1>	12	12	11	16	21	13	0	7	0	0	0	0	0	0	6	0	0	2	0
Bird D1∧	0	0	0	0	0	0	0	0	4	0	0	0	23	19	0	0	7	8	0
Oppossum D1∧	0	0	0	0	0	0	0	0	0	0	0	0	0	0	38	50	0	0	0
Plant, Tree W∧	3	0	4	0	3	13	3	0	0	0	0	0	9	6	0	0	0	0	14
Mountain D3∧	15	12	2	0	0	0	3	0	0	0	0	0	3	0	6	0	0	2	0
Animal Anat. D5∧	6	6	4	10	6	10	6	0	4	0	0	0	0	0	0	0	0	4	0
Butterfly D2∧	3	6	11	23	3	3	0	0	4	6	0	0	0	0	0	50	0	6	0
Tree D3∧	0	0	0	0	9	10	0	0	0	0	0	0	3	0	0	0	4	2	7
Unspec. Animal D1>	0	0	0	0	15	23	0	0	0	0	0	0	0	0	0	0	4	0	0
Flower D2∧	0	0	4	10	3	13	0	4	4	0	0	0	0	0	0	0	0	6	0
Flowers W∨	0	0	2	0	15	7	0	0	0	0	0	0	0	0	0	0	0	0	0
Hu. Anatomy W∧	3	0	0	0	0	0	0	4	0	0	2	17	0	0	6	0	0	4	0
Animal D6∧	12	29	0	0	3	0	0	0	0	0	0	0	0	0	0	0	0	0	0
Lizard, Rodent D1>	0	0	2	0	6	20	0	0	0	0	0	0	0	0	0	0	0	0	7
Hu. Anatomy D5∨	0	0	0	0	0	0	0	0	0	0	0	0	0	0	0	0	0	12	0
Insects D1∧	0	0	0	0	0	0	3	4	0	0	4	0	0	0	0	0	0	0	0

Table X.—Percentage of Various Rorschach Responses in Eleven Cultures: Card X

	NA.		*MEN.*		*MES.*		*MONT.*		*B.C.*		*PAL.*		*IF.*		*N.I.*		*BH.*	*HIN.*	*PAK.*
	M	*F*	*M*	*F*	*M*	*F*	*M*	*F*	*M*	*F*	*M*	*F*	*M*	*F*	*M*	*F*	*M*	*M*	*M*
Hu. Figure D4∧	3	0	4	0	3	3	15	4	19	6	0	0	3	6	44	25	4	10	7
Animal D3∧	33	29	0	3	18	10	3	0	0	0	0	0	0	0	13	0	4	2	0
Tree, Flowers W∧	6	0	2	0	9	7	3	18	4	17	2	7	17	25	13	0	7	2	7
Animals D1∧	0	6	4	7	15	7	0	4	12	17	0	0	0	0	0	0	15	6	14
Clouds W∧	6	0	0	0	0	0	6	7	4	0	16	0	14	17	0	0	0	2	0
Animal D3>	6	0	2	0	18	3	0	0	0	0	0	0	0	0	0	0	0	14	0
Animals D2∧	6	0	7	7	3	0	3	0	4	0	0	0	0	0	0	25	0	10	0
Hand (bet. pi. + gr.)	3	0	0	0	9	3	0	0	0	0	0	0	0	0	13	0	0	6	0
Mountain W∧	0	0	2	0	3	3	3	0	0	0	0	0	11	3	0	0	0	4	7
Animal D1∨	0	6	4	0	12	0	0	0	0	0	0	0	0	0	0	0	0	8	0
Wings D2∧	3	0	0	0	3	0	0	0	15	0	0	0	0	0	0	0	0	0	0
Tree, Flowers W∨	0	6	2	3	0	10	0	0	0	0	0	0	0	0	13	0	0	4	0
Sea Animals D2∧	0	0	0	7	12	0	0	4	0	0	0	0	0	0	0	0	4	0	0
Person(s) D6>	0	0	4	13	3	10	0	4	0	0	0	0	0	0	6	25	0	2	0
Land W∧	0	0	0	0	0	0	3	0	0	0	2	0	3	11	0	0	0	0	0
Flower D1∨ = D5	0	0	0	0	6	7	0	0	0	0	0	0	0	0	0	0	0	0	0

Tables II through XI list 141 different responses. Is there an over-all similarity or homogeneity of response among the eleven cultures throughout these tables? A statistical measure of similarity between groups is Kendall's coefficient of concordance, W. This technique provides a measure of the amount of agreement between the groups in the rank order of frequency of response for the 141 response categories that were selected for analysis. Table XIII indicates that a W of .20 is found between the eleven culture groups.

Table XI.—Percentage of Various Rorschach Responses in Eleven Cultures: Card X

	NA.		*MEN.*		*MES.*		*MONT.*		*B.C.*		*PAL.*		*IF.*		*N.I.*		*BH.*	*HIN.*	*PAK.*
	M	*F*	*M*	*F*	*M*	*F*	*M*	*F*	*M*	*F*	*M*	*F*	*M*	*F*	*M*	*F*	*M*	*M*	*M*
Animal Head D7∧	36	29	42	26	21	10	21	7	12	11	0	0	0	0	19	25	0	0	0
Insects D1∧	9	6	5	36	41	47	0	0	12	6	0	0	9	3	0	25	4	16	14
Flowers, Tree D1∧	3	0	6	3	6	3	3	4	12	11	0	0	14	33	25	25	15	18	7
Flower(s) W∧	9	6	0	0	12	0	0	4	8	6	7	3	17	14	0	0	19	0	7
Dogs D10∧	12	24	18	32	12	17	9	4	12	17	0	0	0	0	6	0	0	0	7
Worms D2∧	6	6	40	13	15	20	0	4	8	6	0	0	0	0	0	0	0	0	0
Sheep, Bulls D13∧	6	6	2	0	9	7	12	0	4	0	0	0	3	0	13	0	0	6	0
Lion, Tiger D10∧	9	12	2	3	6	7	0	0	12	6	0	0	0	0	13	0	0	0	7
Fowl D10∧	6	0	2	10	0	0	3	4	0	6	0	0	3	0	6	25	11	10	7
Insect D1∨	6	0	0	0	3	0	18	36	0	0	0	0	0	0	0	0	0	4	14
2 Animals D3∧	3	0	15	7	12	17	0	0	8	11	0	0	0	0	0	0	0	0	7
Tree D3∧	3	0	4	3	3	7	15	0	4	0	0	0	0	6	13	25	0	0	0
Birds D6∧	3	0	0	0	0	0	0	0	8	6	0	0	6	3	0	0	15	8	0
Insects D6∧	0	0	4	7	0	0	0	0	0	0	0	0	0	0	25	25	0	2	7
Jackrabbit D2∧	21	29	0	0	0	3	9	0	4	0	0	0	0	0	0	0	0	0	0
Flowers W∨	3	0	4	0	9	3	3	18	0	0	0	0	0	0	6	0	0	0	7
Animals D4∧	0	0	0	0	0	0	3	0	12	11	0	0	0	0	13	0	0	4	0
Clouds D9∧	3	6	0	0	0	0	0	0	0	0	4	0	17	3	6	0	0	0	0
Dog D11 <	0	0	2	10	3	0	0	0	0	0	0	0	0	0	0	0	4	20	0
Animals D11∧	9	12	7	13	6	3	0	11	0	0	0	0	3	3	0	0	0	2	0
Rocks, Mt. D9∧	9	6	2	0	3	0	3	4	0	0	0	0	3	0	6	0	0	0	0
Deer D6∧	0	0	0	0	9	13	0	0	8	0	0	0	0	0	0	0	0	8	0
Clouds D9∧ red	9	12	0	3	0	0	0	0	4	0	0	0	6	11	6	0	0	0	0
Animals D6∧	3	0	0	0	0	0	0	0	0	0	0	0	9	0	6	0	4	0	0
Humans, Act. D9∨	0	0	15	3	0	0	0	4	0	0	0	0	0	0	0	0	0	6	0
Seahorses D5∨	0	0	0	0	12	0	0	0	0	0	0	0	0	0	6	0	0	0	0
Map, Land D9∧	0	0	0	0	3	10	6	0	0	6	0	0	3	3	0	0	0	6	0
Small Animals, W∧	3	0	2	0	6	10	0	0	4	17	2	0	0	0	0	0	0	0	0
Insects D4∧	0	0	4	7	3	10	0	4	4	6	0	0	0	0	0	0	0	4	0
Lake, Ocean D1∧	12	6	2	0	0	0	0	0	0	0	0	0	0	0	0	0	0	0	0
Sea Animal D1∧	0	0	6	7	3	13	0	0	0	0	0	0	0	0	6	0	0	0	0
Seed, Leaf D12∨	0	0	4	7	3	0	0	0	0	0	0	0	0	0	6	0	0	2	0
Hu. Anatomy W∧	0	0	0	0	0	0	0	0	0	0	4	10	0	0	0	0	0	8	0
Birds, B-fly D5∨	0	0	0	0	9	3	0	0	0	0	0	0	0	0	0	0	0	0	0
Caterpillars D5∨	0	0	6	3	0	0	0	0	0	0	0	0	0	0	0	0	0	0	0
Seahorse D2∧	0	0	6	7	0	0	0	0	0	0	0	0	0	0	0	0	0	0	0
Wishbone D12∧	3	6	2	7	0	17	0	0	0	0	0	0	0	0	0	0	0	0	0
Horns D13∧	0	0	4	7	0	0	0	0	0	0	0	0	0	0	0	0	0	0	0

This value is significant at less than the .001 level; thus while the amount of agreement between the eleven culture groups is relatively small, this agreement is statistically very reliable.

In order to assess the influence of the geographical area variable, W was computed for the groups within each geographical area as well as between the four geographical areas. If geographical area is indeed a relevant variable, one would expect a greater similarity, or higher W, between the groups within the various geographical areas than between the different geographical areas. That this expectation is substantiated is shown in Table XII. Examining all four geographical areas we find that the average of within area W is .54, indicating a relatively high degree of similarity of responses within the different geo-

Table XII.—Chi-Square Values for Tests between Culture Groups and between Geographical Areas

	Response Category	Between Culture Groups (df = 10)	Between Geographical Areas (df = 3)
Card I	Bat W	52.28***	16.89***
II	Human Figures W	28.61**	9.41*
III	Two People W	146.89***	106.98***
IV	Animal Skin W	90.51***	57.14***
V	Bat W	61.99***	35.95***
V	Bird W	55.81***	11.80**
VII	Cloud W	65.58***	33.83***
VIII	Animals D1	90.04***	31.55***
X	Insects D1	68.90***	44.77***
X	Animal Head D7	75.76***	63.25***
I	Butterfly W	20.19*	8.84*
I	Human Form D1	47.31***	8.08*
II	Bears W	8.31	3.01
III	Two Non-Human Figures D8 or W	34.98***	23.02***
III	Fish D5	43.74***	29.30***
[a] III	Animals D2	31.98***	7.62
[a] VI	Butterfly W	38.22***	17.04***
V	Animal Skin W	10.18	4.37
VIII	Unspec. Animal D1	24.55**	10.99*
VIII	Rodent-like Animal D1	87.90***	44.30***
VIII	Monkeys D1	60.24***	36.88***
IX	Human Figure D4	4.41	1.04
X	Flowers, Tree D1	24.26**	7.49

Key: * = less than .05 level; ** = less than .01 level; *** = less than .001 level.

[a] With these responses, Cochran's recommendation that no cell have an expected value less than 2 was relaxed. No less than 90% of the cells had an expected value of 2 and no cell had an expected value less than 1.

Table XIII.—Similarity between Groups as Indicated by Kendall's W

Between Cultures	*Between Geographical Areas*	*Between Cultures within Geogr. Areas*	
.20***	.33*	Am. Indians	.61***
		West Indies	.63*
		Western Pacific	.42*
		Indian	.52***
		Mean	.54

Key: * = less than .05 level; ** = less than .01 level; *** = less than .001 level.

graphical areas. When the response frequencies for groups within each geographical area were pooled and a measure of the amount of similarity between the four areas was obtained, a value of .33 was found, significant at less than the .02 level. Although it is not possible to obtain a statistical measure of the reliability of the difference between W's, it appears clear that there is a substantially greater similarity of response between the groups within geographical areas than between the geographical areas. Table XIV presents the results of an analysis of variance of within area W's taken card by card. It will

Table XIV.—Analysis of Variance of Within-Area Coefficients of Concordance (W)

Card	*Amer. Ind.*	*West Ind.*	*West. Pacific*	*India*
I	.40	.67	.42	.52
II	.61	.37	.23	.54
III	.60	.57	.30	.58
IV	.55	.58	.35	.48
V	.91	.86	.46	.41
VI	.78	.71	.47	.29
VII	.34	.50	.63	.39
VIII	.77	.78	.43	.70
IX	.25	.75	.54	.38
X	.62	.53	.38	.52
Mean	.583	.632	.421	.481

Source	*ss*	*df*	*Ms*	*F*	*P*
Between areas	.275	3	.092	4.00	.05 signif.
Within areas	.830	36	.023		
Total	1.105	39			

be noted that the difference between the "within-area" variance and the "between-area" variance is significant at the .05 level. This finding indicates that the "between-card" variance is considerably greater than the "between-area" variance and suggests the need for caution in interpreting these findings since the particular blot and its characteristics apparently had a good deal to do with the amount of similarity that is found in various parts of the table. Table XV presents an analysis of coefficients of correlation which parallels

Table XV.—Correlations (r_{sav} Values) in Frequency of Response among Eleven Cultures

Card	*Culture*	*Area*	*Mean within Area*
I	+.19	+.37	+.21
II	+.13	+.23	+.08
III	+.13	+.04	+.21
IV	+.08	+.04	+.16
V	+.11	+.12	+.47
VI	.00	−.03	+.31
VII	.00	.00	+.13
VIII	+.32	+.31	+.47
IX	+.06	−.07	+.19
X	+.08	.00	+.20
Mean	+.11	+.10	+.24

the analysis of W's, the coefficients of concordance. The table indicates that there is considerably greater degree of association between the cultures within a particular area, as indicated by an *r* of .24, than exists either between all of the cultures in the table or among the four areas. Table XVI identifies the geographical areas within which there is the highest degree of association. It may be noted that the American Indian cultures with a mean *r* of .37 are

Table XVI.—Correlations (r_{sav}) of Rorschach Responses within Areas

Card	*Amer. Ind.*	*West Ind.*	*West. Pacific*	*India*
I	+.10	+.34	+.13	+.28
II	+.41	−.26	−.15	+.31
III	+.40	+.14	−.05	+.37
IV	+.32	+.08	+.02	+.22
V	+.86	+.72	+.19	+.11
VI	+.67	+.42	+.20	−.06
VII	+.01	.00	+.44	+.09
VIII	+.65	+.56	+.14	+.55
IX	−.12	+.50	+.31	+.07
X	+.43	+.03	+.07	+.28
Mean	+.37	+.25	+.13	+.22

considerably more similar to each other than the cultures of any of the other geographical areas. By way of summary it may be stated that geographical area does play a very considerable role in the similarities and variances that are found in Rorschach responses.

Discussion

The results in general appear to confirm the expectation of cultural anthropologists that there is a considerable degree of variability in characteristic cognitive structures of different peoples. This can be qualified somewhat to the degree that culture area, and not culture per se accounts for a good part of this variability. Nevertheless, those who entertained the belief that the universals would dominate the perceptual situation and that differences would be relatively infrequent do not find support in these data. Drawing conclusions about the influence of culture on perceptual processes is complicated by the fact that even where such influence is strongest, with a few exceptions, only a minority of individuals in any of the cultures gave the same response. There are in the entire set of tables not more than a half-dozen instances in which more than 50% of the persons in a culture give the same response. We may conclude that culture influence is manifested as a tendency for a particular response to appear in a group more often than in other groups, but not as a force which dominates the perception of everyone in the group. The implication of this is that in every culture, and in some more than others, there is a minority varying in size, which tends to adhere to the "normal" course. Whether the persons found in this modal class are the same from card to card is something that we have not been able to determine. Neither have we been able to determine within the limits of the present analysis whether there is any tendency for certain *types* of response to occur more often in some societies than in others. One has the feeling about these frequently given Rorschach responses that they often lie within the capacities of all members of the group just as, for example, the response Bat on card I does for members of our own society. The fact that a great many individuals do not give this response even though it may occur to them as a possibility seems to be analogous to the perception of a normative expectation which, however, does not absolutely coerce behavior.

As one examines these tables in detail, numerous differences between the groups are perceptible. Some of these differences are difficult to explain. For example, both men and women in the Palau group give the response Bat to card I, 40% of the time, but no Ifaluk or New Ireland individuals do at all; or, on card II, almost 50% of Menomini men give the response Bear to the whole card, a response which is found with substantial frequency in only one other group, the Hindus. The same is true of the D-1 human anatomy response which is given by 50% of New Ireland women but hardly occurs at all anywhere else in the table. Differences such as these seem to be real and important. They provide numerous questions which bear investigating and which may lead directly to the discovery of important cultural and human phenomena. They do not for the most part appear to have obvious explanations and one has the feeling in noting them that only sustained and subtle analysis will clarify their significance.

One limitation to the generality of our conclusions regarding the importance of geographical area should be noted. Several of the cultures within particular geographical areas are either not independent cultures or are close enough to each other so that a question about their independence can be raised. This is true of the Navajo and Apache and of the Ifaluk and Palau groups especially, but may also be true of the Montserrat and Black Caribs and to a limited extent of the Hindu and the Pakistani groups. It is a grave deficiency of our sample of eleven cultures that, being selected more or less at random and on the basis of the available materials, they did not represent the diversity of the cultures that could be found in the given geographical areas. It is to be hoped that future studies conducted on a much larger scale than the present one will remedy this deficiency.

The conclusions that have been reached through this Rorschach analysis may appear to have involved the discovery of the obvious. Certainly the conclusion that the meanings of ambiguous materials vary from one culture to another is not unanticipated, and is in line with the expectations of current ethnological theory. On the other hand it is good to have a rigorous confirmation of this thesis, and the possibility that different results might have been obtained undoubtedly made the study worth doing. In addition to confirming the thesis of cultural differences, however, our results do point to a certain complexity in the matter and suggest that along with these differences there is also an overall tendency toward homogeneity of responses regardless of culture. This finding gives some comfort and support to those workers who are concerned principally with the psychic unity of mankind thesis, indicating as it does that such unity does in fact exist. Thus the results suggest what most anthropologists would find acceptable and congenial, namely, that along with the diversity of meanings in different societies there are tendencies toward universal reactions, and finally that a considerable portion of the reactions that have been noted are more or less idiosyncratic.

References

Erikson, E.
1950: *Childhood and Society* (New York: Norton).

Hallowell, A. I.
1942: "Acculturation Processes and Personality Changes as Indicated by the Rorschach Technique," *Rorschach Research Exchange*, **4**, 42–50.
1945: "Popular Responses and Cultural References: An Analysis Based on Frequencies in a Group of American Indian Subjects," *Rorschach Research Exchange*, **9**, 153–168.
1954: "The Self and Its Behavioral Environment," *Explorations*, **2** (April).

Kaplan, B.
1955 (1956, 1962, 1963): *Primary Records in Culture and Personality* (Madison: University of Wisconsin Press).

Wallace, A.
1961: "The Psychic Unity of Human Groups," in B. Kaplan (ed.), *Studying Personality Cross-Culturally* (Evanston: Row, Peterson).

GEORGE SPINDLER AND LOUISE SPINDLER

Researching the Perception of Cultural Alternatives: The Instrumental Activities Inventory[1]

Purpose and Research Site

Our purpose is to describe the development and application of a research technique that we have chosen to call the "Instrumental Activities Inventory," which we feel to be particularly useful in the study of acculturating communities, and to place it in the context of our study of the relationships between psychological adaptation and culture change in one particular community. The inventory consists of 24 line drawings that depict specific instrumental activities in three categories current on our research site. By instrumental activities we mean those activities that an individual engages in for the achievement and maintenance of a life style and status in the social groups of which he is a member, or aspires to be a member.

1. Grateful acknowledgment of support for this research is hereby given to the Stanford School of Education faculty research fund and to the National Institute of Mental Health. We also wish to acknowledge the help of Anthony D. Fisher, who joined our project in the field near its beginning, did much of the collating of data from the I.A.I., and contributed ideas and interpretations represented at various points in this paper. A shorter analysis of the substance of this paper will be published in the *Southwestern Journal of Anthropology*, spring or summer, 1965.

The research site is the Blood Indian Reserve in Alberta, Canada. It is the largest Canadian reserve, including an area of 540,000 square miles and approximately 3000 Blood Indians. It is a rich reservation, with unusual resources of well-watered grazing and prime wheat-growing land. A tribal herd and wheat leases to white operators provide tribal income. A minority of individual Blood Indians have developed substantial holdings of ranch and wheat land, leased from the tribe, and a few Blood have become entrepreneurs. The majority of the Blood get along with summer and fall haying, perhaps a few head of cattle, intermittent seasonal agricultural and ranch work, and a few are employed as mechanics, carpenters, and painters. Recently the Canadian government instituted a comprehensive economic development study, as a response to growing population pressure within the reserve and a growing awareness on the part of both the Blood and the government that the resources of the reserve must be exploited more efficiently.[2]

The Blood community is culturally conservative in that all Blood speak their native language (even though they are bilingual), nearly all the men belong to functioning age-grade societies, the hand game is the most popular form of gambling, and a relatively large number of individuals own medicine bundles and participate in traditional religious activities. The annual Sun Dance is still held and attracts crowds numbering in the hundreds on the days when the societies put on social dances and giveaways, although the traditional sacred functions of the affair have diminished in recent years, and the Horn Society has decreased both in size and in influence.

In other respects as well the contemporary Blood give evidence of continuity with their cultural past. They are still essentially nomadic. Although all the people have houses somewhere on the reserve they are rarely in them during the summer months when mobility is maximum. They are traveling, visiting, haying, or going to rodeos. Indian names are still acquired as a result of some unusual incident or adventure. Leadership still falls to the man who acts like a chief—one who does not "lead" in the white man sense, but who "helps the people," who "always talks friendly with anyone," and who is generous with his goods as well as his services and is dignified in his demeanor. Formal social affairs are conducted with the grave courtesy and attention to rank that appear to be long-established Blood traits. And in the manner of thinking and judging, as we shall make clear later, the Blood as a whole are quite different than whites and this difference seems to be accountable as an influence of the surviving, though attenuated, traditional culture.

But at the same time the Blood community is in some ways progressive. The successful Blood ranchers and farmers serve as influential models. The

2. The authors, with the assistance of Anthony D. Fisher, have recently given a full report of the research results obtained from our study of the Blood Reserve, at the request of the Division of Indian Affairs, Ottawa, Canada (G. and L. Spindler, 1963a).

Blood are notable for their business acumen in tribal dealings with whites. And the numerous tractors, combines, trucks, frigidaires, and other modern household equipment and furnishings indicate that the Blood are not averse to the material and technological culture of the white man, nor even to certain aspects of his value system.

These characteristics—the culturally conservative base and the selectively progressive elements—make the reserve community ideal for our purposes. We have been engaged since 1958 in a comparative study of the Blood, researching the psychological adaptations to pressures created by the impact of the white man's social and economic system in a situation where there is a high degree of cultural homogeneity but where economic differentiation exists—unlike the Menomini case that we studied in depth where cultural and economic differentiation are concomitant (G. D. Spindler: 1955; L. S. Spindler: 1962). So that we would have data comparable to our Menomini material we have utilized the same techniques, including the Rorschach Projective Technique, autobiographic interviews, socioeconomic schedules, and extensive participant observation. Notwithstanding the collection of these comparable data from 1958 through 1961 we have felt that we did not fully understand how the Blood perceived either themselves, or the white man and his system. It was to this end that we developed the Instrumental Activities Inventory. We selected that aspect of social action that we felt to be most relevant to the way in which a Blood individual behaves as he attempts to cope with the realities of life in his own environment—the activities instrumental to his achievement and maintenance of life styles and socioeconomic statuses recognizable and (in varying degrees) valued in the domain of the Blood community. The IAI, as we shall henceforth term the research technique, is in part a projective technique in the tradition of the Thematic Apperception Test and the several picture techniques that have been developed recently by others, and in part a way of cataloguing the perceptual and cognitive dimensions most directly related to the economic and social behavior of Blood individuals and the Blood community as it moves at an accelerating rate into the Albertan version of the Western industrial and urban world.

Theoretical Orientation

In what has been said up to this point there are certain implications concerning the theoretical position taken in this research, and particularly with respect to the purposes of the IAI. We shall lay these out more explicitly now.

We are indebted to many sources for the ideas that have comingled in our theoretical and methodological orientation in this section and elsewhere in this paper. The works of A. Irving Hallowell have been extremely influential in the course of all our work with both the Menomini and the Blood. A complete bibliographical listing of them would be impossible, since we have read and used, we believe, nearly everything he has written. Perhaps the two most relevant items, since they influenced directly the early formulation of our work, are his "Sociopsychological Aspects of Acculturation" (1945) where he develops so clearly the concept of learning in culture change situations, and his "The Use of Projective Techniques in the Study of the Sociopsychological Aspects of Acculturation" (1951), where he demonstrates the persistence of the Ojibwa personality system through several levels of acculturation. We have also been heavily influenced by the thinking of the structural-functional school of sociology—particularly by Robert K. Merton and Talcott Parsons—and we have received invaluable intellectual aid from the thinking of David Riesman. Our studies with Bruno Klopfer in projective techniques have also played a decisive role. Most recently we have benefited directly from the following: Kaplan (1957, 1961); Goldschmidt (1959); Lindzey (1961); Cohen (1961); Spiro (1961); Weinstock (1963); Inkeles (1958); French (1963); Wallace (1961) as we have attempted to combine a focus on social action with analysis of psychological adaptation in culture change.[3]

In acculturation situations, the established sociocultural system significantly affects the adaptations people can and do make to changes in the conditions of life created by the impact of another culture and its bearers. As changes in the conditions of survival occur, the established sociocultural system loses its meaning and effectiveness in some degree. Under conditions of rapid acculturation it tends to become dysfunctional and therefore threatening to the individual who is trying to adapt to the new situation. The binding of established directives for behavior upon the individual becomes loosened. New alternatives are perceived and reacted to differently by different individuals, but within a spectrum limited in part by the prior sociocultural system. When a successful (i.e., functional) adaptation is reached by a number of persons, new sociocultural systems emerge and are consolidated in coherent form.

We feel that psychological concepts, tools, and methods must be utilized if the strategy of so-called "culture change" studies is to be satisfying. Individuals are thrown upon their own resources of adaptation when previously tight cultural boundaries are weakened or destroyed. Their psychology must be understood as they perceive and grope toward new solutions that require a reorganization of thinking and feeling and result in the generation of new sociocultural systems.

It is for these reasons that we have utilized the Rorschach, and have developed the IAI. We certainly do not regard these or any other "instruments" as sufficient armamentarium for field work on the psychology of culture change, and have given contextual meaning to the data collected with these tools through extensive observations of individuals and groups in social action,

3. For a more complete statement of the rationale for the use of psychology in culture change studies see G. D. and L. S. Spindler (1963b).

personal documents of various kinds, and many interviews as well as ecological, demographic, and historical data.

We regard the Rorschach valuable as a means of gathering information concerning the individual's organization and control of intellectual and emotional resources. It is an abstract and admittedly cryptic map of this organization, but our experience with the Menomini and now with the Blood, and the congruence of Rorschach results with the contextual data we have on each community, convinces us that it is a valuable source of information about this organization that is not as directly available by other means. The IAI gives us quite different information. It gives us information on the cognitive orientations, pervasively influencing the individual's perception of and response to social reality. At a more discreet level the IAI gives us specific, operational perceptions of social reality organized normatively in means-end relationships.

We believe that the most useful dimensions of social reality, for our purposes, are structured into instrumental roles that prescribe activity related to specific and valued social goals. For white man society the most significant instrumental activities are those represented in the occupational structure. Becoming a mechanic, an M.D., or a teacher is an avenue to achievement of a place in the social system with more or less predictable rewards in prestige and economic security. In Blood Indian society the instrumental activities are not usually occupations, as we think of them. Being a "chicken or fancy dancer" is not an occupation, nor is becoming a chief or a medicine man; but they are avenues to recognition in the Blood community. Haying is an activity that has specific rewards—it does not contribute to prestige unless one becomes a middleman for other hayers, but it results in subsistence and a few drinks, and helps one to maintain self-respect.

Blood Indians know well the instrumental activities and the goals to which they are instrumental that are everyday and current in the Blood community. They know less about the occupational roles that are instrumental to rewards in white man society, for they have few prototypic experiences that would allow for learning the appropriate perceptual and cognitive organization, to say nothing of the skills necessary to carry them out. Nevertheless, they are aware of the general prestige hierarchy to which white man occupations are instrumental, and have acquired generalized cognitive and motivational orientations toward white man occupations without acquiring the detailed knowledge of the central and peripheral role requirements associated with them. They have also acquired misperceptions of occupational roles and their complex requirements.

We have therefore developed the IAI as a means of engaging more directly those dimensions of psychological structure that are most influential in determining how the Blood will cope with current social reality. We believe that the technique can be developed and applied in any society, irrespective of degree of acculturation, since all social systems must provide instrumental activities. But the real value of the IAI for us lies in its application to situations where disjunctive instrumental expectations, stemming from two systems quite alien to each other in origin but converging in the same field of social action and achievement are present, and perceived. It is here that we can see most clearly how the individual chooses from possible alternatives—what he chooses, his ordering of his choices, and how he thinks about them.

The IAI and the Research Procedure

Within the Blood community there are three major classes of instrumental activities: (1) Those which are instrumental within the framework of the most traditional aspects of Blood culture—such as being a medicine man, medicine-bundle owner, participating in giveaways, dancing Indian style, etc.; (2) those which are instrumental in the Blood community in its more contemporary and less traditional aspects—such as participating in rodeos, haying, working with stock, being a political leader, etc.; and (3) those which are instrumental within the terms imposed by the Western economy and social system—such as being a white-collar worker, an M.D., a mechanic, an entrepreneur, etc. Certain of this last class of activities, such as being a mechanic or white collar worker, are available in the contemporary community. Others, such as being an M.D., represent activities to which some Blood Indians, particularly the younger generation, may aspire, and of which most Blood are aware, but for which no models exist in the Blood community.

The IAI is built around these three classes. Twenty-four line drawings representing Indians engaged in activities representing these three classes were drawn by Mr. Gerald Tailfeathers, a professional Blood Indian artist who knows the reservation community and the people within it intimately. The activities represented were selected from a broad range of possibilities on the basis of interviews with the Blood themselves, and on the basis of our own knowledge of the community. The drawings are made in such a way that circumstantial detail is eliminated and only the essential features of the activity are retained. The stimulus is concrete but the lack of circumstantial detail focuses attention upon the activity itself. The stimulus value is very different than that of the Rorschach ink-blot test, or the Thematic Apperception Technique (TAT), not only in its more narrow domain, but also in that the stimuli presented are as unambiguous as possible. The subject must understand what the activity is that he is supposed to talk about. The stimulus value is also quite different from that presented to the respondent by the photographic interview technique developed by John Collier (1957) in that specific individuals and surroundings are not represented, so that highly interpersonal interpretations of community life and personalities within it are not elicited. We attempt, therefore, to present the respondent with realistic, concrete activities, instru-

Figure 1.—Medicine man

Figure 2.—Branding

mental in his setting, but decontextualized from the concrete referents of time, place, and person. Four IAI drawings are presented here as examples. Figure 1 (medicine man) is instrumental in the traditional frame of reference; Figs. 2 and 3 (branding and carpentering) are instrumental in the contemporary Blood community; and Fig. 4 (office worker) in the Western-oriented framework. The complete list of activities includes the following: carpenter, farming, mechanic, boxing, branding calves, artist, bronc rider, chicken dancer, barber, haying, oil rig, calf roping, investiture (formal chief-making), cook, medicine man, politician, M.D., office worker, storekeeper, bartender, milking (dairy), priest, mixed marriage, nurse. Indians are pictured in each drawing excepting in the case of the politician, who is speaking to a mixed group of whites and Indians, and the "mixed marriage" situation, where an Indian male is shown marrying a white female. All of the drawings portray males, except in the politician's crowd, the bride in the marriage situation, and the nurse; for it is the males who take the instrumental roles in this culture.

Our techniques of administration were simple. We tried in all cases to stimulate the respondent to choose at least three activities he (or she) valued most highly, and an equal number that he disliked the most. We asked for a response to each of the 24 pictured activities and tried to maintain an open-ended stance to encourage free association. At the end of each administration we asked the respondent to make value-oriented choices from pairs or trios of activities that we selected on the basis of the interview up to that point and probed with questions and comments designed to activate further response that would give us information about the way the subject viewed the activities and the ends to be obtained through them. We asked all female respondents to choose what they would like their sons or husbands (depending upon age and family status) to do. The instrument elicited responses freely, and seemed to "make sense" to respondents. No individual failed to complete the inventory, once he or she started, and no persons refused to respond to it when requested.

We collected responses to the IAI from 48 males and 34 females ranging in age from 18 to 87 years of age and representing all known socioeconomic, religious, and other groupings current in the contemporary Blood community. Of these 72 respondents, 50 of them are people to whom we administered the Rorschach and whom we had interviewed in our previous field research. It was our intention to obtain as much overlap of samples as possible so that we would have a means of interrelating Rorschach and IAI results on an individual as well as a categorical basis, and so that we would have as complete case studies of individuals as possible.[4]

4. Anthony Fisher has collected responses from 40 more males, ranging in age from 14 to 25 years, in a separate but closely related study of the young Blood and their special problems of adaptation. Morgan Maclachan and Gene Reese have collected 80 protocols from the closely related but much more acculturated (and "disorganized") Montana Blackfoot. These data are being analyzed. This paper deals only with the data collected by the Spindlers.

Figure 3.—Carpenter

Figure 4.—Office worker

Antecedents to the IAI

Our research instrument did not spring full-blown from our minds. Like most tools, it is a lineal descendant of others. Many anthropologists have used Henry Murray's Thematic Apperception Test in cross-cultural applications, along with and separate from the Rorschach and a few other projective techniques. As we have stated, the IAI is broadly related to all of these techniques in that the user must make the assumption that what people say in response to visual stimuli bears some significant relationship to their psychic organization on one hand and to their behavior on the other. We believe that the IAI responses are more directly related to actual behavior than the responses generated by the other projective techniques commonly used in anthropological field research.

Starting with William E. Henry's development of a modified TAT for use with Hopi and Navaho (Henry: 1947) there have been a number of other such modifications of the basic Murray cards for research with American Indian, Micronesian, Japanese, and African samples. The assumptions and purposes of the researchers using these modifications are basically similar to those employed by workers who have used the original TAT in anthropological research.[5] These modifications are, however, closer to the character of the IAI in that they are attempts to make the stimuli operationally meaningful in the context of the respondent. They suffer methodologically in the fact that it is very difficult to analog the original Murray TAT interpersonal situations in variable cultural contexts, so the value that might be claimed for standardization of stimuli is destroyed. The Rorschach technique offers a better opportunity for standardization of stimuli, since the inkblots themselves are acultural.

Other anthropologists have invented picture techniques for their specific purposes, stimulated to do so in part at least by the precedents set by the use of the original and modified TAT. Jacob Fried (1954), working with the Tarahumara Indians of southwestern Chihuahua, Mexico, was researching ideal norms exhibited in trial situations. He wanted to find out what norms were applied in other situations, in order to discover what discrepancies might exist between formal trial and everyday norms. He says that "in desperation" (due to difficulties in eliciting relevant responses in interviews) he finally hit upon the solution of drawing up pictures of interpersonal conflicts in family situations, and that this solved his problem.

Walter Goldschmidt and Robert Edgerton developed a picture technique for the study of values (1961) applied to the Menomini Indians of Wisconsin, using the Spindler sample of sociocultural categories in the framework of the broad acculturative continuum defined in our work with this group. They

5. The reader will find a useful summary of these modifications in Barnouw (1963), pp. 263–275.

claim as the most important difference between their technique and the TAT that they are attempting to measure culturally established patterns of behavior rather than individual personality dynamics, and assume that ". . . it is possible to elicit value statements from representative personnel by presenting them with a consistent choice situation between alternate modes of action" (p. 28). Edgerton administered a set of eleven cards to a sample of 44 males. Each card presented alternatives in value choices within the picture on the single card. For example, a man and woman with a child between them are shown looking into store windows. The man is looking at a display of rifles. The woman is looking at new furniture. In another picture two males are fishing with their shoes off, reclining on the banks of the river while off in the distance five other men are going to work in the sawmill. Goldschmidt and Edgerton obtained significant variations in the responses of Menomini individuals in the various acculturative categories.

The IAI and the picture technique for the study of values exhibit certain features in common, and of the various inventions by anthropologists of this general type we owe the most to this antecedent experiment. The IAI is different in certain important respects, however. Our focus upon instrumental activities leads us, we think, to a more total conception of the individual's adaptation to changing conditions. We are asking how the respondent organized his perceptions of a wide range of instrumental alternatives representing the traditional system, the contemporary reservation community, and the white man's system.

Further, each of our pictures represents only one instrumental activity. We do not limit the respondent to dichotomous choices in the stimulus frame of a single picture. We believe that the picture study technique for the study of values presents some false dichotomies—between (for example) ease vs. industry, group participation vs. solitude, guns vs. furniture, buying drinks vs. groceries. But the Blood and the less acculturated Menomini operate in a situation where a medley of choices is available to them. They choose from this medley differently depending upon the situation. The IAI presents 24 specific instrumental alternatives from which the respondent can choose in any order and with any emphasis he wishes. We "force" some choices between pairs and trios of cards, but only after the respondent has had the opportunity of free choice, and on the basis of explicit or fairly clear implicit comparative choices he has already made. Even then we experience some difficulty, for the Blood respondents at least are likely to say that both activities are good—"it depends."

Another difference in the orientation of the researchers is worth mentioning. Goldschmidt and Edgerton state that if they had adequately designed photographs, they ". . . would be ideal for our purposes as we are trying to simulate reality" (p. 28). This would not be true in our application. We want to avoid personalization, so that each respondent can project into the instrumental activity his own motivations and cognitive organization. Photographs are too specific about places, persons, and objects for our purposes. The IAI pictures are, however, not drawn with fuzzy lines or ambiguous detail. Each item in the picture must be technically correct or the respondent becomes so concerned about the technical mistakes that he fails to project much of anything but this concern. And the respondent must know what instrumental activity is being pictured.

Goldschmidt and Edgerton indicate that their pictures have to be redrawn for every culture case. We do not think this is applicable to the IAI. We shall be testing the applicability of the present set of drawings to other situations in the high prairie area of Canada soon. We believe that one can design sets of instrumental activities for culture areas subsuming a number of variant individual communities. And in our usage, the white man-oriented activities remain approximately constant even as we move out of the culture area of North America for which they were designed. Furthermore, instrumental activities are among the most apparent, manifest aspects of any social system. Consequently a researcher should be able to identify the relevant activities fairly quickly, and use such a technique early in his research, provided that the technical difficulties of drawing and reproducing the pictures can be overcome.

The most recent development of a picture technique is by Seymour Parker (1964) in application to two Eskimo villages, one quite isolated and relatively unacculturated, and one very much in the main stream of arctic development and relatively highly acculturated. His purpose has been to delineate motivations about ethnic identity. The responses to his technique enable him to derive apparently useful indications of hostility toward aspects of Eskimo identity versus white man identity, and of inter- and intraethnic social distance. We share with Parker, as with Fried, and with Goldschmidt and Edgerton, an interest in the social action component heuristic to a given situation.

John Collier's experiment (Collier: 1957) with the use of photographs as the stimuli in interviews deserves discussion, for it illustrates a significant methodological point. He regards photographs used in this manner as a "semi-projective" technique. He found that such utilization stimulated sociometric information, attitudes towards work, possessions, activities, and people. He felt that the technique triggered responses and memories that often lie submerged in ordinary verbal interviewing, and that the photographs functioned as a "language bridge." Collier's treatment of the possibilities inherent in photographic interviewing is very persuasive, and we have no reason to doubt that it would be very useful in many situations. We did enlarge and mount 100 selected photographs of people, activities, places, and structures on the Blood Reserve to use as the basis for similar photographic interviewing, and John Collier kindly worked with us in the selection of photographs and gave us advice about how to use them. We cannot be said to have given the technique a fair trial, for after having used the photographs in six formal interview situations we dropped it for that purpose. We did, however, use it for a rather different but related purpose. We found that our suitcase full of photos was the best entree-gaining device that we had ever encountered in our field experience. No matter where we were, when we opened the case and the photographs were passed from hand to hand we had a crowd. The photos made it possible to collect our IAI sample more easily than would otherwise have been the case, and gave us opportunities to observe interactions between the people in the viewing groups that would otherwise have escaped us.

The reason that we dropped the photographic interview technique as such was that though everybody was interested in the photographs the responses were always limited to identifying people or places in the pictures. We observed that this was essentially what the people in the crowds passing the pictures back and forth did also, though frequently nonverbal behavior, or some witty aside gave us clues that the Blood saw more than they verbalized. We feel that the reason the Blood did not talk about the pictures (and we did not succeed in stimulating them to do so) was because in the Blood community one just does not talk about anyone else's business, at least not outside the most intimate social contexts.

The IAI pictures showed the same kinds of people, engaged in the same kinds of activities, as the photographs, but the Blood could respond to them because they were abstracted from the concrete referents that made it impossible to talk about the content of the photographs. One could talk about boxing without talking about the boxer, about white-collar desk work without talking about the administrative clerks in the agency office.

Some Research Results

Preliminary analysis of the IAI data collected by the Spindlers on the Blood has to date centered upon three objectives: (1) to discover how evaluative choices of instrumental alternatives are related to antecedent experience; (2) to describe the specific values projected into the rationales given for choices by our respondents; (3) to isolate persistent cognitive orientations that pervade the specific perceptions and evaluations of instrumental activities.

Before proceeding to the first objective it will be instructive to examine the rank ordering of the 24 instrumental activities by the whole sample. This ordering is presented below:

Chosen as most highly favored activities by one third or more of respondents (in rank order from most frequently selected):

Mechanic
Carpenter
Farming, branding calves, haying
Calf roping

Chosen as most highly favored activities by less than one third but more than one sixth of respondents:

Artist, M.D., office worker
Bronc rider
Chicken dancer, barber

Chosen by less than one sixth of respondents:

Nurse
Milking cows (dairy)
Politician
Priest
Oil rig worker
Chief-making, cook, medicine man, storekeeper
Boxing
Mixed (white-Indian) marriage
Bartender

It is apparent that the aspiration level of the Blood is modest, and reserve-oriented. The instrumental activities chosen by one third or more of the respondents are directly observable and practical in the contemporary reserve environment. Activities, occupations, statuses, that are an integral part of the outside world, are relatively infrequently given high value. Their perception of alternatives is sharply limited by what they see as the realities of their situation, and by their direct experience. The one seeming exception to this is the first-rank choice, "mechanic." This is not the exception it appears to be, however, for as will be seen later, choices of this activity are based upon the notion that such a skill would make it possible to repair one's own car or tractor. Most of the men of fifty and younger are practical mechanics. They have to be, considering the long distances separating virtually every place where one would want or would need to go, and the dependence of the present-day Blood upon motorized transport.

It is significant that chief-making and medicine man are ranked quite low. These activities have high visibility in the reserve community and are a part of the traditional culture. Specific reasons are given by the Blood—being a medicine man is regarded by many of the middle-aged and older people (and by some of the young and apparently wholly secular young men) as "too dangerous" in today's context—where the traditional controls on sacred power are no longer operative. A similar rationale is given for the low placement of chief-making, excepting that the perception of this activity is confused by the fact that in recent years a number of white government officials and distinguished visitors have been made "chiefs" at the Sun Dance and many of the Blood feel that this makes a mockery of the ritual and the status.

The low ranking of dairy work, cook, storekeeper, and barber is due to the low value that the Blood males place upon what they regard as menial, service jobs, and the fact that these jobs involve no demanding physical activity. The activities ranked highest are all highly demanding physically, and none of them involves serving others in a menial or demeaning capacity.

Relating the placement of these instrumental activities to the rationales given by Blood respondents gives us useful insights into the way in which the Blood think of themselves, view their own community and the alternatives available within it, and respond to the alternatives presented to them from the outside world. Even this preliminary level of analysis of the evaluative choices of the whole sample tells us things about the Blood that we had not known from our previous field work, and makes systematic analyses of specific values and instrumental orientations operating in social action contexts possible.

With this background we can proceed to our first stated objective—to discover how choices of instrumental alternatives are related to antecedent experience. By antecedent experience we refer to such variables as sex (male vs. female), extent and type of formal schooling, socioeconomic status, religious affiliation, socialization in tradition-oriented versus "progressive" households, exclusive on-reservation work experience vs. off-reservation work experience, and participation in various informal associations. We have analyzed our data so far with respect to the first four variables, and shall summarize the results briefly.

We have applied simple nonparametric statistical techniques to the data (chi-square and proportions tests) to discover what reliable differences appear at this gross level. Sex differences in choices of most valued instrumental activities appeared in 11 out of 24 possibilities. Without regard for the specific choices made, males appear to be oriented more toward activities current and instrumental within the existent reserve community. Women appear to be oriented more toward movementi nto white man society. There is also a strong masculine identity bias displayed by male choices. The men choose more vital risk-taking activities. Women choose more passive ones (for their sons or husbands). Males are also more pragmatic in their choices—they choose the things that a man actually can do on the reserve, and for which there are concrete models. The women are less reality-centered and more aspiration-oriented.

Socioeconomic differences in choices of most valued instrumental activities appeared in 10 out of 24 possibilities. The differences are in the direction that one might expect. Upper-status men chose more frequently those activities that require goal-orientedness on white man terms, and that are acquisitively oriented in an economic sense. Lower-status men more frequently chose activities that are economically unproductive and that are irrelevant to goal attainment and status on white man terms.[6]

The sample of males was also tested with respect to differences in distribution of responses according to education. Highest grade obtained was used as the differentiating criterion, with those with a fifth grade level or less, and a sixth grade level of attainment or more, constituting the two categories. This cutting point produced four significant differences, with more from the higher education group choosing mechanic and artist, and more from the lower education group choosing haying and bronc rider.

While the differences thus obtained using the education variable make a certain amount of sense, they are not impressive. Education, at least using the criteria indicated, is a weak variable. This may be due to the fact that most of the men in our sample received a residential (on-reserve) school education, so that their perceptions of instrumental activities and associated values relevant to and functional in the existing reserve community are probably reinforced. Parker (1964) also found that years of schooling was a weak variable unless only the highest and lowest grade attainment groups were used. Our sample of these extremes is not large enough to permit statistical tests to be applied. We plan to enlarge the sample in these categories and will retest the variable again.

Religious differences—membership in the Anglican church, the Catholic church, and the Horn Society were tested. No significant differences were discovered. This suggests that the factionalism and differences of opinion associated with religious affiliation do not run deep in a matrix of differences in values. The Blood Indian identity apparently transcends religious factionalism in those areas of outlook and value that are most instrumental in secular social action.

The female sample was tested for internal differentiation using the same variables as in the tests of the male sample. No significant differences and no marked tendencies toward differentiation were discovered. We may conclude from this that the females are more homogeneous in outlook and value orientations than are the males, since the latter are internally differentiated in relatively higher degree. This was our hypothesis, based on our observations among the Menomini (Spindler and Spindler: 1958). The rationale here is that males take the public instrumental roles available in the social system. These roles are

6. We divided the whole sample into four socioeconomic groups on the basis of house type, condition, furnishings, subsistence pattern, possessions (farm and ranch equipment, cattle, land, etc.) collected on a socioeconomic index schedule. Here we have compared the two upper-status groups to the two lower-status groups. A comparison of the socioeconomic extremes would show sharper differences in instrumental choices. Using the present cutting point produces six differences at a P of .05 or less, and four that are close to .05. We are probably safe in regarding these latter as significant, since they are consistent (in kinds of choices made) with the rest.

differentiated in the demands they make upon individual men. In meeting these demands males adopt the appropriate and functional values. This is particularly true in a male-oriented society, and the Blood Indian society can be described as one.

The analysis of data relevant to the second objective—to describe the specific values projected into the rationales for choices by our respondents—has only begun. So far we have remained close to the data, allowing our value categories to grow inductively as we check through individual responses. The distribution of specific values in each group analyzed so far suggests that a great deal of overlap occurs with some differences reflecting the status and experience of individuals in each group. This accords with our general hypothesis that the Blood community is relatively homogeneous in its basic cultural substrata.

The most native-oriented part of our sample value keeping up one's physical appearance; dancing and participating in traditional activities; being active and physically strong; helping others and "talking nice." They disvalue looking awkward or ridiculous; disfiguring the face or crippling the body; getting cheated; telling someone else what to do, or getting told: being "smart" or "cocky." These specific values coincide nicely with what we are led to expect from the descriptions of traditional Blood culture.

The young Blood in our sample (age 18 to 26) value making good money; working outdoors and being active physically; excitement and thrills, particularly in rodeo competition; being able to fix things one's self (fixing a car or tractor, fixing up a house). Only a minority see such skills as leading to status achievement; and only three of the fifteen in the sample see such skills as a channel to adaptation to the outside world. They also value being independent; but at the same time value "easy work" (a job with "sure money" that doesn't require much effort). They disvalue getting crippled or disfigured; telling other people what to do or getting told; and giving up personal freedoms of any sort—they reject confinement.

It is interesting that the overlap between the tradition-oriented sample, including a majority of men over 50, and the young Blood (18 to 25 years old), who have been exposed to supposedly critical acculturative experience during the formative period of their lives should be so great. The hypothesis for underlying cultural homogeneity is reinforced.

The socioeconomic elite—men who run large ranches or are successful entrepreneurs value being one's "own boss" (having own herd, own business, not working for someone else); working outdoors "in the open air"; making money, "sure money"; working hard and planning ahead; being strong and healthy; keeping some traditions, particularly language. They disvalue getting hurt or crippled; being "cooped up with a desk job"; "politicking"; being told what to do.

The striving for independence in this elite group is consistent with the other two groups, as is the concern for being healthy, vigorous, and outdoors. Their conception of independence is different, however, from that expressed by the others. They think of it as a state to be gained by hard work and planning ahead, by acquiring goods and economic security. This appears to be a necessary value orientation, given their success. Their concern with keeping some traditions is interesting, since it is not strong among the younger men. They perceive traditions as something valuable and self-identifying being lost, while many of the young Blood perceive traditions as merely a barrier to acceptance by the dominant society.

In the distribution of specific values revealed in the rationales given by respondents for their choices of instrumental activities one can see large areas of overlap which apparently reflect cultural homogeneity, and certain areas of differentiation appropriate to the demands of different roles and life goals subsumed by subsystems within the Blood community as a whole.

We can now move to what are to us the most interesting results of our analysis to date—the persistent cognitive orientations that pervade specific perceptions and evaluations of instrumental activities.[7] We eliminated the female sample from the analysis. The females are, indeed, most homogeneous but do not represent the major instrumental orientations for the reasons stated. We were thus left with a sample of 48 males. Our analysis required the making of inferential judgments concerning categories of cognitive orientation subsuming individual responses. We attempted to keep the categories as close to the data as possible, and believe that the derivative relationships are clear. The reader can judge for himself, as we have included a sample of responses subsumed by each cognitive orientation below.

AUTONOMY: Every man is his own boss. No one has the right to tell anyone else what to do. One is answerable only for his own actions.

Examples

(Desk worker) OK if he's (son) qualified. But I can't push them into anything they don't want.

(Bronc rider) One of my boys does this. I used to tell him he might get hurt. It's a dangerous job. But I can't tell them they have to quit. They do as they want.

(Mixed marriage) It's up to their own judgment. We're not communists—to have somebody tell them what to do. This is a free country!

7. We are not using the concept of cognition at this point in the same microanalytic way as Wallace, Conklin, Frake, Sturtevant, Hymes, and others who have been working from linguistic analogs to cognitive categories. We feel that our use of the concept is justified, however, for we are concerned with the organization of thought processes in the Blood management of perceived social reality, and by our use of the term "cognitive," focus attention on the intellective rather than affective aspects of personality structure. It is apparent in our usage that "value" orientations are a part of cognitive structuring.

(Chicken dancer) They (sons) were not interested, and I don't try to coax anyone. I was a great dancer in my day. Now I just go there and walk around.

(Politician) I don't like to. . . . I'd rather keep out of politics. I don't think I have the . . . a politician has to be aggressive. They try to change people's ways, or their thinking, and I think people should do their own thinking.

(Desk worker) The subject was speaking of his son's graduating from high school. I asked him "What is he going to do?" Response: "I dunno, I didn't ask him."

ACTIVITY AND HEALTH: An active, vigorous, outdoor life is good. It keeps one young and healthy.

(Storekeeper vs. carpenter) I like the building. It's wonderful. I like to keep movin' all the time. It makes you healthy, makes you lively. If you just sit all the time it makes you old. I'm 60 and I can run ten miles. Keep movin', keep lively.

(Haying) It's my favourite work. It's hard work, but it's a good job—it makes you strong.

(Desk work) I don't mind. It's a source of income. But I don't like being cooped up. I'd be sittin' there day after day, especially in the summertime. But if I had no choice, I'd do it. But being a mechanic, I'd be movin' around on the job.

PRIDE IN PHYSICAL APPEARANCE (AND HEALTH): The physical body should be kept intact and unmarred. Appearance as well as function is important. (Each of the sentences below is an individual response from a separate protocol.)

(Boxing) A guy could get killed and all marked up. It destroys your physical features. Your face can get scarred up doing this. Your nose can get all smashed up.

(Bronc riding) You can lose your body doing this. All you get out of it is broken bones. Some people get crippled for life. Nothing in it, just risk getting hurt. You can get crippled for life this way.

KEEPING TRADITIONS AND IDENTITY: Being an Indian makes one different. An Indian is always an Indian. There is value in keeping this identity, and there is something to the old beliefs, even though they are dying out.

(Investiture) That man ——— who did that last year for the white man (Canadian dignitaries at Sun Dance) is dead. It's dangerous.

(Medicine man) Yeah, that . . . one time I go, when I hurt my back. He sing, drum over me. Yeah, it helped, yup.

(Medicine man) Ahhh . . . they're not . . . just a few of them now. There is five or six of them now. Oh yes, they have some power . . . oh yes! (Tells about specific medicine men on reserve and what they do.)

But according to the younger generation you just go to a doctor and get all butchered up when something goes wrong. (Tells story about prairie bird's wing to remove "cancerous" growth from temple of patient.)

(Chicken dancer) I'd want at least one of my sons to do it. I don't want to lose the Indian language altogether, and this helps. Not that I'd want him to go back to Indian ways. But we're Indians. At least one of us should dance, and we should keep our language.

(Chicken dancer) I think quite a bit about this. My race . . . I think we should keep this up. Our kids go to MacLeod and we wanted to make a float (for the centennial) to show the people that we still want to keep our Indian ways. An Indian will always be an Indian. No matter if I go off to Europe, I'll be an Indian. In some ways I'll be different, even if I'm well educated.

(Medicine man) In the field of medicine I think the white man's medicine has proven to be a better thing. But there is something to the Indian medicine. My father had a nose bleed and couldn't stop it. He went to ——— (an Indian doctor). She said we'd have to take him out of the hospital and we did, and she stopped the bleeding. To this day my Dad hasn't had a nosebleed.

LOW TENDENCY TOWARD STEREOTYPIC THINKING: Each situation has to be judged on its own merits. Avoid sweeping generalizations.

(Politician) If what he is saying is OK, and not against the Indian, then it's OK. Some white men say pretty good . . . other times they put Indian in a bad place, or do something to him—then I'm against him.

(Medicine man) The doctors (M.D.s) are good at operating. But for some sicknesses the Indian doctors are good, and can cure them. Different sicknesses, different herbs and doctors to cure them.

(Politician) It's all right. . . . Some peoples don't know nothing. But telling peoples what to do . . . that could be bad or good. It depends on what they tell them.

IMMEDIACY AND PRACTICALITY: It is good to have skills because they can be used on the spot, to keep things running well, not for distant goal-oriented achievements. Direct, immediate, practical applications are valued. This orientation is connected with the value placed upon autonomy. Skills make it possible to be autonomous, and to survive and maintain one's self independently. But the concept of autonomy and independence is not related (as it would be more often with white men) to achievement of a secure place in the socio-economic structure through an occupation.

(Mechanic) A farmer has got to know how to overhaul a tractor.

(Cook) That's pretty good. If it's like me, my wife is going to the hospital. I'll be all alone. It's good to learn that. You'll be cooking everything you want to eat. Or else you've got to get someone to cook, and pay them.

(Farming: picture of tractor plowing) I sure would like to have my own tractor and work with it. (?) A lot of things. I could cut hay, plow, pull hay racks and trailers, attach a post hole driller. . . .

(Milking) I might use cows for my own use. I'd like to have the milk and butter for my own use.

(Mechanic) I'd rather be a mechanic than this farmer. There's not much good money in crops. A mechanic gets $2 or $3 an hour, and it's handy to have. You don't have to take your car to a garage, you can fix it yourself.

(Milking) Very handy—milking cows. Make butter, milk. We usually had two cows back home. It's nice to have your own milk.

ELITE PRACTICALITY (responses from elite socioeconomic group): What one likes best to do is not always the practical thing to do. One should think of the possibilities in a long-range perspective, and be practical about what is best.

(The difference between the responses above, from the socioeconomic elite, and the practical orientation of the majority of the sample is that the former put the practical considerations in a long-range perspective. But they are still practical.)

(Bronc rider) This is a rough trade. I did it for ten years. I quit before I got busted up. I guess it's all right if you're single all your life. (?) I wouldn't encourage him (son). Some of these cowboys aren't worth anything for any kind of work. They're lazy. And after the season is over they can't do anything for any kind of work. They aren't good for anything. (?) The money and the excitement. But if you go to Calgary it costs $100 for entry fees and $100 to live there a week. In the same time you could put up 100 tons of hay.

(Haying) I love it! The smell of the hay, working out on the prairie, everything. (But why didn't you choose it as a favorite?) Because it's too seasonal. I wouldn't choose it as a way of earning a living.

(Desk work) Chooses this activity as a "favorite" but talked about branding and ranch work more. I asked, "If you could make the same money at both, which would you choose?" Response: I'd rather do this ranch work. I was good at it. I started off rassling calves, at the bottom. This guy (in picture) is a professional. I get good at it, do this. The other (desk work) has more income. This work (branding), you gotta be strong, healthy, good at it. But you always got in the back of your mind—you might get hurt—then you're out of it. This kind (desk work) you always got a good income.

LITERALITY: What is, is, what will be no man knows. Choices are limited by reality. Conditional and conjectural thinking are severely limited.

> (Tractor) When you get tired on a tractor you can fall asleep. When you fall off you get killed.
>
> (Branding) Subject does not choose this picture as a favorite but shows evidence elsewhere in the protocol of liking ranch work and being familiar with it. So I asked him why he didn't choose it. Response: In the olden days I did branding like that (calves). But now I keep horses and have no cattle. I brand only horses. (He didn't have cattle so could not choose the picture of a man branding calves.)
>
> (Haying) I'm one of the hay workers on the prairie. I have the rake, the mower, the team, and the rack. I can make money. (I asked him to choose between haying and ranching.) Response: I have all that I need for haying. I do that. (He could not choose what he could not do. He could not think conditionally.)
>
> (Chicken dancer) When I was fifteen I used to dance. I liked it very much. (But why didn't you choose it as a favorite?) I am old now (50) and I can't dance. (How about your sons?) What they want to do . . . if they want to dance . . . I have no opinion about what they want. (He could not choose what he could not do. He could not venture an opinion about what anyone else would like to do, for he didn't know. He could not think conditionally, or conjecture.)

COMMENT: At first we asked middle-aged men to select what they would like to do if they were twenty years old and starting out again. We gave this up after a few trials because men would choose only pictures of activities they could actually perform when they were twenty, even though later on they had acquired skills that made it possible to do other things. They could not retrospect conditionally any more than they can project into the present and future conditionally. Things are as they are, or were as they were. This is a marked characteristic in many responses. Most Blood simply do not engage in conditional thinking. Despite our previous periods of field work and our Rorschach sample we had not understood this before. This orientation has significant meaning for any economic development plan.

These cognitive orientations constitute a world view: autonomy, activity, keeping identity, nonstereotypic thinking, immediacy and practicality, and literality. It is a world view that is decidedly divergent from that which is an integral part of Western culture. The latter world view overlaps with that of the Blood in certain areas. There is, for instance, value placed upon keeping healthy and active, and being independent in both frames of reference, but the quality of this pattern is quite different in Western culture. The essential differences between the Blood Indian view and the white man view are the long-range achievement orientation, the orientation toward the future, and the strong tendency to project goal-orientations through conditional and conjectural thinking characteristic of the latter. The Blood live in and think about the world as it seems to them to be. Western man lives in the world to a larger extent as he would like it to be, and thinks it should be.

Concluding Remarks

We are not ready for a detailed discussion of what the IAI technique has taught us about the Blood in comparison to the information and understanding afforded through our Rorschach sample. We have not yet finished the exhaustive collating and analysis of Rorschach data from our 118 cases that will be necessary. A few remarks can be made at this time, however.

The two techniques intergrade. The Rorschach responses of the Blood are characteristically nonabstract. The Blood perceive real objects, people, or animals in the ink blots, usually in an action context, the meaning ascribed to them is concrete and specific, and they usually encompass relatively small, sharp details in the ink blots. This pattern is in sharp contradistinction to that most common among the Menomini. The latter, particularly the less acculturated, are inclined to either project rather generalized percepts or use the ink blots as a point of departure for philosophical ruminations, their perceptions of people as well as things are usually in a passive context, and they favor combinatory whole responses that do not fixate on small details. The features of Blood responses described are congruent with what the IAI has revealed about their thinking, particularly with respect to the orientations concerning activity, low tendency toward stereotypic thinking, immediacy and practicality, and literality. The Blood also make extensive use of the brightly colored parts of the ink blots. The majority of the Blood protocols contain dramatic uses of color as a significant determinant in the formation of percepts. This implies, if we accept in general the ascribed psychological meaning of color usage, that the Blood are emotionally open, and capable of aggressive emotional behavior. This is very true of the Blood in everyday behavior. We were jolted by the difference between the Blood and the Menomini when we first started to work in Canada. The Blood "talk nicely" but they are frank, accessible, and aggressive in interpersonal relations when one once gets beyond the façade that is usually put up for white strangers. The native-oriented Menomini are comparatively very passive, extremely reluctant to expose themselves emotionally, and never aggressive excepting under the influence of alcohol. The relationship of this feature of Blood Rorschach responses (and of behavior) to the IAI responses is less direct, but still seems to us to be congruent, particularly with the activity orientation, and the hierarchy of specific values concerning vigorous, nonpassive instrumental roles. Other aspects of Blood Rorschach responses, while not necessarily discongruent with IAI responses, appear to tap different orders of psychological structuring. The Blood, for example, appear to display a larger concentration of percepts in the human movement area, rather than in the animal movement area modally characteristic of the Menomini. At the lowest level of inference this suggests that the Blood are interested in people and their activities (even though they won't talk about their fellows to outsiders). They are anthropomorphic rather than zoomorphic in their world view. If so, this correlates with the intense Blood interest in visiting and in group participation. Both the Menomini and the Blood value autonomy, but the Blood do not surrender their autonomy or individuality to the group. They just seem to take pleasure in being with people, and the bigger the crowd, the better. The Menomini are much more inclined to solitude, and even when together (in the native-oriented group) one has the feeling that each individual is solitary. The tone of Blood life is tumultous, brawling, and exciting compared to the quiet, self-contained character of Menomini life.

The Rorschach may give us an understanding of the psychological resources utilized and channeled in the instrumental choices made in response to the IAI. The Rorschach, we believe, moves us further back into the psyche of the Blood than does the IAI—into the psychic control areas, the management of anxiety and of emotions as well as the intellectual organization, and into the respondent's fantasy life. The IAI moves us directly into the area of the respondent's cognitive management of perceived social realities.

Now that we have the IAI data we do not see how we could have done without them. But we would be reluctant to forego the understandings that the Rorschach data seem capable of giving us. If we had to choose one or the other technique at the present time we would choose the IAI because it told us so much that we did not know, systematized much that we did know, and moved us into an area of dynamic relationships that seems to us to be of great significance in the study of culture change.

But together the two techniques should give us an expanded and sensible interpretation of the psychological concomitants of manifest cultural change. And this is our purpose.

References

Barnouw, V.
1963: *Culture and Personality* (Homewood, Illinois: Dorsey Press).

Cohen, Y.
1961: *Social Structure and Personality: A Casebook* (New York: Holt, Rinehart, & Winston).

Collier, J., Jr.
1957: "Photography in Anthropology: A Report on Two Experiments," *American Anthropologist*, **59**, 843–859.

French, D.
1963: "The Relationship of Anthropology to Studies in Perception and Cognition," in S. Koch (ed.), *Psychology: A Study of a Science*, Vol. 6, *Man in Socius* (New York: McGraw-Hill).

Fried, J.
1954: "Picture Testing: An Aid to Ethnological Field Work," *American Anthropologist*, **56,** 95–97.

Goldschmidt, W.
1959: *Man's Way. A Preface to Understanding Human Society* (New York: Holt).

Goldschmidt, W., & Edgerton, R.
1961: "A Picture Technique for the Study of Values," *American Anthropologist*, **63,** 26–45.

Hallowell, A. I.
1945: "Sociopsychological Aspects of Acculturation," in R. Linton (ed.), *Science of Man in the World Crisis* (New York: Columbia University Press), pp. 171–200.
1951: "The Use of Projective Techniques in the Study of the Sociopsychological Aspects of Acculturation," *Journal of Projective Techniques*, **15,** 27–44.

Henry, W. E.
1947: "The Thematic Apperception Technique in the Study of Culture-Personality Relations," *Genetic Psychology Monographs*, **35,** 3–135.

Inkeles, A.
1958: "Personality and Social Structure," in R. Merton & L. Brown (eds.), *Sociology Today* (New York: Basic Books).

Kaplan, B.
1957: "Personality and Social Structure," in J. B. Gittler (ed.), *Review of Sociology: Analysis of a Decade* (New York: Wiley).
1961: "Cross-Cultural Use of Projective Techniques," in F. Hsu (ed.), *Psychological Anthropology* (Homewood, Illinois: Dorsey Press).

Lindzey, G.
1961: *Projective Techniques and Cross-Cultural Research* (New York: Appleton-Century-Crofts).

Parker, S.
1964: "Ethnic Identity and Acculturation in Two Eskimo Villages," *American Anthropologist*, **66,** 325–340.

Spindler, G. D.
1955: *Sociocultural and Psychological Processes in Menomini Acculturation.* University of California Publications in Culture and Society, Vol. 5 (Berkeley & Los Angeles: University of California Press).

Spindler, G. D., & Spindler, L. S.
1963a: *The Blood Indians of Alberta: A Report to the Economic Development Division, Indian Affairs Branch* (Ottawa, Canada).
1963b: "Psychology and Anthropology: Applications to Culture Change," in S. Koch (ed.), *Psychology: A Study of a Science*, Vol. 6. *Man in Socius* (New York: McGraw-Hill).

Spindler, L. S.

1962: "Menomini Women and Culture Change: Memoir 91," *American Anthropological Association*, **64,** No. 1, Part 2.

Spindler, L. S., & Spindler, G. D.

1958: "Male and Female Adaptations in Culture Change," *American Anthropologist*, **60,** 217–233.

Spiro, M. E.

1961: "An Overview and Suggested Reorientation," in F. Hsu (ed.), *Psychological Anthropology* (Homewood, Illinois: Dorsey Press).

Wallace, A. F. C.

1961: *Culture and Personality* (New York: Random House).

Weinstock, S. A.

1963: "Role Elements: A Link between Acculturation and Occupational Status," *British Journal of Sociology*, **15,** 144–149.

HERBERT H. WILLIAMS AND JUDITH R. WILLIAMS

The Definition of the Rorschach Test Situation: A Cross-Cultural Illustration

During the past few years, the cross-cultural use of projective techniques has been subjected to several critical evaluations (see for instance: J. Henry: 1955; W. Henry: 1961; Kaplan: 1961; Lindzey: 1961). These run the short gamut from harsh disapproval to a somewhat conditional, guarded acceptance.

The Rorschach data presented here were collected almost fifteen years ago and analyzed soon thereafter, during a period when the climate for the cross-cultural use of projective techniques was considerably more benign. They were one aspect of an extensive personality-culture study in a Lebanese Maronite village and were intended to help delineate "basic personality structure" in Abram Kardiner's then already long-established seminar in culture and personality.[1] In addition to the Rorschachs interpreted here, we collected some

1. The Middle East Research Project (1949–51) was sponsored by the Department of Anthropology at Columbia University and was carried out under the direction of Dr. Abram Kardiner and Dr. Joseph Greenberg, and with the financial support of the Kardiner Foundation. In the field it involved, in addition to the two of us, Kepler Lewis, at that time a doctoral student in the Department of Anthropology at Columbia University.

fifty records from children, human figure drawings from both children and adults, finger paintings from a selected group of children, and eight extensive biographies of adult men and women, coming daily for hour-long sessions for anywhere from twenty to thirty days. Our psychological material was embedded in a full village ethnography, the task of the third member of our team.

The Rorschach analysis for Kardiner's seminar was done "blind," by workers who had no knowledge of the culture and no exposure to the other psychological materials. The analysis presented here was earlier and independently completed by us, with full knowledge of the culture and detailed psychological information from all our other sources, of which the biographies were by far the richest.[2] It was presented in A. I. Hallowell's seminar at the University of Pennsylvania for discussion, critical evaluation, and comparison with other cross-cultural Rorschach studies. This is one reason why its updating and inclusion in the present volume seem appropriate. Another reason for airing it now—so many years later and in the chill air of current disapproval—is that our conviction of the usefulness of the Rorschach in cross-cultural studies of personality remains unaltered by recent harsh critiques.

Kaplan raises the problem of the different ways in which the test works from group to group and sees as a chief obstacle to Rorschach interpretation the impossibility of separating "cultural conventions" from "genuine differences in personality processes" (1961, p. 246). We would like to suggest that the impossibility of making this separation is neither cause for despair nor a prerequisite for Rorschach interpretation. Anthropologists have not been able to sift out "culture" from "personality" at the conceptual level with any degree of finality or precision and no empirical device need be dismissed, therefore, for failing to do so. Yet the concern with what is culture-bound—not always as explicitly stated as by Kaplan—has been a plaguing and persistent one and has had a confining effect on the interpretation of cross-cultural Rorschach material. Anthropologists or psychologists have often limited themselves to analyses and comparisons of the strictly quantifiable features of their protocols on the assumption that these are the relatively "culture-free" and, therefore, solely valid and admissible aspects of the Rorschach performance. The many timid and scorebound interpretations have led Lindzey to conclude that ". . . if we removed from this literature all interpretive statements dependent upon Klopfer's specific generalizations, we would probably eliminate three quarters of the results we have examined" (1961, p. 300).

2. The "blind" analysis prepared for Kardiner's seminar never got beyond its original oral form, and detailed comparison with our own is therefore unfeasible. It is a great pity that the "eyes open" and "blind" analyses were not compared in infinite detail. At this point, all that can and need be said is that there was a close correspondence between the two and that each, in turn, closely corresponded to the personality delineations drawn on the basis of the biographies.

We would like to use our own material to illustrate the usefulness of extending the interpretation beyond the easily quantified and so-called "objective" features of the Rorschach, to the qualitative aspects of the records and especially the subjective definition of the testing situation. The way the subject defines and experiences the Rorschach situation has been shown to be a valuable source of insight in clinical practice (for full discussions of the definition of the testing situation and its interpersonal dynamics see Schachtel: 1945; Schafer: 1954). Even in clinical practice, however, it is often viewed only as a source of error and disturbance. In the cross-cultural usage of the Rorschach it has rarely been given detailed consideration. The information gained from a scrutiny of the subject's reactions to the particular interpersonal situation created by the Rorschach administration is both "personality" and "culture" information. Schachtel writes: "The quality of the demand which a person feels to be made on him when he is confronted with [the] task may be considered as consisting of a culturally determined general idea of what he is asked to do, and of the personally determined concretization of this idea. His attitude to the demand corresponds to both these factors, to the broad meaning of 'test-task' as determined by cultural patterns and to the personal meaning, that is, to his own way of experiencing situations in which such a task is given to him. In concrete experience, of course, such a distinction between cultural and personal factors determining the quality of an experience would be artificial; the two are completely merged" (1945, p. 423). When the aim of the study—as was true in our case—is the description of the functioning personality, then this merging need not be any less or more problematic for the cultural anthropologist than for the clinical psychologist. When, however, the sifting out of "personality" and "culture" factors is crucial for research purposes, then the Rorschach is probably an inappropriate instrument to begin with.

The Setting

Lebanon, the smallest of the Near Eastern countries, has an area of but 10,000 square kilometers. Distances are short: about 190 kilometers from north to south, and a maximum of some 80 kilometers from east to west. It is bordered on the south by Israel, on the east and north by Syria, and on the west by the Mediterranean Sea. Its mountains are the most important physical aspect of Lebanon: the Lebanon range along the coast, covering roughly two thirds of the total area; and the anti-Lebanon, down the spine of which runs the eastern border with Syria. Between the two ranges lies the Bekaa valley.

The extreme ruggedness of the Lebanese terrain has been an important factor in the country's historical development. The Lebanon has since ancient times served as a refuge area where persons and peoples could easily defend themselves, with the defiles, cliffs, and heights as allies. The rough nature of the country has probably played a part in the diversity of culture, religion, dialect, and, until recently, of language to be found there.

Lebanon is a country of minorities. It is made up of religious, national, and ethnic minorities with no single group in the majority. Every village, according to folk belief, has its distinctive dialect within clear-cut regional dialects.

Among the thirteen major religious communities of Lebanon, the approximately 400,000 Maronites number more than twice all the other Christian groups combined. They are Catholic Christians who originally formed a branch of the ancient Church of Syria, which in the fifth century was on a par with the Roman and Byzantine Churches. In the thirteenth century, as part of the aftermath of the crusades, the Maronites accepted affiliation with Rome. They remain, however, partly autonomous and retain a distinctive liturgy in the Syriac or Aramaic language and have still a largely noncelibate clergy.

The village which served as the locale of our study, is a quite typical, small (in 1950 about 600 people), and relatively remote community high in the northern mountains. The precipice on which it is situated is ever-present in the minds of the villagers as an important part of their folk belief and as a very real danger: within the last fifty years ten people have "fallen out of the village."

The economy of the village was in 1950 barely above the subsistence level. Agriculture, more diversified than one might suppose, is the mainstay of that economy and everyone in the village is to some degree involved in farming. The chief crops are olives, grapes, wheat, and apples, with the last as the important cash crop. Crafts and home industries are but little practiced. Masonry is the one village speciality. Those who work at it find the largest part of their opportunities outside the village and often in places quite far afield.

The social and political structure of the village is based on nuclear families grouped into largely nonresidential extended families. These extended families, although they practice neolocality, and are not endogamous, are nonetheless important social realities. The village itself is almost perfectly endogamous and there is some tendency to marry within one's lineage, the only unit larger than the extended family which is at all important. Extended families serve important socioeconomic functions even when members are settled as far away as Australia and the United States. Remittances to families from relatives abroad form an important part of village income and help to provide for a continuing stream of emigration.

In its educational facilities, the village was again quite typical of the region. The boys' school is a government school with a government-appointed teacher paid by the Ministry of Education. The girls' school is financed by the church and was in 1950 conducted by three nuns from a teaching order. The curriculum in both schools is spread over three forms requiring three years.

Religion in the village is a very pervasive institution. It is constantly on the lips of the villagers, and a wide range of religious observances are a very prominent part of their daily lives. In conversation there are constant references to God and religion. In addition, the villagers practice their Catholicism in regular institutionalized patterns. For the men, in particular, religion is more a matter of ethnocentric reinforcement than of personal religious feeling. The Maronite faith is an important symbol of unity and identity.

Subjects and Administration

The subjects on whose records this analysis is based are fifty-eight adults, equally divided as to sex and ranging in age from 16 to 63 years for the men, and 15 to 90 years for the women. All sections of the village, all economic and social subgroups are represented, and the sample is certainly reasonably representative of the community.

By the time the Rorschach administration was begun, we had been in the village continuously for almost three months. The people were all well-known to us and accustomed to being asked for information. We simply requested villagers to come to our house for a while and look at some pictures. Only when they did appear for the test, were the purpose and procedure explained. We had only one outright refusal, from a middle-aged woman known in the village as "crazy Mary." She initially consented, but as she was coming toward the house a group of onlookers started to poke fun at her. She ran off and could not be induced to return. A second woman was classified as a refusal: Although she came to be tested, she stared helplessly at the cards and gave a total of three responses.

The method of administration differed somewhat from standard procedures. The most marked difference was the presence of the interpreter, who translated instructions word for word into Arabic and in turn recorded all responses verbatim. We recorded timing, all behavioral responses, as well as most of the response proper in English. By the time we started on the Rorschachs, our Arabic was adequate for understanding almost everything the subjects said, especially since the records were sparse. The performance proper was thus completed. In the inquiry, the interpreter read out the response in English (if necessary), translated our inquiry questions to the subject, and again recorded the reply verbatim. As soon after the subject left as possible—preferably and most often immediately—the entire record was transcribed into English. The disadvantages of working with an interpreter have been reviewed elsewhere (J. Henry: 1941). We did not experience his presence wholly as a disadvantage. We could, for instance, take all the time needed to record behavior, both motor and verbal. Our subjects also often made side remarks to the interpreter which were revealing and which they might not have made to us.

The only other deviation from standard procedure was the somewhat more elaborate introduction to the test than in a clinical-testing situation. In the first few records a testing of the limits was included. In all cases where this was done, it was apparent that it was an extremely threatening procedure. No matter how tactfully, circumspectly, or playfully the limits were probed, the villagers invariably interpreted all questions as a challenge to the "correctness" and "accuracy" of their own original responses and this phase of the test was therefore quickly abandoned.

The Results

In the presentation of results, the purely quantitative features are summarized very briefly. The qualitative aspects of the Rorschach performance and the subjects' reactions to the testing situation are then reviewed in greater detail.

The Quantitative Data—The mean number of responses is 13.5 for the men and 11.3 for the women, with a group mean of 12.4. In comparing these results with the mean productivity of selected groups presented by Hallowell, these subjects are almost at the bottom of the scale (Hallowell: 1956). In only four of the non-American societies reviewed, do adult subjects produce an average of less than 15 responses and only one shows a lower response number than these subjects. The number of additional responses—that is, responses given during the inquiry—is high, particularly so for the men, who give a total of 99 additionals. Twenty-three of the twenty-nine men give one or more additionals. The corresponding figures for the women are considerably lower: 26 additional responses are given by eleven of the twenty-nine female subjects. Fifteen, or more than half of the women, reject one or more cards while only six of the twenty-nine men do.

As for manner of approach, the application of the Klopfer norms shows an overemphasis of W and an underemphasis of D (Klopfer and Kelley: 1942). Twenty-one men and nineteen women have a W% of 31 or more, or within the overemphasized range. Only thirteen of the fifty-eight subjects make any use of the rare location categories. The typical record, then, is the *W*-(D) record.

The most striking features of content are the vague, general quality of most responses, the narrowness of content range, the high percentage of animal responses, and the dearth of human responses. The A% is 53.8 for the men and 61.9 for the women. Again compared to the groups selected by Hallowell, the total mean A% of 57.8 is among the highest. As for human content, the men give a total of 59 and the women a total of 30 H and Hd responses, with percentage values of 15 and 9.9, respectively. Comparing once more to the groups cited by Hallowell, the H% of 12.4 is among the very lowest.

In the group psychograms that were constructed, the towering F column and the general barrenness of the profiles were the outstanding features. The barrenness was even more marked for the women than the men. Next to the F, the FM is the highest column for both groups. Human movement responses are rare: the men give a total of 37; only eight of the twenty-nine women give any M at all; the total for the group is fourteen. The use of all shading is sporadic, with shading as achromatic color relatively most frequent. The means of the color responses would distort the picture even more than the means of other categories. Among the males, at least, there are those who use color and those who do not. Sixteen men, or somewhat more than half of the male group, do use color, and eleven of these have more than one color response. Among the women, the use of color is both less extensive and less intensive: their total thirteen color reactions are given by ten subjects, with no woman giving more than two color responses of any kind. Among the men, CF's are more than twice as frequent than FC's. In sum then, what emerges on the basis of even this very abbreviated presentation of the quantitative results, is an extremely unproductive and barren picture: the response number is low; there is an overemphasis on simple whole responses; the content range is narrow, with an exaggerated A% and a marked paucity of human responses; the psychograms are coartated and constricted. The over-all picture is considerably more impoverished and meager than that found in most other cross-cultural studies.

The Qualitative Features—The kinesthetic responses, their content, character, and quality, are a rich source of information concerning the subject's attitudes toward himself and others. To recapitulate briefly: a total of 51 M responses were given by the 58 subjects. Twenty-six responses are scored additional M: these were either given in the inquiry or are additional by virtue of being F→M. These twenty-six responses are included in the analysis presented in Table I.

The various characteristics and terminology need some explanation. The extensor-flexor dichotomy is Rorschach's own (Rorschach: 1942). It was found that the majority of the M responses fell into a third group, here termed neutral. M's were classified as independent if the people were in actual self-directed motion; as propelled, if they were seen in activities such as riding a boat, a car, or an airplane. The three categories concerned with relatedness are more or less self-explanatory and deal with the kind of relationship involved in the M. The affectivity category deals with the amount of affect the people seen are endowed with, or the amount they express in their activity.

The striking thing about these movement responses is their essential neutrality. Many of them would—if Rorschach's criteria were rigidly applied—not deserve an M score at all. The amount of movement is frequently minimal, the figures are rarely endowed with affect, rarely seen in relation to each other:

Table I.—The Human Movement Responses

	Men	*Women*	*Total*
Extensor	9	4	13
Flexor	3	0	3
Neutral	46	15	61
Independent	44	16	60
Propelled	14	3	17
Positively related	7	6	13
Negatively related	0	0	0
Single or unrelated	51	13	64
Pronounced motor activity	32	13	45
Minimal motor activity	24	5	29
Uncontrolled	2	1	3
Strongly affective	2	8	10
Mildly affective	14	5	19
Non affective	42	6	48

"Here are two girls standing on top of a tree"; "it looks like a man on horseback"; "it looks like human beings, they are standing still"; "and here it looks like a person, he is sitting down." Although the women give M's even less frequently than the men, a larger proportion of the female human movement responses are in independent, vigorous motion, are more often engaging in some form of positive interaction, and more frequently are classified as "strongly affective." It must be kept in mind, however, that only nine of the twenty-nine women gave any M's at all. All that can be said, therefore, is that capacity for M production is even more limited among the women than among the men, but that whenever it does come to the fore, it seems to have a more genuine kinesthetic quality.

It might be worth mentioning here that the difficulties presented by the M analysis were, in themselves, of significance. Various categories, qualities, and schemes came to mind, according to which the M responses could be broken down. Yet when face to face with the movement responses, their most striking quality was their amorphousness and nonclassifiability, as well as their numerical paucity. A number of interesting factors do emerge, however, even on the basis of the minimal analysis that was possible. Seventeen, or almost one fourth of the total M's are what is inadequately termed "propelled." All the people in these responses are somehow not responsible or in control of their activity. They are not moving on their own, but are being moved or carried. Often they are small or insignificant figures, obscured by whatever is doing the moving. To these seventeen belong the three responses where the M is classified as "uncontrolled"—falling, dangling, being lifted. In all of them the key quality is the lack of active control and mastery on the part of the people of their activity or motion. Another area worth dwelling on is that of relationship:

positive affect or relatedness are rarely expressed in the human movement responses, and the thirteen M's that are classified as positively related are, on the whole, of a toned-down quality. Not a single response expressed negative affect. The most common human movement response is of people alone, or, if seen together, side-by-side but not with each other, in the sense of related to each other.

Certain other qualities which are either not obvious or not included in the table should be mentioned. Eleven of the total number of M responses are what might be described as obscured people, either seen in tiny details or seen as insignificant parts of a larger object: people seen far off in the distance; people that are specks on a high rock; people in a tree. They are minutiae on the blot or minutiae in relation to their context.

Fourteen of the total Ms are not actual people but spirits, devils, etc. In addition, nine M responses are marginal in another way: they are brought forth doubtfully and hesitantly. There is considerable uncertainty in the phrasing of the response and much questioning in the subjects' mind as to whether "this is a person." In some of these cases, the response starts out by being an animal and is then changed to a human: "It looks like a frog but not quite. It's more like a seafish or a human being. It looks like a person . . . the hands are lifted up." "This part is like a sea animal. It doesn't look like a human being or bird. The forehead and the neck look like a person, but he has a beak. It's like the shape of a person coming out of the sea."

The villagers' capacity or, rather, lack of capacity for M production is further illuminated by the Levy Movement Blot experiment. The blots, which we administered to only seven biography subjects, are an experimental procedure designed to elicit human movement responses. Although the subjects were specifically instructed to see people in motion, they did so only rarely. Only one of the seven saw moving people spontaneously on the first card. Out of a total of seventy possible responses, twenty-six were human or human-like creatures, and of these, eighteen were seen in motion. Not all of these were spontaneous but were elicited only after some probing or prodding. On this test, where M production is deliberately facilitated both by the instructions and by the nature of the stimulus material, the villagers were essentially unable to do what was asked of them.

Next to the pure F responses, the FM or animal movement is the most common, the mean number for both men and women being 3.3. Only one woman gives no FM at all. The totals are 95 for the men, 96 for the women. The men give 26 additional FMs, the women 25. The additionals are again included in the analysis in Table II.

The same criteria as for M were applied to the first two categories. The last deals with what might be called the purposefulness of the activity in which the animal seen is involved, as, for instance, "a bird flying" and "bears climbing a

Table II.—The Animal Movement Responses

	Men	*Women*	*Total*
Pronounced motor activity	86	81	167
Minimal motor activity	35	41	76
Positively related	7	12	19
Negatively related	7	8	15
Single or unrelated	107	102	209
Activity directed	59	66	125
Activity undirected	62	56	118

tree for food." The first of the examples would be classified as undirected, the second as directed activity.

As with the human movement, a large proportion of the FM are marginal in terms of the amount of movement. Approximately a third show a minimal amount of activity. Again as with the M, the overwhelming majority of the FMs are single or unrelated animals. Only 34 of the total 243 FM responses are animals seen in some kind of relationship to each other, either positive or negative.

The same contentlessness and flatness that was so characteristic of the M responses is, to a large extent, again found here. Nonetheless, of the 243 FMs, 95 had some kind of content other than the animal's natural activity—"butterfly flying," "worm crawling," etc. The content analysis of these 95 responses is given in Table III.

Table III.—Analysis of FM with Content

	Men	*Women*	*Total*
Running away	2	4	6
Threatened	1	7	8
Caught	1	1	2
Burdened	0	2	2
Clinging	2	2	4
Helpless	0	1	1
Threatening	1	6	7
Fighting	4	4	8
Catching each other	2	0	2
Playful	0	6	6
Eating	12	7	19
Open mouths	8	8	16
Going after, looking for food	4	10	14
Total	37	58	95

The totals in Table III show that the women are more prone to give FMs with content than the men. Approximately half of the female FMs do have some content, while the same can be said for only about a third of the male

FMs. As for the kind of content, the largest single area deals with oral activity: 49, or slightly half of the FMs with content and approximately one fifth of the total number of FMs given are animals eating or going after food, or animals with open mouths. If the first six categories of the table are combined, then the next largest area is an expression of some form of inadequacy. Although the manifest content varies—the animals are seen as running away, threatened, caught, burdened, clinging, or helpless—the essential quality of the movement is the animal's inability to cope in one way or another. Only 15 of the total FMs are seen in forthright aggressive activity; and only 8 are engaged in what might be called playful activity.

Any qualitative analysis or breakdown of the total 48 color responses would be not only meaningless but also misleading. Less than half of the subjects make any use of color, with the men being somewhat less reluctant to give color responses than the women as well as more prone to giving uncontrolled color reactions. If additionals are included in the tally, then the men give 10 FCs, 21 CFs, and 3 Cs; the women give 7 FCs, 6 CFs, and no pure C. Twenty-four of the total 48 color responses are plants or flowers. The second largest content category for the men—8 responses altogether—are food responses.

If little could be said about the color responses, there is even less to say about the use of shading. It seems worth pointing out, however, that the "black" responses, which were relatively the most frequent kind of shading used, were among the most affect-laden. There are, in connection with several of them, open expressions of fright or disgust. "It looks like a mud-puppy. It jumps into your hands when you get herbs . . . It's awful. It's black here and it isn't nice to look at. . . . It looks like it's going to bite." "What could this be? You know this looks like the black snail that walks in the night. It's black and it's walking on the road. Its shape is disgusting. I see it with two pointed horns. . . . I am not frightened by these pictures." The blackness of the card seems to have implications of something fearful, ominous, or unpleasant. The heavily shaded and black cards are also the most frequently rejected ones.

There is an almost complete absence of the use of shading to denote softness, furriness, or fuzziness. The total number of Fc or c, both main and additional, is 13 and in all but two of them the textural quality is described as "carved," "engraved," "rough like wood," "wrinkled."

The vagueness, indefiniteness, poor form level, and content impoverishment of the form responses have been referred to earlier. Beyond this, there remains little to be said. Of all the form responses, only 144 had content other than animal, human, plant, or general landscape. The most frequent categories are: stones, rocks or rocky caves (35); religious objects or buildings (32); mechanical objects, tools, machines (32); and much less frequently clouds (9); buildings, ruins (8); ice or icicles (3). There is a barrenness, starkness, and harshness to these F responses, both in terms of what is seen as well as in the verbalization of the responses themselves. Qualifying, descriptive phrases are rare. They are unadorned in every respect. "It looks like rocks. It's like a big rock and stones around it. It's just shaped like a rock and stones." "And this is like a stovepipe. It's shaped like one." "It's like a mountain. Nothing else. This is the top of the mountain. And these look like piles of stone on a mountain. They are shaped like stones and it's shaped like a mountain."

Reactions to the Testing Situation—Tests of any kind are unknown to the villagers. They have no familiarity with them or with the concept of "test" in the Western frame of reference. Yet most of them did feel that they were being tested, that they were on trial, and were being asked to prove themselves. There was a startling uniformity in this appraisal of the situation.

The villagers are unaccustomed to aloneness or isolation. A man may work alone in his field and a woman may gather grass by herself in the valley, but aloneness other than this functional kind is most uncommon. People are constantly with each other, living in groups of one kind or another. Their aloneness in the Rorschach situation was, therefore, as foreign to them as the test itself. The closed door, the deliberate exclusion of others, the inevitable formality of the situation—paper, pencil, recording of all utterances—imposed an additional element of strangeness. The Rorschachs might well have looked different had they been administered in a group, during one of the natural and daily gatherings at our house. The typical barren record must be seen as at least partially a result of "standard" isolated conditions and the villagers' reactions to the objective elements of the testing situation.

Our subjects were not as inexperienced with looking at pictures as the unacculturated Arabs of Bleuler's study (Bleuler and Bleuler: 1935). They have no background in "interpreting pictures," however, and the specific instructions to make the blots "look like" something set up a new and unfamiliar task. Hallowell (1956) points out that the presence or absence of a pictorial graphic art is in no way a prerequisite to the successful use of the Rorschach blots. However, the manner in which the subject relates to the blots does, perhaps, bear some relationship to his previous experience with pictures. Most of the villagers related to the cards in a concrete, immediate way. They did not interpret the blots but recognized them. The blot "is" something—that is the expression most frequently used, despite instructions to tell what the blots "look like, could or might be." This concreteness accounts, perhaps, for the quite frequent fluster and confusion when a detail does not fit what the blot "is." This may also account, in part, for the low number of responses: once the blot is a specific thing, it cannot be something else as well.

For most, the Rorschach situation was essentially a pressure situation. There were only a very few who approached the task with unselfconscious interest and a degree of enjoyment. For the vast majority, it was a puzzling, confusing, immensely difficult assignment for which they felt themselves totally unequipped and unprepared. This overwhelming sense of their own inadequacy which the Rorschach seemed to evoke was the most striking aspect of their response to the situation and, perhaps, one of the key over-all findings. Gestures of helplessness, bewilderment, and confusion, as well as comments to that effect, were extremely frequent. More concrete evidence can be found in the performance proper. The low number of responses is essentially an expression of bewilderment and helplessness, of an inability to react freely and spontaneously when confronted with the unfamiliar, of a deep sense of unease. This leads to a confining and limiting definition of the situation. While the underlying experience seemed to be the same from one person to another, it did not always manifest itself fully or in the same way. The quick, vague, ill-defined single response per card, the hasty return of the card, the obvious eagerness to get finished were one very common expression of the above. Also frequent was the slow, immensely labored, and uncertain response, sometimes uttered with tremendous relief, at other times produced hesitantly and often combined with self-belittling remarks or a reluctance to surrender the card. At other times there was complete bewilderment, resulting either in outright rejections or the production of any response just to comply and get away. There was also, almost exclusively among the men, a kind of bravado which showed itself both in manner as well as in the pretentiousness of response and verbiage and which would often crumble even in our intentionally very gentle inquiry. These reactions, although by no means universal, were typical and obviously not conducive to the production of a great wealth of material.

So far, no differentiation has been made between the men's and women's definitions of the situation. For both groups, the Rorschach was essentially a pressure situation. But while the men, on the whole, showed some capacity to recover and cover up, the women came and remained defeated. The experience of their inadequacy and helplessness was more crippling and enduring. The women's greater tendency to reject cards, to give fewer additionals, as well as their generally more coartated picture substantiate this. Among the men, the inclination to give additionals seems to suggest a reduction of the tension on second contact with the cards. A few words of reassurance at the end of the performance proper, the completion of the first round, so to speak, and the fact that on second contact the cards were no longer totally unfamiliar—all these seemed to have a somewhat liberating effect on the male subjects. The women, on the other hand, showed very little of this capacity to recover. Their sense of defeat and their feelings of insufficiency are much more pervasive and difficult to dispel.

The number of responses points up more sharply than any of the other scoring categories the manner in which our subjects defined the situation. The modes of apperception and the poor quality of the F responses also bear out the above. It was mentioned earlier that the *W*(D) record was very typical. These Ws do not, for the most part, fit Rorschach's W+. They involve little organizational effort and are most often easy Ws. Their form level is usually poor and they are largely made up of vague, indefinite concepts: rocks, ill-defined landscapes. There is a minimal quality to these responses suggesting both lack of involvement in the task and a deep sense of insufficiency. There seemed to be an unwillingness rather than inability to produce which stemmed from a feeling of defeat rather than from genuine resistance.

The pitfalls of making psychopathological analogies in the cross-cultural application of the Rorschach have been pointed out elsewhere (Abel: 1948). Nonetheless, it seems tempting to do so here. The way our subjects defined the Rorschach situation and the effect this definition had on their test performance are strikingly similar to what Schachtel describes as characteristic for depressed subjects: "The depressive personality tends to feel that he is helpless, that he cannot do anything, that every step he takes is really a hopeless step, that the situation confronting him is quite beyond his ability and power. Every act, every attempt to do something, every gesture to cope with the overwhelming weight of the world around him, appears enormously difficult, laborious and also quite useless and futile to him. He cannot hope to do anything adequate" (1945, p. 439).

Interpretation and Conclusion

It now remains to sum up in non-Rorschach terms but on the basis of test findings some of the main features of personality structure. The summary is given not so much for its intrinsic interest but rather to illustrate how very much the personality delineation relies on the qualitative features of the record and the subjects' definition of the test situation.

Perhaps the most striking impression is of the subjects' sense of defeat, their sense of being overwhelmed by their world, a world which most experience as harsh, cold, unrelenting, and ungiving. In this world they feel powerless and dwarfed. There is an almost universal lack of harmony between the individual and his setting: the individual is in constant struggle with the world and he invariably emerges oppressed and defeated. His relationship to the environment is essentially that of victim. There is no sense of mastery or understanding. The subjects feel not only defeated by their world but also confused by it. They are concrete and immediate in their dealings with it—not, however, in the sense of active manipulators. They meet demands from one minute to the next, without basic direction or decisiveness. Since, in their struggle, they never expect to win and feel beaten before they start, their output is always minimal. There is little drive and effort. Typically, the Rorschach was experienced as yet another of the many impositions that they had come to expect—immensely difficult, arduous, and confusing.

Although the individual's overwhelming sense of his own insufficiency and impotence is implied in all of the above, it needs to be reemphasized and elaborated. The villagers think of themselves as inadequate and worthless. They are also frightened and timid, unprepared to cope with their known setting, fearful to the extreme of the unfamiliar and unknown. The difference between men and women in this respect has already been mentioned. It was pointed out that the experience of their own inadequacy and defeat was much more devastating for the women than the men. Perhaps this should be qualified by saying that the women are undisguised in their confession of worthlessness and expressions of defeat. With the men, the underlying experience is the same, or, if anything, even more acute. However, they are much more involved with maintaining or at least trying to create a façade of adequacy and power. There is considerable bravado and pretense at mastery. Theirs is a more strenuous and perhaps precarious adjustment since they feel acutely not only their inadequacy but also their need to deny and hide it.

As striking as the villagers' sense of defeat is the extreme isolation of the individual in relation to his setting and the people around him. In describing the Alorese, Oberholzer spoke of them as "living beside one another but not with one another" (DuBois: 1944, p. 600). Our subjects' interpersonal adjustment could not be summed up in any better way. They are people who live in extreme closeness yet almost complete emotional isolation. They are in constant interaction with each other but have almost no feeling for each other. They never are alone, but always feel alone. They are fearful and mistrustful of each other, gain neither strength nor satisfaction from their interpersonal contacts. They never feel they can rely or depend on each other. There is a lack of certainty and an undercurrent of suspicion in all their human relationships. Many of them are keen and shrewd in sizing up the feelings of others, but this is accomplished in a detached way. It never stems from any experience of empathy or capacity for identifying with the feelings and attitudes of their fellow men. There is hardly any gentleness or softness among people. Just as they expect only harshness from their setting, so do they expect it from each other. This isolation is, if anything, even more complete among the women. They are, if possible, even more leery than the men in all their relationships, even more reluctant to respond to emotion and to show it.

Yet despite their aloneness and isolation from each other, the villagers show little capacity for living within themselves. There is little of the contemplative, inwardly resourceful about them. Furthermore, they feel too fearful, too constantly threatened, too overcome by the weight of the world to use whatever inner resources they might have. There is a lack of purpose and direction, an inability to structure situations, a constant indecisiveness and doubtfulness.

There is among them an expecting and expectant attitude. They show a deep-seated wish and need to be taken care of, to be passive, to be sheltered, and a longing for the omnipotent figure or magical solution and forces that will relieve them of their burden. This expectant attitude is coupled with a simultaneous sense of being deprived and defeated by the harsh and ungiving environment. Perhaps it is this which accounts for the resentment, mistrust, and irritability which are often manifest.

Their fear, unease, and apprehension in the face of the unknown, the new, or the complex have been alluded to already, and extend to a fear of aloneness. Despite their inability to respond to each other, to achieve emotional rapport and closeness, there is, nonetheless, a need for the other person, or, rather, the presence of others. Although there is no warm human interacting among them, they derive a modicum of security from living within the multitude.

Aggressive outbursts, impulsiveness of action, egocentricity can be expected and are not inconsistent with what has been described so far. There is a lack of controls—either purely intellectual, or inward self-control, or the kind of self-restraint that comes from living in a genuinely related way with others. This lack of stabilizing forces in their make-up can lead to much unpredictability of behavior.

What appears, then, on the basis of the Rorschach analysis, is a barren and harsh and not very happy picture. The same barrenness and harshness that the villagers feel all about them in a way characterizes their own make-up. They emerge as hampered and frightened people, limited and unproductive; they feel burdened and deprived and inadequately equipped to cope with their burdens and deprivations.

It is perhaps of interest that the over-all personality picture gained from the Rorschachs is considerably more bleak and impoverished than that which emerged from the biographies. The Rorschach situation was more devastating and crippling in that it presented the subject with the unfamiliar and unknown and left him defenseless. The individual villager appears to the poorest advantage when he confronts the unfamiliar and when he does so alone.

A score-bound analysis by itself could have resulted in little more than a few shallow and barren generalizations. Combined with an assessment of the qualitative features of the protocols and of the subjects' reactions to the testing situation, the yield was considerably richer.

References

Bleuler, M., & Bleuler, R.
1935: "Rorschach's Ink-Blot Test and Racial Psychology: Mental Peculiarities of Moroccans," *Character and Personality*, **4,** 97–114.

DuBois, C.
1944: *The People of Alor* (Minneapolis: University of Minnesota Press).

Hallowell, A. I.

1956: "The Rorschach Technique in Personality and Culture Studies," in B. Klopfer (ed.), *Developments in the Rorschach Technique*, Vol. 2 (Yonkers, New York: World), pp. 485–544.

Henry, J.

1941: "Rorschach Technique in Primitive Culture," *American Journal of Orthopsychiatry*, **11**, 230-234.

1955: "Symposium: Projective Testing in Ethnography," *American Anthropologist*, **57**, 245–270.

Henry, W. E.

1961: "Projective Tests in Cross-Cultural Research," in B. Kaplan (ed.), *Studying Personality Cross-Culturally* (Evanston, Illinois: Row, Peterson), pp. 587–596.

Kaplan, B.

1961: "Cross-Cultural Use of Projective Techniques," in F. L. K. Hsu (ed.), *Psychological Anthropology* (Homewood, Illinois: Dorsey Press), pp. 235–254.

Klopfer, B., & Kelley, D. M.

1942: *The Rorschach Technique* (Yonkers, New York: World).

Lindzey, G.

1961: *Projective Techniques in Cross-Cultural Research* (New York: Appleton-Century-Crofts).

Rorschach, H.

1942: *Psychodiagnostics* (New York: Grune & Stratton).

Schachtel, E. G.

1945: "Subjective Definitions of the Rorschach Test Situation and their Effect on Test Performance," *Psychiatry*, **8**, 419-448.

Schafer, R.

1954: *Psychoanalytic Interpretation in Rorschach Testing* (New York: Grune & Stratton).

Part Seven

History of Anthropology

FRED EGGAN

Some Reflections on Comparative Method in Anthropology[1]

Introduction

In the last decade there has been an unusually large number of theoretical writings in anthropology concerned with comparative method in one form or another. Oscar Lewis, in his comprehensive survey of "Comparisons in Cultural Anthropology" (1955), believes this concentration of interest to be a reflection of "the growing maturity of anthropology as a science, the ever-increasing concern of anthropologists with problems of theory and method, and the accumulation of great masses of data which cry out for systematic comparative analysis" (Lewis: 1955, p. 260). But he also notes that there is considerable variation, and even disagreement, in the conceptions held by different anthropologists as to the nature of the comparative method and how it should be practiced.

1. This paper was originally written for the Conference on the History of Anthropology, April 13–14, 1962, sponsored by the Social Science Research Council, and organized by a committee with A. I. Hallowell as chairman. I am particularly indebted to Milton Singer for materials on comparative studies which he put at my disposal. I have revised the original paper for the present occasion.

Thus he notes that E. H. Ackerknecht and A. L. Kroeber, in a recent volume on *Method and Perspective in Anthropology* (Spencer: 1954), come to quite different conclusions concerning what has happened to comparative method in anthropology. Ackerknecht sees the comparative method as having been generally abandoned in cultural anthropology and believes that anthropologists can ill afford to give up a method with potential usefulness. The only reasonable solution of the problem, in his opinion, "consists, not in abandoning, but in using and improving it" (Ackerknecht: 1954, p. 125). Kroeber, in his commentary, believes "the comparative method has never gone out; it has only changed its tactic" (Kroeber: 1954, p. 273). Lewis' own solution is to abandon the term "comparative method" and "to discuss comparisons in anthropology rather than the comparative method" (1955, p. 259). This he does with great skill for contemporary cultural anthropology, and he finds "a remarkably large number of comparative studies of high quality, a broad coverage of subject matter, a variety of methods and approaches, a wide range of objectives, and a healthy eclecticism which speaks well for anthropology and its future" (1955, p. 279). The problems which such studies face are well described in Schapera's "Some Comments on Comparative Method in Social Anthropology" (1953), and Singer's (1953) summary of the discussion which followed. Here there was general agreement that there is no single method of comparison in anthropology and that method is largely determined by problem. This is also the conclusion which Oscar Lewis comes to on the basis of his empirical survey of contemporary studies using comparison in one form or another.

But it may still be useful to look briefly at the history of the utilization of comparison, and to examine the factors responsible for the development and decline of the comparative method in cultural anthropology. Despite Kroeber's optimism, it has never fully recovered from Boas' attack in "The Limitations of the Comparative Method in Anthropology" (1896), so far as most American anthropologists are concerned, and the change in tactics to which Kroeber refers has added further restrictions on its utilization. Indeed, one might argue that the rehabilitation of the comparative method that has occurred has been largely the result of efforts by British social anthropologists. At this late date we should be able to utilize "the comparative method" as a general cover term, realizing that there are important distinctions within it. Elsewhere (Eggan: 1954, pp. 743–763) I have suggested the method of controlled comparison as one such subdivision in the field of social anthropology.

One of the distinctive characteristics of cultural or social anthropology, as Lewis notes, has been "its simultaneous concern with the intensive and holistic study of small societies and with the comparative analysis of these same societies and cultures over the entire world. Traditionally, the former has been based upon field and comparative analysis, the latter upon library studies, with or without statistical manipulation of huge masses of data" (1955, p. 277). Lewis finds these two concerns to be merging and suggests that we broaden our view of comparative anthropology to include both.

During recent decades anthropology has been broadening its horizons in other directions as well. Edward Sapir, in his famous *Time Perspective* (1916), begins with the statement that "Cultural anthropology is more and more rapidly getting to realize itself as a strictly historical science," a view that was to dominate American anthropology for another two decades. But by the mid-1930's Robert Redfield could write:

> Anthropology finds people all over the earth, at different times in its history, exhibiting structure and behavior of great variety. In the impartial investigation of these by direct observation and in the broadest comparative study, it makes its claim to science. In the integration of local histories into a history of man's body and society as broad as the earth and as deep as the beginnings of the human species, it makes its contribution to history (1962, p. 15).

In his contribution to *Anthropology Today* (1953) A. I. Hallowell sees culture, personality, and society as interrelated variables as well as conceptual types, and notes that "anthropology has always maintained a perspective which has dealt with the evolutionary facts concerning our species, on the one hand, and with the constancies and the widely varying aspects of cultural data, on the other . . ." (1953, p. 600).

Within such a broad framework there is obviously room for almost everything. One of the ways a discipline advances is in terms of a wide range of investigations, depending on the varied interests of scholars, with the hope that the results will add up to something important. But anthropology is far enough along at present to encourage long-term and systematic investigation of particular problems. Whether these be primarily historical or scientific, comparison is essential at almost every step. The greater the control over the conditions affecting the situation, and the more precise the comparison, the more useful are the results. As S. F. Nadel notes in *The Foundations of Social Anthropology* (1951), the comparative method is the equivalent of the experiment for the study of society. "Comparison needs further refinement—planned selections and rigorous checks and controls—to approach the accuracy of a quasi-experimental method" (1951, p. 222). And as A. R. Radcliffe-Brown has stated: "It is only by the use of the comparative method that we can arrive at general explanations" (1952, p. 113).

Historical Survey

The attempt to develop a foundation for a more scientific approach to the study of man had its first impetus in the eighteenth century. The discoveries of the sixteenth and seventeenth centuries, and the resulting accounts of diverse peoples and customs in different parts of the world, attracted the attention of scholars, and the explanations offered for the similarities and the differences provided the first theoretical formulations. Father Joseph François Lafitau, a French Jesuit, is generally credited with the first treatise on comparative ethnology. A missionary among the Iroquois, his procedures were modern in many respects, and the title of his study, *Mœurs des sauvages américaines comparées aux mœurs des premier temps* (1724), foreshadows the major concerns of the nineteenth century with progress and development.

A series of French philosophers and historians—Montesquieu, Rousseau, Condorcet, Turgot, and others—introduced a new note in the study of man. Montesquieu emphasized the importance of searching for general laws behind historical events, and Turgot and Condorcet were primarily concerned with the concept of progress and with its application to the history of mankind, a concept which was to become particularly important in the nineteenth century.

During the same period a group of Scottish writers on moral philosophy were establishing a new basis for the study of man and society. This group, which centered around David Hume, has been studied in detail by Gladys Bryson in *Man and Society* (1945). They were in close touch with their French contemporaries and attempted to develop an inductive study of social institutions in the light of the concept of progress.

The significant developments of the comparative method in anthropology in the nineteenth century were not so much an extension and elaboration of the ideas developed by the French and Scottish philosophers of the eighteenth century, but rather the results of new developments in biology, linguistics, and other disciplines. The science of society which the Scottish philosophers envisaged was further developed by Saint-Simon, Comte, and Spencer as "sociology" and had little direct influence on anthropology until considerably later. Kenneth E. Bock has dealt with the development of the comparative method in the nineteenth century in admirable fashion in *The Acceptance of Histories* (1956). As he notes:

> Use of the comparative method involved acceptance of some principle on which cultural differences in space could be arranged in a presumably temporal series. Comte and his contemporaries had no real doubts that the correct principle lay in the view that change was natural, inevitable, progressive, parallel among distinct societies, from the simple to the complex, and, more specifically, from a condition unlike that represented by modern Western Europe to a condition like it. He was also convinced that change, so far as it was natural, was slow and gradual and proceeded from the nature of man himself, uninfluenced by extraneous elements (Bock: 1956, p. 10).

As Bock points out, these ideas constitute an elaborate philosophy of history, separable from the comparative method as such. But in the ensuing applications of the comparative method to the growing body of ethnographic data the two became inextricably fused. Thus when the results were subjected to critical examination and found wanting the method was thrown out along with the assumptions.

On the biological side the comparative method has had a different history. Ackerknecht has stressed the great popularity of the comparative method during the nineteenth century in physical anthropology and the important role that comparative anatomy played in its development, and in the stimulation of paleontology, geology, and archaeology. In the field of methodology, he suggests, "the influence of comparative anatomy çan hardly be overestimated" (1954, p. 118).

In the meantime important developments were taking place in England and Germany with reference to comparative studies in such diverse fields as linguistics, religion, mythology, and law. Progress seems to have been greatest in the field of linguistics, when the early interest in philology soon shifted to the study of historical relations between languages and the regularities in change which were found. Linguistic data readily lend themselves to comparative procedures, and Sir William Jones suggested the relationship between Sanskrit, Greek, Latin, and German as early as 1786. At about the same time Wilhelm von Humboldt was developing his classification of languages, and advanced the idea that languages were not static, thus opening the way for comparative study of the same language at different periods of time.

These and other contributions paved the way for the formulation of "phonetic laws," or rules of sound change, a development which made it possible to reconstruct ancestral forms of words from a close comparison of modern examples from different branches of a linguistic family. With these developments comparative linguistics and comparative philology were well under way, resulting in genetic classifications of various linguistic stocks by a number of scholars.

The methods of comparison which developed in linguistics proved to be the most successful. Here the interest in "origins" could be partially satisfied because of the genetic character of language families and the regularities in linguistic change. Even the exceptions to the "phonetic laws," which were long a subject of controversy, have largely yielded to more accurate descriptive techniques and studies of diffusion. And the reconstructions of ancestral forms could often be checked by documentary records, particularly in the Indo-European languages. Furthermore, languages proved highly resistant to evolutionary arrangement. Hence, when the evolutionary sequences set up for social institutions on the basis of the comparative method were undermined, the linguistic model was in a strategic position to influence the new anthropology.

Until the middle of the nineteenth century the great majority of comparative studies were carried out without reference to firsthand investigation in the field, or even a critical marshaling of the data available in the library. But during the

1840's Lewis H. Morgan began a study of the Iroquois Indians which was to lead to an expansion of the comparative method in new directions. The work of Morgan is well known, and I have elsewhere (Eggan: 1960, pp. 179–201) detailed the steps in his comparative study of kinship systems which was to result in *Systems of Consanguinity and Affinity of the Human Family* (Morgan: 1871). But, briefly, after his monograph on the Iroquois (Morgan: 1851), he discovered that the Ojibwa Indians, speaking a quite different language, had almost precisely the same pattern or system of kinship terminology. With this discovery, he went on to study at firsthand all available Indian kinship systems, developing an elaborate schedule to ensure comparability. Ultimately, with the help of others, he extended his investigations to other parts of the world, and to the systems of antiquity.

By a careful comparison of the various American Indian terminologies he was able to isolate a broad social type, the "classificatory" system. This he did on the basis of his familiarity with the Iroquois system, which he considered to be closely associated with their clan system; he thought that this system was universal among the American Indians. His early interests were historical, and since he believed that kinship systems were exceedingly stable, he sought to use them to discover the origins of the American Indian, which he assumed were in Asia. His discovery of an apparently identical system to that of the Iroquois among the Tamils of South India seemed to him decisive evidence that he was correct.

As new data came in from other parts of the world, however, there were some surprises. The Hawaiian system was "classificatory" to a much greater degree, and he was forced to look for a set of institutions which might account for it. In this endeavor Morgan laid the basis for his famous series of evolutionary stages which were to dominate anthropology for the next decades. But what is more important for our purposes is the procedure by which he isolated his social types and then looked for correlated phenomena. Here he made his procedures explicit and he organized his field expeditions to specific ends: the testing of his initial hypotheses. That he was wrong in some of his conclusions is to be expected—he had just discovered kinship—but he was far in advance of most of his contemporaries.

In the meantime a group of distinguished scholars in England and on the continent were developing other aspects of anthropology through the comparison of early Indo-European and later sources, with additions from tribal groups in India and elsewhere. Maine, in *Ancient Law* (1861), was primarily concerned with the development of the Indo-European family system, and emphasized the early importance of the patriarchal family. Bachofen, a Swiss scholar, utilized classical mythology in his demonstration of the earlier importance of female descent, and in *Das Mutterrecht* (1861), set up an evolutionary development from communal marriage, through matrilineal institutions, to a patriarchate. At almost the same time, but from a different set of data, McLennan's *Primitive Marriage* (1865) arrived at a similar sequence. Morgan's later work, *Ancient Society* (1877), building on his kinship studies and other works, codified the evolution of culture in three great stages: Savagery, Barbarism, and Civilization, each with several subdivisions; and some fifteen successive stages in marriage and the family.

In working out this unilinear sequence of institutions, the comparative method was utilized to document the various stages on the explicit assumption that existing societies and cultures were surviving examples of earlier stages through which more advanced societies had passed. When comparison within a stage revealed discrepancies these were classed as "survivals," if they could be attributed to an earlier stage, or else attributed to contact with higher cultures. But once the evolutionary structure was established in outline, the comparative method became essentially a procedure by which new information was pigeonholed.

Tylor (1865, 1871), who had developed the first comprehensive definition of culture which included all the "capabilities and habits acquired by man as a member of society," accepted the evolutionary outline as a rough guide to the understanding of the progress of civilization, but "cautioned that comparison is but a guide, not a full explanation" (1881, p. 19). Tylor's procedure in the study of civilization was to classify the details of culture into their proper groups with a view to studying their geographical distribution and the relations which exist among them. Given the conception of culture "at all times and all places," the comparison of traits from different societies did not violate context, and the criticisms advanced by later scholars are based on a different frame of reference.

Tylor was essentially applying the linguistic model to the study of the development of culture, as he makes clear by inference in *Anthropology* (1881). Here he proposes to work from the known to the unknown, and to reconstruct earlier forms of institutions in a fashion analogous to that of the linguist in reconstructing ancestral linguistic forms. Hence, though he worked within a broad evolutionary framework, he was generally concerned with more specific problems, and avoided the excesses of his evolutionary colleagues, for the most part. In his important paper, "On a Method of Investigating the Development of Institutions" (1889), he not only presented a model comparative study but introduced quantitative methods, as well.

The major attack on the comparative method came from Franz Boas. He believed that laws exist which govern the development of society but that the assumptions which the evolutionists made as to their basis were far too simple. In "The Limitations of the Comparative Method of Anthropology" (1896), he pointed out that "anthropological research which compares similar cultural phenomena from various parts of the world, in order to discover the uniform history of their development, makes the assumption that the same ethnological phenomena has everywhere developed in the same manner. Here lies the flaw in the argument of the new method, for no such proof can be given" (1940, p. 273). Boas therefore rejected the grand evolution of society as of doubtful value, and proposed that comparison be limited to the reconstruction of cultural history within small cultural areas, in the first instance. Once histories of particular cultures have been worked out they, in turn, can be compared, and general laws may be found.

> Thus we have seen that the comparative method can hope to reach the results for which it is striving only when it bases its investigations on the historical results of researches which are devoted to laying clear the complex relations of each individual culture. The comparative method, and the historical method, if I may use these terms, have been struggling for supremacy for a long time, but we may hope that each will soon find its appropriate place and function (Boas: 1940, p. 280).

Boas went on to note that the comparative method had been remarkably barren of results and would not be fruitful until comparisons were made on the broader and sounder base which he had outlined.

This criticism effectively killed the classic "comparative method," so far as American anthropology was concerned. Kroeber was technically correct in remarking that all Boas advocated was a change of tactics, but in practice the whole strategy of research was also changed. By the time *General Anthropology* was published in 1938, Boas was still cautious, not only with regard to the comparative method in cultural studies, but also with regard to comparative methods in linguistics, and he was no longer optimistic about finding any laws of historical development (1938, pp. 2–3). As a result not only was the comparative method not rehabilitated in the manner envisaged in 1896, but the work of students such as Kroeber and Sapir in comparative linguistics was severely criticized, and the potentialities of comparison for working out basic concepts were hampered. In the field of social organization, for example, Boas never clarified the Northwest Coast systems, on which he spent so much time; while Spier and Lowie produced some order in regard to kinship terminologies, the essential nature of lineage systems and totemism was long obscured. Goldenweiser, in fact, by the application of Boas' procedures, succeeded in eliminating any central core to totemism, though the concept is currently very much alive.

In England and on the continent there was no such sharp break with the past, so far as the comparative method was concerned. Sir James Frazer continued the search for the origins of various institutions and beliefs, and at Cambridge, A. C. Haddon instituted the first intensive field expeditions and began the training of professional anthropologists. W. H. R. Rivers continued the comparative study of Melanesian society, begun with the Torres Straits expedition, and in *Kinship and Social Organization* (1914), carried forward the earlier researches of Morgan through the correlation of marriage practices with certain types of kinship systems.

In Germany, F. Graebner rejected the evolutionary theory in favor of a historical approach, but attempted to strengthen historical methodology by developing rules of comparison in terms of the criteria of form and quantity. But while the methodology was improved the basic assumptions of the Kulturkreislehre were too rigid and mechanical, and despite W. Schmidt's attempts to salvage the school, it has gradually been abandoned.

The strong historical emphasis in German social science restricted the utilization of comparison, except in the field of jurisprudence and economics, until the advent of Max Weber.[2] In early essays on the methodology of the social sciences he dealt with the relation between history and generalizing social science, and worked out a set of rules for the comparison of social events, and for comparing social systems and subsystems. His procedures involved the construction of ideal types which were set up as a system of interrelated variables, since he believed the application of the comparative method to historical materials is not possible if it is confined to chains of events. In order to utilize the comparative method with historical data, Weber insisted that social systems, or developmental sequences expressed in terms of generalizable variables, be compared with one another. These views have had an important influence on current social science research, but have only just begun to influence anthropology.

In France, Emile Durkheim and his collaborators in the *Année Sociologique* continued the tradition of Comte and Montesquieu, in part, but shifted their attention from problems of origin to the study of social function. They emphasized sociological explanations, rather than psychological or historical ones, and they utilized the comparative method for an understanding of both social and religious phenomena, although their major interest was in examining the function of particular customs in terms of their place in the social system and their significance for social integration.

A. R. Radcliffe-Brown, an early student of Rivers, and later a follower of Durkheim, has made the comparative method central to the study of social anthropology. He defines social anthropology as "the investigation of the nature of human society by the systematic comparison of societies of diverse types" (1958, p. 133), and makes a clear distinction between comparison used in formulating a historical or genetic hypothesis, and comparison to arrive at classifications and generalizations.

2. For the discussion of Max Weber's use of the comparative method I am indebted to an excellent essay "On Comparative History" by Bert F. Hoselitz published in *World Politics*, **9**, 267–279 (1957). Weber's essays on method have been translated in part in *The Methodology of the Social Sciences*, translated by E. A. Shils and H. A. Finch (eds.) (Glencoe, Illinois: Free Press of Glencoe, 1949).

> The use of comparison by the social anthropologist is similar to its use in general linguistics or in comparative zoology. The purpose is to arrive at valid generalizations about the nature of society and social phenomena by the systematic study of resemblances and differences. By the use of abstractive generalization, the more general, essential and permanent characteristics of social life are distinguished from the accidental and variable (Radcliffe-Brown: 1958, p. 165).

Modern Developments

This brief survey suggests that the comparative method is still a useful procedure in cultural anthropology despite the considerable variation in the conceptions held by different anthropologists as to its nature. It should be clear, also, that the comparative method is not a "method" in the broad sense, but a technique for establishing similarities and differences which can be applied with differing degrees of rigor and approximation. It also has had a somewhat different history in America and in England and the continent. The French tradition is the longest and most continuous, and Ackerknecht, who had his training in social anthropology in Paris under Mauss, sees the comparative method as largely abandoned in this country. In America the attack on unilinear evolution was more severe and the comparative method, as the apparent basis for the evolutionary edifice, was thrown out with the evolutionary bath water. Kroeber could say that the comparative method had never gone out, but only changed its tactic, but comparison was largely restricted to culture areas and to limited historical problems. The famous comparative studies of Age Societies and the Sun Dance, initiated by Wissler, were of this character, and we have noted in an earlier section that the development of concepts for cross-cultural comparison and generalization was limited.

The more recent comparative research in the United States has largely stemmed from W. G. Sumner and A. G. Keller, through their influence on G. P. Murdock, or has been stimulated by Radcliffe-Brown, so far as anthropology has been concerned. In other fields Max Weber has stimulated a wide variety of scholars in different disciplines, although his influence is just beginning to be felt in anthropology. Murdock organized the Cross-Cultural Survey in 1937 (see Murdock: 1940) in connection with the interdisciplinary program of research of the Institute of Human Relations at Yale University: and more recently with C. S. Ford and others has developed the Human Relations Area File, as an interuniversity organization devoted to the facilitation of research on the cultures of the world. The files are designed to provide a selected sample of these cultures, organized in terms of a standard system of classification, to provide for comparison, and for the testing of scientific generalizations with regard to cultural behavior.[3]

3. For a convenient summary of studies in this field see Frank W. Moore (ed.), *Readings in Cross-Cultural Methodology* (New Haven: Yale University Press, 1961).

Murdock's *Social Structure* (1949) represents the most important contribution from such organized, large-scale, cross-cultural research which has so far appeared, and Ackerknecht (1954, p. 117) has hailed it as a sign of "a renaissance of the comparative method." Murdock utilized a sample of 250 societies to test a large number of hypotheses concerning the relations between kinship terminology and other aspects of social structure, employing statistical and other methods, and his results have in turn stimulated a great amount of research along similar lines. A parallel study by Whiting and Child (1953) uses ethnographic data from primitive societies to test psychological hypotheses relating to Freudian mechanisms, such as fixation, displacement, projection, and the development of guilt; this and other studies have led to planned field research in some six communities designed to provide better controlled data on the processes of socialization and their relations to personality development.

Hallowell, who began his long anthropological career with a notable comparative study of "Bear Ceremonialism in the Northern Hemisphere" (1926), has in later years concerned himself primarily with the Northeastern Algonkians, and in particular the Ojibwa. Here he has concentrated on the relations between the cultural and the personal, utilizing projective materials as well as observations, and systematically controlling his data in as many ways as possible. Elsewhere (Eggan: 1955, pp. 521ff.) I have discussed his contributions to the study of Northeastern Algonkian social structure; the resulting hypotheses have proved exceedingly important in understanding the variations in kinship patterns and marriage practices in this whole region.

At the same time Hallowell has been concerned with some of the most general problems in anthropology—"questions pertaining to the ultimate roots of human culture and personality structure viewed in the broad horizons of behavioral evolution." He sees this problem in comparative terms, as well:

> When we have more knowledge of the range and variation in the human personality structure in relation to major provincial determinants we shall be able to state with more precision what is common to man everywhere. By that time we may be able to construct a better picture of the psychological structure of man as an evolving primate (Hallowell: 1955, p. 13).

Radcliffe-Brown has exemplified his use of comparison and the comparative method in a number of studies, notably in *The Social Organization of Australian Tribes* (1931), and "The Comparative Method in Social Anthropology" (1952). In the first-mentioned study he finds that all of the social systems in aboriginal Australia can be seen as variants of two types of social structure, the Kariera and the Aranda; and he further advances the hypothesis that the Aranda type has developed from the Kariera. Here by close comparison he was able to generalize so effectively that his hypotheses are still stimulating new research, even though the number of basic types may ultimately have to be enlarged.

In his Huxley Memorial Lecture, "The Comparative Method in Social Anthropology," Radcliffe-Brown begins with exogamous moiety divisions in Australia and shows that the Australian phenomena are instances of certain widespread general tendencies in human societies. He distinguishes the comparative method from the historical method: "only the comparative method can give us general propositions" (1952, p. 21). Ultimately he saw social anthropology as part of a broader comparative sociology.

The present writer, in *Social Organization of the Western Pueblos* (Eggan: 1950) and in some chapters in *Social Anthropology of North American Tribes* (Eggan: 1955) has attempted a comparative analysis of social and cultural systems on the model provided by Radcliffe-Brown, but with a greater concern for change over time. I have preferred to compare on a smaller scale and with a greater control over the frame of comparison. I have worked mainly within social or cultural types and have attempted to take account of both ecological and historical factors, so far as archaeological and documentary data are available. Kimball Romney (1957) has recently presented a similar type of comparative study in his "genetic model" for the study of cultures derived from a known ancestry and linguistically controlled. For a general statement see Oscar Lewis' "Controls and Experiments in Field Work" (1953).

There are a considerable number of other comparative studies that should be mentioned: Margaret Mead's pioneer studies of individual development in several societies and her long-term concern with the nature of human nature; M. J. Herskovits' comparisons of New World Negroes with their African sources, Julian Steward's comparisons of cultural types; among others. Another type of comparative study involves a small group of scholars working intensively on a series of related problems, each bringing their special knowledge to bear on the common problems. Two particularly successful attempts, both based on summer seminars sponsored by the Social Science Research Council, are reported in David M. Schneider and Kathleen Gough (eds.), *Matrilineal Kinship* (1961) and in Edward M. Spicer (ed.), *Perspectives in American Indian Culture Change* (1961).

Of particular importance is the program for the comparative study of civilizations which Robert Redfield was engaged in, with the assistance of Milton Singer and others, at the time of his death. Redfield had earlier made an impressive comparative study of Yucatan Maya communities, *The Folk Culture of Yucatan* (1941); now he turned to the study of historic civilizations. As Singer has recently pointed out in his Foreword to A. L. Kroeber's *An Anthropologist Looks at History* (1963), what Redfield had in mind "was the possibility of studying and comparing civilizations as structures and social organizations of traditions, little and great." (Singer: 1963, p. ix). Kroeber, on the other hand, was more concerned with the historical problems concerning the development and decline of civilizations.

These examples suggest that research design can play a more conscious role in our scholarly programs than it has so far. We still need new ideas and new field data in anthropology, but there is also an increasing need for a more sophisticated testing of ideas and hypotheses behind the front lines. There is sufficient personnel now available in anthropology, and enough research support, to make it possible to plan long-term research programs on important problems. Here we need to evaluate the variant hypotheses now in circulation in terms of the data already available, and to look for field situations which will enable us to select the more promising for further testing and refinement. The comparative method, with the modern controls that are available, is an important instrument for this purpose, and Hallowell's research on the Northeastern Algonkians is one example of what can be accomplished along these lines.

References

Ackerknecht, E. H.

1954: "On the Comparative Method in Anthropology," in R. F. Spencer (ed.), *Method and Perspective in Anthropology* (Minneapolis, University of Minnesota Press), pp. 117–125.

Bachofen, J. J.

1861: *Das Mutterrecht* (Stuttgart: Krais & Hoffman).

Boas, F.

1896: "The Limitations of the Comparative Method in Anthropology," *Science*, **4**, 901–908. Reprinted in *Race, Language and Culture* (New York: Macmillan, 1940), pp. 270–280.

1940: *Race, Language and Culture* (New York: Macmillan).

Boas, F. (ed.)

1938: *General Anthropology* (Boston: Heath).

Bock, K. E.

1956: *The Acceptance of Histories: Toward a Perspective for Social Science* (Berkeley & Los Angeles: University of California Press).

Bryson, G.

1945: *Man and Society: The Scottish Inquiry of the Eighteenth Century* (Princeton: Princeton University Press).

Eggan, F.

1950: *The Social Organization of the Western Pueblos* (Chicago: University of Chicago Press).

1954: "Social Anthropology and the Method of Controlled Comparison," *American Anthropologist*, **56**, 743–763.

1960: "Lewis H. Morgan in Kinship Perspective," in G. E. Dole & R. Carneiro (eds.), *Essays in the Science of Culture* (New York: Crowell), pp. 179–201.

Eggan, F. (ed.)

1955: *Social Anthropology of North American Tribes* (enlarged ed.; Chicago: University of Chicago Press).

Hallowell, A. I.
1926: "Bear Ceremonialism in the Northern Hemisphere," *American Anthropologist*, **28,** 1–175.
1953: "Culture, Personality and Society," in A. L. Kroeber (ed.), *Anthropology Today* (Chicago: University of Chicago Press).
1955: *Culture and Experience* (Philadelphia: University of Pennsylvania Press).

Hoselitz, B.
1957: "On Comparative History," *World Politics*, **9,** 267–279.

Kroeber, A. L.
1954: "Critical Summary and Commentary," in R. F. Spencer (ed.), *Method and Perspective in Anthropology* (Minneapolis: University of Minnesota Press), pp. 273–299.

Lafitau, J. F.
1724: *Mœurs des sauvages américains comparées aux mœurs des premiers temps* (Paris: Chez Saugrain l'aîné, etc.).

Lewis, O.
1953: "Controls and Experiments in Field Work," in A. L. Kroeber (ed.), *Anthropology Today* (Chicago: University of Chicago Press), pp. 425–475.
1955: "Comparisons in Cultural Anthropology," in *Yearbook of Anthropology, 1955* (New York: Wenner-Gren Foundation for Anthropological Research), pp. 259–292.

Maine, Sir H.
1861: *Ancient Society* (London: Murray).

McLennan, J. F.
1865: *Primitive Marriage* (London: Macmillan).

Moore, F. W. (ed.)
1961: *Readings in Cross-Cultural Methodology* (New Haven: Human Relations Area Files).

Morgan, L. H.
1851: *League of the Hodenosaunee, Iroquois* (Rochester: Sage & Brother).
1871: "Systems of Consanguinity and Affinity of the Human Family," *Smithsonian Contributions to Knowledge*, **17,** 1–590.
1877: *Ancient Society* (New York: Holt).

Murdock, G. P.
1940: "The Cross-Cultural Survey," *American Sociological Review*, **5,** 361–370.
1949: *Social Structure* (New York: Macmillan).

Nadel, S. F.
1951: *The Foundations of Social Anthropology* (Glencoe, Illinois: Free Press of Glencoe).

Radcliffe-Brown, A. R.
1931: "Social Organization of Australian Tribes," "*Oceania*" *Monographs*, **1** (Melbourne: Macmillan).

1952: "The Comparative Method in Social Anthropology," *Journal of the Royal Anthropological Institute*, **81**, 15–22.

1958: *Method in Social Anthropology*, ed. by M. N. Srinivas (Chicago: University of Chicago Press).

Redfield, R.

1941: *The Folk Culture of Yucatan* (Chicago: University of Chicago Press).

1962: *Human Nature and the Study of Society*, ed. by M. P. Redfield, Vol. I (Chicago: University of Chicago Press).

Rivers, W. H. R.

1914: *Kinship and Social Organization* (London: Constable).

Romney, A. K.

1957: "The Genetic Model and Uto-Aztecan Time Perspective," *Davidson Journal of Anthropology*, **3**, 35–41.

Sapir, E.

1916: *Time Perspective in Aboriginal American Culture: A Study in Method*, Geological Survey Memoir 90, Anthropological Series No. 13 (Ottawa: Canada Department of Mines).

Schapera, I.

1953: "Some Comments on Comparative Method in Social Anthropology," Wenner-Gren Foundation Supper Conference, *American Anthropologist*, **55**, 353–362.

Schneider, D. M., & Gough, K. (eds.)

1961: *Matrilineal Kinship* (Berkeley & Los Angeles: University of California Press).

Singer, M.

1953: "Summary of Comments and Discussion," Wenner-Gren Foundation Supper Conference, *American Anthropologist*, **55**, 326–366.

1963: Foreward to A. L. Kroeber, *An Anthropologist looks at History* (Berkeley & Los Angeles: University of California Press).

Spencer, R. F. (ed.)

1954: *Method and Perspective in Anthropology* (Minneapolis: University of Minnesota Press).

Spicer, E. H. (ed.)

1961: *Perspectives in American Indian Culture Change* (Chicago: University of Chicago Press).

Tylor, E. B.

1865: *Researches into the Early History of Mankind and the Development of Civilization* (London: Murray).

1871: *Primitive Culture: Researches into the Development of Mythology, Philosophy, Religion, Language, Art and Custom* (London: Murray).

1881: *Anthropology: An Introduction to the Study of Man and Civilization* (London: Macmillan).

1889: "On a Method of Investigating the Development of Institutions," *Journal of the Royal Anthropological Institute*, **18**, 245–272.

Weber, M.

1949: *The Methodology of the Social Sciences*, trans. & ed. by E. A. Shils & H. A. Finch (Glencoe, Illinois: Free Press of Glencoe).

Whiting, J. W. M., & Child, I. L.

1953: *Child Training and Personality* (New Haven: Yale University Press).

JACOB W. GRUBER

Brixham Cave and the Antiquity of Man[1]

During the past fifteen years, human paleontology has been revitalized by a series of discoveries whose interpretation has produced a new excitement in the search for man's ancestry. New paths of human evolution are replacing those which have become rutted through decades of repetition of the same data and the same theories. The current vigor recalls the new spirit of just a century ago when, during the 1850's and early 1860's, the

1. Much of the material upon which this paper is based was gathered during the course of a sabbatical leave granted by Temple University and with the aid of a fellowship from the National Science Foundation and a grant from the American Council of Learned Societies; to these institutions I wish to express both acknowledgment of and gratitude for the aid given. I wish to express particularly my appreciation to Mr. Wilfrid T. Wiatt and to the Torquay Natural History Society of which he is honorary secretary for the cooperation in making available to me the Pengelly manuscripts in the possession of the Society; to the Secretary of the Society of Antiquaries at London; and to Mlle. Lecat, librarian of the Bibliothèque Communal d'Abbeville for making available the correspondence to Boucher de Perthes. In addition, I am grateful to Dr. Walter F. Cannon, Dr. John Cotter, and Dr. John C. Greene for reading earlier versions of this paper and for the liberality of their comments. The inclusion of this paper in this volume cannot, however, pass without my acknowledgment to Dr. Hallowell for the invaluable stimulation of his many conversations with me.

discoveries of the "cave men" revolutionized the concept of man's past and created for him a previously unbelievable antiquity. Like those discoveries, the finds of our generation, culminating in the evidences from Olduvai Gorge, have led to a reexamination of the bases of human behavior and its development. Hallowell's own stimulating examinations of the nature of the human achievement, of human nature itself, have been instrumental in that redefinition of man's uniqueness which underlies the contemporary search for the human threshold in the evolutionary past. And with the reawakening of studies of human evolution both physically and behaviorally, it is perhaps of some interest to examine those events of an earlier period, in an earlier state of the science, which provided the foundations of both data and concept upon which our present knowledge and interests have been built.

Looking backward to events of a seemingly distant past, James Geikie wrote in 1881 that:

> When the announcement was made some years ago that rude stone implements of undoubted human workmanship had been discovered in certain alluvial deposits in the valley of the river Somme under circumstances which argued for the human race a very high antiquity, geologists generally received the news with incredulity. That the advent of man was an occurrence merely of yesterday, as it were, and a matter to be discussed properly by chronologists and historians alone, most of us until lately were taught to believe. So ingrained, indeed, had this belief become, that although evidence of the antiquity of our race similar to those subsequent French discoveries, which succeeded at last in routing the skeptical indifference of geologists, had been noted from time to time . . ., yet it was only noted to be explained away, and in point of fact was persistently neglected as of no importance (Geikie: 1881, p. 3).

The events to which Geikie referred were indeed of his own era; they were less than a generation past. It is true that when Geikie wrote with such certitude, there were still a few scattered voices frantically raised in defense of man's recent origins and recent history; but these were the last laments for the loss of the recency of man's creation. Their very shrillness of tone betrayed the weakness of their position. They were the echoes of a past's prevailing theme, reverberating hollowly in the new chamber into which the new science of prehistory had ushered man.

Geikie was writing during a period of calm which followed one of the great intellectual revolutions of the nineteenth century—the discovery of man's past. It was a revolution the more intolerable because it was so personal, because it struck so violently at man's most hallowed conception of himself. After a time, the threads of history become tangled and the individuality of movements and events become confused and compressed into an unreal simplicity confined within the rubric of an *ism*. Old channels of thought—originally separate and distinct—are covered over and lost as the new cuts its way more deeply into the changing landscape of the mind. It is perhaps, of some value to retrace in some fashion these features of an earlier intellectual horizon.

The ideological conquests during the past century of the idea of organic evolution have led to the general acceptance of an intimate association between the concept of man's high antiquity and that of organic evolution. So closely have these two revolutionary concepts come to be related that the former is often thought to have been but an inevitable conceptual and chronological consequence of the latter. Thus, Graham Clark (1957, p. 32) in surveying the growth of prehistory as a science, notes that "It needed a revolution in man's conception of nature and antiquity of man as an organism before the bare notion of primary prehistory could take birth. Such a revolution was wrought by the publication in 1859 of Charles Darwin's *Origin of Species*;" and he goes on to suggest that it was as a result of the *Origin* that the occasional and previously questioned finds of man's antiquity were reexamined and rehabilitated. The fact that these two intellectual revolutions—the idea that all organic species result, through long periods of time, from a natural process of generational modification and that man's demonstrated history is much different from that which any reconciliation with the scriptural record or Mosaic chronology can justify—the fact that these two great events in the history of human thought occurred almost simultaneously has led to the generally held conclusion that it was the statement of an acceptable theory of organic evolution which made man's antiquity both intelligible and defensible. As a matter of historical fact, however, these two concepts as they emerged a century ago, were the products of two quite separate intellectual traditions—that is, separate to the extent that any two movements within the same intellectual milieu can be said to be separate. The elisions of history, however, have subsequently merged these two separate currents into a single intellectual stream.

For much of the nineteenth century, the concept of the antiquity and/or recency of man had two related but quite different meanings. Of somewhat lesser importance, in the absence of any valid means of measurement, was the absolute age of man's earthly existence. Much more important, however, was the relative period of man's emergence or creation as judged by his faunal associations. It was through the analysis of a whole range of such faunal complexes as they revealed themselves in the accumulating body of fossil remains that the geologists had transformed a succession of lithic strata into a chronologically arranged series of organic communities. Within the limits imposed by credulity as well as by a geology-based chronology, it was possible to expand man's history backward in time so long as the relative position of his emergence was not so altered as to make him a contemporary of fauna foreign to (and therefore assumed to be anterior to) existing forms.

To understand the paramount importance for an interpretation of man's place in nature of this second concept of age based upon faunal association and the significance of its introduction for both the science and the natural theology of a century ago, we must be aware of the accepted synthesis which had emerged from decades of theogeological controversy. It was Cuvier who set the tone for the new science of geology by his insistence on observation and his denigration of speculation. The excellence of his comparative anatomy, the dedication of his empiricism, and the rigor of his logic combined to provide him with that position of authority which directed the thinking of his followers throughout the world long after his death in 1832. Basing his conclusions on his own reconstructions of the strange new mammalian fossils from the Paris basin this "antiquary of a new order" concluded from the obvious evidences, both geological and paleontological, that the earth had been visited by a succession of sudden and cataclysmic revolutions. "Thus we have . . . a series of epochs," he noted (Cuvier: 1817, p. 8), "anterior to the present time, and of which the successive steps may be ascertained with perfect certainty. . . . These epochs form so many fixed points, answering as rules for directing our enquiries respecting the ancient chronology of the earth." And each of these epochs, these "thousands of ages" marching inevitably to the present, bore some characteristic segment of the "thousands of animals" which a succession of revolutions had destroyed. The serious and adventurous efforts of numbers of collectors, following in the path which Cuvier had opened, filled in the outlines of the paleontological past in much the same way and with much the same passion and spirit with which the followers of Linnaeus earlier had expanded beyond prior conception the borders of the living universe. The zeal to observe and to record combined with the tedium surrounding the old controversies to produce a new spirit in geology. "A new school at last arose," wrote Lyell (1855, pp. 58–59) himself one of its most distinguished members, "who professed the strictest neutrality . . . and who resolved diligently to devote their labours to observation. . . . Speculative views were discountenanced. . . . To multiply and record observations, and patiently to await the result at some future period, was the object proposed by them; and it was their favourite maxim that the time was not yet come for a general system of geology, but that all must be content for many years to be exclusively engaged in furnishing materials for future generalizations. By acting up to these principles with consistency, they in a few years disarmed all prejudice, and rescued the science from the imputation of being dangerous, or at best but a visionary pursuit." Nevertheless the very weight of the evidences carved from the superimposed strata of the earth's crust produced a generally accepted theory of its past.

Time—the restricted time of literally interpreted Scripture—was no longer a problem; eons—stretching back beyond the ken of even the most liberal of a prior generation—were there for the asking. And through a large part of that time, living forms had occupied the earth, albeit forms quite different from those now alive. And in this vast new dimension of the organic universe, there was still design and plan and purpose. Although the Noachian deluge, as the one single catastrophe separating the past from the present, had long been abandoned, it had been supplanted by a series of equally destructive forces whose effects could be seen in the tilt of the strata and in the exotic fossils they contained. Although an increasing paleontological sophistication made more subtle the spasms which marked the history of the earth, the idea of catastrophism had both popular and scientific approval. Almost fifty years after Cuvier and just prior to the publication of Darwin's *Origin*, Louis Agassiz, admittedly overly enthusiastic in his catastrophism, but still the most popular American natural scientist, could write:

> Modern science . . . can show in the most satisfactory manner that all finite beings have made their appearance successively and at long intervals, and that each kind of organized beings has existed for a definite period of time in past ages, and that those now living are of comparative recent origin. At the same time, the order of their succession, and their immutability during such cosmic periods, show no causal connection with physical agents and the known sphere of action of these agents in nature, but argue in favor of repeated interventions on the part of the Creator (Agassiz: 1859, p. 84).

One could not speak—nor think—of one organic universe, but only of many, each succeeding the other in a changing order of separate creations. Arguing from his uniformitarianism, Lyell might maintain that the succession was not to be equated with progression; but in the face of the fossil evidence, his cry, if heard at all, went unheeded. For most, a designed improvement within the established types, as an improvement in the types themselves, was a self-evident fact both in the societies of man and in the creations of God. So readily did the doctrine of progression permit the acceptance of the high antiquity of the earth that within a generation this heresy of a former time had become reconciled with—indeed, a part of—prevailing theological belief. The effect of the new reconciliation was the onset of a period of intellectual calm during which the findings of geology and the interpretations of Scripture were made to validate each other to the satisfaction of most of the advocates of both.[2]

On one conclusion, however, all were agreed: The most important of these creations was the last, that in which man appeared, that which Genesis described. Thus, through this new system of belief and its acceptance of a past, man was effectively insulated through the maintenance of what was to become a dogma of his own recent creation. Here lay man's uniqueness, his worth, his tie to God. So long as he could feel himself the product of this last, this most recent, of God's works, he could feel that special kinship to his creator which made him

2. For stimulating, authoritative, although not necessarily compatible accounts of the developments of geology through the first half of the nineteenth century, see Cannon (1960a and b); Eiseley (1958); Gillispie (1951); and Greene (1959).

man and not brute. The recency of man's creation, so readily admitted and so easily accepted, was adduced as one additional support—in fact, the major one—of the progression of the successive creations of life under divine guidance and within a divine plan. In effect, the system was a self-sustaining one: The paleontological succession afforded evidence of a progressive series; man's position as the most recent of the series supported the view of progression; the separations or breaks in the fossil record, those revolutions for which there was no sufficient natural explanation, implied directive creation; Scripture supported the concept of creation, the idea of progressive succession, and, most important, the terminal creation of man as the apex of the series. The clearest expression of this new synthesis, a synthesis which was used to disprove the charge of atheism in science and to validate the truths which science was unveiling, is reflected in the writings of the Scottish amateur geologist, Hugh Miller, who was himself the most active, the most widely read, and probably the most effective advocate of this view.[3]

Within this general interpretation of the paleontological succession—so easy to reconcile with prevailing belief and so consistent with the known geological facts—geology settled down to a premature old-age, eschewing speculation in its zeal to make more specific the nature of each of God's creations. It was a period, known in the history of every science, of relative calm, of synthesis, of consolidation.

Through these years of intensive collecting, the assumption of the continued absence of any evidence for man's antiquity, that is, for the association of his remains with any of those extinct creatures of the past, was the crucial constant which maintained the faith for most progressionists; so delicately balanced and arranged were the various parts of the ideological structure built upon this synthesis of Scripture, progress, and geology that the alteration of any part threatened to collapse the whole.

The absence of such evidences, however, was in fact a myth, a myth which was nurtured with increasing zeal. Frere's often quoted discoveries and lucid interpretation (Frere: 1800) had occurred in the last years of the eighteenth century; but they came too early to introduce even a jarring note into a system which had not yet been constructed. Thus, unexplainable and unexplained, they remained ignored. With increasing paleontological activity, however, particularly in geological deposits of more recent origin, such evidences occurred at an accelerating and alarming rate.

From the cave earths and from the gravel terraces, those leavings of some prior catastrophe, the remnants of man were exposed. Buckland, one of the most ardent of the new geologists, had examined the remains of a human skeleton in Paviland Cave (Buckland: 1822) but was quick to explain it away

3. See particularly Miller (1841, 1857). See also the "popular" presentations of Gideon Mantell (1844).

as that of a courtesan to the soldiers of a Roman camp nearby. But already as he reviewed the early evidences from the cave explorations of Europe in his *Reliquiae Diluvianae* (Buckland: 1824), he was able to record at least seven additional instances in which human bones had occurred in circumstances suggesting their high antiquity; but their associations with extinct fauna were, he argued, fortuitous: "the human bones are not of the same antiquity with those of the antediluvian animals that occur in the same caves with them" (Buckland: 1824, p. 169).[4]

At Kent's Hole in Devon, Father MacEnery in the 1820's had satisfied himself of the contemporaneity of chipped stone implements and the remains of extinct fauna which he had found together below the stalagmite of the cave floor (MacEnery: 1859; Pengelly: 1869); but Buckland in person and Cuvier by reputation persuaded him that both his observations and his inferences were in error.[5]

In the previously undisturbed deposits of the Belgian caverns near Liége, under circumstances of incredible difficulty, Schmerling in the early 1830's had again uncovered human remains in direct association with what had come to be a predictable cave fauna. Against the attacks and ridicule of his associates, forced to defend his own integrity as an excavator, he could only maintain that time alone would prove the correctness of his assertions that man had existed at the time the caves were filled with the mud and fossils they contained (Schmerling: 1833–34, Vol. II, p. 179). And the similar discoveries of the 1820's by Marcel de Serres, Christol, Tournal, and others in the caves of Southern France were widely quoted only to be questioned and repudiated.[6]

The most famous of these early discoverers of man's antiquity was Boucher de Perthes, who lived long enough to see the vindication of his views. Active in the Société d'Émulation of Abbeville at the mouth of the Somme, Boucher de Perthes became interested in the curious chipped flint implements, "*haches*,"

4. For the significance of Buckland's cave researches, which caused something of a sensation at the time of their publication, see *Edinburgh Review* (1828) and North (1942).

5. Kent's Hole or Cavern, at Torquay, is perhaps the most famous of the fossil-bearing caves in England and it had long been known and sporadically plundered (Pengelly: 1868). Moreover, it did supply evidence to support the view of man's contemporaneity with extinct fauna. MacEnery, the most persistent and careful of the early workers at Kent's Hole, did suggest such an association but was never able to commit himself fully to such a view in the face of Buckland's caution regarding the possibilities of excavation errors and/or later intrusions. His conclusions, therefore, as posthumously published by Vivian (MacEnery: 1859) and Pengelly (Pengelly: 1869) were equivocal and do not support the martyrdom granted him by his later admirers. For an interesting controversy over MacEnery's role, see Howorth (1901, 1902); Hunt (1902); and Watson (1902).

6. While the data were widely known, the interpretations followed the pattern established by Buckland in his *Reliqiae* (Buckland: 1824) of disassociating for one reason or another the human materials from the fossils with which they were associated. See, for example, *Edinburgh New Philosophical Journal* (1834), for a rebuttal of de Serres' claims for the antiquity of man in France.

which were found in the Somme gravels. These gave promise of proving the reality of an antediluvian human race of whose existence he had been convinced on logical grounds since 1838. "I have glimpsed," he wrote (Boucher de Perthes: 1857), "for a long time that antediluvian race and during all these years have anticipated the joy which I would feel when in these terraces which geology has so often declared to be barren and anterior to man, I would finally find the proof of the existence of that man, or in default of his bones, a trace of his works." From his first discoveries in 1840, Boucher de Perthes pressed his inquiries and his hypothesis with a good-natured tenacity that resisted the defamation and ridicule of his Parisian colleagues. His extensively illustrated *Antiquités Celtiques et Diluviennes*, although covering the whole range of French prehistory, included the first extensive supports for the existence of man as a contemporary of the extinct fauna whose remains were being discovered with an almost monotonous regularity in both the open gravel terraces and in the stalagmite-covered cave earths. Although he was convinced of the validity of his position by concepts which were even then outmoded, the persistence of his advocacy and his own longevity served to cast him in the role of the prophet of man's prehistory.[7]

Properly interpreted, these accululating data, by thrusting man back into a paleontological past, would have gone far to demolish the carefully raised structure that was British geology in the second quarter of the nineteenth century.

In the excitement following the later documentation of man's antiquity and, I suspect, as a by-product of the attempt to maintain the developing reputation for objectivity and impersonality in science, there was a tendency to regard these earlier discoveries as so obscure as to have gone unnoticed by those who might have interpreted them correctly. This was not the case.

Still a young man with his *Principles of Geology* only recently published, Lyell had visited the Belgian caves in which Schmerling was breaking both his body and heart; but, puzzled himself over the evidences, he could only sympathize with the difficulty of the problem. To Gideon Mantell, he wrote (Lyell: 1881, Vol. I, pp. 401–402) in 1833: "I saw . . . at Liege the collection of Dr. Schmerling, who in *three years* has, by his own exertions . . . cleared out some twenty caves untouched by any previous searcher, and has filled a truly splendid museum. He numbers already thrice the number of fossil cavern mammalia known when Buckland wrote his 'Idola specus'; . . . But envy him not—you

7. As is the case with MacEnery, subsequent events and commentators tended to distort the actual relationship of Boucher de Perthes' work to the times. There can be no doubt as to the value of the tenacity with which he pressed the claims to antiquity of his implements and of the men who made them. His conclusions as well as the discoveries upon which they were based were closely related to his own wide-ranging antiquarian interests, the work of the French cave-explorers of the 1820's and 1830's, and the diluvial concepts which they tended to support (see Aufrere: 1936, 1940; Meunier: 1875).

can imagine what he feels at being far from a metropolis which can afford him sympathy; and having not one congenial soul at Liege, and none who take any interest in his discoveries save the priests—and what kind *they* take you may guess more especially *as he has found human remains in breccia, embedded with extinct species, under circumstances far more difficult to get over than I have previously heard of* . . ." (italics mine). The evidences from Kent's Hole were common knowledge as were the discoveries from the French caves and the interpretations placed upon them by their discoverers.

Nor did the discoveries from the Somme Valley (Boucher de Perthes: 1847, 1857) go unnoticed or unchampioned. Boucher de Perthes engaged in an extensive correspondence with geologists and antiquarians throughout Europe; and he took every available opportunity to send copies of his *Antiquités Celtiques et Antediluviennes* to any one to whom it might have the slightest interest.[8] Darwin wrote to Lyell (F. Darwin: 1887, Vol. 3, p. 15) in 1863 that he "had looked at his [Boucher de Perthes'] book many years ago, and am ashamed to think that I concluded the whole was rubbish!" Boucher de Perthes had sent the British Archaeological Association "a quantity of Celtic antiquities in flint discovered by him in the environs of Abbeville . . . some of which he assigns to an antediluvian date." The Association was to have discussed these discoveries, but apparently never did (*Literary Gazette:* 1849). Roach-Smith, a remarkable English archaeologist and one of the more ardent of Boucher de Perthes' supporters in England wrote to him on April 11, 1850 (*Boucher de Perthes Correspondence*) that "Dr. Gideon Mantell, one of our first geologists, sent to me yesterday to borrow your *Antiquités Celtiques* to lecture on or refer to in one of his lectures"; and on November 26, 1851, he wrote "I expect from Dr. Hume of Liverpool a copy of his paper in which he comments favourably on your '*Antiquités Celtiques*'. . . . Dr. Hume has asked me if I thought you would like to be a member of the Lancashire and Cheshire Historical Society. I have written in the affirmative" (*ibid.*).[9] And another English archaeologist, James Yates wrote on February 12, 1850 (*ibid.*) that "I have not seen the

8. Thus a letter dated December 9, 1857, from Robert Fitch to Ackerman, the secretary of the Society of Antiquaries (*Society of Antiquaries Correspondence*): "I have received a letter from my friend Mr. C. Roach Smith, informing me that M. Boucher de Perthes, was about sending some copies of two antiquarian works to your care, one of which he had kindly presented to the Norfolk & Norwich Archaeological Society . . ."

9. A note from Roach-Smith, dated January 31, 1852, says (*Ibid.*) "The people of Liverpool will elect you into their Society." A footnote in Boucher de Perthes (1857), suggests that Dr. A. Hume published in Liverpool in 1851 a memoir entitled *Stone Period* "where a part of the work of M. Boucher de Perthes 1847 was translated and his figures reproduced." The British Museum does not have a record of this publication nor have I been able to trace it elsewhere. The clustering of these events in the years immediately after 1849 and the inclusion of a slip in my volume of Boucher de Perthes (1847) which reads "Cet ouvrage, imprimé en 1847, n'a pu, en raison des circonstances, être publié qu'en 1849" indicate that despite the date of 1847 on the title page, this volume was not distributed until 1849; its publication date should therefore be the later date.

Dean of Westminster [Buckland] since I sent him your *Antiquités Celtiques.*" Thus, whatever attitudes particular individuals may have entertained with reference to the work of Boucher de Perthes, both man and his work were known and discussed in England. As was the case with Kent's Hole, however, it was the "amateurs" and the archaeologists who tended to support him and the "professionals" and geologists who opposed him.

It was not therefore that these important data were unknown or information concerning them poorly distributed. Rather they were too well known and their advocates too enthusiastic. Consequently all such evidences were examined with extremes of scientific caution and criticism and unnecessarily rejected as, at best, "not proven." The net effect of such caution, laudable as it may be in any abstract judgment of science as an activity, was that with the authority of Cuvier perpetuated by Buckland, it could be maintained that:

> The only evidence that has yet been collected upon this subject [the antiquity of man] is negative; but as far as this extends, no conclusion is more fully established than the important fact of the total absence of any vestiges of the human species throughout the entire series of geological formations. Had the case been otherwise, there would indeed have been great difficulty in reconciling the early and extended periods which have been assigned to the extinct races of animals with our received chronology. On the other hand, the fact of no human remains having as yet been found in conjunction with those of extinct animals, may be alleged in confirmation of the hypothesis that these animals lived and died before the creation of man (Buckland: 1837, Vol. I, p. 103).

Still later, the world of the 1850's, secure now in its traditional faith in revelation and in its new-found allegiance to science, could echo the heartfelt and poetic expression which Hugh Miller gave of the compatability between these two sources of truth:

> It may be safely stated . . . that that ancient record in which man is represented as the last born of creation, is opposed by no geological fact; and that if, according to Chalmers, 'the Mosaic writings do not fix the antiquity of the globe,' they at least *do* fix—making allowance, of course, for the varying estimates of the chronologer—'the antiquity of the human species.' The great column of being, with its base set in the sea, and inscribed, like some old triumphal pillar, with many a strange form—at once hieroglyphic and figure—bears, as the ornately sculptured capital, which imparts beauty and finish to the whole, reasoning, responsible man. There is surely a very wonderful harmony manifested in that nice sequence in which the invertebrates—the fishes, the reptiles, the birds, the marsupials, the placental mammals, and, last of all, man himself—are so exquisitely arranged[10] (Miller: 1857, pp. 132–133).

10. The chapter from which this portion is quoted was delivered as a lecture before the Edinburgh Philosophical Institution in 1853. Miller committed suicide on Christmas Eve, 1856.

Rising above the voices of those whose interests introduced a sometimes strident note into their advocacy of the new palliative was the clear and measured tone of Lyell's authority. Although no progressionist himself, he was firm in his view as he disposed one after another, of the claims for man's antiquity, that "we have every reason to infer that the human race is extremely modern, even when compared to the larger number of species now our contemporaries in this earth" (Lyell: 1855, p. 148). Such recency, stated with such authority and unanimity by those who constituted the professionals of the day, negated any possibility of the contemporaneity of man with any of those exciting forms which had been turning up in the cave deposits and in the gravels of the post-Pliocene and whose existence immediately antedated the last of the earth's great revolutions which sealed off, so to speak, the human epoch and its occupants from the organic events of the past.

Without reference to the scientific merits of the question or the evidences adduced for the support of its solution, this response to the problem of man's past—as well as to his relationship with the organic world as a whole—in a world that had quite suddenly become almost inconceivably old was man's last refuge in the search for his uniqueness and the best hope for the maintenance of his divinity.[11] The defenses constructed to protect his own dignity were sufficient to repel for half a century the occasional assaults of questionable associations of human implements with extinct mammalia; but they fell, at last and in some disorder, before the force of the unanticipated evidences from Brixham Cave.

The men immediately responsible for the discoveries at Brixham Cave, discoveries which were to initiate a revolution, were Hugh Falconer, trained in medicine but active as both botanist and paleontologist, William Pengelly, a provincial school teacher, and Joseph Prestwich, wine merchant. These men themselves are interesting symbols of the ferment which was altering the whole

11. It should be noted, that by the 1840's and 1850's comparative anatomy was making it increasingly difficult to draw clear-cut and unmistakable distinctions between species which had heretofore seemed to occupy discrete steps on the progressionist scale of being. It is highly possible that it was the threat of the elimination of clear-cut distinctions, particularly between man and the anthropoid apes which led Richard Owen (Owen: 1859) to stress man's uniqueness as the occupant of the mammalian subclass *Archencephala*. Because I am concerned here with the geological path which led to the recognition of man's antiquity, I do not refer to the interesting developments in comparative anatomy in particular and in zoology in general which tended to destroy the concept of man's biological separateness and uniqueness, a line of development which culminated in T. H. Huxley's *Essay on Man's Place in Nature* (1863) whose significance in the area of man's biological affinities matched that of Brixham Cave in the area of his temporal or paleontological relations. It must be realized, however, that the two paths were, for the most part, quite separate, converging only occasionally. Within the scientific milieu of the period, the problem of man's antiquity in a geological sense could be and was quite separate from that of man's zoological place in nature. It was the destruction of this kind of separatism—in the whole domain of natural history—that was one of the primary contributions of "Darwinism."

substance of nineteenth-century natural science.[12] Pengelly and Prestwich were both amateurs in the sense that, like most of their co-workers, they lacked formal training in science and were able to "geologize" only during those scant hours stolen from their more mundane pursuits.[13] They formed part of that large and enthusiastic body for whose works John Herschel (1830, pp. 15–16) had written the justification: "The highest degrees of worldly prosperity, are so far from being incompatible with them [scientific researches] that they supply additional advantages for their pursuits. . . . They may be enjoyed, too, in the intervals of the most active business; and the calm and dispassionate interest with which they fill the mind renders them a most delightful retreat from the agitations and dissensions of the world, and from the conflict of passions, prejudices, and interests in which the man of business finds himself continually involved." Their heroes were, during these maturing decades of natural science, the leaders of geology—the Lyells, the Murchisons, the Owens, and the Bucklands—whose extensive publications and commanding positions provided them with the authority of intellectual command. Although Pengelly and Prestwich were exceptional in their command of the field, there were many of their kind whose primarily descriptive articles fill the geological journals of the period. These were initially collectors and observers whose more limited contributions provided the factual bases for the broader syntheses of their leaders. Diffident and often practical, they were in tune with their times; and in their caution they were often led to a conservatism which maintained theoretical views whose fashion had faded under the weight of new evidences and of the theories to which they gave rise.[14] When they did speculate, it was often on the basis of insufficient or provincially circumscribed data or upon general assumptions no longer valid.

Falconer was, however, another sort. Like many of the period, he had been led to a career in natural science through the comparative anatomy of a medical background and through the scientific spirit still perceptible at the Edinburgh University where he had trained. He was one of the new men of nineteenth-century natural science for whom observation was more important than theorizing but who saw in a revived empiricism a virgin field for the

12. All three men have been memorialized in a fashion. Both Prestwich and Pengelly are the subjects of the typical nineteenth-century biographical memoir: Pengelly's by his daughter (H. Pengelly: 1897) and Prestwich's by his wife (Prestwich: 1899). Both are long tributes which conceal more than they inform. Falconer's biographical legacy, unfortunately for so interesting a figure in the history of nineteenth-century science, is a collection of his works, most of them previously unpublished, prefaced by a brief biographical notice, a respectful and judicious treatment which adds little to the knowledge of the man (Falconer: 1868).

13. In 1874, however, Prestwich, at 62, was appointed Professor of Geology at Oxford; but this was little more than an honorary post.

14. Thus, Boucher de Perthes, often regarded as a pioneer in if not the founder of prehistoric studies, interpreted his evidences from the Somme gravels within a diluvial theory which had been completely rejected—and on sufficient grounds—by the "professional" geologists of his time.

collection of the data which would eventually disclose the secrets of nature. He was more a romantic than a rationalist and he approached his work more often with the zeal of the former than the cold logic of the latter. Each new discovery moved him with an excitement to pass on so that he was never able to complete the work he continuously projected for himself.

The literature of Brixham Cave is relatively scant. Death, timidity and delay so postponed the publication of the results of the year-long excavation that by the time the final report at last appeared (Prestwich: 1873), this parent of prehistory had already been devoured, both in interest and in importance, by its more spectacular offspring. Nevertheless the public bickerings over priority of discovery and Pengelly's invaluable manuscript journal of the excavations[15] make it possible to reconstruct the short history during which man's antiquity was for the first time substantiated beyond serious doubt or question through the unlooked for discovery of a few flint implements in direct and indisputable association with the bones of the great extinct mammalia of the Pleistocene.

Like most significant clues to man's past, the cavern on Windmill Hill, at Brixham, overlooking Torquay in South Devon, England, was discovered accidentally. And, significantly for the history of archaeology, it was explored by *geologists* with a view toward the solution of certain *geological* problems. There is no evidence from the contemporary documents that its significance for the "man question" was at all anticipated. As Falconer pointed out, in his request for support from the Geological Society of London, scientific interest in cavern researches had virtually disappeared since the excitement which followed Buckland's publication of his *Reliquiae Diluvianae*. So thorough and so comprehensive had been Buckland's researches and so conclusive and authoritative his conclusions that it seemed nothing more could be added beyond what was contained in that scientific *tour de force*. The results of Buckland's influence were that all caves were

> popularly regarded as containing the debris of the same mammalian fauna, and as having been overlaid with their ochreous loam by the same common agency

15. Now in the possession of the Museum of the Torquay Natural History Society, to whose generosity I am indebted for making the manuscript available through its secretary Mr. Wilfrid T. Wiatt. It is impossible to say when this "journal" was written. It is in Pengelly's handwriting and fills thirteen composition books, of which the second is missing. On the basis of internal evidence, I do not think that it represents a running account written during the actual operations nor is it a series of field notes. Rather, it appears to be the occasional collection and, perhaps abstraction of field journal notes and the letters relating to the excavations combined into one connected narrative. While some of the parts appear to have been written while the researches were in progress, the whole seems to have been completed several months after the conclusion of the excavations. Part of the inspiration for the journal was undoubtedly the already developing, in 1860, conflicts over priority of discovery; and, in part, Pengelly hoped to use this edited version of his notes as the basis for his final report to the Royal Society of London.

> at the same period. The contents of the different caverns were thus considered as being in a great measure duplicates of one another, and the exceptional presence of certain forms in one case, and their absence in another, were regarded more in the light of local accidents than as significant for any general source of difference. Hence it followed that more attention was paid to the extrication of the bones, and to securing good specimens, than to a record of their relative association and the order of succession in which they occurred. The remains have been, in some instances, huddled together in provincial collections—the contents of five or six distinct caves, without a discriminative mark to indicate out of which particular cavern they came. Another consequence has been, that being regarded in the light of duplicates, the contents of some of the most important and classical English caverns have been dispersed piecemeal; and so far as regards them the evil is beyond remedy (Falconer: 1868, Vol. II, pp. 487-488).

During the 1850's, however, with the increasing anatomical discrimination of the expanded number of mammalian species and with the developing awareness of the subtle differences which separated organic types both in time and space, Falconer had become interested in the construction of the temporal and geographical distribution patterns of the cave fauna which might fill in the details of the late, little known and generally neglected period of earth history whose deposits overlay the Pliocene strata; and he felt that controlled investigations of undisturbed cave deposits gave the best promise, through cross-correlation and stratigraphic analysis, for a more comprehensive understanding of the Glacial Age and its faunal variations.

In the course of reconnaissance of the limestone caves in the west of England during the spring of 1858, Falconer stopped off at Torquay, famous for its sporadically plundered Kent's Hole. He had probably been induced to make the detour through a notice in the *Western Times* of April 10 regarding the discovery of Brixham Cave.

The cave itself had been opened, during quarrying operations, by its proprietor, John Philp, on January 15, 1858; and, a short time later, it had been called to the attention of William Pengelly of Torquay, a part-time geologist, and moving force of the Torquay Natural History Society. Pengelly visited the cave as soon as possible, saw some of the fossil material which Philp had hastily dug up for commercial exploitation, noted (Pengelly: 1860, Vol. 1, p. 6) particularly "at 75 feet from the entrance . . . [a] fine antler of some kind of deer lying *on* the stalagmite, attached to, but not imbedded in it"; and immediately discovered (*ibid.*, Vol. 1, p. 7) that the proprietor was "not disinclined to dispose of the Cavern or rather the right of working it to any person prepared to pay him well for it."

Excited at the possibilities of securing specimens for the Torquay Museum, Pengelly, on March 29, called a meeting of a Committee of the Society, the result of which were instructions that a local cave committee should "make such arrangements as they may think desirable for securing specimens for the Museum from the recently discovered Bone Cavern at Brixham (*Ibid.*, Vol. 1, p. 8). Insofar as Pengelly was concerned, the cave was to be one more source of specimens. Philp, it was found, demanded a rental of one hundred pounds, an exorbitant price and far beyond the means of either the Museum or the society which supported it.

It was just at this point that Falconer dropped in, in the midst of his own excitement over the cave researches that had occupied him almost exclusively for five years. After visiting the cave, Falconer met with Pengelly to discuss possibilities. "We were unanimous," Pengelly noted (*ibid.*, Vol. 1, p. 10) in his journal "as to the probability that the cavern was likely to be of importance and also that it was not to be left in Philp's hand, as we had some reason to doubt his veracity. In fact, we had, separately, detected in his glass case, skulls, etc. of animals probably not dead a week, certainly not dead a long time; but which he at first affirmed were found by him in his cavern; subsequently . . . he confessed that they were forgeries, and that he had smeared them with cave earth to give them the requisite colour."

While Pengelly continued to hope that some means might be found to secure the scientific and controlled excavation of this virgin cavern, Falconer had himself been active. Upon his return to London, he addressed a fervent letter to the Council of the Geological Society of London requesting that some means be found to insure the excavation. By the middle of May, the Geological Society had appointed a top-level Brixham Cave Committee, consisting of Sir Charles Lyell, Richard Owen, Joseph Prestwich, A. C. Ramsay, Pengelly, and Falconer; and had obtained a grant of one hundred pounds from the Royal Society. A friend of Pengelly's contributed another fifty pounds. For the next two months, there were lengthy negotiations to secure the lease, to hire the laborer and collector[16] who would do the actual excavation, and to establish the mode of procedures as well as the relations which were to exist between the controlling committee in London and the local enthusiasts at Torquay.

As is not unusual in such situations even today, the local amateurs, excited by the possibility of specimens for local collections fought for the rights of local interests and suggested excavation methods which would most readily and speedily produce the largest number of such specimens without regard to the problems of spatial and temporal relationships whose solution was uppermost in the minds of the members of the London Committee. Pengelly and Falconer were agreed that in order to solve the geological problems involved, the utmost care would have to be exercised in the excavations. "The plan of operations laid down," went the minutes of an early meeting of the London

16. Henry Keeping who had done a considerable amount of fossil hunting, especially on the Isle of Wight, was hired to do the actual excavation under Pengelly's almost daily supervision and instruction.

Committee (*ibid.*, Vol. 5, p. 4) "was to break up the stalagmite floor throughout, and explore the first bed beneath it leaving any inferior beds for subsequent examination;—in this manner the exact extent of the cavern would be ascertained, and the true succession of the beds and the precise position and association of the organic remains would be clearly determined."[17] Thus each bed or stratum would be excavated separately so that there could be no confusion with respect to the actual location of any fossil nor could there be any occasion for the common accusation of the accidental intermingling of specimens through careless cuts through the strata. While the disagreements between the local collectors and the "scientists" in London with respect to this technique were never satisfactorily resolved, it was the latter who were dominant; and despite a developing bitterness among the members of the local committee, the excavations proceeded along the path originally charted.

Fortunately, if accidentally, the excavations were initiated at the original entrance of the cave; consequently, as the overlying stalagmitic covering was taken off, a rich bone bed was exposed below. Each succeeding day of the excavations was excitingly productive so that after a month's work over 1500 bones had been removed.

Within two weeks of the start of operations, the first flint implement was found in the midst of the fossils of the cave earth which underlay the seal of stalagmite. At the end of July, Pengelly noted (*ibid.*, Vol. 4, p. 2): "Bones have been found every day since my last entry. A flint implement was found today about 74 feet from the entrance, just under the spot where the antler lay. It was about 9 inches deep in the 3rd (i.e., bone) bed, and the bed was covered with a cake of stalagmite 3 inches thick. A flint (probably) implement had been found near the same place on the previous day but was not so well formed as that just mentioned." This initial discovery of human implements was followed by other such finds until by the close of the excavations a year later, thirty-six pieces of flint "all more or less white and having a porcellaneous aspect, and, at least some of which are believed to be *human implements*, were met with in various parts of the cavern" (Pengelly: 1874, p. 828). The stratigraphic situation of these implements was such as to leave no doubt that whatever the origin of the contents of the cave, these implements of human manufacture were at least as old as the mammalian remains. And there could be no doubt about the latter. The bone bed in which the flints were found contained the remains of the tichorine rhinoceros, cave bear, and cave hyena. Most significantly, however, both bones and implements lay together, under and sealed off by stalagmite

17. It was this technique, so productively utilized at Brixham, which formed the pattern for the later, more highly publicized and better financed but less significant excavations conducted by Pengelly from 1864 to 1880 at Kent's Cavern (Pengelly: 1884). And it was these latter which a half century later provided the model and impetus for the early controlled archaeology in the United States (Woodbury: 1960).

on the surface of which was imbedded "a fine horn of rein-deer nearly perfect, from the basal 'bur' to the terminal branches of the beam," a discovery which indicated to Falconer that the "Rein-deer continued to be an inhabitant of Britain after the appearance of man in the island." (Pengelly: 1860, Vol. 8, p. 6).

The significance of these discoveries was quickly recognized; and, in Falconer's mind at least, took precedence over the paleontological questions whose hoped for solutions had provided the initial motivation for Brixham's excavation. The discovery of human implements intensified both questions of methodology and interpretation. Falconer wrote (*ibid.*, Vol. 4, p. 11) Pengelly on August 18: "Lyell has written me from Germany that he had shown to him at Maestricht, 'a fossil human skeleton *imbedded in the matrix* dug out of the Loess and that it was stated to resemble the type found by Schmerling at Liege.' We must therefore conduct our Brixham exploration in a careful and guarded manner, keeping an accurate record of the succession of the remains and their association." And upon Pengelly's request that he be permitted to read a paper on the Cave at the up-coming meetings of the British Association in September, 1858 the London Committee "Resolved, that Mr. Pengelly's application . . . be sanctioned; but that in the present early stage of the investigation it is not considered expedient to enter into any discussion or account of the organic or other remains that have been met with" (*ibid.*, Vol. 5, p. 5).

Pengelly's paper which, at his request, appeared only by title in the published proceedings of the Association was cautiously descriptive; but he could not resist the temptation of mentioning the flint implements in order to stress the importance of the excavation. He concluded:

> I cannot take leave of this subject without asking shall the explorations which have been carried on with more than encouraging results be continued or abandoned? Is the Cavern to be fully and systematically investigated, or as in too many cases, partially only? Shall we succeed in exhuming nearly 2,000 bones in about nine weeks, discover previously unsuspected galleries and chambers, disclose new beds of unknown depth, find human industrial remains with the bones of extinct animals, catch a ray of light on this question and that sufficient to stimulate but not to satisfy and prematurely abandon the work? This question resolves itself into one of Ways and Means only. There is the work to be done and there are the men able and willing to do it; but though the Committee are desirous of acknowledging both the public and private liberality which has enabled them to do so much, and though they are most anxious to observe all economy, they cannot conceal from themselves the fact that a very few weeks will exhaust the means now at their disposal (Pengelly: 1860, Vol. 8, pp. 19–20).

While Pengelly could but allude indirectly to the human material, the Committee's own "Report of Progress in Brixham Cave," read to the same meeting immediately afterward was much more direct. Prepared by Falconer, signed by him, Pengelly, and Ramsay, and made public over the protests of the more cautious Prestwich, the Report concluded (Pengelly: 1860, Vol. 8, p. 6; Falconer: 1868, Vol. II, pp. 495–496) with a section entitled "*Human? Industrial? Remains*." Despite the inclusion of the question marks, the text leaves little doubt as to the author's certainty:

> Several well marked specimens of the objects called 'Flint Knives,' and generally accepted at the present day as the early product of Keltic or pre-Keltic industry, have been exhumed from different parts of the cavern, mixed in the ocherous earth with remains of *Rhinoceros*, *Hyaena*, and other extinct forms. One of these so-called 'Flint Knives' was brought up from the deposit No. 2 from a depth of 30 inches below the superficial stalagmite No. 1. We failed in detecting evidence that these so-called flint knives were of different age as regards the period of their introduction from the bones of the extinct animals occurring in the same stratum of cave earth, or that they were introduced into the cavern by different agencies.

Referring to similar discoveries already known from the Continent and the rejection of these evidences because of alleged faulty excavation techniques, the Report further notes that:

> The attention of Mr. Pengelly has been closely directed to a careful and minute observation of the circumstances of the association in Brixham Cavern. The results of the exploration of each day are carefully put aside and labelled; and it may be anticipated that data will be arrived at for settling the disputed question of the contemporaneous introduction, or otherwise, of the supposed human industrial objects into the cavern along with the remains of the extinct mammalia.

Both reports were received by the crowded meeting with excitement, enthusiasm, and some feeling of incredulity. To his wife, Pengelly wrote (H. Pengelly: 1897, p. 80) from the meetings: "I have read my paper [on Brixham Cave] to a crowded house, all the great geologists came in apparently. Owen followed in very eulogistic strains, characterizing exploration of the Cavern, as the only satisfactory and good attempt of the kind that ever had been made. I was very much complimented at the close by sundry persons . . ." There is no evidence, however, that Richard Owen, whose authoritative anatomical investigations for over a generation had corroborated the geological proofs of man's recent creation, was convinced by the Brixham data. Although a gracious endorsement of Pengelly's excavations, his comments were designed to stress the fact that "no discoveries had been made up to this time calculated to show that man is of higher antiquity than has commonly been supposed" (Pengelly: 1860, Vol. 8, p. 9). Whatever the opinion of the various spokesmen, however, for the first time in at least a decade, serious discussion was now entertained—

both among professional geologists and in the popular scientific press—on the subject of man's antiquity.[18]

With a continuing grant from the Royal Society, completion of the Brixham excavation could now be expected, and it was the sense of the Committee that no final interpretive report should be published until the work had been done. But although further implements and bones were discovered in diminished frequencies, none equaled in importance those of the first six weeks, which for the less skeptical at least, had gone so far to establish beyond reasonable doubt the fact of man's contemporaneity with the extinct fauna of the Glacial Period and thus, by presumption, his high antiquity.

Following the Leeds meeting of the British Association, Falconer prepared to leave England for the winter—both for reasons of health and in order to examine at firsthand the cave collections in the south of France and some newly discovered fossiliferous caverns in Sicily. In the few weeks prior to his departure, he was almost completely occupied with the Brixham "flint implements"—comparing them with artifacts in the British Museum, arguing for their authenticity against the "hard sceptics" on his Committee, and, in one case, joining two fragments together to form a relatively complete tool. This preoccupation is evident in a letter to Pengelly, written a week before his departure:

> You will see that the matter of the association of the 'Flint Knives' *under* the Reindeer's antlers, and mixed in the same cave ochre with teeth of extinct animals is now assuming an aspect of grave and serious importance. A part of the case has been adduced before, but the conditions had been so carelessly observed that suspicion was very properly cast on the accuracy of the observations, and the results were considered worthless either as proof of the antiquity or reverse. In the case of our cavern, we had taken the stand that the phenomena would be observed and recorded with a severe fidelity which would place them above suspicion. Trust not, I intreat of you, to Keeping. He is, I have no doubt, a good worthy man of honest intentions, but he is liable like us all to error, and a check ought to be held over him. Tell him, with my love, that if he makes any more

18. See for instance the report of the meeting in the newly established *Geologist* for December, 1858 (**1**, 538):

> The communications of Mr. W. P. Pengelly and Professor Ramsay, on the ossiferous cavern at Brixham in Devonshire, gave an indication of what we may expect when the details of the cave shall be fully worked out. . . .
> In the paper read by Mr. Pengelly . . . it was stated that upwards of 2000 mammalian bones had already been exhumed, amongst which were mingled flint knives and other objects, evidently the work of a primitive race of men.
> M. Boucher de Perthes, of Abbeville, the well-known French antiquary, several years ago pointed out the existence of flint weapons and other such artificial objects in the gravel drifts around that town, and with admirable perseverance that gentleman has accumulated, from various and distant localities, a magnificent suite of these objects. . . .
> For many years past, too, we have had accounts of human remains, from gravel and other deposits, which have been too commonly regarded as apocryphal or as the result of a careless commingling of the contents of proximate strata of very different ages. . . .

> mistakes about the exact position of the Flint Knives, etc., he will be handed down with execrations to the remotest posterity. If this does not touch him, he must have the feelings of a rhinoceros. . . . If not making too great a demand on your valuable time I would suggest that you went over the details of position of every one of the flint knives in such a way that we could give an affidavit to them . . . (*ibid.*, Vol. 9, p. 6).

And in order to emphasize the importance of the exact location of the flints whose authenticity and uniqueness had been affirmed by the authorities of the British Museum, Falconer wrote again a few days later (*ibid.*, Vol. 10, p. 2) that "incredulity is rife about the position of the 'Flint Knives' and every damaging hypothesis that can be thought of will be launched against them," not the least of which was that of forgery. The "incredulity" was occasioned as much by the reluctance of some to recognize man's antiquity as it was by the fact that there were also those who saw in the evidences from Brixham Cave the substantiation of the long-discredited Noachian Flood.[19]

It was with a mind full of the flint knives that Falconer left for the Continent. Remembering an earlier meeting with Boucher de Perthes whose figures in the *Antiquités Celtiques et Diluviennes* he had used to identify the Brixham specimens (Falconer: 1868, Vol. II, p. 593), Falconer decided to break his trip at Abbeville. "Next Saturday," he wrote (*Boucher de Perthes Correspondence*) "I shall be en route to Paris when I shall stop at Abbeville for two hours in the hope that I shall find you there. During the past three months we have found in English ossiferous caves some flint knives probably of very high antiquity."

As always Boucher de Perthes was gracious to his guest; and Falconer, in turn, was tremendously impressed with the mass of materials which the Somme gravels had yielded. After leaving Abbeville, he wrote (Pengelly: 1860, Vol. 11, pp. 6–7) to Pengelly from Avignon: "You remember the book on Celtic Antiquities (Flint knives, etc.) which I took down with me to Torquay. I made a journey to Abbeville purposely to see Mons'r Boucher de Perthes' collection. He showed me very rude flint knives which had been dug up by his own hands mingled in gravel with molars, which I saw, of the Mammoth. I got evidence of the same kind from Professor Jourdain of Lyons. I am now within a few hours distance of the famous caves of Limel-viel near Montpellier, which I shall visit in a couple of days." Earlier, while still at Abbeville and in the flush of excitement which Boucher de Perthes had aroused, he wrote to Prestwich, who was still not fully convinced, still "hesitating" to accept

19. Interestingly enough, the "liberal" position, held by the majority of "professionals" was based upon the rejection of the flood as a geological agent, an hypothesis which had already been abandoned for a generation, and the acceptance of the progressionist system which regarded man as the terminal creation. The "conservatives," still following Buckland's original thesis from which he had been converted in the late 1830's, maintained the diluvial hypothesis; and they saw in the evidences from Brixham Cave both the proofs of the existence of antediluvial man and the deluge which had destroyed him. See, for example, Vivian (1858).

Falconer's conclusions without additional "unmistakable corroboration" (Prestwich: 1899, p. 117). "As the weather continued fine," Falconer wrote:

> I determined on coming here to see Boucher de Perthes' collection. I advised him of my intention from London, and my note luckily found him in the neighborhood. He good-naturedly came in to receive me, and I have been richly rewarded. His collection of wrought flint implements and of the objects of every description associated with them far exceeds anything I expected to have seen, especially from a single locality. He had made great additions, since the publication of his first volume, in the second—which I have now by me. He showed me "flint" hatchets which *he had dug up with his own hands* mixed *indiscriminately* with the molars of *E. primigenius*. I examined and identified *plates* of the molars—and the flint objects, which were got along with them. Abbeville is an out-of-the-way place, very little visited, and the French *savants* who meet him in Paris laugh at Monsieur de Perthes and his researches. But after devoting the greater part of a day to his vast collection, I am perfectly satisfied that there is a great deal of fair presumptive evidence in favour of many of his speculations regarding the remote antiquity of these industrial objects, and their association with animals now extinct. . . . If, during next summer, you should happen to be paying a visit to France, let me strongly recommend you to come to Abbeville. . . . I am sure you would be richly rewarded. You are the only English geologist I know of who would go into the subject *con amore*. I am satisfied that English Geologists are much behind the indications of the materials now is existence relative to this walk of post-glacial geology, and you are the man to bring up the leeway. . . . What I have seen here gives me still greater impulse to persevere in our Brixham exploration (*ibid.*, pp. 119–120).

Stimulated by Falconer's enthusiasm, Prestwich arranged for a group of geologists to visit Abbeville during the Easter holiday of 1859. Of those invited, only John Evans, paper manufacturer, numismatist, and antiquary, came. Upon his return, he described the trip in his journal:

> . . . to Abbeville, where I found Prestwich waiting for me at the Station and very glad to see me. . . . We went straight to bed and soon after 7 the next morning M. Boucher de Perthes, the first discoverer of the stone axes we were in pursuit of, came to take us to some of the gravel pits from whence his collection had been derived. A. M. Marotte, the Curator of the Museum, accompanied us but we did not succeed in finding anything. We then adjourned to the house of M. de Perthes . . . with a wonderful collection of flint axes and implements found among the beds of gravel and evidently deposited at the same time with them—in fact the remains of a race of men who existed at the time when the deluge or whatever was the origin of these gravel beds took place. One of the most remarkable features of the case is that nearly all if not quite all of the animals whose bones are found in the same beds as the axes are extinct. There is the mammoth, the rhinoceros, the Urus—a tiger, etc. etc. . . . Of course our object was if possible to ascertain that these axes had been actually deposited with the gravel, and not

> subsequently introduced; and we had received intelligence from Amiens that in one of the gravelpits there an axe was to be seen in its original position, which made us set off at once. . . . We proceeded to the pit where sure enough the edge of an axe was visible in an entirely undisturbed bed of gravel and eleven feet from the surface. We had a photographer with us to take a view of it so as to corroborate our testimony . . . (Joan Evans: 1943, pp. 101–102).

At Abbeville and Amiens, Prestwich had "worked on the ground" as he had desired and his caution had been overcome by the "unmistakable corroboration" which he required. The trip to Abbeville, spurred on by his responsibility for Brixham and by the excitement of Falconer, marked his conversion. Upon their return from Abbeville, both Prestwich and Evans immediately began to prepare separate papers on their observations. Prestwich's paper read before the Royal Society on May 26, 1859 (Prestwich: 1859) dealt primarily with the geological features of the Somme Valley and the specific associations of the flint implements. Whatever general conclusions might be drawn, he affirmed, upon his position as the foremost student of the post-Pliocene deposits, that the implements were of human manufacture; that they were found in undisturbed ground; that they were associated with the remains of extinct mammalia; and that the deposits themselves were laid down in a late geological period but one anterior to the surface assuming its present outline.[20]

To the Society of Antiquaries a week later, Evans reported more specificially on the implements themselves and the archaeological implications of their discovery. After summarizing Prestwich's geological findings, he demonstrated the human workmanship of the implements and emphasized their distinctness from previously known objects of the so-called "Stone" period. On the basis of his typological separation, Evans hoped that his audience would "be prepared to receive with less distrust the evidence . . . that they are found under circumstances which show that, in all probability, the race of men who fashioned them must have passed away long before this portion of the earth was occupied by the primitive tribes by whom the more polished forms of stone weapons were fabricated, in what we have hitherto regarded as remote antiquity" (Evans: 1859, pp. 293–294). And after predicting that "before many years have elapsed . . . the existence of man upon the earth previously to the formation of these drift deposits will be regarded by all as a recognized fact," Evans concluded his paper with a positive summary designed to stress upon his archaeological colleagues the significance of the discoveries in the Somme gravels:

20. It is important to note here that Prestwich was not convinced of nor was he necessarily arguing for a high *chronological* antiquity of man. What struck him as significant and that to which he was testifying as a geologist was a stratigraphically earlier position of man than that generally recognized, i.e., the contemporaneity of man with an earlier—and conceivably separate—geological and palaeontological horizon.

> This much appears to be established beyond a doubt; that in a period of antiquity, remote beyond any of which we have hitherto found traces, this portion of the globe was peopled by man; and that mankind has here witnessed some of those geological changes by which these so-called diluvial beds were deposited. Whether they were the result of some violent rush of waters such as may have taken place when 'the fountains of the great deep were broken up, and the windows of heaven were opened,' or whether of a more gradual action, similar in character to some of those now in operation along the course of our brooks, streams, and rivers, may be a matter of dispute. Under any circumstances this great fact remains indisputable, that at Amiens land which is now one hundred and sixty feet above the sea, and ninety feet above the Somme, has since the existence of man been submerged under fresh water, and an aqueous deposit from twenty or thirty feet in thickness, a portion of which at all events must have subsided from tranquil water, has been formed upon it; and this too has taken place in a country the level of which is now stationary, and the face of which has been but little altered since the days when the Gauls and the Romans constructed their sepulchres in the soil overlying the drift which contains these relics of a far earlier race of man (*ibid.*, p. 306).

The addresses of Evans and Prestwich, directed to the two Societies most vitally concerned, resurrected in the most forceful fashion the question of man's antiquity. The significance of their conclusions was the greater not only because of the new evidence brought forward but even more because of the acknowledged conservatism and authority of both authors. Falconer's announcement (Falconer: 1859) immediately following, of corroborative evidence from the Sicilian caves only served to emphasize the weight of the evidence pressing man, however resistant, backward into time. In a letter to his wife, Pengelly suggests the growing excitement. "The last *Athenaeum* is worth looking at," he wrote (H. Pengelly: 1897, p. 87). "There is an interesting letter, by Wright the antiquary, on the papers by Prestwich and Evans on their Flint Implements in the drift. In the list of meetings for the ensuing week there is an 'Extraordinary Meeting of the Geological Society at 8 P.M. (yesterday)' to hear 'Further Observations on the Occurrence of Human Art in the Bone Breccia in the Caves near Palermo,' by Dr. Falconer, and 'Reports on the Exploration of the Cave at Brixham,' by Dr. Falconer, also 'On Flint Implements recently obtained from the Gravel near Amiens,' by Flower. Flints are to the fore . . ."

Almost immediately, the excitement infected the whole community of geologists and antiquaries, amateurs and professionals. From Canterbury, one of the members of the Society of Antiquaries wrote the secretary a month after Evans' paper (*Society of Antiquaries Correspondence*): "I feel so much interested by the controversy in respect to the stone axes, arrowheads, etc. found in the Drift, that I feel almost tempted to run up to town to inspect them, but as I fear I cannot leave home for a week or ten days could you inform me how long they will remain in the Library."

Two months later, Sir Charles Lyell—the most eminent geologist of the century and, for the public, the court of last appeal on such matters—having himself made the pilgrimage to Abbeville, announced (Lyell: 1859) his own conversion in his presidential address before a packed meeting of the Geological Section of the British Association for the Advancement of Science at Aberdeen. His address was, according to Pengelly, "a masterpiece of ability and frankness"; and it started Lyell on his three-year search for the materials which formed the substance of the last of his great contributions to science (Lyell: 1863). In Lyell's view, "the facts recently brought to light during the systematic investigation, as reported on by Falconer, of the Brixham Cave, must, I think, have prepared you to admit that scepticism in regard to the cave-evidence in favour of the antiquity of man had previously been pushed to an extreme" (Lyell: 1859, p. 93).

Lyell's address represents something of a watershed in the history of man's conception of his own past. There was still strong opposition at the Aberdeen meeting to the new idea of man's antiquity, but it was even there strongly opposed by the logic of the geological evidence. Pengelly described the reaction to his wife:

> Yesterday was a good day here; . . . The fourth paper was by Rev. Dr. Anderson . . . 'On Human Remains in the Superficial Drift,' in which he attacked all the evidence which has recently been produced of 'Man among the Mammoths,' and a very great deal which no one ever regarded as bearing on the question. After wading through a great amount of rubbish, he boldly attempted to castigate Lyell for his opening address; next he ridiculed Horner's argument of the pottery, etc. in the silt of the Nile . . . Then he ran off to Germany to cudgel Bunsen, then back again, pitched me into Brixham Cave, and did his best to bury the Cave and myself in ridicule, and finally he gave us a yard or two of bad pulpit. There was a considerable amount of orthodoxy in the room, and he got a very undue share of applause. And now *per contra*. Lyell handled him as a gentleman and a philosopher alone can do it. Next Phillips, having rubbed his hands in oil, smoothed him down, but in such a way as to scarify him; then Ramsay seized him by the button-hole, and informed him of a fact or two connected with caverns, and finally handed him over to me upon which I seized him by the collar, dragged him into Brixham Cave, and showed him its facts and their whereabouts. Then came Symonds and pulpited him . . . (H. Pengelly: 1897, p. 90).

The intellectual explosion which had dispersed this skepticism now expanded the corridor of man's past backward into geological time; and, perhaps more significantly, for the studies that were to follow, it made the study of this past a part of a geology which had become not only historical but also developmental.

All of these events occurred prior to the publication of Darwin's *Origin* and without reference to the thesis it expounded; in fact, the critical discoveries of Brixham occurred within so short a time of the first reading of the abstract that it is impossible to see any connection between the two events at all. What is surprising—if not disturbing—is the complete absence in any of Darwin's published correspondence of any reference to the Brixham discoveries which so clearly eased the last and most significant line marking the limits of putative separate creations. Whatever the effect on Darwin, however, the significance of Brixham could not have been lost on a knowing public, a public which had been nourished on the concept of a series of distinct and progressive creations with that of man the last and finest of the series. It was a concept which had had, until Brixham, the force of both logic and observation for its support. Cannon has recently shown (Cannon: 1960a) the sufficiency of the logic and of the evidence as both were marshaled in favor of the progressionism of the catastrophists by the dialectical skill of Whewell, the philosopher of the new science. So long as the discontinuity separating man as a culture-bearing animal from the earlier creations could be supported in the geological record, the defense of the successive creations could be successfully maintained both as a matter of logic and of science. The discoveries at Brixham and the care exercised in their documentation constituted, however, a crushing blow to the defense. With the merging of man's past into creations long gone, with the knowledge of glacial man and the optimistic promise of Tertiary man, evolution, once suggested, must include man. Into the intellectual vacuum made necessary by the demonstration of a continuity, progressionist perhaps, even through man's creation itself, Darwinian evolution was quick to move. For those who could read the evidence of Brixham, Darwin's evolution applied to man with a violence; and for those who still had to maintain man's dignity through the uniqueness of his divinity by virtue of the uniqueness of his creation, such application had to be rejected. With the evidence of man's newly established antiquity, it could be rejected only through a rejection of Darwinian evolution itself.

As an intellectual event, the work of Falconer, Prestwich, and Pengelly at Brixham Cave was rapidly absorbed in the more intensive ferment which accompanied the publication of the *Origin* and the more spectacular discoveries from the caves of France. So ignored, in fact, was the catalytic role of Brixham Cave in the rehabilitation of Boucher de Perthes and his predecessors, so intense the desire to do justice to that aged prophet of man's past, that Brixham Cave was virtually dropped from history.[21] The circumstances of its discovery

21. The French, understandably, have always seen Boucher de Perthes as the great pioneer; see Mortillet (1865, pp. 11–12); Breuil (1945); and Boule and Vallois (1957, p. 15) where, incidentally J. W. Flower, the archaeologist who did visit Boucher de Perthes is confused with J. H. Flower, the anatomist, who did not. However, the same pattern is evident in the English literature; see, for example, Peake (1940) and Brace (1868, p. 333), who, even at that early date, could write: "These discoveries of M. de Perthes at length aroused the attention of English men of science, and during 1859, a number of eminent gentlemen . . . visited M. Perthes' collection and saw the flints *in situ*." See also Joan Evans (1949).

and excavation demand, however, some re-creation, for the value of which Falconer himself provided the justification when, in writing of some other half-forgotten event in the history of science, he noted that:

> The same kind of retrospect which from time to time we cast on the material facts [of science], justice demands of us to apply also to the history of discovery in science. Facts which are now fused in the common mass may have exercised a powerful influence when first brought to light. The impartial historian will regard them in this light, and not merely as they now appear. He will also be scrupulously careful to award to the first observers fairly what is their due; for, apart from the abstract consideration of justice, the only guarantee which we have that our own labours shall be respected in the future is the fairness with which we ourselves deal with the labours of our contemporaries and of those who have gone before us (Falconer: 1868, Vol. I, p. 310).

The establishment of man's geological antiquity was, however, of even greater importance to the emergence of anthropology. I have stressed the role of geology and geologists in the establishment of man's antiquity because it was through that role that prehistory as a discipline—and I believe, by extension, the subsequent synthesis that was to become anthropology—achieved its methodology, its point of view and, most significantly at the time, its status as a science.[22] Even more, much as evolution provided the core around which the several separate biological disciplines were to relate themselves as *Biology*, so prehistory served as the focus at which the already specialized efforts of archaeologists, culture historians, human biologists, and ethnographers could be related as a redefined *Anthropology*. For the varied students of man, already specialized in both techniques and concepts, the ideological world of the mid-nineteenth century was already cramping; the breakthrough into the past provided them with both the opportunity and the materials to build a new science. It was this new dimension to man's existence which provided the stimulus and the meaning for the search for the fossil remains of the past as it did for ordering of the relics of the present.

22. See Daniel (1950, pp. 57–67) for a different view.

References

Agassiz, L.

1859: *An Essay in Classification* (London: Longman, Brown, Green, Longmans & Roberts). First published as an introduction to *Contributions to the Natural History of the United States* (1857).

Aufrere, L.

1936: *Essai sur les premieres découvertes de Boucher de Perthes et les origines de l'archaeologie primitive 1838–1844* (Paris: Staude).

1940: "Figures de préhistoriens: 1. Boucher de Perthes," *Préhistoire*, **7**, 7–134.

Boucher de Perthes, J.
1847, 1857, 1864: *Antiquités Celtiques et Diluviennes* (3 vols.) (Paris: Treuttel et Wurtz).

Boucher de Perthes Correspondence
Correspondence to Boucher de Perthes (MS 682, Bibliotheque Communal d'Abbeville).

Boule, M., & Vallois, H. V.
1957: *Fossil Men*, trans. by M. Bullock (New York: Dryden Press).

Brace, C. L.
1868: *A Manual of Ethnology; or The Races of the Old World* (2nd ed.; London: Murray).

Breuil, H.
1945: "The Discovery of the Antiquity of Man," *Journal of the Royal Anthropological Society of Great Britain and Ireland*, **75**, 21–32.

Buckland, W.
1822: "Account of an Assemblage of Fossil Teeth and Bones discovered in a cave at Kirkdale, Yorkshire, in the year 1821," *Philosophical Transactions of the Royal Society of London*, 171–236.
1824: *Reliquiae Diluvianae* (2nd ed.; London: Murray).
1837: *Geology and Mineralogy Considered with Reference to Natural Theology* (2 vols.) (2nd ed.; London: Pickering).

Cannon, W. F.
1960a: "The Uniformitarian-Catastrophist Debate," *Isis*, **51**, 38–55.
1960b: "The Problem of Miracles in the 1830's," *Victorian Studies*, **4**, 5–32.

Clark, G.
1957: *Archaeology and Society* (3rd ed.; Cambridge: Harvard University Press).

Cuvier, G.
1817: *Essay on the Theory of The Earth*, trans. by Robert Jameson (3rd ed.; Edinburgh: Blackwood).

Daniel, G.
1950: *A Hundred Years of Archaeology* (London: Duckworth).

Darwin, F. (ed.)
1887: *The Life and Letters of Charles Darwin* (3 vols.) (London: Murray).

Eiseley, L. C.
1958: *Darwin's Century* (New York: Doubleday).

Edinburgh New Philosophical Journal
1834: "Proofs that the Human Bones and works of art found in the Caves in the south of France are more recent than the antediluvian Bones in those Caves," **16**, 302–310.

Edinburgh Review
1823: "Geology of the Deluge," **39**, 196–234.

Evans, J.

1943: *Time and Chance: The Story of Arthur Evans and his Forebears* (London: Longmans).

1949: "Ninety Years Ago," *Antiquity*, **23,** 115–125.

Evans, J.

1859: "On the Occurrence of Flint Implements in Undisturbed Beds of Gravel, Sands, and Clay," *Archaeologia*, **38,** 280–307.

Falconer, H.

1859: "On the Ossiferous Grotta di Maccagnone, near Palermo," *Palaeontological Memoirs*, **2,** 543–563 (originally communicated to the Geological Society of London, May 4 & June 22, 1859).

1868: *Palaeontological Memoirs and Notes of the Late Hugh Falconer, A.M., M.D.*, compiled & ed. by Charles Murchison (2 vols.) (London: Hardwicke).

Frere, J.

1800: "Account of Flint Weapons discovered at Hoxne in Suffolk," *Archaeologia*, **13,** 204 205.

Geikie, J.

1881: *Prehistoric Europe* (London: Stanford).

Gillispie, C. C.

1951: *Genesis and Geology* (Cambridge: Harvard University Press).

Greene, J. C.

1959: *The Death of Adam* (Ames, Iowa: Iowa State University Press).

Herschel, J. F. W.

1830: *Preliminary Discourse on the Study of Natural Philosophy* (London: Longman, Rees, Orme, Brown & Green).

Howorth, H. H.

1901: "The Earliest Traces of Man," *Geological Magazine*, n.s., **8,** 337–344.

1902: "The Origin and Progress of the Modern Theory of the Antiquity of Man," *Geological Magazine*, n.s., **8,** 16–27.

Hunt, A. R.

1902: "On Kent's Cavern with Reference to Buckland and His Detractors," *Geological Magazine*, n.s., **9,** 114–118.

Literary Gazette

1849: "Notice of the Meeting of the British Archaeological Association," *The Literary Gazette and Journal of Belles Lettres, Arts, Sciences, etc.*, April 28 & May 5.

Lyell, C.

1855: *Principles of Geology; or the Modern Changes of the Earth and its Inhabitants* (9th ed.; London: J. Murray).

1859: "On the Occurrence of Works of Human Art in Post-Pliocene Deposits," *Report of the British Association for Advancement of Science*, **29,** 93–95.

1863: *The Geological Evidences of the Antiquity of Man* (London: J. Murray).

Lyell, K.
1881: *Life, Letters and Journals of Sir Charles Lyell, Bart.* (2 vols.) (London: Murray).

MacEnery, J.
1859: *Cavern Researches, Discoveries of Organic Remains and of British and Roman Reliques in the Caves of Kent's Hole, Anstis Cave, Chudleigh and Berry Head*, ed. from ms. notes by E. Vivian (London: Simkin, Marshall).

Mantell, G. A.
1844: *The Medals of Creation: or First Lessons in Geology and in the Study of Organic Remains* (2 vols.) (London: Bohn).

Mortillet, G. de
1865: *Matériaux pour L'Histoire Positive et Philosophique de L'Homme.* Première Année, Septembre 1864, à Août 1865 (Paris: Edouard Blot).

Meunier, V.
1875: *Les Ancêtres d'Adam: Histoire de L'Homme Fossile* (Paris: J. Rothschild).

Miller, H.
1841: *The Old Red Sandstone; or New Walks in an Old Field* (Edinburgh: Constable).
1857: *Testimony of the Rocks; or Geology in its Bearings on the Two Theologies, Natural and Revealed* (Boston: Gould and Lincoln).

North, F. J.
1942: "Paviland Cave, the 'Red Lady,' the Deluge, and William Buckland." *Annals of Science*, **5**, 91–128.

Owen, R.
1859: *On the Classification and Geographical Distribution of the Mammalia* (London: Parker).

Peake, H. J. E.
1940: "The Study of Prehistoric Times," *Journal of the Royal Anthropological Institute*, **70**, 103–146.

Pengelly, H.
1897: *A Memoir of William Pengelly of Torquay, F.R.S. Geologist* (London: Murray).

Pengelly, W.
1860: *Journal of the Excavations at Brixham Cave*, ms. (13 vols.) in possession of Torquay Natural History Society, Torquay, England.
1868: "The Literature of Kent's Cavern, Torquay, Prior to 1859," *Transactions of the Devonshire Association for the Advancement of Science, Literature, and Art*, **2**, 470–522.
1869: "The Literature of Kent's Cavern," Part 2, *Transactions of the Devonshire Association for the Advancement of Science, Literature, and Art*, **3**, 191–482.
1874: "The Cavern Discovered in 1858 in Windmill Hill, Brixham, South Devon," *Transactions of the Devonshire Association for the Advancement of Science, Literature, and Art*, **6**, 775–856.
1884: "The Literature of Kent's Cavern," Part 5, *Transactions of the Devonshire Association for the Advancement of Science, Literature, and Art*, **16**, 189–434.

Prestwich, G. A.
1899: *Life and Letters of Sir Joseph Prestwich* (Edinburgh: Blackwood).

Prestwich, J.
1859: "On the Occurrence of Flint Implements, Associated with the Remains of Animals of Extinct Species in Beds of a Late Geological Period in France, at Amiens and Abbeville, and in England at Hoxne" (abstract), *Proceedings of the Royal Society*, **10**, 50-59; *Philosophical Transactions of the Royal Society*, 1860-61, 277-318.
1873: "Report on the Exploration of Brixham Cave, conducted by a Committee of the Geological Society," *Philosophical Transactions of the Royal Society of London*, **163**, 471-572.

Schmerling, P. C.
1833-34: *Recherches sur les Ossemens Fossiles découverts dans les Cavernes de la Province de Liege* (2 vols.) (Liege: Collardin).

Society of Antiquaries Correspondence
In possession of Society of Antiquaries of London, Burlington House, London.

V(ivian), E.
1858: "The Brixham Cavern," *Torquay Register*, September 29.

Watson, J. A.
1902: "Dean Buckland and MacEnery," *Geological Magazine*, n.s., **9**, 85-86.

Woodbury, R. B.
1960: "Nels C. Nelson and Chronological Archaeology," *American Antiquity*, **25**, 400 401.

MELVILLE J. HERSKOVITS

A Genealogy of Ethnological Theory[1]

The purpose of this paper is to suggest a framework for detailed studies of the sequence of ideas that have marked the development of ethnology. Systematic analyses of the relations between successive theoretical positions that have marked the other anthropological subdisciplines are similarly needed—for physical anthropology, archaeology, or linguistics, to say nothing of the more recent specializations in social organization, ethnopsychology, economics, art, and music.

It is also desirable that a scheme of similar dimensions be drawn for anthropology in the large. A genealogy such as the one suggested here, concerned with a single subdiscipline, can only touch the central problems that all anthropologists face. These have to do with such features as the evolution of the hominid forms, the development of man's culture-building ability, the relation of biological endowment and behavior or, as it is conventionally phrased, of race and culture, the interaction between language and culture and,

1. A paper prepared for the Conference on the History of Anthropology, April 13–14, 1962, held at the Social Science Research Council, New York, N.Y.

on a broader plane, between physical type, language, and culture. All these questions have a long and continuing history. Theories about the ecological component in influencing or even determining the form and behavior of man, or which attempt to account for observed psychic similarities and differences, reflect only two of the many more questions which, involving a number of subdisciplines, have been studied since the early days of our science.

Some attempts along these broader lines may be noted. One of the earliest, that of Haddon (1934), was divided into three sections—"Human Biology," "Cultural Anthropology or Ethnology," and "Comparative Sociology." In the next edition, it should be noted, the study of prehistoric cultures and of linguistics is placed in the second section of the book, while the single chapter that makes up the final section is entitled "Sociology (including Religion)." Penniman's later attempt (1936) sought to integrate the several aspects of the discipline, but his book is seriously marred by errors of fact and by numerous omissions of significant developments. Most works are more restricted, tracing developments in an individual subdiscipline, or describing currents of anthropological theory within a given country; Lowie's study (1937) is an example of this. There have also been attempts to further a sense of continuity by publishing collections of papers which have influenced anthropological thought, such as those edited by de Laguna (1960) or by Mead and Bunzel (1960). These have presented principally the writings of American anthropologists. Nonanthropologists, the most recent of whom is Hays (1958), have also been attracted by the richness of the field. The measured appraisal of one such attempt by Hallowell (1962) makes further comment superfluous.

The genealogy of ethnological theory presented here is conceived along broad lines, and has to do only with the major positions taken in the development of the subdiscipline. Obviously, it has not been possible to escape the interplay of theory and method (cf. Herskovits: 1954, *passim*). Practically every theoretical position has been developed by the use of a particular kind of method. In some cases, indeed, methodological considerations have dominated the preoccupations of those who developed a given theory of culture. We may venture the guess that most anthropologists, if asked what ideas they associate with the German-Austrian culture-historical group, would name the principles of form and quantity as criteria of historical relationships. How large the methodological component was in the functionalist approach needs but mention. Indeed, in both these two positions, not only does method dominate, but the theoretical structure is relatively simple.

At this point it should be made explicit that, in indicating the relation between theory and method, there is no implication that ethnology is mostly method and has only a slight armament of theory. In the best scientific tradition, the two have in most cases developed concomitantly, and in this way have followed the inductions demanded by principles of scientific methodology.

There are no "unscientific" anthropologists who study culture without theoretical orientation. Even those who have devoted themselves most assiduously to ethnography mirror in their reports the theoretical frame that has ordered their data. The converse is equally true. There are few anthropologists whose commitment to the study of questions of cultural theory is so complete that they ignore all relevant facts. Indeed, our best theorists are all proved fieldworkers. Anthropologists who, in the past, have been exclusively concerned with theory and have had no experience with field research—"armchair anthropologists," as they were called—have characteristically developed strong psychological compensatory mechanisms.

A caution to be held in mind has to do with the concept of the "school." It is a word that comes easily to the tongue, and if used with understanding, it has a certain utility. Its use is admissible if we assume "school" to mean a group of scholars who, by and large, hold to a given general point of view, and who have come out of a single stream in their training. The principal danger in using the term arises from the temptation to think of such a group as monolithic. As a result, important nuances of theory—the fact that those who hold to a general position rarely agree in detail—tend to be disregarded. If we apply a well-recognized principle of cultural dynamics, we may say that in overlooking these nuances, we neglect the factor of variation which in anthropological theory, no less than in any other element in culture, has been a prime factor in inducing change.

Thus, for example, if we speak of the classical evolutionists as a "school," we overlook the significant differences between Spencer and Tylor, or the controversy between Morgan and McLennan. Certainly it is a misnomer to speak of a "Boas school." Students of Boas were in agreement on certain broad general areas of concept and method. But, to make the point, we need only think of how different were the interests of Sapir and Spier, the kinds of problems they studied and the reasons they studied them. In such a fundamental theoretical position as the meaning of the word "history" in anthropology, the difference between Boas and one of his own students, Kroeber, was large enough so that it could give rise to a controversy that became notable in anthropological history. The several varieties of functionalists, or the differences to be found in the writings of social structuralists, may further be mentioned.

It is important, too, that the identification of particular positions with anthropologists of different nationalities be minimal. In some cases this is unavoidable, as in the three major varieties of diffusion theory, where national identifications have crept into a common parlance that reflects a preponderance of adherents as derived from a given country. On occasion, there is self-identification, as where the group of those in Britain who currently concentrate on the study of social structure tend to refer to their position as that of "British social anthropologists." Yet most of their theory comes from the French sociologists, notably Durkheim, while their contributions have influenced the anthropologists in numerous countries outside Britain who have followed their lead in the study of social organization.

There is, however, one aspect of anthropological history where the factor of nationality does enter. This has to do with area commitment, which became important with the development of the tradition of field research. Perhaps following lines of least resistance, nationals of a given country have tended to study in areas that are a part of that country, or governed by it. Although the International Americanist Congress was founded by European anthropologists, and the tradition of Americanist research continues to be important on the continent of Europe, most anthropologists in the Americanist fields are nationals of the countries of North and South America. For all the development of anthropology in the United States, it was a long time before any appreciable proportion of anthropologists here were concerned to study Asian, or South Seas, or African cultures. Almost none of the anthropologists in India study American Indians. The matter goes further, so that in Africa, French anthropologists conducted their research primarily in French African territories, the Belgians studied Congo peoples, the British those in British possessions, the Portuguese in Guinea, Mozambique, and Angola; and work by anthropologists of these European countries continued to be concentrated in these areas after decolonization.

Closely allied to the "school" concept is that of the "master," its founder and leader, held to be the source of its ideas, whose writings have predominated in developing its position. Here again we must take care if we are to attain a balanced historical perspective. As in any science, there have been outstanding practitioners who have deeply influenced the development of our discipline by their writings, their teachings, and the writings of their students. In some cases, personalities must figure prominently because of the identifications that were in fact established between a man and a position. It is not possible to discuss the heliolithic diffusionist point of view without realizing the almost unique role played by Elliot Smith in devising, developing, and dominating it. On the other hand, it would be extremely difficult to give any single anthropologist an analogous position in discussing psychoethnography. Yet even where one man was dominant in advancing a given position, and has caused his name to be identified with a particular concept or approach, the fact of deviation from his position by those who accepted it in principle cannot ever be overlooked. It is out of such deviations that advances in our discipline have most frequently come.

The genealogy presented here concerns the history of ethnology only since anthropology became a self-conscious science. This implies that anthropology has an intellectual prehistory. As in the case of the development of human culture in general, anthropological prehistory spans a far greater period of time than its history. It is of the utmost importance that this earlier period be thoroughly studied, for otherwise we will be unable to understand how and why anthropology, as a named discipline, with designated aims and specified methodology, came into being. We must search the reports of travelers from the earliest times to find the factual data they yield, and to determine the ideas that influenced their presentation of facts. It is an exercise in scientific humility and historic enlightenment to find that certain questions, currently phrased as to whether anthropology is science or history, were framed as long ago as the fourteenth century (cf. Mahdi: 1957).

Granting the importance of knowledge of forerunners, however, we must recognize that anthropological history, in the strict sense of the term, is not its prehistory. Hence it is at the point where it became a recognized discipline, with all the paraphernalia of explicit theory and method the word implies, that our diagram takes its departure (see Fig. 1). In other words, we are concerned with the history of ethnology from about the middle of the nineteenth century.

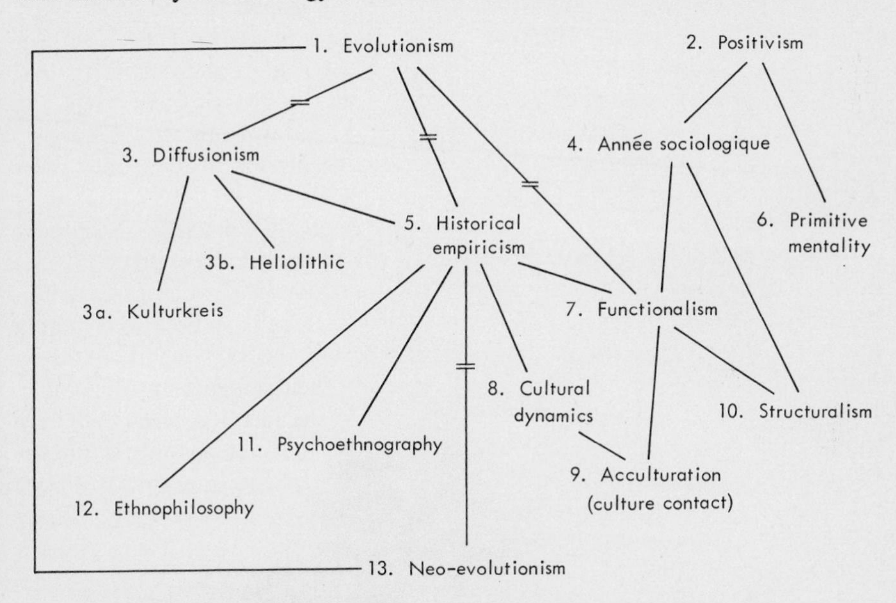

Figure 1.—The development of ethnological theory

The great contribution of the evolutionists was to bring order to the data by reducing to systematic treatment the hodgepodge of facts in the accounts of travelers, missionaries, administrators, and others. If we take the three outstanding exponents of evolutionism, we find their method differed considerably. Morgan, to a degree never before known, drew his theories from field data, either his own, or the observations which others on the spot obtained at his request. Spencer was as complete a deductionist as science has ever seen, documenting his preconceived theories by citing only the supporting evidence. Tylor was between the two, inducing principles from his reading, but stimulated by early, first-hand, cross-cultural experience.

All the classical evolutionists agreed on the orderly progression of human civilization as a guiding principle, and on the level of method, that we could determine the early forms of human civilization by reference to what they termed the "simpler" societies. It was they who established the term "primitive." In their frame of reference their use of the word as the equivalent of "primaeval" showed a sound semantic sense. For them, these peoples, stragglers on the road of progress, were of scientific utility as contemporary ancestors to the more "advanced" civilizations. A grasp of this historic fact brings the realization that they can scarcely be held responsible for the later connotative meanings that have continuously decreased the scientific utility of the word.

Contemporaneous with the classical evolutionists, but in a different current, was the positivism of Auguste Comte. In placing positivism in our genealogy, we move outside the realm of ethnology, strictly speaking. But viewed in terms of the influence exerted on later anthropological thought by theories derived from the positivist position, particularly on two major strands in the development of ethnological theory, it is essential that it be included. It is also significant from another point of view. The sociological aspect of the study of man has always had a place of importance in anthropological thought. This is as it should be, for especially in the study of any given culture, how the members of a given society are organized, and the relationships that exist between them, must be established as a first step in sorting out the data. The line between the study of the sociological aspects of culture and of culture as a whole has always been indeterminate. Another reason why the French sociologists must enter into any historical analysis of the development of ethnological theory is that Lévy-Bruhl (1949), whose thesis of "primitive mentality" stimulated so much anthropological controversy, is to be counted among them.

Later developments of evolutionism, with two exceptions, represented negative reactions. The Heliolithic and Kulturkreis positions took exception to the failure of evolutionary approach adequately to incorporate the factor of cultural borrowing into the study of cultural development. The historical empiricists, who also stressed the importance of investigating the history of culture, were in addition dissatisfied with the ordering of ways of life on a scale of values from lower to higher, with the concept of the "contemporary ancestor," and with the use of the comparative method in its classical form. The functionalist reaction was essentially methodological, and centered its attack on this last point, with which it coupled criticism of the "armchair" approach to the analysis of ethnological data.

So vigorous were all these criticisms, indeed, that there was a tendency to forget the substantial contributions the evolutionists made. Yet in historical perspective, we see that those who took the positions indicated on Fig. 1 by the double-bar—that is, whose reactions were negative—were indebted to their forerunners more than they realized. It was on their contributions, and on the reactions they stimulated, that the later structure of ethnological theory and method was to be erected.

We may at this point break our chronological sequence to consider two later developments which continued in the tradition of classical evolutionism. The first of these, the Marxian position, is only tangentially of anthropological significance, since it is more political than scientific, except as it continues to guide the researches of our colleagues in Communist countries. It is unnecessary here to recount the tale of the discovery, by Marx, of Morgan's work; of Engels' use of the notes Marx made in writing his book *The Origin of the Family, Private Property, and the State*, which became a socialist classic and a basic work in Marxist theory. It thus cannot be ignored because, its conclusions having been ingested by socialist ideology, it constitutes the required framework for the approaches of all Communist anthropologists to their data.

The other development in the tradition of classical evolutionism is neoevolutionism. Except for the studies of Childe, this has thus far been confined to the United States. Here methodology has secondary importance, except insofar as the use of illustrative data, particularly analogies from the physical and biological sciences, is concerned. Neoevolutionism has two major strands. The first is that of White and his associates, who in differentiating "evolution" from "history" base their conception of orderly change on a progressively more effective use of energy, and conceive of culture as an entity existing above and beyond its human carriers. The second, that of Steward and others, is termed "multilinear evolution." The aim of those who espouse multilinear evolution is to seek out, by empirical study, regularities in the development of particular cultural forms. This second variant, it may be said, is mentioned at this point only because its practitioners use the word "evolution" in describing their position; otherwise their work might better be classed with other approaches to the dynamics of cultural change.

It is an interesting fact that two of the three diffusionist schools, so to speak, withered on the vine. The Heliolithic theory fell of its own weight. Much discussed during the decade 1925–35 because of the vigor of the polemics of Elliot Smith, its deficiencies soon revealed themselves, and it disappeared from the anthropological scene. The *Kulturkreislehre* was another matter. On the level of method, indeed, it introduced certain concepts that came to be standard in reconstructions of historic contacts between nonliterate peoples. But its insistence on assuming historic relationships despite the absence of ascertainable paths along which contact between peoples could reasonably be assumed to have taken place, the extreme conservatism attributed to tradition, and the mechanical gathering of traits to form its "complexes" eventually forced its rejection. What has remained is what may be termed the "historic principle," which continues to dominate ethnological research in Germany and Austria.

Historical empiricism, which in one sense may be thought of as a third diffusionist approach, has been one of the most fruitful positions in stimulating the development of ethnological theory, as a glance at our genealogy in Fig. 1 shows. The reason for this must be sought in the breadth of interests of those who worked out its basic tenets—that conclusions must derive from field data, and that these data, gathered without injecting judgments of value or categories derived from the culture of the student, must range the whole gamut of cultural institutions, noting the characteristic behavior in each, and where possible indicating relationships between components. Taking the historic principle as a base, it was held that when attempts were made to reconstruct the past of peoples without written histories, comparisons must be drawn from restricted geographical areas, where actual historic contact can be readily assumed. The most explicit statement of this position was made by Sapir (1916); and its flowering, in the sense of a demonstration of its possibilities for recovering past contacts between nonhistoric peoples, was in Spier's analysis (1921) of field studies of the sun dance among Plains Indians.

Historical empiricism is often labeled "American," but it is correct to do this only because its source of origin was Boas and its influence emanated from the United States. Boas was close to his European contemporaries, however, and influenced many of them. Mauss followed his work closely, and Boas' discussions of many years with Lévy-Bruhl about the concept of primitive mentality was a major factor in causing the latter eventually (Lévy-Bruhl: 1949) to set aside this key concept in his theory. The theoretical position of historical empiricism, and its methodological stance, is also found in the work of the Scandanavian group; through the influence of Bogoras, a revered figured in Russian anthropology, the position can in some measure be thought of as having carried over even to the present generation of Russian anthropologists.

As we have noted, functionalism developed partially out of a negative reaction to evolutionism, partially as a result of the influence of the French sociologists. It has another possible source, which has been given little attention and which, indeed, would perhaps be difficult to document. This has to do with the stimulus that Malinowski, with whose name the term is most associated, derived from contact with developments that were taking place in the early 1920's in the United States. It will be remembered that Paul Radin spent the year 1923–24 in England. His impact is to be discerned in the revolutionary approach to social psychology found in Bartlett's work on the subject (Bartlett: 1928), published at about that time. What is not so well known is that Radin also had long discussions with Malinowski. I may here inject a personal datum.

My initial contact with Malinowski, in London, was in 1924. I first met Radin in Paris, shortly after he had left England for the continent. I was impressed with the vividness of Malinowski's interest in what was being done by American anthropologists, and his awareness of how their concepts and methods fitted in with his own point of view; from Radin, I learned how congenial the points of view of the two men had been. The reasons for the abrupt change in attitude that marked the later intense hostility of Malinowski toward historical empiricism provide an intriguing and important problem in the history of anthropology, and can only be answered when his papers have been subjected to detailed study. I may, however, add that this change was so sudden and so great, that, when I next saw Malinowski, in New York during 1926, I was bewildered by it.

As first enunciated, functionalism was essentially a method; this is clearly to be seen in the discussions of Malinowski's work by those who had studied with him (Firth [ed.]: 1957, *passim*). Extended periods of field work and command of the language of the people studied were held to be prime requisites for anthropological research. The use of informants and interpreters was rejected, and this point was underscored by the emphasis placed on the methodological device described by the phrase, "the participant observer." Because conclusions could be valid only if derived from first-hand observation, historical reconstruction was held to be fruitless. An additional objection to distribution studies was that in many researches the data were fragmented and, after the manner of the classic comparative method, torn out of cultural context.

As Malinowski told it, the designation "functionalism" was coined about 1925. Its theoretical base was not formally set down until almost two decades later, in his two posthumous works. However, the broad lines of its theory were clear when extracted from the ethnographic data in which it was interlarded in the writings of all those who adhered to the functionalist position. On this level, the interaction between cultural elements was emphasized; conversely, the trait-catalog which was being urged by Wissler and later used by Kroeber and Driver was attacked as an exercise in scientific unreality. The teleological role assigned to culture was apparent in the stress laid on its character as an instrumentality to assure the satisfaction of needs, both biological and psychological. Because of the rejection of any possibility of historical reconstruction, the position was ahistorical if not antihistorical, so that, conceptually, the dynamics of culture were quite disregarded, and the unit studied had something of homeostatic stability.

At the outset, Thurnwald and Radcliffe-Brown were associated with Malinowski as functionalists. However, Thurnwald proved to be eclectic in his interests, while for various reasons Radcliffe-Brown found the point of view of Malinowski uncongenial, and came to regard the analysis of social structure to be the fundamental objective of a "scientific"—as against a "historical"—anthropology. He rejected the concept of culture. For him, at best, it was a kind of secondary manifestation of social life whose study could be put aside until the relationships that go to make up the total institutional framework of society were thoroughly investigated.

The functionalist principle of institutional interaction was, however, retained. This is apparent in the reports of field research by the social structuralists, particularly in the organization of their data. The holism in functionalist theory was given over for concentration on the sociological aspects of group life. The ahistoricism of functionalism was not only retained, but emphasized through the dichotomy drawn between "synchronic" and "diachronic" orientations, and the associated concept of the difference between "scientific" or analytical research and "historical" study. The controversies that have centered about this latter formulation, of course, far antedate this particular manifestation of it; it remains a subject for dispute whenever anthropologists oriented to one or the other aspect of the analysis of human behavior discuss common problems.

Because the time factor was so important in historical empiricism, it was natural that the realization grew from the need not only to discover past contacts between peoples, but to establish the mechanisms that had brought about the observed results in the institutions and beliefs of peoples who had been in contact. The logic of this position, however, soon moved those whose research was cast in its theoretical frame of reference to the study of cultural dynamics. In its initial stages the approach was still directed toward recovering the cultures of nonliterate peoples before contact with the industrialized societies of Europe and America and developing hypothetical assumptions about the means by which similarities and differences in observed distribution of cultural elements may have been achieved.

In retrospect, the shift from the hypothetical to the empirical analysis of cultural change can be seen to have been inevitable. The increasing knowledge of nonliterate cultures, especially those of the American Indian, and of the historic contacts between the peoples under study revealed the limitations of earlier aims and procedures and made for an understanding of the actual dynamics of change. It was soon perceived that questions as to the instruments of cultural change, the circumstances under which elements from a new culture become acceptable to a recipient group, and the like, could only be answered by the study of actual situations where change resultant on contact between peoples was taking place. This change in approach may roughly be dated about 1935, when the word "acculturation"—a term that, in actuality, had been known in anthropological usage since about 1880—began to be used.

The shift toward the study of changing cultures is suggested by a concomitant change in the work of the functionalists. In this case, the cause was not the logical development of a theoretical interest, but in factors extraneous to anthropology. The studies out of which functionalism developed were made in societies that were small, isolated, and culturally stable—Malinowski in Melanesia, Radcliffe-Brown in the Andaman Islands, Thurnwald in New Guinea. In all these cases, dynamic factors were remote; there was a character of permanence about them that encouraged analysis of stable systems and pushed questions of innovation to the background.

Concern with Africa was growing, especially in Great Britain, but also in France and Belgium, manifesting the need to obtain the kind of knowledge only anthropologists could provide. With the establishment of the International African Institute in London, research funds became available; with Malinowski as principal adviser, work in Africa was cast along functionalist lines. Here the setting for research was vastly different from the southwest Pacific. Populations were large; contacts between African societies, no less than between Africans and Europeans, had been continuous and on a considerable scale. Against the stability of the cultures that gave the data on which functionalism was reared was posed the dynamics of African societies. Since the word "acculturation" was unacceptable to Malinowski, probably because it was a key concept of the historical empiricists, the designation "culture-contact" was employed.

While it is too much to say that we have here an example of independent development, it is of interest to note how, coming from two different points of view, a total situation encouraged similar responses. This parallel development becomes the more interesting when the differences in approach and in the kind of problem studied are taken into account. The functionalists and the later structuralists, in analyzing culture contact, were concerned mainly with questions of basic kinship and nonkinship units, economics, and political orientation. Those who studied acculturation tended to broaden the field, not only assessing modes of social change, but acculturative adjustments in the fields of language, religion, art, music, and later in the system of values.

The stimulus provided by the historical empiricists, as indicated in our genealogy, gave other new dimensions to ethnological theory. It was not until relatively late that the individual came to figure in the thinking of anthropologists. American students of culture were always aware of the psychological component. The role of cultural learning was implicit in their theory, especially in their insistence on the separation of race and culture as causative factors in behavior. Individual variation within the rubric of patterned traditional forms, while implicit in the theory, however, rarely entered into the research effort of the first quarter of the twentieth century.

If any single figure can be regarded as having first brought the theoretical importance of the psychological component in culture into the forefront of anthropological thinking, it is Edward Sapir. His interest was stimulated by the potentialities he saw in psychiatric-psychoanalytic methods, and his writings encouraged a whole new line of investigation that eventuated in a number of different emphases. One, the configurationist approach, grew into the study of national character. Another was concerned with the manner in which the personality of the individual is affected by his cultural background. A third had to do with the reflection of acculturation in the personality structures of individuals undergoing the acculturative experience. Out of this, too, grew the cross-cultural study of the enculturative process, the conditioning of the individual through the patterned educational processes of training and imitation of his earliest years. And, most recently, have come the experimental studies of the influence of culture on perception of the physical world.

Ethnophilosophy developed out of the realization that, in any holistic approach to ethnography, the role of underlying sanction must be given a prominent place. The most evident source of this interest was the field experience of anthropologists, whereby they learned that over-all evaluation of culture is an intricate matter, which can only be attempted when there is full realization of the ethnocentric component in making judgments cross-culturally. The philosophy of cultural relativism was implicit in earlier writings, but it was not until the depth of cultural conditioning and the devotion of every people to its own way of life was fully realized that there could emerge any systematic study of the place of values in the life of every people or any appreciation of the significance of values for ethnological theory.

At the present time, the field is dominated by two currents: that of historical empiricism in its more recent manifestations, and structuralism. The methodological principles derived from functionalism are so accepted that they are taken for granted by most ethnologists; historical reconstruction has given way to ethnohistory. The recrudescence of evolutionary thought represents an attempt to seek out new types of regularity in cultural change, or to reinterpret those proposed by the classical evolutionists. All these are to be found, frequently, in combination, and in world-wide distribution as interest in ethnology grows. What is important is to realize the derivation of all of them, so that the theorists of the future can build on the achievements of the past.

References

Bartlett, F. C.
1928: *Psychology and Primitive Culture* (New York: Macmillan).

Firth, R. (ed.)
1957: *Man and Culture: An Evaluation of the Work of Bronislaw Malinowski* (London: Routledge & Kegan Paul).

Haddon, A. C.
1934: *History of Anthropology* (2nd ed.; London: Watts).

Hallowell, A. I.
1962: Review of H. R. Hays, *From Ape to Angel*, in *American Anthropologist*, **64,** 174–176.

Hays, H. R.
1958: *From Ape to Angel* (New York: Knopf).

Herskovits, M. J.
1954: "Some Problems of Method in Ethnography," in R. F. Spencer (ed.), *Method and Perspective in Anthropology* (Minneapolis: University of Minnesota Press).
1956: "On Some Modes of Ethnographic Comparison," *Bijdragen tot de Taal-, Land-, en Volkenkunde*, **112**, 129–148.

Laguna, F. de (ed.)
1960: *Selected Papers from the American Anthropologist, 1888–1920* (Evanston, Illinois: Row, Peterson).

Lévy-Bruhl, L.
1949: *Les Carnets de Lucien Lévy-Bruhl* (Paris: Presses Universitaires de France).

Lowie, R. H.
1937: *The History of Ethnological Theory* (New York: Farrar & Rinehart).

Mahdi, M.
1957: *Ibn Khaldun's Philosophy of History* (London: Allen & Unwin).

Mead, M., & Bunzel, R. (eds.)
1960: *The Golden Age of American Anthropology* (New York: Braziller).

Penniman, T. K.
1936: *A Hundred Years of Anthropology* (rev. ed., 1952; New York: Macmillan).

Sapir, E.
1916: *Time Perspective in Aboriginal American Culture: A Study in Method*, Geological Survey Memoir 90, Anthropological Series No. 13 (Ottawa: Canada Department of Mines). Reprinted in D. Mandelbaum (ed.), *Selected Writings of Edward Sapir in Language, Culture, and Personality* (Berkeley: University of California Press, 1949).

Spier, L.
1921: "The Sun Dance of the Plains Indians, Its Development and Diffusion," *Anthropological Papers, American Museum of Natural History*, **16** (Part 7), 451–527.

Bibliography

of A. Irving Hallowell

1921: "Indian Corn Hills," *American Anthropologist*, **23**, 223.

1922: "Two Folk Tales from Nyasaland" (Bantu texts), *Journal of American Folk Lore*, **35**, 216–218.

1924: "Anthropology and the Social Worker's Perspective," *The Family*, **5**, 88–92.

1925: Review of I. H. N. Evans, *Studies in Religion, Folk Lore, and Custom in British North Borneo and the Malay Peninsula*, in *Journal of the American Oriental Society*, **45**, 42–43.

1926a: "Bear Ceremonialism in the Northern Hemisphere," *American Anthropologist*, **28**, 1–175.

1926b: "Following the Footsteps of Prehistoric Man," *The General Magazine and Historical Chronicle* (University of Pennsylvania), **28**, 117–122.

1927: Review of H. H. Wilder, *The Pedigree of the Human Race*, in *Saturday Review of Literature*, April 9.

1928a: "Recent Historical Changes in the Kinship Terminology of the St. Francis Abenaki," *Proceedings, Twenty-Second International Congress of Americanists* (*Rome*), 97–145.

1928b: "Was Cross-Cousin Marriage Practiced by the North-Central Algonkian?" *Proceedings, Twenty-Third International Congress of Americanists* (*New York*), 519–544.

1929a: "The Physical Characteristics of the Indians of Labrador," *Journal de la Societé des Americanistes de Paris*, n.s., **21**, 337–371.

1929b: "Anthropology in the University Curriculum," *The General Magazine and Historical Chronicle* (University of Pennsylvania), **32**, 47–54.

1930: "Editorial Comments: The Results of the Safe Harbor 'Dig,' " *Bulletin, Society for Pennsylvania Archaeology*, **1**.

1932a: "Kinship Terms and Cross-Cousin Marriage of the Montagnais-Naskapi and the Cree," *American Anthropologist*, **34**, 171–199.

1932b: Foreword to H. L. Masta, *Abenaki Indian Legends, Grammar and Place Names* (Victoriaville, P.Q. Canada: La Voix des boisfrancs), pp. 9–12.

1934a: "Some Empirical Aspects of Northern Saulteaux Religion," *American Anthropologist*, **36**, 389–404.

1934b: "Culture and Mental Disorder," *Journal of Abnormal and Social Psychology*, **29**, 1–9.

1935a: "The Bulbed Enema Syringe in North America," *American Anthropologist*, **37**, 708–710.

1935b: "Notes on the Northern Range of *Zizania* in Manitobe," *Rhodora*, **37**, 302–304.

1935c: "Two Indian Portraits," *The Beaver*, No. 3, Outfit 226, 18–19.

1935d: Review of F. E. Clements, *Primitive Concepts of Disease*, in *American Anthropologist*, **37**, 356–368.

1935e: Review of J. M. Cooper, *The Northern Algonquian Supreme Being*, in *American Anthropologist*, **37**, 673–674.

1936a: "Psychic Stresses and Culture Patterns," *American Journal of Psychiatry*, **92**, 1291–1310. Reprinted in M. K. Opler (ed.), *Culture and Mental Health* (New York: Macmillan, 1959), Chapter 1.

1936b: "The Passing of the Midewiwin in the Lake Winnipeg Region," *American Anthropologist*, **38**, 32–51.

1936c: "Anthropology—Yesterday and Today," *Sigma Xi Quarterly*, **24**, 161–169.

1936d: "Two Indian Portraits," *The Beaver*, No. 1, Outfit 267, 24–25.

1936e: Review of R. R. Marett, *Head, Heart and Hands in Human Evolution*, in *American Anthropologist*, **38**, 506–507.

1936f: Review of H. Granqvist, *Marriage Conditions in a Palestine Village*, in *American Sociological Review*, **1**, 991–993.

1936g: Review of F. Kniffen, G. MacGregor, R. McKinnon, S. Mekeel, & M. Mook, in A. L. Kroeber (ed.), *Walapai Ethnography*, in *American Sociological Review*, **1**, 540–541.

1937a: "Temporal Orientation in Western Civilization and in a Preliterate Society," *American Anthropologist*, **39**, 647–670. Reprinted in *Culture and Experience*, 1955.

1937b: "Cross-Cousin Marriage in the Lake Winnipeg Area," in D. S. Davidson (ed.), *Twenty-Fifth Anniversary Studies* (Philadelphia: Philadelphia Anthropology Society), 95–110.

1937c: Introduction, *Handbook of Psychological Leads for Ethnological Field Workers*, prepared for the Committee on Culture and Personality (Chairman, E. Sapir), National Research Council, Division of Anthropology and Psychology. Mimeographed, 60 pp. For printed versions see: *Personal Character and Cultural Milieu*, a collection of readings compiled by D. G. Haring (Syracuse: Syracuse University Press, 1948; 3rd ed., 1956); *The Study of Personality*, a book of readings compiled by H. Brand (New York: Wiley, 1954).

1937d: Review of R. Firth, *We, the Tikopia*, and W. L. Warner, *A Black Civilization*, in *American Sociological Review*, **2**, 558–560.

1937e: Review of R. Linton, *The Study of Man*, in *Annals, American Academy of Political and Social Science*, **190**, 249.

1937f: Review of *Yale University Publications in Anthropology*, Nos. 1–7: C. Wissler, *Population Changes among the Northern Plains Tribes*; P. H. Buck, *Regional Diversity in the Elaboration of Sorcery in Polynesia*; L. Spier, *Cultural Relations of the Gila River and Lower Colorado Tribes*; E. Beaglehole, *Hopi Hunting and Hunting Ritual*; W. W. Hill, *Navaho Warfare*; H. S. Mekeel, *The Economy of a Modern Teton Dakota Community*; C. Osgood, *The Distribution of the Northern Athabascan Indians*; in *American Anthropologist*, **39**, 140–142.

1938a: "Fear and Anxiety as Cultural and Individual Variables in a Primitive Society," *Journal of Social Psychology*, **9**, 25–47. Reprinted in *Culture and Experience*, 1955, and in M. K. Opler (ed.), *Culture and Mental Health* (New York: Macmillan, 1959).

1938b: "Shabwan: A Dissocial Indian Girl," *American Journal of Orthopsychiatry*, **8**, 329–340.

1938c: "The Incidence, Character and Decline of Polygamy among the Lake Winnipeg Cree and Saulteaux," *American Anthropologist*, **40**, 235–256.

1938d: "Notes on the Material Culture of the Island Lake Salteaux," *Journal de la Societé des Americanistes de Paris*, n.s., **30**, 129–140.

1938e: "Freudian Symbolism in the Dream of a Saulteaux Indian," *Man*, **38**, 47–48.

1938f: Review of T. Harrison, *Savage Civilization*, in *Annals, American Academy of Political and Social Science*, **196**, 264–265.

1938g: Review of F. Boas, *The Mind of Primitive Man* (rev. ed.), in *American Sociological Review*, **3**, 580.

1938h: Review of R. Landes, *Ojibwa Sociology* and *The Ojibwa Woman*, in *American Sociological Review*, **3**, 892.

1939a: "Sin, Sex and Sickness in Saulteaux Belief," *British Journal of Medical Psychology*, **18**, 191–197.

1939b: "The Child, the Savage and Human Experience," *Proceedings, Sixth Institute on the Exceptional Child* (*The Woods Schools, Langhorne, Pa.*), 8–34. Reprinted as Chapter 2, "The Recapitulation Theory and Culture," in *Culture and Experience*, 1955.

1939c: "Some European Folktales of the Berens River Saulteaux," *Journal of American Folk Lore*, **52,** 1555–1579.

1939d: "Anthropology" (with D. M. Spencer), in R. Webster (ed.), *The Volume Library* (New York: The Educators Association), pp. 95–110.

1939e: "Growing Up—Savage and Civilized," *National Parent-Teacher*, **34,** 32–34.

1939f: Reviews of E. C. Parsons, *Pueblo Indian Religion*; F. M. Keesing, *The Menomini Indians of Wisconsin*; V. E. Garfield, *Tsimshian Clan and Society*; W. Z. Park, *Shamanism in Western North America*; H. P. Junod, *Bantu Heritage*; A. Guillaume, *Prophecy and Divination Among the Hebrews and Other Semites*; S. M. Zwemer, *Studies in Popular Islam*; in *American Sociological Review*, **4,** 881–883.

1940a: "Aggression in Saulteaux Society," *Psychiatry*, **3,** 395–407. Reprinted in C. Kluckhohn & H. A. Murray (eds.), *Personality in Nature, Society and Culture* (New York: University of Pennsylvania Press, 1948; 2nd ed., 1953); and as Chapter 15 in *Culture and Experience*, 1955.

1940b: "Spirits of the Dead in Saulteaux Life and Thought," *Journal of the Royal Anthropological Institute*, **70,** 29–51. Reprinted as Chapter 7 in *Culture and Experience*, 1955.

1940c: "Magic: The Role of Conjuring in Saulteaux Society," *Papers Presented Before the Monday Night Group, 1939–40* (New Haven: Institute of Human Relations, Yale University, mimeographed).

1940d: Review of M. J. Herskovits, *Acculturation*, in *American Anthropologist*, **42,** 690–692.

1940e: Review of Weston La Barre, *The Peyote Cult*, in *Psychiatry*, **3,** 150–151.

1941a: "The Social Function of Anxiety in a Primitive Society," *American Sociological Review*, **7,** 869–881. Reprinted in *Personal Character and Cultural Milieu*, a collection of readings compiled by D. G. Haring (Syracuse: Syracuse University Press, 1948; 3rd ed., 1956); as Chapter 14 in *Culture and Experience*, 1955; and in *Bobbs-Merrill Reprint Series in the Social Sciences*, A-104.

1941b: "Psychology and Anthropology," *Proceedings of the Eighth American Scientific Congress* (*Washington, D.C.*), **2,** 291–297.

1941c: "The Rorschach Method as an Aid in the Study of Personalities in Primitive Societies," *Character and Personality*, **9,** 235–245.

1941d: "The Rorschach Test as a Tool for Investigating Cultural Variables and Individual Differences in the Study of Personality in Primitive Societies," *Rorschach Research Exchange*, **5,** 31–34 (a prospectus written prior to collection of first Rorschach protocols in 1938).

1941e: Review of W. Vernon Kinietz, *The Indians of the Western Great Lakes, 1615–1760*, in *American Anthropologist*, **42,** 645.

1942a: *The Role of Conjuring in Saulteaux Society* (Philadelphia: University of Pennsylvania Press, 1942).

1942b: "Acculturation Processes and Personality Changes as Indicated by the Rorschach Technique," *Rorschach Research Exchange*, **6,** 42–50. Reprinted in C. Kluckhohn & H. A. Murray (eds.), *Personality in Nature, Society and Culture* (New York: Society for Projective Techniques, 1948); and in M. H. Sherman (ed.), *A Rorschach Reader* (New York: International Universities Press, 1960).

1942c: "Some Psychological Aspects of Measurement Among the Saulteaux," *American Anthropologist*, **44,** 62–77. Reprinted as Chapter 10 in *Culture and Experience*, 1955.

1942d: "Some Reflections on the Nature of Religion," *Crozer Quarterly*, **19,** 269–277.

1942e: "Biological Factors in Family Structure," with E. L. Reynolds, H. Becker, & R. Hill (eds.), *Marriage and the Family* (Boston: Heath), pp. 25–46.

1942f: Review of K. N. Lewellyn & E. A. Hoebel, *The Cheyenne Way*, in *Annals, American Academy of Political and Social Science*, **220,** 272–273.

1943a: "The Nature and Functions of Property as a Social Institution," *Journal of Legal and Political Sociology*, **1,** 115–138. Reprinted in M. R. Cohen & F. S. Cohen (eds.), *Readings in Jurisprudence and Legal Philosophy* (New York: Philosophical Library, 1951), and as Chapter 12 in *Culture and Experience*, 1955.

1943b: "Araucanian Parallels to the Omaha Kinship System," *American Anthropologist*, **45,** 489–491.

1945a: "Sociopsychological Aspects of Acculturation," in R. Linton (ed.), *The Science of Man in the World Crisis* (New York: Columbia University Press), pp. 171–200. Reprinted as Chapter 17 in *Culture and Experience*, 1955.

1945b: "The Rorschach Technique in the Study of Personality and Culture," *American Anthropologist*, **47,** 195–210. Reprinted in *Bobbs-Merrill Reprint Series in the Social Sciences*, A-100.

1945c: " 'Popular' Responses and Culture Differences: An Analysis Based on Frequencies in a Group of American Indian Subjects," *Rorschach Research Exchange*, **9,** 153–168.

1945d: Review of A. Kardiner *et al.*, *The Psychological Frontiers of Society*, in *The Scientific Monthly*, **61,** 394–396.

1945e: Review of L. W. Simmons, *The Role of the Aged in Primitive Society*, in *Annals, American Academy of Political and Social Science*, **244,** 229.

1945f: Review of *Where the Two Came to Their Father: A Navaho War Ceremonial*, given by J. King (text and paintings recorded by M. Oakes, commentary by J. Campbell), *College Art Journal*, **4,** 172–174.

1946a: "Some Psychological Characteristics of the Northeastern Indians," in F. Johnson (ed.), *Man in Northeastern North America: Papers of the R. S. Peabody Foundation for Archeology*, **3**, 195–225. Reprinted as Chapter 6 in *Culture and Experience*, 1955.

1946b: "Concordance of Ojibwa Narratives in the Published Work of Henry R. Schoolcraft," *Journal of American Folk Lore*, **59**, 136–153.

1947a: "Myth, Culture, and Personality," *American Anthropologist*, **49**, 544–556.

1947b: Review of Ruth Underhill, *Papago Indian Religion*, in *Annals*, *American Academy of Political and Social Science*, **253**, 250–251.

1949a: "The Size of Algonkian Hunting Territories, A Function of Ecological Adjustment," *American Anthropologist*, **51**, 35–45.

1949b: "Psychosexual Adjustment, Personality, and the Good Life in a Non-literate Culture," in P. H. Hoch & J. Zubin (eds.), *Psychosexual Development in Health and Disease* (New York: Grune & Stratton), pp. 102–123. Reprinted as Chapter 16 in *Culture and Experience*, 1955.

1950a: "Personality Structure and the Evolution of Man," *American Anthropologist*, **52**, 159–173 (Presidential address, American Anthropological Association, Nov. 18, 1949). Reprinted in M. F. Ashley Montagu (ed.), *Culture and the Evolution of Man* (New York: Oxford University Press, 1962), and as Chapter 1 in *Culture and Experience*, 1955.

1950b: "Values, Acculturation and Mental Health," *American Journal of Orthopsychiatry*, **20**, 732–743. Reprinted as Chapter 20 in *Culture and Experience*, 1955.

1950c: Review of P. A. Schilpp (ed.), *The Philosophy of Ernst Cassirer*, in *American Anthropologist*, **52**, 96–99.

1950d: Review of David Mandelbaum (ed.), *Selected Writings of Edward Sapir*, in *Scientific Monthly*, **72**, 349.

1950e: Review of Sister B. Coleman, *Decorative Designs of the Ojibwa of Northern Minnesota*, in *Journal of American Folk Lore*, **63**, 119–120.

1951a: "Cultural Factors in the Structuralization of Perception," in J. H. Rohrer & M. Sherif (eds.), *Social Psychology at the Cross Roads* (New York: Harper, 1951), 164–195. Reprinted in R. C. Beardslee & M. Wertheim, *Readings in Perception* (Princeton, New Jersey: Van Nostrand, 1955).

1951b: "The Use of Projective Techniques in the Study of the Sociopsychological Aspects of Acculturation," *Journal of Projective Techniques*, **15**, 27–44 (Presidential address, Society for Projective Techniques, October 8, 1950). Reprinted as Chapter 19, "Acculturation and the Personality of Ojibwa," in *Culture and Experience*, 1955.

1951c: "Frank Gouldsmith Speck, 1881–1950," *American Anthropologist*, **53**, 67–75.

1952a: "Ojibwa Personality and Acculturation," in S. Tax (ed.), *Acculturation in the Americas* (Proceedings and Selected Papers of the Twenty-Ninth International Congress of Americanists), 105–112. Reprinted (abridged) in Y. A. Cohen, *Social Structure and Personality Casebook* (New York: Holt, Rinehart & Winston, 1961).

1952b: " 'John the Bear' in the New World," *Journal of American Folklore*, **65**, 418.

1953a: "Culture, Personality and Society," in A. L. Kroeber (ed.), *Anthropology Today* (Chicago: University of Chicago Press). Translated into Arabic, Social Science Section, UNESCO, Middle East Office, 1960. Reprinted in S. Tax (ed.), *Anthropology Today: Selections* (Chicago: University of Chicago Press, 1962), and in P. B. Hammond (ed.), *Cultural and Social Anthropology: Selected Readings* (New York: Macmillan, 1964).

1953b: Review of A. Joseph & V. F. Murray, *Chamorros and Carolinians of Saipan*, in *Journal of Projective Techniques*, **17**, 106–108.

1954a: "The Self and Its Behavioural Environment," *Explorations*, **2** (April). Reprinted (revised) as Chapters 4 and 8 in *Culture and Experience* (1955).

1954b: "Psychology and Anthropology," in J. Gillin (ed.), *For a Science of Social Man* (New York: Macmillan).

1954c: Comments on C. Kluckhohn, "Southwestern Studies of Culture and Personality," *American Anthropologist*, **56**, 700–703.

1954d: "Daniel Sutherland Davidson, 1900–1952" (with E. Gunther), *American Anthropologist*, **56**, 873–876.

1954e: Review of H. Palmer, *The Philosophy of Psychiatry*, in *American Anthropologist*, **56**, 336.

1955a: Comments on "Symposium: Projective Testing in Ethnography," *American Anthropologist*, **67**, 262–264.

1955b: *Culture and Experience* (Philadelphia: University of Pennsylvania Press).

1956a: "The Structural and Functional Dimensions of a Human Existence," *Quarterly Review of Biology*, **31**, No. 2. Reprinted in M. F. Ashley Montagu (ed.), *Culture and the Evolution of Man* (New York: Oxford University Press, 1962), and in *Bobbs-Merrill Reprint Series in the Social Sciences*, A-105.

1956b: "The Rorschach Technique in Personality and Culture Studies," in B. Klopfer *et al.* (eds.), *Developments in the Rorschach Technique*, Vol. 2, pp. 458–544. Portions of this chapter appear in Chapter 3, *Culture and Experience*, 1955.

1957a: "The Impact of the American Indian on American Culture," *American Anthropologist*, **69**, No. 2. Reprinted in H. P. Beck (ed.), *Folklore in Action* (Philadelphia: American Folklore Society, 1962), and in *Bobbs-Merrill Reprint Series in the Social Sciences*, A-102.

1957b: "The Backwash of the Frontier: The Impact of the Indian on American Culture," in W. D. Wyman & C. B. Kroeber (eds.), *The Frontier in Perspective* (Madison: University of Wisconsin Press). Reprinted with illustrations added in *Annual Report, Smithsonian Institution*, 1958, and in paperback edition, *The Frontier in Perspective*, 1964.

1957c: "Rorschach Protocols of 151 Berens River Adults and Children and 115 Adults from Lac du Flambeau," in B. Kaplan (ed.), *Microcard Publications of Primary Records in Culture and Personality*, No. 6 (Madison, Wisconsin: Microcard Foundation). Preface to this series in Vol. 1, 1956.

1957d: Review of W. N. Fenton, *American Indian and White Relations to 1830: Needs and Opportunities for Study*, in *American Anthropologist*, **59,** 118–119.

1957e: Review of C. Hall & G. Lindzey, *Theories of Personality*, in *American Anthropologist*, **59,** 936–937.

1958: "Ojibwa Metaphysics of Being and the Perception of Persons," in R. Tagiuri & L. Petrullo (eds.), *Person Perception and Interpersonal Behavior* (Stanford: Stanford University Press).

1959: "Behavioral Evolution and the Emergence of the Self," in B. J. Meggers (ed.), *Evolution and Anthropology, A Centennial Appraisal* (Washington, D.C.: Anthropological Society of Washington, D.C.). Reprinted in *Bobbs-Merrill Reprint Series in the Social Sciences*, A-100.

1960a: "Algonkian Tribes"; "Ojibwa"; "Frank G. Speck"; *Encyclopaedia Britannica.*

1960b: "Self, Society, and Culture in Phylogenetic Perspective," in S. Tax (ed.), *Evolution After Darwin*, Vol. 2, *The Evolution of Man* (Chicago: University of Chicago Press).

1960c: "Ojibwa Ontology, Behavior, and World View," in S. Diamond (ed.), *Culture in History* (New York: Columbia University Press). Reprinted in *Bobbs-Merrill Reprint Series in the Social Sciences*, A-101, and in S. Diamond (ed.), *Primitive Views of the World* (New York: Columbia Paperbacks, 1964).

1960d: "The Beginnings of Anthropology in America," in F. de Laguna (ed.), *Selected Papers from the American Anthropologist, 1888–1920* (Evanston, Illinois: Row, Peterson), pp. 11–90.

1961a: "The Protocultural Foundations of Human Adaptation," in S. L. Washburn (ed.), *Social Life of Early Man.* Viking Fund Publications in Anthropology, No. 31 (New York: Wenner-Gren Foundation for Anthropological Research).

1961b: Review of P. Teilhard de Chardin, *The Phenomenon of Man*, in *Isis*, **52,** Part 3.

1962a: Review of H. R. Hays, *From Ape to Angel*, in *American Anthropologist*, **64,** 174–176.

1962b: Review of S. Koch (ed.), *Psychology: A Study of a Science*, Vols. 1, 2, 3, in *American Anthropologist*, **64,** 204–207.

1962c: Review of E. F. Hammer, *The Clinical Application of Projective Drawings*, in *American Anthropologist*, **64,** 207–208.

1962d: Review of T. Kroeber, *Ishi in Two Worlds: A Biography of the Last Wild Indian in North America*, in *Annals, American Academy of Political and Social Science*, **340,** 164–165.

1963a: "Personality, Culture, and Society in Behavioral Evolution," in S. Koch (ed.), *Psychology: A Study of a Science*, Vol. 6 (New York: McGraw-Hill), pp. 429–509.

1963b: "The Ojibwa World View and Disease," in I. Galston (ed.), *The Image of Man in Medicine and Anthropology* (New York: International Universities Press).

1963c: "American Indians, White and Black: The Phenomenon of Transculturalization," *Current Anthropology*, **4,** 519–531.

1963d: Review of D. G. Mandelbaum, G. W. Lasker, & E. M. Albert (eds.), *The Teaching of Anthropology and Resources for the Teaching of Anthropology*, in *Science*, **141,** 144–145.

1963e: Review of R. Kluckhohn (ed.), *Culture and Behavior: The Collected Essays of Clyde Kluckhohn*, in *Journal of Higher Education*, **34,** 237–238.

1964a: Review of *Human Nature and the Study of Society: The Papers of Robert Redfield*, Vol. 1, in *American Sociological Review*, **29,** 464.

1964b: Review of E. D. Evans-Pritchard, *Essays in Social Anthropology*, in *American Sociological Review*, **29,** 424–425.

1964c: Review of E. R. Service, *Primitive Social Organization: An Evolutionary Perspective*, in *American Sociological Review*, **29,** 314–315.

Index

Name Index

Subject Index